NOVELL'S

Guide to NetWare® 5
and TCP/IP

NOVELL'S

Guide to NetWare® 5 and TCP/IP

DREW HEYWOOD

Novell Press, San Jose

Novell's Guide to NetWare® 5 and TCP/IP

Published by
Novell Press
2211 North First Street
San Jose, CA 95131

Library of Congress Catalog Card Number: 99-60193

ISBN: 0-7645-4564-7

Printed in the United States of America

10 9 8 7 6 5 4 3 2 1

1B/RX/QT/ZZ/IN

Distributed in the United States by IDG Books Worldwide, Inc.

Distributed by CDG Books Canada Inc. for Canada; by Transworld Publishers Limited in the United Kingdom; by IDG Norge Books for Norway; by IDG Sweden Books for Sweden; by Woodslane Pty. Ltd. for Australia; by Woodslane (NZ) Ltd. for New Zealand; by TransQuest Publishers Pte Ltd. for Singapore, Malaysia, Thailand, Indonesia, and Hong Kong; by ICG Muse, Inc. for Japan; by Norma Comunicaciones S.A. for Colombia; by Intersoft for South Africa; by Le Monde en Tique for France; by International Thomson Publishing for Germany, Austria and Switzerland; by Distribuidora Cuspide for Argentina; by Livraria Cultura for Brazil; by Ediciones ZETA S.C.R. Ltda. for Peru; by WS Computer Publishing Corporation, Inc., for the Philippines; by Contemporanea de Ediciones for Venezuela; by Express Computer Distributors for the Caribbean and West Indies; by Micronesia Media Distributor, Inc. for Micronesia; by Grupo Editorial Norma S.A. for Guatemala; by Chips Computadoras S.A. de C.V. for Mexico; by Editorial Norma de Panama S.A. for Panama; by American Bookshops for Finland. Authorized Sales Agent: Anthony Rudkin Associates for the Middle East and North Africa.

For general information on IDG Books Worldwide's books in the U.S., please call our Consumer Customer Service department at 800-762-2974. For reseller information, including discounts and premium sales, please call our Reseller Customer Service department at 800-434-3422.

For information on where to purchase IDG Books Worldwide's books outside the U.S., please contact our International Sales department at 317-596-5530 or fax 317-596-5692.

For consumer information on foreign language translations, please contact our Customer Service department at 1-800-434-3422, fax 317-596-5692, or e-mail rights@idgbooks.com.

For information on licensing foreign or domestic rights, please phone +1-650-655-3109.

For sales inquiries and special prices for bulk quantities, please contact our Sales department at 650-655-3200 or write to IDG Books Worldwide, 919 E. Hillsdale Blvd., Suite 400, Foster City, CA 94404.

For information on using IDG Books Worldwide's books in the classroom or for ordering examination copies, please contact our Educational Sales department at 800-434-2086 or fax 317-596-5499.

For press review copies, author interviews, or other publicity information, please contact our Public Relations department at 650-655-3000 or fax 650-655-3299.

For authorization to photocopy items for corporate, personal, or educational use, please contact Novell, Inc., Copyright Permission, 1555 North Technology Way, Mail Stop ORM-C-311, Orem, UT 84097-2395; or fax 801-228-7077.

For general information on Novell Press books in the U.S., including information on discounts and premiums, contact IDG Books Worldwide at 800-434-3422 or 650-655-3200. For information on where to purchase Novell Press books outside the U.S., contact IDG Books International at 650-655-3021 or fax 650-655-3295.

® John Kilcullen, *CEO, IDG Books Worldwide, Inc.*
Steven Berkowitz, *President, IDG Books Worldwide, Inc.*
Brenda McLaughlin, *Senior Vice President & Group Publisher, IDG Books Worldwide, Inc.*
The IDG Books Worldwide logo is a registered trademark or trademark under exclusive license to IDG Books Worldwide, Inc., from International Data Group, Inc. in the United States and/or other countries.

Marcy Shanti, *Publisher, Novell Press, Novell, Inc.*
Novell Press and the Novell Press logo are trademarks of Novell, Inc.

Welcome to Novell Press

Novell Press, the world's leading provider of networking books, is the premier source for the most timely and useful information in the networking industry. Novell Press books cover fundamental networking issues as they emerge — from today's Novell and third-party products to the concepts and strategies that will guide the industry's future. The result is a broad spectrum of titles for the benefit of those involved in networking at any level: end user, department administrator, developer, systems manager, or network architect.

Novell Press books are written by experts with the full participation of Novell's technical, managerial, and marketing staff. The books are exhaustively reviewed by Novell's own technicians and are published only on the basis of final released software, never on prereleased versions.

Novell Press at IDG Books Worldwide is an exciting partnership between two companies at the forefront of the knowledge and communications revolution. The Press is implementing an ambitious publishing program to develop new networking titles centered on the current versions of NetWare, GroupWise, BorderManager, ManageWise, and networking integration products.

Novell Press books are translated into several languages and sold throughout the world.

Marcy Shanti
Publisher
Novell Press, Novell, Inc.

Novell Press

Publisher
Marcy Shanti

Administrator
Diana Aviles

IDG Books Worldwide

Acquisitions Editor
Jim Sumser

Development Editor
Kurt Stephan

Technical Editors
Neil Cashell
Chuck Flood
Ken Neff

Copy Editors
Eric Hahn
Lauren Kennedy

Project Coordinator
Karen York

Graphics and Production Specialists
Angie Hunckler
Brent Savage
Janet Seib
Michael A. Sullivan

Proofreaders
Christine Berman
Kelli Botta
Nancy Price
Rebecca Senninger
Rob Springer
York Production Services

Indexer
York Production Services

About the Author

Drew Heywood is a networking professional who has been working with NetWare since 1987. He has managed WANs and LANs in government and industry, and now spends most of his time writing books and articles about networking. As sole or contributing author, Drew has written more than a dozen books about NetWare and Windows NT, and has nearly a million books in print. Drew holds CNE and MCSE certifications.

For Lauren, ma petite danseuse

Preface

With NetWare 5, TCP/IP moves to the forefront. For the first time, NetWare Core Protocols (NCP) can operate natively over a TCP/IP protocol stack without resorting to IPX encapsulation — a capability Novell has dubbed *Pure IP*. Now administrators can build NetWare networks that are truly based on a single protocol stack. Clients can access NetWare services and the Internet using only TCP/IP. Life is great, isn't it?

Novell's Guide to NetWare 5 and TCP/IP covers Pure IP, the most significant new feature included in NetWare 5. There are a lot of tweaks and new features in NetWare 5, but Pure IP is the big enchilada. In my opinion, Novell has done an outstanding job of meeting its Pure IP design goals. Without sacrificing the ease of use we have come to expect from NetWare, Pure IP is considerably leaner than IPX. Gone, for example, are the periodic SAP broadcasts we have learned to dread. In place of SAP is a much less bandwidth-hungry protocol named the Service Locator Protocol (SLP), a protocol designed to function on WANs without detracting from performance. Pure IP is a giant step forward for NetWare, and you will learn all about it in this book.

Who Should Read This Book?

TCP/IP knowledge is a vital job skill for any network administrator. If you need your PCs to talk to a UNIX computer through your LAN, you need to know TCP/IP. Heck, if you need to talk to just about any computer, you need to know TCP/IP. And if you want to connect your LAN to the Internet — and who doesn't these days? — you need to know TCP/IP. Don't try to avoid it — TCP/IP is everywhere, and every LAN administrator's resume should include TCP/IP as a skill.

This book is intended to help administrators of NetWare 5 make the transition to TCP/IP. I'll assume that you know the basics of administering your NetWare server and that utilities such as SYSCON and NWADMIN aren't mysteries to you. But I don't assume that you know anything about protocols or communication theory. Don't worry if you don't know the difference between a protocol and a protractor. It's my job to orient you with the right data communications knowledge.

NetWare and TCP/IP

Novell has known about TCP/IP for a long time and began including support in NetWare 3 in 1987. Since that time, a comprehensive set of products has been introduced that enables NetWare servers to provide many of the services that are generally associated with UNIX.

For this book, I chose to cover the most central aspects of TCP/IP, and focus on setting up and managing Pure IP on NetWare 5 servers and clients (workstations). Further, due to the intricacy of Pure IP, I had to select among its features. My goal is to give you the background to understand Pure IP, and then show you the essentials everyone needs to know about running TCP/IP on NetWare 5 LANs. Basically, I follow the old proverb of teaching you to fish so that you can feed yourself. When you finish this book, you will have the skills you need to comprehend any of Novell's TCP/IP-related products.

Learning TCP/IP

When you consider the complexity of the job it performs, NetWare is really a very simple product to administer. On a simple network, IPX (Novell's counterpart to TCP/IP) is practically invisible. Typically, the only configuration information you need to enter is network numbers for the internal and external networks. Everything else comes automatically. Routing, the capability of forwarding data through complex networks, is built into NetWare. You don't have to do a thing to turn routing on other than add a second network card to a server. The folks at Novell are justifiably proud of their network architecture, which performs well and practically snaps together.

All this changes with TCP/IP. The wonderful plug-and-play world of IPX is left behind and you enter the realm of a protocol where everything—and I mean everything — can, and often must, be configured. In other words, you can't do TCP/IP unless you know how and, in most instances, why TCP/IP works.

And that's where this book comes in. Within these covers you will find everything you need to know to put TCP/IP to work on your NetWare network.

What's in This Book

Novell's Guide to NetWare 5 and TCP/IP provides you with two kinds of knowledge: theoretical knowledge about what TCP/IP is and how it works, and practical knowledge about the NetWare products that implement TCP/IP. In fact, these two types of knowledge define the organization of this book.

Part I: TCP/IP Concepts

This section provides the theory. The overall organization is taken from the structure of the TCP/IP protocol model, with its four layers: network access, Internet, host-to-host, and process/application. These layers break down the functionality of TCP/IP into chunks that are bite-sized as opposed to TCP/IP as a whole, although each layer still has a lot to chew on. Here's how the chapters are organized.

▶ Chapter 1, "Introduction to TCP/IP," prepares you to do your own research on TCP/IP. The many protocols that make up the TCP/IP protocol suite are documented in Request for Comment (RFC) documents, which now number over 2,000 and date back to the origins of the ARPANET in 1969. To appreciate and understand this rich set of documentation, you need to understand how the ARPANET has evolved, ending up as the Internet we know today. More importantly, you need to know how standards are established on the Internet. Then, you can retrieve RFCs for yourself and learn about TCP/IP from the horse's mouth.

▶ Chapter 2, "TCP/IP and Network Communication," builds some theoretical models of network communication. Starting with the 7-layer OSI Reference Model and moving to the 4-layer TCP/IP model, you will learn how network communication works. My goal in this chapter is to provide you with a rich set of conceptual hooks on which you can hang the many facts you encounter in the next four chapters.

▶ Chapters 3 through 6 provide layer-by-layer coverage of the TCP/IP protocol suite. You might react to the lengths of these chapters, saying perhaps, "I don't need to know much at all about IPX. Why are there over 50 pages about the network access layer alone?" The unfortunate answer is that TCP/IP was designed with functionality in mind and not simplicity; TCP/IP is considerably more complex to configure and manage than the Novell IPX/SPX protocols. TCP/IP administrators perform tasks that are unheard of with IPX/SPX, such as manually addressing each TCP/IP computer with a network and host identification number. In answer to how you may react: No, all of the information in these chapters isn't essential. I could have helped you get started with a bit less, but then I wouldn't have answered the many questions that are sure to arise as you become more deeply involved in TCP/IP.

Part II: Implementing NetWare TCP/IP

Part II is where theory meets practical fact, where you put your knowledge from Part I to work building TCP/IP into your NetWare network.

▶ Chapter 7, "Introducing NetWare TCP/IP," builds the bridge, demonstrating how, in general, TCP/IP is realized with NetWare products. Here we review the NetWare protocol architecture, and briefly examine the various NetWare products that provide TCP/IP support.

▶ Chapter 8, "Configuring a Pure IP Network," shows how TCP/IP works on NetWare 3 and NetWare 4 servers. You learn how to install, configure, activate, and manage the protocols on both types of NetWare servers.

▶ Chapter 9, "Configuring NetWare 5 Clients," shows how to get TCP/IP running on Windows 95/98, Windows NT, and DOS/Win 3.x clients.

▶ Chapter 10, "Internetworking NetWare TCP/IP," moves beyond simple networks to show how TCP/IP is configured on large, routed networks. You learn how to configure static routing as well as the routing protocols RIP and OSPF.

▶ Chapter 11, "Managing a Domain Name Service (DNS)," explains how to configure a TCP/IP name server using the shiny new DNS server Novell has added to NetWare 5. Now at last, NetWare has a full-capability, standards-compliant name server, and you will learn all about it.

▶ Chapter 12, "The Dynamic Host Configuration Protocol," shows you how to simplify TCP/IP client management using the Dynamic Host Configuration Protocol (DHCP). NetWare 5 includes a dandy DHCP server that offers a variety of client configuration options that are specially attuned to NetWare.

▶ Chapter 13, "Managing NetWare TCP/IP," explains how to configure Simple Network Management Protocol (SNMP) management on your NetWare TCP/IP network. You will learn how to configure NetWare servers and clients so that they can be managed using SNMP, and how to use the management consoles that are included with NetWare 3 and Netware 4 as well as LAN WorkPlace.

Part III: Supporting TCP/IP Services

▸ Chapter 14, "Locating Services on Pure IP Networks," describes the Service Location Protocol (SLP) that substitutes for SAP in the Pure IP environment. You need to know some SLP design issues before you implement a large network using Pure IP.

▸ Chapter 15, "Migrating to Pure IP," examines the tools included with NetWare 5 that enable you to migrate smoothly from IPX to Pure IP, or to support networks that are IPX and IP hybrids. You will learn about IPX Compatibility Mode, which enables IPX-dependent applications to run on a Pure IP network, and about the Migration Gateway, which enables you to internetwork IPX and Pure IP network segments.

▸ Chapter 16, "Managing an FTP Server," shows you how to add a File Transfer Protocol server to your NetWare network. Everything you need is included with NetWare 5, and the procedure is straightforward and painless.

▸ Chapter 17, "Building a Web Server," explains how to get a World Wide Web server running on your network. NetWare 5 includes the Netscape FastTrack server, an easily managed but powerful Web server.

▸ Appendixes A through C provide valuable reference material about working with binary, decimal, and hexadecimal numbers and their equivalents, as well as supply a handy list of top-level Internet domain codes.

Keep in Touch

Thanks for choosing this book. I sincerely hope it meets your needs, and that you will turn to it many times as you learn about and operate NetWare TCP/IP on your LAN. I've been a LAN administrator for a long time and believe I have a good idea of what my colleagues need to know. But I also know there is always room for improvement.

This is about the twelfth book on NetWare that I've written or co-authored, and I haven't written the perfect book yet. There's always something I should have included or a better way to make a point, and so help me, there is an occasional error as well. The fastidious editors at Novell Press and my excellent technical editors have already done a lot to help me fine-tune this manuscript, but I'm sure there is more to be done.

Nothing tests a book like having a few thousand readers tear through it. You, the readers, are a vital part of the process of making my books — and the computer book industry as a whole — better and more responsive to your needs. So please, if you have a comment, be it praise or poison, let us know.

At the time this book is published, my Internet address is `drheywo@ibm.net`. Please feel free to write with your comments and questions. I'll do my best to answer all your e-mail promptly.

Acknowledgments

My sincere gratitude goes out to the following persons, without whom this book could not have come into being:

To Jim Sumser, thanks for keeping the book alive for a new edition and for your many acts of random, and not so random, kindness.

To Kurt Stephan, thanks for keeping this new edition on track.

To Marcy Shanti, thanks for helping the first edition see the light of day.

To Kirk Kimball, special thanks for help above and beyond the call of duty. Without the information you provided and the support you arranged, this book could not have been written.

To all at Novell who responded to my urgent pleas for technical support, please receive my heartfelt appreciation. With apologies to any whose names I have forgotten, I would like to specifically express my gratitude to Molly Allen, Chuck Flood, Juan Luciani, Tom Miller, Todd Rupper, Rich Shone, and Richard Tenney.

To my technical editors Neil Cashell, Chuck Flood, and Ken Neff, my profound thanks for rooting out my errors. This is a significantly better book thanks to your efforts.

And finally, to everyone else at Novell, thanks for making products worth writing about.

Contents at a Glance

Contents

PART I

TCP/IP Concepts

## CHAPTER 1

Introduction to TCP/IP

Imagine a room filled with people from different countries — a German, a Finn, an Italian, a Korean, a Saudi Arabian. All have an urgent need to communicate, but there is a problem: no two people speak the same language.

Until recently, the realm of computer networking resembled that room. Computers communicate with one another using languages called network protocols. Unfortunately, unless all of the computers in a network use the same protocols, communication may be impossible.

For example, IBM computers have traditionally used *System Network Architecture* (SNA) network protocols to exchange data. Computers made by Digital, however, have traditionally been connected through *Digital Network Architecture* (DNA) networks. As a result, exchanging data between IBM and Digital computers can be quite difficult. In the 1970s and 1980s, different computer vendors such as IBM, Digital, Sperry, Burroughs, Honeywell, and Tandem (among others) promoted their own protocols. Although a few vendors supported other vendors' network protocols, the majority did not. A particular vendor may have decided not to support competing protocols for a variety of reasons:

▶ Certain protocols may not have coincided with the vendor's own particular network design philosophy.

▶ The vendor may have regarded its own protocols as superior to others.

▶ Proprietary protocols could serve to tie customers to one brand of equipment.

▶ Changing protocols for a computer network architecture involved a major effort.

▶ By and large, customers were loyal to a particular computer brand and had no need to connect with other brands.

Local area networks (LANs) led the computing world into a new age. However, LANs tended to remain strongly tied to their own homegrown protocols. LANs were essentially isolated islands, much like their mainframe cousins. Although Novell promoted an excellent set of protocols called the IPX/SPX protocol suite early on, those protocols were not implemented by many vendors for quite some time. Microsoft and IBM relied on NetBEUI. Apple introduced its own AppleTalk. Even though Novell began supporting other protocols such as AppleTalk and SNA, variations in the architectures of IPX, AppleTalk, and SNA continue to hinder smooth interoperability between different computer systems. For example, an IBM mainframe cannot connect seamlessly with a NetWare LAN that uses only IPX protocols.

All of this "netspeak" — SNA, DNA, AppleTalk, NetBEUI, and so forth — may seem a little puzzling to you at first. I simply want to demonstrate all of the confusion that existed in the early years of the network industry.

The Need for Common Protocols

When people need to overcome language barriers, they often use translators. For example, the United Nations General Assembly uses a large body of language translators to facilitate communication among the representatives. A similar approach can be used to allow different kinds of computers to communicate.

Translation is a common tool for enabling network communication. Certain kinds of translators, called *gateways*, exchange data between different environments — for example, between a NetWare and an SNA environment. One simple way to allow different vendors' networks to interconnect uses different gateways for the various types of networks, just as the UN employs different translators for communication among the various nations.

Although using gateways is an effective means of connecting networks, in the long run it is not a very practical solution. Gateways are difficult to design, and they are seldom foolproof. Furthermore, each gateway must be purchased, installed, and maintained. Finally, gateways complicate LAN communication, which should be kept as simple as possible. In short, gateways do not provide the kind of seamless communication that most networks require.

An alternative approach solves many of the problems presented by gateways. That approach involves agreeing on common protocols that can be used by *all* computers to communicate through a network. Although having a common set of protocols would seem to be an obvious solution, it nevertheless took a long time for that solution to be realized. For the reasons mentioned above, manufacturers continued to adhere to their own protocol suites.

Until very recently, the most common means of transporting data between different computer brands was to store the data on a disk or magnetic tape and then physically transport the magnetic media to another computer. It was not uncommon for a computer system in a small- to medium-sized company to resemble the example shown in Figure 1.1. In this configuration, the accounting, sales, and finance data are stored on an IBM mainframe, engineering data are stored on a VAX, and end users are connected to a Novell LAN, which supports the company's personal productivity programs. This kind of setup caused many problems. For example, for a long time, only one way existed to take data from a report produced by an IBM mainframe and use it in a Lotus spreadsheet: Someone had to reenter the figures manually from a green-bar printout into the spreadsheet.

▶ . . . . ◀

FIGURE 1.1

A Multiprotocol Network

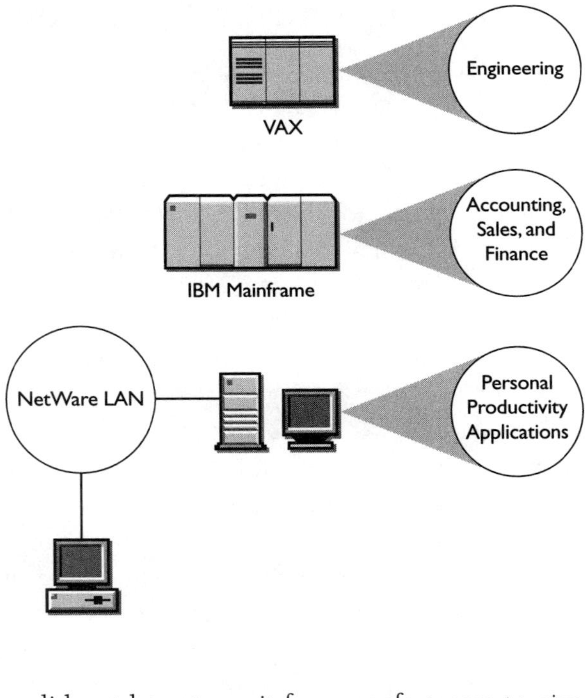

VAX

Engineering

IBM Mainframe

Accounting, Sales, and Finance

NetWare LAN

Personal Productivity Applications

Fortunately, users did not have to wait for manufacturers to give in and agree on common protocols. By the late 1980s, those protocols already existed in the form of the TCP/IP protocol family developed for the Internet. The name TCP/IP derives from the two most prominent protocols in the suite: *Transmission Control*

Protocol (TCP) and *Internet Protocol* (IP). The TCP/IP protocols are mature, robust, and extensive. They are open protocols, defined in public forums. They were not designed to meet the specific requirements cf a particular company. As organizations began to see the potential of TCP/IP to unify their network environments, they began to push for TCP/IP support in all of their computing environments. One by one, vendors have yielded. Today, TCP/IP is available on virtually every computing platform.

NOTE

The term TCP/IP is derived from the two most prominent components of a vast suite of protocols: the Transmission Control Protocol (TCP) and the Internet Protocol (IP). You will learn more about TCP, IP, and many other related protocols in this book.

To understand why the TCP/IP protocol suite has become the common language of the modern network, you need to understand a little about the evolution of TCP/IP and how TCP/IP standards are set. The remainder of this chapter explores the processes by which TCP/IP continues to evolve to meet the changing needs of its users.

The Origins of TCP/IP

The U.S. Department of Defense (DoD) was one of the first organizations to realize a need for wide area networking. As far back as the 1960s, the DoD infrastructure included hundreds of computers around the world. Some of these computers were operated by the DoD itself, but many belonged to defense contractors and universities that were doing work for the DoD.

In the early 1960s, computers exchanged data through dedicated communication channels. If a pair of computers needed to communicate, they were connected by a dedicated circuit. As more computers were added, separate lines were installed to connect each computer to every other computer in the network. This setup is called a *mesh*. (See Figure 1.2.) A mesh network functions very well but it is costly. Today, many mainframes still use dedicated communication channels. The problem with this approach is that the number of required lines increases rapidly as the number of computers grows. The configuration quickly becomes unwieldy.

FIGURE 1.2

A Mesh Network

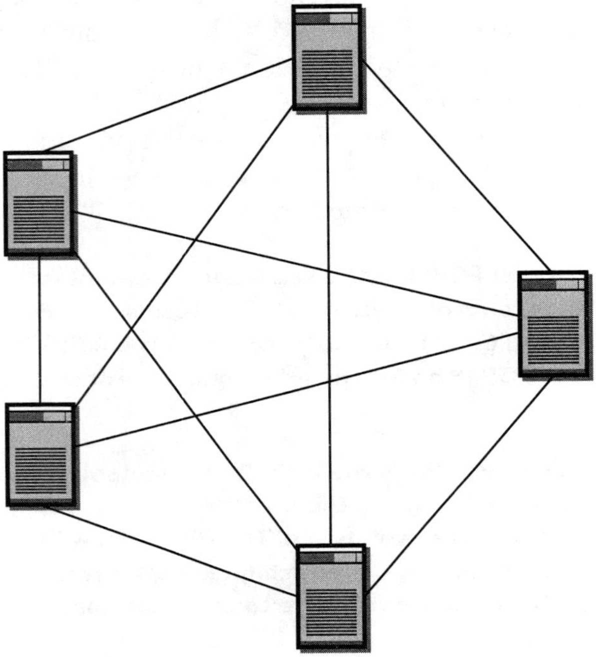

The next step in the evolution of networking was to have some hosts route messages between other hosts, as shown in Figure 1.3. This strategy enabled network designers to reduce the number of communication links, but it also created complications because it required several computers to share the same communication lines. Figure 1.3 shows how a system that uses hosts requires shared communication lines.

Communication lines can be shared in two ways:

▶ By permitting a single computer to monopolize a line until its message has been sent. This technique is known as *circuit switching*. With circuit switching, extra channels are needed to allow several conversations to take place at the same time.

> ► By breaking messages into small units so that parts of different messages can take turns on the same line. This technique is called *packet switching*. It enables many computers to share a single communication channel.

In the late 1960s, the Advanced Research Projects Agency (ARPA) of the DoD decided to focus its research on the second technology — that is, packet switching.

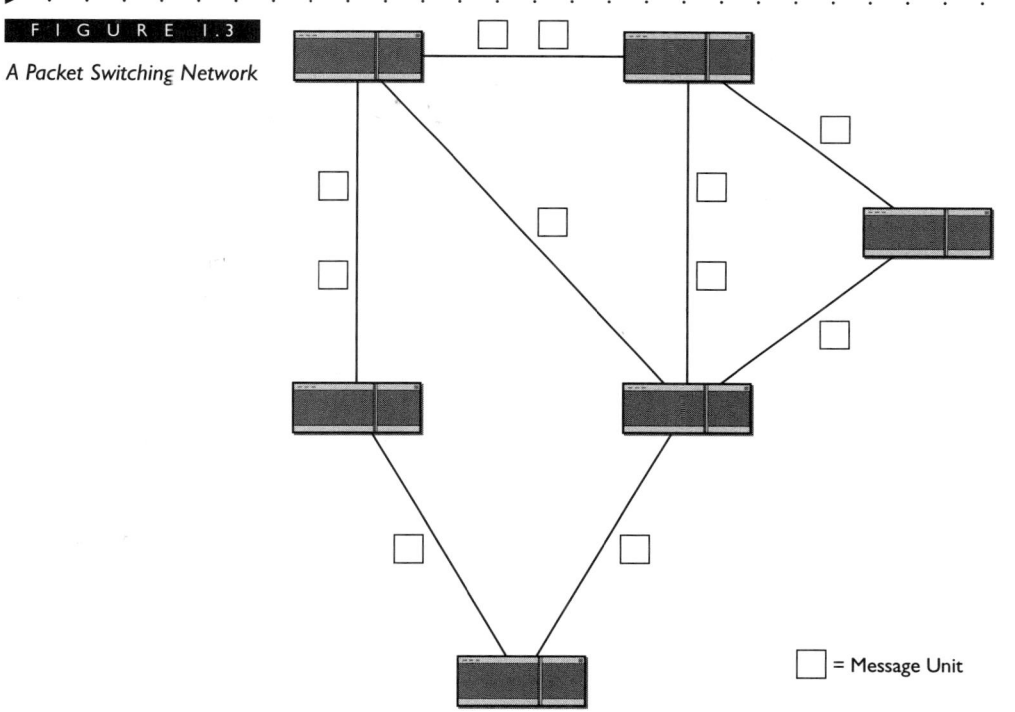

FIGURE 1.3

A Packet Switching Network

☐ = Message Unit

The DoD required several items from its networks:

> ► **Standard protocols.** The DoD purchases computer equipment from the lowest bidder. Therefore, the DoD required a standard set of protocols that could be used for all computer configurations. It was essential to develop protocols that enabled different computer brands to interoperate.

► **Reliability.** The DoD needed to be prepared for wartime conditions. At the time ARPA decided to initiate packet switching research, long-distance communication technologies were primitive and prone to trouble. Consequently, ARPA required protocols that could cope with a lot of stress.

► **Flexibility.** Networks constantly change, and the protocols had to allow the changes to be made smoothly without interrupting service.

History of the Internet

The particular wide area network that eventually became the Internet began in 1968. It connected four sites: SRI International, the University of California at Santa Barbara (UCSB), the University of California at Los Angeles (UCLA), and the University of Utah. Dubbed the ARPANET, the network grew to include 20 hosts by 1972.

Remember that in 1972 all computers were so-called *host* computers: mainframes and minicomputers that serviced large numbers of people through time-sharing or batch processing. At that time, it was hardly imaginable that an individual person could have his or her own computer on which to work. The convention of calling all computers on a TCP/IP network "hosts" derives from those early days of shared computers.

As the ARPANET grew, it gradually came to function as much more than simply a means of communication between the DoD and its contractors. Soon, the ARPANET connected a majority of colleges and graduate schools, as well as a large number of technology vendors. By the mid-1980s, the ARPANET had expanded far beyond its DoD origins and had gained a momentum of its own.

Consequently, in the mid-1980s, ARPA (now called DARPA, or the Defense Advance Research Project Agency) decided to end the ARPANET experiment. The DoD had established MILNET for U.S. military data communication, and the ARPANET was left to its own devices.

In 1986, the ARPANET was replaced by a higher-performance network funded by the National Science Foundation (NSF). This network, called NSFNET, now serves as the backbone of the Internet. NSFNET is managed by Advanced Network Services (ANS).

NSFNET represented the first step toward privatizing the Internet. Since NSFNET was established, management of the network has become more and more privatized, although oversight of network standards still belongs to a public organization — the Internet Activities Board (IAB).

Development of the TCP/IP protocols began in the early 1980s, and in 1983 the ARPANET converted to TCP/IP. Availability of the TCP/IP protocols received a significant boost when TCP/IP was included in Version 4.2 of Berkeley Standard Distribution (BSD) UNIX. Because use of BSD UNIX was free to educational institutions, it was widely adopted by universities and in a variety of industries. Additionally, BSD UNIX became the foundation of several commercial UNIX products, including Digital's Ultrix and Sun's SunOS. As BSD UNIX was disseminated through the educational and research computing communities, TCP/IP soon became the dominant network protocols in those environments.

By the mid 1980s, TCP/IP had two big advantages:

▶ It was readily available to those who needed it (primarily industrial and educational researchers).

▶ It was the protocol of the ARPANET, to which those researchers were connected.

The result was widespread use of TCP/IP in communities of users who were on the leading edge of computing technology. TCP/IP's evolution took off accordingly. By 1990, TCP/IP had gained momentum and was poised for the next critical stage in its evolution: TCP/IP was ready to enter the business world.

TCP/IP and Open Computing Standards

As TCP/IP was maturing, another trend was emerging. Although corporate information systems departments were still relying heavily on mainframe computing, the personal computer had begun to infiltrate business operations. The business world began to explore new ways of using computers beyond the established paradigm of computing using shared hosts.

By about 1985 (the year the IBM AT computer was introduced), the number of personal computers on corporate desktops had reached critical mass, and companies began to demand network connectivity. Users were no longer willing to transfer files via "sneakernet" and modems. LANs, which previously had been niche products, began to flourish. Some of the more reliable and versatile LAN products — most notably NetWare — began to change the way organizations did their computing.

Soon managers of information systems (often collectively referred to as MIS) began to realize that they had a problem. Users wanted to expand the range of their desktop computers. They wanted to access the corporate mainframe from their PCs. For example, some users wanted to obtain sales data from a VAX so that they could manipulate it using Lotus 1-2-3. Other users wanted to send files to branch offices without having to set up dial-in and dial-out modems. Basically, users were asking for seamless communication — that is, they wanted their computers to be able to communicate freely with all other computers. The problem of integrating computing had to be addressed.

No single vendor had a comprehensive strategy for dealing with the problem. In fact, as the demand for connectivity grew among users, computer vendors tended to focus on improving their own protocols rather than building bridges with other protocol suites.

To achieve their goal of interconnecting their companies, MIS needed protocols that were not tied to a particular vendor's network. Out of this need developed a movement that came to be called *Open Computing*, which sought to establish non-proprietary computing standards.

Even though TCP/IP was available as an open standard, many people viewed TCP/IP with skepticism because it is not governed by an international standardization body. Therefore, many industry authorities supported a different approach for developing open network standards. For a while, the most popular interconnectivity movement was *Open Systems Interconnection* (OSI), a set of network standards being developed by the International Organization for Standardization (ISO). The government of the United States was deeply involved with OSI, and at one time it announced that all agencies of the U.S. government would convert to Government OSI Profile (GOSIP), which is a set of standards derived from OSI.

However, the excitement about OSI soon dissipated. As with many international negotiations, it has proved difficult to establish a final product that satisfies everyone involved. Work on the OSI protocols has progressed slowly. The GOSIP initiative has foundered, and the DoD has continued to use TCP/IP for its networks.

As OSI bogged down, MIS came to realize what the TCP/IP community had known all along: TCP/IP could be used to integrate the computer world. People began to realize that TCP/IP standards are not as unreliable as previously thought. Although TCP/IP is not standardized by an official international body, the standardization process is exceptionally responsive to input. There are no closed-door decisions, and all standards are available to the public. In short, TCP/IP has the two main features the corporate world desired: openness and connectivity independent of any particular computer brand or brands.

Later in this chapter, you will see how TCP/IP standards are developed. The process is extraordinarily inclusive. In fact, you yourself could get involved. TCP/IP has attracted some of the brightest and most imaginative people in network computing, and the protocols have achieved a remarkable richness. Here are just a few of the services that are readily available through TCP/IP protocols:

▸ **FTP (File Transfer Protocol).** Used to transfer and manage files among networked computers. This is a widely implemented service.

▸ **Telnet.** Provides remote terminal service that enables users to log onto remote computers.

▸ **DNS (Domain Name Service).** Makes TCP/IP networks more comprehensible by providing a hierarchical directory of usernames that identify network hosts.

▸ **SMTP (Simple Mail Transfer Protocol).** Delivers electronic mail through internetworks.

▸ **SNMP (Simple Network Management Protocol).** Used for managing network devices.

▸ **HTTP (Hypertext Transfer Protocol).** This protocol, the core of the World Wide Web, facilitates retrieval and transfer of hypertext documents.

This book examines all of these protocols, among others.

TCP/IP and Internet Standards

Standards for TCP/IP are set somewhat indirectly. Unlike other protocols, the TCP/IP protocols are not standardized by an international treaty organization. Under the authority of the NSF, the Internet Activities Board (IAB) sets all standards for the Internet and therefore sets standards for TCP/IP, which is used on the Internet. Anyone who wants to connect to the Internet — which today is practically everyone — must use protocols approved by the IAB. As a result, the TCP/IP protocols running on most networks are standardized by a group that has no real authority, other than its charter, to manage the Internet. The process may not be ideal, but as you will see, it works very well.

In 1983, the IAB received its charter to design, engineer, and manage the Internet. The IAB charter describes the organization as "an independent committee of researchers and professionals with a technical interest in the health and evolution of the Internet system." The IAB has established two groups to oversee the short-term and long-term evolution of the Internet: the Internet Engineering Task Force (IETF) and the Internet Research Task Force (IRTF). The various groups involved in Internet standards are shown in Figure 1.4.

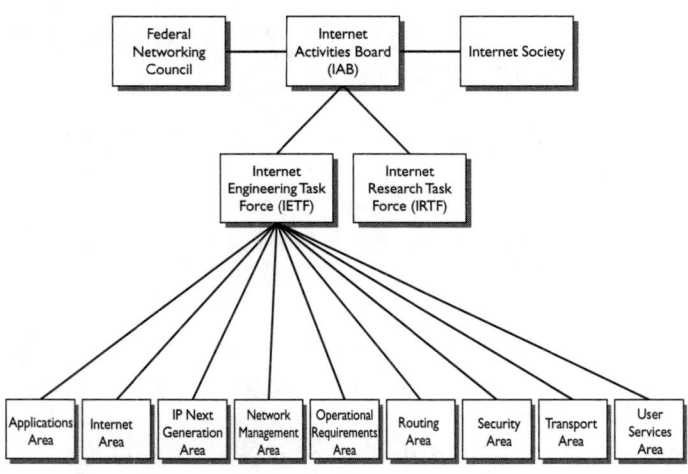

The most prominent organization is the Internet Engineering Task Force, which is responsible for specifying the Internet architecture and protocols. The charter of the IETF describes the organization as follows:

> The IETF is not a traditional standards organization, although many specifications are produced that become standards. The IETF is made up of volunteers who meet three times a year to fulfill the IETF mission. There is no membership in the IETF. Anyone may register for and attend any meeting.

A document named *The Tao of IETF* provides insight into the organization and function of the IETF as well as a description of the organization's meetings. This chapter, in the subsequent "Obtaining Internet Documentation" section, explains how to find this document on the Internet, along with other related documents.

The IETF is organized into a number of technical areas. The specific areas evolve with the needs of the Internet community. At present, the IETF's technical areas are:

- ► Applications

- ► Internet

- ► IP Next Generation

- ► Network Management

- ► Operational Requirements

- ► Routing

- ► Security

- ► Transport

- ► User Services

The Internet Engineering Steering Group (IESG) oversees the IETF and is responsible for formally recommending standards to the IAB. The IESG members are the directors of the various IETF technical areas.

The Internet Research Task Force conducts Internet research. In reality, it is difficult to draw a line between the IRTF and the IETF because membership overlaps considerably. Membership overlaps not only because the participants have similar interests, but also because this overlapping promotes the transfer of technology among participants.

Two outside organizations have close ties with the IAB. The Federal Networking Council represents agencies of the U.S. government and coordinates the agencies' use of the Internet. The Internet Society is a public organization made up of people from education, industry, government, and the general Internet-user community. The Internet Society promotes use of the Internet and gives its members a forum for contributing input into the Internet standards process. For information, contact:

The Internet Society
Suite 100
1895 Preston White Drive
Reston, VA 22091
USA
E-mail: isoc@isoc.org
703-648-9888

Internet Documentation

Discourse related to the development of the Internet is open to the public. All documents are freely available on the Internet through a variety of access methods. Among the public documents are minutes of IETF meetings, existing standards, standards under development, and miscellaneous memoranda that are of interest to the Internet community.

Requests for Comments

The documents you hear about most often are *Requests for Comments* (RFCs). All Internet standards are published as RFCs. For example, the *Transmission Control Protocol* (TCP) is documented in RFC 793, and "The Tao of IETF" is published in RFC 1718. The official document that lists all Internet standards is itself an RFC entitled *Internet Official Protocol Standards* (currently RFC 2200). This document is updated periodically.

If you scan the index of RFCs, you will find documents on a wide variety of subjects. (I'll tell you how to access the index a little later in this chapter.) Here are some typical entries from the index:

```
1866  PS    T. Berners-Lee, D. Connolly, "Hypertext Markup

            Language - 2.0", 11/03/1995. (Pages=77)

            (Format=.txt)

1850  DS    F. Baker, R. Coltun, "OSPF Version 2 Management

            Information Base", 11/03/1995.

            (Pages=80)(Format=.txt) (Obsoletes RFC1253)

1132  S     L. McLaughlin, "Standard for the transmission of

            802.2 packets over IPX networks", 11/01/1989.

            (Pages=4)(Format=.txt)

1796  I     C. Huitema, J. Postel, S. Crocker, "Not All RFCs

            are Standards", 04/25/1995. (Pages=4)

            (Format=.txt)

1791  E     T. Sung, "TCP And UDP Over IPX Networks With Fixed

            Path MTU", 04/18/1995. (Pages=12) (Format=.txt)

0968        V. Cerf, "Twas the night before start-up",

            12/01/1985. (Pages=2) (Format=.txt)

0740  H     R. Braden, "NETRJS Protocol", 11/22/1977.

            (Pages=19) (Format=.txt) (Obsoletes RFC0599)
```

The letter to the right of each RFC number indicates the category to which the RFC belongs. There are several formal RFC categories, as follows:

▶ **Standard (S).** An official standard Internet protocol.

▶ **Draft Standard (DS).** A protocol that is in the final stages of development and is nearing approval as an Internet standard.

▶ **Proposed Standard (PS).** A proposal that is under consideration as a possible future standard.

▶ **Experimental (E).** Protocols that are being tested but are not yet on the standards track.

▶ **Historical (H).** Obsolete protocols or protocols that are no longer standards.

▶ **Informational (I).** RFCs that provide the Internet community with general information. Some of these RFCs document standards that, although not actual Internet standards, are commonly used on the Internet.

▶ **Unclassified (no code).** RFCs of a miscellaneous, sometimes frivolous nature (for example, RFC 968).

It is important to understand that not all RFCs are standards. For example, the *Network File Service* (NFS) protocol developed by Sun Microsystems is in widespread use on the Internet, but NFS is not an Internet standard. Making NFS an Internet standard would place it under the jurisdiction of the IETF, rather than Sun, which licenses the protocol to many vendors of TCP/IP products. Nevertheless, there is a need for the Internet community to be informed about the protocol. Therefore, NFS v. 3 is documented in RFC 1814, which is an informational RFC. For a list of the RFCs that document Internet standards, consult the RFC named *Internet Official Protocol Standards*.

Not all Internet standard protocols are mandatory. Instead, the protocols are assigned varying degrees of requirement. The different levels are:

▶ **Required.** All systems on the Internet must implement the protocol.

▶ **Recommended.** The protocol should be implemented.

▶ **Elective.** The protocol may be implemented.

▶ **Limited.** The protocol may be useful in some situations. This requirement level may be assigned to historical, experimental, and specialized protocols.

> ► **Not recommended.** Historical, experimental, and specialized protocols that are not recommended for use on the Internet.

Only certain levels are associated with each category of RFC. Table 1.1 summarizes the levels that correspond to each category.

TABLE 1.1 Levels of Requirement Associated with RFC Categories	REQUIRED	RECOMMENDED	ELECTIVE	LIMITED	NOT RECOMMENDED
Standard	✓		✓	✓	
Draft Standard	✓		✓	✓	
Proposed Standard			✓	✓	
Experimental					✓
Historic					✓

You should keep in mind that specific RFCs are never updated. After a document is assigned an RFC number, it is effectively cast in stone. Any modifications that are approved by the IETF result in a new RFC with a new number. The RFC index entries shown earlier include two examples of RFCs that make previous RFCs obsolete. Although the obsolete RFCs remain in distribution, they are typically categorized as historic. Therefore, while you need to be sure that you use the most recent RFC that describes a given protocol, you never need to worry that there may be a more recent version of a particular RFC, such as RFC 793.

The procedure for establishing Internet standards is conservative, and is described in RFC 2026, *The Internet Standards Process — Revision 3*. An entity as enormous as the Internet cannot afford to be governed by rash decisions. Many proposed protocols do not survive, but the ones that do tend to have a broad consensus of support. Those protocols also tend to be fairly long-lived. The TCP protocol described in RFC 793 has existed since September 1981. Figure 1.5, adapted from a diagram in RFC 1920, illustrates the life cycle of an Internet protocol. Each transition to a new classification requires an explicit decision of the IAB based on the recommendations of the IESG.

FIGURE 1.5

The Internet Protocol
Standards Process

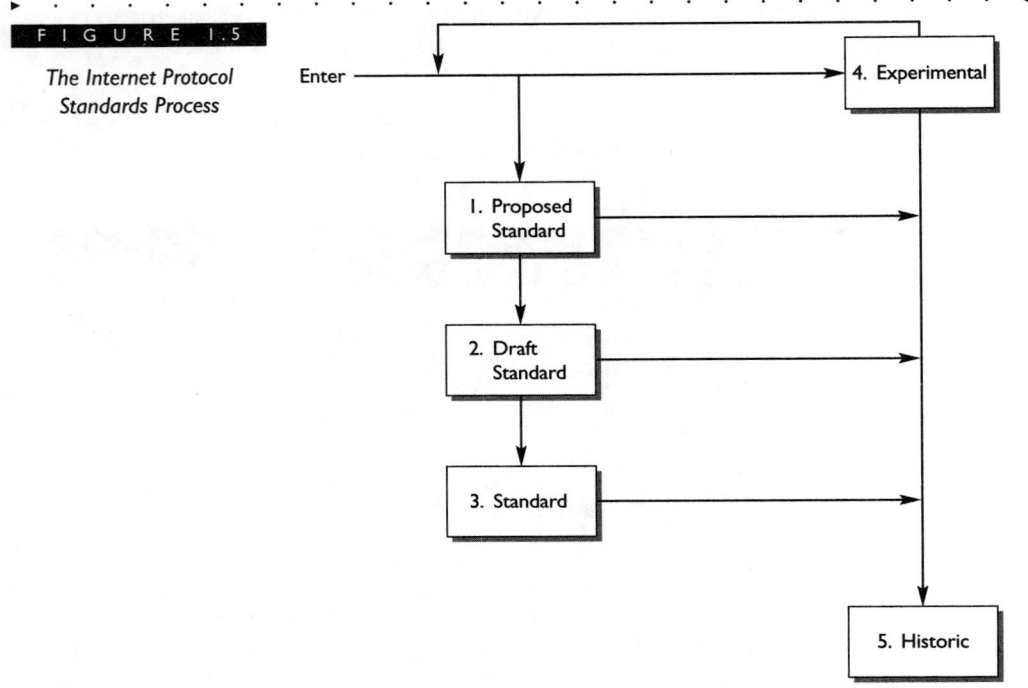

The stages in the cycle are as follows:

1. When a proposal enters the standards process it is assigned an initial status, often as a proposed standard. Many protocols undergo extensive scrutiny by the IETF before they enter the standards track. That is why certain subjects are never introduced into the RFC cycle. You won't find experimental RFCs related to IP next generation (IPng), a very hot topic at the IETF, because the RFC process is too slow and cumbersome for topics that generate a lot of debate.

Classification of a protocol as a proposed standard places the protocol on track as a candidate for future standardization. A proposal may enter the standards track only with the approval of the IESG.

2. A proposed standard can only be promoted to a draft standard by specific action of the IESG. A protocol must remain a proposed standard for at least six months. In general, a proposed standard is only promoted after there have been at least two independent implementations of the protocol and after the IESG has made a recommendation.

Classification of a protocol as a draft standard notifies the Internet community that the protocol is nearing standardization. Unless significant objections are made, a protocol that is a draft standard will most likely become a standard after about six months.

3. A draft standard is promoted to a standard only by approval of the IESG. The protocol must have been a draft standard for at least six months. In order to be promoted to a standard, a protocol must have operational experience, and it must demonstrate interoperability in at least two implementations.

4. Protocols classified as experimental are not on the standards track. The IESG may assign an experimental classification to a protocol that is under consideration when it feels the proposal is not yet ready for standardization. Experimental protocols may reenter the standards track as they mature, or they may be removed from consideration altogether and classified as historic.

5. When a protocol becomes obsolete or when it is declassified as a standard for some other reason, it is designated as historic. Any experimental or standard protocol can be removed from further standards evaluation in this way.

The Internet standards process is a cautious one, and considerable time may be required for a standard to emerge from the standards track. The careful nature of the standards process ensures that protocols that become standards are thoroughly tested for reliability and features.

The explosion of activity on the Internet, particularly that associated with the World Wide Web, has burst the limits of the Internet standards process. Some new protocol features are awaited so eagerly that they are placed in widespread use long before they have emerged from the standards track. HTTP, for example, has been deployed extensively for several years, but HTTP Version 1.0 has never become an official Internet standard (its specification is published in an Informational RFC). HTTP Version 1.1 is, however, undergoing the rigors of the Internet standards process and is currently on the standards track. World Wide Web developments are overseen by the World Wide Web Consortium (W3C). A good place to track Web developments is the W3C home page at http://www.w3.org.

Increasingly, the Internet standards process is being dominated by heavy hitters such as Sun, Microsoft, Netscape, and Novell that regard Internet protocols as key contributors to their competive strategies. In the future, expect to see the Internet standards process bypassed by numerous protocols and protocol extensions.

Internet-Drafts

Much of the work being done on protocols is published in documents called Internet-Drafts. Protocols that are not yet ready to enter the standards track are typically documented in Internet-Draft form. Unlike RFCs, Internet-Drafts are subject to modification at any time, so you need to keep up with the latest versions. A great deal of the IETF's work is ongoing. The information may be hard to find, but documentation is generally available.

Obtaining Internet Documentation

RFCs, Internet-Drafts, and other Internet documents are readily available through the Internet. The majority of documents may be acquired using a variety of methods, including FTP, electronic mail, the World Wide Web, and WAIS. This section discusses several approaches (see Chapter 6 for more detailed information).

RFCs are stored in *primary* and *secondary repositories*. Primary repositories receive RFCs immediately after they are published. Secondary repositories receive copies of RFCs from primary repositories. Updates of secondary repositories may, therefore, be delayed to some degree, depending on the site.

An index of RFCs, available from the InterNIC Directory Services, is extremely useful for finding out more information about the Internet and TCP/IP. The index file named rfc-index.txt can be obtained via e-mail or anonymous FTP. Both methods are discussed in detail in the following subsections.

The most recent guidelines for retrieving RFCs are given in the file `rfc/retrieval.txt`, which is available from many sources, including the RFC Editor's Web site (`http://www.rfc-editor.org/`). This site is one of the most convenient places to access RFCs and related information.

Electronic Mail

An excellent way to get started is to use the RFC-INFO service, which lets you obtain RFCs, FYI documents, and Internet Monthly Reports (IMRs) using e-mail. This technique is available to anyone who can send e-mail to the Internet directly or through an Internet gateway. To obtain current instructions on obtaining RFCs and other documents, send e-mail addressed to `rfc-info@isi.edu`. The message text should be `help: ways_to_get_rfcs`. A help document will be returned to you via e-mail. The document returned to you lists the current primary repositories for RFCs and explains how to use FTP to retrieve RFC files.

Requests made to the RFC-INFO service consist of keywords placed in the message text. To obtain help documents, start with the following requests:

▶ `Help: Help`. Obtains a brief command list.

▶ `Help: Manual`. Obtains a complete manual for the service.

▶ `Help: List`. Shows you how to use the List request.

▶ `Help: Retrieve`. Shows you how to use the Retrieve request.

If your primary goal is to retrieve RFCs, you just need to know how to use the Retrieve request. The message you would use to retrieve RFC 793 is:

```
Retrieve: RFC

Doc-ID: RFC0793
```

Notice that the RFC number must be four digits. (If necessary, you may need to add a zero at the beginning.) Consult the help documents for ways to retrieve documents using standards numbers, as well as methods for retrieving FYIs and other Internet documents. Documents will be sent to you in text format. If you require files that are preformatted for PostScript printers, you may want to retrieve them from an FTP site.

Besides the help documents, you may wish to obtain directories of available documents. Because there are so many documents available, different search criteria can be used to narrow the search. (These criteria are described in the help documentation.) For example, to obtain a list of FYI documents published in 1994, the message would be:

```
List: FYI

Dated-after: Dec-31-1993

Dated-before: Jan-01-1995
```

You can also use the `List: RFC` and `List: IMR` requests to obtain lists of FYI and IMR documents.

NOTE

Another way to obtain RFCs via e-mail is to send a message to `mailserv@ds.internic.net`. **In the message include the text** `file/ftp/rfc/rfcnnnn.txt`, **where** *nnnn* **is the RFC number. Do** *not* **include leading zeros in the RFC numbers.**

FTP

Probably the most common way that documents circulate on the Internet is via `file transfer protocol` (FTP). FTP is a protocol used to configure FTP servers, which make parts of their file systems available to users running FTP client software. Although FTP can be used to manage remote file systems—for example, to create and remove directories—the most common use of FTP is to transfer files. Today, it is likely that the majority of FTP file retrievals are performed using a Web browser.

RFCs and other Internet documents are widely available on anonymous FTP servers. These servers are called "anonymous" because they permit anyone to log in without a specific user account. Users simply enter `anonymous` as a login name. Typically, a user is requested to enter his or her e-mail address as a password (although Web browsers that make FTP connections do not prompt for a username or password unless they are required by the FTP server). Anonymous FTP users are very limited in what they can do, but anonymous FTP is a convenient way for organizations to make files readily available to Internet users. Chapter 6 shows you how to use FTP to obtain documents from the InterNIC document service.

The most up-do-date sources of RFCs are the primary RFC repositories. You can obtain a listing of the primary repositories and procedures for retrieving files at `http://www.isi.edu/in-notes/rfc-retrieval.txt`. Worldwide FTP repositories include: `NIS.NSF.NET`, `NISC.JVNC.NET`, `FTP.ISI.EDU`, `WUARCHIVE.WUSTL.EDU`, `SRC.DOC.IC.AC.UK`, `FTP.NCREN.NET`, `FTP.SESQUI.NET`, `FTP.NIC.IT`, and `FTP.IMAG.FR`.

Often, RFCs are stored with the path `rfc/rfcnnnn.txt`, where *nnnn* is the number of the RFC. Leading zeros are not included in the filename. Thus, RFC 793 would be stored in the file `rfc793.txt`.

You can also obtain RFCs in PostScript format by replacing the `.txt` filename extension with `.ps`.

World Wide Web

The World Wide Web is probably the easiest way to obtain Internet documentation and other information about TCP/IP. The best place to start is the RFC Editor's Web page at `http://www.rfc-editor.org/`. At that site, you can search for RFCs by number or by full-text searches for characters appearing in the filename or the description.

The IETF also maintains a Web server, which you can access with the URL `http://www.ietf.org/`.

► · ◄

What Is Inside the RFCs?

This chapter has given you an overview of the origins of TCP/IP, the processes that help TCP/IP to evolve, and ways to gain access to the enormous amount of information available about TCP/IP. You now know what an RFC is, and you know how to get all the RFCs you could ever desire. Now we can discuss the contents of RFCs. However, before I get too specific, you need some background on what communications protocols do and how they are organized. Therefore, in the next chapter I examine different models of network communications.

## CHAPTER 2

TCP/IP and Network Communication

If you have been working with NetWare for any length of time, you may take for granted the ease with which network protocols can be configured. Adding IPX protocol support to a network card is as simple as typing the command `BIND IPX TO NE2000 NET=1234`. You have probably never had to configure IPX routing, supply the addresses of computers on a network, or enter tuning parameters for network protocols. One source of NetWare's reputation as an easy-to-manage network operating system is the plug-and-play nature of NetWare's protocols.

As you work with TCP/IP, however, you must deal with a more complex environment — not impossible, just complex. You need to be more knowledgeable and you need to plan more for setting up the network, because each computer on the network must be assigned an address that conforms to a master address scheme. On each host, you must configure files that enable it to locate gateways (routers) and to access directories of host names. With NetWare, you never have to worry about computer names because NetWare takes care of the names for you. With TCP/IP, names must be administered. Also, you need to know more about your own specific network because TCP/IP functions differently on some networks than on others.

The chapters in Part I prepare you to work as a TCP/IP administrator. In these chapters, you will learn, layer-by-layer, how TCP/IP functions, how it relates to the network, and how it relates to NetWare and the IPX protocol. This chapter provides valuable background information about the layers of a TCP/IP network and how network protocols work.

You have probably seen layered models of networks before — most likely the *Open Systems Interconnection* (OSI) seven-layer reference model. Layers are exceptionally useful tools for understanding network communication. Networks are built in layers because layers make networks easier to understand, easier to design, and easier to reconfigure.

This chapter begins with a discussion of communication in general. I use a layered model to describe an example of real-world, human communication in order to illustrate basic principles of network design. If you are not comfortable with the concept of network protocol stacks, you should take some extra time to review the communication process described here.

After you thoroughly understand network protocol stacks, you will be ready to look at some real network models. This chapter covers not just one, but two network models. I first introduce you to the OSI Reference Model, because Novell uses this model to discuss NetWare protocols. The *Open Datalink Interface* (ODI) standard, which guides design of network protocol drivers for NetWare, follows the OSI model. Therefore, in order to understand NetWare TCP/IP, you must understand the seven layers of the OSI model.

However, the OSI model did not exist when TCP/IP was created. The designers of TCP/IP instead used their own four-layer model. Although the TCP/IP protocols can be forced to fit the OSI model, they can be better understood in the context of their original four layers.

Layered Communication

You can learn a lot about data communication by looking closely at how people exchange information. Many seemingly simple everyday processes are more complicated than you may realize.

When people converse, there is always the possibility that they will misunderstand each other. Subtleties in choice of words, in the inflection of voice, and in body language can affect the way others interpret your meaning. That is why many people prefer the telephone to electronic mail. Because subtle cues are left out when you send an e-mail message, your precise meaning is more likely to be misunderstood.

Techniques have been devised to improve communication in a number of different settings. Diplomats have long been aware of the need for clear communication, and diplomatic protocols have been established to reduce miscommunication. *Robert's Rules of Order* is a set of guidelines that in part are intended to reduce the potential for miscommunication inherent when communication becomes disorderly. In business letters, certain conventions are used so that readers can quickly see what's important. In electronic correspondence, a whole system of symbols (called *emotion icons* or *emoticons*) has developed to ensure that the writer's meaning is properly understood. You have undoubtedly come across a :-) or a ;-) at one time or another.

Model of Everyday Communication

Consider a complex human process that closely parallels network data communications: the process of bringing clothes along on an airplane trip.

The process starts when you place your clothes in a suitcase. You attach an identification tag so that your luggage will not be lost. At the airport, you hand your suitcase to an attendant, who attaches a tag that indicates your destination. When you have arrived at your destination, you pick up your suitcase. But how does your luggage get to the same place? What steps need to be taken?

The complete process is surprisingly complex — especially because so many different people are involved. Here are the steps when you travel from, say, Indianapolis to Los Angeles:

1. You place your clothes in a suitcase.

2. You label the suitcase with an identification tag.

3. You take the suitcase with you to the airport and hand it to an attendant.

4. The attendant examines your ticket to determine your destination and then attaches another tag that indicates the appropriate airport code. The attendant then sends the suitcase to the airplane.

5. Baggage handlers examine the suitcase's destination information to decide on which plane it belongs.

6. If you need to change planes along the way — for example, at Denver — baggage handlers at the intermediate airport must examine the suitcase's routing information to determine what to do with your suitcase. (For example, they determine that your suitcase must be transferred to another plane headed for Los Angeles.)

7. When your plane arrives in Los Angeles, baggage handlers again must examine the tag to determine where to route your suitcase. At this point, your suitcase is sent to a luggage carousel.

8. You retrieve your suitcase and take it with you to your hotel room.

9. You open the suitcase and unpack your clothes.

I've gone through these steps in detail because the process provides a useful analogy to many of the concepts applied to data networks. Figure 2.1 shows a model of the baggage-handling process.

FIGURE 2.1

Example of a Layered Model

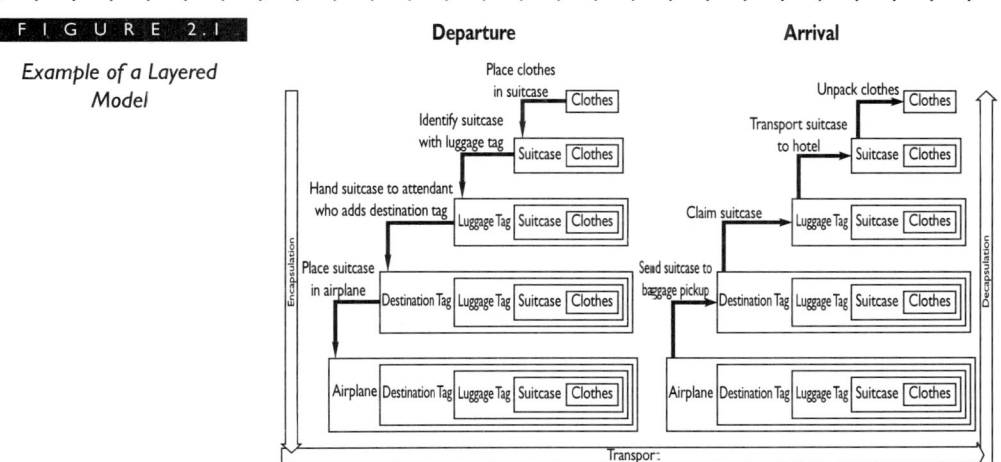

The first concept to note is *encapsulation* — that is, placing something inside a container. You place your clothes in a suitcase so you can keep them all together and label them all at once. Likewise, your suitcase is encapsulated in the plane. All of the suitcases for your flight are placed on the same plane so that they all arrive at the proper destination at the same time.

NOTE

> **The encapsulation/decapsulation process ensures that the identical data unit is present at corresponding layers in the sending and receiving protocol stacks. That is to say, the network layer data unit at the sending node is identical to the network layer data unit at the receiving node.**

The reverse of encapsulation is *decapsulation* — that is, opening containers and removing their contents. When you arrive at your destination, the luggage from your plane is removed so that each suitcase can be individually routed. Similarly, when you arrive at your hotel, you remove your clothes from the suitcase that you used to encapsulate them.

Another important concept is *routing*, which takes place at three points in the scenario:

- In Indianapolis, the suitcase is routed to your plane.

- At the intermediate airport in Denver, your suitcase is routed again. Baggage handlers examine the suitcase and decide whether it should remain in Denver or be forwarded to another flight.

- In Los Angeles, baggage handlers again examine the suitcase and determine that it has reached its final destination. They, therefore, route the suitcase to the local baggage claim area.

Figure 2.2 shows the big picture. The diagram should look familiar to you. If you substitute computers for airports, the picture resembles a typical network diagram. The difference is that, on the one hand, suitcases and airplanes are used to route clothes from one location to another. On the other hand, computer networks route data through cables. The general principles, however, are the same.

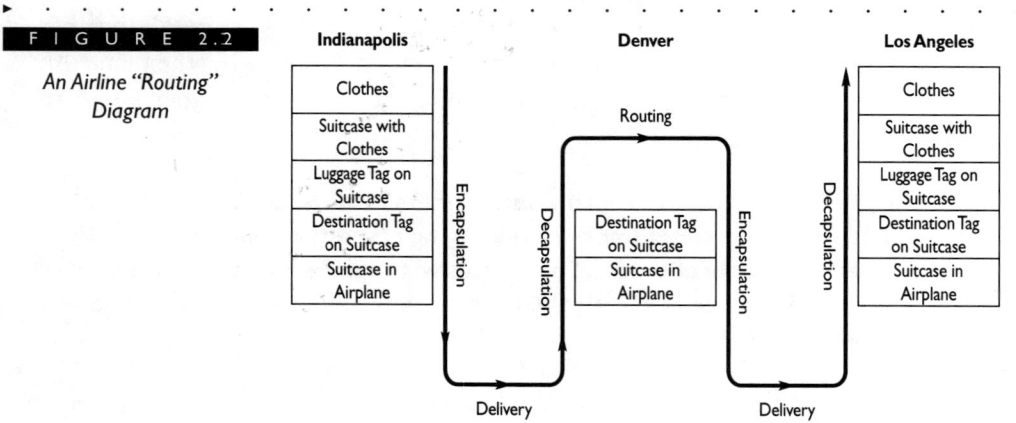

FIGURE 2.2
An Airline "Routing" Diagram

In Figure 2.2, you can see that the routing in Denver does not require complete decapsulation. Your clothes are partially decapsulated when your suitcase is unloaded from the plane, but your clothes nevertheless remain encapsulated in your suitcase. Only enough decapsulation occurs to enable baggage handlers to properly route your clothes. Keep this analogy in mind later on when I discuss network routers. (Later, you will see that routers need not always implement a complete set of protocols. They only need to implement enough protocols to allow routing to occur.)

Another key concept is *addressing*. In the suitcase analogy, routing depends on one critical piece of information: the destination tag placed on your suitcase at the beginning of the trip. This tag indicates where your suitcase needs to be delivered. The tag can be regarded as yet another form of encapsulation: Your clothes become encapsulated in a suitcase bearing a destination tag.

Routing can be performed efficiently only if a consistent labeling system is recognized at all of the locations through which luggage must be routed. Imagine the confusion that international travel would cause if every country in the world had its own unique tagging system that was not recognized in other countries. At best, travel would be much slower. At worst, your luggage would wind up lost forever. Fortunately, international agreements have resulted in fairly uniform standards for regulating commercial air travel. The common standards work fairly well because they are universally recognized.

The concept of *layering*, subdividing a complex task into multiple distinct steps, can also be understood in light of the luggage analogy. The task of transporting your suitcase from one place to another can be broken into discrete steps that occur more or less independently. The interfaces between the steps must be clearly defined. When you hand your suitcase to an attendant at your departure airport, you must present a ticket that identifies your destination. When the attendant transfers the suitcase to baggage handlers, it must have a destination tag. At each step along the way, certain previously defined conditions must be met before a transfer from one layer to another can occur.

Layering is a key concept. It involves compartmentalizing complex processes into elementary steps. Imagine how complicated baggage handling would be if each passenger had to devise a method for delivering his or her bags and personally had to execute that plan. Each passenger would want to do things differently, and chaos would ensue. As it is, the passenger is only responsible for starting and ending the process. Someone else takes care of the intermediate steps.

Layering enables you to deal with the individual processes at each layer separately. Different layers can function in their own unique ways. For example, the baggage handling in Indianapolis may proceed differently from the baggage handling in Denver. Indianapolis could use a system in which people manually transfer luggage from a conveyor belt to a cart and then onto the airplane. Denver might instead use an automated system that transfers luggage mechanically and performs routing with a computer. As long as common interfaces are used, the steps that occur at each layer can be different.

Another concept illustrated by the luggage analogy is *peer-to-peer communication*. Each layer communicates with corresponding layers at other locations. When the airline attendant places a destination tag on your suitcase, the attendant is not using the tag to communicate with you. The attendant is communicating with other baggage handlers at other airports. In other words, the baggage handler is communicating with peers.

Finally, you should be familiar with the concept of *error handling*. Given the volume of luggage transported every day, mistakes naturally occur. Those mistakes can be very costly, especially when valuable items are lost. In almost every case, more effort must be expended to correct an error than to deliver an item properly the first time. Although the airline industry spends far less on its error correction mechanisms than on its primary luggage-delivery system, its error handling system is nevertheless important.

Summary of Layered Communication

Here is a summary of the concepts that the luggage analogy helped illustrate:

▶ **Encapsulation.** The process of enclosing messages in packages so they can travel through different layers during communication.

▶ **Routing.** Procedures that ensure packages follow the most efficient paths through complex systems.

▶ **Addressing.** Conventions that are used to identify packages.

▶ **Layering.** The organization of complex processes into discrete steps that are connected to each other by certain well-defined interfaces.

▶ **Peer-to-peer communication.** Communication between corresponding layers in different locations.

▶ **Error handling**. Mechanisms that are used to detect and, if possible, correct errors.

By looking at a computer-based model (namely, the OSI Reference Model), you can see more clearly how these principles apply to network data communication.

The OSI Reference Model

Unless you understand the OSI model, you will have trouble understanding the organization of Novell protocols. Novell's Open Datalink Interface (ODI) technology is based on the OSI model, and discussion of the IPX and TCP/IP protocols necessarily involves OSI terminology. Therefore, you must be familiar with the OSI model if you want to understand NetWare TCP/IP fully.

Figure 2.3 illustrates the OSI model. At the risk of enraging OSI purists, I use a nine-layer model instead of a seven-layer model. I feel the additional layers are necessary for the following two reasons:

▶ The OSI Reference Model does not address network cabling or other media. The physical layer describes only the protocols, interfaces, and signaling for the medium. It does not include the hardware and cabling. I have added the media layer (layer 0) to represent hardware and cabling in network communication.

▶ The OSI Reference Model does not include end-user applications, such as word processors. The application layer describes the interface between user applications and the network. It does not deal with the applications themselves. I have added the user layer (layer 8) to show how end-user applications fit into the picture.

		8	User
Drew's Extended Reference Model	The Official OSI Reference Model	7	Application
		6	Presentation
		5	Session
		4	Transport
		3	Network
		2	Data Link
		1	Physical
		0	Media

The following sections describe my extended OSI Reference Model layer by layer.

NOTE   **Figure 2.3 shows why suites of protocols are commonly called protocol stacks. A suite of protocols consists of several protocols that are grouped by layer to fulfill a specific network communication function.**

The Media Layer (Layer 0)

All communication requires a medium through which the communicated information can travel. For speech, the medium is the air. For sight, the medium is light. For electronic data, the medium can be just about anything that scientists find a way to adapt.

By far the most common medium is copper cable, but fiber optics, infrared light, radio waves, and microwaves are all alternative media. Each particular medium has its own advantages and disadvantages. For example, copper is cheap and easy to install, and it performs well for most applications. But copper is not as effective when data rates are too high. Microwave, by contrast, supports high data rates and can be used to send data anyplace within the line of sight, but microwave is unbelievably expensive. Therefore, very few organizations can afford private microwave links.

The different media use a variety of methods to convey information. Information may be transmitted using high and low voltages, voltage transitions, light pulses, or changes in analog carriers. However, regardless of the method used, computer data must be transmitted as bits. One signal represents a 1; another represents a 0. That is all that is going on as far as the medium is concerned.

You need not understand how the different media operate. The basic point is: The medium is only important at the physical layer. TCP/IP couldn't care less whether messages are routed through a coax Ethernet or a laser beam. Layers make it unnecessary to adapt TCP/IP to the medium because TCP/IP isn't even aware of the medium.

The Physical Layer (Layer 1)

The first layer of the traditional OSI model is the physical layer. The physical layer is responsible for transmitting data bits to the network medium and receiving data bits from the medium. Protocols at the physical layer perform two functions that complement each other, as follows:

▶ When data moves down the protocol stack toward the network medium, the physical layer receives streams of bits from the data link layer and sends the data in electrically encoded form to the medium.

▶ When data moves up the protocol stack from the medium to the upper layers, the physical layer receives bits from the network and sends them to the data link layer.

Figure 2.4 shows how the physical layer functions. The message unit at the physical layer is the bit. The physical layer receives a stream of bits from the data link layer, which it transmits as an electrical waveform on the network. The physical layer deals only with the mechanical, electrical, and procedural interfaces required to send bits to the medium and to receive bits from the medium. Examples of issues that relate to the physical layer include:

▶ What voltages (or other signal conditions) should represent different bit values?

▶ How long should a bit last?

▶ Is communication one-way or two-way?

▶ Which wires should carry specific signals?

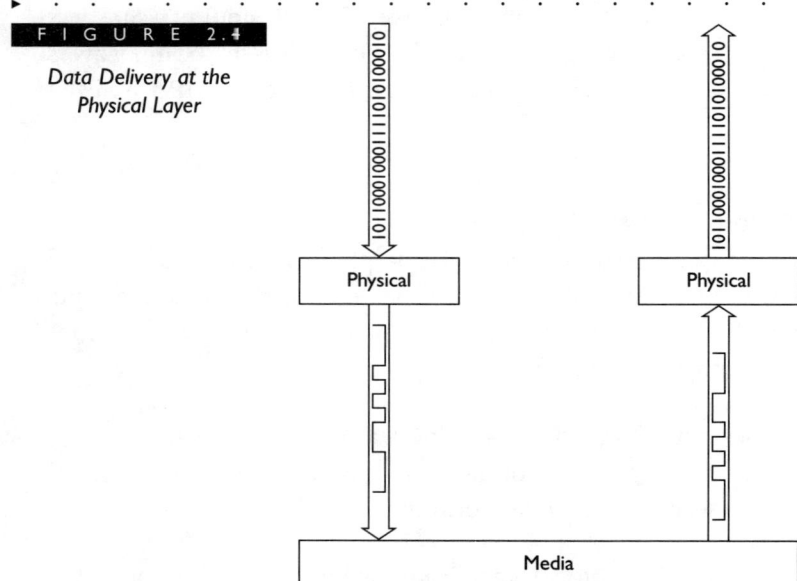

FIGURE 2.4

Data Delivery at the Physical Layer

The Data Link Layer (Layer 2)

The data link layer is responsible for delivering message units between devices on the same network. Several different names are used to describe network devices. The most common name for network devices is probably *nodes*. The data link layer is responsible for node-to-node delivery of message units. Message units are usually called *frames* at the data link layer, but they are also commonly referred to as *packets*.

The data link layer performs two functions:

▶ It provides an address mechanism that uniquely identifies each node on the local network.

▶ It receives message units from upper layers, formats the data into frames, and sends the frames as bits to the physical layer.

In *local area networks* (LANs), many nodes are attached to the same network medium. Therefore, each node sees every message that is transmitted. A node addressing scheme allows each node to tell which messages are intended for it. Node addresses uniquely identify every piece of hardware connected to a network.

In Figure 2.5, node B sends a frame to node C. To do so, node B merely creates a frame addressed to C and passes the frame to the physical layer. The frame travels through the network to nodes A and C. Node A does not recognize the node address as its own, so it discards the frame. Node C recognizes the address and therefore receives the frame.

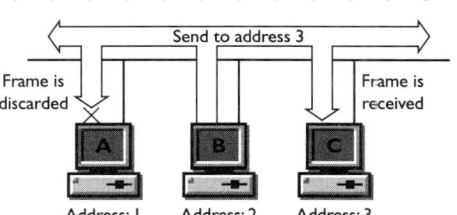

FIGURE 2.5

Delivery of a Frame on the Network

Node addresses are often referred to as *physical addresses* because these addresses are typically coded into the network interface's hardware. Node addresses are also sometimes called *MAC addresses* because the Institute of Electrical and Electronics Engineers (IEEE) protocols such as 802.3 (IEEE Ethernet) and 802.5 (Token Ring) define a *medium access control* (MAC) sublayer at which addressing takes place. I prefer to use the term "physical address."

The information needed to deliver data is encoded into frames, which the data link layer constructs. The format of a typical frame is shown in Figure 2.6. A frame consists of several parts called fields. The various fields are as follows:

▶ **Start Indicator.** A bit pattern that indicates where a frame begins.

▶ **Destination Address.** The physical address of the destination node.

▸ **Source Address.** The physical address of the node that sent the frame.

▸ **Control Information.** Protocol-dependent data that serves a variety of control functions.

▸ **Data.** Data received from upper layers. This is the frame's payload.

▸ **Error Control.** A value that can be used to determine whether a frame has been damaged during transmission.

Start Indicator	Destination Address	Source Address	Control Information	Data	Error Control

FIGURE 2.6

Structure of a Typical Frame

Because the physical layer can only handle bits, the data link layer must organize bits into the proper message structure. The data link layer accomplishes this by adding special bit patterns to the beginnings and ends of frames. After adding the framing information to a frame, the data link layer transmits the frame to the physical layer in the form of a stream of binary digits.

Examples of data link–layer protocols are Ethernet and Token Ring. (Both protocols are also used at the physical layer.) Chapter 3 explains Ethernet and Token Ring, along with other protocols.

The Network Layer (Layer 3)

The message delivery depicted in Figure 2.5 is very basic. But what happens when more than one network is involved? Figure 2.7 shows what happens when data travels from one network to another. When B sends a frame to E, the frame circulates throughout network 1, where it originated. However, none of the devices on network 1 will find its address in the destination address field. Although C is connected to both network 1 and network 2, some functionality above and beyond the data link layer must be added to enable C to forward the frame from one network to another. The term *bridging* is used to describe the transfer of frames between networks. (Bridging is discussed in more detail later in this chapter.)

The network shown in Figure 2.7 is typically called an *internetwork* because it is a network of networks. Node C, which is connected to both networks, is called a *router* because it routes messages from one network to another. Often, routing involves the selection of the best route through a complex internetwork.

In order for routers to work, each network must have its own unique *network address*. Routers build tables that contain network addresses for all of the networks on an internetwork. These network addresses must be encoded into messages at the network layer. When a router finds a network address in a message, it sends the message on its way to the appropriate destination network. Each node on an internetwork can be identified by the combination of its network address and its physical address.

FIGURE 2.7

Delivering a Frame on an Internetwork

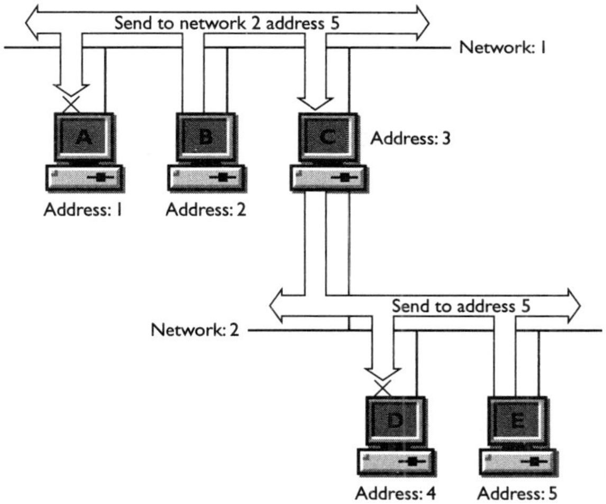

Consequently, nodes on an internetwork can be categorized in two ways:

► *End nodes* are the endpoints of a communication. At the network layer, end nodes add network addresses to message units. End nodes do not perform routing. The OSI term for an end node is *end system*. The traditional TCP/IP term for an end node is *host*.

▶ *Intermediate nodes* are routers. They forward messages through internetworks. Intermediate nodes must be equipped with a routing function so they can determine routes and forward messages. A router can be a dedicated piece of equipment, or it can be a device that also serves another purpose (such as a NetWare server or a TCP/IP host to which a routing function has been added). The OSI term for intermediate node is *intermediate system*. The TCP/IP term has traditionally been *gateway*, but the term *router* has recently become more popular.

Network-layer message units are usually called *packets*. Novell's network-layer protocol is *Internet Packet Exchange* (IPX). The TCP/IP network-layer protocol is the *Internet Protocol* (IP). IP's message units are called *datagrams*, which is discussed later in this chapter under the heading "Packet Switching."

The Transport Layer (Layer 4)

Here are some of the transport layer's functions:

▶ If a message is too big for layers 0 through 3 to handle, the transport layer breaks the message into smaller units that the network can handle.

▶ The transport layer can make delivery more reliable by detecting errors and requesting that damaged message units be resent.

▶ On multitasking hosts, the transport layer ensures that messages are delivered to the correct processes.

Each of these important functions are discussed in the subsections that follow.

Message Fragmentation and Reassembly

When you are determining the maximum message size that your network will accommodate, you must strike a balance. If the maximum message size is too large, a single transmission could monopolize the network for too long. Therefore, a relatively small cap is usually placed on network frame size. An Ethernet data frame, for example, accepts a maximum of 1500 bytes of data.

Because the majority of messages on your network will probably exceed 1500 bytes in length, you need some way to break up large messages into small pieces. That method is called *message fragmentation*. The transport layer accepts a continuous stream of data from upper-layer protocols and buffers the data until the amount reaches the maximum that a frame can accommodate. Each message fragment, called a segment, is tagged with a sequence number. The sequence numbers are used at the receiving end to reassemble the segments in their original order and recover the message. Segment numbers are necessary on packet switching networks because segments may not arrive in the order they were sent. Figure 2.8 illustrates how segments may take different routes through an internetwork and arrive out of order.

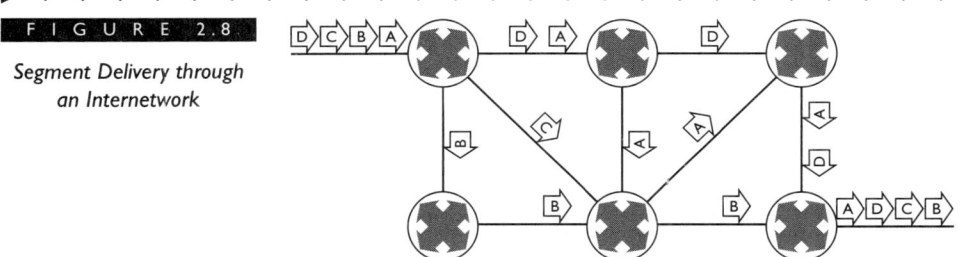

FIGURE 2.8

Segment Delivery through an Internetwork

Error Detection and Recovery of Data

Although error detection and recovery of data may occur at any protocol level, these functions are usually performed by the transport-layer protocols. The transport-layer protocols ensure that all the segments related to a message are received without error. That task makes the process of detecting errors and recovering data extremely complicated. Typically, transport-layer protocols employ a system of acknowledgments. The transport layer at the receiving node must acknowledge that it has received individual segments or groups of segments. The sending transport layer then resends segments for which it has not received acknowledgments.

When a network's messages need to be absolutely free of errors, that network can employ *reliable delivery* protocols. When you use reliable delivery protocols, errors may still occur, but the errors are detected and then corrected. Certain costs are associated with reliable delivery. Acknowledgments take up network bandwidth, and additional processing is required when the sending and receiving nodes must track each segment and determine whether it has been acknowledged.

Because reliable delivery can be costly, sometimes it makes sense to assume that messages will be delivered properly. For example, if messages are short and relatively unimportant, it probably does not matter if a few messages are occasionally lost. You probably don't need reliable delivery for your network-management data. If a device sends an alert that is lost, it can always resend the message after a delay. Also, reliable delivery can unnecessarily add overhead to networks that are basically pretty reliable, such as LANs.

When the cost of reliable delivery outweighs the benefits, network designers turn to *unreliable delivery* methods. With unreliable delivery, errors are not automatically detected and corrected. However, if the transport layer does not perform error recovery, a higher-level protocol (or even an application) can take on the responsibility of detecting errors.

Usually, NetWare does not provide reliable delivery at its transport-level protocol. Because LAN delivery is generally error-free, NetWare's designers decided not to sacrifice performance for the sake of reliable delivery. Error recovery is performed by the *NetWare Core Protocols* (NCP), which work in conjunction with IPX at the network layer. When reliable delivery is required, NetWare uses the *Sequenced Packet Exchange* (SPX) protocol.

In the TCP/IP protocol suite, the *Transmission Control Protocol* (TCP) provides reliable delivery. Because TCP/IP is commonly used in relatively unreliable *wide area network* (WAN) environments, the majority of TCP/IP services rely on TCP for reliable delivery. When unreliable delivery is acceptable, the *User Datagram Protocol* (UDP) can be substituted for TCP.

Protocol Multiplexing

The majority of computers are multitasking devices, meaning that they can run several processes at once. Multitasking complicates matters on a network. Not only does a network need to deliver messages to the right computers, each message must also be directed to the correct process on each computer.

The OSI protocol model solves this problem by assigning a *service access point* (SAP) to each protocol. A SAP is a number that serves as an address. Each message has three identifiers: a network address, a physical address, and an SAP. The combination of these three numbers ensures that the message will reach the correct process on the correct computer. Figure 2.9 illustrates how SAPs are used to deliver messages to processes.

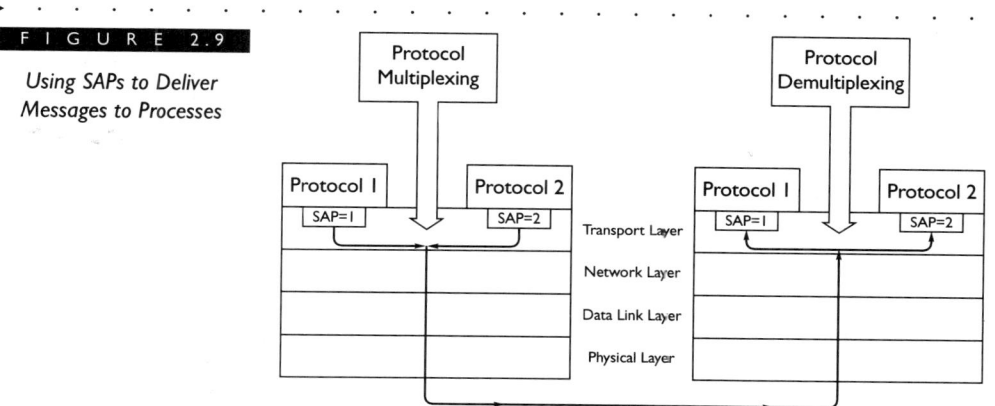

FIGURE 2.9

Using SAPs to Deliver Messages to Processes

Service access points allow the transport layer to combine messages from several processes and send those messages through a common network interface. That process is called *multiplexing*. At the receiving end, the transport layer does the reverse: it recovers separate messages from the single incoming stream of data. The process of recovering the original messages is called *demultiplexing*.

The Session Layer (Layer 5)

Usually, network computers engage in two-way communication. In other words, computers typically have *dialogs*. The primary function of the session layer is to control those dialogs.

The three modes of communication between computers are:

▶ **Simplex.** Data travels in one direction. One node transmits and the other receives.

▶ **Half-Duplex.** Data travels in both directions. Both nodes can transmit and receive. However, the nodes must take turns because the medium cannot accommodate simultaneous transmissions.

> **Full-Duplex.** Data travels in both directions. Both nodes can transmit and receive data simultaneously. (Each node can send and receive at the same time.)

Figure 2.10 illustrates the three modes.

Full-duplex operation is the most desirable mode of network communication. To make full-duplex work, a network needs some form of flow control so that a node does not send data more rapidly than the data can be received. On data networks, the orderly exchange of data between two nodes is called a *session*. (In reality, most LANs do not permit multiple messages on a medium at a given time. Therefore, full-duplex communication is not — strictly speaking — simultaneous. Nevertheless, from the end nodes' standpoint, full-duplex communication does appear to be simultaneous.)

A session establishes a *virtual connection* between two computers on a network. The computers behave as though a dedicated communication channel existed between them, even though they are sharing a medium with many other computers. A virtual connection is necessary for reliable delivery.

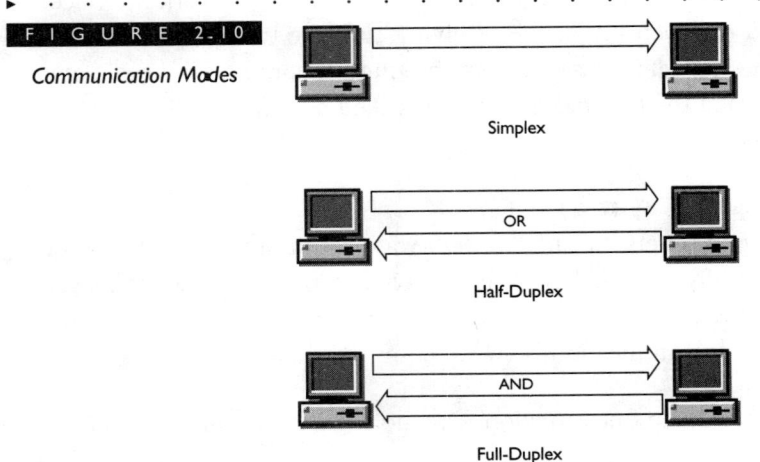

FIGURE 2.10

Communication Modes

Simplex

Half-Duplex

Full-Duplex

The session layer's primary job is management of sessions. Each session has three phases:

1. **Connection establishment.** This is the special process during which two computers agree to communicate. Many things can be decided during connection establishment, including the protocols to be used, the error control parameters, and the limitations on the size of messages.

2. **Data exchange.** During most of the session, the computers exchange data in an orderly manner. A session may last a short time or it may be of indefinite duration.

3. **Connection release.** This is the distinct process in which the computers terminate the connection. (The process is also sometimes called *tear down.*) Failure to release a connection can invalidate the data transmitted, or it can leave the processes in limbo.

Connections often make considerable demands on a system. Those demands may be justifiable when network errors are likely — for example, on WANs — or when errors cannot be tolerated. However, sometimes the cost of having connections cannot be justified. For example, if a node only transmits short, infrequent messages, it may require more effort to build, maintain, and tear down connections than to send the data. That would be a disproportionate use of network bandwidth. In cases where the cost of having connections cannot be justified, *connectionless delivery* can be used. With connectionless delivery, a connection need not be established or released. The sending computer simply transmits data without any assurance that it will be received.

The Presentation Layer (Layer 6)

Not all computers are alike. For example, most computers use ASCII character codes, but IBM mainframes use a system called EBCDIC. The numerous differences among computers make it difficult for computers to exchange data.

The presentation layer's job is to overcome those differences by presenting data to upper-layer protocols in a uniform format. This often involves using a standard to represent data so that the data can be understood by different computer hardware and software systems. Computers typically do not arrive from the factory with the standards included, but all computers can be programmed to understand standard formats. In the OSI realm, the standard is called *Abstract*

Syntax Notation, Revision 1 (ASN.1). In TCP/IP, an example of a standard format is the *External Data Representation* (XDR) format, which Sun's *Network File System* (NFS) protocol uses. You will learn more about NFS in Chapter 6.

The presentation layer can also be used for encryption and decryption and for compression and decompression of data. When data formats are converted as data travels from an application to a network, the conversion can be performed at the presentation layer.

In practice, presentation-layer protocols are seldom implemented. The presentation layer often simply passes data unaltered between the session and application layers. For example, data encryption and decryption are often performed by the applications themselves. Likewise, data compression and decompression are often performed by network hardware, such as compression modems. In reality, presentation-layer protocols are very rare.

The Application Layer (Layer 7)

From its name, you might assume that the application layer involves familiar applications like WordPerfect and Lotus 1-2-3 — that is, the applications that users operate directly. However, you would be mistaken. In the OSI Reference Model, the term *application layer* means something else. The application layer is the interface that allows applications to connect to the network.

Some application-layer protocols provide the foundation of network services. For example, Novell's *Message Handling Service* (MHS) and TCP/IP's *Simple Mail Transfer Protocol* (SMTP) are protocols that enable e-mail applications to send, receive, and manage electronic mail.

Application program interfaces (APIs) are an important component of the application layer. An API is an interface that programmers use to connect their programs to a system. For example, Novell's *NetWare Core Protocol* (NCP) is an API that programmers use to build NetWare-aware applications. In TCP/IP, some common APIs are:

- ▶ Berkeley Sockets (or BSD Sockets), popularized by 4.3BSD UNIX

- ▶ Streams *Transport Layer Interface* (TLI), developed by AT&T

- ▶ Windows Sockets (Winsock), designed for the Microsoft Windows environment and based on BSD Sockets

NetWare servers support applications written for the Sockets and TLI APIs. Application-level protocols are associated with a wide variety of network services in addition to electronic mail. Here are some others:

- **Remote file services.** Application-level protocols are necessary for the remote file services provided by systems such as Novell's NetWare and Sun's NFS. NetWare enables user applications to access files on NetWare servers. NFS enables TCP/IP hosts to mount remote file systems and use them as if they were local.

- **Remote job execution.** This service enables users to initiate programs that execute on remote computers.

- **Naming services and directories.** These services provide a catalog of a network's computers and shared resources. The catalogs use logical names so users and applications do not need network and node addresses.

- **Network management.** Some protocols — for example, *Simple Network Management Protocol* (SNMP) — enable computers to send alerts and statistics to management consoles. These protocols also allow management consoles to change operating parameters of network devices.

The User Layer (Layer 8)

The final layer of my extended version of the OSI model is the user layer. The user layer consists of the programs that the end users run. Depending on the interface with the application layer, certain programs may be able to access the network without being network-aware. Because networks have become so popular, most applications now conform to one or more APIs. You may have already specified API calls without realizing what you were doing. For instance, when you install WordPerfect and specify NetWare operation, you are in fact indicating which API calls you want WordPerfect to use.

The DoD Protocol Model

Although there are several different names for the protocol model associated with TCP/IP, the model is often referred to as the DoD model because the protocols originated at the U.S. Department of Defense. It is also frequently referred to as the Internet model.

The DoD model was created before the OSI model existed. Consequently, the four-layer Internet model does not fit neatly into the OSI model. Nevertheless, in Figure 2.11 you can see how the layers of the Internet model correspond more or less to the layers of the OSI Reference Model.

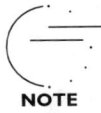

NOTE **Because the layers of the two models do not correspond exactly, you may find variations on this diagram in other sources. Different people are bound to conceptualize the layers differently. There is not a single "right" way to compare the two models.**

FIGURE 2.11

Comparison of the DoD and OSI Protocol Models

OSI Reference Model	Internet Model
Application	Process/Application
Presentation	
Session	
Transport	Host-to-Host
Network	Internet
Data Link	Network Access
Physical	

The following paragraphs give you an overview of the layers of the DoD protocol stack. Later chapters examine each layer in more detail.

The network access layer enables TCP/IP hosts to communicate with other hosts on a network. The network access layer corresponds roughly to the data link and physical layers of the OSI model. At the network access layer, hosts are identified by physical addresses that are used for local delivery of messages. You should keep in mind that TCP/IP was designed to operate over existing network types. The creators of TCP/IP have not defined their own network types. You may occasionally need to adapt TCP/IP to a particular type of network (several RFCs discuss adaptation issues). The network access layer is the subject of Chapter 3.

The internet layer — covered in Chapter 4 — delivers messages through internetworks. The internet layer corresponds to the network layer of the OSI model. The internet layer is primarily associated with one protocol, the *Internet Protocol* (IP), which delivers messages (called *datagrams*) between hosts on an internetwork. The internet layer uses logical addresses to identify hosts. The logical addresses (called *IP addresses*) incorporate both network and host identifiers that IP uses for routing. An *address resolution protocol* (ARP) is used to map IP addresses to the network access layer's physical addresses.

The host-to-host layer corresponds to the OSI transport layer. The host-to-host layer performs message fragmentation and assembly, as well as message multiplexing. The host-to-host layer may provide reliable delivery. The Internet uses two protocols at this level. The *Transmission Control Protocol* (TCP) provides fully reliable service, and it is therefore used most often. When unreliable service is acceptable, the *User Datagram Protocol* (UDP) can be employed. You learn more about the host-to-host layer in Chapter 5.

The process/application layer — discussed in Chapter 6 — includes a wide variety of protocols, processes, and applications that depends on the host-to-host layer to provide a network interface. You can see the richness of TCP/IP at the process/application layer. Here are just a few examples of the many services supported by TCP/IP:

- ▶ **File Transfer Protocol (FTP).** Supports transfer of files between systems and lets users access file systems remotely.

- ▶ **Telnet.** Provides remote terminal capability. With Telnet, users can utilize different networked computers for terminal sessions.

- ▶ **Simple Mail Transfer Protocol (SMTP).** Serves as the standard protocol for delivering electronic mail over the Internet.

- ▶ **Simple Network Management Protocol (SNMP).** Enables network administrators to collect network-management information and to manage network devices remotely.

▶ **Network File System (NFS).** Enables users to mount remote file systems as if the files were local. NFS lets users share file systems on remote computers.

The process/application layer does not correspond exactly to the layers of the OSI model. Some applications perform functions that correspond to several OSI levels. FTP, for example, manages user sessions. As I mentioned earlier, session management is a function of the session layer in the OSI model. FTP also converts file formats when they are transferred between different systems. In the OSI model, format conversion is handled by the presentation layer. FTP can also be used for file transfers, which is a function of the application layer in the OSI model.

Figure 2.12 shows several important TCP/IP protocols and how they correspond to the DoD protocol model.

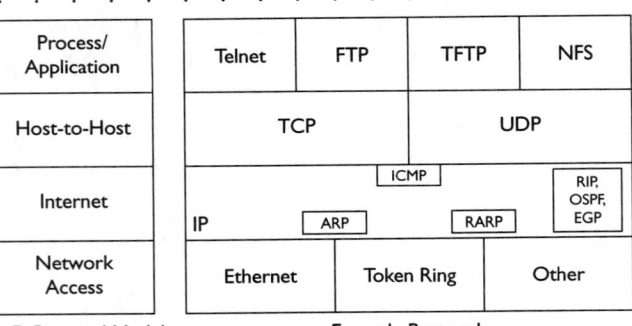

F I G U R E 2.12

Relationship of TCP/IP Protocols to the DoD Protocol Model

More on Protocol Models

Now that you have seen two different protocol models, a few additional observations may be made.

As you know, protocol layers must communicate with each other. For example, the network layer of one computer sends network addresses to the network layers on other computers. In order for communication between corresponding layers to take place, you need to use message formats that can be understood by all of the layers in the sending and receiving protocol stacks. Effective communication between all of the layers is possible because each layer builds on what it receives from other layers.

The OSI term for the messages that a protocol layer sends to the next lower layer is *protocol data units* (PDUs). Each layer adds its information in the form of a header that is appended to the start of the PDU received from an upper layer. Figure 2.13 illustrates the process for the network and transport layers. The network layer constructs a network PDU by appending its header information to the transport layer PDU that is to be sent. When the network layer receives a frame from the network, it strips off the network header to recover the original transport layer PDU, which is forwarded to the transport layer.

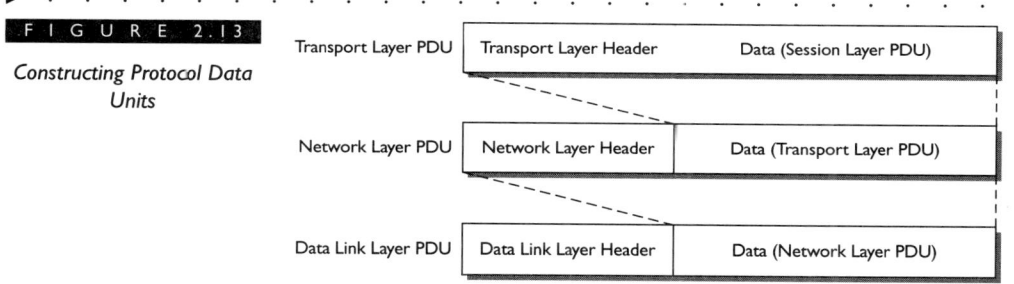

FIGURE 2.13

Constructing Protocol Data Units

The process of packaging information from higher layers into new PDUs is called *encapsulation*. In Figure 2.13, transport layer data is encapsulated in the network layer PDU, and network layer data is encapsulated in the data link layer PDU. The processes of encapsulation and decapsulation take place at each layer of sending and receiving protocol stacks. Figure 2.14 illustrates the complete process. Notice that the data link layer typically adds a trailer as well. This trailer contains codes that can be used to detect network transmission errors.

Each layer (except possibly the physical layer) has a specific header format. This header information is used by the corresponding layer at the receiving end. In other words, each protocol communicates with its peer protocol in the receiving computer. This type of communication is called *peer-to-peer communication*.

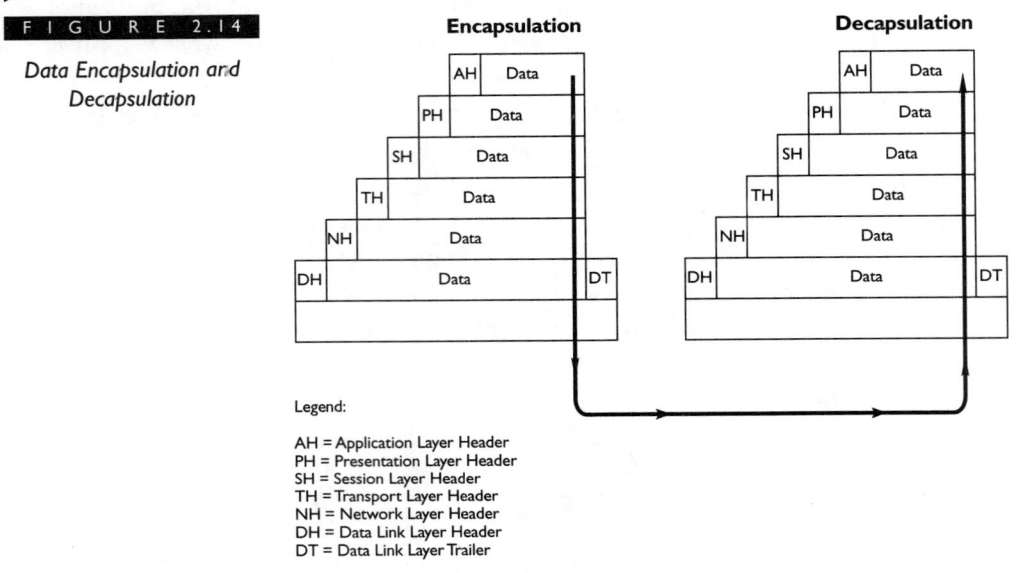

FIGURE 2.14

Data Encapsulation and Decapsulation

Legend:

AH = Application Layer Header
PH = Presentation Layer Header
SH = Session Layer Header
TH = Transport Layer Header
NH = Network Layer Header
DH = Data Link Layer Header
DT = Data Link Layer Trailer

Data Communication Technologies

Network communication is a complex process. Large networks can have many computers that all need to communicate with each other. Combinations of different network types can make network communication even more complicated. This section discusses several important technologies that make complex networks possible with the following questions in mind:

▶ When several messages must be sent through a single communication channel, how can the messages share the channel yet still retain their distinct identities?

▶ When messages travel through complex networks, how can the messages be switched through the available paths?

▶ When messages are switched through different paths, how does the network determine the best route for messages to take?

Multiplexing

Often, many data streams need to share the same communication channel. Sometimes only a single channel is available. Or it may be too costly to pay for more than one channel. Or a channel may have very high bandwidth, and it may be inefficient to dedicate the entire channel to a single data stream. The technology that allows multiple streams of data to share a single communication channel is called *multiplexing*.

This section examines two types of multiplexing: *protocol multiplexing*, which occurs in protocol stacks, and *signal multiplexing*, which takes place in data communication channels.

Protocol Multiplexing

You saw an example of protocol multiplexing earlier in this chapter's transport layer section. Using service access points, the transport layer delivers messages to the appropriate protocols in higher layers. But the transport layer is not the only layer that uses protocol multiplexing. For example, protocol multiplexing is used in other layers in each of the following cases:

▶ When the data link layer must recognize several different types of Ethernet frame types and enable them to share a network interface card.

▶ When the data link layer must determine where to deliver messages (that is, which is the appropriate protocol stack). For example, both IPX and TCP/IP protocol stacks may be present.

▶ When the network layer must determine where to deliver messages (that is, which is the correct transport protocol). For example, the network layer might have to decide between TCP and UDP.

▶ When the transport layer must deliver messages to the correct upper-layer application, such as FTP, Telnet, or SMTP.

Figure 2.15 illustrates how protocol multiplexing can take place at virtually any protocol level.

Protocol Multiplexing

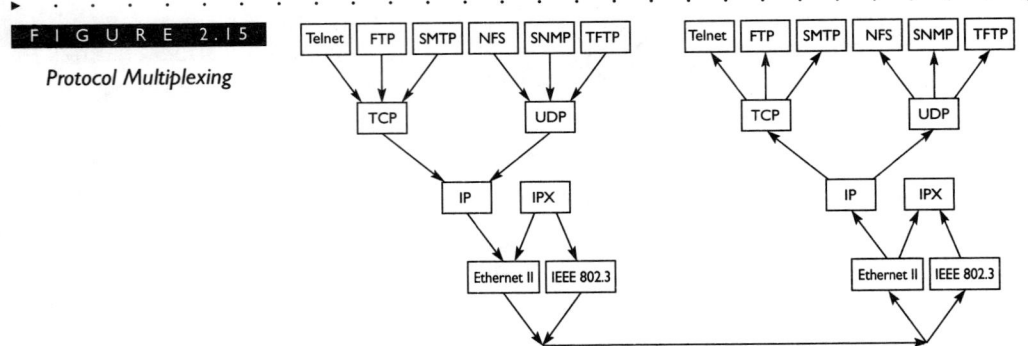

Signal Multiplexing

Baseband media are media that support a single data stream. LANs often use baseband media. Ethernet and Token Ring assume a baseband medium is in use, and they both employ mechanisms to ensure that only one node can transmit at a time.

Broadband media are media that can carry multiple data steams simultaneously. Broadband media are common as well. Microwaves, fiber optics, and coaxial cables are all examples of broadband media. With these media, multiplexing is necessary so that multiple data streams can share the bandwidth of the medium at the same time.

Digital data can be multiplexed using a technique called *time-division multiplexing* (TDM). The bandwidth of the medium is broken into multiple time slots, which are allocated to the data streams transmitted. Figure 2.16 illustrates how TDM works. The multiplexer and demultiplexer are synchronized. They associate each time slot with the correct data stream. The data streams take turns using the data capacity of the medium.

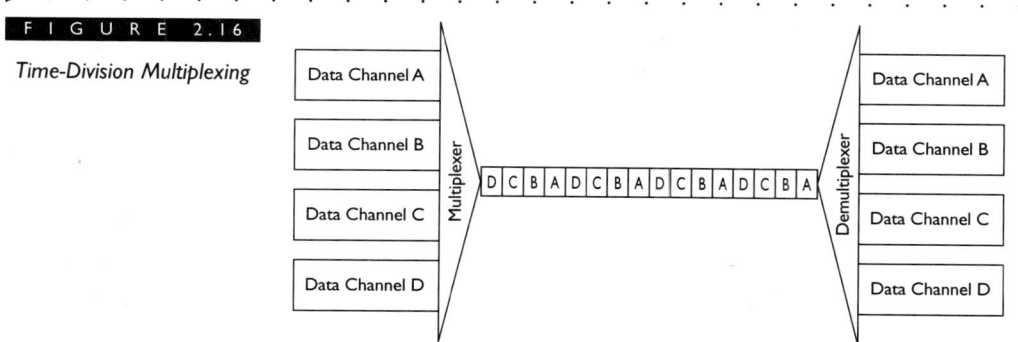

FIGURE 2.16

Time-Division Multiplexing

Time-division multiplexing works well if all data streams are equally busy. If the traffic levels in the data streams are uneven, however, some time slots may be underutilized, and other time slots may not be able to handle the data streams that are allocated to them. A technique called *statistical TDM* allocates time slots based on how busy the data streams are. Figure 2.17 illustrates statistical TDM. In Figure 2.17, the time slots are no longer allocated in a fixed sequence. Each time slot is assigned a data stream based on need. In the diagram, data stream B is the busiest, and therefore it receives the most time slots. Data stream D is silent, and so it does not receive any time slots.

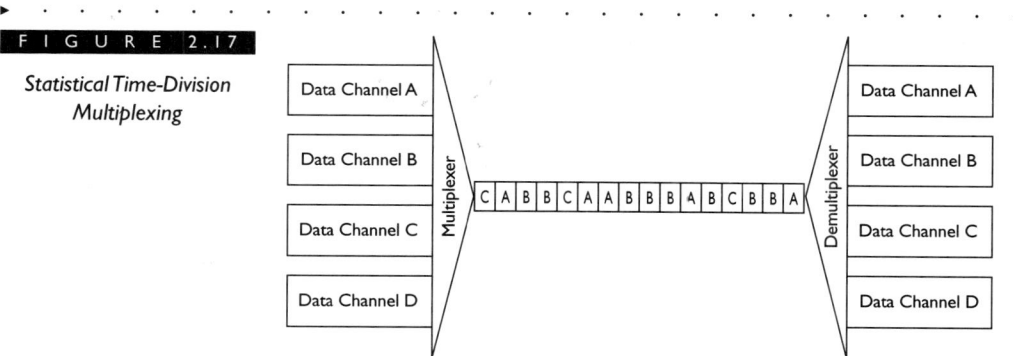

FIGURE 2.17

Statistical Time-Division Multiplexing

Switching Data through Internetworks

Networks are frequently designed so that two or more paths are available between nodes. Having multiple paths provides a backup in case one of the paths fails. Furthermore, having multiple paths can increase network data capacity because you then have the option of using all of the pathways simultaneously, if necessary. However, multiple paths present a problem: How should messages be switched through the available pathways to reach their destinations? There are two common techniques for switching messages: circuit switching and packet switching.

Circuit Switching

Circuit switching works much like the public telephone system. When you pick up a phone and call a friend, the telephone system creates a path between your phone and your friend's phone. A circuit is established between the two telephones. (At one time, the circuit consisted of an actual copper wire that you could trace from one phone to the other. Today, several types of media are used.) From your point of view, a portion of the network is dedicated completely to your personal use.

A circuit-switched data network is shown in Figure 2.18. When two nodes establish a session, a circuit is created through the internetwork. All traffic between the endpoints travels through this circuit. The connected computers are guaranteed a certain amount of bandwidth devoted to their use. Also, circuit switching pre-establishes a path through the network. Because there is a pre-established path, circuit switching delivers messages reliably and with few delays.

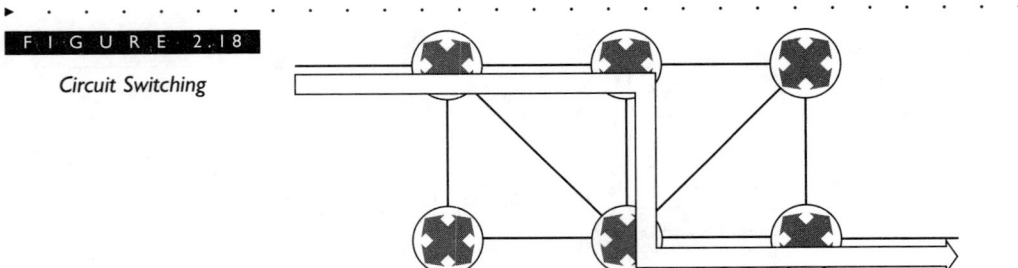

FIGURE 2.18

Circuit Switching

Circuit switching has disadvantages, however. If the circuit's dedicated bandwidth is not fully used, a portion of the network's overall bandwidth is wasted. Furthermore, if the network temporarily requires extra capacity, the circuit may need to be torn down and reestablished with greater bandwidth. Therefore, circuit switching is seldom used for data communication. One exception is *asynchronous transfer mode* (ATM). Chapter 3 demonstrates how ATM is able to benefit from the advantages of circuit switching without the problem of inefficient bandwidth utilization.

In real-world implementations, it is highly unlikely that a dedicated physical circuit could ever be traced through a network. Circuits are usually multiplexed through high-bandwidth media. Nevertheless, from the standpoint of the users at both ends, a dedicated circuit appears to exist.

Packet Switching

Because circuit switching typically wastes network capacity, the vast majority of LANs and WANs employ *packet switching*. With packet switching, messages are broken into pieces, and each piece contains information that identifies the source and destination computers. (In the early days of the technology, the pieces were usually called *packets*. Today, they are often called *frames*.) The identification information is used by the switches to route the pieces through the network. Refer back to Figure 2.8 for a diagram of how packet switching works.

Packet switching has several advantages over circuit switching. With packet switching, bandwidth is available on demand. Bandwidth is not dedicated, and therefore bandwidth is never wasted. Also, because a circuit is not established through the network, switches may change the routes they use from time to time. If a switch·discovers that a new route would be more efficient (for example, when the current route is congested), the switch can choose the new path.

Two types of service are available on packet switching networks:

▸ *Connectionless* service does not establish a formal connection between the end nodes. Each packet is treated as a separate entity, and is routed through the internet independently, based on address information embedded in the packet. Packets that are treated in this manner are referred to as *datagrams*, and connectionless service is sometimes called datagram service. Because a formal connection is not established, connectionless service is unreliable. In other words, the network cannot be counted on to detect errors. With connectionless service, error detection and correction are the responsibility of upper-layer protocols.

▸ *Connection-oriented* service establishes a formal connection that gives the packet switching network the appearance of a dedicated circuit (at least from the perspective of the endpoints). Because this type of service behaves like a dedicated connection, the circuits established are called *virtual circuits*. Virtual circuits provide reliable delivery, and errors are detected and corrected.

An example of unreliable (connectionless) communication in the real world occurs when a company sends out a direct mail advertisement. The recipients do not expect to receive the communication. Furthermore, short of calling everyone who receives the mailing, there is no way for the company to confirm delivery. The individual pieces of mail sent out by the company are comparable to the datagrams transmitted during connectionless service.

Physical versus Virtual

The terms *physical* and *virtual* are often used when networks are discussed. As a rule, you can distinguish the physical from the virtual by following these rules:

▶ If you can see or touch it, it is physical.

▶ If you can't see or touch it, it is virtual.

What you see on a network isn't always what you get. For example, you may think a computer is using a dedicated circuit, but the circuit may in fact be multiplexed. In that case, the circuit is called a virtual circuit.

Bridging and Routing

You have learned that packets can be switched through internetworks. However, this chapter has not yet explained how routes are selected. The two main techniques used to select routes are bridging and routing. The protocol layer where the routing decision takes place determines which term should be applied.

Bridging

At the data link layer, *bridging* uses physical addresses to make routing decisions. Figure 2.19 illustrates a typical bridging network. Bridges examine all of the frames that pass by them. Eventually, a bridge can ascertain the physical addresses that can be reached from the various networks connected to the bridge.

In the diagram, bridge A cannot tell whether node B is attached to a nearby network or a distant network. Bridge A knows only that if it receives a frame from network 1 that should go to node B, the frame should be forwarded to network 2. Bridge A is totally unaware that B is on a remote network.

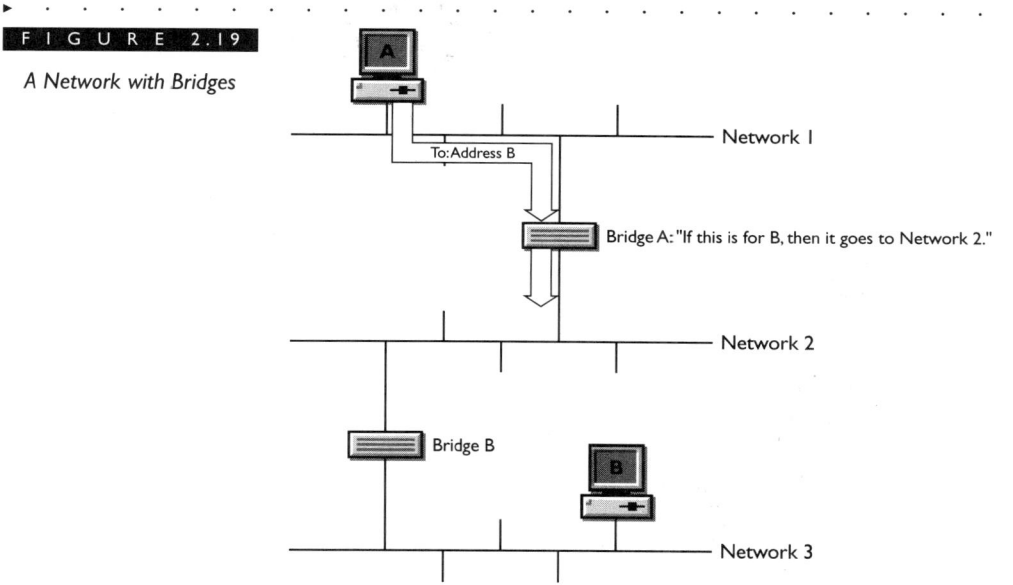

FIGURE 2.19

A Network with Bridges

Bridging takes place at the data link layer of the protocol stack. Figure 2.20 illustrates what takes place at the bridge. An incoming frame is forwarded to the data link layer, where the address information is recovered. The address information is used to select the interface that should be used to forward the frame, which is then sent down through the protocol stack and on to the appropriate destination.

Notice that the bridge implements a separate protocol stack for each attached network. In theory, these protocol stacks could be different and a bridge could be used to connect one type of network to another — for example, an Ethernet to a Token Ring. In practice, this is seldom the case. As you will see in Chapter 3, networks at the physical layer are quite different from networks at the data link layer. Consequently, few bridges have been developed that can successfully connect different types of networks.

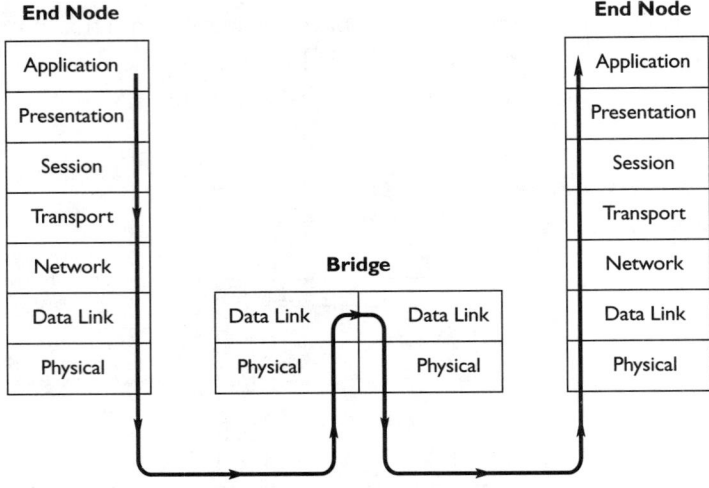

FIGURE 2.20

A Protocol Stack Model of Bridging

NOTE

A growing trend is to deploy devices called *LAN switches* to improve network bandwidth. In its simplest form, a **LAN** switch is a high-speed bridge that is equipped with large numbers of ports. Several techniques improve the speed with which switches can forward frames. Unlike bridges, switches typically do not bother to buffer the entire packet before forwarding. Instead, the switch examines the frame only until the destination physical address field is reached, at which point, the **LAN** switch begins to forward the packet immediately. The remainder of the frame is forwarded without processing, other than regeneration of the signal.

Because most of the frame contents are ignored, a **LAN** switch cannot use the error control field to detect errors in transmission. This tradeoff between speed and reliability is frequently worthwhile on **LANs**, which are typically very reliable. Because switches, like bridges, ignore network addresses, they cannot be used as the connecting points to create internetworks.

Bridging has some limitations. The principle limitation is that bridging cannot handle networks that provide multiple routes to a destination. Loops develop, and the network clogs with endlessly circulating traffic. An approach called the *spanning-tree algorithm* enables bridging networks to include redundant paths, but the network is logically configured so that redundant paths are only used if one of the paths fails. Then the extra paths are used to provide new routes. Spanning-tree neither enables bridges to select the best possible routes, nor gives bridges the ability to use different routes when network conditions change.

Network addresses, visible at the OSI network layer, are used to create internetworks consisting of multiple, distinctly identified networks. Internetworks are necessary for a variety of reasons. Many network topologies impose limits on the number of nodes that can be attached to the same cable segment. To expand beyond that limit, an internetwork is required. Also, TCP/IP allocates node addresses in classes, which have a limited number of available addresses. A class C address, for example, supports a maximum of 254 node addresses. To expand beyond the node limits of a class, multiple network addresses are required and an internetwork must be deployed. Bridges ignore network layer information and are ignorant of network addresses. As a result of this ignorance, bridges cannot be used to create internetworks. Therefore, there is always a limit on the extent to which a bridged network can expand.

Source routing is an alternative to traditional bridging. With source routing, a node broadcasts a frame called a *discovery frame* to the network. Each time the discovery frame crosses a bridge, it collects the route information. When a discovery frame reaches the destination node, it has collected enough information to describe a complete route between the endpoints. The discovery frame then returns to the original node, which adds the route information to each frame it transmits. Although Token Ring uses source routing to route packets, processing takes place at the data link layer. Therefore, Token Ring really uses bridging. However, because each Token Ring frame includes complete routing information, bridging decisions need not be made en route.

NOTE

Hybrid devices exist that perform various combinations of bridging and routing. These devices are called bridging routers, or routing bridges, or *brouters*. There is no one accepted method to combine bridging and routing functions. Therefore, this book discusses only bridges and routers, and does not attempt to describe all of the variations that exist.

Routing

At the network level, route decisions are made by a process called *routing*, which uses the network addresses. Network address information is used to build a logical picture of a network in the form of a *routing table* that describes how messages should be routed to destination networks. Because routers deal with relatively few networks, routing tables can make fairly complex routing decisions. A routing table can build a detailed picture of where networks are and the best way to reach them.

Figure 2.21 shows an internetwork consisting of six distinct networks.

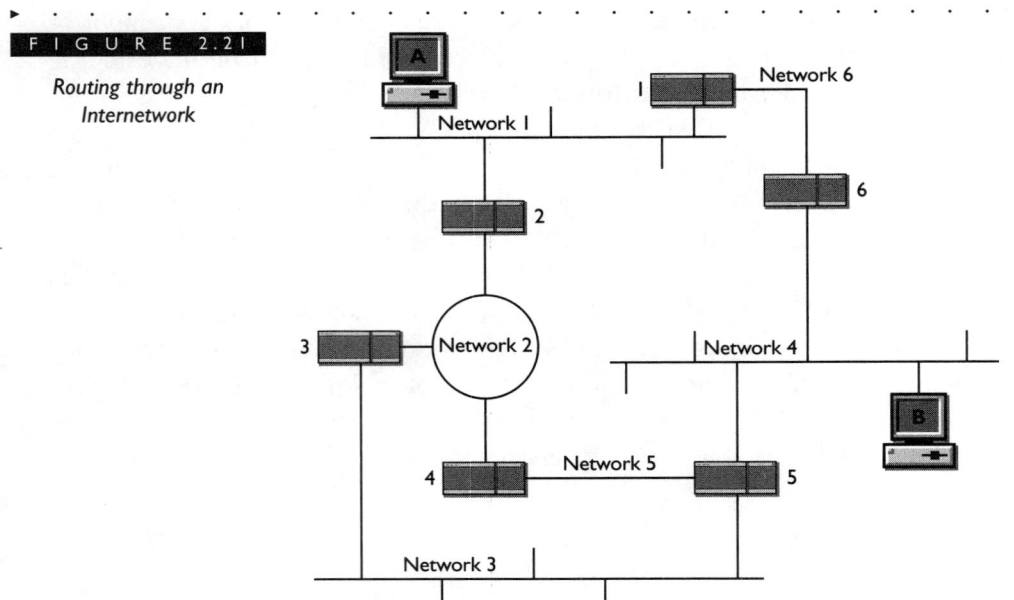

FIGURE 2.21

Routing through an Internetwork

The most common algorithm for making route decisions uses *hop count*, which involves counting the number of networks that must be crossed to reach the destination network. Consider a packet being routed from computer A to computer B. When counting hops, the originating network counts as one hop. Therefore, the hop counts for the various possible routes are:

ROUTE	NUMBER OF HOPS
A-1-6-4-B	3 Hops
A-1-2-5-4-B	4 Hops
A-1-2-3-4-B	4 Hops

An estimation of the cost of routing is called a *metric*. By the hop count metric, the shortest route would be through routers 1 and 6. This simplistic approach could lead to poor choices, however, if the lines connecting the various routers operate at different speeds. Suppose network 6 operates at 56 kilobits per second while all the other lines operate at 1.2 megabits per second. In that case, the A-1-2-5-4-B route would probably deliver data faster. This problem can be corrected by assigning larger metrics to certain paths. For example, a hop count of ten might be assigned to network 6. The slow connection would then be used only if the other routes were unavailable.

As I mentioned earlier, routing operates at the network level. Figure 2.22 shows a protocol stack model of routing. The router implements a protocol stack for each network interface. The advantage of routing is that the network level is independent of the physical network. Different kinds of networks can share exactly the same network layer. This makes it easy for routers to forward data from one type of network to another. A common network layer could operate over an Ethernet data link layer for one interface and a Token Ring layer for another interface. Because of this capability, routers are the primary tool for connecting different types of networks.

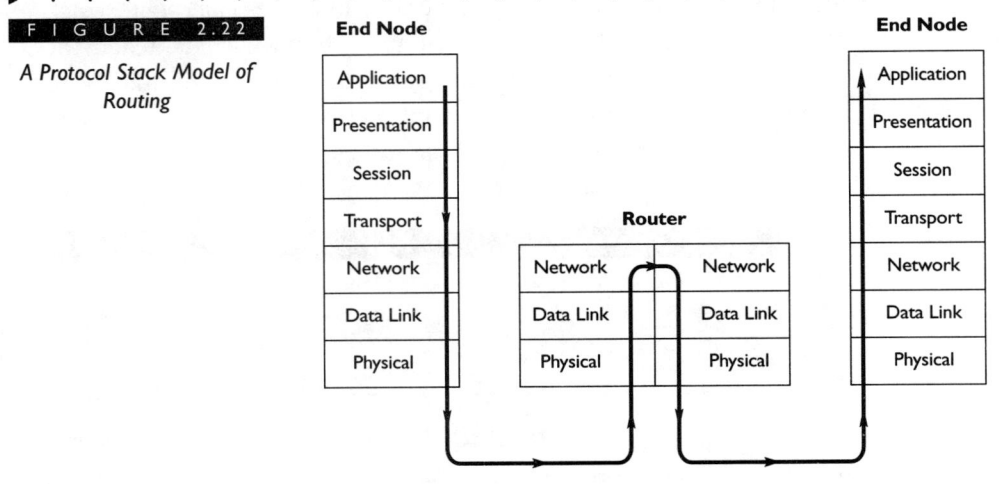

FIGURE 2.22

A Protocol Stack Model of Routing

Unicasting, Broadcasting, and Multicasting

Nodes can communicate with one another in three ways: unicasts, broadcasts, and multicasts. These three styles of messaging are primarily defined by the ways the messages are addressed. A unicast message is addressed to a single node, a broadcast is addressed to every node in a defined area, and a multicast is addressed to every node that is a member of a pre-defined group. Let's examine these styles of messages to see their individual advantages and disadvantages.

Broadcast Messaging

Figure 2.23 illustrates the transmission and reception of a broadcast message. The network is a broadcast-style network like an Ethernet. When a node transmits a message, the packets containing the message propagate throughout the network. Every node can, if it wants, eavesdrop on the packets — which is exactly what happens with a broadcast message. The destination address of the message is a special broadcast address that instructs every node that sees the message that it should receive the entire message and process it.

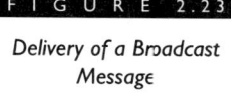

FIGURE 2.23

*Delivery of a Broadcast
Message*

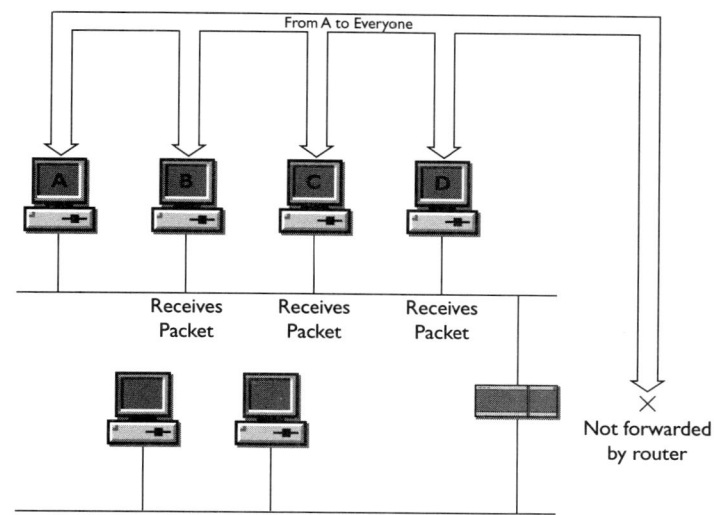

Broadcast messages are useful in at least two situations. If a message needs to be delivered to every node on the network — a warning that a server is shutting down, for example — a broadcast accomplishes the goal as efficiently as shouting "fire." A broadcast is also useful if a node wishes to communicate with a specific device but does not know the address of the device. Suppose that a workstation needs to locate an available NetWare server. A broadcast may be the only way to get the word out so that the servers can respond with a service announcement.

Broadcasts can be costly, however. Every node that sees the broadcast message is obligated to receive the entire message and process it to some degree, if only to determine that the message can be ignored. Because each broadcast message requires processing overhead on every node, excessive amounts of broadcast messages can waste a lot of the collective processing power on a network. That's why Novell's SAP protocol often gets a bad rap. SAP relies heavily on broadcast messages.

Broadcast messages have another liability in that it is dangerous to allow them to cross routers. Most routed networks contain redundant paths so they can continue to function when a router fails. When broadcast messages are allowed to cross routers on such a network the redundant paths form loops. The broadcast messages tend to cross and recross the same routers, resulting in a storm of messages that rapidly eats into network bandwidth and processing power on the nodes. Because of this behavior, most network implementations do not permit broadcast messages to be routed. Consequently, they cannot be used to communicate with nodes on different networks in an internetwork.

Some networks, such as X.25 and ATM, do not support broadcast messages. All communication between devices on these networks takes place between two nodes that form a virtual circuit. Because virtual circuits always communicate directly between two nodes, other nodes do not listen in and broadcast messaging is not possible. On such networks, other means must be devised to simulate the effect of a broadcast message.

Unicast Messaging

Figure 2.24 illustrates the transmission and reception of a broadcast message. As above, the network is a broadcast-style network like an Ethernet. When a node transmits a unicast message, it includes in the message the network address of the one node that should receive the message. Other nodes will ignore the message as soon as they determine that they are not the intended recipients. In Figure 2.24, node A sends a unicast message addressed to E. Notice that a unicast message is forwarded to its destination network by a router. All nodes except E reject the packet.

But wait a moment. This is a broadcast network. Every node sees every packet that is sent on the network. Just how is a unicast message more efficient than a broadcast message?

The difference is that a unicast message is accepted or rejected in the network interface. The network interface knows the node's address. It decodes just enough of the packet to learn whether it is the intended destination of the packet. If it is not the recipient, the network interface simply ignores the packet. The packet data stops at the interface and requires no processing by the CPU.

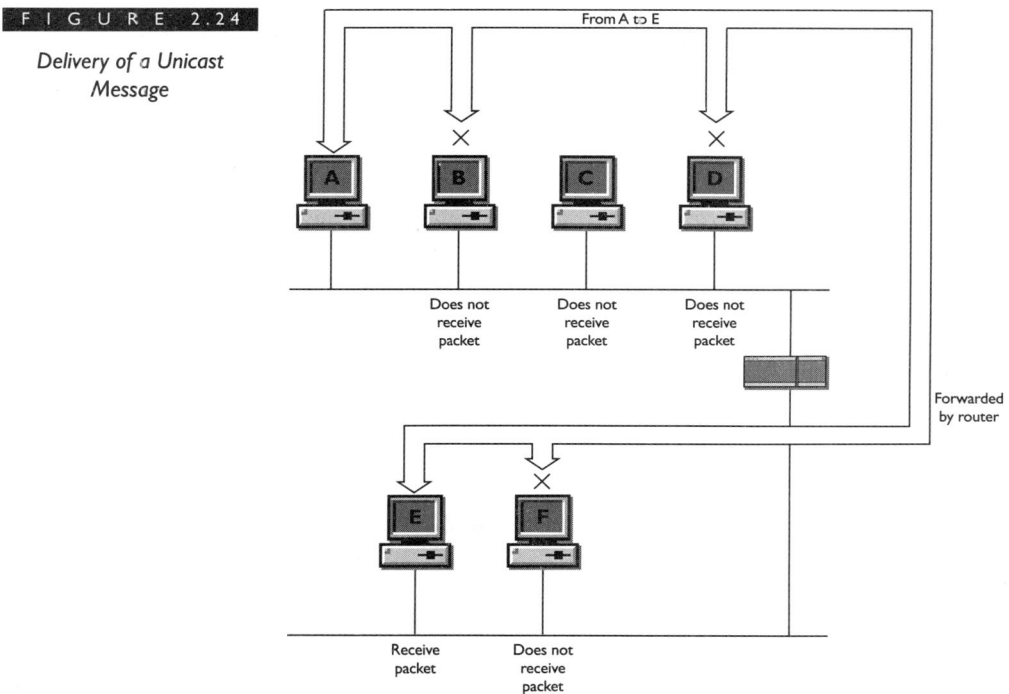

FIGURE 2.24

Delivery of a Unicast Message

By contrast, every broadcast packet requires at least some CPU time. The broadcast address matches every node on the network and cannot be used to determine whether the packet should be received. To learn if it should receive the packet, the node must examine the data in the packet. "Let's see now. I'm a NetWare server. Is this the kind of packet to which I should pay attention? Is it an NCP packet? No, it is a UNIX packet. Shucks, that's no good to me. I'll ignore it." A bit of thought was required before the server could safely ignore the packet.

Nearly all network communication makes use of unicast packets because the majority of network communication takes place between two nodes that know each other's network address. On IPX, nodes are always identified by their network addresses. On TCP/IP, helper protocols such as the Address Resolution Protocol enable nodes to learn the network addresses of the stations with which they want to communicate.

Multicast Messaging

Figure 2.25 illustrates the transmission and reception of a multicast message. Multicast messaging serves a middle ground between unicasts and broadcasts. Suppose that a node needs to send multiple messages to some but not all of the devices on a network. It could send a unicast message to each destination, but that wastes network bandwidth. It could send a broadcast, but that wastes processing power, and a broadcast message would not reach a node on the other side of a router. What we want is a message that will be received only by the intended systems, regardless of their location on the internetwork.

Delivery of a Multicast Message

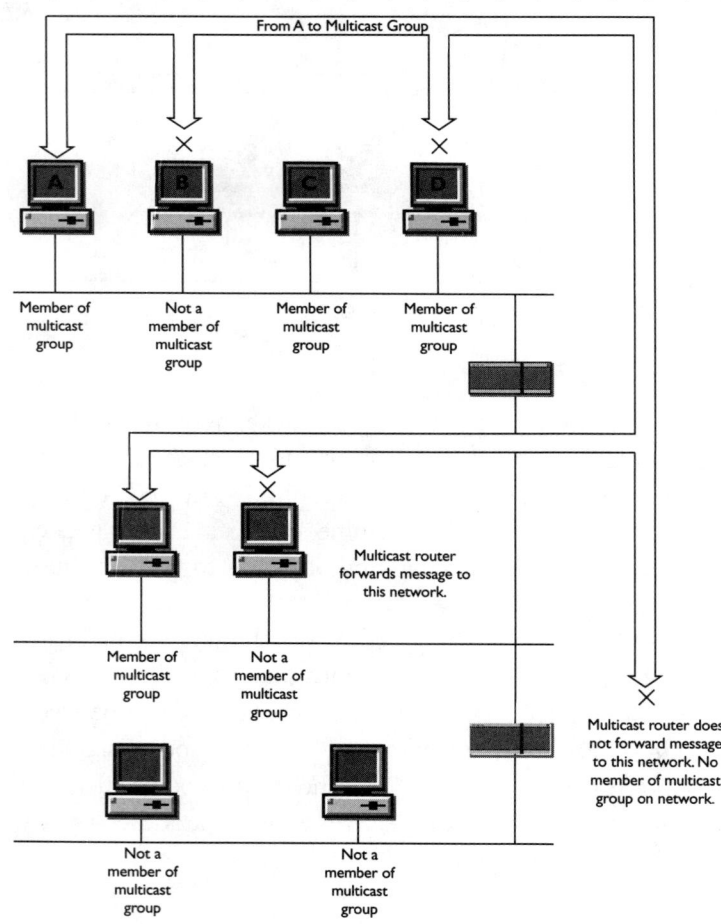

When multicasting is used, nodes join multicast groups and notify special multicast routers that they belong to the groups. Nodes that do not belong to the multicast group will ignore messages addressed to the group, rejecting the packets either in their network interfaces or very low in their protocol stacks. Multicast routers can forward multicast messages because the messages are forwarded only to network segments that contain members of the multicast group. In Figure 2.25, no nodes on the bottom network segment have registered as members of the multicast group. As a result, the multicast router does not forward the message to that network.

Multicasting is not a new technology, but it has been sparingly used until recently. Now multicasting is just what we need for a whole new category of services that rely on limited broadcasting. For example, multicasting is the technology that makes the multimedia MBONE realistic, enabling it to deliver multimedia bandwidth (lots of packets) to subscriber nodes without dragging every other node down in the process. Multicasting is a great way to deliver news to only those users who want it. And multicasting is used by the Service Locator Protocol employed in NetWare 5 to replace SAP broadcasts on Pure IP networks.

From Theory to Practice

This chapter has given you a theoretical context for the next four chapters. Although you have seen in general terms how networks function layer-by-layer, you have not yet encountered any real protocols in this book. Now it is time to get down to specifics. Chapter 3 discusses TCP/IP in detail, and shows you how TCP/IP network designers have built these functions into real networks and real protocols. Chapter 4 examines the network access layer, which is at the bottom of the DoD protocol model.

The Network Access Layer

TCP/IP comes into play at the network access layer. The United States Department of Defense did not design a network architecture specifically for TCP/IP. Rather, TCP/IP was designed with a layered approach so that it could be adapted to future network standards. As you will see in this chapter, TCP/IP has been used with many different types of networks. The following network standards are discussed in this chapter:

- Ethernet II

- IEEE 802.3 Ethernet

- IEEE 802.5 Token Ring

- Digital Data Services

- X.25 Packet Switching

- Frame Relay

- Asynchronous Transfer Mode (ATM)

The primary goal of this chapter is to show how TCP/IP can be adapted to these different networks. This chapter also explains a bit about how each network works.

Ethernet II

Ethernet and TCP/IP have had a long history together. Ethernet grew out of work by Robert Metcalf, Daniel Boggs, and their colleagues at the Xerox Palo Alto Research Center (Xerox PARC), and Ethernet was already well-defined when TCP/IP was being developed for the ARPANET. Ever since the inception of TCP/IP, the two have been closely related. The vast majority of TCP/IP implementations are designed with Ethernet II in mind.

NOTE

The name *Ethernet* was coined at Xerox. It refers to "luminiferous ether," a substance physicists once believed to be the medium through which light travels.

There have been two generations of Ethernet. The first generation emerged in 1980, and was developed through the cooperation of Digital, Intel, and Xerox. This first generation is generally referred to as Ethernet I (or DIX 1.0). An updated version was introduced in 1982. The updated version was dubbed Ethernet II (or DIX 2.0). Nowadays, Ethernet I is seldom used, although you may still encounter it on older hardware. Ethernet II, by contrast, is very common on TCP/IP networks.

The death of Ethernet has been predicted many times, as experts have anticipated Ethernet succumbing to the lures of token ring, FDDI, and ATM. But Ethernet survives for a number of reasons. 10-Mbps Ethernet offers service that is adequate for all but the most demanding LAN applications. Simply segmenting the network with bridges, routers, or switches can keep local traffic levels down to levels that provide suitable performance. Besides its basic soundness, Ethernet has proven to be extensible thanks to the efforts of many dedicated engineers and vendors. Coax Ethernet made the move to unshielded twisted-pair wiring. 100-Mbps Ethernet is now readily available and costs much less than FDDI or ATM, enabling LAN administrators to have speed without leaving the comfortable Ethernet environment. Now gigabit Ethernet looms on the horizon, enabling Ethernet to take advantage of all the bandwidth offered by fiber optic cable. Although it may one day be eclipsed by a technology such as ATM, Ethernet will likely remain the most popular LAN cabling method for years to come.

How Ethernet Networks Work

The majority of LANs use baseband media, which allow only one computer to transmit data at a time. Therefore, network designers must decide how to enable multiple computers to share a medium. A mechanism that determines how computers share a medium is called an *access control method*.

The access control method that Ethernet uses is very basic. Essentially, a node that needs to transmit on an Ethernet network simply listens to the network before sending. If the network is silent, the node begins to transmit. The official name for this type of access control method is *carrier-sensing multiple access* (CSMA). *Carrier-sensing* merely means that the nodes listen before they talk.

If that were the whole story, Ethernet would be simple indeed. Unfortunately, it takes time for electrical signals to travel through wires, and that delay causes a problem. Two different nodes may sense a quiet network at the same time and then begin to transmit simultaneously, producing two signals on the network. That event is called a *collision*. Figure 3.1 shows how collisions can happen.

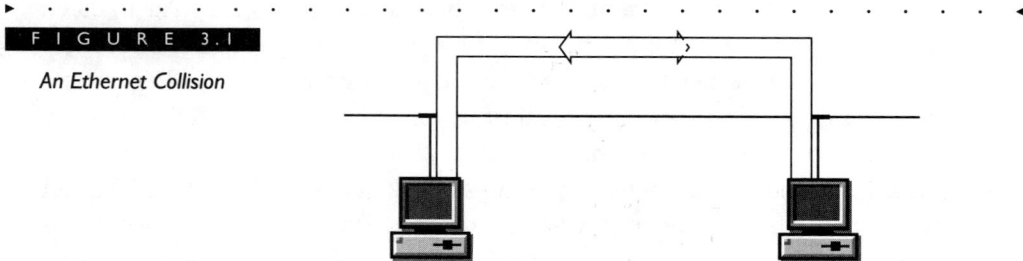

FIGURE 3.1

An Ethernet Collision

When a collision occurs, no valid data is transmitted. Each node continues to listen to the network as it transmits and senses that a collision has occurred. (A collision can be easily sensed because the two signals result in higher than normal voltages.) If a transmitting node senses a collision, it transmits a *jamming* signal that invalidates the frame and notifies all other nodes that a collision has taken place. Then the sending nodes stop transmitting for a while. The period of time each node waits before transmitting again is determined randomly. The random delay makes it less likely that the nodes' transmissions will collide again. The mechanism for detecting collisions is called *collision detection* (CD). The full name of the access control method developed for Ethernet is *carrier-sensing multiple access with collision detection*. Because that name is a mouthful, the mechanism is usually referred to as CSMA/CD for short.

One problem with collision detection mechanisms is that collisions between very short frames might not be detected. Nodes listen for collisions only during transmission. If the transmission ends before a collision occurs, the collision will not be detected. Figure 3.2 shows how a collision might be undetected. To ensure that all collisions are detected, a minimum frame length must be specified. The minimum length ensures that all frames reach all nodes in the network before transmission is complete. The transmitting nodes will therefore always detect collisions before the nodes stop transmitting.

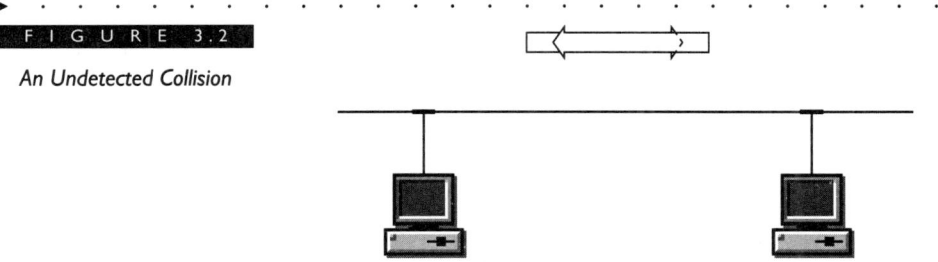

FIGURE 3.2

An Undetected Collision

Ethernet CSMA/CD is an elegant and efficient protocol. On a properly loaded network, very little of the network bandwidth needs to be devoted to Ethernet's operation. When there are relatively few collisions, the collisions do not critically impair network performance.

However, when many collisions occur, they can become a problem. CSMA networks are commonly called *contention-based networks* because nodes contend for network access. When too many nodes contend for network access, collisions start to dominate the network, and performance deteriorates (see Figure 3.3). Eventually, transmission becomes difficult because the majority of attempts produce collisions. In theory, collisions could prevent all nodes from accessing the network. Because nodes are not guaranteed an opportunity to transmit (in other words, because there is only a probability that a node will be able to transmit), Ethernet is sometimes referred to as a *probabilistic network*.

FIGURE 3.3

Performance of Ethernet as Demand Increases

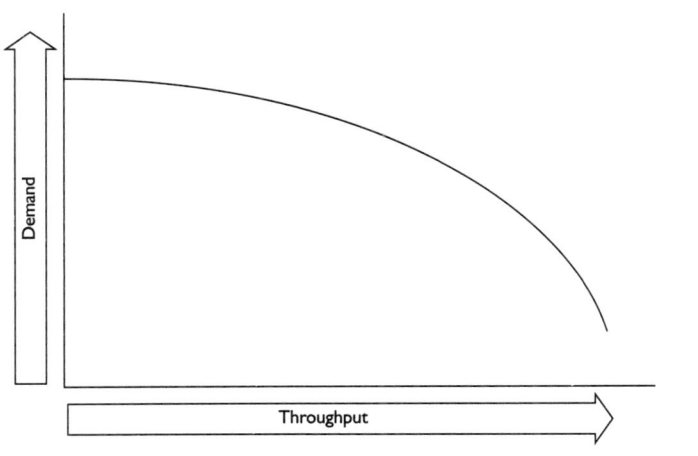

Nevertheless, Ethernet (that is, Ethernet II and IEEE 802.3, which is discussed in a following section) remains the most popular network standard. It works well in the vast majority of situations. Furthermore, it is simple, and the network components it requires are relatively inexpensive.

Ethernet Media

The original Ethernet medium is a thick coaxial cable referred to as *Thick Ethernet* or simply *ThickNet*. The cable can be used for network segments up to 500 meters in length. The cable can support up to 100 nodes, and it operates at 10 megabits per second (Mbps). However, Thick Ethernet's cables—and the hardware components it requires—are fairly costly. The popularity of Thick Ethernet has waned as cheaper alternatives have become available.

The other medium developed specifically for Ethernet consists of a thinner coaxial cable. Not surprisingly, this cable is called *Thin Ethernet* or *ThinNet*. Networks that use Thin Ethernet are limited to 185-meter segments and 30 nodes. Like Thick Ethernet, Thin Ethernet operates at 10 Mbps. The hardware required for Thin Ethernet is much simpler than the hardware required for Thick Ethernet. Therefore, Thin Ethernet costs considerably less.

Both varieties of Ethernet media—thick and thin—were adopted for standardization when the IEEE sought to develop an industry standard for CSMA/CD networks. These Ethernet media are explained in more detail in this chapter's IEEE 802.3 standard section.

The Ethernet Frame Format

The Ethernet II frame format is particularly relevant to TCP/IP. Ethernet II and TCP/IP fit together perfectly. When you adapt TCP/IP to other types of networks, you must do some extra work.

Figure 3.4 shows the Ethernet II frame format. In general, frame format diagrams show a frame's first bit on the left-hand side. Therefore, you should read the diagram from left to right to see the frame format from start to end. Table 3.1 summarizes the fields in an Ethernet II frame. The term *octet* is used in many protocol standards to describe a group of eight bits. (Because an octet is the same thing as a byte, many newer standards use the term *byte* instead.)

	Preamble (8 octets)	Destination Address (6 octets)	Source Address (6 octets)	Type (2 octets)	Data (46-1500 octets)	FCS (4 octets)

F I G U R E   3.4

Format of an Ethernet II Frame

If you add up the lengths of all fields, you find that an Ethernet frame has a maximum length of 1518 octets (6 + 6 + 2 + 1500 + 4 = 1518) and a minimum length of 64 octets (6 + 6 + 2 + 46 + 4 = 64). The 64-octet minimum combined with the 8-octet preamble results in a minimum frame length of 576 bits, which is long enough to ensure detection of all collisions.

T A B L E   3.1

Fields in an Ethernet II Frame

FIELD	PURPOSE
Preamble	An 8-octet (64-bit) field signals the beginning of an Ethernet frame. It begins with 7 octets that have the bit pattern 10101010 and ends with 1 octet that has the bit pattern 10101011. This distinctive pattern marks the beginning of a frame, but the preamble is not part of the frame and it is not counted in the frame length.
Destination address	A 6-octet (48-bit) address indicates the physical address of the node that is the frame's destination. The receiving node examines this field to determine whether it is the destination of the frame.
Source address	A 6-octet (48-bit) address indicates the physical address of the node where the frame originated. This address is used by receiving nodes to address reply frames.
Type	A 2-octet (16-bit) field describes the type of data that the frame carries. The information in this field is generally referred to as the EtherType.

Continued

TABLE 3.1	FIELD	PURPOSE
Continued	Data	This field contains the protocol data unit received from upper layers. This field has a minimum length of 46 octets and a maximum length of 1500 octets. If the data field is shorter than 46 octets, upper-layer protocols must pad it with octets of 0 value to achieve the minimum length.
	Frame check sequence (FCS)	A 4-octet (32-bit) code detects errors during transmission. The code is derived using an algorithm called a *cyclic redundancy check* (CRC). The receiving node recalculates the CRC and compares its result to the value to the frame check sequence. A match indicates the frame was not corrupted.

Ethernet Addressing

Ethernet uses a very simple mechanism to deliver frames on a network. The sending node inserts the destination node's address in the destination address field. The frame is then placed on the network where it is examined by all nodes. The node that recognizes its own address in the destination address field receives the frame.

For this scheme to work, each node on a network must have a unique number. The designers of Ethernet created a scheme that ensures every Ethernet device *in the whole world* has a unique number.

Figure 3.5 shows the format of an Ethernet address, which consists of 48 bits arranged in three fields. Bits are numbered from bit 0 (the low-order bit) to bit 47 (the high-order bit). The first bit on the left of the address is the high-order bit, and addresses are arranged like conventional binary numbers — going from higher-bits to lower-bits as you read left to right.

FIGURE 3.5

Structure of an Ethernet Address

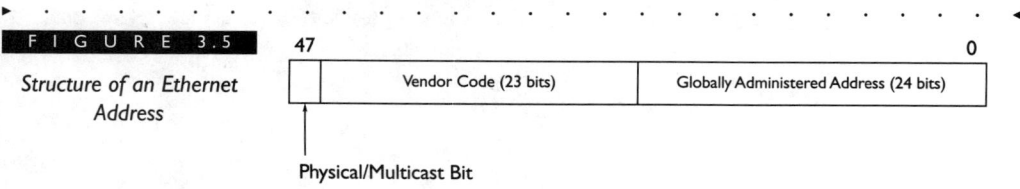

47   Vendor Code (23 bits)   Globally Administered Address (24 bits)   0

Physical/Multicast Bit

Typically, Ethernet addresses are expressed as six two-digit hexadecimal numbers. This expression is easy to do because each group of 8 bits maps to two hex digits. An example would be 06 02 AD 01 20 1D. Hex representation makes it easier for humans to scan the addresses. Figure 3.6 illustrates how to create a hexadecimal representation of an Ethernet address. Hex is so easy to use that it is seldom necessary to worry about the binary form of an Ethernet address.

FIGURE 3.6

Format of an Ethernet II Address

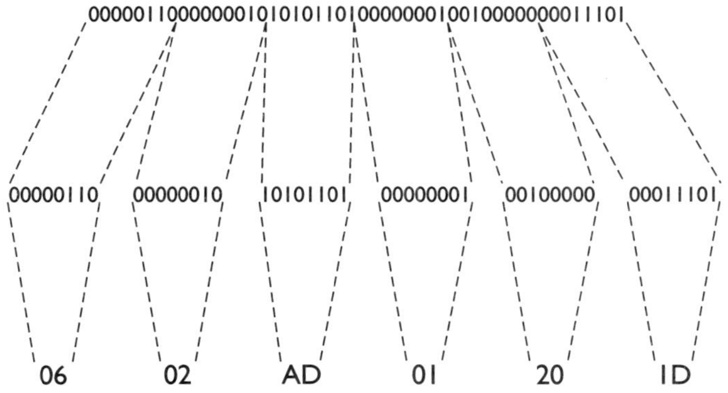

000001100000001010101101000000010010000000011101

00000110 00000010 10101101 00000001 00100000 00011101

06   02   AD   01   20   1D

Bit 47 (the high-order bit) is the Physical/Multicast (P/M) bit. When this bit has a value of 0, the frame specifies the physical address of a node on the network. The P/M bit is set to 0 for unicast messages. When this bit has a value of 1, the address is a multicast address. (Refer to the discussion in Chapter 2 for the distinction between unicast and multicast messages.)

The first three octets of an Ethernet address comprise a vendor code. Each manufacturer of Ethernet equipment is assigned one or more 24-bit identification codes by a central registry. (All vendor codes begin with a P/M bit value of 0.) Registration originally was performed by Xerox but has been delegated to the IEEE. Table 3.2 lists some typical vendor codes, which are documented in RFC 1700, entitled *Assigned Numbers*.

When vendors need to use a multicast address, they will frequently use their vendor codes, toggling only the P/M bit.

NOTE

TABLE 3.2	VENDOR CODE	VENDOR
Examples of Ethernet Vendor Codes	00 80 C2	IEEE 802.1 Committee
	00 AA 00	Intel
	08 00 09	Hewlett-Packard
	08 00 14	Novell
	08 00 2B	DEC
	08 00 56	Stanford University
	08 00 69	IBM

The remainder of the address is a 24-bit code that uniquely identifies each device the vendor manufactures. The combination of the unique vendor codes and a unique code for each piece of hardware results in a unique Ethernet address for each piece of hardware created. These addresses are typically burned into the hardware and are often called *physical addresses*. Because the addresses are registered on a global basis, they are also called *globally administered addresses*.

NOTE **It is possible to override the physical address of an Ethernet adapter by changing parameters in the network drivers. Addresses that are created locally are called locally administered addresses.**

One more Ethernet address should be mentioned. An address consisting entirely of 1s is the standard Ethernet *broadcast address*, which is represented in hex as FF FF FF FF FF FF. The route of messages sent using the broadcast address depends on the network layer. Typically, broadcast messages are not permitted to cross routers and are distributed to the local network only.

To summarize, there are three categories of Ethernet addresses:

▶ Globally administered addresses (physical addresses burned into hardware), which have a Physical/Multicast (high-order) bit value of 0.

▶ Multicast addresses, which have a Physical/Multicast (high-order) bit value of 1.

▶ Broadcast addresses, which consist entirely of 1s.

EtherType

The *type* (or *EtherType*) field plays a significant role in relation to TCP/IP. This field identifies the type of data that is carried in the data field. The EtherType value is used in protocol multiplexing to ensure that data is delivered to the correct upper-layer protocol stack. The Assigned Numbers RFC (RFC 1700) lists EtherType numbers that have been assigned to specific protocols and organizations. Table 3.3 shows some common EtherType values listed in RFC 1700.

TABLE 3.3	ETHERTYPE	ETHERTYPE	DATA TYPE (DECIMAL)
Examples of EtherType Values	2048	0800	Internet IP (IPv4)
	2053	0805	X.25 Level 3
	2054	0806	ARP
	33023	80FF – 8103	Wellfleet Communications
	32873	8069	AT&T
	33079 – 33080	8137 – 8138	Novell, Inc.

NOTE In the IEEE 802.3 version of Ethernet (see the following section), the type field has been replaced by a length field, which has a maximum value of 1500. All EtherType values are 1501 (5DDh) or greater. Therefore, systems can distinguish between 802.3 and Ethernet II frames by examining the value of the type or length field.

IEEE LAN Standards

The main organization that sets international LAN standards is the Institute of Electrical and Electronics Engineers (IEEE), the largest professional organization in the world. Network standards are handled by the 802 committee — so called because the committee first met in 1980 during the month of February. The International Standardization Organization (ISO),which establishes international LAN standards, has adopted the IEEE 802 standards in ISO standard 8802. (The ISO standard based on IEEE 802.3 is called ISO 88023.)

Figure 3.7 illustrates the architecture of the IEEE 802 standards. Notice that the OSI data link layer has been subdivided into two sublayers in the diagram. The subdivision allows the IEEE to designate a common layer above all LAN protocols. The responsibilities of the data link layer have been divided between the sublayers as follows:

▶ *Logical link control* (LLC) provides a common interface between lower-level IEEE protocols and the network layer. The LLC sublayer delivers data between nodes that reside on the same network segment.

▶ *Medium access control* (MAC) is the mechanism that enables nodes to share a common network medium.

Only the standards discussed in this chapter are shown in Figure 3.7. This chapter examines three of the 802.x standards:

▶ 802.2, which defines the LLC sublayer.

▶ 802.3, which defines the MAC and physical layers for a CSMA/CD network derived from Ethernet II.

▶ 802.5, which defines the MAC and physical layers for a token-passing network derived from IBM's Token-Ring network.

Notice in Figure 3.7 that the 802.2 LLC protocol serves as a common protocol that is used above 802.3 and 802.5 networks. This approach simplifies adaptation of network layers to different types of LANs. Each of these protocols is discussed in following sections. First, however, let's examine the addressing scheme of 802 networks.

IEEE 802 Addressing

Node physical addresses are used for local delivery of data frames. When the physical address format was being developed, the IEEE required a format that could be used for all 802 protocols. The address format that was chosen closely resembles the address format of Ethernet II. In the IEEE model, physical addresses are functions of the MAC protocol sublayer. Therefore, physical addresses are frequently referred to as *MAC addresses*.

F I G U R E 3.7

*Organization of the IEEE
802 Standards*

Application
Presentation
Session
Transport
Network
Data Link
Physical

IEEE 802.2 LLC	
MAC	MAC
IEEE 802.3 CSMA/CD	IEEE 802.5 Token Ring

The IEEE defined both 16- and 48-bit address formats. However, because 16-bit addresses are seldom used, they are not discussed here.

All nodes on a network must be configured to use the same address format. Figure 3.8 illustrates the format of a 48-bit address. This address format has been adopted for IEEE 802, ISO 8802, and other network standards such as Frame Relay. Although the format resembles addresses for Ethernet II, some differences exist.

The high-order bit (bit 47) designates the address as an *individual* or a *group address*, and it is therefore called the *I/G bit*. If the value of the I/G bit is 0, the address is an individual address. (An individual address is comparable to an Ethernet II physical address.) If the value of the I/G bit is 1, the address is a group address. (A group address is comparable to an Ethernet II multicast address.) In other words, apart from the difference in terminology, the I/G bit has the same purpose and function as the Ethernet II P/M bit.

F I G U R E 3.8

*Format of IEEE 802
Addresses*

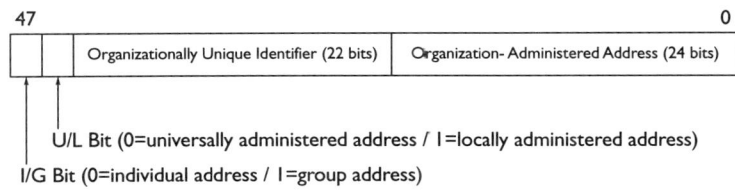

47			0
		Organizationally Unique Identifier (22 bits)	Organization- Administered Address (24 bits)

U/L Bit (0=universally administered address / 1=locally administered address)

I/G Bit (0=individual address / 1=group address)

Bit 46 designates the address as either a *universally* or a *locally administered address*. Therefore, bit 46 is referred to as the U/L bit. If the value of the U/L bit is 0, then the address is universally administered. A universally administered address is based on a 22-bit identifier that is unique to a particular organization and a 24-bit address that is assigned by the organization to each device it manufactures. Universal addresses can be overridden by parameters that configure the drivers for the network adapter. If the value of the U/L bit is 1, then the address is locally administered.

The combination of an organizationally unique identifier and a unique address assigned by the organization results in global uniqueness for each device that is assigned an IEEE 802 address. The IEEE now assigns organizationally unique identifiers—a responsibility that was transferred to the IEEE from Xerox. In general, universally administered addresses are preferable because they prevent conflicts from occurring.

IEEE 802.2 Logical Link Control

The LLC sublayer performs two basic functions: frame delivery and protocol multiplexing and demultiplexing. Many of the services at the LLC sublayer are optional and can be performed instead by upper-layer protocols.

Protocol Multiplexing and Demultiplexing

The multiplexing capability of the LLC sublayer enables it to support multiple upper-layer protocol stacks. This function is performed by the EtherType value in an Ethernet II frame. 802.2 LLC uses a different mechanism called the *link service access point* (LSAP). Each upper-layer protocol is assigned an LSAP, which functions as a logical address. The LSAP identifies the protocol stack that is associated with each frame and enables LLC to deliver frames to the correct protocol stack.

The most significant difference between the IEEE protocols and Ethernet II is the difference between the LSAP and EtherType mechanisms. To support TCP/IP, an extension of the LLC protocol called the *Subnetwork Access Protocol* (SNAP) must be employed. (SNAP is discussed later in the section "IEEE 802.3 CSMA/CD.")

Delivery Services

LLC is responsible for delivering data between computers. The delivery services have two functions: flow control and error recovery. LLC provides three levels of delivery services that offer different degrees of communication integrity.

Flow Control   Communication devices are equipped with *receive buffers* — memory that can store data while it is waiting to be processed by a device. If data arrives faster than the device can pull the data from its receive buffers, some of the data may be lost. One responsibility of LLC is to prevent buffer overflow. Two primary mechanisms are used to manage communication flow:

> ▶ *Stop-and-wait* is an uncomplicated method that requires the receiving device to acknowledge each frame it receives. An acknowledgment signals the receiver's ability to receive more data. The sending device waits for an acknowledgment before it sends more data. This technique is effective, although it is inefficient because the acknowledgment process slows down transmission. Also, because each data frame spawns an acknowledgment frame, this technique almost doubles the amount of network traffic.

> ▶ *Sliding-window* enables the receiver to acknowledge several frames at once. A window is the number of frames that can be traveling at any given time. When two devices connect for an exchange of data, they agree on an appropriate window. The sending device can transmit only as many frames as the window designates. When that number is reached, the sending device must pause. The receiving device can acknowledge more than one frame with the same message. When frames are acknowledged, the window moves forward so that the sender can transmit more frames. In a full-duplex dialog that enables the sender to both send data and receive acknowledgments simultaneously, sliding-window results in a more regular data flow. Because multiple frames can be acknowledged with a single message, the increase in network traffic is not as noticeable as with stop-and-wait.

Error Recovery   Error recovery may be performed by LLC, depending on the service that is selected. The MAC sublayer detects errors but does not perform error recovery.

LLC error recovery uses an *automatic repeat request* (ARQ) technique. With ARQ, the receiving node must acknowledge each frame that it receives correctly. There are two types of ARQ:

▶ **Stop-and-wait ARQ.** The sending device waits for an acknowledgment of each frame that is received intact. Any unacknowledged frame is retransmitted after a short delay.

▶ **Go-back-N ARQ.** The receiving device can request retransmission of specific frames. Connection-mode service is required.

Delivery Service Modes　　LLC has three different delivery-service modes, which implement different combinations of flow control and error recovery techniques. The available services are:

▶ **Unacknowledged datagram service (Type 1 service).** This mode is connectionless. It supports point-to-point, multipoint, and broadcast transmission. Flow control and error recovery are not performed.

▶ **Virtual circuit service (Type 2 service).** This mode is connection-oriented. It provides flow control, frame sequencing, and error recovery.

▶ **Acknowledged datagram service (Type 3 service).** This mode is a combination of Type 1 and Type 2 services. It supports point-to-point datagram service with message acknowledgments.

Type 1 service is the most common. LLC is seldom implemented with Type 2 or Type 3 service. Type 1 service promotes efficiency in lower-layer protocols. In the TCP/IP protocol suite, the TCP protocol provides reliable service when it is necessary. It would be redundant to perform the same service at both the network layer and the data link layer.

Format of LCC Data　　The protocol data unit (PDU) constructed by the LLC sublayer is shown in Figure 3.9.

FIGURE 3.9	DSAP	SSAP	Control	Data

Format of an LLC Protocol Data Unit

Table 3.4 describes the different fields of an LLC PDU.

Fields of an LLC Protocol Data Unit

TABLE 3.4	FIELD	DESCRIPTION
	Destination Service Access Point (DSAP)	The link service access point specifying the protocol stack on the receiving node at the data's destination.
	Source Service Access (SSAP)	The link service access point specifying the protocol stack on the sending node where the data originated.
	Control	Control information that varies depending on the function of the PDU.
	Data	The payload of the PDU. In other words, the data received from the network layer.

IEEE 802.3 CSMA/CD

Digital, Intel, and Xerox — who jointly developed Ethernet II — submitted the new technology to the IEEE for standardization. The 802.3 committee took on the task of developing LAN standards based on Ethernet CSMA/CD technology. IEEE 802.3 is similar to Ethernet II in most respects. However, there are some differences between the two, which result from the IEEE's decision to implement 802.2 as a common LLC layer for all LAN protocols.

IEEE 802.3 LANs use the same signaling techniques and — with a very minor exception — the same hardware as Ethernet II. As a result, the two Ethernet varieties coexist fairly smoothly. 802.3 and Ethernet II frames can be multiplexed on the same medium without difficulty, and Novell's ODI architecture supports both frame types on the same network adapter. (The Ethernet_802.2 frame type supports standard Ethernet 802.3 frames. The older Ethernet_802.3 frame type does not comply with IEEE standards, omitting the IEEE 802.2 LLC information.)

There has been considerable debate about whether IEEE 802.3 should in fact be called Ethernet. The dispute is likely to continue as long as both Ethernet II and IEEE 802.3 are in use. Xerox long ago surrendered the Ethernet trademark, and some people (including Robert Metcalf) argue that the term should be applied to the latest version of Ethernet, which is IEEE 802.3.

I use the term *Ethernet* to describe both standards. When I need to point out a difference between the standards, I refer specifically to Ethernet II or Ethernet 802.3.

NOTE

The IEEE 802.3 Frame Format

The format of an IEEE 802.3 frame is shown in Figure 3.10.

Table 3.5 describes the fields in an IEEE 802.3 frame.

FIGURE 3.10

Format of an IEEE 802.3 Frame

Preamble (7 octets)	Start Frame Delimiter (1 octet)	Destination Address (6 octets)	Source Address (6 octets)	Length (2 octets)	Data (46-1500 octets)	FCS (4 octets)

TABLE 3.5

Fields in an IEEE 802.3 Frame

FIELD	DESCRIPTION
Preamble	A 56-bit field consisting of 7 octets with the bit pattern 10101010.
Start frame delimiter	A single octet field with the bit pattern 10101011 that signals the start of a frame.
Destination address	A 6-octet (48-bit) address that indicates the physical address of a frame's destination node. Receiving nodes examine this field to determine which frames they should receive.
Source address	A 6-octet (48-bit) address that indicates the physical address of the node where the frame originated. Receiving nodes use this address to send reply frames.

FIELD	DESCRIPTION
Length	A 2-octet (16-bit) field that specifies the number of octets in the LLC data field. The number of octets can vary from 46 to 1500.
LLC data	The field that contains the protocol data unit received from the LLC sublayer. This field has a minimum length of 46 octets and a maximum length of 1500 octets. If the protocol data unit is shorter than 46 octets, 0-value octets are added to attain the minimum length.
Frame check during sequence (FCS)	A 4-octet (32-bit) code used to detect errors during transmission. The code is derived using an algorithm called a *cyclic redundancy check* (CRC). The receiving node recalculates the CRC and compares the result to the value of the frame check sequence. A match indicates that the frame was not corrupted.

Figure 3.11 compares the formats of Ethernet II and IEEE 802.3 frames. The most significant difference is that an IEEE 802.3 frame has a length field instead of a type field. Otherwise, the two frame types are essentially the same. If 48-bit addresses are used, the length of both IEEE 802.3 and Ethernet II frames can range from 64 through 1518 octets.

In an IEEE 802.3 frame, the combination of the 7-octet preamble and the 1-octet frame start sequence is comparable to the 8-octet preamble of an Ethernet II frame.

Although 16-bit MAC addresses are possible with IEEE 802 LANs, they are seldom used. Because the IEEE address format was adapted from Ethernet II, address fields are functionally identical when 48-bit address are used.

The one functional difference between the frame formats is the distinction between an Ethernet II frame's type field and an IEEE 802.3 frame's length field. These two fields perform different functions in the different networks. The protocol multiplexing function of the EtherType field is performed by the 802.2 LLC protocol for IEEE LANs. As previously mentioned, it is easy to distinguish Ethernet II frames from IEEE 802.3 frames. If the value of the type or length field is 1501 or greater, then that field represents an EtherType value, and the frame is therefore an Ethernet II frame. If the frame's length is anywhere from 46 through 1500, then the frame is an IEEE 802.3 frame.

FIGURE 3.1

Comparison of Ethernet II and IEEE 802.3 Frame Formats

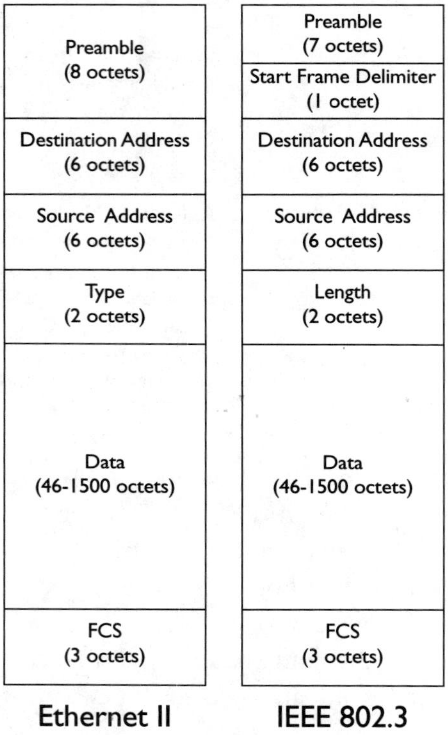

Ethernet II	IEEE 802.3
Preamble (8 octets)	Preamble (7 octets)
	Start Frame Delimiter (1 octet)
Destination Address (6 octets)	Destination Address (6 octets)
Source Address (6 octets)	Source Address (6 octets)
Type (2 octets)	Length (2 octets)
Data (46-1500 octets)	Data (46-1500 octets)
FCS (3 octets)	FCS (3 octets)

Implementing TCP/IP over IEEE 802.3 Networks

Although TCP/IP may be adapted to any network, it fits most naturally on Ethernet II LANs. NetWare TCP/IP is typically implemented using Ethernet II frames.

To run TCP/IP with networks that do not incorporate the type field of Ethernet II, the EtherType information must be encoded using the Subnetwork Access Protocol (see RFC 1042), which extends the LLC header to include the EtherType. Figure 3.12 shows the format of an LLC PDU with the Subnetwork Access Protocol (SNAP) extensions. To indicate that the PDU utilizes SNAP encapsulation, the values of the Destination Service Access Point (DSAP) and Source Service Access Point (SSAP) fields must be set to 170, the control field must be set to 3 (unnumbered information), and the organization code must be set to 0.

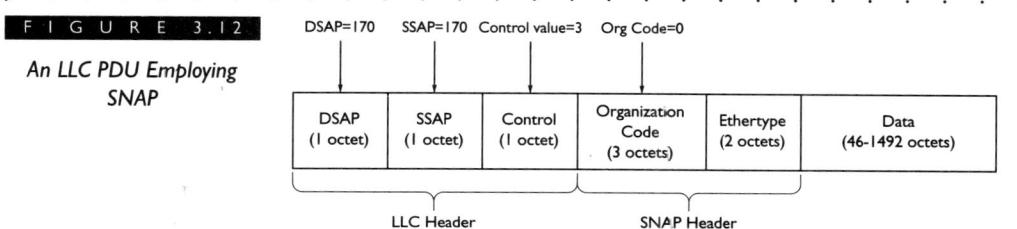

FIGURE 3.12

An LLC PDU Employing SNAP

The SNAP data is encoded as the first 8 octets of the data field. This unfortunately reduces the number of bytes that an IEEE 802.3 frame can carry when SNAP encapsulation is used. The maximum length of an Ethernet frame is 1518 octets. The maximum length allows at most 1500 octets for data. When SNAP encapsulation is employed, 8 octets in the data field are co-opted to store SNAP data. As a result, 1492 octets remain available for data, as opposed to the 1500-octet payload supported by Ethernet II. This may complicate matters if frames are routed between Ethernet II and IEEE 802.3 networks.

SNAP is a general-purpose extension that is applicable to all IEEE 802.x LANs. NetWare uses SNAP encapsulation to run TCP/IP over token ring physical layers, for example. SNAP can also be used to mate TCP/IP to networks such as Frame Relay and ATM.

IEEE 802.3 Media

The IEEE has assumed responsibility for standardizing all Ethernet media. Both Thick Ethernet and Thin Ethernet have been adopted as part of the IEEE 802.3 media options. However, the committee has broadened Ethernet media choices considerably. The most notable addition is a standard that enables Ethernet to run on unshielded twisted-pair cable. More recently, 100-megabit-per-second (Mbps) networks based on CSMA/CD have been added.

This book does not discuss the different media options at great length because the type of cable used is irrelevant to the way TCP/IP works. Therefore, the different media options offered by the 802.3 standard are only briefly mentioned here.

Each option is identified by a three-part name (for example, 10BASE5). The first number in the name indicates the nominal speed of the network—for instance, 10 signifies 10 Mbps. The middle part (for example, BASE) indicates the network's operating mode (for example, baseband). The final characters reflect the physical characteristics of the network. For example, 5 indicates that a 10BASE5 network accommodates cable segments up to 500 meters in length. The current IEEE 802.3 media options are listed in Table 3.6.

T A B L E 3.6 *IEEE 802.3 Media Options*	MEDIUM	DESCRIPTION
	10BASE5	The IEEE version of Thick Ethernet. It employs a thick, 50-ohm coaxial cable and operates in baseband mode. Cable segments can extend to 500 meters without bridges or routers. It operates at 10 Mbps.
	10BASE2	The IEEE version of Thin Ethernet. It employs a thin, 50-ohm coaxial cable and operates in baseband mode. Cable segments can extend to 185 (the 2 in 10BASE2 indicates approximately 200) meters without bridges or routers. It operates at 10 Mbps.
	10BASE-T	Ethernet using unshielded twisted-pair (UTP) cable. It operates at 10 Mbps. It is wired in a star. Cables connecting nodes to wiring concentrators may be up to 100 meters in length.
	10BROAD36	Broadband Ethernet. Supports multiplexing of multiple 10 Mbps Ethernet channels through a single 75-ohm coaxial cable.
	100BASE-TX	One of several 100-Mbps standards being considered by the IEEE. Many of the 100-Mbps standards being considered use unshielded twisted-pair cable. These standards differ in the number of pairs and in the quality of cable they require. Also being considered is 100BASE-TF, for use with optical fiber cable.

IEEE 802.5 Token Ring

The technology standardized in the IEEE 802.5 token ring network originated out of research at IBM. Token ring is the second most popular LAN physical layer. Although at one time token ring was poised to surpass Ethernet, the plummeting cost of Ethernet components has helped Ethernet to remain the market leader. Ethernet is more popular than token ring for several reasons:

▶ Ethernet's mechanisms are much simpler than token ring's mechanisms. As a result, the hardware required for Ethernet is significantly cheaper.

▶ For a long time, token ring was perceived as proprietary technology of IBM, despite its availability as an IEEE standard. Buyers have perceived Ethernet as more open — that is, not as controlled by a single vendor.

▶ TCP/IP has grown in popularity. Many buyers recognize that TCP/IP fits most naturally with Ethernet.

There are, however, compelling reasons to consider token ring in some cases. To understand when token ring might be appropriate, it is necessary to examine how token ring functions.

How Token Ring Networks Work

The basic operation of token ring is easy to understand. Nodes are arranged in a ring, as shown in Figure 3.13. Frames pass from station to station around the ring. To control access to the network, a special *token frame* is circulated around the network. A node needing to transmit must wait until it receives the token frame. Only the node that has control of the token may transmit. This restriction prevents more than one node from accessing the network at a given time. After a node has transmitted its frame, the node transmits a new token frame around the ring so that other nodes can transmit.

Token ring access control is complicated by several factors. Frames can become lost or damaged. More importantly, if a token were lost, the network would grind to a halt. The token ring designers therefore had to design a mechanism that could create a new token if the old one were lost. Another complication in token ring stems from the fact that one node is designated as an *active monitor* that oversees network operation. Token ring designers had to create a mechanism for designating a new active monitor if the old one were to fail. There are at least a dozen other problems that further complicate token ring's design.

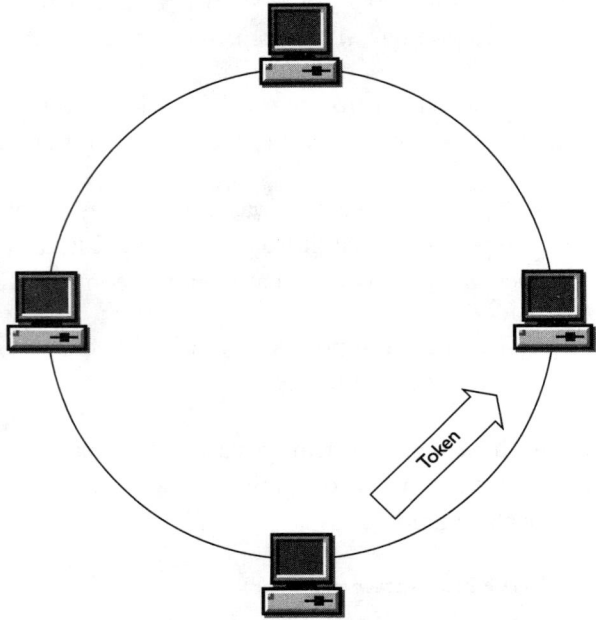

FIGURE 3.13

Operation of a Token Ring

Why did IBM bother to design a more complicated network than Ethernet? To understand the answer to that question, you need to understand one of Ethernet's main weaknesses. Each time a node transmits, there is a chance that a collision will occur. The probability of collisions rises as the network gets busier. Eventually, the network can reach a point where nodes experience transmission delays — or even complete failures. In many systems, the uncertainty inherent in Ethernet transmissions cannot be tolerated. For example, in manufacturing, a delay or a failure of a warning signal could cause expensive equipment to be damaged.

Token ring is immune to such problems. Every node on the network is guaranteed a chance to transmit each time the token goes around the ring. There is no chance that a node will be unable to transmit because of collisions. Moreover, token ring has a priority mechanism that allows you to designate certain critical systems. (That feature is not available in Ethernet.)

It is hard to compare the general performance of token ring with Ethernet's performance. Nevertheless, I'll venture to say that when demand on a network is within reasonable limits, a 16-Mbps token ring and a 10-Mbps Ethernet have similar performance. Ethernet is extremely simple. Apart from collisions, no network bandwidth is used solely for the purpose of operating the network. A high percentage of Ethernet's capacity is available to transmit data. Token ring, on the other hand, requires a variety of control mechanisms to keep the network running. The control mechanisms use network bandwidth and therefore reduce the capacity of the network to carry data. However, token ring performs better on heavily loaded networks. With Ethernet, busy networks can experience gridlock when too many collisions are occurring.

In general, the capabilities of Ethernet — coupled with its low cost — make Ethernet more popular. Token ring is usually only chosen by buyers who have a need for its special capabilities and can justify the additional expense.

Token Ring Media

Although the IEEE 802.5 standard specifies certain things like data rates and interface requirements, the standard does not include the details of cabling a token ring network. As a result, the majority of vendors and customers use the IBM Cabling System, which was designed with token ring in mind.

IBM's approach to cabling token ring is called a *star-wired ring*. Frames circulate around a ring, but the ring is concealed by a star wiring plan. Figure 3.14 illustrates how wiring hubs can be configured so that a network can be wired as a star but still function as a ring.

The majority of early token rings were cabled with IBM Type 1 cable — a fairly heavy cable that featured two twisted-pairs of wires enclosed by a shield. IBM approved of having token ring networks operate at 4-Mbps and 16-Mbps data rates over Type 1 cable. IBM also recommended 4-Mbps operation over Type 3 cable (data grade, unshielded twisted-pair). However, IBM was reluctant to approve 16-Mbps networks using UTP cable. IBM introduced a higher-speed standard for UTP only after several other vendors brought out networks that offered 16-Mbps operation over Type 3 cable. IBM has since revised its cable system to support operation up to 100 Mbps.

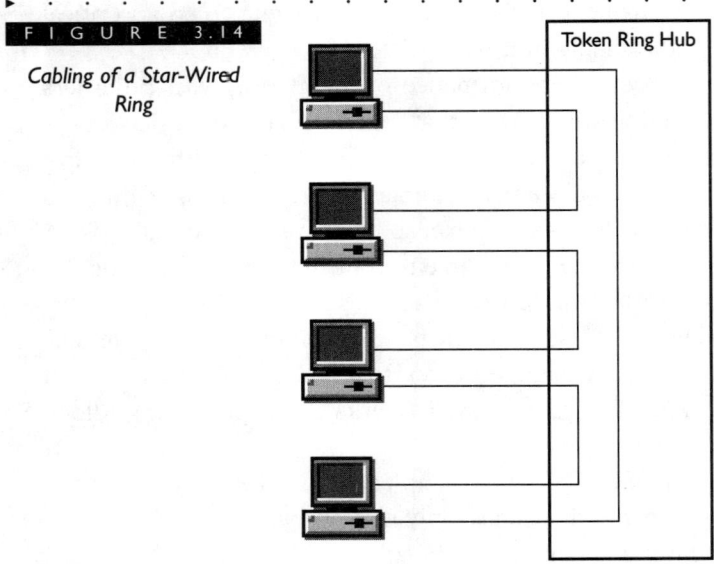

FIGURE 3.14

Cabling of a Star-Wired
Ring

Token Ring Hub

The IEEE 802.5 Frame Format

Figure 3.15 shows the format of an IEEE 802.5 frame. The frame is divided into three major sections:

- **Start-of-frame sequence (SFS).** Indicates the beginning of a frame.

- **Data section.** Includes control information, upper-layer data, and the frame check sequence.

- **End-of-frame sequence (EFS).** Indicates the end of the frame and includes several control bits.

Table 3.7 describes the fields of an IEEE 802.5 frame. As you can see, a token ring frame contains no counterpart to an Ethernet II frame's type field. SNAP encapsulation allows TCP/IP to run over a token ring network. NetWare uses the TOKEN-RING_SNAP frame type for this purpose.

*Format of an IEEE 802.5
Frame*

SD (1 octet)	AC (1 octet)	FC (1 octet)	DA (2 or 6 octets)	SA (2 or 6 octets)	Information (0 or more octets)	FCS (4 octets)	ED (1 octet)	FS (1 octet)

Start-of-Frame   Data Section   End-of-Frame
(FCS Coverage)

Legend:

SD = Starting Delimiter   SA = Source Address
AC = Access Control   FCS = Frame Check Sequence
FC = Frame Control   ED = Ending Delimiter
DA = Destination Address   FS = Frame Status

*Fields in an IEEE 802.5
Frame*

FIELD	PURPOSE
Starting delimiter (SD)	A 1-octet field comprising electrical signals that are not permitted elsewhere in the frame. The SD field purposely violates data encoding rules (it stands out like a sore thumb) and it contains no data. The SD signals the beginning of a frame.
Access control (AC)	A 1-octet field that includes control bits used to set priority and to carry out a variety of token ring control functions.
Frame control (FC)	A 1-octet field that indicates whether the frame is a MAC control frame. MAC control frames are used to manage operation of the token ring network.
Destination address (DA)	A 2- or 6-octet field that contains the 802-format address of the destination node.
Source address (SA)	The 802-format address of the node that originated the frame.
Information	Contains LLC data or data related to the control operations of a MAC protocol frame.

Continued

TABLE 3.7	FIELD	PURPOSE
Continued	Frame check sequence (FCS)	A 32-bit cyclic redundancy check value used to detect errors in transmission.
	Ending delimiter (ED)	A 1-octet field comprised of electrical signals that are not permitted elsewhere in the frame. The ED field purposely violates rules for encoding data and contains no data. The ED signals the end of a frame.
	Frame Status (FS)	A duplicate of the ED. Because the ED field is not covered by the FCS, this copy of the ED is used to check for errors.

Digital Data Services

This section discusses the protocols used to build WANs, which can range in size from networks that cover a radius of only a few miles to networks that cover the whole world. To build a private WAN — or to connect to a public one — you need a way to set up data communication lines across large distances. In virtually all cases, this means leasing a communication line from a digital data service (DDS). This chapter introduces you to available options, including dedicated and switched digital services.

Dedicated Leased Lines

A *dedicated leased line* is a communication line that permanently connects two points. Users are usually unaware of the specifics of connections, which make use of a variety of technologies including copper cables, fiber optics, and microwaves. From a user's perspective, the important thing is that a certain capacity for data transmission has been dedicated exclusively to the user's needs.

Dedicated leased lines are expensive. The cost is significantly greater for higher data rates. Typically, data rates on dedicated leased lines are substantially lower than on the average LAN. Although a wide variety of services are available in both analog and digital, the use of high-speed modems and analog lines to connect computer sites is becoming increasingly less common. The majority of lease lines are digital, and data rates are usually 56 Kbps or higher.

T1, originally developed for digital voice channels, is the most widely available DDS. A T1 line can multiplex 24 digital voice channels, but T1 is useful for computer data, as well. T1 supports point-to-point full-duplex communication at a data rate of 1.544 Mbps. The international equivalent of T1 is E1, which operates at a data rate of 2.048 Mbps.

Because T1 supports multiple, discrete channels, some service providers offer leases on part of the capacity of a T1 line. Fractional T1 enables customers to lease one or more of the 56-Kbps channels at a reduced cost. Other digital data rates in the United States are T2 (6.312 Mbps), T3 (44.736 Mbps), and T4 (274.176 Mbps). The comparable international services — standardized by the International Telecommunications Union (ITU) — are 8.848, 34.304, and 139.264 Mbps. (The ITU was formerly known as the International Telegraph and Telephone Consultative Committee, or CCITT.)

It is entirely possible to build a private network using only leased lines. However, usually only large corporations can afford to pay the high cost. The Internet consists largely of dedicated lines, but the cost of ownership has been spread across the entire Internet community. In the past, an organization that wanted to connect to the Internet would lease a line that connects to a willing host. In turn, the organization would let other organizations connect to the Internet through its network.

Leased lines are also used to connect to public data services, such as X.25 and Frame Relay networks. (See the following sections "X.25" and "Frame Relay" in this chapter.) When a network provider is local, you can usually save money by leasing a local line to a network provider rather than leasing private lines to all of your remote sites.

Leased lines are both costly and inflexible. When you lease a line, you need to lease a fixed data capacity that allows for your peak demands. During quiet periods, much of the capacity you are paying for is unused. If your network demands are irregular, you may want to consider a switched digital connection. (See the following subsection.)

Several pieces of equipment are required to connect a network to a digital leased line. Figure 3.16 shows how a leased line can be used to connect two LANs. The wide-area connection consists of the following components:

▶ A bridge or router configured to direct traffic from the LAN to the leased line.

▶ A channel service unit/digital service unit (CSU/DSU) to translate LAN signals into the format required by the leased line.

▶ A network interface supplied by the communication provider.

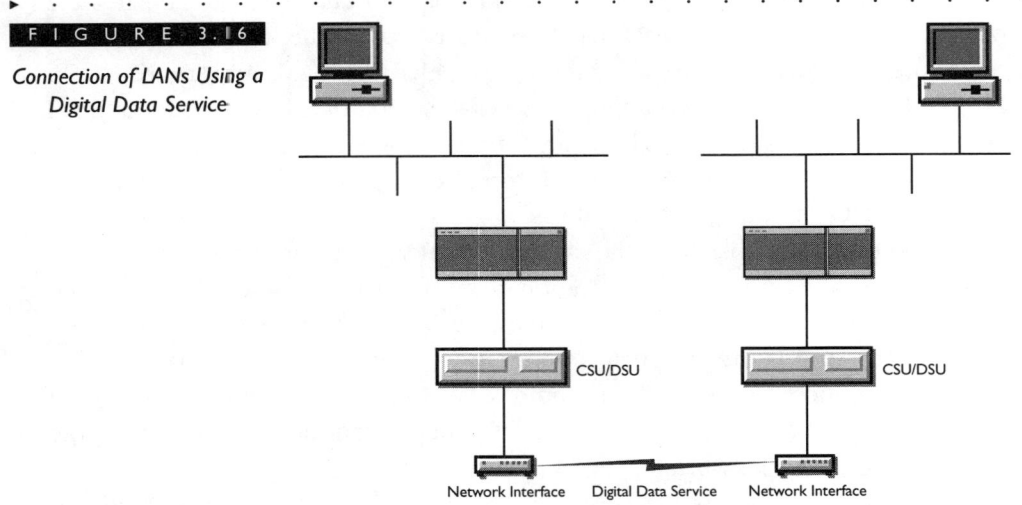

FIGURE 3.16

Connection of LANs Using a Digital Data Service

Novell's MultiProtocol Router can be used to connect to a DDS (see Chapter 10).

Switched Digital Services

At one time, a *switched data connection* meant a standard analog telephone line and a modem. Unfortunately, analog modems seldom provided the performance required to connect LANs. As a result, most organizations were forced to lease dedicated lines — even though their communications might have been infrequent.

In recent years, however, a variety of services have made switched connections possible. Switched digital services and switched 56-Kbps CSU/DSUs are both now available.

The emerging technology that seems likely to replace the analog modem is the *Integrated Services Digital Network* (ISDN), which is a fully digital service designed for switched connections. Many levels of ISDN service are available. A common service provides two 64-Kbps digital channels. These channels offer a potential bandwidth of 128 Kbps, but they must be aggregated by equipment at the customer site. ISDN has the potential to make switched digital service available at reasonable cost. Recently, several major communication providers have committed to making ISDN available in their service areas. At present, however, ISDN's availability remains spotty.

X.25

Leased circuits have many significant disadvantages. Dedicated lines are costly. Furthermore, it is expensive to reconfigure a network based on leased circuits, because the setup fees are high. That is why the majority of organizations obtain their wide-area connectivity from public data networks.

Public data networks are owned and operated by network providers, who establish a high-capacity network to cover a specific geographic area. Customers lease bandwidth on the network. The only leased lines involved are the lines that connect the customers' sites to the local network's point of presence. Although public data networks aren't cheap, they can be much more cost-effective than networks based on leased lines — particularly when a number of sites must be connected.

 **Some public data networks offer dial-in capacity, which can make it easy to implement a mobile computing strategy.**

NOTE

X.25 was one of the earliest WANs. Despite unspectacular performance by today's standards, X.25 remains widely available. Virtually any network environment can be connected to an X.25 network. X.25 is a packet switching network that supports both switched and permanent virtual circuits. *Permanent virtual circuits* can be established to provide reliable connections between computers that must remain in constant communication. *Switched virtual circuits* enable devices to establish temporary connections that are torn down when no longer needed, much like the connection you have when you make a telephone call.

NOTE

X.25 is a connection-oriented network and requires a connection to be established between any two computers that need to communicate. Connection-oriented networks make no provision for broadcast-mode communication and consequently, offer no mechanism that enables one node to communicate with many nodes without formally establishing a connection with each node. Many TCP/IP protocols depend on broadcast transmissions. Such protocols must be specially adapted if they are to operate on connection-oriented networks, or some other mechanism must be put in place to provide the functions supported by the protocols.

X.25 was developed when communication lines were slow and not very trustworthy. The upper limit on X.25 data rates is 64 Kbps, which was more than enough when the majority of networks carried traffic between dumb terminals and host computers. Today, however, the performance constraints of X.25 make it unsuitable for linking LANs.

Because X.25 networks initially often relied on unreliable analog media, the X.25 protocol was designed for robust error detection and recovery. Each X.25 switch is responsible for detecting and recovering errors. Therefore, error checking occurs many times along the way as a packet is switched through the network. Modern digital lines are far more reliable, so X.25's frequent error checking is often unnecessary. Further, the modern preference is to perform error checking high in the protocol stack. Because TCP performs its own error checking, the redundant error checking by X.25 only slows network performance.

Figure 3.17 illustrates LANs connected through a packet-switching network. Packet-switching networks are commonly represented by a cloud because the inner workings of the network are hidden from outside observers. Data enters the network at one point and exits at another point. What happens in between is the packet-switching network's concern.

The networks shown in Figure 3.17 can run any protocols. When they run TCP/IP protocols, for example, the IP messages are encapsulated in X.25 frames and are decapsulated at the receiving end. The encapsulation and decapsulation process is very transparent.

Devices connect to an X.25 network using a *packet assembler-disassembler* (PAD). The PAD could be located at the customer site, interfaced to a LAN through a router, and linked to the X.25 network through a leased or dial-up connection.

Another option could locate the PAD at the network service provider and make it available through a dial-up modem connection.

FIGURE 3.17

Connection through an X.25 Public Data Network

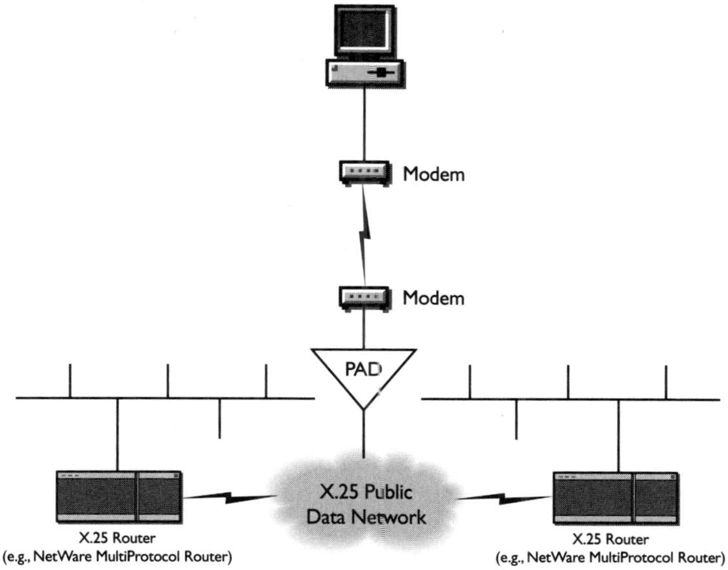

X.25 is recommended by the *International Telecommunications Union* (ITU), which is the agency of the United Nations responsible for international communication standards. The protocol model for X.25 is shown in Figure 3.18.

FIGURE 3.18

The X.25 Protocol Stack

Application	
Presentation	
Session	
Transport	
Network	X.25 Packet Level Protocol
Data Link	Link Access Protocol Balanced (LAPB)
Physical	X.21 or X.21 *bis*

The protocol model for X.25 consists of three layers:

▸ X.21 provides the physical layer for digital circuits. X.21 is the comparable standard for analog circuits.

▸ *Link Access Procedure Balanced* (LAPB) is the data link layer protocol. It provides full-duplex, synchronous communication.

▸ X.25 is a network layer protocol that provides flow control and reliable delivery.

As already indicated, X.25 is an extremely limited protocol that remains popular primarily because it is readily available. But X.25 is not well-suited to LANs for a variety of reasons. LANs tend to produce traffic that is characterized as *bursty* — that is, traffic that has extremely variable data requirements. Frame Relay, which was derived from X.25, offers bandwidth on demand and therefore works better for most LAN communication.

▶ · ◀

Frame Relay

Frame Relay is essentially a modernized X.25 network. The ITU designed Frame Relay as a streamlined packet-switching network that could provide broadband service. Frame Relay accommodates bursty LAN traffic by offering bandwidth on demand. Therefore, Frame Relay can adjust to varying rates of data flow.

Subscribers to a public Frame Relay network contract for a guaranteed data rate called a *committed information rate* (CIR). Depending on the service provider, subscribers may be permitted to exceed the CIR on a temporary basis. Subscribers pay for additional bandwidth as necessary. This flexibility enables customers to purchase Frame Relay service that closely matches their normal requirements. At the same time, customers still have the option of obtaining more bandwidth on a temporary basis.

Frame Relay is connection-oriented. It supports *switched virtual circuits* (SVCs) and *permanent virtual circuits* (PVCs). Establishing a PVC configures a fixed path through the network that enables devices to communicate efficiently, because very little processing is needed to move each frame through the network. A PVC can multiplex up to 1024 logical connections.

The data field of a Frame Relay frame is called the *payload*. The capacity of the payload field is configurable. Therefore, when you implement a Frame Relay network, you can fine-tune the network to different requirements.

 **SNAP encapsulation must be used to support TCP/IP over Frame Relay.**

NOTE

Frame Relay accommodates much higher data rates than are available with X.25. Also, Frame Relay can operate over high-speed digital services such as T1 and T3. In fact, data rates of up to 44.6 Mbps are possible.

Frame Relay's performance is better than X.25's because Frame Relay's designers were able to assume that data communication lines would be reliable. This assumption frees Frame Relay of the need to perform error detection and recovery each time a frame is switched. Although Frame Relay detects errors and discards bad frames, upper-layer protocols are responsible for requesting retransmission of bad or missing frames. In general, moving error recovery to upper-layer protocols enhances network performance. Figure 3.19 shows the Frame Relay protocol stack, which corresponds to the data link and physical layers of the OSI Reference Model.

FIGURE 3.19

The Frame Relay Protocol Stack

| Application |
| Presentation |
| Session |
| Transport |
| Network |
| Data Link |
| Physical |

Frame Relay

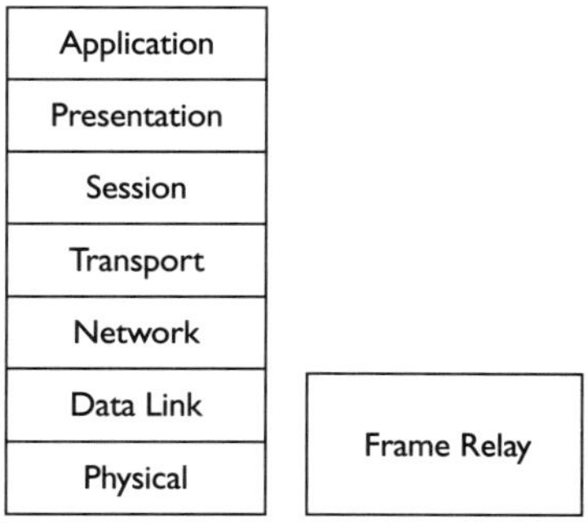

A typical Frame Relay network is shown in Figure 3.20. LANs connect to the Frame Relay network using a *Frame Relay Interface* (FRI), which often is incorporated into a router. Frame Relay is one of the WAN options of the Novell MultiProtocol Router. Frame Relay networks can be either public or private data networks.

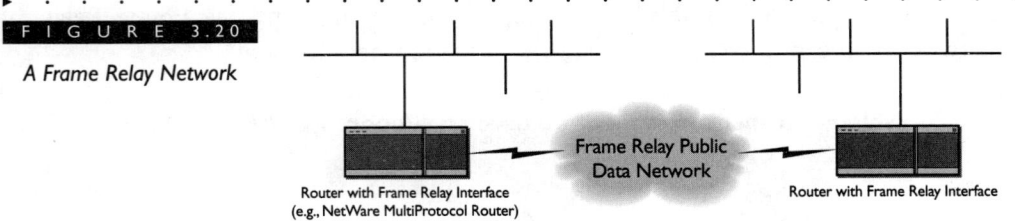

FIGURE 3.20

A Frame Relay Network

Router with Frame Relay Interface
(e.g., NetWare MultiProtocol Router)

Frame Relay Public
Data Network

Router with Frame Relay Interface

Asynchronous Transfer Mode

If there were such a thing as a high school yearbook for networks, *asynchronous transfer mode* (ATM) would undoubtedly be voted Most Likely to Succeed. ATM is an emerging technology that promises to solve a host of problems faced by computer network administrators. To understand why there is currently so much interest in ATM, you need to know something about the different kinds of services that LANs are now being asked to provide.

In the mainframe era, network traffic consisted primarily of character data being transferred between terminals and host computers. Terminal traffic could be supported with limited bandwidth, and 56-Kbps data links were pretty hot stuff. But the emergence of LANs has changed all that. New technologies such as Ethernet and token ring (which operate at about 10 Mbps) have changed the way distributed processing is done. In the early days of LANs, users primarily transferred files, ran programs, and printed documents through the network. The networks that emerged in the 1980s were capable of handling all of those tasks satisfactorily.

Now, however, new LAN applications are emerging. The problem isn't just that more data must be handled. Today, users want their LANs to support new types of data such as voice and video. Video, in particular, places heavy demands on a network. Not only does video require a great deal of bandwidth (as much as 6 Mbps for a single channel), but video also relies on two different streams of data (video and audio) that must remain synchronized as data is delivered through the network. Traditional LANs — even fast ones — simply aren't up to the task of delivering synchronized data streams.

ATM has unique capabilities that position it to satisfy these new requirements. All types of data can be accommodated by ATM, including data, voice, and video. ATM offers bandwidth on demand, very high throughput, and the ability to synchronize the delivery of multiple data streams, such as the components of a video signal.

ATM evolved from broadband ISDN (B-ISDN), a technology that is an extension of the narrowband ISDN developed in 1983 by the CCITT (now known as the ITU). The ITU governs the primary standards of ATM but has not addressed issues of LAN implementation.

The ATM Forum is a consortium of network industry partners that addresses the issues involved in employing ATM with LANs. The *Internet Engineering Task Forum* (IETF) also looks at ATM issues, and several Internet-Drafts address topics related to ATM.

How ATM Works

ATM stands for *asynchronous transfer mode*. To understand how ATM works, you must first know something about transfer modes in general. A transfer mode is a method of transporting data units through a network. Transfer modes are closely related to the concepts of multiplexing and packet switching, which are discussed in Chapter 2.

Synchronous transfer mode (STM) makes use of time-division multiplexing. Multiple data streams are assigned time slots. The data streams share the communication bandwidth by taking turns. STM allocates each data stream a guaranteed bandwidth and offers synchronous delivery of multiple data streams. As such, STM is well suited to voice and video. However STM is too inflexible to support data. Also, because time slots must be configured, STM has trouble accommodating variable data transfer requirements.

Packet transfer mode (PTM) employs packet switching, which provides the kind of flexible service required for computer data. PTM is not bound by time slots that have fixed sizes, so it can accept data units of varying sizes. However, PTM cannot provide synchronous delivery.

In many ways, ATM is a hybrid of STM and PTM. ATM can be adapted to data, voice, and video. ATM employs fixed-size data units called *cells*, which are switched through virtual circuits. ATM cells are 53 bytes in length. With ATM, switching operations are more efficient, because switching can be optimized for a standard-size data unit. Virtual circuits ensure that cells arrive in the order in which they were transmitted, because all cells are switched through the same path.

To accommodate the needs of voice and video, ATM provides *cell synchronous service*. ATM can synchronize delivery of multiple data streams, as well as provide guaranteed bandwidth. In especially critical situations, ATM can provide *constant bit rate service* — in other words, service that delivers data at a constant rate that compensates for delays in transmission. For computer data, ATM offers bandwidth on demand and is highly responsive to bursty LAN traffic.

ATM is connection-oriented, and devices must establish a virtual circuit in order to communicate. The virtual circuit defines a path through the ATM network that is dedicated to the use of the connected devices. Figure 3.21 illustrates how a virtual circuit is defined.

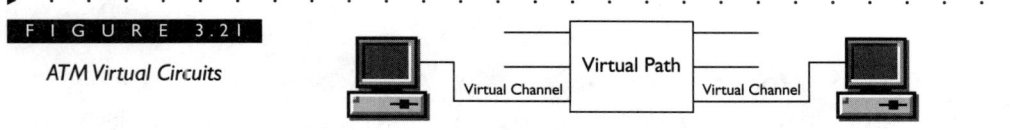

FIGURE 3.21

ATM Virtual Circuits

In a virtual circuit, two ATM devices are connected by at least one *virtual path*, which typically corresponds to a media channel. The path is called virtual because it does not correspond to a specific dedicated physical path through a medium. Bandwidth is dedicated to the virtual path only when the connection is used to transfer cells. Because bandwidth is not dedicated to any connections, bandwidth is available to all connections on demand.

A virtual path can accommodate more than 16 million virtual channels, although most equipment accommodates fewer than this amount. A virtual circuit between two switches is defined by the virtual path and virtual circuit assigned to it. As shown in Figure 3.22, each pair of switches may assign a different virtual path and virtual circuit to the connection. Virtual path and virtual circuit information is encoded in the header of the ATM cell. Figure 3.23 shows the format of an ATM cell.

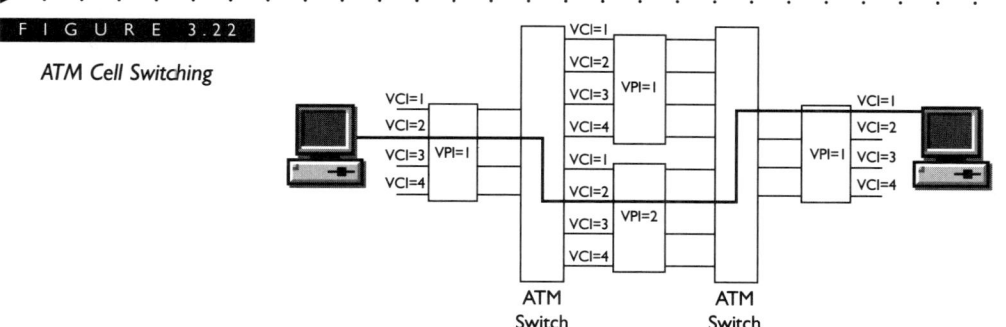

ATM Cell Switching

The cell's connection information is encoded in the *virtual path identifier* (VPI) and *virtual channel identifier* (VCI) fields. The VPI and VCI fields are the only fields discussed here because these two fields are key to understanding how ATM routes cells. Figure 3.22 shows how cells are switched through an ATM network. The bold line indicates the path associated with a particular virtual circuit. Between each pair of switches, a VPI and a VCI are associated with the virtual circuit. Each switch maintains a database that describes how cells for each connection should be switched. The VPI and VCI fields are updated as cells are forwarded from switch to switch using data stored in databases maintained by the switches. Switches consult their databases to determine which path to use when forwarding a cell that arrives from a virtual circuit.

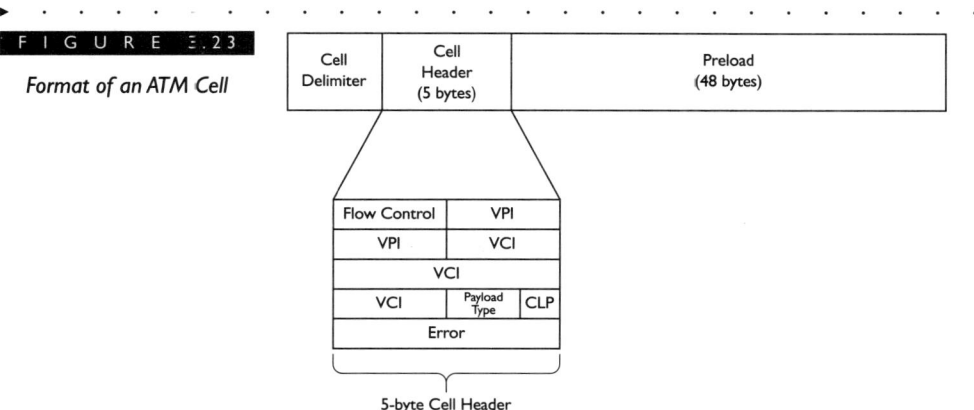

Format of an ATM Cell

The ITU has defined the protocol model for B-ISDN. That protocol model is shown in Figure 3.24. Although ATM protocols correspond to the first three layers of the OSI Reference Model, all switching is performed below the network layer in order to achieve greater efficiency.

F I G U R E 3 . 2 4

The ATM Protocol Stack

ATM Adaptation Layer (AAL)
ATM Layer
ATM Physical Layer

The layers of the ATM protocol model are as follows:

- **ATM adaptation layer (AAL).** This layer provides an interface between upper-layer protocols and ATM switching. When multiple protocols are multiplexed through the same virtual channel IEEE 802.2 LLC encapsulation is used. SNAP must be used to support TCP/IP. The AAL is responsible for message fragmentation and reassembly. The AAL provides either connection-oriented or connectionless service. Variable and constant bit rate services are supported.

- **ATM layer.** This layer defines cell formats. It is responsible for cell delivery. The ATM layer supports permanent virtual circuits (PVCs) and switched virtual circuits (SVCs).

- **ATM physical layer.** This layer transports cells through the network and defines signaling requirements.

The ATM physical layer does not define data rates or media types. ATM can be adapted to virtually any medium and any performance level.

ATM Media
There are no inherent restrictions on ATM data rates or media, and different combinations of media and data rates are bound to appear. IBM, for example, has offered a 25-Mbps ATM product that is designed to bring ATM to the desktop.

Four ATM interfaces have been defined by the ATM Forum:

► 45-Mbps DS3 WAN

► 155-Mbps OC-3 SONET

► 155-Mbps multimode optical fiber based on Fiber Channel

► 100-Mbps multimode optical fiber based on *Fiber Distributed Data Interface*
(FDDI)

The DS3 service interface supports copper and fiber media and can be used to
interface LANs to telecommunications networks.

Synchronous Optical Network (SONET), developed by BellCore, is a common
ATM carrier. SONET data rates are specified by *optical carrier* (OC) levels.
Available data rates range from 52 Mbps (OC-1) to 2.5 Gbps (OC-48).

The FDDI interface is most likely to be incorporated into LANs. This interface
is designed to take advantage of newer developments in FDDI, such as FDDI over
copper (CDDI). FDDI is a fault-tolerant network based on token ring operating at
100 Mbps.

A unique benefit of ATM is that networks can incorporate a mix of data rates.
A 25-Mbps desktop connection could be switched to a 100-Mbps FDDI backbone,
which could in turn be switched into a 466-Mbps public network. This scalability
could make ATM the dominant network standard in coming decades.

Architecture of ATM LANs

The ATM Forum has been most responsible for defining an ATM LAN
architecture. Figure 3.25 shows a typical ATM LAN. ATM networks consist of
endstations and switches. The ATM Forum has defined two network interfaces:

► **User-Network Interface (UNI).** An endstation is connected to a switch
through this interface.

► **Network-Network Interface (NNI).** A switch connects to another switch
through this interface.

FIGURE 3.25

Architecture of an ATM LAN

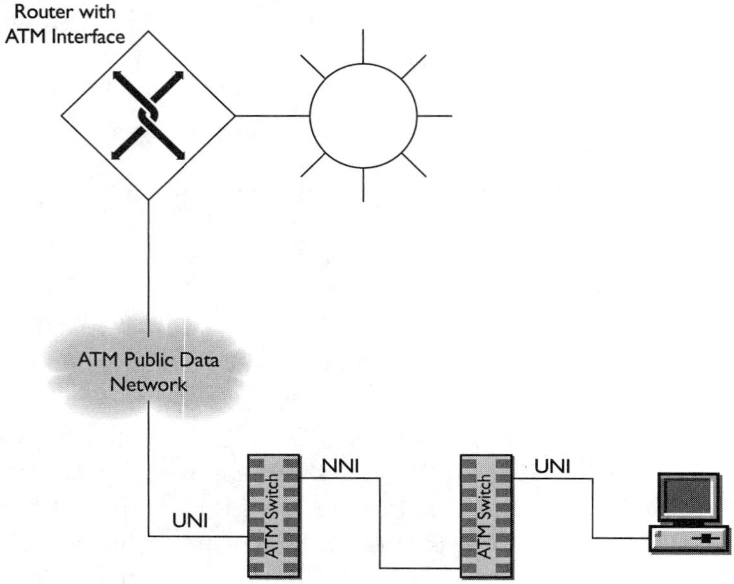

ATM sounds great, but don't rush out and sell your Ethernet boards. ATM LANs are still nascent. Several years will be required before you will see standards that can be turned into cost-effective products. ATM remains an expensive technology that is ready only for those organizations that require ATM's unique capabilities.

ATM is a connection-oriented network, requiring a connection between each pair of communicating nodes. As you discovered in the section about X.25, connection-oriented networks do not provide direct support for the broadcast (one-to-many) transmissions that are broadly employed by TCP/IP and other protocol stacks. To enable ATM to coexist with LAN protocols, the ATM industry has developed LAN emulation, which enables an ATM network to present the appearance of a more typical LAN protocol such as Ethernet. While this may enable ATM to edge its way into LAN environments, LAN emulation has its price. Considerable network bandwidth is lost to the LAN emulation process. Consequently, a fast ATM infrastructure with LAN emulation may be equivalent in performance to a slower LAN. The performance overhead of LAN emulation has let fast Ethernet technologies easily keep pace with ATM while maintaining a lower cost-per-node.

A Note on Network Evolution

The needs of network users are evolving rapidly. There is no sign that a few trusted standards will be universally adopted anytime soon. In fact, the market is expanding for network products that satisfy specific market niches. Some of the network standards that have been around for a while are still emerging technologies. Even good old Ethernet continues to evolve into ever-faster versions. This chapter has tried to make you aware of the many different options available.

Chapter 2 explained that the function of the network access layer is fairly limited. The network access layer is responsible for delivering frames (or other small message units) between nodes on a network. There are many other tasks that the network layer does not perform. TCP/IP can be used to carry out many of those tasks. The next chapter examines the internet layer, which is the first TCP/IP protocol layer.

## CHAPTER 4

The Internet Layer

The Internet Protocol (IP) is a required protocol at the internet layer. IP is really at the heart of the DoD protocol stack. At other layers, you will learn about alternative protocols that serve specialized purposes. At the internet layer, however, there is only IP, which has three key responsibilities:

▶ Addressing

▶ Delivery of datagrams on the internetwork

▶ Datagram fragmentation and reassembly

RFC 791, as amended by RFCs 919, 922, and 950, sets forth the IP specifications.

Although IP is the powerhouse protocol at the internet layer, several other protocols assist IP. The protocols that assist IP are discussed in detail later in this chapter, but here is a general overview of the services they provide:

▶ The *Internet Control Message Protocol* (ICMP) enables destination hosts to communicate errors to source hosts. ICMP also allows destination hosts to provide other hosts with limited routing information.

▶ The *Internet Group Messaging Protocol* (IGMP) supports IP multicasting, enabling members of multicast groups to register their presence with multicast routers.

▶ The *Address Resolution Protocol* (ARP) and the *Reverse Address Resolution Protocol* (RARP) help IP resolve (match) addresses used at the internet level to physical addresses used at the network access level.

▶ The *Routing Information Protocol* (RIP) and the protocol called *Open Shortest Path First* (OSPF) assist IP with routing. IP uses information from routing tables to route data, but IP cannot gather routing information to update routing tables. RIP and OSPF are designed to gather network path information and maintain the routing tables used by IP.

In order to understand IP itself, you must first learn a little about IP addressing. TCP/IP uses distinctive addresses called *IP addresses* to identify hosts at the internet level and at higher layers. IP addresses are unique to TCP/IP.

NOTE

Many TCP/IP concepts have no counterparts in the IPX/SPX protocols that support standard NetWare communication. IPX relies on physical addresses, and NetWare uses dynamic mechanisms such as the *Service Advertising Protocol* (SAP) to advertise the availability of services. With NetWare, node names are collected and updated automatically.

IP Addressing

TCP/IP predates many other protocols and, in fact, predates the vast majority of physical network standards. When IP was first conceptualized, there were no network node identification standards like IEEE 802's globally administered addresses. TCP/IP needed an addressing scheme that could be independent of network hardware so that a uniform address scheme can be applied to all hosts, regardless of type.

Consequently, at the layers above the network access layer, hosts are identified by logical IP addresses. Each IP address includes a network address and a node address so that every host on an internetwork can be uniquely identified by its IP address.

TCP/IP's logical IP addresses have some administrative benefits. When a TCP/IP host is set up, its configuration includes information that identifies several critical hosts on the network. For example, each host is configured with the address of a default router. Also, when a naming service is operating, each host is configured with the address of the host operating as a name server. Suppose that dozens of hosts have been configured using the physical address of a particular router. The address would change if the network board in the router were replaced. In that case, you would need to reconfigure all of the hosts that use the router. However, a router can retain the same logical IP address even though its network board is changed. If the router's IP address is used in the hosts, no other hosts need to be reconfigured when the network board in the router is replaced.

As you can see, IP addresses promote stability in the network. This stability is important to end users as well as administrators because the end users may need to access hosts using addresses. When commonly used host addresses are changed, all users on the network must be informed or else the users will not be able to access the hosts.

NOTE

Using a name service alleviates this problem. A name service enables users to access hosts by name rather than address. The TCP/IP Domain Name Service is discussed in Chapter 6.

Formats of IP Addresses

An IP address consists of 32 bits arranged in two fields. The two fields of IP addresses are as follows:

▶ The *netid* field specifies the address of the network to which the host is attached.

▶ The *hostid* field specifies a unique logical identifier for each host on a given network.

The netid is used to route data through the internetwork. An IP network consists of a group of hosts that share the same netid. All hosts with a given netid should be attached to a common network segment so that they can communicate directly. Hosts separated by a router will be unable to communicate even though they have the same netid. Hosts with different netids must communicate through a router — even though they may be attached to the same network segment.

When the IP addressing scheme was designed, its creators assumed that networks would vary greatly in size and number. This assumption led them to create several IP address classes that could support networks of different sizes. The five address classes are as follows:

▶ *Class A* addresses were designed to support a few very large networks. The netid is contained in the first octet. The hostid is contained in the remaining three octets. Class A addresses begin with the high-order bit set to 0.

▶ *Class B* addresses were designed to support a moderate number of networks of intermediate size. The first two octets are devoted to the netid. The remaining two octets are the hostid. Class B addresses begin with the high-order bits 10.

▶ *Class C* addresses were designed to support a large number of small networks. The first three octets are the netid. Only the final octet is devoted to the hostid. Class C addresses begin with the high-order bits 110.

▶ *Class D* addresses support multicasting, enabling messages to be sent to defined groups of hosts. The use of multicast addresses is defined by the network implementation. Class D addresses begin with the high-order bits 1110.

▶ *Class E* addresses are reserved for experimental purposes and begin with the high-order bits 11110.

Figure 4.1 shows the classes of IP addresses. Notice that a 32-bit IP address is divided into four octets, which form the basis of the address classes.

FIGURE 4.1

Structure of IP Addresses

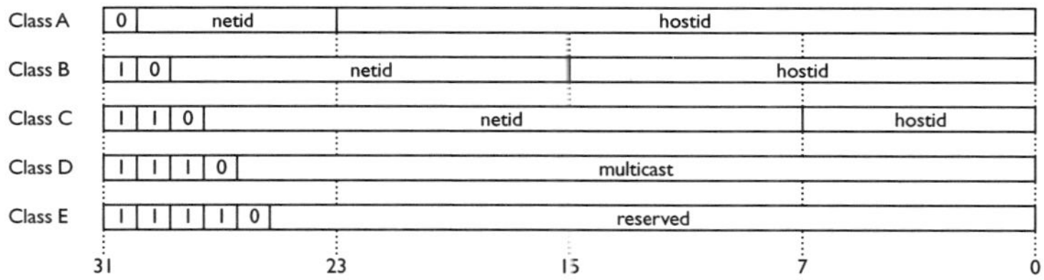

Using Dotted-Decimal Notation

You will discover that there are times when it is necessary to work with IP addresses in their binary form. However, bit patterns of IP addresses aren't easy to read or remember. An address that reads 10001111 01010111 11000111 00100001 is not likely to stick in your memory.

Because binary numbers are not easy to deal with, an alternative format has been developed for representing IP addresses. The majority of IP addresses you see are expressed in dotted-decimal notation. The conversion is simple. Each of the four octets is converted to an equivalent decimal value from 0 through 255. The complete address is represented by separating the decimal numbers with periods. The dotted-decimal equivalent of the address previously listed is:

143.87.199.33

Dotted-hexadecimal notation is also used for IP addresses, but it is not as common. In dotted-hex, the above address is represented as follows:

8F.57.CF.21

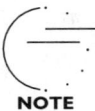

NOTE

The calculator that ships with Microsoft Windows has a scientific mode that converts hex, binary, and decimal numbers. Turn on scientific mode by selecting the Scientific command in the View menu. Alternatively, Appendix B includes a table that lists decimal, binary, and hexadecimal equivalents. (Appendix A explains briefly how the numbering systems work.)

Rules for Assigning IP Addresses

Some IP addresses are designated for special purposes. Therefore, certain addresses cannot be assigned to hosts. Here are some of the addresses that cannot be used for hosts:

▶ A hostid with all bits set to 0 identifies the network itself. (For example, the IP address 128.1.0.0 refers to the network with the netid 128.1.) A hostid cannot consist entirely 0 bits.

▶ A hostid with all bits set to 1 is a limited broadcast address. Consequently a hostid cannot consist entirely of 1 bits.

▶ A netid with all bits set to 0 refers to "this network." (For example, the IP address 0.5.127.240 refers to host 5.127.240 on the current class A network.) Therefore, a netid cannot consist entirely of octets with the value 0.

▶ An octet that is all 1s (decimal 255, hex FF) indicates a broadcast address. Thus, the IP address 255.255.255.255 identifies a message that is to be broadcast to all hosts on the current network, and the IP address 199.38.87.255 identifies a message that is to be broadcast to all hosts on network 199.39.87.

▶ The netid 127 (binary 01111111) is reserved for use as a loopback address. If a host sends a message to 127.0.0.1 (or any address on network 127), the message will not reach the network. The message will be reflected back to the sending process. The loopback address is a useful troubleshooting tool.

These restrictions limit the addresses that are available in each address class. Table 4.1 summarizes the IP addresses that are available for addressing hosts.

T A B L E 4.1
Available IP Addresses

CLASS	FROM (BINARY)	FROM (DECIMAL)	TO (BINARY)	TO (DECIMAL)	AVAILABLE NETWORKS	AVAILABLE HOSTS
A	00000001	1	01111110	126	126	16,777,214
B	10000000	128	10111111	191	16,384	65,534
C	11000000	192	11011111	223	2,097,152	254

NOTE

The only network likely to run out of available IP addresses is the Internet. However, recent fears that the Internet would run out of IP addresses have turned out to be unfounded, due in part to a classless approach to addressing (Classless Inter-Domain Routing or CIDR; RFC 1518/1519). CIDR is described later in this chapter.

Assigning IP Addresses to Hosts

In most cases, IP addresses are manually assigned to host computers by entering the IP address into the host configuration files. This manual procedure is perhaps the single most time-consuming task an administrator faces when setting up a TCP/IP network. The network administrator must devise a plan for assigning each network a unique netid and each host a hostid that is unique on the host's network.

In many cases networks are segmented to form internetworks. Figure 4.2 shows an example of a TCP/IP internetwork that incorporates network segments with class A, B, and C addresses. Address classes can be mixed freely on an internetwork.

Notice that routers are essentially TCP/IP hosts that interface to two or more networks. Each interface must be assigned an IP address that is correct for the network to which it attaches.

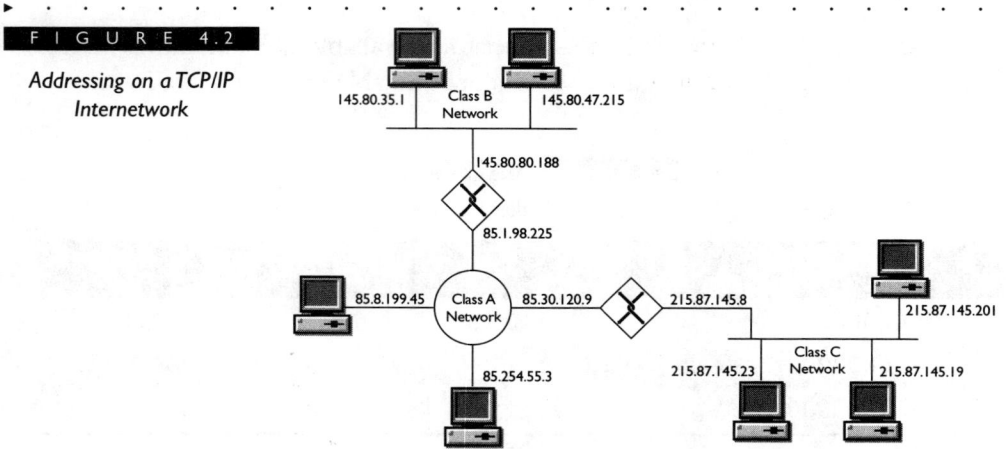

F I G U R E   4.2

Addressing on a TCP/IP
Internetwork

There are a number of reasons to segment a network. Here are a few:

► If a network is congested, properly designed segmentation reduces traffic on each segment. With the best design, the majority of traffic will be between hosts on the same network segment.

► LAN cabling systems accommodate maximum numbers of connected devices. To exceed those limits, the network must be segmented.

▸ LANs can accommodate different LAN technologies to meet different requirements. A token ring network may be required in manufacturing, for example, whereas Ethernet is used elsewhere. Routers can interconnect different types of LANs.

▸ WAN technologies enable a network to grow beyond local limits. Routers are used to keep unnecessary traffic off the wide-area connection.

▸ Security may be enhanced by isolating parts of the network. Routers can be configured to filter traffic so that critical data does not reach other local or remote networks.

Routing theory is addressed later in this chapter, under the heading "Delivering Datagrams on Internetworks." Chapter 10 covers the installation and configuration of NetWare routers for TCP/IP.

Obtaining Addresses for the Internet

The Internet can run smoothly only if each network and each host is uniquely addressed. So if you want to connect your network to the Internet, you need to apply for enough addresses to support your network.

The authority for registering IP addresses is the responsibility of the following organizations:

▸ APNIC (Asia-Pacific Network Information Center):
`http://www.apnic.net`

▸ ARIN (American Registry for Internet Numbers): `http://www.arin.net`

▸ RIPE NCC (Reseau IP Europeens): `http://www.ripe.net`

The majority of IP addresses are assigned by Internet Service Providers (ISPs), however. ISPs are allocated blocks of IP addresses, which they in turn assign to their clients. Only clients with large networks obtain their IP addresses directly from an Internet address authority. See the section "Classless Inter-Domain Routing" for more about how IP addresses are allocated on the Internet.

Subnetting

A class A or B address can accommodate a lot of users. Not many networks can physically support 65,534 hosts without a few routers. So what's an administrator to do? Should you use a class B address for a 500-node LAN and let the rest of the available addresses go to waste? If you're attached to the Internet, you can't really do that because your organization probably won't be assigned sufficient IP addresses to let you configure every network with a separate netid. So what should you do?

Subnetting is a technique that enables you to spread a single network IP address more thinly so that its address pool can be shared by several network segments. Even if your organization has a single class C network address, subnet addressing enables you to support a LAN with several segments. Subnetting is defined in RFC 950.

Figure 4.3 shows the theory behind subnetting. Ordinarily, an IP address is read like this:

netid + hostid

When subnetting is used, an IP address has three fields:

netid + subnetid + hostid

The bits necessary to create the subnetid field are borrowed from the hostid field. You lose some of the bits that could be used to configure hosts, but you gain in the number of network segments your lone IP address can support.

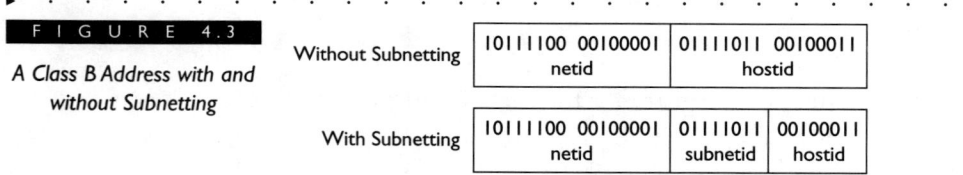

FIGURE 4.3
A Class B Address with and without Subnetting

Without Subnetting	10111100 00100001	01111011 00100011
	netid	hostid

With Subnetting	10111100 00100001	01111011	00100011
	netid	subnetid	hostid

Introduction to Subnet Masks

Subnetting is achieved using a subnet mask. Subnet masking is the tool that designates bits for the subnet mask. I'll warn you right now: Subnet masking is an area where there's no substitute for getting down to the bit level. Dotted decimal equivalents just don't allow you to see what's going on. So if you're uncomfortable with binary, now is the time to review number notation schemes in Appendix A.

Figure 4.4 shows how subnet masking can be applied to class A, B, and C addresses. Of course, you have more bits available for subnetids with a class A or B address, but class C addresses can be productively subnetted.

▶ . . . . ◀

FIGURE 4.4
Subnetting with Different Address Classes

Class A Network With Subnetting	00100011	11010000 0000	0011	11010010
	netid	subnetid		hostid

Class B Network With Subnetting	10111100 00100001	1C10000	0 00100011
	netid	subnetid	hostid

Class C Network With Subnetting	11011101 01100011 01111011	1010	0010
	netid		

subnetid ─┘   └─ hostid

The subnet mask is simply a 32-bit binary number that matches an IP address digit-for-digit. A 1 in the subnet mask indicates that the corresponding bit in the IP address is part of the netid or subnetid. A 0 in the subnet mask indicates that the corresponding bit in the IP address is part of the hostid.

Like IP addresses, subnet masks are frequently represented in dotted-decimal form. However, dotted-hex is also common. In fact, NetWare generally represents subnet masks in dotted-hex notation. See Appendix A for further explanation.

In most cases, the 1s in a subnet mask are adjacent, high-order bits. (In fact, many hardware vendors require subnet masks to be constructed with 1s in contiguous, high-order bits. Contiguous bits aren't required by RFC 950, but I have never seen an example that requires a non-contiguous subnet mask.) As a result, there are only eight subnet masks you will commonly encounter. If you memorize the information in Table 4.2, you will know the most popular subnet masks.

TABLE 4.2	BINARY	DECIMAL
Common Subnet Masks	00000000	0
	10000000	128
	11000000	192
	11100000	224

Continued

. . . . .

TABLE 4.2	BINARY	DECIMAL
Continued	11111100	252
	11111110	254
	11111111	255

The majority of TCP/IP implementations require that IP addresses be assigned a subnet mask even though the network may not be segmented into subnets. When IP addresses are used without subnetting, a default subnet mask must be specified, which simply includes a 1 that corresponds to each digit in the standard netid field. Table 4.3 lists the default subnet masks for the three IP address classes.

TABLE 4.3

Default Subnet Masks

ADDRESS CLASS	BINARY SUBNET MASK	DOTTED-DECIMAL MASK	DOTTED-HEX MASK
A	11111111 00000000 00000000 00000000	255.0.0.0	FF.00.00.00
B	11111111 11111111 00000000 00000000	255.255.0.0	FF.FF.00.00
C	11111111 11111111 11111111 00000000	255.255.255.0	FF.FF.FF.00

The subnet mask must contain as many bits as are required to define the hostid field for the address class of the IP address. A subnet mask of 255.255.0.0 is invalid for a class C IP address.

Identifying Subnetids and Hostids

Here are a few examples to help you understand subnet masks (see also Figure 4.5). Suppose a class A network identified by 65.0.0.0 is to be subnetted with the subnet mask 255.255.0.0. What are the subnetid and netid for host 65.210.185.33? To determine the values, the numbers must be examined in binary form:

IP Address	01000001	11010010	10111001	00100001
Subnet Mask	11111111	11111111	00000000	00000000
Subnetid		11010010		
Hostid			10111001	00100001

Therefore, the IDs for this host are as follows:

Netid	65
Subnetid	210
Hostid	185.33

FIGURE 4.5

Determining the Subnetid for a Class A Address

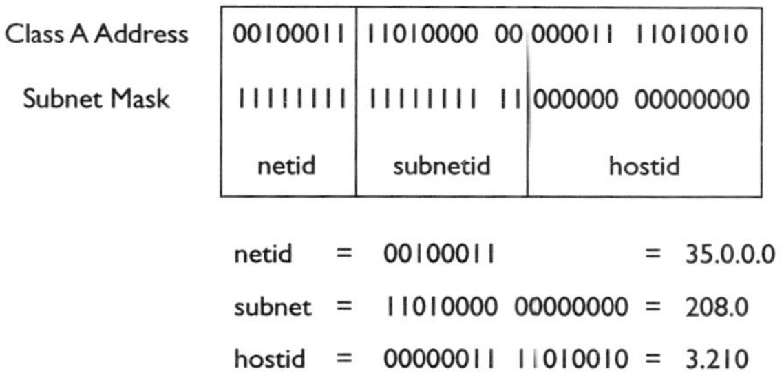

Class A Address	00100011	11010000 00	000011	11010010
Subnet Mask	11111111	11111111 11	000000	00000000
	netid	subnetid		hostid

netid = 00100011 = 35.0.0.0

subnet = 11010000 00000000 = 208.0

hostid = 00000011 11010010 = 3.210

Things get a bit more complicated when the subnet mask doesn't fall on an even octet boundary. Here are some more examples. Suppose a class B network with the address 128.100 is to be given the subnet mask 255.255.240. What will be the subnetid and netid for host 128.100.158.200? Here are the binary equivalents:

IP Address	10000000	01100100	10011110	11001000
Subnet Mask	11111111	11111111	11110000	00000000
Subnetid			10010000	
Netid			00001110	11001000

When the subnetid is expressed in decimal form, trailing zeros are added to complete an octet. In decimal form, the IDs for this host are:

Netid	128.100
Subnetid	144
Hostid	14.200

Here is another example. A class C network with the address 200.85.123 will be subnetted with the mask 255.255.255.224. What are the subnetid and hostid for host 200.85.123.45?

IP Address	11001000	01010101	01111011	00101101
Subnet Mask	11111111	11111111	11111111	11100000
Subnetid				00100000
				(32 decimal)
Netid				00001101
				(13 decimal)

Therefore, the IDs in decimal form are:

Netid	200.85.123
Subnetid	32
Hostid	13

NOTE

RFC 950, which defines IP subnet addressing, specifies that subnetids should not consist entirely of 0s or 1s. This significantly reduces the number of subnets that can be defined, particularly for class C addresses.

A number of TCP/IP vendors (including Novell, Cisco, Bay, Ascend, and Microsoft), permit use of the all-0s and all-1s subnets. If you choose to implement the all-0s or all-1s subnets on your network, be sure that all systems on the network support them. (Examples in this book do not use the all-0s or all-1s subnets.)

When subnetting is applied, the rule remains in effect that the hostid cannot consist entirely of 0s or 1s.

Example A Class C Network with Subnets

Because so few bits are available for subnetting, class C addresses present the greatest challenge when setting up subnets. Therefore, here is a more complex example of a class C network that consists of an internetwork with four subnets. The subnetid must occupy three bits, giving a total of six subnets with which to work. The subnet mask, therefore, is 255.255.255.224. Table 4.4 lists the ranges of addresses that a three-bit subnet mask makes available (assuming that subnet 0 will not be supported). Remember the following rules, which restrict the available subnetids and netids:

▶ The subnetid should not be all 0s or all 1s. (According to RFC 950, although most vendors permit the all-0s and all-1s subnets).

▶ The netid cannot be all 0s or all 1s.

TABLE 4.4

IDs Available on a Class C
Subnet with Subnet ID
255.255.255.224

SUBNETS (BINARY)	FIRST IP ADDRESS (BINARY)	LAST IP ADDRESS (BINARY)	FIRST IP ADDRESS (DECIMAL)	LAST IP ADDRESS (DECIMAL)	AVAILABLE HOSTID
00000000*	00000001	00111110	1	30	30
00100000	00100001	00111110	33	62	30
01000000	01000001	01011110	65	94	30
01100000	01100001	01111110	97	126	30
10000000	10000001	10011110	129	158	30
10100000	10100001	10111110	161	190	30
11000000	11000001	11011110	193	222	30
11100000	11000001	11011110	225	254	30

If subnet 0 is not used, the three-bit subnet mask enables you to configure six subnets with 30 hosts each for a total of 180 hosts. With subnet 0, you can configure 210 hosts on seven subnets. Although you lose between 45 and 75 potential hostids in the process, that may be a small price to pay if it can allow your class C address to handle a WAN.

Figure 4.6 shows an internet with four subnets. The internet is configured with a class C address, and the subnet mask is 255.255.255.224.

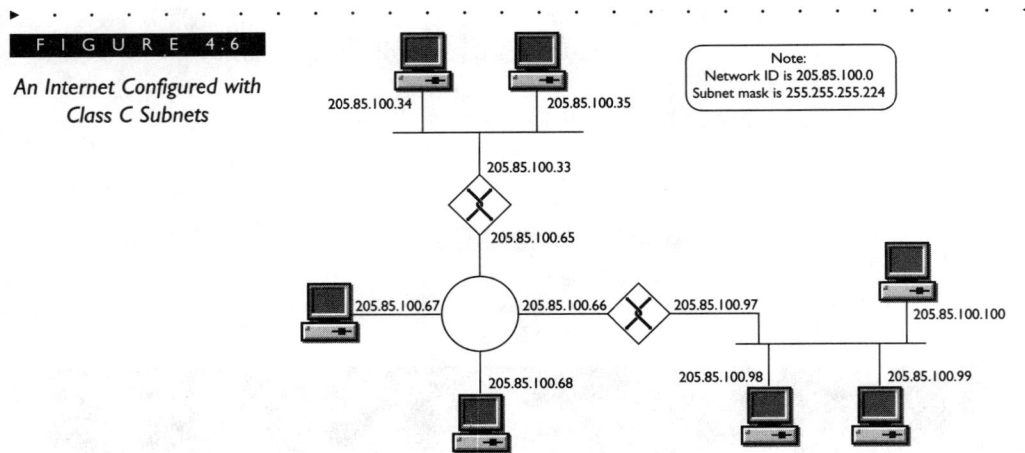

FIGURE 4.6

An Internet Configured with Class C Subnets

Class C subnets are pretty quirky, and there are some subnet masks that aren't very useful. Table 4.5 shows what different subnet masks (not including subnet 0) can achieve.

TABLE 4.5

Effects of Class C Subnet Masks

NUMBER OF MASK BITS	MASK (BINARY)	MASK (DECIMAL)	AVAILABLE SUBNETS	HOSTS PER SUBNET	TOTAL HOSTS AVAILABLE
1	10000000	128	0	N/A	0
2	11000000	192	2	62	124
3	11100000	224	6	30	180
4	11110000	240	14	14	196
5	11111000	248	30	6	180
6	11111100	252	62	2	124
7	11111110	254	126	0	0
8	11111111	255	254	0	0

Calculating Available Subnets and Hostids

You can use two simple formulas to determine the number of subnetids and hostids-per-subnet you can configure with a given subnet mask:

Available subnets = $2^{(\text{number of masked subnet bits})}-2$

Available networks = $2^{(\text{number of unmasked bits})}-2$

 **NOTE** **If all devices on your network permit the all-0s and/or all-1s subnets, you can omit the "-2" from the above formulas and in the formulas that follow.**

To demonstrate, I will apply the formulas to a class B address with the subnet mask 255.255.248.0. This mask designates five bits for the subnetid and leaves eleven bits for the netid. Here are the calculations:

Available subnets = $2^5 - 2 = 30$

Available networks = $2^{11} - 2 = 2046$

Shortcuts for Calculating Subnets

Subnet calculations can be greatly simplified by using a few shortcuts to determine the number of subnets that result from a given subnet mask, and what the host ID range will be for each subnet.

Calculating the Number of Subnets First determine the number of 1 bits in the subnet portion of the subnet mask and call that number n. Then calculate the number of subnets the mask will create using the formula 2n–2. If the subnet mask contains four 1 bits in the subnet portion of the subnet mask, 6 subnets are available (24–2 or 8–2). (8 subnets are permitted if the all-0s and all-1s subnets are supported.)

Calculating the Netid Values Follow these steps:

1. Identify the rightmost 1. bit in the subnet mask and convert its value to decimal notation. The number you obtain is referred to as Delta.

2. Add Delta to the original network ID to obtain the first subnet ID.

3. Add Delta to the last subnet ID you obtained to determine the next subnet ID. Continue the process of adding Delta to the most recently determined subnet ID to calculate further subnetids.

Let's see how these calculations work in an example using the class C network 205.98.103.0 with a subnet mask of 255.255.255.224.

▶ To obtain Delta, examine the subnet mask, which in binary is 11111111 11111111 11111111 11100000. The decimal equivalent of the rightmost bit is 32, which will be used as Delta.

▶ If your network does not support the all-0s subnet, determine the first netid, add Delta to the network ID 200.100.50.0. The result is that the first subnetwork ID is 200.100.50.32.

If your network supports the all-0s subnet, the first subnetwork ID starts with hostid 0. The result in this example is that the first subnetwork ID is 200.100.50.0.

▶ Repeatedly add Delta to the IP addresses that result to determine further subnets:

205.98.103.0	+	32	= 205.98.103.32 (The all-0s subnet.)
205.98.103.32	+	32	= 205.98.103.64
205.98.103.64	+	32	= 205.98.103.96
205.98.103.96	+	32	= 205.98.103.128
205.98.103.128	+	32	= 205.98.103.160
205.98.103.160	+	32	= 205.98.103.192
205.98.103.192	+	32	= 205.98.103.224
205.98.103.192	+	32	= 205.98.103.254 (The all-1s subnet.)

This calculation generates the same network IDs that you saw in Table 4.3. Compare the results to better familiarize yourself with the technique.

Planning for Growth

If you are not careful when planning your IP address scheme, it is possible to paint yourself into a corner. Let's see what can happen by using the example of the class B address 130.5.0.0. Because we need six subnets, we use the subnet mask 255.255.224.0. That leaves 13 bits available for netids.

As we begin to assign IP addresses, we aren't very careful, and we assign addresses such as 130.5.210.80. What sorts of problems could arise from this address assignment?

Suppose that the company expands and more than six subnets are required. If you examine the bit patterns, you will notice that IP addresses such as 130.5.210.80 assign the fourth bit of the third byte to the netid. Consequently, we cannot expand the subnetid field without freeing up a bit or two by reassigning any IP addresses that encroach on those bits. On a large network, this can require reconfiguration of many hosts, a process that requires planning, visiting the hosts, and updating the network records.

You can simplify your life by applying two guidelines when planning IP addresses:

▶ Assign bits to subnetids starting from the leftmost (high-order) bits. You should assign subnetids after the following fashion: 1, 01, 10, 11, 001, 010, 011, 101, 111, 0001, and so forth.

▶ Assign bits to hostids starting with the rightmost (low-order) bits. You should assign hostids in the following order: 1, 10, 11, 100, 101, 110, 111, 1000, and so forth.

This technique preserves a buffer zone of 0s between the subnetids and the hostids. This gives you room to maneuver if you need to modify your subnetting. You can add bits to the subnet field without colliding with bits that have already been assigned to hostids.

Subnets and Outside Hosts

At first glance, it may appear that subnetting greatly complicates internetworks. Consider Figure 4.7. Suppose that host 155.8.33.108 needs to contact host 128.1.2.100, which is located on a subnet with the subnet mask 255.255.255.0. You might be concerned that 155.8.33.108 would need to know the subnet mask as well as the IP address of the host to be contacted. That would certainly complicate things on a large network, but in most cases it turns out to be an unnecessary concern.

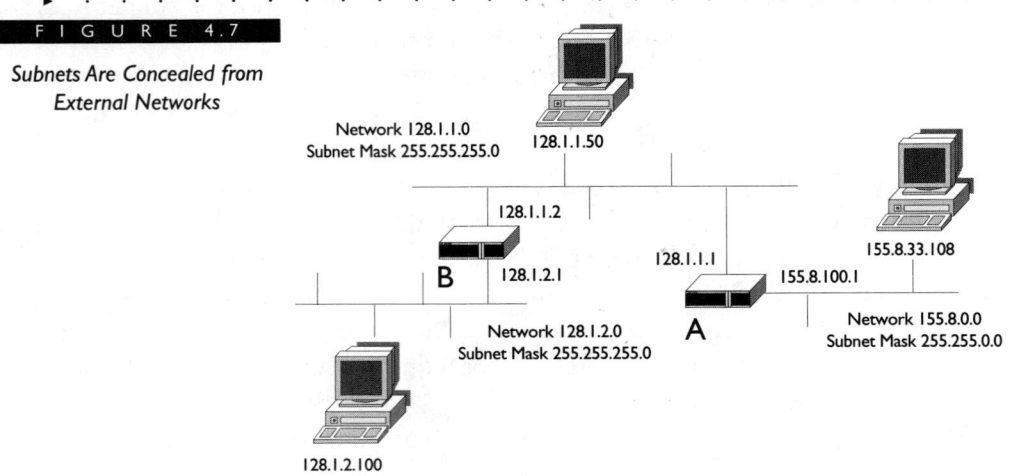

FIGURE 4.7

Subnets Are Concealed from
External Networks

On the network shown in Figure 4.7, it turns out that the subnetting of network 128.1.0.0 is completely transparent to outside networks. Router A serves as a connection point that can route to all of the subnets of 128.1.0.0. To deliver a datagram to 128.1.2.100, host 155.8.33.108 simply routes the datagram to router A, which has the responsibility for routing to the correct subnet. As it turns out, the subnetting of network 128.1.0.0 is completely invisible to host 155.8.33.108.

When A receives a datagram for network 128.1.0.0, it simply forwards the datagram via interface 128.1.1.1. It can take this simpleminded approach because all hosts on network 128.1.0.0 are located on the far side of that interface.

Because it resides between subnets, Router B has a somewhat more complicated job. When it must direct a datagram to a host on network 128.1.0.0, router B must be able to determine the subnet on which the host is located. Without a knowledge of subnets, B cannot determine which interface should be used to route the datagram.

This simplicity is shattered if the subnets of a network are not contiguous. In Figure 4.8, subnets 128.1.1.0 and 128.1.2.0 connect to network 155.8.0.0 through separate routers. Suppose that host 155.8.33.108 uses router A as its default router and needs to route a datagram to host 128.1.2.100. Unless A's routing table contains information about subnet addressing, A will be unable to route the datagram to B for delivery to the correct subnet. You may encounter a similar situation if your organization is assigned a single class B address, which must be subnetted to support hosts in several cities. In such circumstances, it is impossible to configure the subnets so that they are contiguous.

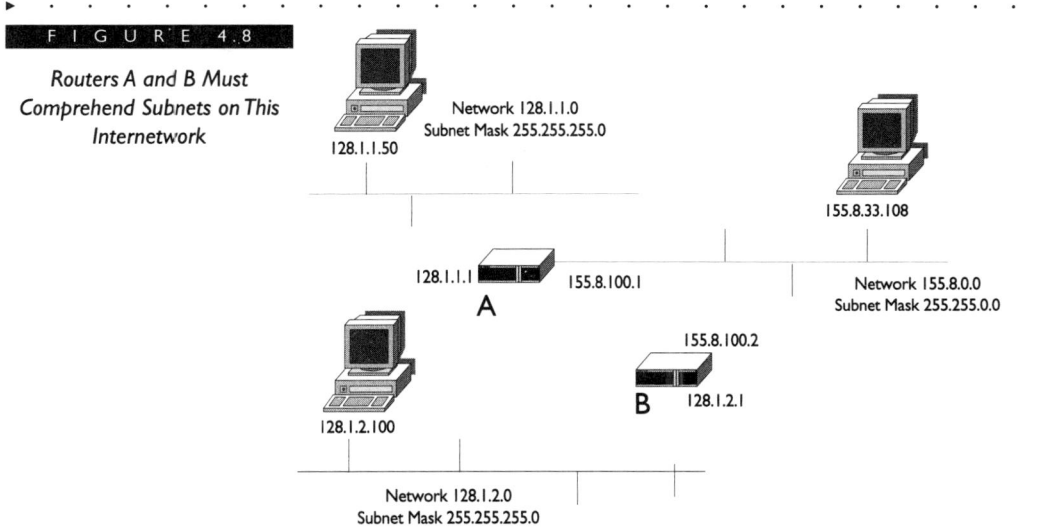

FIGURE 4.8

Routers A and B Must Comprehend Subnets on This Internetwork

Network 128.1.1.0
Subnet Mask 255.255.255.0

128.1.1.50

155.8.33.108

128.1.1.1   155.8.100.1
A

Network 155.8.0.0
Subnet Mask 255.255.0.0

155.8.100.2

B   128.1.2.1

128.1.2.100

Network 128.1.2.0
Subnet Mask 255.255.255.0

Later in this chapter, you will learn about two routing protocols, Routing Information Protocol (RIP) and Open Shortest Path First (OSPF). OSPF was designed to include subnet information in routing tables. RIP, on the other hand, comes in two versions. RIP I was designed before subnetting was added to the IP address scheme and has a limited ability to work with subnetted networks. RIP II understands subnets. Unfortunately, a great many RIP routers are still running RIP I.

In many implementations, RIP I routers can learn subnet information from the configurations of their network interfaces. In Figure 4.7, suppose that router B is running RIP I. Because B is directly attached to both subnets of network 128.1.0.0, it is probably capable of routing between the two subnets. To be certain in such situations, you need to run tests on the router being used.

Networks such as the one shown in Figure 4.8 are beyond the capabilities of RIP I, however. Because no router is directly attached to all the subnets of 128.1.0.0, it is impossible for the routers to learn the subnets. RIP II or OSPF would be required for such networks.

Classless Inter-Domain Routing

The systems of IP addresses and subnetting were arrived at long before the Internet's explosive growth in the 1990s. In recent years, two trends have complicated Internet address assignment:

▶ Class B addresses have nearly been exhausted, requiring large organizations to obtain (and juggle) many class C addresses.

▶ Class C addresses are at risk of exhaustion, and small organizations that don't need a full class C allocation should receive only what they require.

Classless inter-domain routing (CIDR; RFC 1518) is a technique for assigning blocks of addresses to accommodate organizations larger and smaller than 254 hosts. With CIDR, address ranges can be allocated without the constraints imposed by the traditional A, B, and C address classes.

If your organization is small, you might be allocated a portion of a class C address. If you require 50 addresses, for example, you might be assigned addresses 192.168.8.64 through 192.168.8.127 to be used with the subnet mask 255.255.255.192. This arrangement gives you 6 bits for host IDs and results in 62 usable addresses.

Recall the rule stated earlier that subnet masks must include 1s corresponding to all bits in the netid portion of the address. For many rules there are exceptions, and an exception called *supernet addressing* permits subnet masks to define a shorter network mask than the default mask for a given network class. Supernet addressing provides a means for large organizations to aggregate multiple class C addresses so that they can be managed as a larger address space.

Suppose you want to attach a network with 800 nodes to the Internet. At this time, the organization must accommodate this many nodes by registering four class-C addresses. Unfortunately, with standard addressing, these four class-C addresses define four distinct networks, and routing is required to enable data to be transferred between the networks.

If the class C addresses are carefully chosen, however, supernet addressing permits an administrator to treat four class C addresses as one network. To see how this works, apply the net mask 255.255.252.0 to the following addresses, shown with their binary equivalents:

192.168.180.0 (11000000 10101000 10110100 **00000000**)
192.168.181.0 (11000000 10101000 10110101 **00000000**)
192.168.182.0 (11000000 10101000 10110110 **00000000**)
192.168.183.0 (11000000 10101000 10110111 **00000000**)

In the list, the hostid bits are set in bold type. You will see that the supernet mask enables the administrator to use 10 bits for hostids, supporting a total of 1046 hosts. Because sequential class C addresses are being used, all hosts share a common netid.

CIDR addresses are classified by the number of bits that are allocated for the netid portion of the address. A CIDR address that allocates 22 bits to the netid portion (as in the above example) is referred to as a /22 ("slasu 22") address.

At present, most Internet customers obtain their IP address allocations from their Internet Service Providers. ISPs are assigned blocks of IP addresses by the Internet address authority. In turn, the ISPs allocate IP addresses to their customers according to the customers' requirements. Under guidelines in effect while this book is being written, all IP addresses that are /19 or greater (19 or more netid bits) are obtained from ISPs. Customers who need address spaces that are /18 or less (18 or fewer netid bits) must apply directly to an Internet address authority (listed in the preceding "Obtaining Addresses for the Internet" section).

NOTE

Supernet masks are not supported under all TCP/IP implementations. Be sure to check your system specifications for all affected devices before attempting an implementation.

CIDR is, at best, a workaround for our present IP address woes. Suppose a customer relocates or begins connecting to the Internet through a different provider. Two disturbing choices are possible. The provider can retain the addresses for use by future customers, in which case the organization must re-address its entire network. Or the provider can generously permit the organization to retain its assigned addresses, in which case the customer has "punched a hole" in the provider's CIDR block, complicating future address allocations. Clearly, CIDR has not eliminated the need for a revised IP addressing scheme.

▶ · ◀

Delivering Datagrams on Internetworks

IP provides connectionless delivery of messages through an internetwork. RFC 791, which outlines the IP standard, refers to IP messages as *datagrams*. A datagram is a message that is sent individually — without any formal connection or error checking. When connection-oriented delivery is necessary, TCP provides it at the host-to-host layer.

Routing is performed at the IP protocol layer. Originally, IP routers were called gateways, but the term *gateway* is also used to describe an upper-layer protocol translator that connects dissimilar systems (for example, a gateway may be used to connect a LAN to an IBM SNA network). Therefore, there has been a trend away from using the term to describe devices at the IP protocol layer. Instead, the devices are simply called *routers*.

IP is responsible for delivering datagrams to the correct network, but the data link layer handles delivery of the data to the correct computer. Consequently, two different address schemes are involved: IP addresses are used to route datagrams to the right network, and physical addresses are used to deliver the message to the proper computers. The following subsection explains how data delivery is carried out in a simple scenario involving a single network segment.

Basic Datagram Delivery

When a frame's source and destination nodes are connected to the same network, a simple mechanism can handle delivery of the data. The source codes the physical address of the destination into the destination address field (or DA field) of the frame and sends the frame out on the network. Every node on the network looks at the frame and checks the DA field. If a node recognizes its own address in the DA field, it receives the frame and passes it to the network layer. If the node's address does not match the address in the frame, the frame is ignored.

However, as previously mentioned, IP works with IP addresses, which are not used by the data link layer. Before IP can send a datagram on its way, IP must know the physical address of the destination computer. To get that information, IP relies on an auxiliary protocol called the *Address Resolution Protocol* (ARP).

Address Resolution Protocol

ARP has one purpose: to supply IP with physical addresses. Figure 4.9 shows how IP and ARP work together.

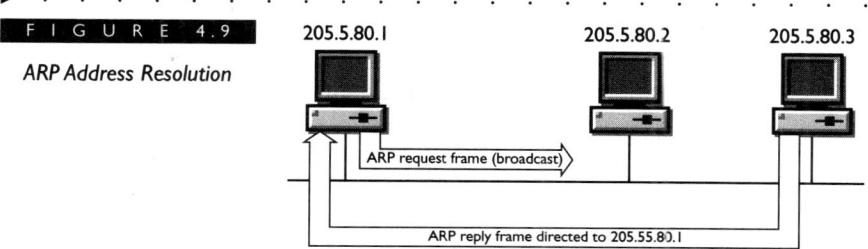

F I G U R E 4 . 9

ARP Address Resolution

Here are the steps that allow IP to obtain the physical address of the host 205.5.80.3:

1. IP calls ARP, passing ARP the address 205.5.80.3.

2. ARP generates an ARP request frame, which is broadcast to the local network. (Broadcasts to Ethernets and IEEE LANs are sent to the physical address FF FF FF FF FF FF.) The ARP request frame includes the sending host's IP address and physical address. The frame also includes the IP address ARP is attempting to resolve.

3. The broadcast ARP request frame is received by all hosts on the local network. (IP broadcasts do not cross routers.) Each host attempts to match its own IP address to the IP address in the ARP request frame.

4. If a host discovers a match, it generates an ARP response frame by adding its own physical address in a space provided in the ARP request frame. The ARP response frame is then returned directly to the host that originated the ARP request frame.

5. ARP in the original host receives the ARP response frame, extracts the physical address, and passes the address to IP.

ARP maintains a cache table of recently resolved addresses. Before generating a request frame, ARP consults the table to see whether the address has been recently matched. This reduces the network traffic that would be generated if ARP were required to resolve addresses for each datagram sent. Entries in the cache table remain there for a limited period of time, which is determined by the network administrator. ARP regains addresses that have expired.

Reverse Address Resolution Protocol (RARP) complements ARP by resolving physical addresses to their corresponding IP addresses.

Delivering a Datagram Locally

After IP has identified the physical address of the destination host, IP uses the network access layer to deliver the datagram.

The process of delivering a datagram locally is as follows:

1. IP receives data from an upper-layer protocol, which includes the IP address of the destination host.

2. IP examines the netid portion of the destination IP address and compares it to its own netid. If the destination and source netids match, the data can be delivered on the local network.

3. IP queries ARP to obtain the physical address of the destination host.

4. IP constructs a datagram that includes the source and destination IP addresses.

5. IP passes the datagram to the network access layer. With the datagram, IP passes the source and destination IP addresses.

6. The network access layer builds a frame that includes the source and destination physical addresses. The datagram received from IP is stored in the data portion of the frame.

7. The network access layer sends the frame on the network.

8. The host whose physical address matches the destination address in the frame receives the frame. Delivery is accomplished.

IP's job is quite simple when it must deliver a datagram to a local network. Understanding local delivery is essential to understanding internetwork delivery. Every hop through an internet is accomplished through local datagram delivery.

Delivering a Datagram to a Remote Network

When data is delivered to a remote network, delivery involves routing. Figure 4.10 shows a simple internetwork consisting of two network segments separated by a single router. Note: An IP router is essentially a TCP/IP computer that is equipped with two network interfaces. A TCP/IP host that is connected to two or more networks is called a *multihomed host*. A router may be a dedicated device, in which case, protocols above the internet layer will probably not be implemented. There is no need for TCP when you have a dedicated router because the datagrams are never sent above the internet layer. However, a router can also be a working computer. A NetWare server, for example, can route IP datagrams as well as perform file services.

Routers need routing information that pertains to all of the remote destinations where the datagrams are to be sent. This information is stored in a routing table, which lists the destination networks and the best IP address to use for each network. Information can be added to routing tables in three ways:

▶ By an automated route discovery program

▶ Manually

▶ In response to ICMP messages

NetWare uses all three methods. This chapter discusses two different route discovery programs: RIP and OSPF. Chapter 10 discusses manual and automated routing.

When a routing table does not contain information about a destination, a router may check a *default router* (also called a *default gateway*). The IP address of a default router is usually entered manually when a host is configured. Default routes can also be defined using ICMP, RIP, or OSPF.

Figure 4.10 depicts delivery of a datagram to a remote destination.

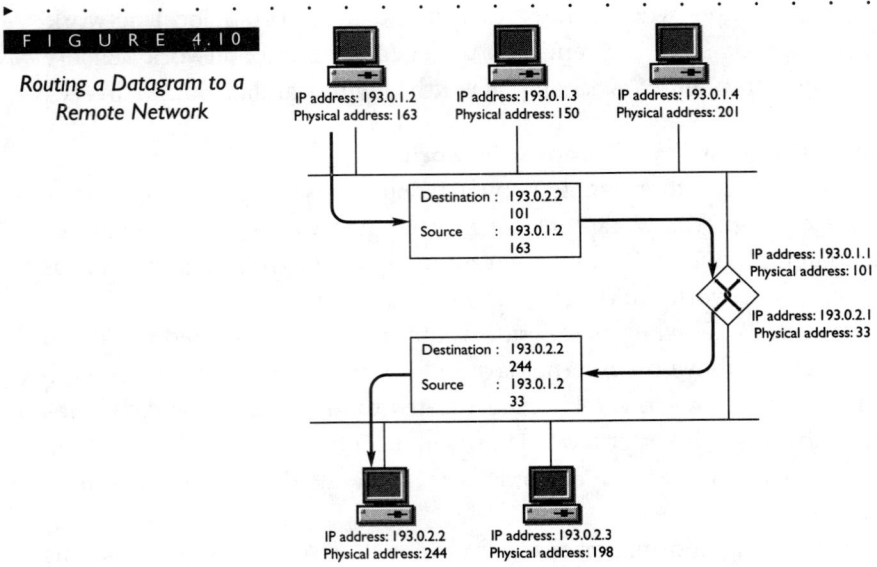

Routing a Datagram to a
Remote Network

IP address: 193.0.1.2
Physical address: 163

IP address: 193.0.1.3
Physical address: 150

IP address: 193.0.1.4
Physical address: 201

Destination : 193.0.2.2
101
Source : 193.0.1.2
163

IP address: 193.0.1.1
Physical address: 101

IP address: 193.0.2.1
Physical address: 33

Destination : 193.0.2.2
244
Source : 193.0.1.2
33

IP address: 193.0.2.2
Physical address: 244

IP address: 193.0.2.3
Physical address: 198

In Figure 4.10 a datagram is routed from host 193.0.1.2 to host 193.0.2.2. Delivery is performed as follows:

1. IP in host 193.0.1.2 examines the datagram and determines that it must be routed to a remote network. (The netid portion of the destination IP address is not 193.0.1.)

2. IP consults its routing table to obtain the IP address of the interface that should receive datagrams destined for network 193.0.2. The best next interface is 193.0.1.1.

3. IP performs an ARP request to determine the physical address of interface 193.0.1.1. ARP responds with the physical address 101.

4. IP constructs an IP datagram and sends it to the network access layer, along with the hardware address obtained from ARP. The address information sent to the network access layer is as follows:

- Destination IP address: 193.0.2.2

- Destination physical address: 101

- Source IP address: 193.0.1.2

- Source physical address: 163

NOTE **The destination IP address and the destination physical address do not correspond to the same host. When the datagram is routed, the IP address always refers to the ultimate destination. The physical address refers only to the source and destination interfaces for the current hop.**

5. The network access layer constructs a frame and deposits it on the network. The router recognizes its physical address and receives the frame.

   IP on the router recovers the datagram, examines the IP address, and learns that the destination is on network 193.0.2. Because the destination netid does not match the netid of the interface that received the datagram, the frame must be routed. IP consults its routing table and learns that the network can be reached from interface 193.0.2.1.

6. If IP on the router determines that the netid in the destination address matches the netid of the interface that received the datagram, the datagram is discarded. Only datagrams destined for other networks are routed.

7. IP calls ARP to obtain the physical address of the destination host. ARP responds with the physical address 244.

8. IP constructs a datagram and sends it to the network access layer with the physical address information as follows:

   - Destination IP address: 193.0.2.2

   - Destination physical address: 244

   - Source IP address: 193.0.1.2

   - Source physical address: 33

Here again, the IP addresses refer to the original source host and the ultimate destination. The physical addresses reflect the current hop only.

9. The network access layer constructs a frame and forwards it to the network.

10. The network layer of host 193.0.2.2 recognizes its physical address, receives the frame, and recovers the original datagram.

As you can see, the IP address remains constant when a frame is routed. In order to send its reply, the receiving host does not need to know the physical address of the source host. Only the source IP address is necessary.

Routing Tables

Routing tables and the programs that maintain them are vital tools on internetworks. They determine how efficiently datagrams are delivered and how well routers adjust to changes in the network. There are two approaches to maintaining routing tables: static and dynamic.

Static Routing

When relying on *static routing*, the network administrator uses a software tool to manually maintain the information in the routing table. Any changes made to the network must be entered in the routing tables of all routers on the network. Consequently, static routing can be a tedious task. However, static routing may be appropriate in some cases. Here are some examples of cases where static routing makes sense:

▶ The network is small enough that network administrators are comfortable with manual maintenance.

▶ The network changes infrequently.

▶ The network does not have alternative routes to destinations. (Static routing cannot take advantage of alternative routes when a primary route fails.)

Another reason for turning to static routing is that static routing generates no network overhead. Dynamic routing protocols require routers to communicate to exchange routes. In some instances, the traffic generated to maintain routing tables can overwhelm the network, particularly when slow, wide-area links are involved.

With NetWare, static routing table entries can be entered in two ways:

▸ Using the INETCFG NetWare Loadable Module (NLM)

▸ Using the INETCFG NLM

▸ Adding the route to the SYS:\ETC\GATEWAYS file and reloading TCPIP.NLM with the STATIC=YES parameter

In the vast majority of cases, the difficulty associated with static routing outweighs whatever advantages it may offer, especially now that efficient routing protocols are widely available for use in dynamic routing.

Dynamic Routing

Dynamic routing involves using protocols to monitor the network, identify routes, and create entries in routing tables. Dynamic routing protocols can automatically adjust to changes in the network. These protocols enable hosts to take advantage of alternative paths when primary paths become unavailable. NetWare supports four TCP/IP protocols related to routing:

▸ *Routing Information Protocol* (RIP)

▸ *Open Shortest Path First* (OSPF)

▸ *Exterior Gateway Protocol* (EGP)

▸ *Internet Control Message Protocol* (ICMP)

RIP and OSPF are classified as *interior gateway protocols* (IGPs) or *interior routing protocols* (IRPs). An IGP is used to determine routes within an autonomous system (AS) — that is, within a group of hosts that share the same routing protocol. You can use these protocols to configure routing on your NetWare TCP/IP networks.

Exterior gateway protocols (EGPs), also called *exterior routing protocols* (ERPs), perform routing between autonomous systems. Figure 4.11 illustrates the relationship of IGPs and EGPs.

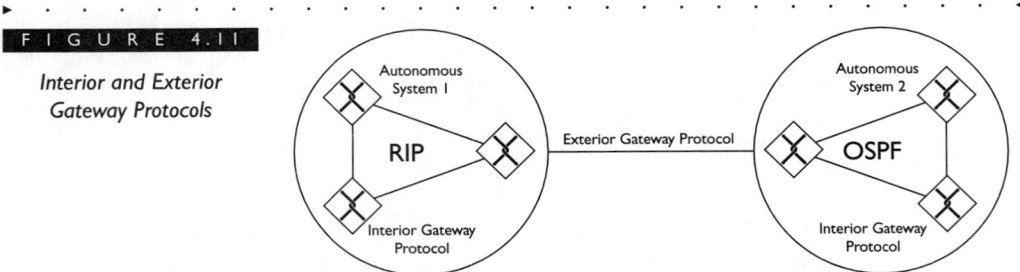

FIGURE 4.11

Interior and Exterior Gateway Protocols

Routing Information Protocol

Routing Information Protocol (RIP) is a widely used internet routing protocol. RIP is classified as a "distance vector routing" protocol. Distance vector routing is a technique for describing routes to a destination network in terms of the cost to reach the destination using a particular IP address. Cost is simply a metric ranging in value from 1 to 15. Typically, cost represents the number of hops required to reach the destination via a particular route. One hop is counted for each network that must be crossed.

The original implementation of RIP, now known as RIP I (RFC 1058), was written prior to several RFCs that extended the functionality of IP. A particularly problematic limitation of RIP I is that it does not support subnet addressing. This limitation prevents RIP I from advertising subnet routes. Although RIP I can be used with subnets, RIP I advertises only network routes, and numerous restrictions apply. (For example, RIP I does not support variable-length subnets.)

RIP II (RFC 1723) is a draft standard that is supported by NetWare TCP/IP. RIP II extends RIP I by adding support for subnet masks and also supports the use of subnet 0. RIP II incorporates the following enhancements:

▶ Passwords may be used for authentication.

▶ Subnet masks are supported. A subnet mask is associated with each destination, supporting use of variable-length subnet masks.

▶ RIP II routing packets can be multicast, reducing the load on hosts that are not listening for RIP packets. The RIP II multicast address is 224.0.0.9.

NetWare 4.1 and the NetWare MultiProtocol Router can support RIP I and RIP II simultaneously.

A RIP routing table entry must include — at a minimum — the following data:

▶ The IP address (or host name) of the destination

▶ A metric representing the total cost to reach the destination

▶ The IP address (or host name) of the next router used to reach the destination

▶ A flag indicating that the route has been recently updated

▶ Timers

Each routing table must contain an entry specifying a default router. When the routing table does not contain enough information to forward a particular datagram, the datagram is relayed to the default router. By convention, the default router is specified by the destination IP address 0.0.0.0. Typically, the routing tables of nonrouting hosts (such as user workstations) are configured with the default router only, specifying a router on the local network. The routing tables of routers contain routes for all destinations in the internet.

IMPORTANT

The TCP/IP RIP routing protocol is not the same as the NetWare IPX RIP protocol with which you may be familiar. Both RIP implementations were derived from the Xerox XNS protocol, but they function separately and operate somewhat differently. For example, NetWare RIP advertises routing information at 1-minute intervals, whereas TCP/IP RIP advertises routes at 30-second intervals. Of course, they are also designed to route different protocols.

RIP Route Convergence The basic RIP mechanism is extremely simple. Each router periodically broadcasts its entire routing table. Other routers use these broadcasts to update their own routing tables. Eventually, each router learns all of the available routes in the internetwork. The process that enables each router to arrive at an accurate picture of the internetwork is called *route convergence*.

Before you can understand the shortcomings of RIP, it is necessary to examine how route convergence takes place. Figure 4.12 illustrates an internetwork consisting of five segments (N1 (N5) connected by four routers (R1 (R4).

F I G U R E 4.12

Route Convergence

The following steps explain how R1 initializes its routing table and how the R1 information is propagated throughout the internet (assuming that all routers have been newly initialized with empty routing tables):

1. When a router is initialized, it has information only about the networks to which it is directly attached. R1 is aware of N1 and N2, and, because they are directly attached, R1 knows them to be one hop away.

2. R1 broadcasts a RIP response packet stating that R1 is one hop from N1 and one hop from N2.

3. R2 receives the RIP response packet from R1. Because R2 has a direct attachment to N2, R2 discards the information it receives about N2.

4. R2 now knows that it is one hop away from R1 because they are both one hop from N2. To determine the distance to N1, R2 adds its cost to reach R1 to R1's cost to reach N1. R2 concludes that it can reach N1 through R1 at a cost of 2.

5. R2 broadcasts a RIP response packet with its routing table entries. From R2's broadcast, R1 learns that it has a route to N3 at a cost of 2. Also, R3 learns that it has a route to N2 (cost of 2) and to N1 (cost of 3).

Each router broadcasts its routing table at 30-second intervals. While the above exchanges are taking place, R4 has also been at work transmitting its routing table so the other routers can learn about routes to N5. Eventually, each router receives information about every other destination in the internet, along with the costs to reach those destinations. If multiple routes exist, the router selects the route that has the lowest cost. If a new, lower-cost route later becomes active, the router discards the old route.

The preceding scenario asks you to assume something that is very unlikely — namely, that all routers have been newly initialized. In practice, this is seldom the case. A newly started router can converge on the network fairly quickly by issuing a RIP request packet soliciting routing information from established routers.

RIP Convergence Problems   The basic RIP algorithm is not perfect. In particular, it can take a long time for routers to converge after a network change occurs.

Figure 4.13 shows a typical network. Notice that a cost of 1 has been assigned to all connections except the connection between R2 and R4, which has a cost of 10. There are two main reasons why a network administrator may assign a higher cost to that connection. The cost at that link may be higher because of a slower WAN link that ought to be avoided if a more efficient path exists. The cost at that connection might also be higher because several other routers (not shown in the diagram) come between R2 and R4.

When all channels are functioning properly, the routers have the following entries in their routing tables:

- R1 can reach N6 via R3 at a cost of 3

- R2 can reach N6 via R3 at a cost of 3

> ▸ R3 can reach N6 via R4 at a cost of 2

> ▸ R4 can reach N6 directly at a cost of 1

What happens if the link between R3 and R4 fails? Then the routers' cost information becomes invalid. R1, for example, must now route through R2 to reach N6, at a cost of 12. The routers cannot quickly adjust to the network change.

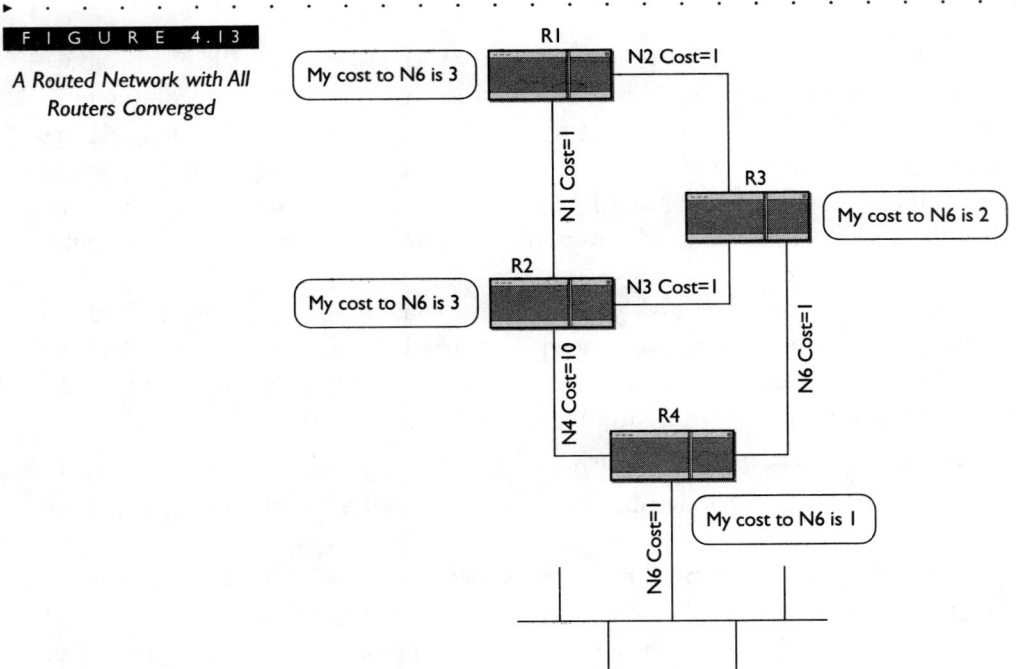

F I G U R E 4.13

A Routed Network with All Routers Converged

R3 would become aware of the problem fairly quickly through a time-out mechanism. If it has not received a route response packet from R4 within 180 seconds, R3 purges any routes in its table that are directed through R4. When that happens, R3 must find a new route to N6.

Finding a new route is more complicated than discovering the original route because, under the basic RIP algorithm, R1 and R2 have both advertised that they can reach N6 at a cost of 3. R1 and R2 do not know the cause of the failure. When after 180 seconds R3 advertises that its route to N6 is gone, R1 and R2 begin searching for a new route. And that's the root of the problem. A route advertisement announces only that a route exists. An advertisement does not identify the path that the data takes. When R1 advertises that it can reach N6 in 3 hops, the other routers are ignorant of the fact that the advertised route may depend on a failed network segment.

Suppose R2 continues to advertise that it can reach N6 at a cost of 3. R1 may pick up on this and conclude that R1 can now reach N6 through R2 at a cost of 4. R1 now advertises that it can reach N6 at a cost of 4. R3 sees these advertisements and assumes that it can reach N6 through R1 at a cost of 5. Figure 4.14 shows how each of the routers would advertise its cost at this point.

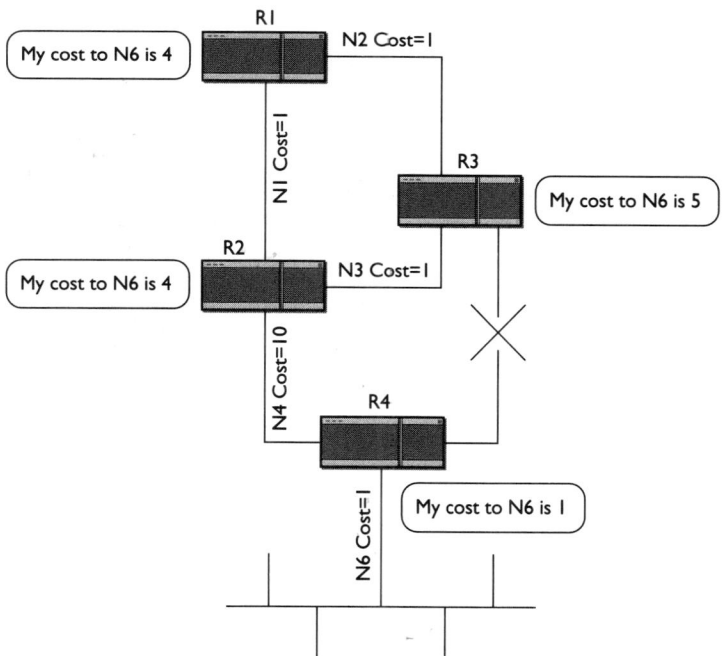

FIGURE 4.14

A Network with Obsolete Routing Information

Suppose now that R1 and R2 receive the R3 routing advertisement and use it to update their routing tables. Using the R3 misinformation, R1 and R2 assign a cost of 6 to the routes. This prompts R3 to update its routing table to reflect a route through R1 at a cost of 7, forcing R1 and R2 to update their cost estimates.

In this way, the costs slowly ratchet up until R2 concludes that its route through R4 is the most efficient route available. This causes R2 to advertise that it can reach N6 in 11 hops. R1 and R3 recognize that R2 is now the low-cost route to N6 and update their routing tables as shown in Figure 4.15.

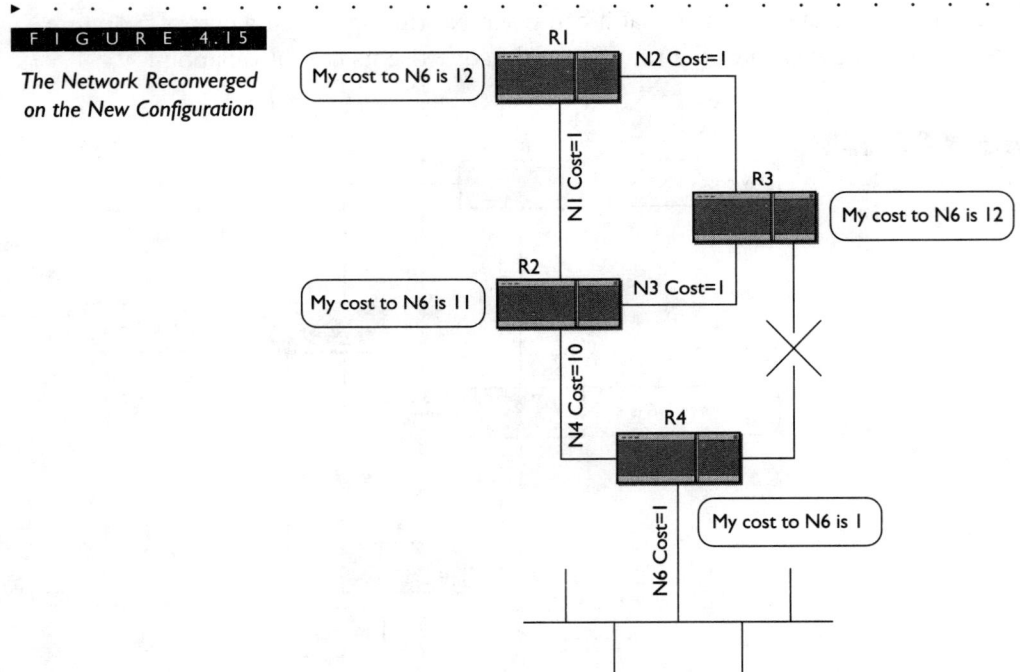

FIGURE 4.15

The Network Reconverged on the New Configuration

Routing tables gradually converge on the new values as RIP advertisements are sent at 30-second intervals. Eventually, if a valid route exists, the routers converge on the new configuration. This process could take a considerable amount of time and, in the meantime, no datagrams would be routed to N6.

The Count-to-Infinity Problem   A more serious problem occurs when a network failure renders a destination unreachable. Consider the simple network in Figure 4.16. Under normal operation, R1 can reach N2 through R2 at a cost of 2.

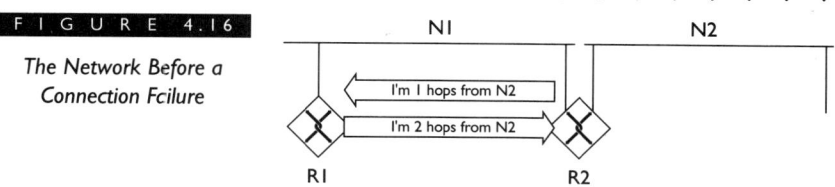

FIGURE 4.16

The Network Before a Connection Failure

Now, consider what happens when R2's connection to N2 fails, as shown in Figure 4.17.

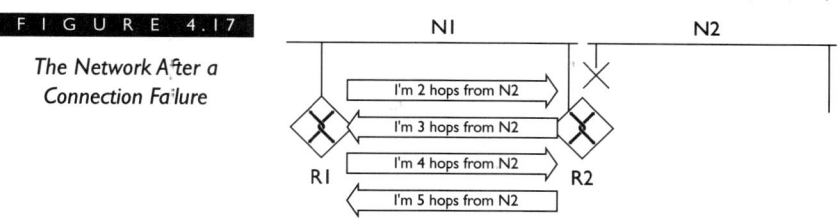

FIGURE 4.17

The Network After a Connection Failure

R2 immediately discovers the failure and searches its routing tables for an alternate route. Because R1 has been advertising that it can reach N2 in 2 hops, R2 decides to use that route. Now, R2 announces that it can reach N2 in 3 hops.

When R1 learns that the R2 cost to N2 is 3, R1 concludes that its cost to reach N2 must now be 4. Therefore, R1 begins to advertise that its cost to reach N2 is 4. But R2 has assumed it can reach N2 through R1. Now R2 learns that its cost to reach N2 is 5.

In reality, N2 is no longer reachable. (This is a sinister scenario indeed.) R1 and R2 can never converge on a correct route to N2 because no such route exists, and their hop counts continue to escalate as the routers count to infinity. The solution to this problem is to designate a certain number as infinity — in other words, to set a limit on the number of counts. For RIP, the limit is 16. Any route that is advertised with a cost metric of 16 is assumed to be unreachable. However, it can take a while for the routers to realize that the destination is unreachable.

In the preceding examples, when a router realizes that a route is no longer available, it simply purges the entry from its routing table. Nothing indicates to the other routers that the destination is unreachable. A simple modification could greatly reduce the time it takes the routers to realize a destination is unreachable. Instead of simply discarding the table entry, R2 could also announce that its cost to reach N2 is now 16. Then, R1 would immediately realize that the network cannot be reached. The routers would never even begin the time-wasting count to infinity.

With distance-vectors algorithms, the value of infinity represents a design compromise between the time it takes routers to converge and the size of network that can be supported. Because RIP designates a metric of 16 as infinite, no two destinations on the internet may be more than 15 hops apart. This limits the size of the networks that RIP can support. The designers of the RIP protocol did not feel that it could adequately support networks with diameters larger than 15 hops.

NetWare TCP/IP supports three techniques that help avoid loops and speed convergence:

▸ Split horizon

▸ Triggered updates

▸ Poison reverse

The following subsections explain how these techniques work.

Split Horizon   If you refer back to Figure 4.15, you see that problems arise because R1 advertises routes to R2 that have been obtained from R2. This leads R2 to the erroneous conclusion that R1 has its own route to N2, independent of R2.

Split horizon is a technique based on the observation that it is never advantageous for a router to advertise a route back to the interface from which the route was received. In other words, if R1 has received a route from a network, R1 should never advertise that route back to the same network. Split horizon prevents routers like the ones shown in Figure 4.15 from entering a self-referential loop because R1 would never inform R2 that R1 can reach N2.

Figure 4.18 shows split horizon in action. R1 advertises to network N3 R1's cost to N2. However, R1 does not advertise that cost to N1 because R1 based its calculation of the cost on information received from N1.

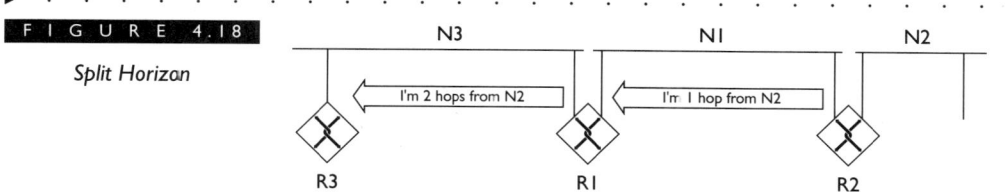

FIGURE 4.18

Split Horizon

Split horizon works best when routers are adjacent. Figure 4.19 illustrates a more complex network. If the connection between R3 and N4 fails, N4 becomes unreachable and R3 stops advertising its route to N4. Because R1 and R2 no longer receive information about the route to N4, after about 90 seconds the route times out (expires), and information about the route is removed from the routing tables of R1 and R2.

Even so, a loop might still be created. Thanks to split horizon, R1 and R2 cannot advertise routes they learn from R3 back to R3. However, a path between R1 and R2 is still possible, which is all it takes for a loop to get started. Here's how:

1. R1 times out its route to N4 before R2.

2. R2 continues to advertise its route to N4, and the route is picked up by R1, which now assumes that it has a route to N4 via R2 at a cost of 2.

3. R1 advertises to N2 that it can reach N4 at a cost of 3 hops.

4. R3 receives the route advertisement from R1, adds the route to its routing table, and advertises the route to N3.

5. R2 times out its route entry for N4.

6. R2 receives a route advertisement from R3 and assumes that it can reach N4 through R3 at a cost of 4 hops.

7. R2 advertises its new route to N1 and a loop is created.

As you can see, split horizon does not solve the count-to-infinity problem when network routers are arranged in loops. In Step 1, the routers update their routing tables at different times, so phantom routes persist in routing tables. To solve this problem, vestiges of old routes must be eliminated as quickly as possible. *Triggered updates* is a technique that can be used to speed up the removal of old routes.

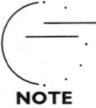

NOTE

Routing loops can be avoided by eliminating redundant pathways in your networks. However, that means sacrificing fault tolerance. The best way to prevent routing loops is to avoid RIP altogether. The *Open Shortest Path First* (OSPF) protocol, discussed in the next section, does not suffer from the routing-loop problem and has many additional benefits.

▶ . . . . ◀

FIGURE 4.19

A Routing Loop with Split Horizon

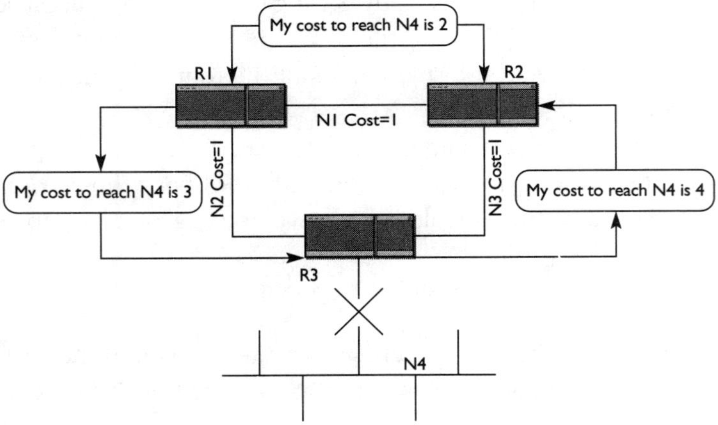

My cost to reach N4 is 2

R1

R2

N1 Cost=1

N2 Cost=1

N3 Cost=1

My cost to reach N4 is 3

My cost to reach N4 is 4

R3

N4

Triggered Updates   *Triggered updates* force a router to send a RIP update immediately after learning of a route change. The router does not wait to broadcast its regular router response packet. The update contains information only about the change. In Figure 4.19, R3 would immediately advertise that N4 is unreachable. That advertisement would force R1 and R3 to update their routing tables almost simultaneously. If necessary, triggered updates propagate to other routers in the network so routers converge on the new configuration rapidly.

WARNING

Triggered updates can cause excessive broadcast traffic and should be used with caution. Also, because RIP uses UDP as a transport protocol, triggered updates are not reliable and may be lost.

Poison Reverse *Poison reverse* is an alternative to split horizon. With poison reverse, when a router receives information about a route from a particular network, the router does advertise the route back to that network. However, the router advertises a metric of 16, which indicates that the destination is unreachable. In Figure 4.20, if R1 reaches N2 through R2, then R2's route to N2 must not go back through R1. To reinforce this, R1 advertises to R2 that R1's cost to reach N2 is 16 (virtual infinity). Therefore, R2 concludes that N2 is unreachable through N1. Poison reverse informs routers of invalid routes immediately, eliminating the delay caused when routing table entries must time out.

▶ · ◀

FIGURE 4.20

Poison Reverse

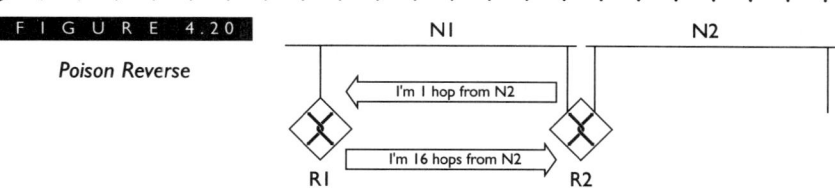

Although poison reverse enables networks to converge on changes more rapidly than split horizon, poison reverse also increases router traffic. Every route that is learned must be advertised back with a metric of 16. This is especially a problem on networks where many routes must be advertised. In those cases, split horizon may work better.

NOTE

With NetWare, split horizon is automatically invoked if poison reverse is deactivated.

Conclusions About RIP Many people believe that OSPF has made RIP obsolete. Nevertheless, RIP remains in wide use partly because of the many operating routers that support RIP but not OSPF. Fortunately, RIP remains a viable protocol that operates reliably. RIP provides fairly rapid convergence, and the overhead it requires is not unreasonable on a properly configured network. However, if your network uses RIP, you should be aware of the following limitations:

▸ RIP imposes a maximum network diameter of 15 hops, limiting the scope of your network.

▸ Convergence can take considerable time.

▸ RIP routers advertise their complete routing tables every 30 seconds. On a large internet having many routers, considerable traffic can be generated, monopolizing an unacceptable amount of network bandwidth. This is especially troublesome when router traffic must cross WAN links.

For all these reasons, you should consider migrating your network to a link-state routing protocol such as OSPF. As the next subsection indicates, link-state protocols do not suffer from any of RIP's aforementioned disadvantages.

Open Shortest Path First

OSPF (RFC 2328) is a protocol on the Internet Standards track. OSPF is becoming increasingly popular as the Internet community becomes less willing to cope with the limitations of RIP. Perhaps the most significant problem in moving to OSPF is that although OSPF is more network-friendly and uses less bandwidth, it requires more processing capability in the router. Therefore, many older routers cannot be upgraded to support OSPF.

OSPF is a link-state routing protocol. Unlike RIP routers, which view networks merely in terms of adjacent routers and hop counts, OSPF routers build a comprehensive picture of networks that fully describes all possible routes along with their costs. This picture, called a *topological database*, takes the form of a hierarchical tree. Each router places itself at the root of a database tree and constructs a complete picture of the network from the router's own perspective.

Building the Topological Database   The network shown in Figure 4.21 illustrates the process by which link-state algorithms build topological databases. Each link between routers is identified with a cost. Because OSPF is not subject to routing loops, a much more flexible cost metric can be used than with RIP. In fact, with OSPF you can use costs that range up to 65,535. Administrators can assign costs to each link and adjust the costs to fine-tune network traffic patterns.

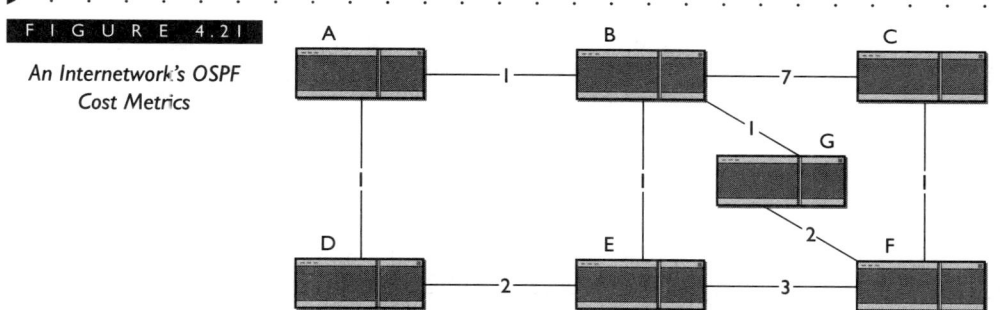

FIGURE 4.21

*An Internetwork's OSPF
Cost Metrics*

The information that routers require to build their databases is provided in the form of link-state advertisements. Routers do not advertise entire routing tables. Instead each router advertises only its information regarding immediately adjacent routers. These link-state advertisements are used to build a hierarchical database, similar to the one shown in Figure 4.22, which describes the network in Figure 4.21 from the perspective of router F.

FIGURE 4.22

*Representation of a
Topological Database*

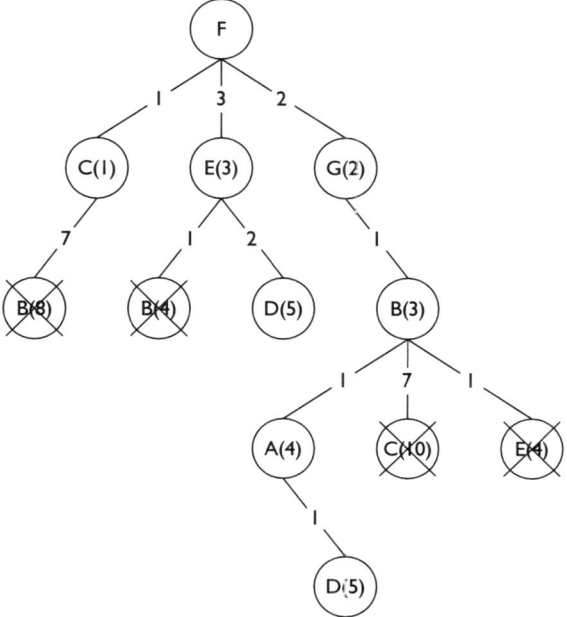

A topological database describes the most efficient route to each destination. Efficiency is determined by the total of all cost metrics encountered on the path. Only the most efficient route is maintained. As Figure 4.22 shows, less efficient routes are discarded. Therefore, F retains the route F-G-B (with a total cost of 3) as the least costly route to B, and F discards the route F-E-B (which has a total cost of 4).

What happens if several equally efficient routes are available? F has two routes to D that have a cost of 5: F-E-D and F-G-B-A-D. Then, OSPF can perform load balancing, which distributes traffic across the available routes. This capacity, which RIP lacks, is a big advantage of the OSPF protocol.

Relationships Among OSPF Routers   With OSPF, routers form two types of relationships with one another. The two kinds of relationships are as follows:

▶ A neighbor relationship exists between two routers that connect to the same network segment and successfully exchange HELLO packets in both directions.

▶ *Adjacency* exists between neighboring routers that share routing information. Not all neighbors form adjacencies. Adjacent routers exchange routing information that enables them to synchronize their databases.

When an OSPF router starts up, it first uses a protocol called the hello protocol to discover which routers are its neighbors on the network segment. On networks that support broadcasts (such as Ethernet and token ring), a router can dynamically identify its neighbors by multicasting hello packets to all routers on the local network. On networks that do not support broadcasts (for example, connection-oriented networks such as X.25 and frame relay), neighbors must be manually entered into the router configuration.

After a router identifies its neighbors, the router attempts to form adjacencies with its neighbors. After adjacencies have been established, the router advertises its information to adjacent routers by transmitting link-state update packets. A router's link-state advertisements include only firsthand information about the specific networks to which the router is directly attached. (This prevents routers from advertising routes about which they have no direct knowledge.) As a link-state update packet is passed from router to router, each router adds its own link-state advertisements to the packet.

One router on each network acts as the designated router (DR). The DR performs two functions:

- ► It generates link-state advertisements on behalf of the network.

- ► It coordinates the distribution and synchronization of advertisements.

When there is no DR, neighbors select a new DR based on priority values carried in hello packets. At that time, a backup DR is also selected. Both the DR and the backup DR maintain adjacency relationships, but only the DR is responsible for generating network advertisements.

DRs simplify the process of synchronizing routers. Refer back to Figure 4.21. If router A and the DR are synchronized, and router B and the DR are synchronized, there is no need for A to synchronize with B. Therefore, if all neighbors synchronize with either the DR or the backup DR, the neighbors obviously must be synchronized with each other. In practice, therefore, routers establish adjacencies with the DR and the backup DR but not with other routers on the network. The DR serves to keep all routers in the network synchronized.

Administrators can designate areas, which are groups of routers that may or may not be on the same local network. Routers advertise their current state to all routers in their area by means of link-state update packets that are flooded throughout the area. The packets are propagated to all routers that belong to the area. A reliable delivery mechanism ensures that all routers in the area receive the advertisements.

Each router uses the information in the link-state update packets to construct its own topological database. Although the database is customized from the perspective of each router, all routers have exactly the same information. This is in sharp contrast to RIP, in which each router has an eccentric and incomplete knowledge of the network.

OSPF generates considerably less traffic than RIP for a variety of reasons:

- ► Routers transmit link-state advertisements at infrequent intervals. RIP requires each router to broadcast its entire routing table every 30 seconds.

- ► Between periodic updates, OSPF router advertisements only take place when a change is observed in the network.

▶ Link-state update packets are sent to adjacencies and are not broadcast. Adjacencies forward link-state update packets to other routers in the area. All packets are transmitted point-to-point, eliminating broadcast traffic.

▶ Link-state update packets are flooded within an area, but the area may be defined by the network administrator to control the impact of OSPF updates on the Internet.

▶ A single link-state update can carry link-state advertisements for many routers.

Autonomous Systems and Areas An *autonomous system* (AS) is a group of routers that exchange information using a common routing protocol under the authority of a single organization. When an AS is joined to a network that uses a different protocol, the router connecting the dissimilar networks is called an *autonomous system border router* (ASBR). Figure 4.23 shows an ASBR used to connect an OSPF AS to a RIP AS.

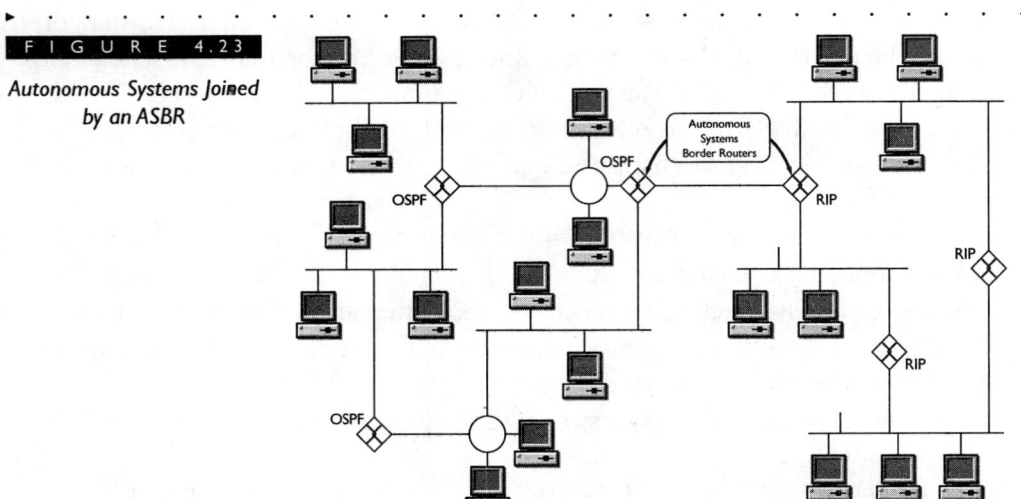

Autonomous Systems Joined by an ASBR

Areas are administrative subdivisions of an OSPF autonomous system. By defining areas, administrators can determine which routers will participate in exchanging link-state updates.

By default, the entire AS is configured as a single area. It is possible, however, to subdivide the AS logically into two or more areas. When link-state updates are flooded, they will only be flooded to routers that participate in the same area. This selectiveness has several benefits:

▸ The amount of internetwork traffic is reduced.

▸ The routers maintain a smaller database, reducing memory and other CPU requirements.

▸ Routers can process changes more quickly because they have less to process.

Two rules must be followed when defining areas:

▸ An area must consist of contiguous routers. In other words, parts of an area cannot be separated by another area. (Although virtual links can be used to connect two separate parts of an area through the backbone area.)

▸ The organization must be hierarchical. There must be one top-level area to which all other areas are connected. The top-level area is called the *backbone*.

NOTE **Link-state routing applies only within each area. If the areas are not organized hierarchically, loops can develop. A NetWare router acts as an intra-area router within each area. A NetWare router does not pass route information between nonbackbone areas, and it therefore does not cause loops.**

Figure 4.24 illustrates an AS that is organized in three areas. Connections between areas are made using *area border routers* (ABRs). Routers within the areas receive routing information for other areas from the ABRs, and ABRs are responsible for exchanging routing information with the backbone. ABRs serve as filters to determine what routing information should be propagated to adjoining areas. (Because ABRs carry heavy workloads, Novell recommends not using low-end computers as ABRs.)

Figure 4.24 illustrates the relationship of the backbone area (area B) to the areas it joins. All other areas must be directly connected to the backbone. If nonbackbone areas are joined, loops may develop. Area C is connected to the backbone through two ABRs. This arrangement provides redundant paths, enabling the area to sustain a single router failure. Areas fall into two categories:

▶ *Stub areas* are connected to the backbone through a single ABR. To reduce routing network traffic, the ABR advertises itself as the default router within the area. No ASBRs are permitted within a stub area. In Figure 4.24, area A is an example of a stub area.

▶ *Transit areas* have two or more connections to the backbone. Area C in Figure 4.24 is an example of a transit area.

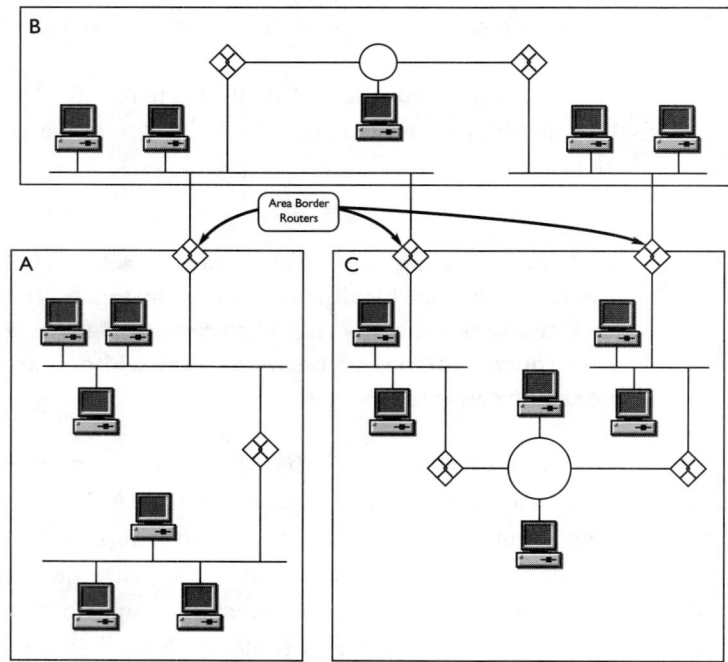

FIGURE 4.24

An Autonomous System Organized in Three Areas

Conclusions About OSPF

The network world is headed in the direction of link-state routing, although the remaining base of older routers is slowing the transition. NetWare supports two link-state protocols:

▸ NLSP (NetWare Link Services Protocol) for IPX

▸ OSPF for IP

Regardless of the protocols your network is running, you should consider implementing link-state routing. Even if your network is modest in size, you will observe a reduction in routing traffic. In summary, the advantages of link-state routing protocols over distance-vector protocols (such as RIP) are as follows:

▸ Network size is virtually unlimited.

▸ Bandwidth utilization is significantly lower.

▸ Packet sizes are smaller and increase in size less rapidly as the network grows.

▸ Updates are infrequent.

▸ Loops cannot develop within areas.

▸ Network changes propagate rapidly.

The primary disadvantage of link-state routing is that routers require more powerful hardware. Essentially, OSPF removes much of the responsibility for routing from the network and increases the responsibilities of the router. RIP uses a simpler algorithm that places greater demands on the network.

Exterior Gateway Protocol

RIP and OSPF are examples of interior routing protocols, which support routing within an autonomous system. Most administrators deal with this type of routing protocol.

External routing protocols are used to route between autonomous systems. Figure 4.25 illustrates an internetwork that uses an exterior gateway protocol to route between an OSPF AS and the Internet.

FIGURE 4.25

An Internetwork That Uses an Exterior Gateway Protocol

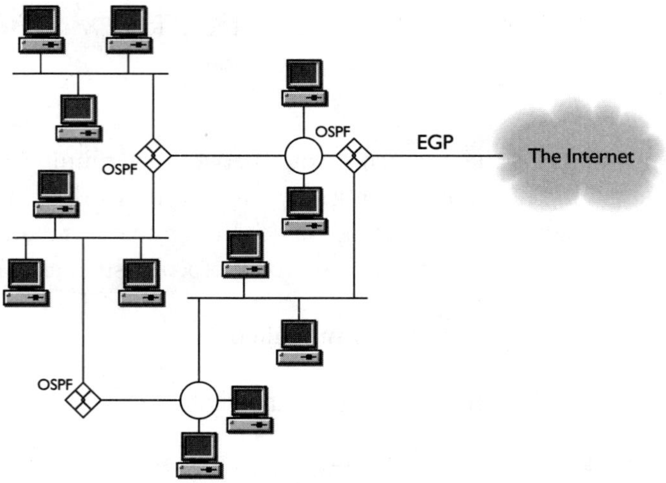

NetWare supports the Internet *Exterior Gateway Protocol* (EGP) (RFC 827/904), which was introduced in 1982. EGP functions in a very simple manner. First, EGP establishes neighbor relations with other directly connected routers. Then EGP determines which networks can be reached through each of its neighbor routers. Finally, EGP advertises route availability. EGP routers exchange periodic routing update messages to maintain current reachability databases.

EGP is extremely limited in its operation. An EGP router advertises only that it can reach a given remote network. No cost metric is used and no load balancing or route optimization is performed. This limitation also limits use of EGP to tree-shaped network configurations. All networks must connect to a central backbone.

EGP obtains its information about an AS from the IGPs within the AS. The information EGP receives must be specified by means of route filters — a precaution that prevents unwanted data from being propagated to external networks.

Datagram Fragmentation and Reassembly

IP accepts fairly large datagrams from upper-layer protocols (as large as 65,535 bytes). This size far exceeds the size limits imposed by most networks. Ethernet, for example, can accommodate at most 1500 octets of upper-layer data in a frame.

One of IP's functions is to fragment large datagrams into smaller datagrams that are compatible with the network access protocols in use. The header of the IP datagram contains fields that let receiving hosts identify the position of each datagram in the overall structure and reassemble the original datagram.

The *maximum transfer unit* (MTU) describes the maximum frame size that a network can accommodate. Datagram fragmentation is complicated when data must be routed through internetworks consisting of networks having different MTUs. The internet in Figure 4.26 serves to illustrate the difficulty. Data must be routed through an Ethernet (MTU 1500), a token ring (MTU 3000), and a WAN link (MTU 520, allowing for 500 octets of data and 20 octets of header). Attached to the token ring, host 1 can initiate the process by transmitting a datagram up to 3000 octets in size. In that case, router A must refragment the datagram for transfer over the WAN. Then, router B must reassemble the fragments to recover.

FIGURE 4.26

Networks on This Internet with Different MTUs

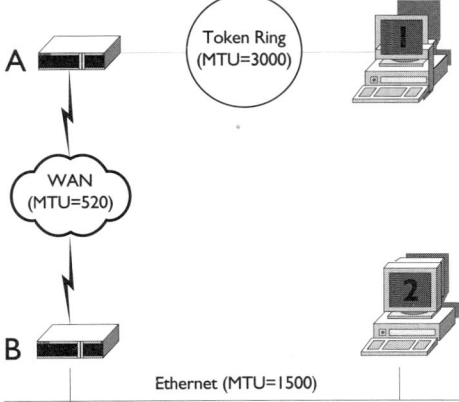

The IP specification sets minimum ground rules for the sizes of datagrams that hosts and routers are expected to handle. All hosts must be prepared to accept and reassemble datagrams of at least 576 octets. IP routers must be prepared to handle datagrams up to the MTUs of the networks to which the routers are attached and must always be able to handle datagrams up to 576 octets.

IP has the responsibility for fragmenting datagrams into datagrams that are compatible with the networks through which the datagrams are sent. When a datagram is fragmented, the header contains data that enables the receiving IP to determine the position of the fragment in the overall datagram so that the datagram can be reassembled.

The header of a fragmented datagram includes an *offset* parameter that indicates where the first octet in the fragment belongs in the complete datagram. Figure 4.27 illustrates the process of fragmenting a datagram containing 1300 octets in its data field. The datagram must be fragmented for a network with an MTU of 520. To accommodate a 20-octet header, each fragment can contain 500 octets of data. Consequently, fragments are generated with offsets of 0, 500, and 1000.

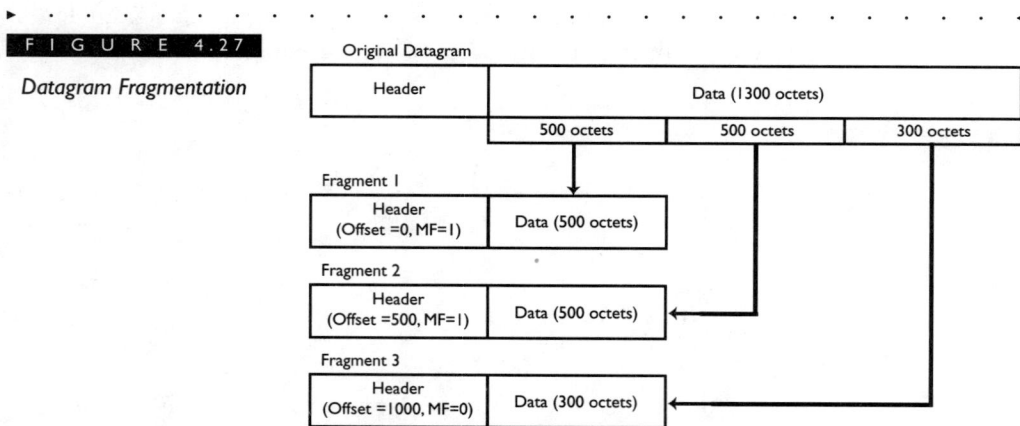

FIGURE 4.27

Datagram Fragmentation

The resulting fragments are themselves IP datagrams. Their headers differ from the header in the original datagram in that the MF bit in the flags field specifies whether the datagram is an intermediate fragment or the last fragment in the overall datagram. You learn about the MF bit when the IP header format is discussed later in this chapter.

IP does not implement any error detection or recovery. Consequently, if a single fragment of a datagram is damaged, the entire datagram is lost. No mechanism exists that permits IP to resend the fragment. When an error such as a missing fragment is detected, IP notifies the upper-layer protocol, which must retransmit the entire datagram. Because the entire datagram is retransmitted, IP fragmentation can result in inefficient communication.

Many implementations of TCP enable TCP to identify the MTU between the source and destination host using a technique that is described in Chapter 5. With this information, TCP can provide IP with datagrams that do not require fragmentation as they are routed.

IP Datagram Format

Figure 4.28 shows the format of an IP datagram header. Many operational characteristics of IP can be tuned by placing different values in these fields.

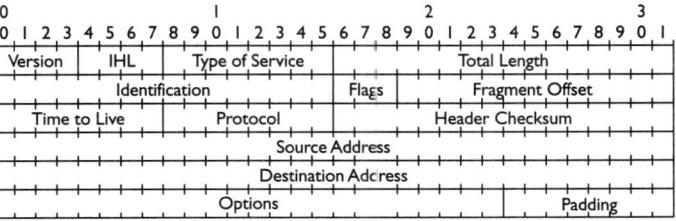

FIGURE 4.28
Format of the IP Datagram Header

Table 4.6 summarizes the fields in an IP datagram header.

TABLE 4.6	FIELD	DESCRIPTION
Fields of an IP Datagram Header	Version	A 4-bit field that specifies the format of the Internet header. The current version of IP is Version 4 as specified in RFC 791.
	Internet Header Length (IHL)	A 4-bit field that specifies the length of the Internet header in 32-bit words.

Continued

TABLE 4.6	FIELD	DESCRIPTION
Continued	Type of Service	An 8-bit field that specifies the quality of service that is required. Figure 4.29 expands the details in this field.
		The effect of values in the precedence fields depends on the network in use. These values must be configured accordingly.
		Some of the options are incompatible. Low delay, high reliability, and high throughput are mutually exclusive because better performance in one area degrades performance in another.
	Total Length	A 16-bit field that specifies the length of the datagram in octets, including the header and data. The size of this field limits IP datagrams to a maximum size of 65,535 octets. The IP standard recommends that all hosts should be configured to receive datagrams with a minimum size of 576 octets in length.
	Identification	A 16-bit field containing information used to reassemble fragmented datagrams.
	Flags	A 3-bit field test that contains the following control flags:
		Bit 0. Reserved; must be 0.
		Bit 1 (DF). 0 = may fragment; 1 = do not fragment.
		Bit 2 (MF). 0 = last fragment; 1 = more fragments.
		If a datagram is fragmented, the MF bit will be 1 in all datagram fragments except the last.

FIELD	DESCRIPTION
Fragment Offset	A 13-bit field that specifies the position of a fragment within the complete datagram if a datagram has been fragmented.
Time to Live	An 8-bit field that specifies the length of time a datagram may remain on the network. Typically, this value represents seconds. Each IP module that handles the datagram is required to decrement time to live by at least one. When time to live reaches zero, the datagram must be discarded. This ensures that undelivered datagrams cannot circulate endlessly on the network.
Protocol	An 8-bit field that specifies the upper-layer protocol associated with this datagram. See the RFC titled *Assigned Numbers* for the numbers associated with many protocols.
Header Checksum	A 16-bit error checksum that covers the header only. Whenever the header is modified, the checksum must be recalculated.
Source Address	Specifies the 32-bit IP address of the host that originated the datagram.
Destination Address	Specifies the 32-bit IP address of the host that should receive the datagram.
Options	May contain 0 or more 32-bit words that contain options as specified by RFC 791.

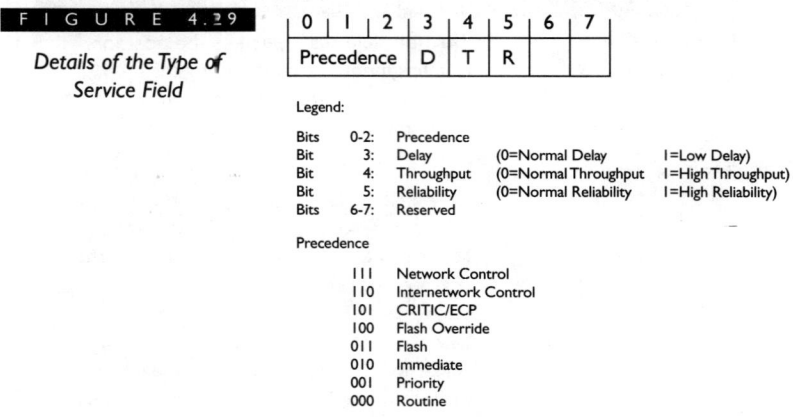

FIGURE 4.29

Details of the Type of Service Field

0	1	2	3	4	5	6	7
Precedence			D	T	R		

Legend:

Bits	0-2:	Precedence		
Bit	3:	Delay	(0=Normal Delay	1=Low Delay)
Bit	4:	Throughput	(0=Normal Throughput	1=High Throughput)
Bit	5:	Reliability	(0=Normal Reliability	1=High Reliability)
Bits	6-7:	Reserved		

Precedence

111	Network Control
110	Internetwork Control
101	CRITIC/ECP
100	Flash Override
011	Flash
010	Immediate
001	Priority
000	Routine

The Internet Control Message Protocol

The Internet Control Message Protocol is one of the features that makes the TCP/IP protocol suite so sweet. IP was not designed as a reliable protocol, and numerous potential problems can arise. ICMP (RFC 792) is a standard protocol that provides a messaging capability for IP. Although ICMP is described separately from IP, ICMP is an integral part of the internet protocol, and ICMP messages are carried as data in IP datagrams.

For a complete list of messages, consult RFC 792. A glance at some of the potential messages is sufficient for this discussion.

▶ **Destination Unreachable.** These messages provide information when a host, net, port, or protocol are unreachable.

▶ **Time Exceeded.** These messages notify the source if a datagram is undeliverable because its time to live expired or if a datagram is not reassembled within a specified minimum time.

▶ **Parameter Problem.** These messages report a parameter problem and the octet in which the error was detected.

▸ **Source Quench.** These messages may be sent by destination routers or hosts that are forced to discard datagrams due to limitations in available buffer space or if for any reason a datagram cannot be processed.

▸ **Redirect.** These messages are sent to a host when a router receives a datagram that could be routed more directly through another gateway. The message advises the host that was the source of the datagram of a more appropriate router to receive the datagram.

▸ **Echo Request and Echo Reply Messages.** These messages exchange data between hosts. The ping utility, used to test communication between TCP/IP hosts, makes use of echo request and echo reply messages.

▸ **Timestamp Request and Timestamp Reply.** These messages exchange timestamp data between hosts.

▸ **Information Request and Information Reply.** These messages can be used to enable a host to discover the network to which it is attached.

NOTE

ICMP provides a mechanism for reporting errors to the host that originated an IP datagram, but ICMP has no capability of correcting the error. The original host must associate the error message with the application that produced the datagram and take steps to correct the problem.

ICMP Router Discovery Messages (RFC 1256) are an extension to ICMP that extend the capabilities of hosts to discover routes to gateways. Router Advertisements are multicast at periodic intervals, announcing IP addresses for its interfaces to networks. Hosts obtain route information by listening for these announcements. When a host starts up, it may send a Router Solicitation to request immediate advertisements. This technique provides information about available routers but cannot provide best-path information.

Unfortunately, Router Discovery Messages cannot substitute for a routing protocol such as RIP and OSPF. All ICMP messages are sent to the host that originated the datagram inspiring the message. Intermediate routers do not learn of a routing error and do not have the opportunity to update their routing tables. Therefore, you can rely on ICMP as a routing protocol only on very simple networks.

IP Multicasting and the Internet Group Messaging Protocol

IP multicasting is the transmission of an IP datagram to devices belonging to a *host group*. A multicast datagram is delivered to all members of the host group using the same best-effort approach used for unicast IP datagrams. That is to say, delivery of the datagram is not guaranteed to be delivered to all members of the multicast group.

The Internet Group Messaging Protocol (IGMP; RFC 1112) provides a mechanism for registering the members of host groups with multicast routers. Multicast routers may be implemented as stand-alone devices that work in addition to any IP routers that are on the network. More commonly, multicast routers are incorporated into IP or multiprotocol routers, such as the router built into NetWare 5.

Registering Multicast Group Members

All IP devices that are capable of receiving multicast messages are automatically made members of multicast group 224.0.0.1. This is the only permanent multicast group. Devices must specifically join and leave other host groups, and multicast routers keep track of whether any multicast group members are present on each network that they support.

The procedure for refreshing the list of active multicast groups is as follows:

1. At periodic intervals, the multicast router multicasts a Host Membership Query message (simply referred to as a Query) to address 224.0.0.1.

2. At one-minute intervals, the multicast router multicasts a Query to address 224.0.0.1. The message has a time-to-live of 1, ensuring that it will not be forwarded by other multicast routers attached to the network.

3. Each host that receives a Query starts a timer for each multicast group to which it needs to belong. Each timer is set to a different random value so that all hosts' timers will not expire at the same time.

4. When a timer expires, the host generates a Host Membership Report (or, more simply, a Report) that it sends to the address of the host group of which it is a member.

5. Other members of the host group receive the first Report generated on the network. Because the multicast router only needs to know that at least one member of the multicast group is present on the network, other members need not respond. They stop their timers and do not generate Reports. As a result, under normal circumstances only one Report will be generated on the network for each multicast group.

6. The multicast router receives the Report and notes that the network supports members of the multicast group. If no Reports are received after a number of Queries, the multicast router concludes that no members of the multicast group are present on the network.

When a host initially joins a multicast group, it should immediately generate a Report informing the multicast router of its presence.

Mapping Multicast Addresses to MAC Addresses

As you have seen, all IP datagrams are delivered using the physical (MAC) addresses of the destination hosts. Chapter 3 discussed the mechanism for defining multicast addresses for Ethernet nodes. Similar techniques are defined for other broadcast networks.

RFC 1112 describes the approach for mapping IP multicast addresses to Ethernet physical addresses. An IP host group address is mapped to an Ethernet multicast address by placing the low-order 23-bits of the IP address into the low-order 23-bits of the Ethernet multicast address.

This technique has limits because there are 28 significant bits in an IP host group address. Consequently, it is possible for multiple IP multicast addresses to map to the same Ethernet address. System implementors must be aware that this is a potential problem, and must work to ensure that conflicts are resolved.

IP Version 6

The current version of IP, Version 4 (IPv4), has done an admirable job of supporting the Internet for more than 17 years. However, this protocol is starting to show its age, particularly in light of the rapid expansion of the Internet in recent years. IP addresses are becoming scarce, the chief motivation behind the effort to design an updated Internet Protocol. Furthermore, IP is ill-suited to some tasks many people are demanding from the Internet.

The IP next generation (IPng) working group of the IETF has developed a successor to IPv4. The new protocol, IP Version 6 (IPv6; RFC 1883), is currently an elective protocol on the standards track. Among the improvements offered by IPv6 are the following:

▶ The current 32-bit addresses are extended to 128 bits. Address hierarchies are supported. Automatic configuration of addresses are improved.

▶ Authentication support enables IP to support private, secure data and to ensure data integrity.

▶ The header format is simplified, with several fields being dropped.

Greater support is provided for extending the protocol and adding options.

Who Could Ask for Anything More?

IP is the central protocol in all TCP/IP configurations. It is the one protocol that will always be present. From this central position, IP bears the crucial responsibility of delivering message units through both simple and complex internetworks. IP can provide all of the message delivery necessary to run applications on a network.

It could, that is, if all applications had the same delivery requirements. If all applications could withstand unreliable delivery of 64KB messages, IP would suffice. But often applications must transfer huge amounts of data, and application designers don't always want to divide the data into 64KB chunks. Also, applications usually cannot tolerate faulty message delivery.

So IP isn't enough. Several additional features are necessary for a complete and versatile set of message-delivery capabilities. Those features include reliable data delivery and fragmentation of large messages. The next chapter, which deals with the host-to-host layer, explains how those capabilities can be added to a network.

## CHAPTER 5

The Host-to-Host Layer

We have reached the point in our tour of TCP/IP where the network has the capability of probably delivering any message up to 65,535 bytes in size anywhere in any size internetwork. That's an amazing capability when you think about it, but I can see you're not all that excited. You'd probably like to transfer a 5MB file with all the data for your office football pool, or you just don't think "probably" is good enough when the data going through the network is used to cut you a paycheck. Well, relax, because relief is at hand in the guise of the host-to-host layer.

The host-to-host layer builds on the capabilities of the internet layer by adding two features to the network protocol stack:

▶ A network interface that enables upper-layer protocols to utilize the network without worrying about the logistics of message fragmentation.

▶ The capability of delivering messages between hosts either reliably or unreliably, as the situation demands.

The host-to-host layer is not one protocol but two. *Transmission Control Protocol* (TCP) provides reliable delivery, and *User Datagram Protocol* (UDP) provides unreliable delivery. These two protocols provide network protocol designers with a choice of host-to-host services: slower and practically bulletproof, or fast and unreliable.

TCP provides for reliable host-to-host communication. TCP uses every trick it knows to deliver your data, and it lets you know if the attempt fails. TCP checks for errors and resends data as required to accomplish delivery. If delivery cannot be performed (for example, if the only router is down), TCP lets upper-layer processes know that the delivery attempt failed. TCP has had to be good, because it was given the task of delivering data on the ARPANET at a time when WAN technology was pretty iffy. Unfortunately, all this reliability comes at a price — TCP has a lot of overhead that generates network traffic and slows performance. At times, these disadvantages are too costly, which is why there are two protocols at the host-to-host layer.

UDP provides unreliable delivery when efficiency is more important than foolproof delivery. Datagrams are independent messages delivered on a best-effort basis. UDP sends the datagram down the protocol stack but doesn't spend any effort to determine if the datagram reaches the destination host. If an upper-layer protocol wants to know about failed delivery attempts, the upper layer must check things out on its own. Before you decide that UDP is good only for casual communications, guess again. Sun's *Network File System* (NFS) uses UDP as the host-to-host protocol. NFS performs extremely sophisticated remote file services, but its designers wanted the most efficient transport mechanism available and chose to implement NFS over UDP, providing reliable messaging in NFS itself.

The host-to-host layer is in the middle of the TCP/IP protocol stack and ties together upper-layer processes and the network. Figure 5.1 illustrates the TCP/IP protocol stack, showing several prominent protocols at the process/application layer. This figure gives you an idea of how the pieces fit together and also demonstrates which protocols rely on TCP and which rely on UDP. So that you can understand how TCP and UDP service upper-layer protocols, this chapter initially addresses protocol multiplexing.

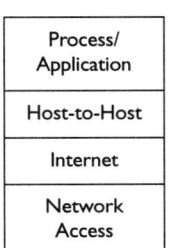

FIGURE 5.1

The TCP/IP Protocol Stack

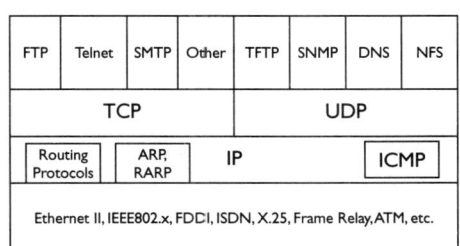

Process/Application	FTP	Telnet	SMTP	Other	TFTP	SNMP	DNS	NFS
Host-to-Host	TCP				UDP			
Internet	Routing Protocols	ARP, RARP	IP				ICMP	
Network Access	Ethernet II, IEEE802.x, FDCI, ISDN, X.25, Frame Relay, ATM, etc.							

Host-to-Host Layer Protocol Multiplexing

Chapter 2 introduced you to the concept of *protocol multiplexing*, which enables lower-layer protocols to maintain message streams for multiple upper-layer protocols. If you look at Figure 5.1, you can see that TCP and UDP must have access to a mechanism that enables them to sort out the data that is received from and that must be delivered to each upper-layer protocol.

But TCP must do more than just deliver data. TCP is a connection-oriented protocol that enables processes to engage in reliable, full-duplex dialogs with the corresponding protocols on another host. This turns out to be a pretty demanding job.

The interface between the host-to-host layer and upper-layer processes is the *port*, which is simply a mechanism for identifying data associated with specific protocols. TCP and UDP use the ports to deliver data to the correct protocol.

A port is identified by a *port number*. Although protocol designers can specify custom port numbers, a large number of port numbers, called *well-known ports*, have been reserved for specific protocols and organizations. Well-known ports and other official Internet numbers are assigned by the Internet Assigned Numbers Authority (IANA) and are specified in an RFC titled *Assigned Numbers* (RFC 1700).

A process is specified fully by the port together with the IP address of the host on which the process is running. The combination of a port number and IP address is called a *socket*. Because each host on an internetwork has a unique IP address, each process running on the internetwork has a unique socket.

A connection between two processes is specified fully by the sockets assigned to the processes. With sockets, the host-to-host layer provides a mechanism that supports full-duplex dialogs between end processes. Figure 5.2 shows how process-to-process communication takes place.

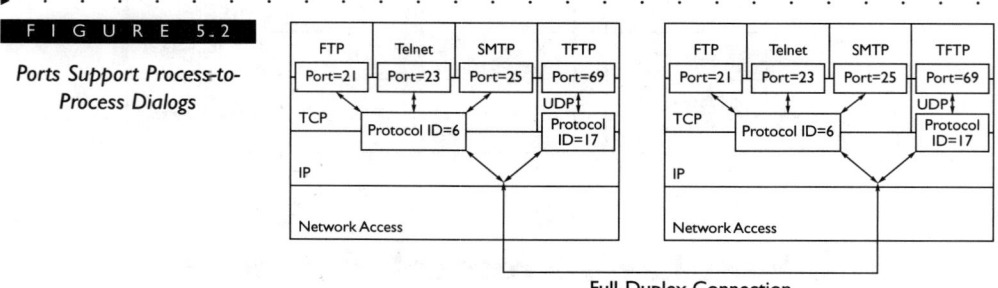

FIGURE 5.2

Ports Support Process-to-Process Dialogs

Two types of sockets are used in TCP/IP:

▸ TCP uses *stream sockets* to provide reliable, sequential, bidirectional data exchange.

▸ UDP uses *datagram sockets* to provide unreliable, bidirectional data transfer.

Sockets provide an *application program interface* (API) between processes and TCP and UDP. Programmers use the API to enable their applications to interface with the network. NetWare supports two common APIs:

- **Sockets.** An API that gained wide distribution in Berkeley Standard Distribution (BSD) UNIX.

- **STREAMS Transport Layer Interface (TLI).** An API developed by AT&T.

Transmission Control Protocol

TCP (RFC 793) provides a connection-oriented transport mechanism that enables hosts to engage in reliable dialogs. TCP communicates through the network in much the same way that we communicate through a telephone, with complete indifference to the complex mechanisms that enable communication to take place. Although TCP establishes connections pretty much by "dialing" the remote computer's number, TCP knows nothing about the network. In fact, TCP is quite indifferent to the network. Instead, IP worries about the network. TCP concerns itself with communicating with its peer TCP protocols on other hosts. This capability enables TCP to provide reliable delivery on any network, regardless of size or technology.

The philosophy behind TCP's design is spelled out in RFC 793: "Be conservative in what you do, be liberal in what you accept from others." TCP modules should be designed to accept a certain amount of variation in incoming data so that processes don't malfunction because of trivial errors. TCP is intended to be a forgiving protocol, but a protocol that provides rock-solid reliability.

TCP has several responsibilities:

- Enabling upper-layer processes to send streams of data through the network

- Maintaining connections between processes

- Providing reliable communication

Let's take a look at each of these capabilities before moving on to the TCP data format.

Data Stream Maintenance

In comparison with TCP, processes and applications know even less about the network. They aren't used to fragmenting messages into byte-size pieces, for example. When they need to send data, they pretty much just send data, in a continuous stream. One of TCP's responsibilities is to enable those streams of data to be delivered through the network so that the peer process receives the same data in the same stream. Figure 5.3 shows how the entire process works. Here is what happens as data flows down the protocol stack of the sending host, through the network, and up the protocol stack of the receiving host:

1. TCP receives a continuous stream of data from the upper-layer process.

2. If the amount of data exceeds what IP can handle in a datagram, TCP fragments the data stream into segments sized to meet the maximum size requirements of IP.

3. IP receives the segments and, if necessary, fragments the segments into datagrams that conform to the maximum data capacity of a network frame.

4. Network protocols encapsulate the datagram in a frame and transmit the frame to the network as a series of bits.

5. Network protocols at the receiving host capture the bits and reconstruct the original frame.

6. The datagram is extracted from the frame and passed up to IP.

7. If the datagram is a fragment, IP reconstructs the original segment from the fragments. The segment is passed up to TCP.

   TCP reconstructs the original data stream from the segments that it receives and presents the data stream to the upper-layer process.

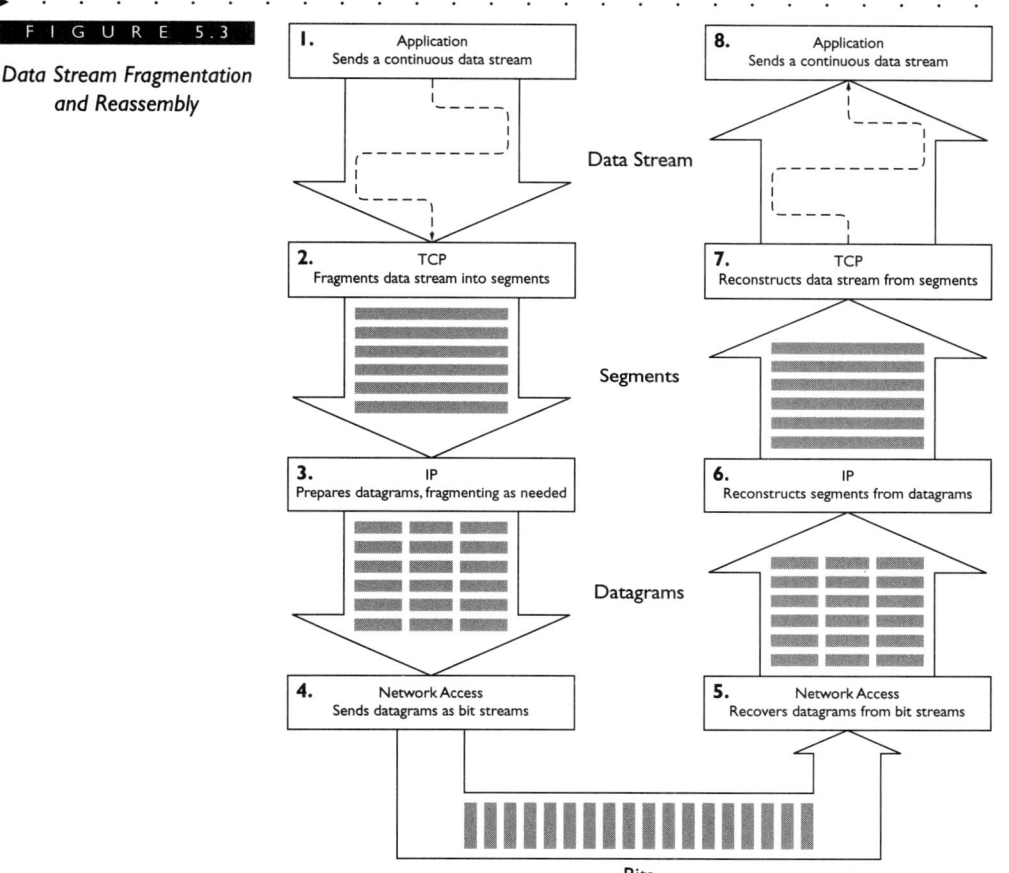

FIGURE 5.3

*Data Stream Fragmentation
and Reassembly*

Windowing

As all this data is being transferred between hosts, TCP is responsible for managing flow control via a process called *windowing*. When hosts set up a connection, they agree on a *window*, the number of unacknowledged octets of data that can be outstanding. If the sending host reaches the limit imposed by the window, it ceases transmitting until acknowledgments are received for some or all of the outstanding data. Acknowledgments move the window forward so that more data may be transmitted.

When a TCP connection is established, each host establishes a receive window size that specifies the amount of data the host can accommodate in its receive buffer and, therefore, the maximum amount of data a sending host can have outstanding at a given time.

Message transfer is most efficient when messages are fragmented to match the *maximum transfer unit* (MTU), the largest message size supported by the internetwork that joins the hosts. When TCP establishes a connection, the MTU of the network is used to determine a *maximum segment size* (MSS), which is typically 40 bytes less than the MTU to allow for the TCP and IP headers.

RFC 1191 defines the PMTU discover process used to establish the MTU when a connection is established. TCP transmits segments with the *don't fragment* bit set. If a router handling the segment encounters a network with a smaller MTU, it returns an ICMP error that informs the sender that the destination is unreachable because fragmentation would be required. In most cases, the router includes in this message the MTU of the network that forced the error. The sending TCP adjusts its MSS to the MTU of the intervening network and continues to try until the MTU for the overall route is determined.

RFC 1191 is supported by the vast majority of routers, but you may encounter so-called "black hole" routers that simply drop segments that have the don't fragment flag and that exceed the MTU of the next hop.

Connection Maintenance

TCP enables processes to establish connections with peer processes on other hosts. A connection must be explicitly opened or closed. When TCP issues an OPEN call, the call includes the local port and the remote socket. When the connection is established, the process that requested the connection is provided with a name that identifies the connection.

Connections may be active or passive:

> ▶ An *active open* is an explicit attempt to establish a connection with a remote process. In other words, an active open is one host reaching out to touch another.

▸ A *passive open* configures TCP to await incoming connection requests, enabling the process that requested the passive open to accept connections from remote processes. Passive opens are the tools that servers use to make services available on the network. Outside processes can then issue active opens to establish a connection.

The desirability of well-known ports becomes especially clear when considered with regard to passive opens. A remote host that wishes to connect to a service must be able to grab a handle on that service. That handle is the well-known port. For example, a remote FTP user's program knows that it can connect to an FTP server by requesting an active open using port 21.

When an open request is generated, TCP constructs a segment with the SYN (synchronize) control bit set. (Control bits are discussed in the section "TCP Header Format" later in this chapter.) When the remote TCP module receives the segment, it matches the remote socket to a local socket to establish a connection. The peer TCP modules exchange sockets and synchronize segment sequence numbers to complete the connection.

Connections must be explicitly closed. When a process asks TCP to close a connection, TCP constructs a segment with the FIN control bit set. Both ends must participate in closing the connection. The TCP that sends a CLOSE may continue to receive data until it receives a CLOSE from the remote TCP. This system accomplishes a smooth shutdown that enables both hosts to flush any outstanding data. Reliable data delivery continues until all data is received and both partners have closed the connection. Applications can also close connections in a less elegant way by sending a RST, which forcibly resets the connection.

Reliable Delivery

TCP provides reliable delivery using a system of *segment sequence numbers* and *acknowledgments*. Every octet that is sent must be acknowledged, or TCP will retransmit the data. When delivery begins, each octet is assigned a segment sequence number. The segment header specifies the segment sequence number of the first data octet along with an acknowledgment number. When a segment is sent, a copy is retained in a hold queue until the segment is acknowledged. Unacknowledged segments are resent.

When a receiving TCP acknowledges a particular segment sequence number, the sending TCP is relieved of responsibility for the data up to that point. The receiving TCP bears responsibility for reliably delivering data to the upper-layer process. These acknowledgments also form part of the windowing flow-control mechanism.

TCP Header Format

TCP applies a header to each segment that it constructs. The format of this header is shown in Figure 5.4. TCP segments are organized in 16-bit words and must contain an even number of octets. If the segment contains an odd number of octets, it is padded with an octet consisting of zeros. Table 5.1 describes the fields in the TCP header.

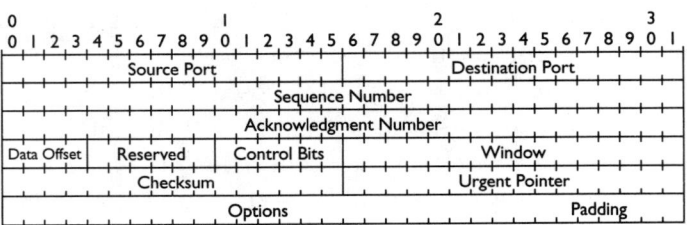

FIELD	PURPOSE
Source Port	A 16-bit field that specifies the port on the sending TCP module.
Destination Port	A 16-bit field that specifies the port on the receiving TCP module.

FIELD	PURPOSE
Sequence Number	A 32-bit field that specifies the segment sequence number of the first octet in the data field. If this segment opens a connection, the SYN control bit is set, the sequence number is the initial sequence number (ISN), and the first data octet is at sequence ISN+1.
Acknowledgment Number	A 32-bit field that specifies the next segment sequence number that the sending TCP expects. When a connection is active, TCP always sets the ACK control bit.
Data Offset	A 4-bit field specifying the number of 32-bit words in the TCP header. When options do not end on a 32-bit word boundary, the header is padded with 0-value octets.
Reserved	A 6-bit field reserved for future use. Its value must be 0.
Control Bits	A 6-bit field consisting of 6 control bits as follows: URG. 1 = Urgent pointer significant; 0 = ignore urgent pointer. ACK. 1 = Acknowledgment number is significant; 0 = ignore acknowledgment number. PSH. 1 initiates a push function. RST. 1 forces a connection reset. SYN. 1 = first segment of connection; synchronize counters. FIN. 1 = no more data; close the connection.

Continued

TABLE 5.1	FIELD	PURPOSE
Continued	Window	A 16-bit checksum that provides error control for the header and data fields but does not cover padding that is added to make the header come out on an even 32-bit boundary. A 96-bit pseudo header is also covered.
	Checksum	A 16-bit field used to detect errors in transmission.
	Urgent Pointer	A 16-bit field that identifies the sequence number of the octet that follows urgent data. This pointer is a positive offset from the segment sequence number.
	Options	A variable-size field that incorporates options.
	Padding	A variable number of 0-value octets used to pad the header to an even 32-bit boundary.

In Table 5.1, the explanation of the window field mentioned a *pseudo header*. TCP uses a 12-octet data structure called a pseudo header to communicate with IP and to protect TCP from misrouted segments. The length of the pseudo header is not included in the value of the segment length field. The pseudo header format is shown in Figure 5.5.

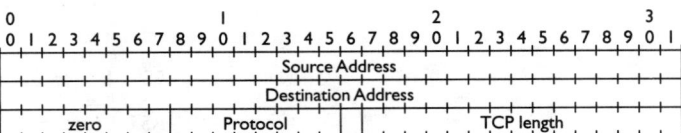

FIGURE 5.5

Format of the TCP Pseudo Header

User Datagram Protocol

TCP is an aggressively conservative and formal protocol that communicates only in a connection-oriented environment. The overhead required to establish, maintain, and release a connection is justified in many situations when significant amounts of data must be communicated reliably. In many cases, however, the overhead is difficult to justify.

UDP (RFC 768) is a less fanatical protocol used by many processes that want to communicate with a minimum of fuss and bother and that can either tolerate an occasional error or provide error control themselves. UDP is a datagram protocol that does not need to process streams of data from upper layers. Because UDP is freed of the responsibilities of developing segments and maintaining connections, UDP is an extremely simple and efficient protocol.

When is UDP useful? Here are some examples:

▸ When messages are sporadic, the effort to establish and tear down a connection can exceed the effort required to transport the data. A good example of sporadic messaging is provided by SNMP, which generates network alerts called *traps* when specific network conditions occur. If a connection were established for each trap, overhead would slow delivery of traps and bog down the network.

▸ When messages require no acknowledgment, a connection is wasted effort. SNMP traps are simply sent on the network. If network managers don't correct the cause of the trap, it will be generated again when necessary.

▸ When a protocol has special needs that don't fit with TCP, protocol designers may choose UDP because it imposes fewer limits. Sun's *Network File System* (NFS) was implemented over UDP so that the designers had more freedom to design the complete communication process.

Figure 5.6 shows the header format for a UDP datagram. The fields in the header are described in Table 5.2. Like TCP, UDP generates a pseudo header, which guards against misrouted datagrams. Figure 5.7 shows the data format of the pseudo header.

FIGURE 5.6

Format of the UDP Datagram Header

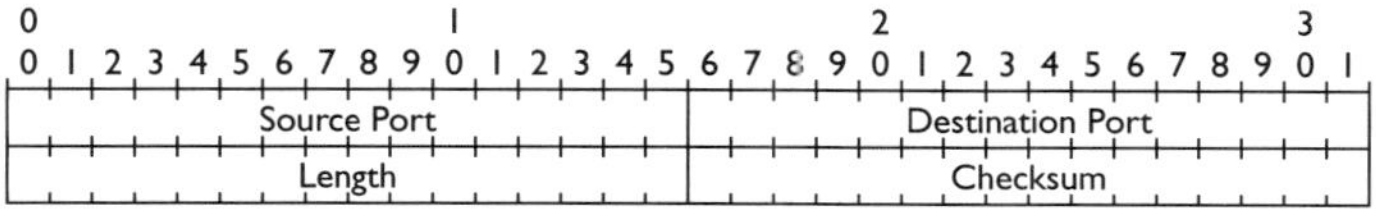

```
 0                   1                   2                   3
 0 1 2 3 4 5 6 7 8 9 0 1 2 3 4 5 6 7 8 9 0 1 2 3 4 5 6 7 8 9 0 1
+-+-+-+-+-+-+-+-+-+-+-+-+-+-+-+-+-+-+-+-+-+-+-+-+-+-+-+-+-+-+-+-+
|            Source Port        |        Destination Port       |
+-+-+-+-+-+-+-+-+-+-+-+-+-+-+-+-+-+-+-+-+-+-+-+-+-+-+-+-+-+-+-+-+
|              Length           |            Checksum           |
+-+-+-+-+-+-+-+-+-+-+-+-+-+-+-+-+-+-+-+-+-+-+-+-+-+-+-+-+-+-+-+-+
```

TABLE 5.2	FIELD	PURPOSE
Fields in a UDP Datagram Header	Source Port	An optional 16-bit field that specifies the port on the sending module when a reply is anticipated. When a reply is not required, the source port is 0.
	Destination Port	A 16-bit field that specifies the port on the receiving UDP module.
	Length	A 16-bit field that specifies the length of the datagram in octets, including the header and data fields. The minimum value of this field is 8. The maximum value imposes a maximum datagram size of 65,535 octets, with 56,527 octets available for data.
	Checksum	A 16-bit checksum that provides error control for the header, data, and pseudo header.

FIGURE 5.7

Format of the UDP Pseudo Header

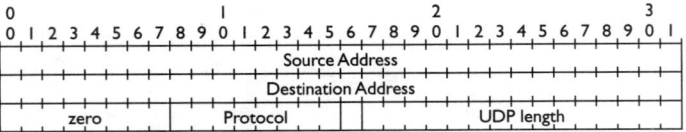

Ready for Work

Now, depending on the choice of transport protocol, the network can deliver huge messages with very high reliability. Or, if desired, the network can deliver small messages with great efficiency. The overall architecture of TCP/IP provides this versatility by offering a choice of host-to-host layer protocols.

The network is ready to go to work, but it doesn't yet have any work to do. Without taking one more step, the delivery capabilities of TCP/IP resemble an automobile without a driver's seat and steering wheel. The car can move, but it can't carry a payload. Unless we add some applications that enable end-users to "ride" the network, all we have is a technical curiosity. In the fourth and final protocol layer, we at last encounter the reason for TCP/IP's existence: processes and applications that enable the network to accomplish real tasks.

## CHAPTER 6

The Process/Application Layer

The previous three chapters have shown you how TCP/IP can be used to build networks that can deliver messages reliably through a variety of media to anywhere in the world. That's all very impressive, but I'll tell you a secret: The network we've built to this point is a far cry from finished. It has no data to deliver, so even though the network is operational, it can't do useful work. We have built the infrastructure of the information highway, but we have yet to set a single vehicle in motion.

The process/application layer is the reason the lower layers exist. At this layer you find numerous protocols that support users directly or indirectly. At the process/application layer, it can be difficult to draw the line between a protocol and an application. Take the *file transfer protocol* (FTP) as an example. FTP enables hosts to offer a file transfer service to other hosts on an internet. FTP also enables remote users to connect with an FTP server and perform file operations. So FTP refers to both the server- and the client-side protocols. It also behaves somewhat like an application, in that users can enter protocol commands directly from the keyboard. You will see an example of this function later in this chapter when FTP is demonstrated.

NetWare client-server protocols function quite differently. Most NetWare services are made available via the *NetWare Core Protocol* (NCP). Users never see NCP protocols and never enter NCP commands directly. Instead, users interact with NetWare via familiar application and operating system commands. A NetWare shell or requester running on the workstation intercepts requests for network services and issues the proper NCP commands to the network. In NetWare, network protocols are practically invisible.

With TCP/IP, users may interact directly with protocols at the process/application layer, or they may use applications that in turn access the network protocols. For example, you will seldom send TCP/IP e-mail by entering Simple Mail Transport Protocol (SMTP) commands directly, although you could. You are more likely to use an e-mail application that will generate the SMTP messages for you.

The process/application layer provides a protocol interface that enables upper-layer processes such as user applications to obtain network services. This chapter examines several protocols that are used widely on TCP/IP networks, including:

▶ File Transfer Protocol (FTP)

▶ Trivial File Transfer Protocol (TFTP)

▶ Telnet

▶ Simple Network Management Protocol (SNMP)

▶ Simple Mail Transport Protocol (SMTP)

▶ Network File System (NFS)

▶ Hypertext Transfer Protocol (HTTP)

To provide a network interface for users, the process/application layer must put a friendly face on the network. How friendly would the network be if you had to access every host by its IP address? Could you remember the addresses of each of the dozens (or hundreds) of Internet hosts that you access to retrieve files, view Web pages, or send e-mail? Well, neither can anyone else, and the Internet community has long realized that if the Internet is to be usable, it must be possible to specify hosts by names rather than numbers. Because host naming is so central to using virtually all TCP/IP applications, we will examine how TCP/IP host naming is performed before looking at the applications themselves.

· ◀

Naming TCP/IP Hosts

NetWare administrators tend to take naming for granted. After a name is specified in a server's AUTOEXEC.NCF file, the server takes over the job of advertising the name to users. But TCP/IP lacks a protocol like the NetWare *Service Advertising Protocol* (SAP). Instead, host names are made available only if network administrators provide a naming service. Thanks to host naming, you can use the name DS.INTERNIC.NET instead of 198.49.45.10 to specify the InterNIC FTP host.

Naming is provided by two mechanisms — static hosts files and the Domain Name Service — that may be used separately or in conjunction. Because DNS grew out of the static hosts files system, we'll look at the use of static files first.

Hosts Files

Would you believe that the Internet was once fairly quiet? The ARPANET included a few hundred hosts and was fairly stable, at least compared to the recent frantic pace with which sites have been added to the Internet. Although current Internet growth is measured in hosts added per day, only a few hosts were added to the ARPANET in a given year. But even with a smaller, more stable network, it was important to provide users with a mechanism for naming hosts.

The mechanism involved a file named HOSTS.TXT, which provided a database that matched IP addresses to host name aliases. The master file was maintained at the Stanford Research Institute's Network Information Center (NIC). ARPANET site administrators would e-mail their name changes to the NIC, where they would be edited into the master HOSTS.TXT file. This file would be compiled every few days to build a file named hosts, which would be made available on a host named SRI-NIC. System administrators would then use FTP to retrieve the master hosts file for use on their local hosts.

Each host at a site required access to the hosts file. For UNIX hosts, the convention was to store the file in the /etc directory on each host. Host processes would access the file to match hostnames to IP addresses. The hosts file is a text file with contents similar to the following:

```
#IP Address       Aliases
127.0.0.1         localhost loopback lb      #this host
192.168.100.1     eng1 bob.widgets.com bob
192.168.100.2     eng2 fred.widgets.com fred
192.168.150.1     sales1 mary.widgets.com mary
```

Entries in the hosts file contain three information fields separated by one or more spaces:

▸ An IP address.

▸ One or more aliases that serve as host names. Among the names included in the example are Internet domain names, such as mary.widgets.com.

▶ An optional comment, consisting of all text that follows the # character. Comments describe hosts file entries but are ignored when the file is processed.

Although hosts files could theoretically provide naming support on networks of any size, static naming files ran out of steam very early in the life of the ARPANET. Because the entire system depended on a single centrally administered file, updates could not take place as rapidly as was desired. Also, because one host served as the distribution point for the master file, FTP traffic to that host quickly became overwhelming. Even when the Internet consisted of a few hundred hosts, it became evident that static hosts files would soon be unsupportable. Today, when the Internet supports millions of personal computers, all configured as hosts, in a configuration that changes hourly, static naming would not be functional. That is why, in 1983, the ARPANET adopted the Domain Name Service as a more automated technology for providing a host naming service.

NOTE

Static hosts files remain a viable means of providing naming services on local TCP/IP networks, particularly if the networks are small in scope and change infrequently. Using static files, hosts can match names to addresses without generating network traffic. Administration of hosts files may be less labor-intensive than maintaining a dynamic naming service. NetWare TCP/IP servers and clients use hosts files to map names to IP addresses.

Domain Name Service

The *Domain Name Service* (DNS; RFC 1034/1035) was designed to maintain a hierarchical database of host names. You are already familiar with another example of a hierarchical database: the system of directory and subdirectory trees that is used to organize files on DOS-based PCs and NetWare servers. Before looking at DNS, let's look at the characteristics of hierarchies in the familiar context of a file directory tree.

Example of a Hierarchical Data Structure

Figure 6.1 illustrates a hierarchical file system, using a portion of the directory structure on the sys: volume of a NetWare 5 server. Before looking at the rules for constructing trees, let's name the components of a hierarchy.

► **Nodes.** These are the places where lines intersect. Each node is assigned an identifying name.

► **Root node.** One node, typically shown at the top of the tree, is called the root node, or the *root directory* when it is part of a file system. Because there is only one root node, it is often unnamed. The DOS root directory is represented by a backslash (\). UNIX uses a forward slash (/). NetWare recognizes either.

► **Intermediate nodes.** Any node below the root is an intermediate node. With DOS and NetWare, intermediate nodes in the file system are called directories. In a hierarchy, intermediate nodes can contain subnodes. Each node is assigned a name, such as SYSTEM or PUBLIC.

► **End or leaf nodes.** A leaf node is the last node in a branch.

File systems typically permit files to reside in both intermediate and leaf nodes. When moving up and down the hierarchy, nodes are often referred to as *parents* and *children*. A parent node is a node that contains one or more subordinate nodes, referred to as children. A child of one node can be the parent of another. Leaf nodes, however, are always children. Nodes that are children of the same parent are called *siblings*.

Figure 6.2 illustrates two rules about naming nodes. First, no two siblings may have the same node name. For example, the PUBLIC directory cannot contain two NLS directories. Second, two nodes may have the same name if the nodes are children of different parent nodes. If you browse around a NetWare 4 server, you will find several NLS subdirectories, but all will be under different directories.

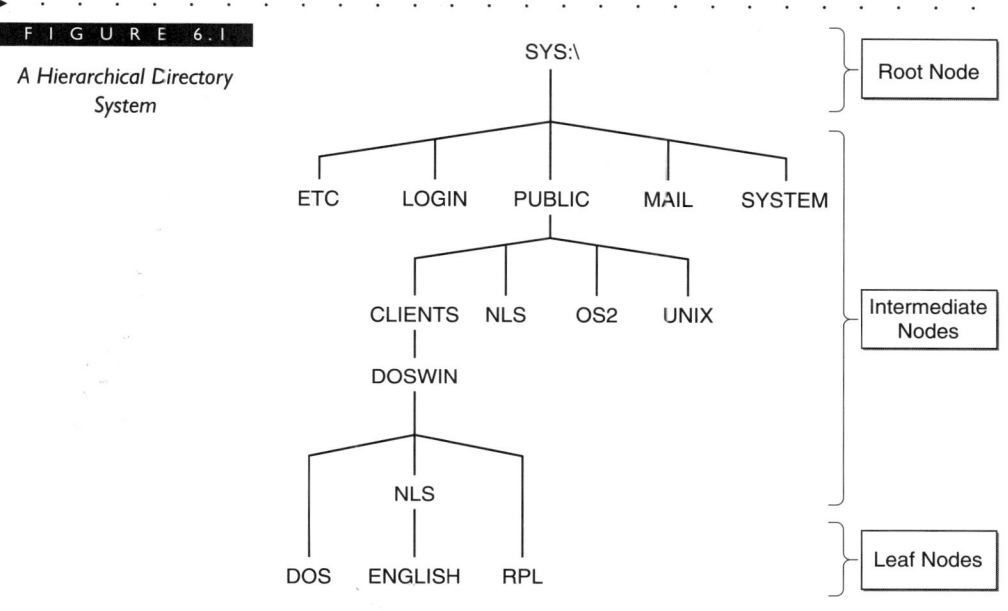

FIGURE 6.1

A Hierarchical Directory System

FIGURE 6.2

Siblings Must Have Unique Names

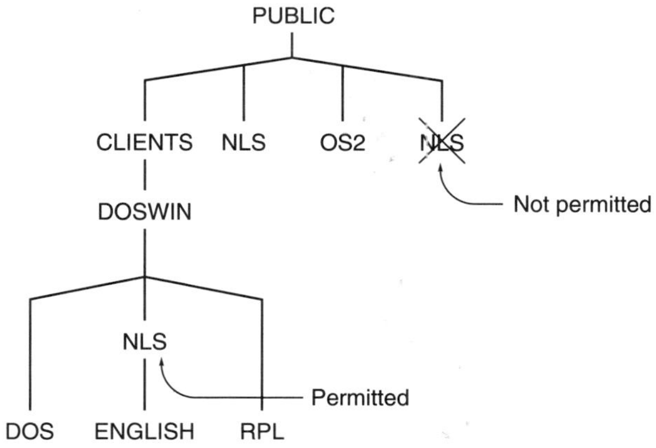

A node can be specified by listing its node name along with the intermediate nodes between itself and the root. In Figure 6.3, the directory containing English message files can be specified with the directory path \PUBLIC\CLIENTS\ DOSWIN\NLS\ENGLISH. The complete name of a node, starting from the root and including every intermediate node name, is called *a fully qualified name*. Because siblings cannot have the same node name, each node in the tree will have a unique fully qualified name.

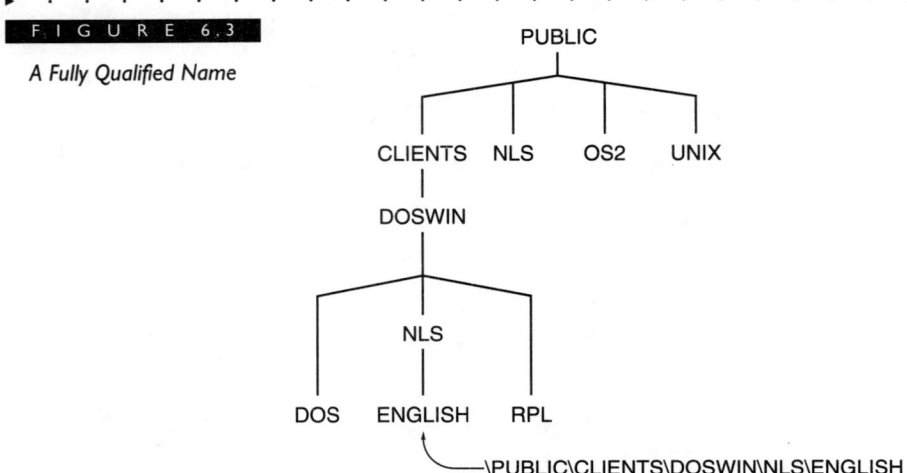

FIGURE 6.3

A Fully Qualified Name

Organization of the Domain Name Space

The DNS uses a hierarchical database called the *domain name space*. Figure 6.4 shows a simple domain name space that would be suitable for a small organization. Nodes in the domain name space are called *domains*. At the top of the hierarchy is a single root node called either *root* or the *root domain*. The root domain does not have a name and is often specified with a pair of empty quotation marks (" ").

Each node in the tree is assigned a name that may be up to 63 characters long. As with file systems, sibling nodes must be named differently. The full name of a node is specified by its *fully qualified domain name* (FQDN). Two important differences between DOS and DNS fully qualified names should be emphasized:

> ▶ Reading left-to-right, DNS names begin with the leaf node and proceed up the tree to the root. The period separating node names is read as "dot." DOS names begin with the root node on the left and proceed down through the tree to the subdirectory.

► A DNS fully qualified name does not usually include a symbol for the root. The root may be specified with a trailing dot (for example, `rose.hwr.eng.`), but the trailing dot is usually omitted. A DOS fully qualified name always specifies the root with a leading backslash (\) character.

F I G U R E   6.4

A Simple DNS Tree

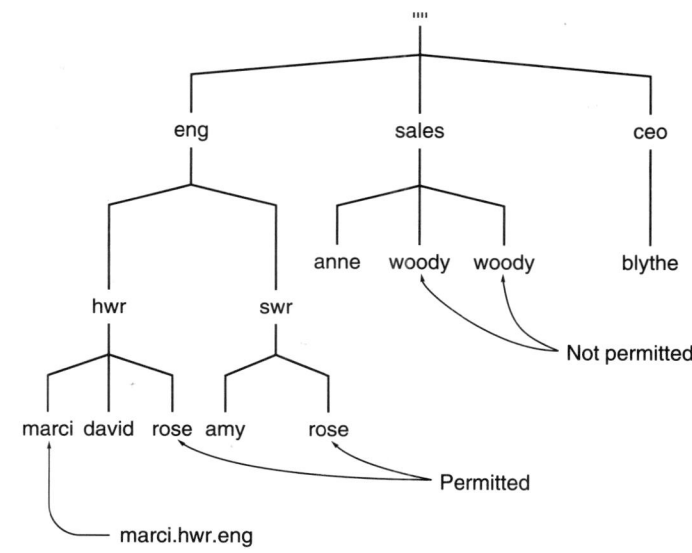

A *domain* is simply a subtree of the domain name space, and you can change your perspective on the domain name space by selecting a different domain. The name of a domain is simply the FQDN of the topmost node in the domain. For example, in Figure 6.4, `swr` can be viewed as a subdomain of the `eng` domain. Alternatively, `marci` can be viewed as a subdomain of the `swr.eng` domain.

A domain cannot, however, consist of a part of a subtree. In Figure 6.4, you cannot define a domain that includes nodes from `hwr.eng` and `sales`. A domain must consist of a parent node together with all nodes that are below the parent node in the hierarchy.

NOTE

DNS names are not case-sensitive. The domain names `hwr.eng`, `HWR.ENG`, **and** `Hwr.Eng` **are interchangeable. However, domain names are most frequently expressed in lowercase characters.**

As you can see, the term *domain* is relative, depending on your perspective on the domain name space. Although every node can be viewed as a subdomain of the root domain, it is more convenient to identify an intermediate node as the domain that anchors a set of names. When it is necessary to classify domains based on their positions in the hierarchy, the following terms are used:

▶ A first-level domain is a child of the root domain. First-level domains are more commonly referred to as top-level domains.

▶ A second-level domain is a child of a first-level domain.

▶ A third-level domain is a child of a second-level domain (and so forth).

A domain name can serve multiple purposes. As the name of a node in the domain name space, the domain name serves as a point around which domain names can be defined. But a domain name can also provide a mapping to an IP address. On the Internet, for example, `novell.com` is associated with the IP address 192.31.114.4.

The Internet Domain Name Space

In some cases, an organization may implement a private DNS on an isolated network. A DNS is required on a network running NetWare/IP, for example. However, the largest incentive to implement a DNS usually comes from a desire to integrate a private network with the Internet. Although name space administration is distributed fairly broadly, all organizations that want to advertise a domain on the Internet must register a domain name. Registration prevents duplication of names and enables the process of resolving names to IP addresses to be coordinated among the many name servers on the Internet.

Ultimate authority for assigning Internet domain names belongs to the Internet Assigned Numbers Authority (IANA), which is administered by the Internet Registry (IR). Because the Internet name space is vast and changes daily, IANA has delegated registration authority for most lower-level domains to other organizations. Top-level domains are administered directly by Internet authorities.

The Internet name space can be divided into subdomains and zones to distribute administration. When a new second- or third-level domain is added, a management authority for the domain must be designated. In many cases, management of the domain will be performed by the organization that requested the domain, but management can also be delegated to other organizations as required.

The configuration of the Internet domain name space is described in RFC 1591, *Domain Name System Structure and Delegation*. This document describes the overall domain name structure as well as guidelines for administering delegated domains. Figure 6.5 illustrates major features of the Internet domain name space. Top-level domains (TLDs) fall into three categories:

► Generic worldwide domains

► Generic United States domains

► Country domains

Before you can request a domain name, you need to decide where your organization fits in the overall scheme of things.

FIGURE 6.5

Internet Domain Name Space

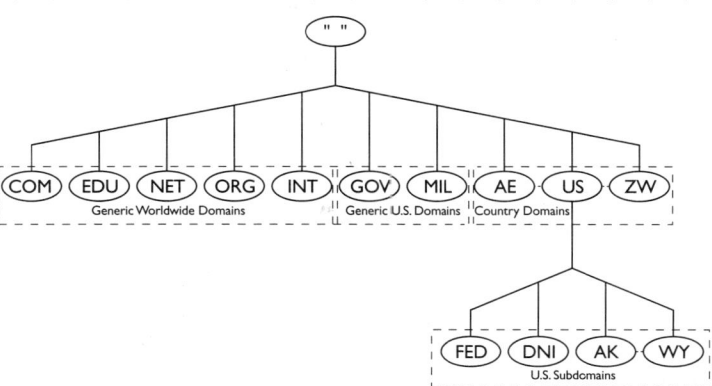

Generic Worldwide Domains   You will encounter generic worldwide domains with the greatest frequency. Although each country is assigned a country domain, many organizations outside the United States are represented in these generic domains. To a degree, the place an organization registers is a matter of choice. The five generic worldwide domains are:

- **COM**. This domain is for commercial (business) organizations. The vast majority of companies with an Internet presence are registered in this domain. Because the COM domain is growing rapidly, there has been some discussion of subdividing it. Example: `novell.com`.

- **NET.** This domain includes network service providers and Internet administration authorities. Example: `internic.net`.

- **EDU.** This domain originally was intended for all educational institutions. But like COM, EDU has become quite extensive, so registration is now limited to four-year colleges and universities. All other schools are registered in their country domains. Example: `berkeley.edu`.

- **INT.** A domain for organizations established by international treaties. Example: `nato.int`.

- **ORG.** A miscellaneous domain for organizations that don't fit in the other domains. Example: `ietf.org`.

Secondary domains beneath the generic world wide domains are the responsibility of the InterNIC. Contact `hostmaster@internic.net` via e-mail for registration information. The InterNIC is also responsible for registering new top-level domains.

Generic United States Domains   Two top-level domains have been created for use by the Unites States government:

- **GOV.** Although at one time any government organization could register in this domain, the GOV domain is now restricted to agencies of the United States federal government. State and local government agencies may register in state domains under the U.S. country domain. Example: `nsf.gov`.

- **MIL.** This domain is used exclusively by the United States Department of Defense. Example: `dca.mil`.

Second-level subdomains in the GOV domain are registered by the InterNIC. Second-level domains under the MIL domain are registered by the DDN registry at `nic.ddn.mil`.

Country Domains   The IANA has no desire to get involved in international politics. Rather than attempting to decide whether a country is entitled to a country domain, the IANA defers to the ISO, an international organization with mechanisms in place to identify bona fide countries. Country top-level domains are derived from ISO 3166.

Registration of country domains has been delegated as follows:

- For Europe, the authority is RIPE NCC. Contact `ncc@ripe.net`.

- For the Asia-Pacific region, the authority is APNIC. Contact `hostmaster@apnic.net`.

- For North America and undelegated regions, the authority is InterNIC. Contact `hostmaster@internic.net`.

Later in this chapter, I show you how to use WHOIS to obtain domain information.

Organization of the US Domain   The majority of United States organizations that are statewide in scope (as opposed to national) are organized under the US country top-level domain, described in RFC 1480. Each state is assigned a second-level domain under US, named using the abbreviations established by the postal service. For example, `CA.US` is the domain assigned to California.

Two special subdomains of US designate organizations that have national scope:

- **FED.** Agencies of the U.S. federal government.

- **DNI.** Organizations that have a presence in multiple states or regions.

Although Internet administration does not manage state subdomains, RFC 1480 includes recommendations for organizing state domains. RFC 1480 describes the following state subdomains:

▶ **Locality.** A designation for the city, county, parish, or other locality in which the organization resides. Examples: `Marvista.CA.US` and `Portland.OR.US`.

▶ **CC.** Community colleges with a state-wide presence. Example: `<school>.CC.MA.US`.

▶ **CI.** As a subdomain of a locality, CI designates city government agencies. Example: `Fire-Dept.CI.Los-Angeles.CA.US`.

▶ **CO.** As a subdomain of a locality, CO designates county government agencies. Example: `Fire-Dept.CO.San-Diego.CA.US`.

▶ **GEN.** Entities that do not fit in the other categories. Example: `<organization>.GEN.KY.US`.

▶ **K12.** Public school districts. The PVT name may be included to designate private schools. Examples: `<school>.K12.IL.US` or `<school>.PVT.K12.AZ.US`.

▶ **LIB.** Libraries only. Example: `<library>.LIB.OR.US`.

▶ **STATE.** State government agencies. Example: `<agency>.STATE.TX.US`.

▶ **TEC.** Vocational and technical schools and colleges with a state-wide presence. Example: `<school>.TEC.OR.US`.

Figure 6.6 illustrates the organization of the US domain, including recommended subdomain names.

Administration of US subdomains has been delegated to local contacts. If you want to register a domain under US you will need to determine the appropriate contact person. Start by using FTP to retrieve the file `in-notes/us-domain-delegated.txt` from `venera.isi.edu`. This file can also be obtained via e-mail using the RFC-INFO service described in Chapter 1. Send e-mail to `rfc-info@isi.edu` with the following message:

```
help: us_domain_delegated_domains
```

▶ • ◀

Structure of the US Domain

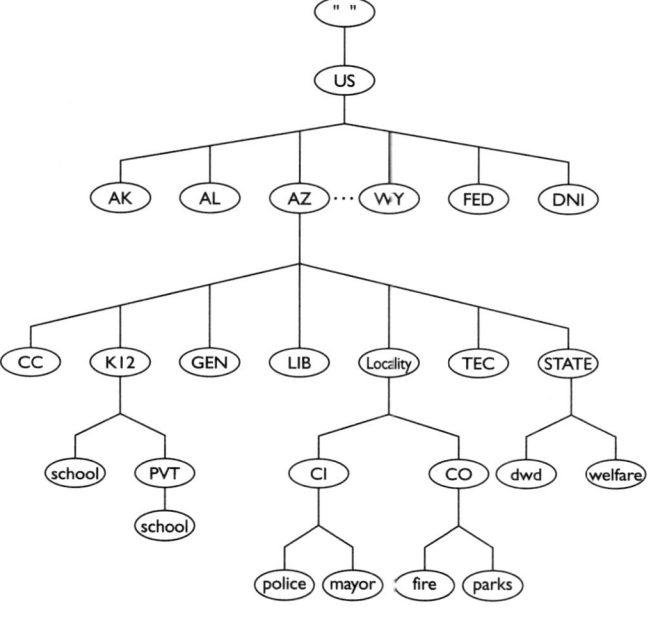

LEGEND

(UPPER) = RFC1480 domain names

(Mixed) = Replace with local name

(lower) = Example subdomains

Structure of Organization Domains   An organization that registers a domain on the Internet has complete freedom to design the domain as the organization sees fit. Of course, the organization's database tree must be configured within the organization's Internet domain. Figure 6.7 illustrates an example of a name space that might be established for the organization Widgets, Inc. This organization has been assigned the domain widgets.com and is responsible for managing the name space below that domain. Widgets will be required to maintain a DNS name server to handle all name resolution requests within its portion of the directory name space.

Because each organization is assigned a unique second-level domain name, every host in the Internet directory name space is identified by a unique FQDN.

For example, no other host on the Internet will have the FQDN `marci.swr.eng.widgets.com`.

Using WHOIS to Obtain Domain Information   WHOIS is a service that provides a "white pages" directory of people and organizations on the Internet. The information available is somewhat limited and reaches only the first two or three levels of the Internet name space. For example, only the second and third levels below the US domain are listed (for example, down to `K12.CA.US`). Nevertheless, WHOIS can be a valuable tool for obtaining information about domains and their contacts.

▶ · ◀

FIGURE 6.7

A Sample Organization's
Name Space

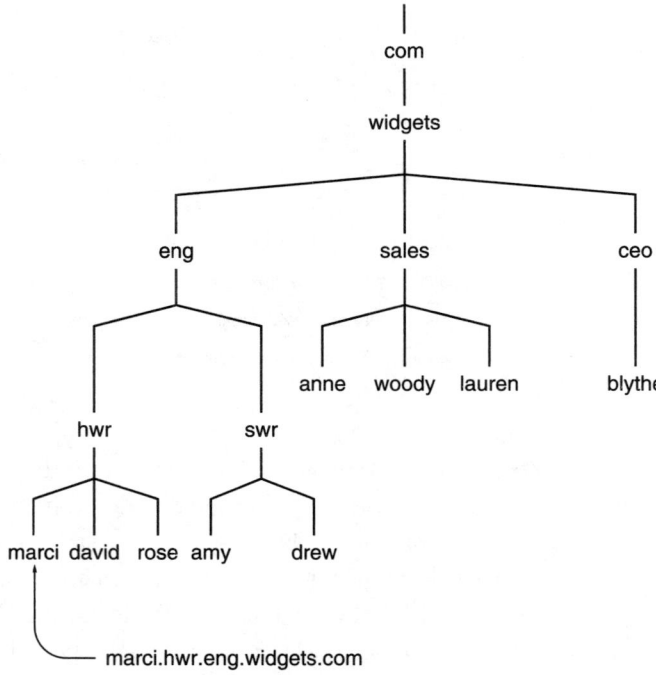

Entities within WHOIS are indexed by keywords. Top-level domains are indexed by the domain name followed by -DOM. To search for the EDU domain, you would search for EDU-DOM.

WHOIS searches may be conducted using client software, via the World Wide Web, or by using Telnet to access a WHOIS client on an InterNIC host.

If your host is equipped with a WHOIS client — many UNIX hosts are — you can conduct queries directly from the command line. The query to identify the contact for the COM domain is:

```
whois -h rs.internic.net com-dom
```

The InterNIC Web site can be used to conduct WHOIS searches. Reach the site with the URL http://www.internic.net. This Web page includes a field where you can enter WHOIS queries. Enter a search word in the query form, and press Enter. The following databases will be searched and results will be displayed:

- InterNIC Directory and Databases Services (ds.internic.net), for domains other than MIL and for information other than point-of-contact.

- InterNIC Registration Services (rs.internic.net), for point-of-contact information.

- DISA NIC (nic.ddn.mil), for the MIL domain.

Using Telnet to access a WHOIS client on the InterNIC host is an efficient way to obtain detailed WHOIS reports. After using Telnet to access rs.internic.net (no login is required), enter the command **whois** to access a WHOIS client. The following dialog shows a Telnet session with the results of querying for EDU-DOM:

```
Whois: edu-dom


Registrant:

Education top-level domain (EDU-DOM)

    Network Solutions, Inc.

    505 Huntmar park Dr.

    Herndon, VA 22070
```

```
Domain Name: EDU


   Administrative Contact, Technical Contact, Zone Contact:

     Network Solutions, Inc.  (HOSTMASTER)
hostmaster@INTERNIC.NET

     (703) 742-4777 (FAX) (703) 742-9552


   Record last updated on 17-Jan-97.

   Record created on 01-Jan-85.

   Database last updated on 12-Jan-99 11:33:42 EST.


   Domain servers in listed order:


   A.ROOT-SERVERS.NET              198.41.0.4

   H.ROOT-SERVERS.NET              128.63.2.53

   B.ROOT-SERVERS.NET              128.9.0.107

   C.ROOT-SERVERS.NET              192.33.4.12

   D.ROOT-SERVERS.NET              128.8.10.90

   E.ROOT-SERVERS.NET              192.203.230.10

   I.ROOT-SERVERS.NET              192.36.148.17

   F.ROOT-SERVERS.NET              192.5.5.241

   G.ROOT-SERVERS.NET              192.112.36.4
```

Besides information about the EDU domain, this report lists the domain name servers that service top-level domains on the Internet. You can learn more about a specific host by searching on the host's IP address. An example in the following section shows details about one of the root name servers.

How DNS Works

DNS name resolution is performed by name servers, which are programs running on network hosts. Because the Internet is so extensive, DNS was designed so that many name servers could share the responsibility for resolving names. This is accomplished by dividing the complete name space into zones. Each zone can be serviced by its own name servers.

A name server that manages data for a zone is said to have *authority* for that zone. A name server has authority for at least one zone, but a single name server can have authority for many zones, if required. Figure 6.8 illustrates a name space that has been organized into zones. Notice that zones need not follow domain structures. Although a domain must consist of a connected subtree of the overall name space, zones need not consist of contiguous nodes. This flexibility enables a single name server to provide name resolution for multiple domains.

▶ • ◀

F I G U R E 6.8

A Name Space Divided into Three Zones

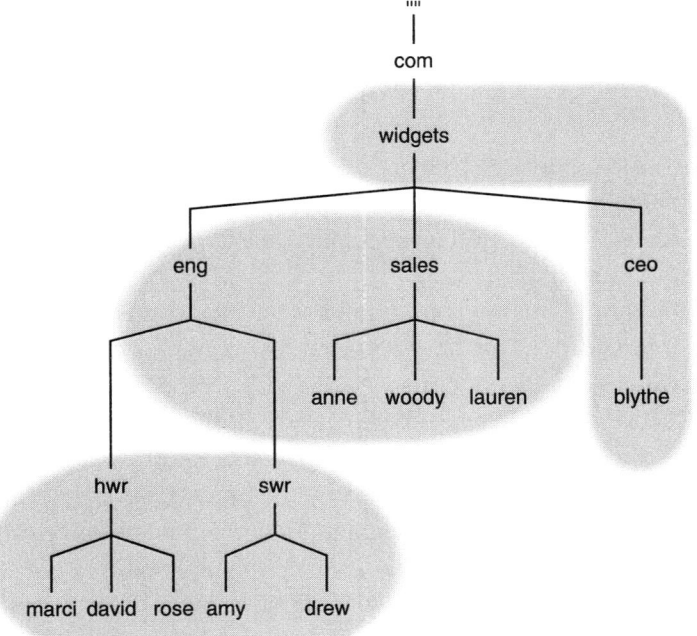

The principle name server for a zone is the *primary master name server*, which collects data for the zone from its configuration files. *Secondary master name servers* are redundant backups to primary servers and obtain data for the zones they service by performing *zone transfers* from other name servers for the zone. The source name server for a zone transfer is referred to as a *master name server.* Either primary or secondary name servers can function as master name servers. Secondary masters perform periodic zone transfers to keep up to date with changes in the zone. Configuration of two or more name servers for a zone provides fault tolerance and improves performance by distributing name-resolution processing across several hosts.

NOTE

Name servers can also be configured as *caching-only* name servers. Caching-only name servers do not store a complete copy of the zone database. They simply act as intermediaries between DNS clients and DNS name servers and cache any name resolution data that they receive. This has the effect of offloading name queries from primary and secondary name servers because the caching-only name server remembers frequently-resolved names and can fulfill client requests itself.

Assignment of primary and secondary master name servers is quite flexible. A name server can be authoritative for one or for several zones, and a given name server can function as a primary master for one zone and as a secondary master for another.

Because many name-resolution attempts must begin with the root domain, the Internet root domain is serviced by many root name servers (13 as I am writing), which include systems on NSFNET, MILNET, SPAN (NASA), and in Europe. These root-domain servers are authoritative for all top-level domains on the Internet. Authority for secondary- and lower-level domains is distributed across many name servers operated by the organizations that inhabit the Internet.

When an organization obtains a domain name and establishes a presence on the Internet, a name server must be designated that is authoritative for the domain. In most cases, the name server will be maintained on a host that is operated by the owner of the domain. It is not necessary for an organization to operate its own name server, however. Most Internet connections are now obtained from commercial Internet access providers. Many of these providers maintain their clients' zones on the provider's name servers. Contracting an Internet access provider to manage your domain name space is particularly desirable if your organization is small and cannot justify the cost of labor to have DNS experts on staff or the cost of the hardware required to maintain a primary and a backup name server.

The complete Internet domain name space is maintained by many distributed name servers that have some degree of awareness of one another. This distributed network of name servers cooperates to provide name resolution for the complete Internet.

The client side of the name service is provided by *resolvers*, which are components of TCP/IP processes and applications that make use of DNS host names. The resolver is embedded in the software of each application, such as FTP or Telnet, enabling the application to contact one name server to initiate a name resolution query. The resolver in the application can construct a DNS query, but resolution of the query is the responsibility of the network name servers.

Figure 6.9 illustrates the process of resolving a query. The configuration of a TCP/IP host will include the IP address of at least one DNS name server. When an application requires name resolution service, it constructs a name service query and sends the query to a known name server. If the name server that is queried cannot resolve the name, it initiates a search starting with one of the available root name servers. The root name server provides the address of a name server that is authoritative for the first-level domain in the query. The search proceeds from first- to second- to lower-level domain name servers until a server is found that can respond to the query.

The name search process depends on access to an intact hierarchy of name servers. If a functioning name server is unavailable at any level, name resolution fails. That is why it is so important to have primary and secondary name servers available and why the Internet is serviced by nine servers at the root domain. Although lower-level servers reduce name resolution traffic by maintaining a cache of recently resolved names, if all root name servers on the Internet were to fail, all name resolution would eventually cease.

The most commonly used implementation of DNS is BIND (*Berkeley Internet Name Domain*), which is included in 4.3BSD UNIX. Now at Version 4.8.3, BIND has been ported to a variety of UNIX and other platforms. BIND supports tree depths up to 127 levels, sufficient even for the Internet. In fact, all Internet root name servers are running an implementation of BIND.

▶ · ◀

FIGURE 6.9

Resolution of a Name
Query

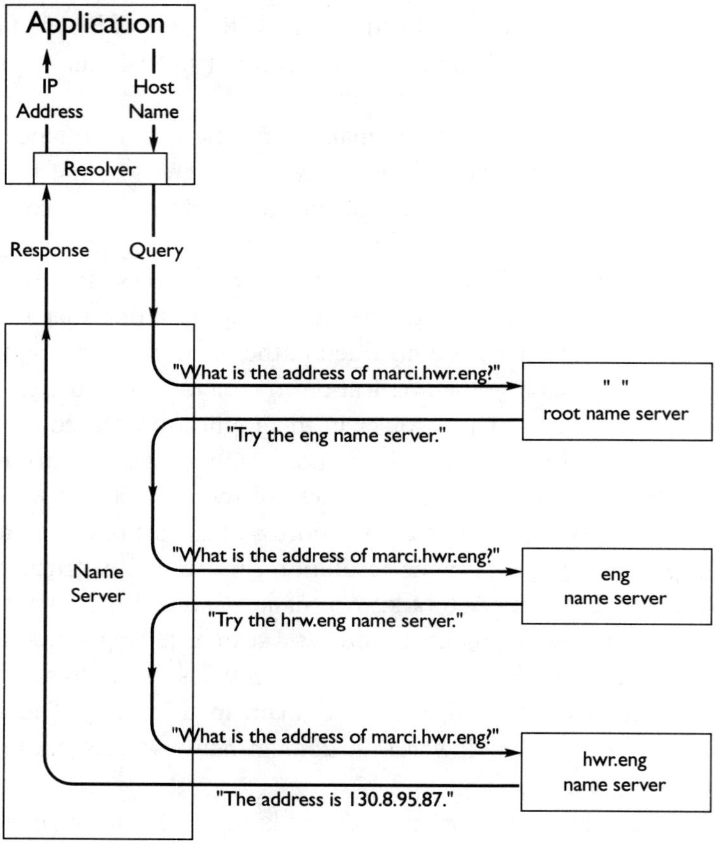

Application

IP
Address

Host
Name

Resolver

Response   Query

"What is the address of marci.hwr.eng?"

root name server

"Try the eng name server."

Name
Server

"What is the address of marci.hwr.eng?"

eng
name server

"Try the hrw.eng name server."

"What is the address of marci.hwr.eng?"

hwr.eng
name server

"The address is 130.8.95.87."

BIND is a complex product, and DNS is an involved technology. This chapter should contain enough information for you to be able to configure and administer a basic DNS implementation. If you require more extensive information, I recommend the book *DNS and BIND* by Paul Albitz and Cricket Liu (O'Reilly & Associates).

NetWare 5 includes an excellent, full-featured DNS server that is neatly integrated with NDS. You will learn how to manage the NetWare 5 DNS service in Chapter 11.

Common TCP/IP Applications

The remainder of this chapter examines some of the TCP/IP process protocols and applications you are most likely to encounter. Some, such as Telnet and FTP, are end-user tools that you will probably use frequently. Others, such as SMTP and SNMP, are protocols that support the functionality of end-user applications such as e-mail (SMTP) and network management (SNMP). We examine the following process/application layer protocols:

- File Transfer Protocol (FTP)

- Trivial File Transfer Protocol (TFTP)

- Telnet

- Simple Network Management Protocol (SNMP)

- Simple Mail Transfer Protocol (SMTP)

- Network File System (NFS)

File Transfer Protocol

FTP is the primary protocol used to move files around TCP/IP networks and is heavily used on the Internet. The name FTP refers to the protocol itself as well as to the program that users access to perform file operations. The FTP protocol can also be used by applications that need to perform network file operations.

FTP is a reliable, session-oriented protocol that operates over TCP. Users must log in before gaining access to the remote file system. Although FTP logins can be coordinated with user account names and passwords, FTP security is impaired because usernames and passwords are not encrypted and, therefore, are accessible through the network. The majority of FTP sites you are likely to encounter offer *anonymous* FTP service, which means that any user can log in with the username anonymous and a password that is usually the name of the user's e-mail account.

FTP Architecture

As shown in Figure 6.10, FTP operation requires client and server components. The host that makes its file system available to users runs FTP server software. Users run FTP client software that lets them establish a network connection and perform file operations.

When the FTP server software is run on the server host, it performs a passive open, establishing a socket that can accept outside connections. When an FTP client issues an active open request, a virtual circuit is established between the sockets on the server and the client. A virtual circuit functions like a pipe through which data can be transferred reliably. The FTP connection lets the remote client manipulate part of the server's file system as though the client were accessing the server directly.

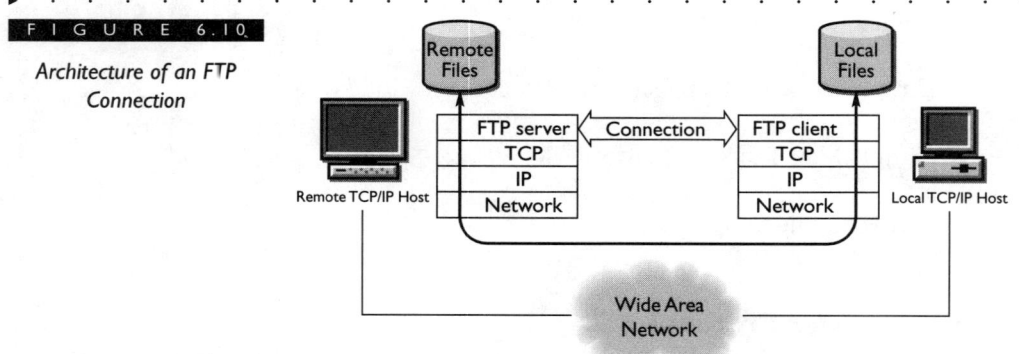

F I G U R E   6.10

Architecture of an FTP Connection

NOTE

NetWare 5 includes an FTP server in the UNIX Print Services. Installation and configuration of the NetWare 5 FTP server is discussed in Chapter 16.

Guidelines for Using FTP

Most FTP servers are UNIX-based, and the UNIX file system is somewhat different from the DOS file system with which you are probably familiar. When you use FTP on the Internet, you need to be aware of the following differences between UNIX and DOS or NetWare:

▶ With NetWare and DOS, file and directory names are not case-sensitive. For example, the filenames `salesrpt.txt`, `SalesRpt.TXT`, and `SALESRPT.TXT` are functionally identical and in a given directory refer to the same file. UNIX filenames and commands, in contrast, are case-sensitive. The file `This-Is-A-File.txt` is different from `this-is-a-file.txt`, for example. Directory names also are case-sensitive. In the UNIX environment, FTP commands are entered almost exclusively in lowercase. The examples in this chapter follow that convention.

▶ UNIX supports longer filenames than are possible with DOS-based file systems. The latter are limited to the familiar 8.3 naming convention (up to eight characters, followed by a period and an extension of up to three characters).

▶ Finally, DOS uses backslashes (for example, \DATA\REPORTS\SALES). When manipulating files on Novell servers, you have the option of using backslashes or forward slashes. In UNIX, however, forward slashes are used (for example, /data/reports/sales).

Sample FTP Session

These days, most FTP file retrievals are performed using an Internet browser such as Microsoft Internet Explorer or Netscape Navigator. Browsers, however, are typically used for file retrieval. Because you may want to use command-line FTP to send or retrieve files, the following example is a dialog that shows you the basics.

Before starting FTP, an Internet connection is required. The connection can be a network connection through a LAN that has a direct interface, or it can consist of a dial-up session through an Internet access provider. After the connection is established, you can begin an FTP session. The following commands assume that you are using command-line FTP software on a DOS host.

Starting FTP   To begin, start the FTP client software by typing **ftp** at the command prompt. In the following dialog examples, bold text is typed by the user:

```
C:> ftp

ftp>
```

When the FTP client software is activated, the prompt changes to `ftp>`, indicating that FTP is active. At this point, only FTP commands are accepted.

Opening a Connection with an FTP Server   The next task is to connect with a remote FTP server and log in. The following example accesses an RFC repository on `FTP.ISI.EDU`. I learned about the site using the e-mail RFC-INFO service described in Chapter 1.

The session is initiated by using the `open` command (text entered by the user appears in boldface type):

```
ftp> open ftp.isi.edu

Connected to VENERA.isi.edu.

220 venera.isi.edu FTP server (Version s/key wu-2.4(6) Mon
Feb 26 C9:43:41 PST 1

996) ready.

User (VENERA.isi.edu:(none)): anonymous
```

The previous dialog excerpts started the FTP client and opened a connection in two steps. You can perform both tasks in a single step by including the name of the FTP server as a command-line parameter. The following command starts the FTP client and attempts to connect to the InterNIC server:

```
C:> ftp ftp.isi.edu
```

Logging In   Many Internet FTP servers accept anonymous logins, allocating limited FTP privileges to users who do not have a personal username and password. To accomplish an anonymous login, type **anonymous** when prompted for your username. Most anonymous FTP sites request that you use your e-mail name as a password. Here is an example of an anonymous login process dialog:

```
User (VENERA.isi.edu:(none)): anonymous

331 Guest login ok, send your complete e-mail address as
password.

Password: I entered my e-mail address, which does not echo
back

230-
```

```
230 Guest login ok, access restrictions apply.

ftp>
```

NOTE

The FTP login process is not particularly secure. Usernames and passwords are not encrypted as they travel through the network, and anyone who has a network protocol analyzer (such as Novell's LANalyzer for Windows) can examine the packets and recover the login information. If you implement an FTP server that is accessible through a public network such as the Internet, you should ensure that the account names and passwords used for FTP are different from the names and passwords used to access secure systems. Anonymous FTP isn't as risky as it may seem. All anonymous FTP users can be assigned strictly defined access to files and directories, limiting the damage they can do. In most cases, anonymous FTP users are given read-only access to public directories.

Getting Help During an FTP session, you can obtain help about the available commands by typing **help**, as in the following dialog:

```
ftp> help

Commands may be abbreviated.  Commands are:
```

!	delete	literal	prompt	send
?	debug	ls	put	status
append	dir	mdelete	pwd	trace
ascii	disconnect	mdir	quit	type
bell	get	mget	quote	user
binary	glob	mkdir	recv	verbose
bye	hash	mls	remotehelp	
cd	help	mput	rename	
close	lcd	open	rmdir	

The exact commands you see depend on the commands available on the FTP software with which you are connected (Windows 98 in my case). Many of these commands remind us of FTP's origins in the UNIX community. Some are familiar to DOS users, such as `dir`, `delete`, and `cd`. Others are quite unfamiliar, such as `ls` (*list files*) and `pwd` (*print working directory*). Most commands are easy to grasp if you understand the logic behind the command name.

To obtain a brief description of a command, type **help** followed by the command name. For example:

```
ftp> help help

help            Print local help information
```

Verbose and Sparse Responses   LAN WorkPlace FTP is configured so that by default it does not echo the command response messages that are produced by the FTP server. This chapter shows these responses by typing the command **verbose** at the `ftp>` prompt. Verbose mode is helpful when you are learning to use FTP, because some messages contain information confirming that the command was carried out.

Navigating FTP Server Directories   When using FTP, you are concerned with two current directories: one on your FTP client and another on the FTP server. Any files you copy are copied between those two directories. The commands for changing directories are:

- ▶ `cd`, which changes the current directory on the FTP server

- ▶ `lcd` (local cd), which changes the current directory on the FTP client

The current directory on a UNIX computer is referred to as the `working directory`. When you first connect with an FTP server, your working directory is the root directory. The RFC documents on `ds.internic.net` are located in the /in-notes directory. (How did I know the directory name? I obtained it from the e-mail reply I received from the RFC-INFO service.) The following dialog takes place when changing the working directory to /rfc:

```
ftp> cd /in-notes
250 CWD command successful.
```

Notice the use of the forward slash to specify a UNIX directory. You must always enter file and directory specifications using the conventions of the host that the command is manipulating. You can determine the identity of the working directory with the pwd (*print working directory*) command, as in the following dialog, entered in the /rfc directory:

```
ftp> pwd
257 "/in-notes" is current directory.
```

Here are some techniques that are useful when changing directories:

▸ To change to the parent directory of the working directory, issue the command cd up or cd .. (where .. is shorthand for the parent directory).

▸ To change to any directory in the file system, use a fully qualified directory name that starts from the root directory. The command cd /ietf/ipngwg changes the working directory to the ipngwg directory regardless of the current working directory. A fully qualified directory path is called an *absolute reference*.

▸ To change to a subdirectory of the working directory, you can use a *relative reference*. If your working directory is ietf and you want to change to the /ietf/ipv6mib subdirectory, enter the command cd ipv6mib.

Figure 6.11 illustrates the use of absolute and relative directory references.

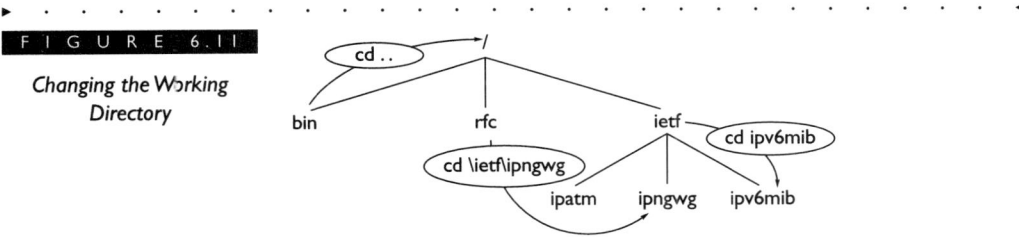

FIGURE 6.11

Changing the Working Directory

Navigating FTP Client Directories   Before copying files, you also need to set the current directory on the DOS client. If the files are to be copied to C:\RFCDOCS, enter the following command:

```
ftp> lcd \rfcdocs
```

```
Local directory now c:\rfcdocs
```

You can use absolute and relative directory references with the lcd command.

Examining Directories   In the above dialogs, the working directory on the FTP server is set to rfc. You can now transfer files if you like, but suppose you don't know the exact names of the files you want? How can you examine directory contents?

The ls command produces a basic listing of directory contents. But don't rush to enter an ls command, because the rfc directory contains about 2000 files. To display only a few of the files, you can use wildcard characters. FTP recognizes DOS * and ? wildcard characters. The following listing selects a filename parameter that will retrieve several important files:

```
ftp> ls rfc-*.txt
```

```
200 PORT command successful.
```

```
150 Opening ASCII mode data connection for file list.
```

```
rfc-index.txt
```

```
rfc-instructions.txt
```

```
rfc-retrieval.txt
```

```
226 Transfer complete.
```

```
ftp>
```

The parameter rfc-* produced a listing of all files starting with the characters rfc-. The * character matches any series of characters and found several files in this example. The rfc-index.txt file is mentioned in Chapter 1. This file includes an index to the current set of RFC documents. The other documents provide useful information on retrieving RFCs.

If the FTP server is a UNIX host, you can use several parameters with the ls command (see Table 6.1). Note that some of the following parameters must be entered in uppercase:

	PARAMETER	RESULT
T A B L E 6.1	-a	All files are listed, including hidden files.
Parameters for the ls Command	-C	A multicolumn listing is produced.
	-d	Only directory names are listed.
	-F	File types are included in the listing (directory or executable).
	-l	A long listing is displayed.
	-R	A recursive (continuous) listing is produced.

Users familiar with the UNIX ls command may expect other options to be available as well. During an FTP session, however, the ls command is handled by FTP, not by the UNIX shell. Only the options supported by FTP are available.

Getting Files   At this point, we have set the working directories on the client and the server, and we have obtained a directory listing to confirm that the file we need resides in the working directory on the server. After the working directories are set, retrieving a file is a piece of cake, as in this example:

```
ftp> get rfc-index.txt

200 PORT command successful.

150 Opening ASCII mode data connection for rfc-index.txt
(354926 bytes).

226 Transfer complete.

ftp: 363344 bytes received in 38.28Seconds 9.49Kbytes/sec.

ftp>
```

Files can be transferred in ASCII or binary modes. A binary transfer is a verbatim, byte-for-byte transfer of data that preserves the exact structures of program and data files. When transferring text files, however, it is preferable to use ASCII mode.

Text files have varying formats under different operating systems. UNIX files represent the end of a text line with a linefeed character. DOS represents the end of a line with the combination of a carriage return followed by a linefeed. If a text file is transferred between UNIX and DOS, a verbatim binary transfer produces a file that does not conform to the file format of the destination system. An ASCII-mode FTP transfer compensates for file format differences by translating the end-of-line characters so that they are correct for the destination file system.

If you want to perform an ASCII-mode transfer but don't want end-of-line character translation, use the cr command to disable character translation. Turn off character translation if a file will eventually end up on a system with an operating system that differs from the current FTP client. Suppose, for example, that you are using a DOS FTP client to retrieve a file from a UNIX FTP server. The file you retrieve, however, will eventually be copied to a UNIX computer. Use the cr command to turn off character translation so that the file will remain in UNIX format.

To switch to binary transfer mode, use the command binary. Switch back to ASCII mode with the command ASCII.

Closing the FTP Session When you have completed operations, you should close the FTP session. Enter the **close** command to close the connection to the FTP server, followed by the **bye** command to exit the FTP client software:

```
ftp> close
221 Goodbye
ftp> bye
C:\
```

Alternatively, you can simply enter the command **bye**, which both closes the connection and exits FTP.

FTP Command Reference

Although you probably have access to a program that provides a graphical FTP interface, such as the Rapid Filer utility included with Novell's LAN WorkPlace product, you may need to use the command-line approach at some point. In some cases, the command-line approach is more efficient because less data must be transferred to produce directory listings on the graphic client. Table 6.2 lists some of the commands available during FTP sessions.

NOTE

NetWare and DOS commands are not case-sensitive. The example dialogs show the commands in lowercase, but uppercase could be and is used in Table 6.1. When using FTP on a UNIX host, however, commands are case-sensitive, and virtually all commands are entered in lowercase. Be sure to check the conventions of the environment in which you are using FTP.

T A B L E 6.2	COMMAND	FUNCTION
Summary of FTP Commands	APPEND *local remote*	Appends the contents of the workstation file local to the end of the server file remote. If the file specified by remote does not exist, the file is copied to a new file named *local*.
	ASCII	Sets file transfer to ASCII mode, the default transfer mode. End-of-line characters will be translated as appropriate for the destination file system.
	BELL	Turns on or off (toggles) a bell that sounds after completion of an FTP operation.
	BINARY	Sets file transfer to binary mode. This mode should be used for data, program, and 8-bit ASCII text files.
	BYE	Closes any active sessions and exits the FTP client to DOS.
	CD *remote_path*	Changes the current working directory on the FTP server to the directory specified in *remote_path*.
	CLOSE	Closes the host session but remains in FTP command mode.

Continued

TABLE 6.2	COMMAND	FUNCTION
Continued	COPY [-A] [-B] [F] [-I] [-R] *source destination*	Copies files. If *source* is a file, *destination* may be a directory or a file. If *source* specifies multiple files or directories, *destination* must be a directory. Options are:
		-A Specifies ASCII file transfer. If the file has binary file characteristics then the -A option is overridden and the transfer will be binary, unless the -F option is specified.
		-B Specifies binary file transfer. If the file has ASCII file characteristics then the -B option is overridden and the transfer will be ASCII, unless the -F option is specified.
		-F Forces files to be transferred as specified by the -A and -B options. If an -A or -B flag is absent and COPY uses an open connection, COPY will use the same mode that was used for the previous COPY operation. If this is the first transfer, COPY defaults to ASCII.
		-I Forces COPY to ignore files that will be copied to a DOS computer if the files do not have valid DOS filenames.
		-R Copies recursively, including all subdirectories of the source directory. The source parameter may not include wildcards.
	DEBUG	Sets debugging mode, during which FTP displays commands sent to the FTP server during a session. The default setting is off.
	DEFAULTS	Restores DEBUG, SENDPORT, and VERBOSE to their default settings.
	DELETE *remote_file*	Deletes the file named *remote_file* from the FTP server.

COMMAND	FUNCTION
DIR [*remote_directory*]	Displays a detailed list of files in the working directory on the FTP server. If a directory parameter is included, displays a detailed list of files in the working directory specified by *remote_directory*.
FILE	Sets file transfer to file mode, unstructured byte streams.
FORCE	Determines whether file transfer parameters in effect for the connection are set automatically (the default setting), forcing FTP to transfer files according to the setting of the type parameter. When FORCE is off, FTP attempts to determine the file type prior to transfer. Setting FORCE to off has the same effect as specifying the -F option for the COPY command. Repeated entry of the FORCE command toggles the state between on and off.
GET *remote_file* [*local_file* |*local_directory*]	Retrieves the file *remote_file* from the FTP server and stores it either with the name *local_file* on the local host or with the name *remote_file* in the *local_directory*.
HASH	Prints a # character as each block of data is transferred. This slows file transfers. HASH is a toggle command, with the default value of off.
HELP [*command*]	Displays list of available commands, or, if a command is specified, a brief message about that command.
LCD [*local_directory*]	Changes the working directory on the local computer.
LDIR [*local_directory*] [*local_file*]	Produces a detailed list of files in the current local directory or in the local directory specified by *local_directory*. Include a *local_file* parameter, which may include wildcards, to limit the display to specific files.

Continued

TABLE 6.2	COMMAND	FUNCTION
Continued	LEXEC ["command"]	Escapes to a DOS command shell. If a command parameter is included, the command will be executed. If the command includes spaces, enclose it in quotation marks ("").
	LLS [local_directory] [local_file]	Lists files in the current local directory or in the local directory specified by local_directory. Includes a local_file parameter, which may include wildcards, to limit the display to specific files.
	LPWD	Displays the name of the working directory on the DOS workstation.
	LS [{remote_directory | remote_file} local_file]	Lists files in the remote_directory on the FTP server, or files in the working directory on the FTP server that match the filename, which may include wildcards. Includes a local_file parameter to direct the results to a file on the DOS computer. On a UNIX host, accepts UNIX ls options.
	MDELETE remote_file	Deletes all files on the FTP server that match remote_file, which may include ? and * wildcards.
	MDIR [{remote_directory | remote_file} local_file]	Lists detailed contents of the remote_directory on the FTP server, or files in the working directory on the FTP server that match the filename remote_file, which may include wildcards. The last filename is interpreted as a local_file parameter, computer. On a UNIX host, accepts UNIX ls options, specifying a file that will receive the results reported by MDIR. Enter a hyphen (-) as the local_file to direct output to the screen.
	MGET remote_file	Copies files from the FTP server that match remote_file, which may include ? and * wildcards.

COMMAND	FUNCTION
MKDIR *remote_directory*	Creates the subdirectory named `remote_directory` on the FTP server.
MLS [{*remote_directory* | *remote_file*} [*local_file*]]	Lists contents of the *remote_directory* on the FTP server, or files in the working directory on the FTP server that match the filename *remote_file*, which may include wildcards. The last filename is interpreted as a *local_file* parameter, specifying a file that will receive the results reported by MDIR. Enter a hyphen (-) as the *local_file* to direct output to the screen.
MPUT *local_file*	Copies one or more files specified by *local_file* to the FTP server. The *local_file* parameter may include ? and * wildcards.
OPEN *hostname* [*port*]	Opens a connection to the specified *hostname*, which must be running FTP server software to accept the connection. The default FTP port is 21. If another port is used by an FTP server, it can be specified by the *port* parameter.
PROMPT	Switches prompting on or off during operations on multiple files (wildcards are used). You may find prompting irritating for routine operations such as MPUT and MGET, but may prefer to have prompting active for deleting files with MDELETE.
PUT *local_file* [*remote_file* | *remote_directory*]	Copies the local file *local_file* to the FTP host with the filename *remote_file* or to the *remote_directory* with the filename *local_file*.
PWD	Prints the working (current) directory on the FTP server.
QUIT	Terminates all FTP sessions and exits FTP to DOS.

Continued

T A B L E 6.2	COMMAND	FUNCTION
Continued	RENAME *remote_old* | *remote_new*	Renames a file on the FTP host from the name *remote_old* to the name *remote_new*.
	RMDIR *remote_directory*	Deletes the directory named *remote_directory* from the FTP server.
	TYPE [*type_name*]	Displays the current file transfer setting. Include a *type_name* parameter to change the settings. Valid settings are ASCII (7-bit ASCII), BINARY (bit image) and LOCAL 8 (8-bit ASCII).
	USER *username*	Initiates a login to the FTP host with the username specified. FTP prompts for a password.
	VERBOSE	Switches verbose mode on or off. Verbose mode provides information you may not want, such as file transfer statistics.

Trivial File Transfer Protocol

FTP was designed to provide robust file transfer service, with a measure of security, that could operate over unreliable WANs. Consequently, the designers of FTP selected TCP as the host-to-host protocol. But providing reliable service with TCP comes at a cost. Network overhead is required to establish a virtual circuit, maintain a reliable dialog, and close the virtual circuit when the dialog is complete.

On some networks and for some purposes, the overhead associated with FTP is undesirable. When file transfer is informal and is performed on reliable networks, for example, a simpler protocol may do. That is why the *Trivial File Transfer Protocol* (TFTP; RFC 1350) was developed. TFTP operates in an unreliable, datagram environment using the UDP host-to-host protocol. No formal connection must be established or released, and no login is required.

TFTP is of particular value because it can be embedded into computer boot ROMs. This makes it possible to construct diskless, remote booting computers that operate in the TCP/IP environment. Sun UNIX workstations, for example, can use TFTP to download an operating system image from a central server when the computer is started.

But TFTP's complete lack of security can make it a security risk when a host is attached to a public network. Many system administrators disable TFTP on their network hosts. If TFTP is enabled, careful attention should be paid to the areas of the file system that TFTP users can access. (Incidentally, TFTP is included with Novell's NFS Services.)

Telnet

Another TCP/IP application you are likely to use is *Telnet* (RFC 854/855), a remote terminal program that lets users engage in terminal dialogs with remote hosts on TCP/IP internetworks. The effect is much like using a telecommunications package and a modem to dial into an information service, but the entire process happens within the internetwork, without needing a dial-up connection.

Architecture of Telnet

Like FTP, Telnet operates in a client-server configuration. As Figure 6.12 illustrates, a host must run Telnet server software, which enables it to maintain a virtual terminal image that represents the connecting client. This virtual image is the key to making Telnet work, because the processes running on the Telnet server interact with the virtual terminal just as though they were talking with a hardware terminal attached to a terminal port.

To initiate a Telnet connection, a user runs Telnet client software and logs onto the Telnet server. The Telnet server software receives keystrokes from the client and forwards the keystrokes to the virtual terminal where they become available to the application being used. When the application directs screen display data to the virtual terminal, the data is forwarded to the Telnet server process, which passes the characters on to the client. This process is a *double fooler*. The applications running on the server think they are interacting with a local terminal, and the user can behave as though the processing were taking place on the local client.

Telnet is a pretty basic telecommunications program, designed around text-based terminals, typically the Digital VT220, VT100/VT102, or VT52. Although these terminals are quite sophisticated as text terminals go, they will seem like pretty old technology to users who have come to know graphic user environments.

Architecture of Telnet

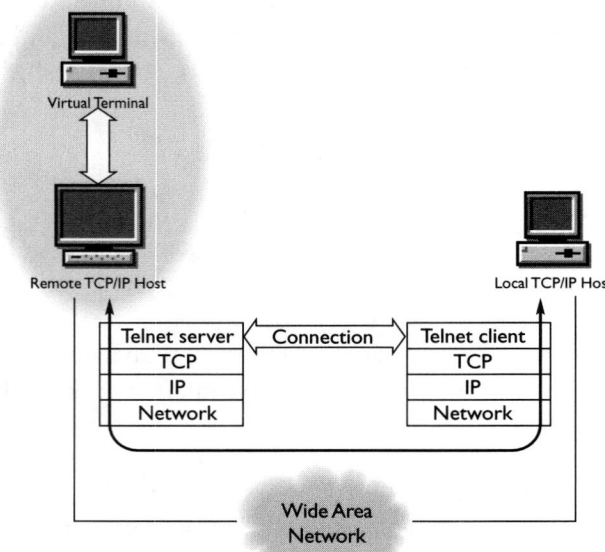

Although Telnet has a client and a server side, all the processing takes place at the server side. The client host may as well be a terminal, because it operates in a pretty "dumb" mode. Telnet is not the first step toward distributed processing. So, if Telnet is dumb and text-based, why use it?

As it turns out, Telnet has been largely eclipsed by the World Wide Web. The chief remaining use for Telnet is network management. Many network devices have Telnet interfaces that enable them to be managed remotely. You can also Telnet into a NetWare 5 server that is running an xconsole.

Simple Network Management Protocol

The "Network Management" in Simple Network Management Protocol (SNMP) refers to the task of collecting, reporting, responding to, and in some cases remotely changing data about devices on the network. SNMP is the most widely used network management protocol, and it is supported by many NetWare software products.

Actually, SNMP is one of three components that together make up the network management strategy for the Internet:

▶ SNMP is the protocol that supports communication between managed and managing devices.

▶ MIB is the *management information base*, which is the database that stores information about managed devices.

▶ SMI is the *structure and identification of management information*, which describes how object records in the MIB are constructed.

Chapter 13 teaches you how to use SNMP to monitor and manage a NetWare network. Before you can configure SNMP, you need to know the components of an SNMP management system and how they are related.

The Management Information Base

A MIB is a management database consisting of *objects*. The MIB states what the objects are, but the structures of the objects are described by the SMI.

Three RFCs describe SNMP MIB standards:

▶ MIB-I (RFC 1156) was the first MIB specification and was originally published in 1988 as RFC 1066. MIB-I defines 8 object groups and 114 objects.

▶ MIB-II (RFC 1213) is the current Internet standard. MIB-II defines 10 object groups and 171 objects. NetWare 3, 4, and 5 servers support MIB-II.

▶ RMON-MIB (RFC 1513/1217) defines objects oriented around managing network media rather than network devices.

MIBs are extensible and can be defined for special purposes. Vendors provide MIBs to support their products, for example, and a number of experimental MIBs are available. Experimental MIBs are MIBs that are undergoing trials for possible inclusion in the standard MIB-space.

Architecture of SNMP

Two types of devices make up the SNMP architecture. Figure 6.13 shows how the devices are related:

▸ Devices managed by SNMP run an SNMP *agent*, which is a background process that monitors operation of the device and communicates with the outside world. Each SNMP agent maintains a MIB that contains data about the device.

▸ SNMP agents are managed by SNMP *managers*, which are network management stations that collect messages from SNMP agents, generate reports, and in some cases manipulate data in the MIBs of managed devices.

A network management station gets its information either by requesting agents to send their data (a process called *polling*), or through *trap messages*.

FIGURE 6.13

Architecture of SNMP Network Management

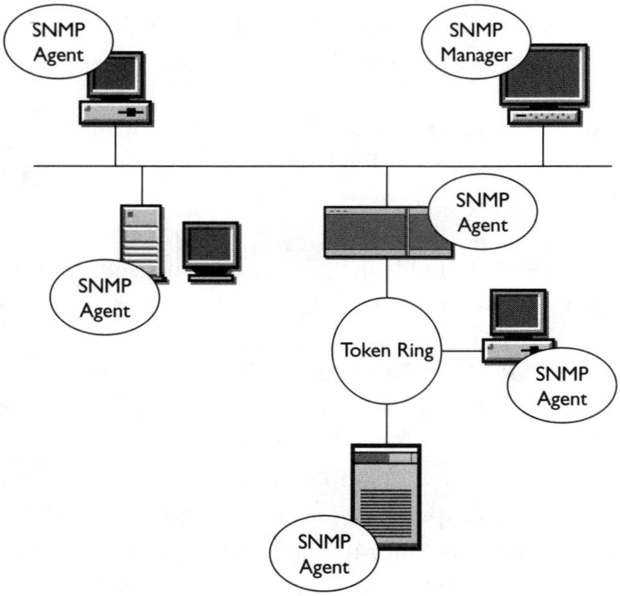

SNMP Functions

The use of SNMP (RFC 1157) is not limited to the Internet or even to TCP/IP. SNMP can be implemented independently of the TCP/IP protocols and can, for example, operate over IPX. In the TCP/IP environment, SNMP runs over the UDP transport

All SNMP functions are based on the following five operations:

- ▸ **GetRequest.** The manager uses this command to poll an agent for information.

- ▸ **GetNextRequest.** The manager uses this command to request the next item in a table or array. The command is repeated to obtain all data in the table or array.

- ▸ **SetRequest.** The manager uses this command to change a value within an agent's MIB.

- ▸ **GetResponse.** An agent uses this command to satisfy a request from a manager.

- ▸ **Trap.** An agent uses this command to inform a manager of an event.

These messages enable SNMP computers to exchange data in two ways. Managers can poll agents for information, as shown in Figure 6.14. Polling occurs at spaced intervals to prevent network management traffic from using excess network bandwidth. Polling enables the SNMP manager to collect data about the network during normal operation. This data provides a baseline that can be used as a basis of comparison when performance degrades.

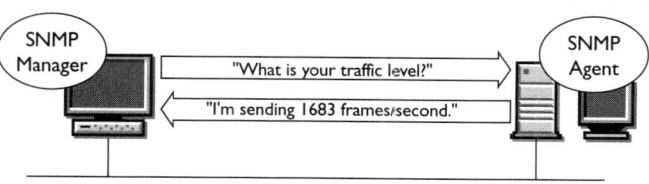

FIGURE 6.14

Polling for Network Management Data

When things go wrong, however, agents need to be able to make the problem known. As shown in Figure 6.15, agents can generate messages in response to events called *traps*. Network administrators configure traps that result when utilization thresholds are exceeded. The trap messages convey the information to the SNMP manager.

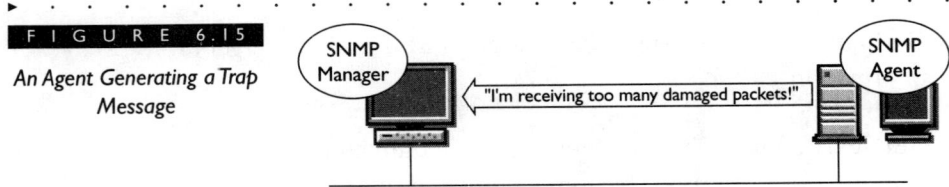

FIGURE 6.15

An Agent Generating a Trap Message

SNMP messages are exchanged within designated groups of computers that are identified by community names, which are 32-character, case-sensitive identifiers that serve much the same purpose as passwords, although they are not encrypted when transmitted and therefore are not secure. Three types of communities can be defined:

▶ The *monitor community* grants read access to MIBs. A manager must include the monitor community name in requests. The default monitor community is named *public*.

▶ The *control community* grants read and write access to MIBs.

▶ The *trap community* identifies all messages originated by agents in response to traps. An SNMP manager will receive those trap messages that match its trap community name.

The current SNMP standard, Version 1, has significant limitations. Perhaps most significant is that community names are not encrypted as they are transmitted. As a result, anyone snooping the network with a protocol analyzer can learn the community names and gain access to considerable information about the network as well as gain the capability to manage network devices.

SNMP Version 2 (RFC 1441–1452) is a proposed standard that encrypts messages to enhance security. SNMP improves the ability of the manager to retrieve network data by providing commands to retrieve entire tables without the need to read the table one record at a time with the GetNextRequest command.

NetWare 5 includes SNMP support in server and client components. SNMP configuration and management is discussed in Chapter 13.

NOTE

Simple Mail Transfer Protocol

If the majority of Internet users were to name the application that they use most frequently, it would almost certainly be electronic mail. The protocol that supports Internet e-mail is the *Simple Mail Transfer Protocol* (SMTP), defined in RFCs 821 and 822. Generally speaking, users do not interface directly with SMTP. Access is generally gained through a *mail transfer agent* (MTA). The relationship between SMTP and MTAs is described in the following section.

Architecture of TCP/IP E-mail

Figure 6.16 shows the relationships of the components of a TCP/IP electronic mail system. Overall management of messages is the responsibility of an MTA running on an e-mail server (also called a *mail exchanger*). The MTA performs three functions:

▸ Providies an interface that enables users and applications to interact with the mail system

▸ Sends and receiving messages

▸ Forwards messages between mail servers

MTAs communicate with one another using the SNMP protocol.

▶ · ◀

FIGURE 6.16

*Architecture of TCP/IP
E-Mail*

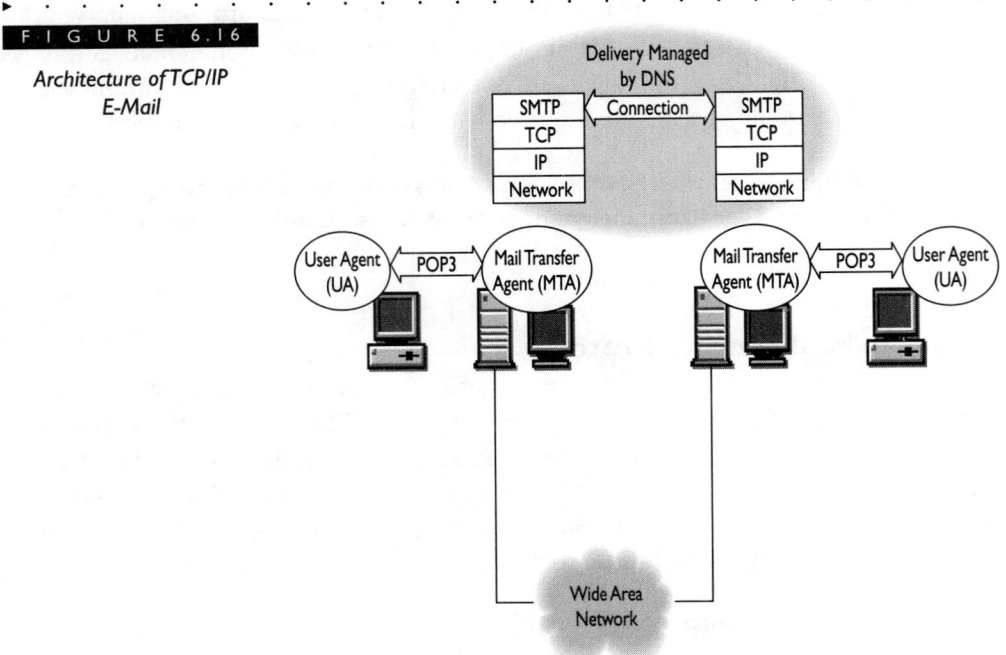

The familiar Internet e-mail addresses, such as GOOBER@foobar.com, are provided by MTAs. DNS does not know anything about GOOBER, but it does know about foobar.com. Also, DNS knows the addresses of mail exchangers that are running the MTAs that service the foobar.com domain. The division of labor is as follows:

▶ DNS delivers messages between mail exchangers. DNS maintains a directory of host names and of mail exchangers servicing a domain.

▶ Mail exchangers receive messages from user client software and enable user clients to receive messages.

End users interact with MTAs via *user agents* (UAs), which communicate with the MTA using a mail protocol such as the *Post Office Protocol Version 3* (POP3; RFC 1460). A wide variety of Uas are available. Novell's GroupWise clients include SMTP UA capability.

Internetwork Mail Delivery

Unlike data that supports applications such as FTP and Telnet, e-mail data is not routed through the internetwork in real-time. E-mail routing is designed to be able to transfer high volumes of data in a reasonable period of time while minimizing the impact on network performance. The Internet delivers a lot of e-mail. If all of it traveled at top priority, the Internet would quickly be overwhelmed.

E-mail is transferred using a *store-and-forward* technique, illustrated in Figure 6.17. In this figure, *mail exchanger 2* (MX2) is forwarding messages between MX1 and MX3. To improve efficiency, MX2 may wait until it has several messages to send to MX3, storing waiting messages on a hard drive until the data volume justifies opening a connection. MX2 may also improve efficiency by waiting until the network is quiet before transmitting, to minimize its impact on network performance. If messages in MX2 have waited more than a specified time, MX2 may be configured to send the messages even if the message volume is below the configured threshold. The goal is to produce a compromise between timeliness and network traffic impact.

FIGURE 6.17

E-Mail Delivery through an Internetwork

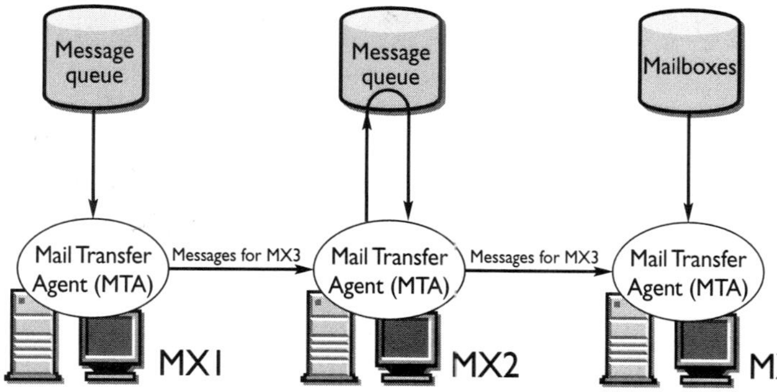

Limitations of SMTP

SMTP grew up in the days when terminals were text-only and when the fact that you could send electronic mail at all was pretty cool. Today e-mail is referred to as *messaging*, and all sorts of data that were unknown in 1982 (when SMTP became a standard) are riding on e-mail. Voice, graphics, and video are becoming part of the electronic messaging picture.

SMTP still has a few limitations, though. Because SMTP was designed around 7-bit ASCII text, we need to tap-dance a bit to send binary data this way. The binary data must be encoded so that it fits into 7-bit ASCII messages. For UNIX, this typically involves a coding scheme called uuencode (UNIX-UNIX encode) to build the messages and the companion uuencode to recover the original binary data.

The *Multipurpose Internet Mail Extensions* (MIME; RFC 1521) are an elective Internet protocol that enables SMTP to carry nontext messages. Many e-mail packages for DOS and Windows support uuencode and MIME.

Another limitation of SMTP is that all messages are sent in open text. Security just wasn't a priority when the Internet resembled a friendly community of users rather than today's method of doing business electronically. If you need to send sensitive data via SMTP, the data files should be encrypted.

Network File System

You've learned about FTP, which enables you to transfer files and manage remote file systems. And you've learned about Telnet, which lets you enter a remote terminal session with a remote host. But let's consider other activities. Suppose a remote computer has the files for a program that you want to run on your local computer. Or you want to place a spreadsheet file in a common location so that users can open it and enter their sales data. Neither of these scenarios presents any problem for NetWare. You simply store the files on a volume of the server, give users the required rights, and voilà, the files are shared. Users don't need to run FTP, retrieve the files, and FTP them back when the job is done. With NetWare, a shared file works like a local file, but it can be a local file for hundreds of users.

In the TCP/IP environment, the product that permits file volumes to be shared is the *Network File System* (NFS), developed by Sun Microsystems. An NFS server can export part of its directory tree. The exported directories can be mounted on NFS client workstations, where they function as part of the local file system. A DOS user accessing files shared by a UNIX NFS server perceives the shared directories and files as though they were stored using the DOS FAT file system. Figure 6.18 shows how NFS works.

FIGURE 6.18

How NFS Exports Directories

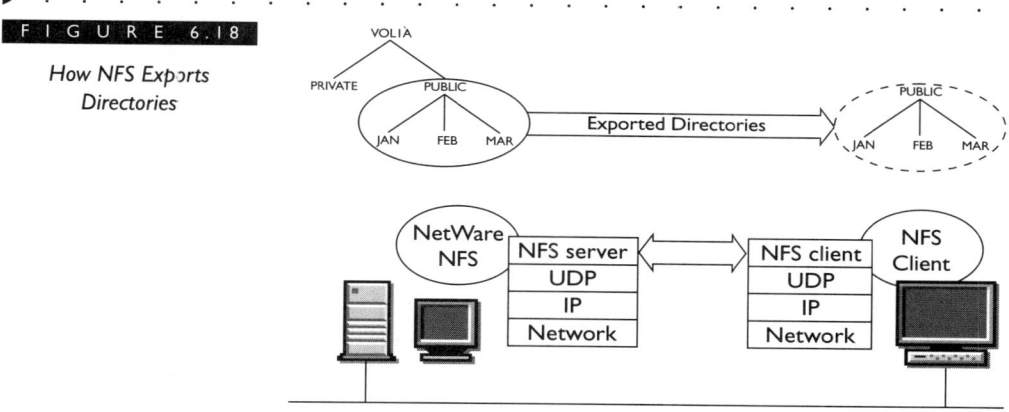

Novell offers NFS products for NetWare 3, 4, and 5. Visit www.novell.com for current information about these products.

Hypertext Transmission Protocol

The *Hypertext Transmission Protocol* (HTTP) is the backbone protocol for the World Wide Web. Standards for the World Wide Web are established by the World Wide Web Consortium (W3C), although recent developments of HTTP have taken place under the auspices of the IETF in cooperation with W3C. You can learn about W3C from their Web site at http://www.w3.org.

HTTP is an application-level protocol that, in the words of RFC 2068, supports "distributed, collaborative, hypermedia information systems." HTTP is a versatile protocol that supports communication between user agents and proxies or gateways to other Internet systems, including servers supporting the SMTP, FTP, Gopher, and WAIS protocols. Typical user agents or clients are Web browsers such as Netscape Navigator and the Microsoft Internet Explorer. Internet servers include Web, FTP, Gopher, and WAIS servers. Novell's HTTP server offering is the Novell Web Server, which is included in IntranetWare.

Unlike mail or file transfer protocols, HTTP supports hypermedia access to resources. Hypermedia are complex documents that can consist of combinations of text, graphics, sound, video, formatting, and other information. All you need to appreciate the flexibility of HTTP is to compare the complexity of a Web page to the contents of a typical, text-only e-mail message.

The first version, referred to as HTTP/0.9, was a stripped-down protocol that supported raw data transfer through the Internet. HTTP/1.0 was the next release, and is described in the informational RFC 1945. HTTP/1.0 extended the protocol to support messages in MIME-like format, but is in many ways an inefficient protocol. For example, HTTP/1.0 does not support persistent connections, and each connection that is established can be used to transfer only a single message. The most recent version is HTTP/1.1, a proposed standard defined in RFC 2068. Among the new features of HTTP/1.1 is a provision for persistent connections, enabling extended dialogs to take place with a single connection.

Figure 6.19 shows a typical HTTP communication exchange. A *user agent* (UA) initiates a request chain over TCP, establishing a connection with the *origin server* (OS). The CS generates a response chain, which is sent to the UA.

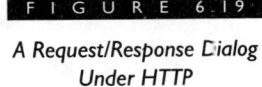

F I G U R E   6.19

A Request/Response Dialog Under HTTP

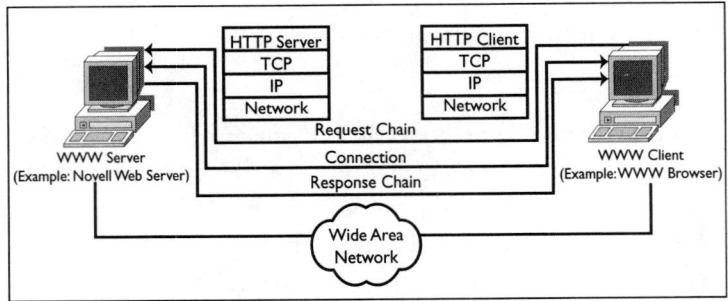

Three types of entities can separate the UA from the OA:

▶ A *proxy* acts as a forwarding agent that receives a request from a UA, reformats the message, and forwards the request to the OS. Proxy servers serve a firewall function, isolating UAs from the Internet while enabling them to access Web services.

▶ A *gateway* is a receiving agent that translates HTTP requests into another protocol. Gateways enable the UA to access services that are not directly supported by HTTP.

▶ A *tunnel* is a relay point between two connections. Tunnels do not change messages but enable messages to pass through intermediary entities such as firewalls.

The World Wide Web protocols are hotbeds of competition as vendors seek to introduce client and server products that generate interest in the user community. Many of the features of HTTP/1.1 were found in commercial products well in advance of the standard's publication, and we can expect vendors to keep pushing the envelope established by HTTP/1.1, introducing features in products that are just entering discussion in the standards process. Unlike many other Internet protocols which are characterized by stability and controlled evolution, HTTP will likely be at the center of a revolution for some time to come.

That's It for Theory

You now know the theory behind the complete TCP/IP architecture. You have seen how:

▶ The network access layer enables nodes to communicate.

▶ The internet layer extends communication throughout the internetwork.

▶ The host-to-host layer makes communications reliable and handles message fragmentation and reassembly.

▶ The process/application layer enables users to take advantage of the services that the lower layers provide.

The time has come to put theory into practice. In other words, you are about to put TCP/IP into action on your NetWare network. First, I'll tell you a bit about how Novell has implemented TCP/IP, and then we'll move on to the fun stuff. Just one more (short, I promise) chapter of background information, and then it's hands on!

## PART II

Implementing NetWare TCP/IP

## CHAPTER 7

Introducing NetWare TCP/IP

NetWare has included a TCP/IP protocol stack for quite some time. So what's the big deal about NetWare 5? With NetWare 5, the NetWare Core Protocols (NCP) can now inter-operate directly with the TCP/IP protocol stack without recourse to IPX. Novell has dubbed this capability *Pure IP*.

Before Pure IP, IPX always showed up somewhere in the protocol stack. With NetWare/IP, Novell's older technology for providing NetWare services using an IP transport, only IP datagrams appeared on the network. However, if you looked inside the IP datagrams, you found that they encapsulated IPX protocol packets. Encapsulation works, but it is inefficient — and encapsulated IPX doesn't qualify TCP/IP as a native NCP protocol stack. With NetWare 5, however, TCP/IP support has been fully integrated with NCP. In normal communication, NCP packets ride in IP datagrams, without encapsulation. Now NCP doesn't care whether it is operating over IPX or IP. In fact, if both IPX and IP are available, NetWare will actually prefer IP.

But wait! If your organization has been using NetWare for any amount of time, you probably have one or two applications dependent on the IPX protocol stack. BTRIEVE is an example of an IPX-dependent application, as are several network backup applications, which use SPX to detect and recover from communication errors. If IP has gone native, do you have to jettison all your IPX-dependent utilities to shift to Pure IP? That's where the innovation of Novell's Pure IP solution becomes apparent, because Pure IP offers seamless, on-demand IPX support. It's all very clever and painless. You'll see how NetWare 5 simplifies the transition from IPX to Pure IP a bit later.

Before learning about Pure IP, you need to know the background: How do all the components of NetWare's protocol support fit together? To get that part of the story, we need to look at the NetWare protocol architecture: the Open Datalink Interface.

▶ . . . . ◀

Open Datalink Interface

The OSI Reference Model and the DoD protocol model are just that: models. They present a general picture of network protocol stacks, but they do not describe specific implementations of the protocols. In other words, they don't tell you how a particular vendor has implemented the protocols in specific hardware and software modules.

One of the theoretical justifications for layered models is that different protocols can be plugged into different layers with a minimum of fuss. When vendors seek to develop a protocol environment that can integrate multiple protocol stacks, they must turn the theory into reality, and that turns out to be a bit complicated.

Novell's architecture for enabling NetWare servers and clients to support multiple protocol stacks flexibly is called *Open Datalink Interface* (ODI). As you will see, ODI enables NetWare servers to mix a variety of protocols and network interfaces, providing the flexibility required on a multiprotocol, enterprise internetwork. Because NetWare TCP/IP networks are typically multiprotocol networks, you need to understand how the parts of ODI fit together to grasp how protocols on your LAN are interrelated.

ODI Layers

Figure 7.1 illustrates the ODI architecture, filled in with some protocols that NetWare supports. The ODI architecture enables NetWare to support three protocol stacks (IPX, TCP/IP, and AppleTalk), which in turn support three classes of services. Our discussion will ignore AppleTalk, which is beyond the scope of this book. IPX is integral to our discussion, however, and you need to understand both IPX and IP configuration.

NOTE

If you have seen Figure 7.1 in earlier editions of this book, you will notice a significant change. NetWare Services specifically the NetWare Core Protocols (NCP), now interface directly with the TCP/IP protocol stack. That small change in the diagram is the result of a big change in NCP, which has been redesigned to eliminate any dependencies on IPX. The new capability of NCP to operate directly over TCP/IP is the key enabling technology that makes Pure IP possible. Unless an application specifically requires a feature in the IPX protocol stack, no IPX packets appear on the Pure IP network, even as IPX encapsulated in IP datagrams.

Anyone who has spent time managing a NetWare server has had to load and unload *NetWare Loadable Modules* (NLMs), the building blocks used to add features to NetWare 3, 4, and 5 servers. Each box in Figure 7.1 corresponds roughly to an NLM loaded automatically or manually on a server. To start the TCP/IP protocols running on the server, for example, you load a TCP/IP NLM packaged in the file TCPIP.NLM. As you load modules on a server, or start drivers on a workstation, you can think in terms of where in the ODI model those modules and drivers fit. Let's start at the bottom of the figure and examine the layers.

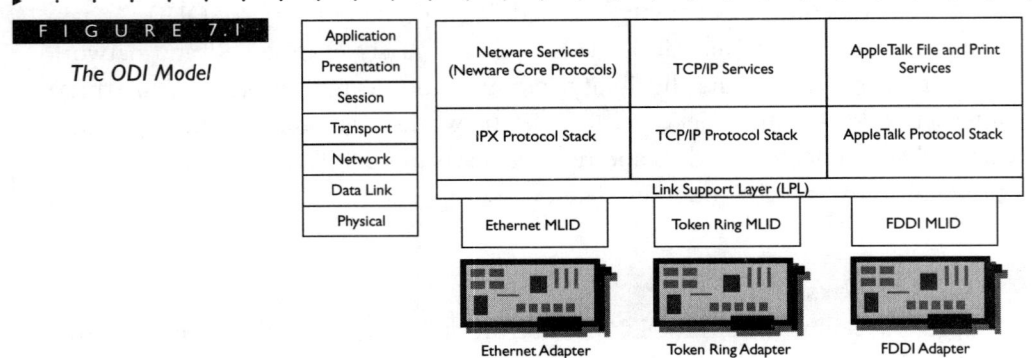

FIGURE 7.1

The ODI Model

Network Hardware

At the bottom of the model is the physical hardware, the network interface board, or other communications hardware that enables the server to communicate with the outside. This hardware is not formally part of the ODI model, any more than Layer 0 is a part of the OSI Reference Model introduced in Chapter 2. However, the hardware must be included in the picture to illustrate ODI's ability to link a given upper-layer protocol stack to given network hardware.

NetWare network drivers are able to support multiple network boards in a given computer. Why would you want to do that? With multiple network boards, you could segment your network to control traffic flow. Alternatively, you could connect one network to another, which may or may not be the same network type.

NetWare servers are particularly adept at supporting multiple LAN adapters. Any NetWare server connected to two or more network adapters is able to function as a router, forwarding network traffic between different attached networks.

Multiple Link Interface Drivers (MLIDs)

The next layer up the ODI model provides the software that enables upper-layer protocols to communicate with the network hardware. From the top of the model, all MLIDs look alike. At the bottom, each MLID provides a custom fit to a particular make and model of network board. This capability is the key feature that enables NetWare servers to mix and match network hardware.

The MLID completely isolates upper-layer protocols from the network hardware. IPX has no idea whether it is running over an Ethernet network or an FDDI network. As far as IPX is concerned, the network is irrelevant.

MLIDs must be able to support multiple network boards of the same type and multiple frame types. Remember from Chapters 2 through 6 that protocol multiplexing is an important activity as message units travel up and down the protocol stack. At the MLID layer, protocol multiplexing is required to enable messages with different frame types to travel through the same MLID and the appropriate network interface. MLIDs have to be able to keep the various message streams sorted out.

Supporting Multiple Network Interfaces   When, as in Figure 7.2, a NetWare server needs to support two or more network interfaces that use the same driver, it can use a neat trick called *reentrant loading*, which enables the server to reuse the program code in an MLID. For example, suppose that a server has two NE2000 network adapters. The first time you load the NE2000.LAN network driver software, the driver program is loaded into memory. The second time you load the NE2000.LAN driver, NetWare is able to reuse the program loaded previously. This bit of programming magic uses memory more efficiently than loading the module two or more times.

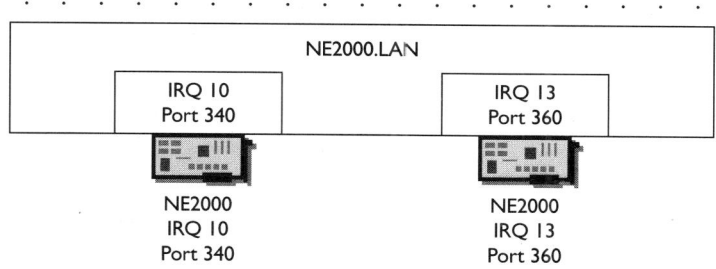

FIGURE 7.2

Supporting Multiple Network Interfaces

The MLID must have a way to direct message units to the appropriate network board. This process is enabled by identifying each board with unique interface parameters. At minimum, these parameters consist of a unique interrupt (IRQ) and a unique I/O address (called a *port*) for each board. The MLID module is loaded each time with a unique set of interface parameters that enables it to keep the various network boards sorted out.

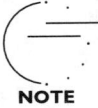

NOTE

The trend now is to use PCI network adapters rather than ISA adapters, such as the NE2000 that I used when I wrote first wrote this chapter. PCI adapters are usually configured automatically by the system when it boots up. Typically, you don't need to worry about the specific adapter settings because PCI adapters are identified by their slot numbers.

Supporting Multiple Frame Types   Chapter 3 demonstrated that many types of networks support multiple frame types. Nowhere is this more evident than with Ethernet. NetWare supports no less than four Ethernet frame types, which are as follows:

- ► **ETHERNET_II.** The original Ethernet frame type and still the champion on TCP/IP networks.

- ► **ETHERNET_802.2.** A frame type that fully complies with IEEE 802 specifications.

- ► **ETHERNET_802.3.** A frame type that Novell developed before the IEEE 802.2 specification was nailed down. Although this frame type is still available on all NetWare platforms, it is not recommended.

- ► **ETHERNET_SNAP.** The IEEE 802.2–compliant Ethernet frame type with SNAP encapsulation to support TCP/IP and other SNAP-compliant protocols.

NetWare also supports two token ring frame types:

- ► **TOKEN-RING.** The standard token ring frame type used in most environments.

▶ **TOKEN-RING_SNAP.** Token ring with SNAP encapsulation for use with TCP/IP and AppleTalk.

Many other frame types are supported for other network interfaces, but the above examples illustrate the problem faced by NetWare. If messages with several frame types are arriving from a single network through a single network adapter, NetWare must be able to send the appropriate frame type to the appropriate upper-level protocols.

This capability is accomplished by creating *virtual network adapters*. A given network adapter, identified by its hardware IRQ and I/O address, is virtualized by identifying each virtual adapter with a frame type. Figure 7.3 illustrates an MLID maintaining two physical adapters, which are installed as four virtual adapters. Each virtual adapter is identified by a combination of an IRQ, a port, and a frame type. For any given MLID, these identifiers must be unique. Therefore, you can't load the same driver with the same parameters more than once.

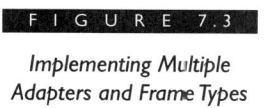

FIGURE 7.3

Implementing Multiple Adapters and Frame Types

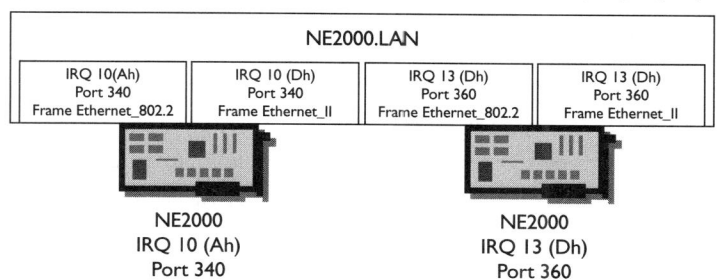

Loading MLIDs on the Server Server MLIDs are found in NLM files that have a LAN filename extension. Like all NLMs, the MLIDs are installed on the server with the LOAD command. Parameters entered on the command line specify the unique network board hardware characteristics as well as the frame type. Here is an example of a LOAD command for an NE2000 network board:

```
LOAD NE2000 INT=A PORT=340 FRAME=ETHERNET_802.2
```

A LOAD command for a PCI adapter would specify its slot number as in the following example:

```
LOAD E100B SLOT=3 FRAME=ETHERNET_II
```

Because each virtual network board must be unique, the LOAD command can be entered only once with a particular set of parameters on a given server.

To provide a shorthand for referring to a specific virtual network board, each is typically given a name, which is assigned with a NAME parameter in the LOAD command, as in this example:

```
LOAD NE2000 NAME=NE2000_1_E82 INT=A PORT=340
FRAME=ETHERNET_802.2
```

Although you can name your boards in any way, the above example follows the convention of a three-part name:

▸ The name of the board driver.

▸ A number identifying each board of that type. If the NE2000 driver is loaded for a different hardware adapter, the second adapter will be board 2.

▸ A shorthand for the frame type. E82 is, for example, shorthand for the ETHERNET_802.2 frame type.

The Link Support Layer

Take another look at Figure 7.1. The *Link Support Layer* (LSL) appears above the MLIDs. The LSL acts as a switch, performing protocol multiplexing to ensure that the appropriate message units from the various MLIDs are directed to the appropriate upper-layer protocols. When MLIDs and upper-layer protocols are loaded, they register with the LSL, which assigns a logical identifier to each MLID and protocol stack. The LSL uses these logical identifiers to route incoming data from an MLID to the appropriate protocol stack, or to route outgoing data from a protocol stack to the correct MLID.

A given upper-layer protocol stack is associated with a given virtual network adapter through a process called *binding*. For example, a binding may declare that the frame type Ethernet_II loaded on adapter NE2000 number 2 will be associated with the IP protocol.

Recall from the discussion in Chapter 2 that the OSI network layer identifies each network using a unique network identifier. The situation is a bit more complicated in reality, because many MLIDs can support two or more frame types.

The LSL's life is complicated by the need to route data between a given frame type in a given MLID to the appropriate protocol stack.

When ODI prepares a frame for the network, a *protocol ID* (PID) is appended to the start of the frame. The 6-byte PID identifies the frame type and the communication protocol that the frame encapsulates. For example, a PID of 8137h identifies an Ethernet II frame containing IPX data. A PID of 800h identifies a frame with IP data. These PID values are used by the LSL to route data to the correct protocols and MLIDs, which are identified by LSL-maintained registration tables. Although you may be able to see only one network cable, that cable may be supporting two or more *virtual networks*. Let's see how virtual networks work.

Virtual Networks   To deliver frames to the correct virtual LAN adapter, each adapter/protocol combination must be identified. As far as NetWare is concerned, each virtual LAN adapter is connected to a separate network cabling system. Each of these networks is identified by a *network number*, which is specified when the adapter is loaded. The IRQ, port, slot, and frame parameters are utilized within the MLID; outside the MLID, by contrast, the virtual network is identified by a network number unique within the entire internetwork. All NetWare servers that connect to this virtual network must identify the virtual network with the same network ID.

Figure 7.4 illustrates a network that consists of a single LAN cable segment. As far as NetWare is concerned, this physical network consists of three networks, associated with the Ethernet II, Ethernet 802.3, and Ethernet 802.2 frame types. Here is how the network functions from the perspective of each of the servers:

- ▸ NetWare server A (a NetWare 2 server) is connected to the Ethernet 802.3 virtual network.

- ▸ NetWare server B (a NetWare 3 server) is connected to the Ethernet 802.2 virtual network.

- ▸ NetWare server C (a NetWare 5 server) is connected to all three virtual networks.

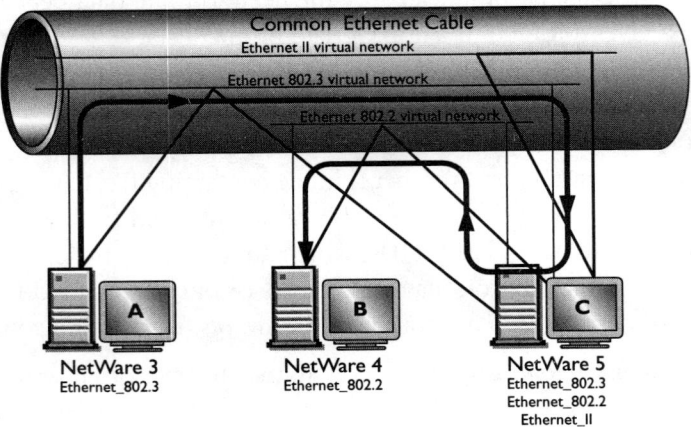

FIGURE 7.4

A Single-Segment LAN with Three Virtual Networks

Server C is the hub of the virtual network, serving as an IPX protocol router. If server A needs to communicate with server B, frames must be routed through server C. Even though A and B are attached to the same network cable, they cannot talk directly because they are using different frame types and therefore exist on different virtual networks.

You will seldom if ever encounter a TCP/IP analog to the IPX network shown in Figure 7.4. Because Ethernet_II frames are supported on all TCP/IP implementations, it is difficult to conceive of a situation that would require both the Ethernet_II and Ethernet_SNAP frame types on the same internetwork.

NOTE

Simply because Figure 7.4 depicts a network that has three frame types, please don't get the notion that multiple frame types are desirable. On IPX networks, each frame type generates its own SAP and RIP traffic, so you should settle on one frame type for all your IPX network segments whenever possible, preferably Ethernet_802.2. The Ethernet_802.3 frame type is required only if your network includes a NetWare 2.x server.

Binding Protocols to Networks Before a protocol may be bound to a network, two conditions must be met:

▸ An MLID must be loaded that defines a virtual network adapter for the physical adapter and frame type that will be used.

▸ The upper-layer protocol stack must be loaded.

By default, the IPX protocol stack is always loaded on a NetWare server, and no manual intervention is required on the part of the LAN administrator. IPX is even loaded on Pure IP servers, although IPX is not bound to a network adapter. As you will discover later in the chapter, the IPX protocol stack supports Compatibility Mode, which makes it possible to execute legacy, IPX-dependent applications on Pure IP networks.

The NLM that supports TCP/IP must be explicitly loaded before the protocol stack can be bound to a network adapter. This process is accomplished with the following LOAD statement:

```
LOAD TCPIP
```

Now that the network adapters and protocols are defined, a binding can take place. Here is a complete sequence:

```
LOAD TCPIP

LOAD NE2000 NET=NE2000_1_EII FRAME=ETHERNET_II INT=A PORT=340

BIND IP NE2000_1_EII ARP=YES MASK=FF.FF.0.0 ADDRESS=128.1.0.1
```

Figure 7.5 illustrates the logical path that this command sequence establishes. Notice that the protocol being bound is IP, the lowest-level protocol in the TCP/IP protocol stack. The meaning of each parameter may already be clear to you if you have followed the discussion in the preceding chapters. Chapter 8 examines the parameters in greater detail.

Now that binding has taken place, upper-layer processes can communicate with the network through the various network protocol layers.

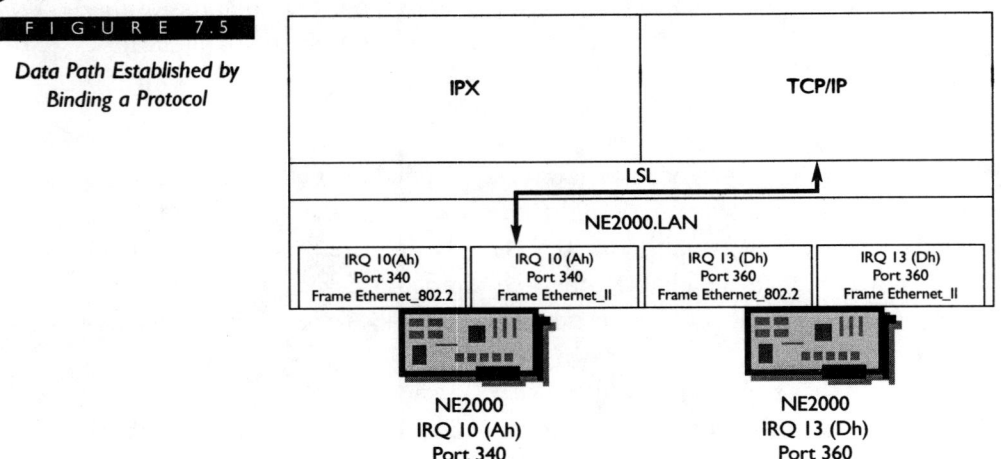

FIGURE 7.5

Data Path Established by
Binding a Protocol

Data Path Established by Binding a Protocol
Upper-Layer Process

Specific upper-layer processes are associated with each upper-layer protocol stack. As a result, users who access NetWare servers function in distinct process environments depending on the protocol stack employed. Figure 7.6 illustrates which upper-layer processes are supported for each protocol stack.

For the IPX protocol stack, upper-layer processing is supported by the NetWare Core Protocol (NCP), sometimes referred to as *NCP/IPX* when operating over IPX. NCP provides all of the services traditionally made available to users by NetWare servers, including creating and releasing connections, directory and file services, access to NetWare Directory Services, and printing. NCP is the default NetWare service protocol and is loaded automatically on the server.

As mentioned earlier, the most significant new feature of NetWare 5 is that NCP now has the capability of interfacing directly with the TCP/IP protocol stack, a feature sometimes referred to as *NCP/IP*. Figure 7.6 ignores some of the subtleties that enable NCP/IP to provide IPX compatibility. We'll take a look at IPX Compatibility Mode in the next section.

*Processes Associated with
NetWare-Supported
Protocols*

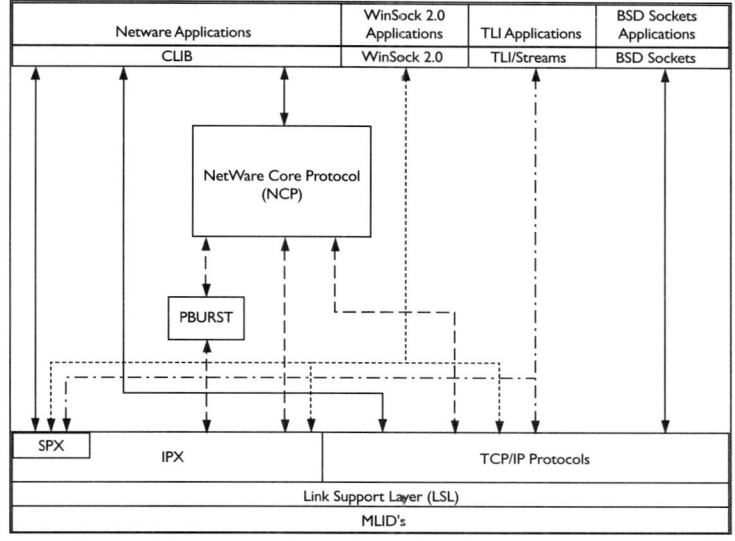

NCP/IP makes use of both UDP and TCP transport protocols, selecting the appropriate protocol for its current purpose. UDP is useful for connectionless-mode communication normally executed by IPX. TCP may be selected to perform large data transfers, taking advantage of TCP's sliding window and error-recovery capabilities. The Internet Assigned Numbers Authority (IANA) has assigned port 524 to Novell for NCP over UDP and TCP.

NetWare 5 TCP/IP supports four *application program interfaces* (APIs):

▶ *WinSock 2.0* support is a new NetWare 5 feature. WinSock originated as an implementation of BSD Sockets for the Microsoft Windows environment and is now a public standard. NetWare supports all features of WinSock 2.0 applicable to the server environment. Unlike other APIs, WinSock 2.0 architecture is not dependent on a particular protocol stack, and WinSock 2.0 applications can access multiple protocol stacks simultaneously, including UDP, TCP, IPX, SPX, and SPX2. Consequently, Novell regards WinSock 2.0 as the preferred API for NetWare applications that require transport protocol independence.

▶ *CLIB* is the standard program interface to NCP. Under Pure IP, developers don't need to be concerned with any layers below the NCP API level. Applications written to the CLIB API library will be compatible with IPX or Pure IP without change.

▶ *Transport Layer Interface* (TLI) is an API developed by AT&T. Using the Streams interface, TLI applications can be made compatible with IPX and IP transports.

▶ *4.3 BSD Sockets* is the widely used API popularized by BSD UNIX. BSD Sockets applications operate only over the TCP/IP stack.

This choice of APIs provides developers with many options when porting programs to the NetWare environment. Figure 7.6 illustrates the NetWare API architecture. Both TCP/IP APIs are supported by the Streams interface, which provides a uniform interface to the transport layer protocols.

AppleTalk has its own upper-layer services. On a NetWare server, AppleTalk services are supported by two protocols: the *AppleTalk Filing Protocol* (AFP) and the *AppleTalk Print Services* (ATPS). These protocols enable users of AppleTalk-based computers to access files and printers on NetWare servers, and are included with NetWare 3.12 and 4.1.

▶ • ◀

Service Location on Pure IP Networks

Service location is a crucial technology on any network. On IPX networks, service location is practically invisible to the end user thanks to SAP, which advertises services and responds to client queries, and RIP, which enables clients to discover a route to a desired server. On IP networks, however, service location must be enabled manually. NetWare 5 offers a variety of technologies that support service location on Pure IP networks.

Let's demystify service location. To connect to a service, a client must know two things:

▶ The address of the computer where the service is located. On IP networks, that address is the IP address of the server. On IPX networks, the address is formed by the combination of the server's network address and its node address.

▶ The identification of the specific process that offers the desired service. On an IP host, services are identified by port numbers. On IPX servers, services are identified by socket numbers.

Typically a client knows the port or socket number of the desired service. For example, NCP is associated with IPX socket 0x0451. To log on to an IPX server, a NetWare client only needs to identify the server's network and node addresses by issuing a SAP query (specifically a Get Nearest Server query).

A NetWare client seeking to log in on a Pure IP network knows that NCP is assigned the well-known port number 524, so all it needs to determine is the IP address of the server. However, the SAP protocol doesn't work over IP. When Novell planned Pure IP, they needed to devise mechanisms that would do the work of SAP. They did a thorough job, enabling clients to locate services using four possible methods:

▶ **Service Location Protocol** (SLP; RFC 2165) is a new Internet protocol that provides the benefits of SAP but is much more efficient and scaleable. SLP is discussed in detail in Chapter 14.

▶ **Domain Name Service** (DNS) can be used to locate the IP address of a server. DNS is discussed in Chapters 6 and 11.

▶ **Dynamic Host Configuration Protocol** (DHCP) can provide the locations of NDS servers to DHCP clients. DHCP is discussed in Chapter 12.

▶ **Static configuration database files** also enable clients to map names to IP addresses. TCP/IP clients obtain static address mappings from a file named HOSTS. The format of the HOSTS file is discussed in Chapter 11.

Of these service location methods, the greatest market buzz surrounds SLP. This method is regarded as a milestone TCP/IP protocol that heralds a new era in ease-of-use, and NetWare 5 is the first implementation of SLP in a commercial product.

Supported by SLP, users can browse the network for services such as file and print services, for example, without first knowing the name of the server. SLP was also crucial to supporting Novell's goal to support legacy IPX applications transparently.

Actually, many networks can get along just fine without SLP, and many administrators may choose to remove SLP support from their NetWare 5 servers. Nevertheless, SLP is a key ingredient in Novell's strategy to provide a smooth transition from IPX to Pure IP. The next section shows how SLP supports IPX compatibility on Pure IP networks.

IPX Compatibility and Pure IP

Novell didn't forget the installed NetWare base when they designed Pure IP. They were well aware that there are dozens of important applications dependent on the IPX protocol stack. These applications fall into two categories:

▶ Some applications make legitimate calls to NCP that request services from the IPX protocol stack. For example, some applications call on SPX services to provide error detection and recovery.

▶ Some applications use so-called "dirty hooks" to bypass NCP and go directly to IPX or SPX.

NetWare 5's IPX Compatibility Mode supports IPX applications under both scenarios and also performs a few other tricks. When a NetWare 5 Pure IP client is configured with the Compatibility Mode Driver, it essentially has on-demand access to a virtual IPX network (called the *CMD network*) that supports IPX communication by encapsulating IPX traffic in IP datagrams. This is a far cry from NetWare/IP, which encapsulated all NetWare server traffic. On a CMD network, encapsulation is performed only when IPX-specific support is required. All normal NCP traffic is communicated through IP without requiring encapsulation.

NetWare 5's Compatibility Mode drivers have some other tricks as well. The CMD drivers can be configured to act as a gateway between IPX and IP network segments. This feature is referred to as the *Migration Gateway*, because it enables you to migrate your network from IPX to Pure IP in easy stages. With the Migration Gateway, you can configure networks as in Figure 7.7. While the IPX and NetWare/IP network segments integrate seamlessly using features provided by NetWare/IP, the NetWare 5 Migration Gateway enables the IPX and NetWare/IP network segments to inter-operate with Pure IP.

Service Location Protocol is integral to the transparent operation of Compatibility Mode. When an IPX-dependent application issues a call to SAP, the Compatibility Mode Drivers redirect the query to SLP, enabling the CMD network to function with the same service location transparency as on IPX networks. There is a lot more to IPX compatibility, and I'm deliberately skipping the details until Chapter 15, where we will take a close look at strategies for migrating from IPX to Pure IP.

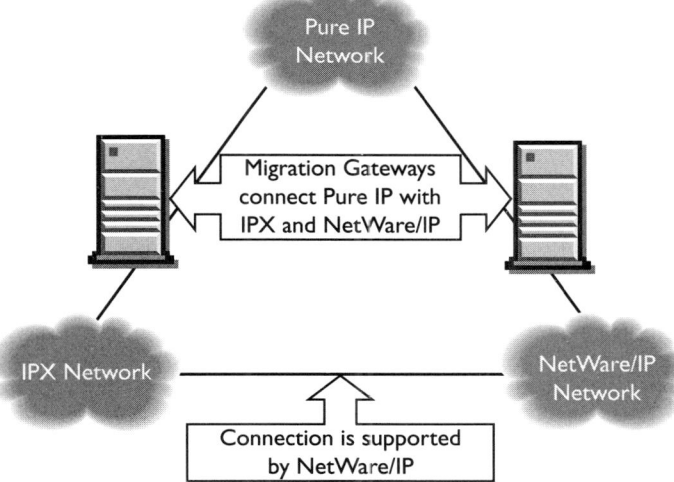

F I G U R E 7.7

The Migration Gateway enables IPX and NetWare/IP network segments to inter-operate with Pure IP.

Let's Get Going

I promised this chapter would be short and (protocol) suite. Now, at last, you are ready to put theory into practice. The next two chapters focus on installing TCP/IP protocol support on NetWare servers and clients.

## CHAPTER 8

Configuring a Pure
IP Network

In earlier editions of this book, this introductory chapter had to cover the configuration of a NetWare server with both IPX and IP protocol stacks. IPX was always required (although it wasn't necessary to bind IPX to a network adapter), even when the network was using NetWare/IP, because NCP-based services had to run over IPX while TCP/IP services ran over IP. With the advent of Pure IP, however, dual protocol stacks can be eliminated.

This chapter will examine a fairly basic configuration, a Pure IP network that ultimately will include two LAN segments and a single router. Chapter 10 (Internetworking NetWare 5 Clients) will extend the discussion to include more complex routed internetworks. Chapter 15 (Migrating to Pure IP) will cover the issues that arise when the NetWare environment includes both IPX and IP protocols.

The first part of this chapter covers planning. You will examine issues such as planning addresses and host names, make some decisions, and fill in some planning forms that will guide the rest of the process.

The second part covers configuration of TCP/IP database files. You will learn about the various files used to store TCP/IP configuration information.

The final part covers configuration and activation of TCP/IP. This section discusses how to configure and load the TCP/IP protocols and bind them to network adapters. After completing this step, your NetWare server will be ready to talk TCP/IP.

Planning

Preceding chapters have addressed many of the implementation planning issues, but now it is time to get real and plan an actual LAN. Here are the planning tasks that will be examined:

▶ Planning IP addressing

▶ Planning host names

▶ Planning the server hardware configuration

▶ Planning frame types and bindings

None of these tasks is terribly difficult on a single-segment LAN, but it is useful to see how the entire process works before getting into more complex cases. To illustrate the planning process, we will build a network for a hypothetical company, Pseudo Corporation, which has registered the Internet domain name pseudo-corp.com. Management of this small company has set the following goals:

1. The network's primary file services will be provided by a NetWare file server.

2. The network will eventually obtain an Internet connection so that it can offer a Web server.

3. Only IP protocol will appear on the network.

4. The Web server will be run locally for now, functioning as a company bulletin board.

5. Users will access the network using NetWare 5 clients.

At present, the following employees need to use the network:

► Drew, president

► Blythe, manufacturing manager

► Woody, security

► Cyd, corporate communications

► Lauren, product testing

Figure 8.1 illustrates the network configuration, which consists of five workstations, a NetWare 5 server, and a UNIX host running the Web server software. Our task is to plan and implement the protocols on the network. Workstation installation will be covered in Chapter 9. In this chapter, we will configure and activate TCP/IP on the NetWare server.

▶ • ◀

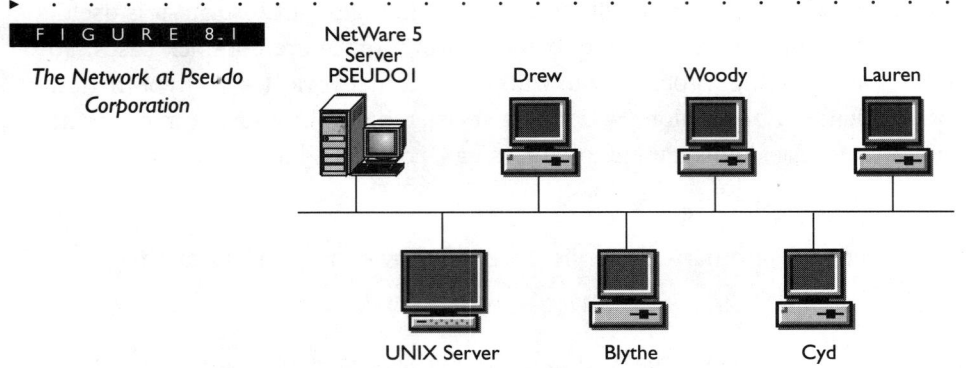

FIGURE 8.1

The Network at Pseudo Corporation

Planning IP Addressing

Your first decision is whether you want to attach your network to the Internet, in which case you must obtain a range of Internet IP addresses. If you will be connecting through a commercial Internet access provider, as is most common these days, the InterNIC expects you to obtain addresses from your service provider, which has been assigned blocks of IP addresses for use by their customers. You may want to begin, even at an early stage, to identify Internet service providers in your area and perhaps lease an IP address range so that you can configure your network with its final IP addresses. If you will never connect to the Internet, you have the luxury of selecting your own IP addresses. Go ahead, be a big shot and configure your office with a class A address. Why not?!

Now that you have an IP address, you need to decide whether your network will require subnetting. If the network will be segmented by routers, and you will have more segments than IP addresses, subnetting is a necessity. But you may want to plan for subnetting in the future even if you won't be subnetting now. To make your network subnetting easy to reconfigure, assign hostids starting with the low-order (rightmost) bits of the hostid field. For a class B address, you should begin assigning hostids in the following order:

```
00000000 00000001    0.1

00000000 00000010    0.2

00000000 00000011    0.3

00000000 00000100    0.4
```

. . . and so forth. If you will be employing subnets, number your subnets from left to right. Again, looking at the hostid portion of a class B address, you would create subnets in the following order:

```
10000000 00000000    128.0

01000000 00000000    64.0

11000000 00000000    192.0

00100000 00000000    32.0

01100000 00000000    96.0

11100000 00000000    224.0
```

This approach creates a buffer of unassigned bits in the center of the hostid field. You have considerable freedom to add or remove bits from the subnetid field without running into bits that are already assigned as parts of existing subnetids or hostids. Yes, you have to change the subnet masks on your hosts, but the IP addresses you have assigned remain valid.

Figure 8.2 shows the example network, including the IP addresses that will be assigned to each host. When planning, you may find it convenient to reserve a few low hostids you can easily remember to identify routers, servers, and other hosts you need to access frequently.

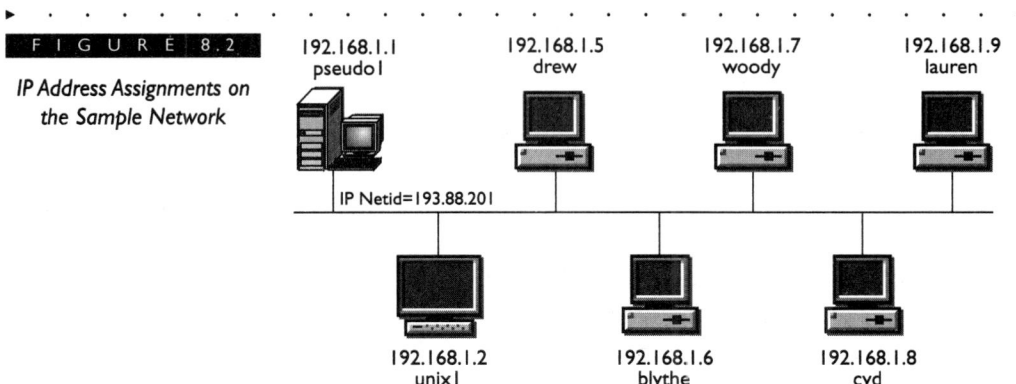

F I G U R E 8.2

IP Address Assignments on the Sample Network

192.168.1.1
pseudo1

192.168.1.5
drew

192.168.1.7
woody

192.168.1.9
lauren

IP Netid=193.88.201

192.168.1.2
unix1

192.168.1.6
blythe

192.168.1.8
cyd

Planning Host Names

Host names make the network easier to use and are required in some instances. Each host can be assigned a name along with up to ten aliases. Aliases are handy if the primary names are lengthy — if, for example, they are fully qualified domain names. Here are the IP addresses, host names, and aliases that will be configured in our example:

```
192.168.1.1 pseudo1.pseudo-corp.com pseudo1
192.168.1.2 www.pseudo-corp.com www unix1
192.168.1.5 drew.pseudo-corp.com drew ws1 pres
192.168.1.6 blythe.pseudo-corp.com blythe ws2 manuf
192.168.1.7 woody.pseudo-corp.com woody ws3 security
192.168.1.8 cyd.pseudo-corp.com cyd ws4 corpcom
192.168.1.9 lauren.pseudo-corp.com lauren ws5 testing
```

Use of aliases clearly provides considerable flexibility, enabling you to identify hosts by function, location, primary user, and by other characteristics as well. Some, such as the ws names, will be useful for network administrators. Others provide alternative names for users.

Next, you must decide how naming information will be made available. For a small network as in our example, you may choose to use static HOSTS files. However, because the goal is to connect to the Internet eventually, this is a good time to contemplate establishing a name server.

If your network doesn't already have a DNS name server, the NetWare 5 DNS server is an ideal name service for your TCP/IP network. The NetWare 5 DNS service is tightly integrated with NDS, as you will see in Chapter 11, which provides several benefits. And the NetWare 5 DNS service can work in conjunction with the NetWare 5 DHCP service, enabling DNS to update its name database as DHCP assigns and revokes IP address assignments, a feature that is dubbed *Dynamic DNS* (DDNS).

If your network already has a DNS name server in operation, such as a UNIX server running the Berkeley Internet Name Domain (BIND) DNS server, you may want to continue using your tried-and-true name server. You will give up DDNS, but otherwise BIND will meet your DNS name service requirements.

If you will be configuring your hosts to obtain names from a name server, you will need to configure each host with the IP address of the name server. For our example, we will assume that the name server will be the UNIX host with the IP address 192.168.1.2.

Okay, you have decided that your network will be using a DNS name service. Should you go to the trouble of creating static HOSTS files as well? It may not be a bad idea. If you are running a single name server (two is the preferred minimum) and the name server is down for any reason, your users can use HOSTS files to resolve names. If you are on the Internet, your local HOSTS files won't enable outside users to continue to resolve your domain names, but HOSTS files enable your local users to continue to function locally. Therefore, static HOSTS files that list at least the most critical hosts may be a good safety precaution — but HOSTS files quickly become unmanageable as networks grow in scope.

Planning the Server Hardware Configuration

The only hardware characteristic of concern in this chapter is the type of network adapter along with its hardware settings. You need to record the hardware settings of all your adapters, including IRQs, port addresses, and so forth. The adapter in the server is a PCI adapter that requires only the following configuration parameters:

▶ Driver: E100B.LAN

▶ Slot: 3

Planning Frame Types and Bindings

This network will be a Pure IP network and only TCP/IP must be bound to the E100B adapter. NetWare TCP/IP is most commonly configured with the Ethernet_II frame type, although Ethernet_SNAP may also be used. Ethernet II frames are required for the Internet, however, so that is the correct choice for this network. In fact, there is seldom a good reason to select the Ethernet_SNAP frame type.

Each frame type will be assigned a name when it is loaded. This book uses adapter names that follow Novell's conventions. For my Intel EtherExpress adapters, the adapter name E100B_1_EII would be used for the first network adapter bound with the Ethernet_II frame type.

▶ . . . . ◀

Configuring TCP/IP Database Files

Some features of TCP/IP are configured by entering data into database files that are stored in the directory SYS:ETC. The files are:

- ▶ SYS:ETC\HOSTS

- ▶ SYS:ETC\NETWORKS

- ▶ SYS:ETC\GATEWAYS

- ▶ SYS:ETC\PROTOCOL

- ▶ SYS:ETC\SERVICES

When NetWare is installed, samples of these files are placed in the SYS:ETC\SAMPLES directory. Although you could create your own files from scratch, it is easier to use the sample files as templates. Some of the sample files may be used with little or no alteration. Before you begin to create the configuration database files for your network, copy the sample files from SYS:ETC\SAMPLES to SYS:ETC. All of the database files are simply text files that may be edited with any text editor.

The following sections will examine each of the configuration files along with any modifications required for the example network.

SYS:ETC\HOSTS

The HOSTS file associates IP addresses with host names and aliases. The sample HOSTS file illustrates the file format:

```
#
# SYS:ETC\HOSTS
#
#   Mappings of host names and host aliases to IP address.
#
```

```
127.0.0.1  loopback lb localhost # normal loopback address


#

# examples from Novell network

#

130.57.4.2    ta tahiti ta.novell.com loghost

130.57.6.40   osd-frog frog

130.57.6.144  sj-in5 in5

192.67.172.71 sj-in1 in1


#

# interesting addresses on the Internet

#

192.67.67.20  sri-nic.arpa nic.ddn.mil nic

26.2.0.74     wsmr-simtel20.army.mil simtel20
```

An entry in a HOSTS file has the following format:

```
ipaddress hostname [alias1] [alias2] [alias10] #comment
```

Each field must be separated from the next by at least one space or tab character.

The *ipaddress* is the IP address of the host, which is ordinarily expressed in dotted decimal form. It can also be stated in dotted-hexadecimal. Using dotted-hex, the IP address 192.168.1.2 would be 0xC3.0x53.0xC9.0x2.

The *hostname* is a name for the system that owns the IP address. Host names cannot contain space, tab, or # characters. The *alias* is simply a nickname that may be used in place of the host name. Aliases follow the same character rules as host names and up to ten aliases may be specified. Host names and aliases must be unique within the HOSTS file. In other words, a given host name or alias must not be associated with more than one IP address.

A # character indicates the beginning of a comment. Any text between the # and the carriage return/line feed characters at the end of the line will be ignored.

Here is the HOSTS file for the PSEUDO1 server:

```
#
# SYS:ETC\HOSTS
#
#IP Address      HOSTNAME               Aliases
127.0.0.1        loopback               lb localhost


192.168.1.1      pseudo11.pseudo-corp.com     pseudo1 fs1
192.168.1.2      www.pseudo-corp.com     www unix1
192.168.1.5      drew.pseudo-corp.com     drew ws1 pres
192.168.1.6      blythe.pseudo-corp.com     blythe ws2 manuf
192.168.1.7      woody.pseudo-corp.com     woody ws3 security
192.168.1.8      cyd.pseudo-corp.com     cyd ws4 corpcom
192.168.1.9      lauren.pseudo-corp.com     lauren ws5 testing
```

NOTE **The HOSTS file conventionally includes an entry for the address 127.0.0.1, which is used for testing host TCP/IP configurations. Any datagrams sent to address 127.0.0.1 are reflected back and do not reach the network. This looping back demonstrates that lower-level protocol layers are properly configured and functioning.**

The same HOSTS file may be used on all of the TCP/IP hosts on your network. You may wish to configure users' login scripts so that their local HOSTS file is updated periodically by copying it from a master file on the server.

SYS:ETC\NETWORKS

The NETWORKS file supplies logical names for networks much as HOSTS provides logical names for hosts. Following is the sample NETWORKS file. (If I remind you that the Bears are the football team at the University of California, Berkeley, can you guess the environment that originated this file?)

```
#
# SYS:ETC\NETWORKS
#
#              Network numbers
#
loopback    127      # fictitious interral loopback network
novellnet   130.57  # Novell's network number


#
# Internet networks
#
arpanet     10   arpa # historical network
milnet      26        # not so historical military net
ucb-ether   46        # Go bears!
```

The format of an entry in the NETWORKS file is as follows:

```
netname netid[/netmask] alias #comment
```

The *netname* is simply a logical name for the network. Network names must adhere to the the same rules as host names. The *alias* field enables each network name to be assigned an alias if desired.

The *netid* is the netid portion of the IP address associated with the network, expressed in dotted-decimal or hexadecimal form. If desired, a subnet mask can be specified using the optional mask parameter. If a subnet mask is not specified, the default subnet mask is used.

Networks don't really need names, but they can make the network administrator's life a lot easier. Among other things, network names can be used to identify routes in the GATEWAYS database, which is described in the next section. A NETWORKS file is not required for the Pseudo Corporation network, but the following NETWORKS file will serve as an example:

```
#
#  SYS:ETC\NETWORKS
#
#
loopback            127
pseudonet1          192.168.1
```

NOTE

> **When a network is described in SYS:ETC\NETWORKS, it is identified by name in TCPCON. (You can use the Tab key to switch between name and IP address formats.) TCPCON is described in Chapter 13.**

SYS:ETC\GATEWAYS

The GATEWAYS database file includes static routing information. If a dynamic routing protocol (RIP or OSPF) is not loaded, static routes can be read into the server's routing tables by loading the TCPIP NLM with the option STATIC=YES. Here is the sample GATEWAYS file:

```
#
#  SYS:ETC\GATEWAYS
#
#  List of unusual routes that must be added to the routing
#  database statically.
#
#  Normally you will not need this file, as most routing
```

```
# infcrmation should be available through the routing

# protocols.

#


# Examples.   These entries will not be useful to you.

#net milnet gateway sj-in5 metric 3 active  # to milnet
through in5.

#net arpa gateway sj-in1 passive   # to arpanet.  in1 is
passive.

#host 130.57.6.40 gateway 192.67.172.55   # route with
numbers.
```

This file can define routes to remote hosts and networks. The syntax for a host route is as follows:

```
HOST {ipaddress | hostname} GATEWAY routeraddress
[METRIC cost] [ACTIVE | PASSIVE]
```

The syntax for a network route is as follows:

```
NET {netid | netname} GATEWAY routeradaress
[METRIC cost] [ACTIVE | PASSIVE]
```

Each entry states "to reach this remote destination, here is the next gateway to use." The HOST and NET keywords describe the type of address that the destination defines:

▸ For a HOST entry, the destination can be a host IP address, or it can be a host name that is defined in the HOSTS file.

▸ For a NET entry, the destination can be a netid (the network address portion only of the IP address), or it can be a network name defined in the NETWORKS file. To include a subnet mask with the netid, enter the address with the format *netid/netmask*, for example: 10.1.0.0/255.255.0.0.

The *routeraddress* is the IP address of a router attached to a network that is connected directly to this host. Any datagrams that are directed to the destination network or host will be forwarded to this IP address. The optional cost represents the cost of this route. If a METRIC parameter is not specified, the default cost is 1.

By default, routes that the host receives from the GATEWAYS database are PASSIVE, meaning that they do not expire. Routes that are flagged as ACTIVE must be refreshed through ICMP protocol messages received from other routers. Active routes that are not refreshed will expire eventually and be purged from the database.

NOTE

Typically, each TCP/IP host will be defined with a default route, which states "any time I don't have a defined route to a destination, I will send the datagram to this default IP address." A default route is specified in a NET database entry with a netid of 0. The following entry defines a default route:

```
Net 0 Gateway 128.2.00.2 Metric 1 Passive
```

For an IP host attached to a single network (a host referred to as an *end node*), typically the GATEWAYS file will contain only a default route entry.

The GATEWAYS file has been described here so that all the configuration database files are defined together, but it is not required for the sample network. Static routing will be revisited in detail in Chapter 10. Unlike the other database files, which may be usable by all hosts without modification, the GATEWAYS file must be explicitly tailored to each host, depending on the host's location in the network topology.

SYS:ETC\PROTOCOL

The PROTOCOL database file identifies the names and numbers of TCP/IP protocols. Protocol numbers are used to complete the protocol ID field in the IP header, which identifies the upper-layer protocol associated with the datagram. For many protocols, the Internet Assigned Numbers Authority (IANA) has assigned official protocol numbers, which are recorded in the RFC titled *Assigned Numbers* (currently RFC 1700).

An entry in the PROTOCOL file has the following syntax:

protocol_name number [alias] [#comment]

The *protocol_name* states the name of the protocol. A protocol name cannot contain tab, space, or # characters. An alternate name for the protocol can be specified with the alias parameter. Service names and aliases must be unique within the PROTOCOL database. The number is the protocol number. Most are taken from the *Assigned Numbers* RFC. However, the PROTOCOL database file can be used to configure the host for new protocols that have not been assigned numbers by IANA. All characters between a # character and the end of a line are regarded as comment text and are not processed.

The sample PROTOCOL file follows. The sample file can typically be used without alteration but will require modification if additional TCP/IP protocols are installed.

```
#
# SYS:ETC\PROTOCOL
#
#   Internet (IP) protocols
#
ip      0    IP    # internet protocol, pseudo protocol number
icmp    1    ICMP  # internet control message protocol
igmp    2    IGMP  # internet group multicast protocol
ggp     3    GGP   # gateway-gateway protocol
tcp     6    TCP   # transmission control protocol
pup     12   PUP   # PARC universal packet protocol
udp     17   UDP   # user datagram protocol
```

You should be able to use the sample PROTOCOL file without alteration.

SYS:ETC\SERVICES

Entries in the SERVICES file define services along with the transport protocols and ports the services utilize. For example, an entry in the SERVICES file for FTP indicates that FTP will use port 21 with the TCP protocol. The syntax of an entry in the SERVICES file is as follows:

```
service port/transport [alias] [#comment]
```

The *service* parameter is the name of the service defined by the entry. Service names may not contain tab, space, or # characters, and each service must be uniquely named. The port parameter states the port number that will be used when the service uses the transport protocol defined by transport. All characters between a # character and the end of a line are regarded as comment text and are not processed.

The sample SERVICES file included with NetWare is lengthy, but you will get the gist of the file contents from the following sample:

```
#

# SYS:ETC\SERVICES

#

# Network service mappings.  Maps service names to

# transport protocol and transport protocol ports.

#

echo       7/udp

echo       7/tcp

discard    9/udp      sink null

discard    9/tcp      sink null

systat     11/tcp

daytime    13/udp

daytime    13/tcp

netstat    15/tcp
```

```
ftp-data      20/tcp

ftp           21/tcp

telnet        23/tcp

smtp          25/tcp      mail

time          37/tcp      timserver

time          37/udp      timserver

name          42/udp      nameserver

whois         43/tcp      nicname      # usually to sri-nic

domain        53/udp

domain        53/tcp

hostnames     101/tcp     hostname     # usually to sri-nic

sunrpc        111/udp

sunrpc        111/tcp

#

#

# Host specific functions

#

tftp          69/udp

rje           77/tcp

finger        79/tcp

link          87/tcp      ttylink

supdup        95/tcp

iso-tsap      102/tcp

x400          103/tcp                  # ISO Mail

x400-snd      104/tcp
```

```
csnet-ns    105/tcp

pop-2       109/tcp                      # Post Office

uucp-path   117/tcp

nntp        119/tcp     usenet          # Network News Transfer

ntp         123/tcp                     # Network Time Protocol

NeWS        144/tcp     news            # Window System

#

# UNIX specific services

#

# these are NOT officially assigned

#

exec        512/tcp

login       513/tcp

shell       514/tcp     cmd             # no passwords used

printer     515/tcp     spooler         # experimental

courier     530/tcp     rpc             # experimental

biff        512/udp     comsat

who      513/udp     whod

syslog   514/udp

talk     517/udp

route    520/udp     router routed

new-rwhc     550/udp     new-who    # experimental

rmonitor     560/udp     rmonitord  # experimental

monitor 561/udp             # experimental
```

```
ingreslock     1524/tcp

snmp      161/udp          # Simple Network Mgmt Protocol

snmp-trap      162/udp     snmptrap     # SNMP trap (event)
messages
```

Notice in the sample file that some services are listed twice, in association with both TCP and UDP. These services may run over either transport protocol, depending on the implementation. You should be able to use the sample SERVICES file without alteration.

When a service is described in SYS:ETC\SERVICES, the service is identified in TCPCON by name rather than by port number. You can press the Tab key to switch between service name and port number formats. TCPCON is described in Chapter 13.

NOTE

Tuning Communication Parameters

You should be aware of at least two server tuning parameters that can affect network performance. These parameters determine the maximum number of packet receive buffers and the maximum packet size that the server can receive.

Maximum Packet Receive Buffers

Receive buffers are used to temporarily store incoming data that must await server processing. If insufficient buffers are available to handle incoming data, frames may be lost, requiring upper-layer protocols to request retransmission. Clearly, retransmission of frames is inefficient and should be avoided.

You should have at least one packet receive buffer for each user and one for each application accessing the server. Each application accessing the server opens up a communication channel that requires an available packet receive buffer. For users of multitasking operating systems such as Windows and OS/2, who may have several applications running, you may need to allocate several packet receive buffers per user.

You can observe free packet receive buffers in the NetWare console MONITOR utility. On a NetWare 5 server, examine the *Packet receive buffers* field in the General Information window. If the value you observe consistently approaches the configured maximum, the value of Maximum Packet Receive Buffers should be increased.

The command to set the maximum number of packet receive buffers is

SET MAXIMUM PACKET RECEIVE BUFFERS=n

where n is a number in the range of 50–4294967295 (NetWare 5), 50–4,000 (NetWare 4) or 50–2000 (NetWare 3). The default value is 500 for NetWare 5. Configure higher values as required based on the number of users and running applications on your network. The SET command can be added to the AUTOEXEC.NCF file, or you can configure it in MONITOR as described later in this chapter (see the section "Setting Communication Parameters Using MONITOR").

Maximum Physical Receive Packet Size

Different physical networks have different maximum packet sizes. The Maximum Physical Receive Packet Receive Size should be configured to accommodate the largest frames possible for the network types employed. If the value is too small, large frames will be lost. If the value is too large, system memory will be used inefficiently.

As you learned in Chapter 3, the maximum size of an Ethernet packet is 1518 bytes, which is also Novell's recommendation for the Maximum Physical Receive Packet Size parameter with Ethernet Networks. The recommended value for token ring networks is 4202. If a server is connected to two network types, this parameter must be configured for the network with the largest maximum packet size

Because the example network for Pseudo Corporation currently is exclusively Ethernet, this parameter should be changed from its default value to a value of 1518.

The command to increase the physical receive packet size is

SET MAXIMUM PHYSICAL RECEIVE PACKET SIZE=n

where n is a number between 618 and 24682 (for NetWare 4.1 or 3.12). The default value is 4202 for both NetWare versions. This parameter is entered in the

STARTUP.NCF file. To change the parameter, you must add the above SET command to the STARTUP.NCF file. The easiest way to modify STARTUP.NCF is to use the NWCONFIG utility. In NWCONFIG, select the path *NCF File Options* ⇨ *Edit STARTUP.NCF file* to open the editor. You can also adjust SET parameters in the MONITOR utility as described later in this chapter.

You must restart the server to activate any changes made in the STARTUP.NCF file.

Setting Communication Parameters Using MONITOR

The NetWare 5 MONITOR utility is a more convenient way to update many SET parameters. (NetWare 4 uses the SERVMAN utility in much the same manner.) You cannot make an error in the command syntax or in the value assigned, and MONITOR ensures that the changes are stored in the correct NCF file. To edit a communication parameter:

1. Start MONITOR with the console command **LOAD MONITOR**. (Start SERVMAN in NetWare 4.)

2. Select *Server parameters* in the Available Options menu. This will open the Select a parameter category menu.

3. Select *Communications* in the Select a parameter category menu. This will open the Communications Parameters window shown in Figure 8.3.

4. To edit a field, highlight the field and press Enter. A box at the bottom of the screen briefly describes the parameter, along with the range of values that can be assigned.

5. After changing the field, press Enter.

6. When changes have been completed, press Esc twice.

Parameters modified by MONITOR are stored in a hidden configuration file that can be modified only by using MONITOR. Settings stored in the configuration file are persistent and are reactivated when the NetWare server is restarted.

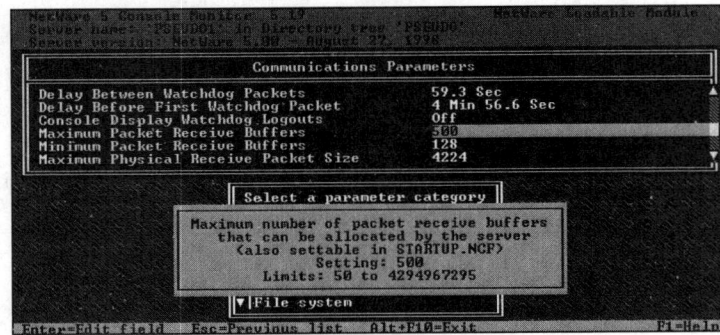

F I G U R E   8.3

Managing Communications
Parameters in MONITOR

If required, you can reset most parameters to their default values by executing the command RESET ENVIRONMENT. This command resets all parameters in the hidden configuration file to their default values and restores default values of most parameters in the running configuration.

Some parameters, such as Maximum Physical Receive Packet Size, can be changed only by placing the SET command in the STARTUP.NCF file and restarting the server. Commands that must be placed in STARTUP.NCF and parameters that are manually added to AUTOEXEC.NCF are unaffected by the RESET ENVIRONMENT command.

Configuring and Activating TCP/IP

Now that you have made your plans and configured the server database files, TCP/IP can be activated on the server. Activation is a three-step process:

1. Loading the required protocols

2. Loading MLIDs

3. Binding protocols to MLIDs

When you install NetWare 5, you select one of the following protocol configurations:

▸ **IP only.** You specify the IP address and subnet mask of at least one network adapter. Optionally, you can specify a default gateway IP address. IPX protocols are installed but not bound to a network adapter. The server is configured to support IPX compatibility mode.

▸ **IPX only.** No IP protocols are configured.

▸ **IP and IPX.** Both IP and IPX are installed. Both are bound to network adapters. The server is configured to support IPX compatibility mode.

For any of these options, server installation configures basic support for the selected protocols, placing the required LOAD and BIND commands in AUTOEXEC.NCF. The commands added to AUTOEXEC.NCF during server installation are very basic. They enable the server to communicate with the protocol stack you specified during installation, but they don't enable any advanced capabilities such as routing.

The protocol commands in AUTOEXEC.NCF can be manually edited by an administrator. The approach of manually adding commands to AUTOEXEC.NCF works, but leaves something to be desired. The syntaxes of the commands are a bit involved, and administrators must understand the details of the command structure to make things work. Manual entry does not ensure that all necessary parameters will be present or that commands will execute in the correct order. And, because features like MLID logical names are entered as plain text, administrators often use different names and command sequences, making it difficult to maintain configuration consistency in a multiserver environment. Wouldn't it be nice if configuring networks was as easy as, say, managing users with SYSCON or NWADMIN? Of course, I wouldn't be asking that question if such a tool was not included with NetWare 5. Its name is INETCFG.

INETCFG (Internetworking Configuration) is a menu-driven utility included with the MultiProtocol Router bundled with intraNetWare 4.11 and NetWare 5. The INETCFG utility is quite comprehensive and eliminates the need to edit the commands directly in a NetWare command file. Additionally, INETCFG is the only way to configure advanced protocol capabilities such as RIP II and OSPF routing.

Understanding TCP/IP LOAD and BIND Commands

Before we delve into INETCFG, you need a basic understanding of the syntax and usage of the protocol configuration commands required for TCP/IP. This knowledge can be very important when troubleshooting the configuration of a NetWare server. Also, you may want to examine the commands generated by INETCFG and review them for correctness. And, because lots of NetWare 3 servers remain in operation, you need to know how the manual commands work. So let's start by configuring the server manually. Let's examine the procedures for loading TCP/IP protocols and binding network adapters assuming that no protocols are currently configured.

The Network Configuration Before Loading TCP/IP

Until a protocol stack is loaded and bound to a network adapter, the NetWare server's network configuration consists of three disjointed components. At the top are NetWare Services—the home of the NetWare Core Protocols. Figure 8.4 also contains a box to indicate the presence of TCP/IP processes such as World Wide Web or FTP servers.

Somewhere in the middle is the Link Support Layer (LSL), which is the "glue" that enables network protocols to communicate with network adapters. At the bottom is the network adapter hardware, installed in a slot but dormant because no drivers enable it to communicate with NetWare. The next few sections fill in the gaps so that a communication path exists between NCP and the network adapter.

FIGURE 8.4		
Server Configuration Before Installing the TCP/IP Protocol Stack	NetWare Services (NetWare Core Protocol)	TCP/IP Services (WWW, FTP, etc.)

Link Support Layer (LSL)

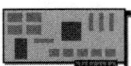

Configuring and Loading TCPIP.NLM

The TCP/IP protocols are packaged in the file TCPIP.NLM. To load the TCP/IP protocol stack, the command LOAD TCPIP is added to the AUTOEXEC.NCF file. Loading TCP/IP, or any NLM for that matter, dynamically links the NLM with the operating system. Figure 8.5 shows the server configuration after TCP/IP protocol support has been installed.

FIGURE 8.5

Server Configuration After Installing Transport Protocols

NetWare Services (NetWare Core Protocol)	TCP/IP Services (WWW, FTP, etc.)
TCP/IP Protocol Stack (TCPIP.NLM)	
Link Support Layer (LSL)	

The syntax of the LOAD TCPIP command is as follows:

```
LOAD TCPIP [FORWARD = {YES | NO}]
    [DIRBC = {YES | NO}]
    [LOADSHARING = {YES | NO}]
    [RIP = {YES | NO}]
    [STATIC = {YES | NO}
    [TRAP = ip_address]
```

Table 8.1 describes the LOAD TCPIP parameters.

	PARAMETER	VALUES	PURPOSE
TABLE 8.1 *Parameters for TCPIP.NLM*	FORWARD	YES or NO	If this host has interfaces on two TCP/IP network segments, it will forward datagrams between network segments FORWARD=YES. The default value is NO.
	DIRBC	YES or NO	Specifies whether the router will forward directed broadcasts, ie. a broadcast directed to a specific network. An example directed broadcast address is 172.16.255.255. Directed broadcasting is active only when forwarding is enabled (FORWARD=YES). The default value is NO.
	LOADSHARING	YES or NO	Load sharing enables traffic to be divided over equal-cost routes learned from OSPF. The maximum number of routes to a destination network is 4. The default value is NO.
	RIP	YES or NO	If RIP=YES, this host will function as a RIP router. The default value is YES.
	STATIC	YES or NO	If STATIC=YES TCP/IP includes static routes in its routing table. Static routes are stored in SYS:ETC\GATEWAYS and can be defined by editing the GATEWAYS file directly or through the INETCFG or TCPCON utilities. The default value is NO.
	TRAP	IP address	The IP address of a host to which SNMP trap messages should be sent.

NetWare servers that have a single network interface are referred to as *end nodes*. An end node cannot forward datagrams to other networks, which explains why the default value of FORWARD is NO. A host that is connected to two or more TCP/IP networks is referred to as a *multihomed host*. Multihomed NetWare servers can function as routers, and the value of FORWARD should be YES.

Because even an end node NetWare server may be a communication hub for the internetwork, it makes tremendous sense for the majority of NetWare servers to keep their routing tables up-to-date by running a routing protocol. This explains why the default value of the RIP parameter is YES. In Chapter 10, you will learn more about configuring RIP (and about configuring OSPF as well).

The TRAP parameter enables the server to direct SNMP trap messages to an SNMP console. Chapter 13 will discuss SNMP management using the TCPCON utility, and you will see the TRAP parameter in action at that time.

To load TCP/IP with forwarding and RIP on, add the following command to the AUTOEXEC.NCF file:

```
LOAD TCPIP FORWARD=YES RIP=YES
```

Loading MLIDs

The next step is to fill the gap between the LSL and the network adapter hardware. This is done by installing driver software that communicates between the LSL and the network adapter hardware.

Each network interface adapter must be serviced by an MLID. As you learned in the previous chapter, an MLID is a multiple link interface driver, Novell's term for LAN driver software. NetWare includes a large number of MLIDs, packaged in NetWare Loadable Modules with the filename extension LAN. Like all NLMs, the LAN modules are activated on the server with the LOAD command. (As with standard NLMs, NetWare 5 permits you to omit the LOAD command when loading an NLM with the LAN extension.) The syntax for loading an MLID is as follows:

```
LOAD [path]LAN_driver [parameter=value...]
```

The *LAN_driver* parameter is the filename of the NLM file containing the driver. The LAN extension is assumed. If the LAN file is not stored in the SYS:SYSTEM directory, the path to the driver file can be included as a path parameter.

Nearly all LAN driver modules are configured with default parameters, and you may be able to load the driver without parameters if the adapter is configured for the default settings. In practice, however, it is much better to include each parameter explicitly when the command is stored in the AUTOEXEC.NCF file, documenting the driver configuration.

Table 8.2 lists most MLID parameters. Consult the documentation for your hardware to determine which hardware parameters apply to your configuration. (Note: All hardware parameters for the TOKEN driver are optional.)

TABLE 8.2	PARAMETER	VALUES	PURPOSE
Parameters for LAN Driver NLMs	DMA	Hardware defined	Reserves a DMA channel for use by the network board.
	FRAME	Ethernet_802.2 Ethernet_802.3 Ethernet_II Token-Ring Token-Ring_SNAP	Specifies the frame encapsulation that is to be used with this logical network. For Ethernet drivers shipped with NetWare 3.12 and 4.1, the default frame type is Ethernet_802.2. For the TOKEN driver, the default frame type is Token-Ring. ARCnet has a single frame type for all transports.
	INT	Hardware defined	Reserves an interrupt for use by the network board.
	LS	Hardware defined	Specifies the number of 802.5 link stations to be configured for the TOKEN driver.
	MEM	Hardware defined	Reserves a memory address for use by the driver.
	NAME	Up to 17 characters	A name that identifies this logical network interface.

PARAMETER	VALUES	PURPOSE
NODE	Node address	Can be used to override the physical addresses of some network adapter hardware.
PORT	Hardware defined	A memory address that is reserved for input/output use by this adapter.
RETRIES	0–255	Determines the number of times a LAN driver will attempt to retransmit a packet.
SAPS	Hardware defined	Specifies the 802.2 service access point for the TOKEN driver.
SLOT	1–8	On an EISA computer specifies the slot in which the target network board is installed. Hardware configuration parameters are taken from the EISA configuration.
TBC	0–2	Specifies the transmit buffer count for the TOKEN driver. The default value is 2.
TBZ	0 (use default) 96–65535	Specifies the transmit buffer size for the TOKEN driver. The default for this parameter is the value of the Maximum Physical Receive Packet Size parameter.

An example of a command that loads a LAN driver is:

```
LOAD E100B NAME=E100B_1_E82 FRAME=Ethernet_802.2 SLOT=3
```

Many drivers will prompt for required parameters that have not been specified. This is fine when the driver is entered from the command line, but the goal is to configure AUTOEXEC.NCF to start the server's communications automatically. Therefore, all parameters must be specified in the command line.

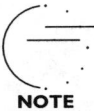

NOTE

In practice, you will almost never be directly editing the commands that load network drivers. Instead, you will be configuring the drivers in INETCFG. In that case, the forms that configure your network drivers will automatically prompt you for the required parameters.

Binding a Protocol to an MLID

At this point, the server is configured as shown in Figure 8.6. All of the communication layers are in place, but a crucial piece is missing. The LSL must be configured to serve as a communications link between specific network adapters and transport protocols.

FIGURE 8.6

Server with All Protocol Layers Installed

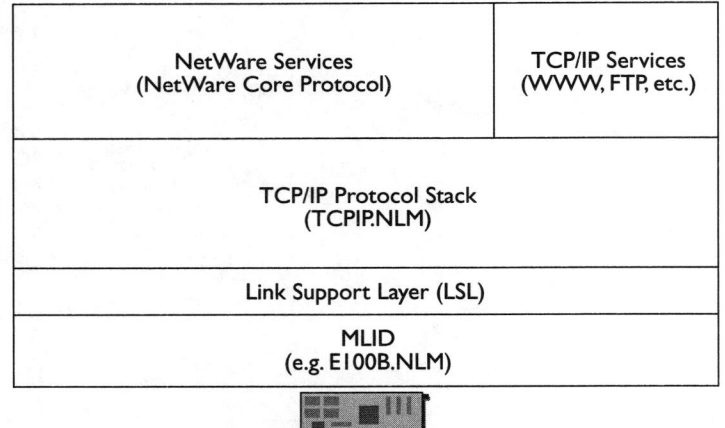

NetWare Services (NetWare Core Protocol)		TCP/IP Services (WWW, FTP, etc.)
TCP/IP Protocol Stack (TCPIP.NLM)		
Link Support Layer (LSL)		
MLID (e.g. E100B.NLM)		

That link is established by binding a protocol stack to a virtual LAN adapter, a function performed by the BIND command.

When binding the IP protocol, a variety of parameters must be considered. The parameters for the BIND IP command are listed in Table 8.3. The syntax of the BIND IP command is as follows:

```
BIND IP TO board_name

        [ADDR=ip_address]

        [MASK=subnet_mask]

        [GATE=gateway_address]

        [BCAST=broadcast_address]

        [DEFROUTE={YES | NO}]

        [ARP={YES | NO}]

        [POISON={YES | NO}]

        [COST=hop_count]
```

The *board_name* parameter must match the board name established when the corresponding MLID was loaded.

T A B L E 8.3	PARAMETER	VALUES	PURPOSE
Parameters for BIND IP	ADDR	IP address	The value of `ip_address` specifies the IP address assigned to this interface.
	MASK	Subnet mask	The `subnet_mask` specifies the subnet mask used for addressing on the attached network.
	GATE	IP address	The `gateway_address` specifies a default gateway to be used on this network. If a default gateway is not specified, RIP is the source of routing information. This parameter may be entered in dotted decimal or dotted hexadecimal notation.

Continued

T A B L E 8.3 Continued	PARAMETER	VALUES	PURPOSE
	DEFROUTE	YES or NO	If TCPIP was loaded with the FORWARD=YES parameter, DEFROUTE=YES configures this server to advertise itself as a default gateway through RIP. The default value is NO.
	ARP	YES or NO	Specifies whether ARP is to be used to resolve IP addresses to hardware addresses. The default value is YES.
	POISON	YES or NO	Specifies whether this node will use poison reverse for routing updates sent to this interface. If POISON=NO, split horizon will be used. The default value is NO.
	COST	1–16	Specifies the cost metric for this interface. The default cost is 1.

An example of a BIND IP command is the following:

```
BIND IP TO E100B_1_EII ADDR=192.168.1.8 MASK=255.255.255.0
```

After protocols have been bound to network adapters, associations are established in the LSL layer that enable network adapters and protocols to communicate. NetWare communication configuration is complete, as shown in Figure 8.7. Notice that the TCP/IP protocol stack directs messages to the appropriate upper-layer process. Recall from Chapter 5 that each application-level process is assigned a port number. TCP and UDP use these port numbers to deliver message units to the appropriate upper-level process.

Enabling Support for Compatibility Mode

The configuration depicted in Figure 8.7 enables a NetWare 5 client to communicate with the NetWare 5 server using only TCP/IP protocols. Because NCP can now interoperate directly with TCP/IP, it is unnecessary to load IPX to enable normal NetWare 5 functionality. Clients can log on, access files, print, and execute NCP-based applications.

As you learned in Chapter 7, a variety of applications are written directly to the IPX and SPX protocols. To support these applications on a Pure IP network, a compatibility mode network must be configured. This procedure is extremely simple. After loading TCPIP.NLM, the SCMD.NLM is loaded. SCMD configures the compatibility mode component and, if necessary, loads IPX.

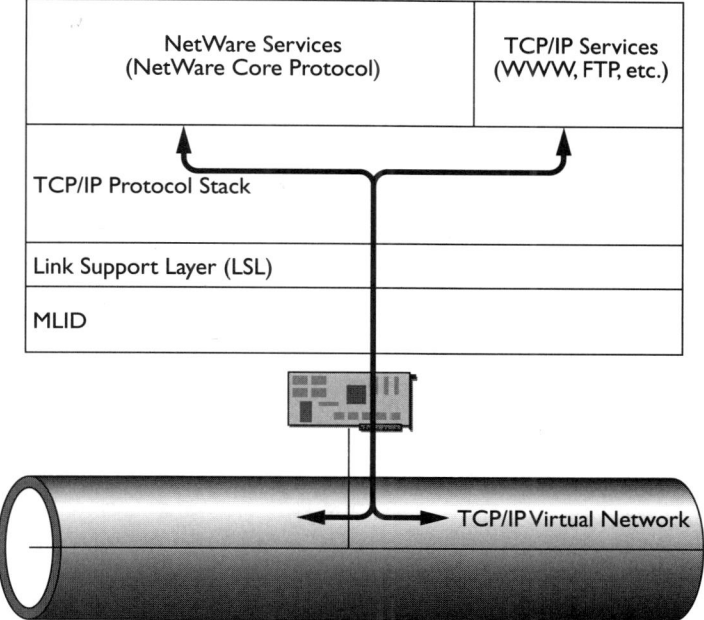

FIGURE 8.7

Completed TCP/IP Configuration of NetWare Server Communications

At the server end, the compatibility mode driver (SCMD.NLM) maintains a virtual IPX network. The command LOAD SCMD.NLM is added to the AUTOEXEC.NCF file whenever TCP/IP is configured during NetWare 5 installation. When SMCD.NLM is loaded, the protocol architecture of the NetWare 5 server has the configuration shown in Figure 8.8.

The compatibility mode process encapsulates and decapsulates IPX datagrams so that they can be transmitted through the Pure IP network. For example, when NCP is communicating through an IPX-dependent application, it routes outbound messages through IPX to the compatibility mode process, which encapsulates the messages in UDP datagrams. (TCP encapsulation can be configured optionally.) The encapsulated IPX datagrams are transported through the Pure IP network and are decapsulated by a compatibility mode process at the client end.

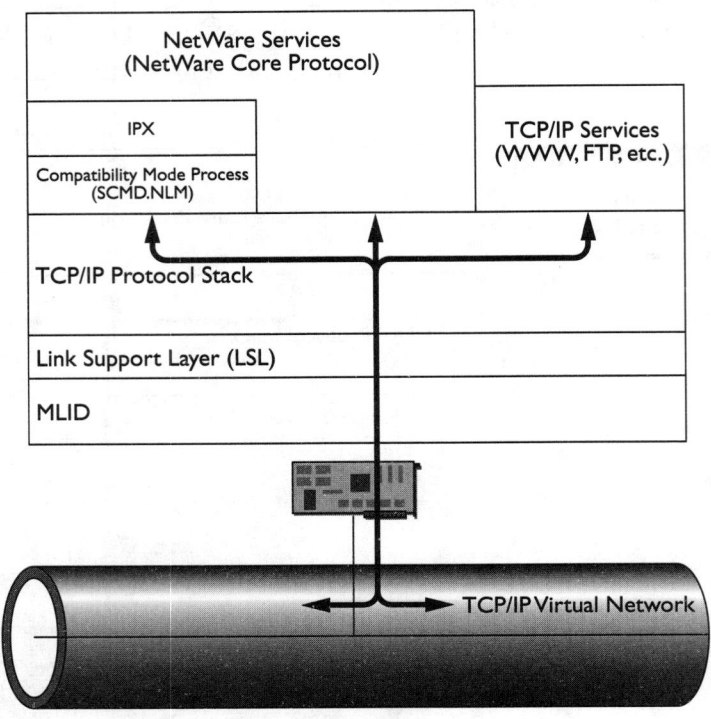

F I G U R E 8.8

Compatibility Mode Added to the TCP/IP Configuration

It is instructive to view the description of the compatibility mode driver included in the report generated by the console CONFIG command:

```
Compatibility Mode Driver

        Version 1.04c   August 13, 1998

        Hardware setting: I/O Port A55h

        Node address: 7E01C0A80102

        Frame type: CMD

        Board name: CMD Server

        LAN protocol: IPX network FFFFFFFD
```

The CMD network is configured with the default IPX network number FFFFFFFD. Notice that the CMD network is entirely virtual—it is not bound to a hardware network interface. SCMD.NLM is dependent on IPX and will load IPX.NLM if it is not loaded already.

SCMD.NLM also supports the migration gateway component that enables NetWare 5 IPX and IP networks to interoperate. We will return to SCMD.NLM and to its gateway capabilities in Chapter 15 ("Migrating to Pure IP"), in which we will examine the topics of networks that incorporate both IPX and IP protocol stacks.

NOTE

If you are disabling IPX protocols to establish a Pure IP network, you must manually add the command LOAD SCMD to AUTOEXEC.NCF. Add the command after LOAD TCPIP or, if the configuration is being managed via INETCFG, after the statement SYS:ETC\INITSYS.NCF. If TCP/IP support is added when NetWare 5 is installed, the LOAD SCMD command is added to the AUTOEXEC.NCF file.

Examples of Network Configurations

Now let's look at some complete examples of server configurations. We will start with the basic configuration for Pseudo Corporation, and then enhance the configuration as the network grows.

A Single-Segment Network

The server configuration for the network in Figure 8.2 represents a simple case. Because the network has a single cable segment, TCPIP will be configured without RIP or forwarding. Forwarding is off by default, but RIP must be disabled with the RIP=NO parameter.

The TCP/IP database files that apply to this network were shown in the preceding "Configuration" section. For this network, the server requires the files HOSTS, PROTOCOL, and SERVICES. Only the HOSTS file requires customization.

Because this server is connected to an Ethernet, the following command can be added to STARTUP.NCF:

```
SET MAXIMUM PHYSICAL RECEIVE PACKET SIZE=1518
```

The following commands are used to configure the network:

```
LOAD TCFIP RIP=NO

LOAD E1C0B INT=B PORT=340 FRAME=ETHERNET_II

NAME=E1C0B_1_EII

BIND IP TO E100B_1_EII ADDR=192.168.1.1
```

Because subnet masking is not employed, a MASK parameter is not required, and the default class C subnet mask will be used (255.255.255.0). All other parameters can be left at their default values as well.

Configuring a Routed Network

Few networks are as simple as the one shown in Figure 8.8, and we need to examine some more involved examples. Let's see what happens when Pseudo Corporation expands. Because the expanded network will support manufacturing operations, the company decides to use a token ring.

Pseudo Corporation is still constrained to the original class C address. Therefore, it becomes necessary to subnet the network. To allow room for future growth, the MIS department has decided to allocate three bits for the subnet mask, resulting in a subnet mask of 255.255.255.224. The Ethernet will be subnet 192.168.1.32, and the token ring will be subnet 192.168.1.64. For each host on the network, the IP address must be updated and a subnet mask must be added to the configuration. The new network configuration is shown in Figure 8.9. (Refer to Table 4.4 in Chapter 4 for a summary of the available IP addresses for a class C network that allocates three bits for the subnetid.)

The NetWare server will function as a router between the two networks. All employees need to access the Web server, so the NetWare server must route IP. Forwarding must be turned on (FORWARD=YES). It is not necessary to load RIP, however. RIP is responsible for exchanging route information between routers but does not perform the actual routing. Because the network has a single router, RIP is not needed — loading RIP would just waste memory.

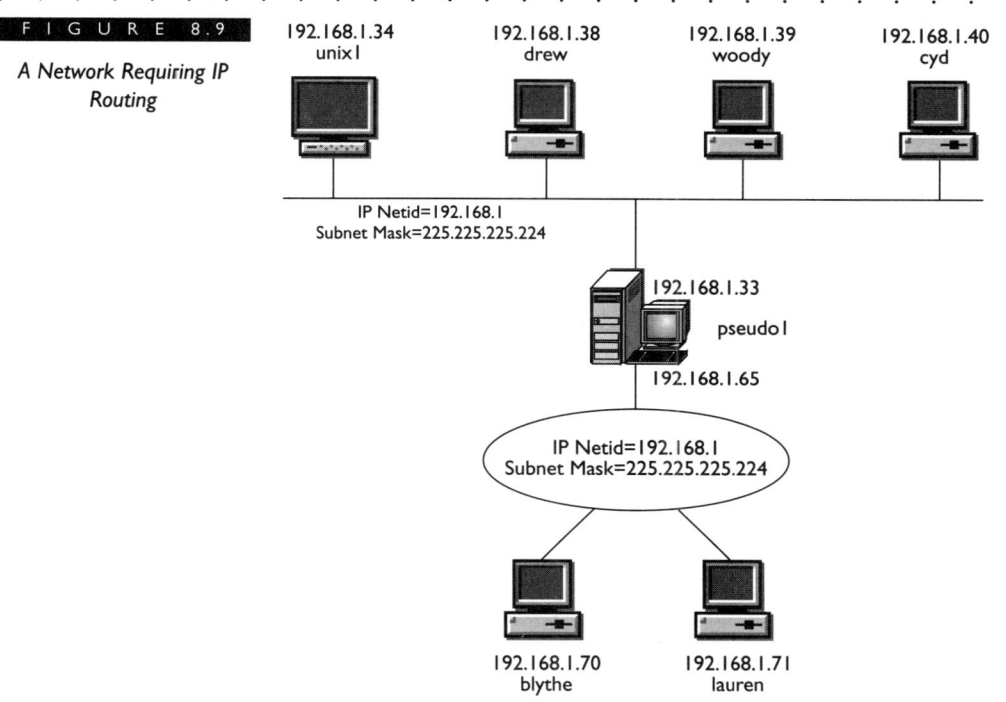

FIGURE 8.9

A Network Requiring IP Routing

192.168.1.34
unix1

192.168.1.38
drew

192.168.1.39
woody

192.168.1.40
cyd

IP Netid=192.168.1
Subnet Mask=225.225.225.224

192.168.1.33

pseudo1

192.168.1.65

IP Netid=192.168.1
Subnet Mask=225.225.225.224

192.168.1.70
blythe

192.168.1.71
lauren

As the token ring functions best with a larger frame, the following command will be entered in STARTUP.NCF to optimize the server for token ring:

```
SET MAXIMUM PHYSICAL RECEIVE PACKET SIZE=4202
```

Be aware that enlarging this parameter allocates somewhat more server memory to packet receive buffers. The administrator should pay close attention to server memory utilization to ensure that the server does not require additional memory in the new configuration. However, the administrator should always pay close attention to server memory utilization, so this admonition should be unnecessary.

The following configuration commands are used:

```
LOAD TCPIP    FORWARD=YES    RIP=NO

LOAD E100B....SLOT=3    FRAME=ETHERNET_II

NAME=E100B_1_EII
```

```
LOAD TOKEN                    FRAME=TOKEN-RING_SNAP

NAME=TOKEN_1_TSP

BIND IP  TO  E100B_1_EII  ADDR=192.168.1.33
MASK=255.255.255.224

BIND IP  TO TOKEN_1_TSP   ADDR=192.168.1.65
MASK=255.255.255.224
```

If this network had been configured with two Ethernet segments, serviced by two E100B adapters, the configuration commands would resemble the following:

```
LOAD TCPIP FORWARD=YES RIP=NO

LOAD E100B SLOT=3 FRAME=ETHERNET_II    NAME=E100B_1_EII

LOAD E100B SLOT=2 FRAME=ETHERNET_II    NAME=E100B_2_EII

BIND IP  TO E100B_1_EII  ADDR=192.168.1.33
MASK=255.255.255.224

BIND IP  TO E100B_2_EII   ADDR=192.168.1.65
MASK=255.255.255.224
```

Because the host IP addresses have changed to accommodate subnetting, the HOSTS and NETWORKS files must be updated. Here is the new HOSTS file:

```
#

# SYS:ETC\HOSTS

#

#IP Address      HOSTNAME              Aliases
127.0.0.1        loopback              lb localhost
192.168.1.33     fs1.pseudo-corp.com   pseudo1 fs1e  #Ethernet
192.168.1.34     www.pseudo-corp.com   www unix1
192.168.1.38     drew.pseudo-corp.com  drew ws1 pres
192.168.1.39     woody.pseudo-corp.com woody ws3 security
192.168.1.40     cyd.pseudo-corp.com   cyd ws4 corpcom
```

```
192.168.1.65    fs1t                              #token ring

192.168.1.70    blythe.pseudo-corp.com   blythe ws2 manuf

192.168.1.71    lauren.pseudo-corp.com   lauren ws5 testing
```

Pseudo1 is a multihomed computer. A given host name can be resolved to only one IP address. For testing purposes, the network administrator chose to add an entry for the token ring interface on pseudo1. When you learn about testing network communications, you will appreciate the convenience this name offers.

To reflect the use of subnetting and the added network segment, the NETWORKS file would be updated to include the subnetid:

```
#

# SYS:ETC\NETWORKS

#

#

loopback    127

pseudcnet1        192.168.1.32

pseudcnet2        192.168.1.64
```

A Network Segment with Two NetWare File Servers

The Information Technology department at Pseudo Corporation has decided to add a file server used for testing new network hardware and software. Figure 8.10 shows how the IT server will be attached. On a Pure IP network, the primary configuration concern is routing.

The communications configuration for the new server would be established with the following commands in AUTOEXEC.NCF:

```
LOAD TCPIP RIP=YES

LOAD E100B SLOT=3 FRAME=ETHERNET_II    NAME=E100B_1_EII

BIND IP  TO E100B_1_EII ADDR=192.168.1.35
MASK=255.255.255.224
```

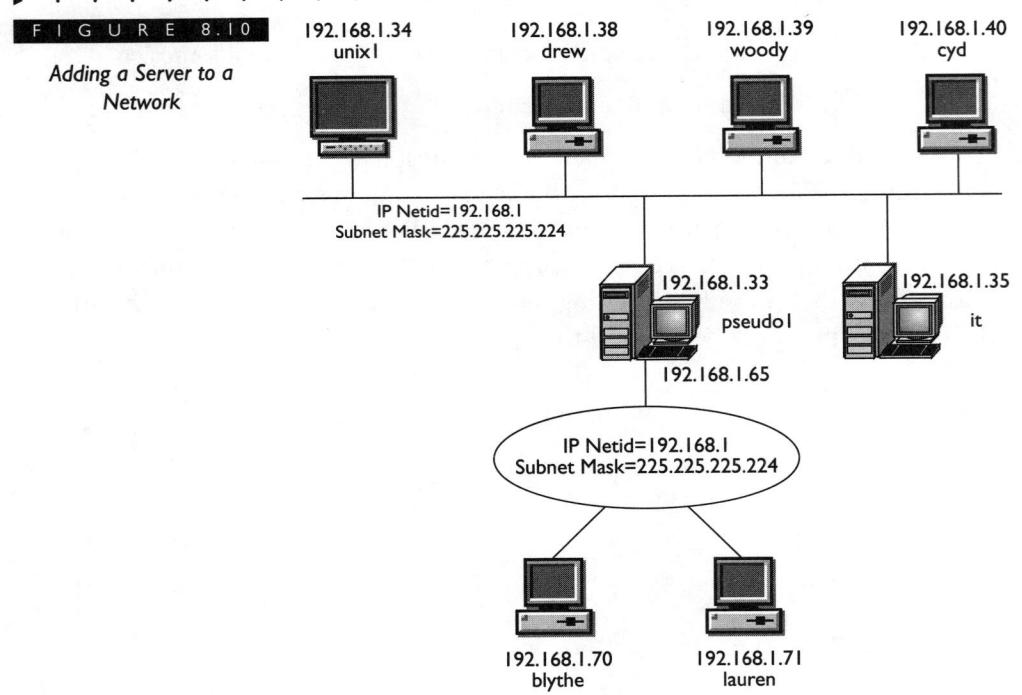

F I G U R E   8 . 1 0

Adding a Server to a Network

RIP has been turned on, even though this is an end node, which enables it1 to learn routes from pseudo1. Alternatively, static routes could be configured, a procedure described in Chapter 10.

Because RIP is being used, it must be enabled on pseudo1. The AUTOEXEC.NCF file on PSEUDO1 must be updated to load TCP/IP as follows:

```
LOAD TCPIP FORWARD=YES
```

The final required change is that the network HOSTS files must be updated with an entry for the new computer.

NOTE

The NetWare MultiProtocol Router included with NetWare 5 supports use of the ICMP Router Discovery Protocol, which would enable it1 to discover pseudo1 as an available router. This arrangement would generate less overhead traffic than RIP, and might be the preferable configuration. You will see how to configure ICMP router discovery in the Chapter 10.

Network Configuration with INETCFG

You should not even consider defining network communications for NetWare 5 from the command line. Manual configuration is tedious and error-prone, and many of the more advanced features offered by NetWare 5 cannot be configured from the command line.

Configuring network communication for NetWare 5 follows the same three steps used to configure the network from AUTOEXEC.NCF, although a slightly different order will be followed here:

1. Load and configure network boards.

2. Load and configure network protocols.

3. Bind protocols to network boards.

How INETCFG Configuration Works

The best way to configure NetWare 5 is to use INETCFG, which puts a menu-driven interface on NetWare communications configuration. The first time you load INETCFG, it will ask you if you want to "Transfer LAN driver, protocol and remote access commands?" If you choose *Yes*, INETCFG will examine the AUTOEXEC.NCF file to identify the statements that load and bind protocols and adapters. This configuration information is stored in the configuration database maintained by INETCFG. Then, the commands in AUTOEXEC.NCF are commented out. You are prompted to restart the server after transferring commands to the INETCFG configuration files.

The next time you start INETCFG, you are shown the prompt, "Use the fast setup method?" You can respond with the following choices:

▸ **No, use the standard method.** INETCFG will start and you can configure all options manually, as described in the sections below.

▸ **Yes, use the fast setup method.** INETCFG will configure IPX and TCP/IP protocols using default settings. Fast setup supports all LAN boards, but supports only permanent, synchronous WAN connections.

Fast setup doesn't accomplish much, especially in terms of the goals of this book. You will need to use standard configuration procedures to set up most of the features we will discuss. You can switch from fast setup to the standard method using an option in the fast setup menu.

INETCFG stores communication configuration data in several files. The following files are maintained by INETCFG and should not be modified with any other utility or editor:

- ► TCPIP.CFG

- ► IPXSPX.CFG

- ► NLSP.CFG

- ► NETINFO.CFG

- ► AURP.CFG

- ► IPWAN.CFG

- ► NLSPSTAT.CFG

In place of the original communications configuration commands, the following command is added to AUTOEXEC.NCF:

```
SYS:ETC\INITSYS.NCF
```

This NetWare command file contains the INITIALIZE SYSTEM command, which loads the communications configuration from the INETCFG database files.

Start INETCFG with the LOAD INETCFG command. The startup window is shown in Figure 8.11. In this section, you will use four of the options in this menu:

- ► The **Boards** option will be used to used to add and configure network board drivers.

- ► The **Protocols** option will be used to add and configure network protocols.

▶ The *Bindings* option will be used to bind protocols to boards.

▶ The *View Configuration* option will be used to view the configuration settings you choose.

The INETCFG Startup Window

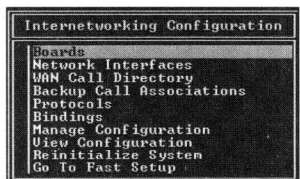

You can access INETCFG directly or from the NIASCFG utility, which is a menu front-end to the various utilities that are part of the NetWare Internet Access Server. To reach INETCFG, start NIASCFG and select the path Configure NIAS ➪ Protocols and Routing.

Managing Boards

To add a network board to the server configuration:

1. Ensure that the network drivers for your network boards are in the SYS:SYSTEM directory. These files are identified by the filename extension LAN.

2. Select *Boards* from the Internetworking Configuration menu. This will open the Configured Boards window, which shows one configured network board (see Figure 8.12).

Configured Boards in INETCFG

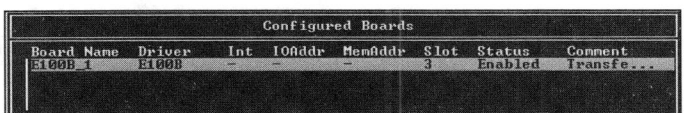

3. Press Insert to open an Available Drivers window that lists all drivers stored in SYS:SYSTEM. Select the driver you wish to configure, and press Enter to open a configuration dialog box.

Figure 8.13 shows the configuration dialog box for the TOKEN driver, and Figure 8.14 shows the configuration dialog box for the E100B driver. In each case, INETCFG has specified a name for the driver, consisting of the driver name and a number that identifies this particular board. Don't try to specify the protocol part of the name in this window. The protocol part will be added when the bindings are defined.

Many settings fields can be opened to produce lists of parameters. To choose parameters for a field, select the field and press Enter. Select the parameter from the list that is provided and press Enter.

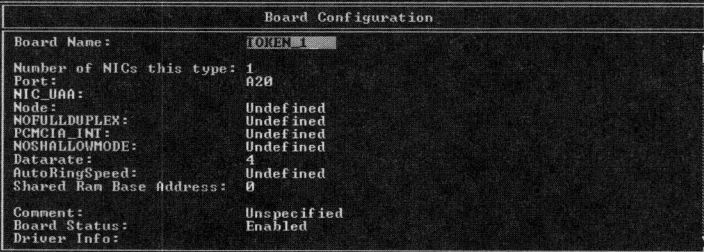

F I G U R E   8.13

The Configuration Dialog for the TOKEN Driver

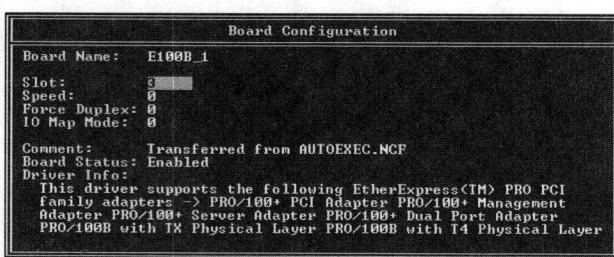

F I G U R E   8.14

The Configuration Dialog for the E100B Driver

4. After configuring the board, press Esc to exit the dialog window. To add the board to the server configuration, choose Yes when the Save Changes dialog box appears.

INETCFG Configuration

Changes made in INETCFG are not activated as they are configured. To activate a communications configuration, you must exit INETCFG (press Esc several times) and do one of the following:

- Select the **Reinitialize Server** command from the INETCFG main menu.

- Type the command **REINITIALIZE SERVER** at the server console.

- Type **DOWN** to stop the server. Type **EXIT** to return to DOS. Type **SERVER** to restart the server. (This procedure takes longer than REINITIALIZE SERVER and is seldom necessary.)

Either of these procedures will disrupt network communication. If users are connected to the server, have them log out before you shut down communication.

Managing Protocols
To load and configure TCP/IP:

1. Select the *Protocols* option from the Internetworking Configuration menu to display the Protocol Configuration window, shown in Figure 8.15. This window lists the protocols along with a status: Enabled, Disabled, or Unconfigured.

The Server Protocol Configuration

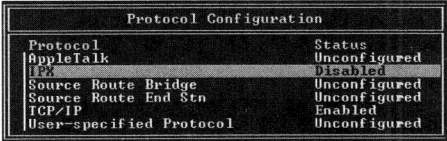

2. Select *TCP/IP* in the Protocol Configuration window to open the dialog box shown in Figure 8.16. The options in this dialog box are described in Table 8.4. The following fields are required to configure the network for Pseudo Corporation (as shown in Figure 8.9):

- TCP/IP Status (Enabled)

- IP Packet Forwarding (Enabled)

- RIP (Disabled)

3. After entering the TCP/IP configuration, press Esc.

4. To save the new configuration, choose *Yes* when you see the prompt "Update TCP/IP Configuration?" Choose *No* to cancel changes.

FIGURE 8.16

TCP/IP Protocol Configuration Options

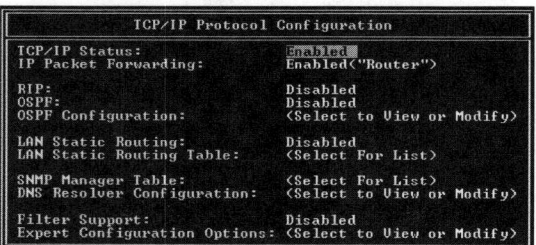

TABLE 8.4	PARAMETER	VALUES	PURPOSE
INETCFG TCP/IP Configuration Options	TCP/IP Status	Enabled/Disabled	Must be set to Enabled to activate TCP/IP protocols.
	IP Packet	Enabled/Disabled	If two or more network boards are installed on this server and IP Packet Forwarding is set to *Enabled*, the server functions as an IP Forwarding router. On an end node (single adapter) host, this feature should be set to *Disabled*.

PARAMETER	VALUES	PURPOSE
RIP	Enabled/Disabled	If RIP is set to *Enabled*, this server will exchange routing updates with other hosts running RIP.
OSPF	Enabled/Disabled	If OSPF is set to *Enabled*, this server will participate in OSPF routing. An OSPF configuration must be established. See Chapter 10 for information about configuring OSPF.
OSPF Configuration		Select this field to open the OSPF Configuration dialog window. (See Chapter 10.)
Static Routing	Enabled/Disabled	If set to *Enabled*, the server will read static routes from the static routing table when it is started or reinitialized.
Static Routing Table		Select this field to open the TCP/IP Static Routes list and manage the static routing table.
SNMP Manager Table		Select this field to open the SNMP Manager Table list and manage the list of hosts that will receive SNMP alerts from this host. (See Chapter 11.)
Filter Support	Enabled/Disabled	If set to *Enabled*, TCP/IP supports packet forwarding filters and routing information filters. (See Chapter 10.)
Expert Configuration Options		Select this field to open the TCP/IP Expert Configuration dialog window. (See Chapter 10.)

Binding Protocols to Network Boards

To bind TCP/IP to a network board:

1. Select *Bindings* from the Internetworking Configuration menu to open the Configured Protocol to Network Interface Bindings window shown in Figure 8.17.

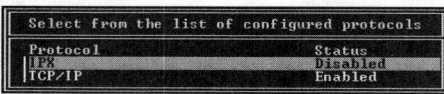

FIGURE 8.17

Configured Network
Protocols

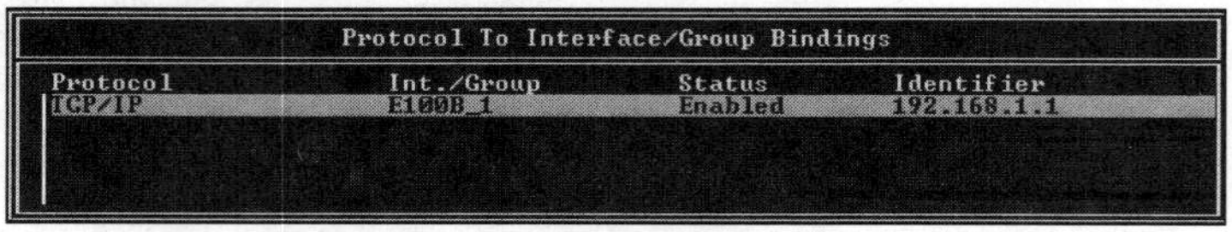

2. To add a binding, press Insert to open a list of protocols enabled on the server (see Figure 8.18).

FIGURE 8.18

Enabled Protocols Are
Available for Binding

3. Select *TCP/IP* from the list of enabled protocols to open a list of configured network interfaces (see Figure 8.19).

FIGURE 8.19

Configured Network
Interfaces

4. Select one of the configured network interfaces and press Enter to open a dialog box for binding the protocol (see Figure 8.20). Entries are required in the *Local IP Address* and *Subnetwork Mask of Connected Network* fields.

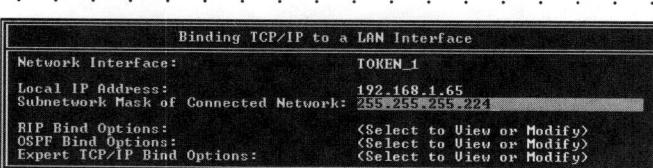

FIGURE 8.20

Options for Binding a
Protocol

5. Select the *Local IP Address* field and press Enter. Edit this field to reflect the IP address to be assigned to this host.

6. Select the *Subnetwork Mask of Connected Network* field and press Enter. Edit this field to reflect the subnet mask to be applied to this interface.

7. By default, TCP/IP will be bound using the Ethernet_II frame type for Ethernet and the Token-Ring_SNAP frame type for token ring, so you don't need to do anything else to configure TCP/IP on a basic network. To change the Ethernet frame type to Ethernet_SNAP, select Expert TCP/IP Bind Options. In the Expert TCP/IP LAN Options window, change the value of the Frame Type to the desired frame type. Remember: Ethernet_II is the overwhelming choice on TCP/IP networks!

8. When binding parameters are entered, press Esc to exit the window. Respond *Yes* when you are asked, "Update TCP/IP Configuration?"

Some of the other available options, such as RIP and OSPF bind options, will be examined in Chapter 10.

NOTE

Figure 8.21 shows the status of the Configured Protocol to Network Interface Bindings window when all of the bindings have been entered for the network shown in Figure 8.9.

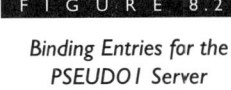

Binding Entries for the PSEUDO1 Server

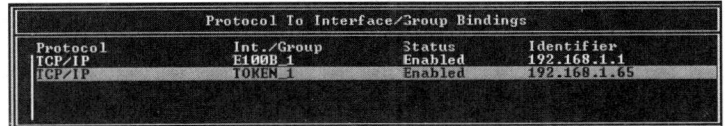

FIGURE 8.21

Protocol	Int./Group	Status	Identifier
TCP/IP	E100B_1	Enabled	192.168.1.1
TCP/IP	TOKEN_1	Enabled	192.168.1.65

Viewing the Network Configuration

After configuring communications in INETCFG, you can view the commands that INETCFG will generate. To view a menu of available options, choose View Configuration from the Internetworking Configuration menu. This choice will bring up the menu shown in Figure 8.22.

▶ · ◀

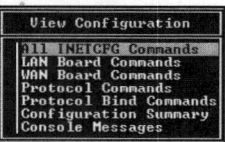

F I G U R E   8.22

*Options for Viewing
INETCFG Configurations*

The option *All INETCFG Commands* generates a display similar to the one in Figure 8.23. Most of the commands will be familiar to you if you think back to the discussion about entering configuration commands manually. Some are added automatically by INETCFG and do not concern us. Some of the parameters that can be configured through INETCFG will not be reflected in this list. These parameters are stored in the various configuration files maintained by INETCFG and cannot be modified except by using INETCFG.

▶ · ◀

F I G U R E   8.23

*Commands Generated by
INETCFG*

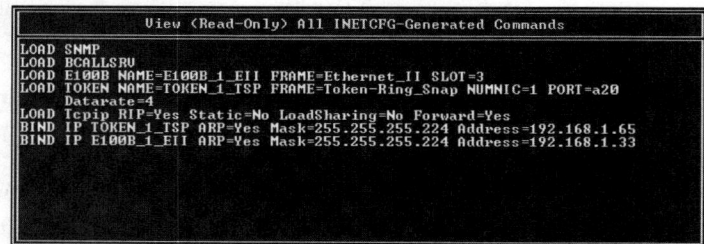

Activating the Network Configuration

Changes made in INETCFG are not activated as they are configured. After saving changes in INETCFG, you can put changes into effect in two ways.

In most cases, changes can be activated typing **REINITIALIZE SYSTEM** at the server console or by selecting the **Reinitialize Server** option in the INETCFG main menu. This command performs the following tasks:

▶ It compares the current NETINFO.CFG file to the NETINFO.CFG that was last used to start the system.

▶ If changes are identified, REINITIALIZE SYSTEM executes the new commands. REINITIALIZE SYSTEM is limited in two ways:

- If the new command is a LOAD command, REINITIALIZE SYSTEM must first unload the affected NLM. If the NLM cannot be unloaded because other loaded NLMs are dependent on it, the change cannot take effect. After unloading the NLM, it will be reloaded with the new configuration.

- Some communications changes are not reflected in the NETINFO.CFG file and will not be put into effect. Therefore, restarting the server remains the most effective way to put changes into effect.

In some cases it may be necessary to restart the server. Type **DOWN** to stop the server; type **EXIT** to return to DOS, and then type **SERVER** to restart the server. Of course, this will disrupt all communication with the server. Be sure to warn your users.

Testing Connectivity

Before you go to a lot of trouble hooking up client software, it's a good idea to establish that basic TCP/IP connectivity exists between your hosts. Once you have configured two or more hosts you should make sure they can talk to one another. The most common tool for testing TCP/IP connectivity is PING.

PING uses ICMP messaging to establish that hosts can communicate. Because PING can resolve host names, it is a useful tool for testing out your name resolution mechanism as well. Ordinarily, PING is a command-line tool. To test connectivity with 192.168.1.38, you would enter the command **PING 192.168.1.38** and wait for a reply.

The PING utility for a NetWare server has the capability of continuously pinging multiple hosts. PING sends an ICMP request packet at periodic intervals and waits for the target to return an ICMP response packet. If a response arrives, PING reports the statistics. If not, PING lets you know the host is unavailable.

Figure 8.24 shows PING in action. To start PING on a NetWare server, enter the command **LOAD PING**. Then, press the Insert key to add a target to be pinged. In Figure 8.24, the administrator is in the process of adding woody as a target. You can specify the interval at which pinging is to take place. Long intervals enable you to keep an eye on the network without generating outrageous traffic levels.

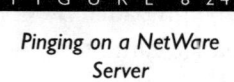
▶ ·   ◀

F I G U R E   8 · 24

*Pinging on a NetWare
Server*

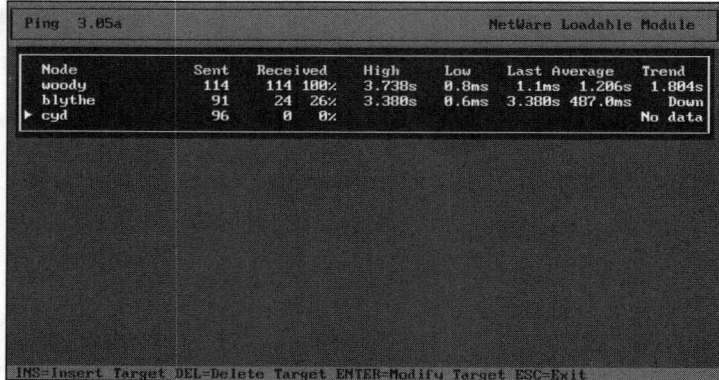

In this figure, two hosts are not responding to pings. blythe responded initially, but has stopped. You can see that received packets are far fewer than sent packets. Also, the Trend column indicates that this host is down. cyd has never responded to a ping, and the Trend column shows no data.

For the responding hosts, PING reports high, low, last, and average response time. These values, with the trends, can tip you off on changes in network performance.

To run a quick PING test, use TPING.NLM (trivial PING). TPING simply reports whether a destination is reachable as in the following dialog:

```
PSEUDO1:load tping 192.168.1.2

Loading module TPING.NLM

 TCPIP TPING Utility

  Versicn 4.00   Mar 5, 1998

  Copyright 1994-1998 Novell, Inc.  All Rights Reserved

   TPINC-1.02-8: 192.168.1.2 is alive
```

How Simple Can It Get?

Pure IP is almost trivially easy to get running. TCP/IP also configures quite easily. In fact, it's already configured if you selected it during NetWare setup. But there's quite a bit of work remaining. You probably need to do some work with routing, and you almost certainly want to set up a DNS server. The basic infrastructure, however, is in order. The next chapter will show you how to configure TCP/IP clients, and the rest of the book will address enhancements to the basic network, such as DNS, DHCP, and basic TCP/IP services like the World Wide Web.

This chapter doesn't present a completely realistic picture if you are already running NetWare, because you will have to deal with IPX as well as IP. Do you run a dual-protocol network or do you migrate? If you decide to migrate, how do you migrate without disruption? The questions that arise on multiple protocol networks will be addressed in Chapter 15, "Migrating to Pure IP."

## CHAPTER 9

Configuring NetWare 5 Clients

The servers on your network now can talk TCP/IP, but the network still lacks two crucial ingredients: applications to be used and workstations on which to use them. Half of the client-server equation is missing. You have the servers; now you need to add the clients.

NetWare 5 represents somewhat of a break with the past in that a variety of older client technologies have not been updated to support Pure IP. LAN WorkPlace and LAN WorkGroup have not been updated, for example. However, they have not been updated in part because they are not needed. The really helpful feature of LAN WorkGroup was its support for BOOTP client configuration, but NetWare 5 includes DHCP, a client configuration technology that is superior to BOOTP. LAN WorkGroup did not make the transition because it is no longer needed.

We are left, therefore, with only three client technologies that need to be considered in this book:

▸ Novell Client for Windows NT

▸ Novell Client for Windows 95 and 98

▸ Novell Client for DOS and Windows 3.1*x*

We will not attempt thorough discussions of any of the clients. Installation is straightforward, and should present no problems. Instead, we will concentrate on TCP/IP-related issues. You will see how to install and configure the TCP/IP protocol stack and how to configure any client parameters that are specific to TCP/IP.

Novell Client for Windows 95 and 98

All of the NetWare clients install through a wizard. Most Windows 95 and 98 systems will automatically start the installation program when the Novell Client Software CD-ROM is inserted. Installation is managed through a Wizard that prompts for installation parameters and installs the protocol stacks that you request.

You should be familiar with the procedures for manually adding and removing protocol stacks and for configuring protocol parameters. If you are managing a transition from an IPX environment to Pure IP, you will need to reconfigure client protocol stacks one or more times during the course of change.

Client Installation Options

The Novell Client for Windows 95/98 installation program supports three client protocol configurations:

- ▶ **IP only.** Only IP will be installed. You can direct the client setup program to remove IPX if it is present. There will be no support for Compatibility Mode and IPX-dependent applications are not supported.

- ▶ **IP with IPX Compatibility.** TCP/IP protocols are installed and bound to a network adapter. IPX is installed to support Compatibility Mode, but IPX is not bound to a network adapter. The client can communicate only with NetWare 5 servers configured to support TCP/IP. All communication is in the form of Pure IP packets.

- ▶ **IP and IPX.** Both IPX and TCP/IP protocol stacks are installed. The client will use either stack depending on the type of communication and the configuration of the server.

- ▶ **IPX only.** No support for TCP/IP. The client can communicate with all NetWare servers configured to support IPX.

The following sections illustrate how each option affects the configuration of the client.

IPX-Only Installation

The Novell Client integrates tightly with the standard network features of Windows 95/98 and is managed from the Network applet in the Control Panel. Other entries may appear in the installed components list. The entries appearing in Figure 9.1 are for a client configured with IPX only. When an IPX-only installation is performed, the client is configured as follows:

▸ The *Novell NetWare Client* is installed.

▸ The *IPX/SPS compatible protocol* is installed and bound to the Novell NetWare Client. This protocol is Microsoft's implementation of the Novell IPX/SPX protocol stack, also known as NWLink.

▸ The *IPX 32-bit Protocol for the Novell NetWare Client* is installed and bound to the Novell NetWare Client. This component includes Novell's enhancements to the Microsoft IPX/SPX compatible protocol.

▸ The network adapter is bound to the IPX/SPX compatible protocol and to the IPX 32-bit Protocol for Novell NetWare Client.

▸ . . . . ◀

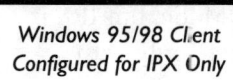

F I G U R E   9.1

Windows 95/98 Client
Configured for IPX Only

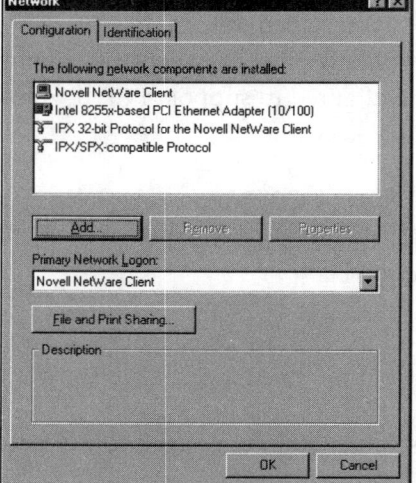

NOTE

An IPX-only installation does not remove TCP/IP if it was installed previously. If you want to completely remove TCP/IP, you must do so yourself by removing the TCP/IP entry in the Network applet.

With this configuration, only IPX communication is supported and only IPX packets will appear on the network.

NOTE

The Microsoft Network Client is always installed when you install the Novell NetWare client. This is probably a side effect of installing the Microsoft protocol stacks. If you use the Network applet to add either the IPX/SPX-compatible protocol or TCP/IP, the Microsoft Network Client is automatically installed. You can remove the Microsoft client if your network does not include Microsoft servers or peer-to-peer network groups. Because it does not apply to this chapter, the Microsoft Network Client was removed before the figure screen captures were taken.

You can examine the properties of any of the network components by selecting the component and clicking *Properties* to open a Properties dialog box. All protocol properties dialog boxes will have a *Bindings* tab such as the one shown in Figure 9.2 This tab can be used to determine which bindings are active for the protocol. You can also remove the check mark to disable the protocol binding.

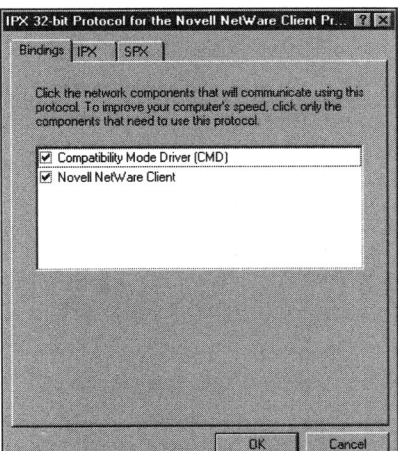

F I G U R E   9 . 2

The Properties for Every Protocol Will Have a Bindings Tab

IPX and IP Installation

The entries appearing in Figure 9.3 are for a client configured with both IPX and IP. When an IPX-only installation is performed, the client is configured as follows:

► The *Novell NetWare Client* is installed.

► *TCP/IP* is installed and bound to the Novell NetWare Client. If TCP/IP was not previously installed, it is configured with default settings that should be reviewed after installation is completed.

► The *IPX/SPS-compatible protocol* is installed and bound to the Novell NetWare Client. This is Microsoft's implementation of the Novell IPX/SPX protocol stack, also known as NWLink.

► The *IPX 32-bit Protocol for the Novell NetWare Client* is installed and bound to the Novell NetWare Client. This component includes Novell's enhancements to the Microsoft IPX/SPX compatible protocol.

NOTE

When installed by the Novell Client installation program, TCP/IP is configured with default settings. The client is configured to use DHCP to obtain its IP address. If your network is not running a DHCP server, you must manually configure the TCP/IP protocols with a static IP address and subnet mask.

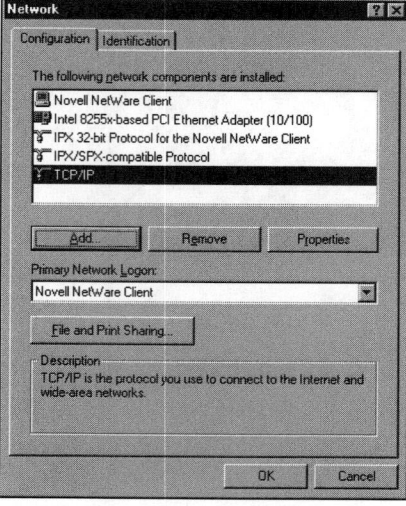

F I G U R E   9 . 3

Windows 95/98 Client Configured with IPX and IP

The client can now communicate with a NetWare server using either TCP/IP or IPX. If a given server supports both protocols, the client will prefer TCP/IP unless an application is IPX-dependent.

IP with IPX Compatibility Installation

The entries appearing in Figure 9.4 are for a client configured with IP and support for IPX Compatibility Mode. When IP is installed with support for IPX compatibility, the client is configured as follows:

▶ The *Novell NetWare Client* is installed.

▶ The *Compatibility Mode Driver (CMD)* is installed. By default, the CMD is configured to obtain its configuration from DHCP.

▶ *TCP/IP* is installed and bound to the Novell NetWare Client. If TCP/IP was not previously installed, it is configured with default settings that should be reviewed after installation is completed.

▶ The *IPX/SPS-compatible protocol* is installed and bound to the Novell NetWare Client and to the Client for Microsoft Networks.

▶ The *IPX 32-bit Protocol for the Novell NetWare Client* is installed and bound to the Novell NetWare Client and to the Compatibility Mode Driver. This component includes Novell's enhancements to the Microsoft IPX/SPX compatible protocol.

When the Compatibility Mode Driver is configured, all communication between client and server is Pure IP. IPX communication is not supported. The client can communicate with IPX-only servers only through a migration gateway. Packets for applications that are IPX-dependent will be encapsulated at the client for transport on the network and decapsulated by the Compatibility Mode component on the NetWare server.

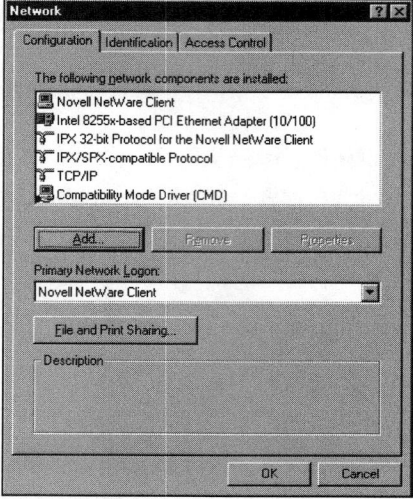

FIGURE 9.4

Windows 95/98 Client Configured for IP with IPX Compatibility

IP-Only Installation

The entries appearing in Figure 9.5 are for a client configured with the IP protocol stack only. IPX applications are not supported with this configuration.

When IP is installed without support for Compatibility Mode, the following components are installed:

▸ The *Novell NetWare Client* is installed.

▸ *TCP/IP* is installed and bound to the Novell NetWare Client. If TCP/IP was not previously installed, it is configured with default settings that should be reviewed after installation is completed.

▶ . . . . ◀

F I G U R E 9.5

*Windows 95/98 Client
Configured for IP Only*

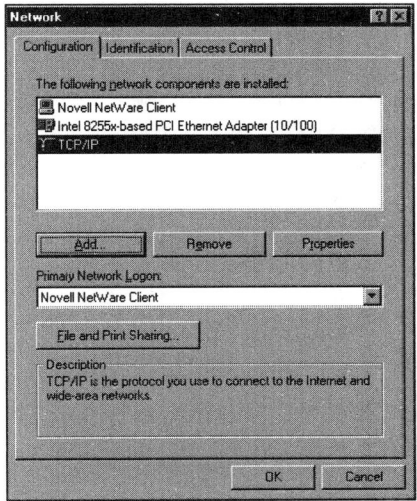

Installing and Removing Protocol Stacks

The NetWare 5 clients make use of the IPX and IP protocol stacks that are included with Windows 95/98. You can manually add, remove, and reconfigure most protocols without running the Novell Client installation program. (The *IPX 32-bit Protocol for the Novell NetWare Client* must be installed from the Novell Client installation program.) We will focus on the configuration of the TCP/IP protocol stack. Configuration of the IPX/SPX protocol stack is similar.

To install the TCP/IP protocol stack:

1. Open the Network applet in the Control Panel.

2. In the *Configuration* tab, click *Add*.

3. In the *Select Network Component Type* list, select *Protocol* and click *Add* to open the Select Network Protocol dialog box.

4. In the *Manufacturers* list, select *Microsoft* to open a list of Microsoft protocols.

5. In the *Network Protocols* list, select *TCP/IP*. Then click *OK*.

6. When you are returned to the Network dialog box, TCP/IP will appear in the list of installed components.

7. Choose OK in the Network applet to install the required files. You may need to supply the path to the Windows 95/98 CD-ROM from which files are copied.

8. Restart the computer to activate the changes.

Configuring TCP/IP

After installing TCP/IP, you need to configure it. Open the Network applet in the Control Panel and examine the *Configuration* tab. Figure 9.6 shows an example of a Configuration tab for Windows 98. The Windows 95 Configuration tab is similar. Before TCP/IP can operate properly, it must be configured with appropriate addressing information.

A protocol stack may be bound to more than one network adapter. In fact, Windows will automatically bind every installed protocol stack to every installed network adapter. In such cases, each protocol will be listed more than once in the Configuration tab, along with the adapter bindings associated with each entry. Figure 9.6 displays the installation of the Dial-Up Adapter to show you what to expect. When multiple network adapters are installed, their entries will resemble the following, which binds TCP/IP to an Intel E100B EtherExpress adapter:

```
TCP/IP -> Intel 8255x-based PCI Ethernet Adapter (10/100)
```

Each protocol-adapter pair is individually configured. To edit the properties for a protocol-adapter binding, select a TCP/IP-to-interface entry and click the Properties button to open the TCP/IP Properties dialog box shown in Figure 9.7. Let's review three of the tabs in this dialog box.

The *IP Address* tab determines how the client receives its IP address. If you select *Obtain an IP address automatically*, the client attempts to obtain its address from DHCP. This is the default configuration when TCP/IP is installed using the Novell NetWare Client installation.

Network Protocols Bound to
Multiple Network Adapters

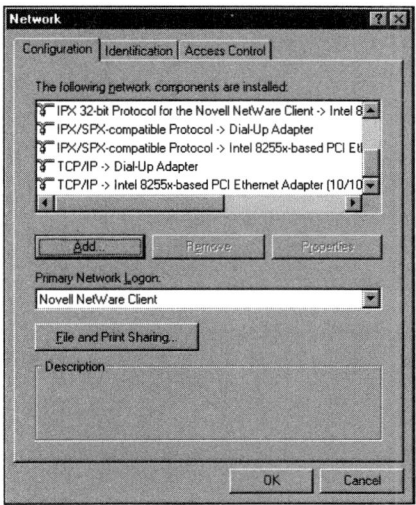

TCP/IP Address Properties

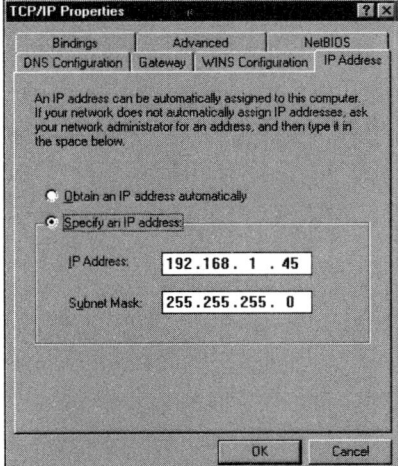

If you select *Specify an IP address*, you must enter a static IP address and subnet mask. DHCP is the only address configuration service supported by the Microsoft TCP/IP protocols. BOOTP and RARP are not supported. Consequently, you cannot use the LAN WorkGroup BOOTP server to provide addresses for your Windows 95 clients. Of course, the NetWare 5 DHCP server will probably be your preferred client configuration protocol.

The *Gateway* tab, shown in Figure 9.8, is used to specify default gateways. To enter the address of a default gateway, type it in the *New gateway* field and click *Add*. If multiple addresses are entered, add them in the order of priority. The first address entered will always be the primary IP gateway. You cannot adjust the order of entries without removing them and starting over.

▶ · ◀

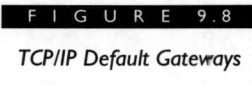

F I G U R E   9 . 8

TCP/IP Default Gateways

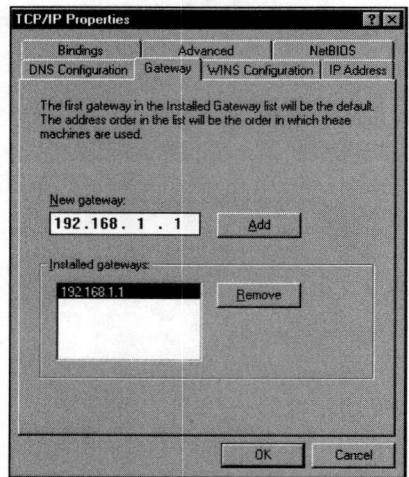

The *DNS* tab, shown in Figure 9.9, determines how the client will resolve names in the TCP/IP environment. If you select *Disable DNS*, the client must resolve names using static hosts files. If you select Enable DNS, the client will consult DNS when attempting to resolve names. The following entries can be configured:

- ▶ **Host**. This field specifies the host name.

- ▶ **Domain**. This field specifies the domain in which the host resides. The host name together with the domain name comprise the fully qualified domain name for the host.

▸ **DNS Server Search Order**. Here you can specify the IP addresses of up to three DNS name servers. Add the addresses in the order of preference, with the first address entered having the highest preference.

▸ **Domain Suffix Search Order**. This field is optional. Here you can specify domain name suffixes that will be added to names in an attempt to resolve simple names. Suppose that you are attempting to resolve blythe, a host that is in the mayberry.com domain. If you include mayberry.com in the domain suffix search order, you can resolve blythe.mayberry.com by entering just the name blythe. The domain suffix will be applied automatically by the DNS name resolver.

FIGURE 9.9

Configuring DNS Name Resolution

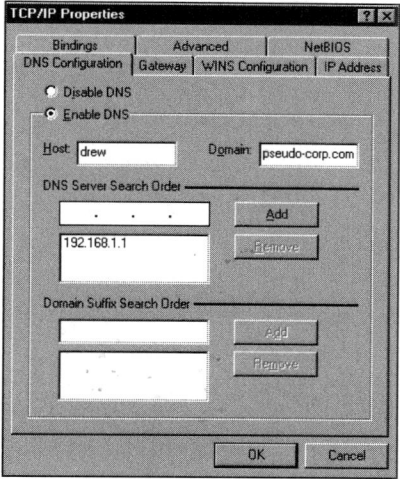

After configuring the TCP/IP protocols, restart the computer to activate the changes.

Configuring the Compatibility Mode Driver

By default, the Compatibility Mode Driver is configured to obtain its configuration information from DHCP. CMD parameters can also be manually configured in the Network applet. To change the CMD configuration, select the

Compatibility Mode Driver (CMD) entry in the Network applet *Configuration* tab and click *Properties* to open the Compatibility Mode Driver (CMD) Properties dialog box shown in Figure 9.10. The following entries can be configured:

▶ **Use DHCP**. If this box is checked, the CMD obtains its configuration parameters from DHCP. This box is checked by default. If the check is removed, the CMD obtains its configuration from SLP or from static entries in the CMD property page. CMD configuration via DHCP is described in Chapter 14.

▶ **IPX Compatibility Scope**. This field can be used to specify an SLP scope for the client. SLP scopes are discussed in Chapter 14.

▶ **Network Number (Hex)**. This field specifies the IPX network number of the CMD network used by the client. This number must match the CMD number that is configured on the servers used by this client.

▶ **Agent List State Time**. This setting is used only when the client is configured to discover Migration Agents dynamically. It specifies the minimum time the client must wait before attempting to refresh its Migration Agent addressing information. A setting of 0 disables the timeout so that the client does not attempt to refresh Migration Agent addressing information. If the setting is too high, the client will have difficulty recovering when a Migration Agent becomes unavailable. If the setting is too low, the client may generate excessive network traffic.

▶ **Migration Agents**. This field can be used to list up to ten Migration Agents that can be used by the client. Migration Agents can be specified by dotted-decimal IP address, fully-qualified DNS host name, or by a name that appears in the client's HOSTS file. If this field is blank, the client uses SLP to discover Migration Agents.

F I G U R E   9 . 1 0

Compatibility Mode Driver
Properties

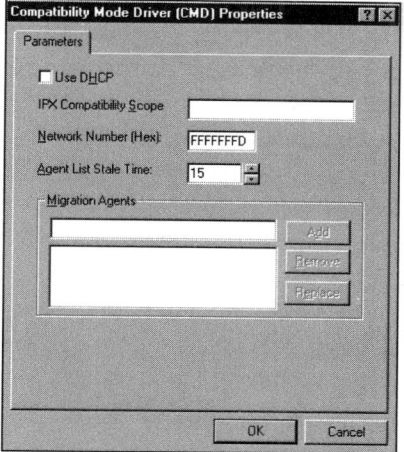

Configuring the Novell NetWare Client

Several configuration parameters for the Novell NetWare Client are relevant to Pure IP. You will find them on the Service Location and Protocol Preferences tabs. We will examine the *Service Location* tab in Chapter 14 when we discuss the Service Location Protocol.

The *Protocol Preferences* tab is shown in Figure 9.11. This tab has two configurable areas:

- **Protocol order**. Each configured protocol will appear in this list. The Novell client will attempt to use protocols in the order specified. If the list contains the entries IP and IPX in that order, the client will first attempt to connect using IP. If the client cannot connect using IP, it will attempt to connect using IPX. If the client cannot connect using IPX, it will again attempt to connect using IP. To change the protocol order, select a protocol and click the Up or Down buttons.

- **Name Resolution Order**. The Novell NetWare client can use a variety of name service technologies to resolve names. This list specifies the order in which the client will use those technologies. The available naming services are described in Table 9.1. Entries appear in the table according to their default order in the *Name Resolution Order* list.

FIGURE 9.11

Protocol Preferences for the
Novell NetWare Client

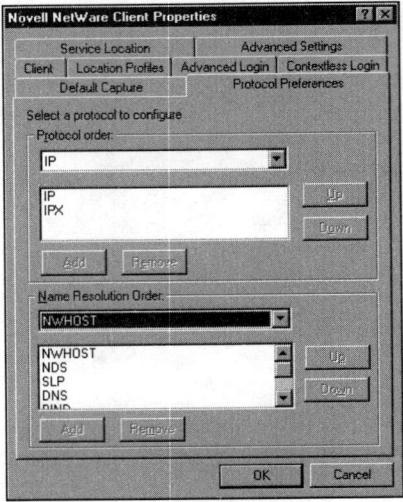

	SERVICE	DESCRIPTION
TABLE 9.1		
Available Name Services	NWHOST	This is a file found in the directory c:\novell\client32 directory. The file is a text file database. Each entry consists of a name and an IP address. This file can be used to establish aliases for servers.
	HOSTS file	This is a TCP/IP HOSTS file. The file is a text file database. Each entry consists of a name and an IP address. HOSTS files are described in Chapter 11. HOSTS files are options for the Windows NT client, but are not listed in the options for Windows 95/98.
	NDS	Novell Directory Services. Can be used to resolve both IP and IPX addresses.
	SLP	Service Location Protocol. Can be used to find NetWare 5 servers and trees. SLP replaces SAP in the Pure IP environment.
	DNS	Domain Name Service. This service is described in Chapters 6 and 11.
	BIND	Bindery. When connected to a server, a client can scan the bindery for IPX addresses and names.

SERVICE	DESCRIPTION
SAP	Service Addressing Protocol. Used to advertise services on IPX networks. IPX clients can use SAP queries to establish connections and to resolve names. In the NetWare 5 environment, SAP is placed toward the end of the name resolution order.
DHCP	Domain Host Configuration Protocol. The client can use options 85, 86, and 87 to establish an initial connection and determine a preferred tree and context. See Chapter 12 for a discussion of DHCP.

NetWare Client for Windows NT

This section covers configuration of the NetWare 5 Client for Windows NT and configuration of the client to support TCP/IP. This client requires Windows NT Version 4.0. Like the Windows 95/98 client, the installation Wizard for the Windows NT client offers four installation options.

Because the installation results are distributed on several tabs of the Network applet, it is less easy to show you graphically what happens when the Novell Client is installed on Windows NT. As a result, the installations are summarized briefly to start. Then, we'll look more closely at the Network applet.

IPX only installation makes the following changes to the system configuration:

▸ The NWLink IPX/SPX Compatible Transport is installed.

▸ The Novell Client for Windows NT is installed.

▸ The Novell Client for Windows NT is bound to NWLink.

IPX and IP installation does the following:

▸ The NWLink IPX/SPX Compatible Transport is installed.

▸ TCP/IP is installed.

- ▶ The Novell Client for Windows NT is installed.

- ▶ The Novell Client for Windows NT is bound to TCP/IP.

- ▶ The Novell Client for Windows NT is bound to NWLink.

IP with IPX Compatibility makes these changes to the client configuration:

- ▶ The NWLink IPX/SPX Compatible Transport is installed.

- ▶ TCP/IP is installed.

- ▶ The Novell Client for Windows NT is installed.

- ▶ The Novell IPX Compatibility Adapter is installed.

- ▶ The Novell Client for Windows NT is bound to TCP/IP.

- ▶ NWLink is bound to the Novell IPX Compatibility Adapter.

IP only installation makes the following changes:

- ▶ The NWLink IPX/SPX Compatible Transport is optionally removed.

- ▶ TCP/IP is installed.

- ▶ The Novell Client for Windows NT is installed.

- ▶ The Novell IPX Compatibility Adapter, if present, is removed.

- ▶ The Novell Client for Windows NT is bound to TCP/IP.

Many of the components installed with the Novell Client for Windows NT require configuration. The following sections examine client configuration issues.

Configuring the TCP/IP Protocols

The TCP/IP protocols must be configured when first installed and can be reconfigured at any time. Open the Networks applet in the Control Panel and select the *Protocols* tab, shown in Figure 9.12. Select *TCP/IP* and click *Properties* to open the *IP Address* tab.

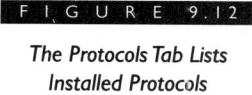

FIGURE 9.12

The Protocols Tab Lists Installed Protocols

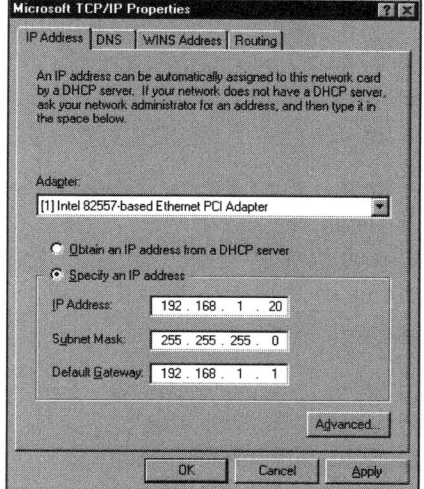

The *IP Address* tab determines how the client will obtain its IP address configuration. If this is a multihomed host, you must configure each interface. If the computer has more than one adapter, first select the interface in the *Adapter* field. Then enter the appropriate configuration settings. If you do not select *Obtain an IP address from a DHCP server*, you must specify an IP address and a subnet mask. The *Default Gateway* entry is optional.

If you click the *Advanced* button in the *IP Address* tab, the Advanced IP Addressing window opens. Figure 9.13 shows this window, which has the following settings:

▶ **IP Addresses**. You can associate a given adapter with multiple IP addresses. Use the Add button to add addresses to the list and the Remove button to erase addresses.

▶ **Gateways**. This field enables you to specify the addresses of multiple default gateways. The first gateway in the list will be used unless the client determines that the router is dead, in which case a fallback router will be used if it appears in the list. The order in which addresses appear in the list determines the router priority. Use the Up and Down buttons to adjust the order.

▶ **Enable PPTP Filtering**. The Point-to-Point Tunneling Protocol enables protocols such as IPX to be transported through TCP/IP networks by encapsulating the IPX messages within IP datagrams. Consult the Windows NT Server documentation for more information. (PPTP is not supported by Windows NT versions prior to Version 4.)

▶ **Enable Security**. If this field is checked, filters can be applied that limit the ports supported by the interface. See the Help messages for more information.

▶ · ◀

F I G U R E   9.13

Configuring Advanced TCP/IP Addressing

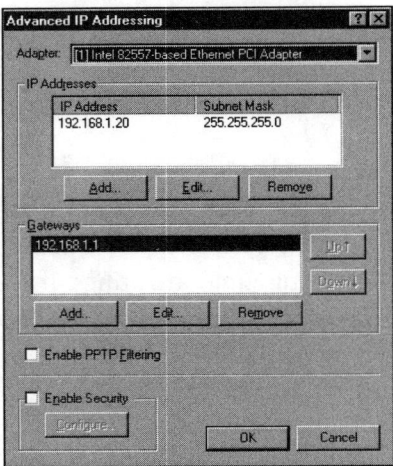

The *DNS* tab, shown in Figure 9.14, determines how the client will resolve names in the TCP/IP environment. If you select Disable DNS, the client must resolve names using static hosts files. If you select Enable DNS, the client will consult DNS when attempting to resolve names. The following entries can be configured:

- **Host**. This field specifies the host name.

- **Domain**. This field specifies the domain in which the host resides. The host name together with the domain name comprise the fully qualified domain name for the host.

- **DNS Server Search Order**. Here you can specify the IP addresses of up to three DNS name servers. Add the addresses in the order of preference, with the first address entered having the highest preference.

- **Domain Suffix Search Order**. This field is optional. Here you can specify domain name suffixes that will be added to names in an attempt to resolve simple names. Suppose that you are attempting to resolve blythe, a host that is in the mayberry.com domain. If you include mayberry.com in the domain suffix search order, you can resolve blythe.mayberry.com by entering just the name blythe. The domain suffix will be applied automatically by the DNS name resolver.

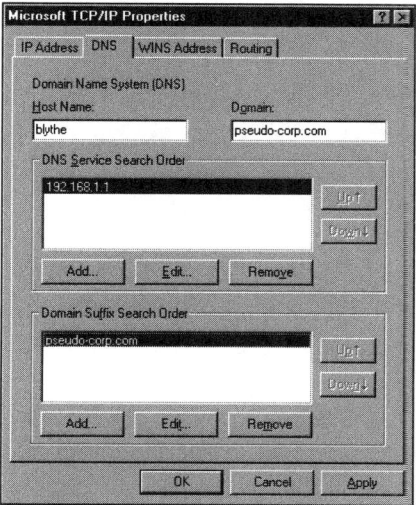

F I G U R E   9.14

Configuring TCP/IP DNS Settings

The *WINS* tab determines how the client will resolve names in the Microsoft networking environment and has no impact on NetWare operation.

The *Routing* tab enables multihomed hosts to function as IP routers. Check *Enable IP Forwarding* to establish a multihomed host as a router.

After entering the desired changes to the TCP/IP configuration, restart the computer to activate the new settings.

Configuring the Novell IPX Compatibility Adapter

The Novell Client for Windows NT configures a virtual network adapter to support IPX Compatibility Mode. To configure the Novell IPX Compatibility Adapter, open the Networks applet in the Control Panel and select the *Adapters* tab, shown in Figure 9.15.

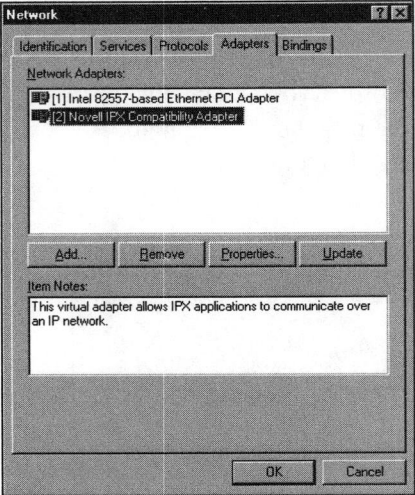

The Novell IPX Compatibility Adapter Appears in the Adapters Tab

Select *Novell IPX Compatibility Adapter* and click *Properties* to open the Novell IPX Compatibility Adapter dialog box shown in Figure 9.16. This dialog box has the following configurable properties:

▶ **Server Resolution Time**. The compatibility client will first attempt to connect with a server using an IP connection, even though the server is known by its IPX address. After the Server Resolution Time expires, the client will revert to a CMD connection using IPX encapsulated in IP. This setting is used when IPX applications request that the client establish a NetWare connection or when the user wants to connect to an IPX server.

▶ **IPX Compatibility Scope**. Optionally specifies an SLP scope that contains only Compatibility Mode information. If a scope is specified, the same scope must be specified on all nodes that use Compatibility Mode. It is usually unnecessary to define an IPX Compatibility scope. If a scope is not specified, the client uses the SLP scope specified in the *Service Location* tab of the Novell Client Configuration property page.

▶ **Adapter**. This box selects the adapter being configured. If the computer has multiple network adapters, each can be configured with separate settings. Parameters defined for the *Default Settings* adapter apply to all adapters for which the *Use Default Settings* checkbox is checked.

▶ **Use DHCP**. If this box is checked and the client is configured to use DHCP, the client will obtain its IPX Compatibility configuration from DHCP options. If the box is not checked, the client will obtain its configuration from SLP. This box is checked by default.

▶ **Use Default Settings**. If a network adapter is selected in the *Adapter* field (*Default Settings* is not selected) and this box is checked, the adapter will be configured with properties assigned to the *Default Settings* adapter.

▶ **Enabled**. If this box is checked, IPX Compatibility Mode is enabled for the adapter selected in the *Adapter* field. Remove the check mark to disable Compatibility Mode support for the selected adapter. On a computer with multiple network adapters, use this field to determine which adapter will provide Compatibility Mode support.

▶ **Network Number (Hex)**. This field specifies the IPX network number of the CMD network used by the client. This number must match the CMD number that is configured on the servers used by this client.

▸ **Agent List Stale Time**. This setting is used only when the client is configured to discover Migration Agents dynamically. It specifies the minimum time the client must wait before attempting to refresh its Migration Agent addressing information. A setting of 0 disables the timeout so that the client does not attempt to refresh Migration Agent addressing information. If the setting is too high, the client will have difficulty recovering when a Migration Agent becomes unavailable. If the setting is too low, the client may generate excessive network traffic.

▸ **Migration Agents**. This field can be used to list up to ten Migration Agents that can be used by the client. Migration Agents can be specified by dotted-decimal IP address, fully-qualified DNS host name, or by a name that appears in the client's HOSTS file. If this field is blank, the client uses SLP to discover Migration Agents.

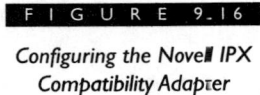

FIGURE 9.16

*Configuring the Novell IPX
Compatibility Adapter*

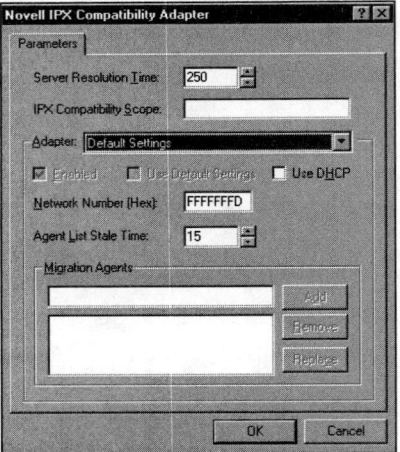

Configuring the NetWare Client

Several configuration parameters for the Novell NetWare Client are relevant to Pure IP. You will find them on the *Service Location* and *Protocol Preferences* tabs. Chapter 14 examines the Service Location tab while discussing the Service Location Protocol.

The Protocol Preferences tab is shown in Figure 9.17. This tab has four configurable areas:

- ▶ **Preferred Network Protocol**. If multiple protocols are installed on the client, use this field to select the protocol that should be used first when attempting to connect with a NetWare server.

- ▶ **Protocol**. Select the protocol to be configured in the *Protocol* box.

- ▶ **Component**. Select the component to be configured in the *Component* box. The only component installed with the Novell client is *Naming*.

- ▶ **Protocol component settings**. Configure the selected component. In the case of the *Naming* component, select the naming services that will be used by this client for the specified protocol. The naming services are briefly described in Table 9.1.

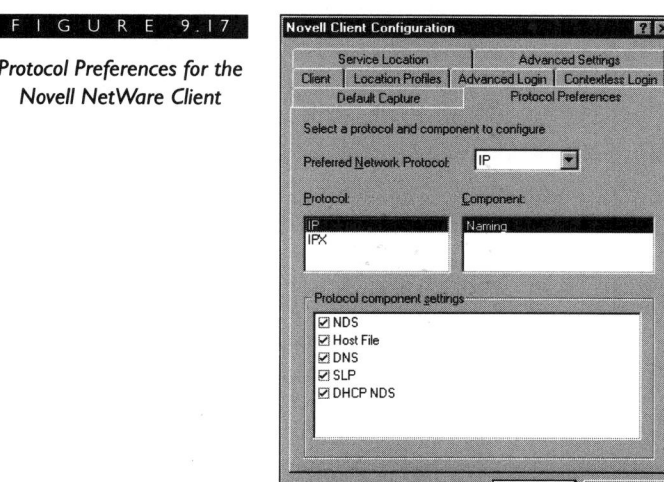

F I G U R E   9 . 1 7

Protocol Preferences for the Novell NetWare Client

NetWare Client for DOS and Windows 3.1x

As this book is being written, the official line at Novell is that Pure IP is not supported on the DOS client. The NetWare 5 documentation states that the DOS client can operate in an IP-only configuration. However, if you select an IP installation, the client doesn't work.

Perhaps that policy will change by the time you read this book, because the NetWare 5 distribution CD-ROMs contain everything you need to operate a DOS client on a Pure IP network. Thanks to some help from support staff at Novell, I learned the secret to making the combination work, and I'm going to pass the technique on to you.

Two factors determine the configuration of communication protocols on the DOS client:

▶ The order in which the drivers are loaded. This order is defined in a file named STARTNET.BAT.

▶ The configuration settings for the individual drivers. Most configuration settings are stored in a file named NET.CFG.

Most protocol modules can be configured by editing parameters in the NET.CFG file, which is usually stored in the same directory as the program files. Most of the work of configuring a NetWare client lies in editing the NET.CFG file. After looking at how STARTNET.BAT loads protocols on the client, we'll take a close look at the NET.CFG file.

The STARTNET.BAT File

All of the 32-bit clients are based on an architecture borrowed from NetWare 3 and later servers, which enables loadable modules to be bound dynamically to the network software infrastructure. The main component of Client 32 is the NetWare I/O System (NIOS), which is derived from the SERVER.EXE module that serves as a module launcher on NetWare servers. A significant difference is that NIOS works in conjunction with the extended memory manager that is active in the environment it supports.

Under DOS, NIOS loads as a conventional EXE file, but all other modules are activated using a LOAD command that functions much like the LOAD command on a NetWare server. Under Client 32, the LSL layer, the MLIDs, the protocol stacks, and the NetWare client all are implemented as loadable modules.

An interesting feature of Client 32 is that the same LAN drivers can be used on the NetWare server and the client. All LAN NLMs written for NetWare 4.1 and later can be used as LAN drivers under Client 32. If a 32-bit LAN driver is not available for your network interface card, Client 32 permits you to use conventional 16-bit ODI LAN drivers, although 16-bit drivers load as conventional DOS programs and require memory below 1 MB.

The layers in the protocol stack are established by executing driver programs in a specific order. The DOS client installation program builds a file named C:\NOVELL\CLIENT32\STARTNET.BAT that includes the required commands. To execute the STARTNET.BAT file, INSTALL places a CALL statement in the AUTOEXEC.BAT file similar to the following:

```
CALL C:\NOVELL\CLIENT32\STARTNET.BAT
```

A CALL statement enables batch files to execute other batch files. Each NetWare client package creates different batch files and different client directory structures, but the principle remains the same from package to package.

As mentioned earlier, the installation program does not configure IP to support NetWare login. To configure the NetWare server connections, you must copy the file SRVLOC.NLM to the directory C:\NOVELL\CLIENT32. SRVLOC.NLM is distributed on the Novell Client Software CD-ROM in the directory \PRODUCTS\DOSWIN32\CLIENT32.

You must edit the STARTNET.BAT file to activate CMD support. Here is a STARTNET.BAT file configured for IP with Compatibility Mode:

```
REM ******************************************


REM this section is not to be modified manually
```

```
@ECHO OFF


C:\NOVELL\CLIENT32\ISINPATH C:\NOVELL\CLIENT32
if errorlevel 1 goto skippath
PATH=C:\NOVELL\CLIENT32;%PATH%
:skippath
SET NWLANGUAGE=ENGLISH
C:
CD C:\NOVELL\CLIENT32


C:\NOVELL\CLIENT32\NIOS.EXE
LOAD C:\NOVELL\CLIENT32\NBIC32.NLM
LOAD C:\NOVELL\CLIENT32\LSLC32.NLM
LOAD C:\NOVELL\CLIENT32\CMSM.NLM
LOAD C:\NOVELL\CLIENT32\ETHERTSM.NLM
rem LOAD C:\NOVELL\CLIENT32\E100B.LAN FRAME=Ethernet_802.2
SLOT=3
LOAD C:\NOVELL\CLIENT32\E100B.LAN FRAME=Ethernet_II SLOT=3
LOAD C:\NOVELL\CLIENT32\TCPIP.NLM
LOAD C:\NOVELL\CLIENT32\SRVLOC.NLM
LOAD C:\NOVELL\CLIENT32\TRANNTA.NLM
rem LOAD C:\NOVELL\CLIENT32\IPX.NLM
rem LOAD C:\NOVELL\CLIENT32\SPX_SKTS.NLM
LOAD C:\NOVELL\CLIENT32\CLIENT32.NLM
REM *******************************************
```

The above listing comments out the lines that would enable IPX support. The batch file loads the following modules:

- **NIOS.EXE.** Always the first module loaded, this loads the NetWare I/O System, which in turn is used to load and unload other client modules. These other client modules are added and removed with LOAD and UNLOAD commands, as on the NetWare server.

- **NBIC32.NLM.** Enables ODI drivers to detect advanced bus hardware and provides a mechanism for retrieving hardware configuration information.

- **LSLC32.NLM.** The 32-bit implementation of the Link Support Layer. Enables one network adapter to be associated with multiple protocol stacks. The 16-bit implementation is LSL.NLM.

- **CMSM.NLM.** Loads the media support layer.

- **ETHERTSM.NLM.** The *topology specific module* for Ethernet. Configures Ethernet-specific network support. Load TOKENTSM.NLM for token ring networks.

- *adapter*.**LAN.** A network adapter driver: E100B.LAN in this example. LAN adapter modules can be loaded multiple times, once for each required frame type. Note the LAN driver parameters must be included on the command line. They are not read from NET.CFG, as with earlier Novell DOS clients. Thinking about the format of the LOAD commands on the NetWare server will help the inclusion of parameters on the command line make sense.

- **TCPIP.NLM.** Loads the TCP/IP protocol stack.

- **SRVLOC.NLM.** Provides CMD network support.

- **TRANNTA.NLM.** Loads the Transport NetWare Transport Agent. Provides an interface for the Microsoft TCP/IP stack, the Novell TCP/IP stack, and the Novell IPX stack so that packets are sent and received, regardless of the stack that is employed.

- **CLIENT32.NLM**. Loads the DOS client software.

NOTE The drivers for Client32 have been rewritten in the C programming language to enhance portability. The 32-bit versions of many drivers are identified by appending C to the beginning of the driver name. For example, CNE2000.LAN is the 32-bit version of the NE2000 driver.

After configuring the STARTNET.BAT file, you will want to review the Protocol section in the NET.CFG file to ensure that TCP/IP settings are correct for your network. For example, the default setting for client configuration is DHCP. You will want to change the client configuration method if DHCP is not in use on your network.

The NET.CFG File

The NET.CFG file is a text file maintained with any standard text editor. If you install NetWare client software using any of the automated installation programs, a basic NET.CFG file will be created for you, but you must be prepared to edit the file. Almost any change to client protocols requires you to modify NET.CFG.

This discussion of the NET.CFG file focuses on features that come into play when multiple protocol stacks or multiple drivers are employed — when you configure TCP/IP alongside IPX on a workstation, for example.

In a significant departure from the older VLM architecture, 32-bit LAN drivers do not obtain configuration parameters from the NET.CFG file. In fact, if a Link Driver section appears in NET.CFG, it is ignored when the LAN modules are loaded. Instead, the parameters that configure the LAN module are included in the LOAD command line, exactly as the parameters are included in the LOAD command line when entered on the NetWare server.

The NetWare DOS Requester (CLIENT32.NLM), IPX, and TCP/IP modules continue to obtain configuration information from the NET.CFG file. Consequently, the NET.CFG file still includes NetWare DOS Requester and Protocol sections.

Take a look at the following sample NET.CFG file. For the sake of clarity, the sample omits a variety of options that don't apply to the material covered in this book. See the Novell product documentation for information about parameters in the NetWare DOS Requester section.

Link Support

    Buffers 8 1500

    MemPool 8192

    Max Boards 4

    Max Stacks 4

Netware DOS Requester
    First Network Drive = F
    NETWARE PROTOCOL = NDS,BIND
    VLM = AUTO.VLM
    Preferred Tree pseudo
    Name Context "o=pseudo"
    SHORT MACHINE TYPE = IBM

Protocol TCPIP
    IF_CONFIGURATION STATIC LAN_NET
    IP_ADDRESS 192.168.1.145 LAN_NET
    IP_NETMASK 255.255.255.0 LAN_NET
    IP_ROUTER 192.168.1.1 LAN_NET
    BIND E100B #1 Ethernet_II LAN_NET

```
PATH TCP_CFG C:\NOVELL\CLIENT32\TCP

TCP_SOCKETS 15

UDP_SOCKETS 15

TCP_WINDOW 10240


NIOS

    LINE DRAW CHARS = "_¿þØ_Ž"


Link driver E100B

    FRAME Ethernet_802.2

    FRAME Ethernet_II
```

The NET.CFG file format must follow these rules:

► Each section is identified by a header, which is entered flush with the left margin.

► The options within the sections must be indented using at least one space or tab character.

► Only one option should be entered per line.

► Parameters within the options must be separated by at least one space or tab character.

► Commands are not case-sensitive, so you can use uppercase and lowercase letters to improve legibility.

The following sections discuss the parameters relevant to configuration of TCP/IP protocol support.

The Link Support Section

Options in the Link Support section configure the ODI Link Support Layer (LSL), which is implemented by the files LSLC32.EXE and LSL.EXE. Table 9.2 describes the options that can appear in the Link Support section.

TABLE 9.2	OPTION	PARAMETER	PURPOSE
Link Support Section Options	BUFFERS *number* [size]	*number*	Specifies the number and size of the receive buffers maintained by the LSL. The *number* parameter must specify enough buffers to hold all media headers together with the maximum amount of data specified by the size parameter. The buffer size is 618 bytes. The total buffer space (*number* × *size*) must be less than approximately 59K.
		size	Specifies the maximum amount of data accommodated by a receive buffer.
	MAX BOARDS *number*	number	Specifies the number of logical boards the LSL will support. Each logical LAN driver uses one board resource. Any driver configured in a Link Driver section uses board resources. Range = 1–4. Default = 4.

Continued

TABLE 9.2	OPTION	PARAMETER	PURPOSE
Continued	MAX STACKS number	number	Specifies the maximum number of logical protocol stack IDs the LSL can support. Each protocol stack uses one or more stack ID resources. Increasing the number of stacks increases the memory requirements of the LSL. Range = 1–16. Default = 4.
	MEMPOOL number [K]	number	Specifies the size of the memory pool buffer maintained by the LSL. The number parameter specifies memory in bytes unless the optional K parameter is included, indicating that the number parameter is multiplied by 1024. This parameter is ignored by the IPXODI protocol stack.

Pay close attention to the MAX BOARDS and MAX STACKS options when configuring multiple protocol stacks. You can run out of resources fairly quickly. Suppose that you configure an NE2000 driver to support all four Ethernet frame types (Ethernet_II, Ethernet_802.3, Ethernet_802.2, and Ethernet_SNAP). That driver requires four board resources.

The Link Driver Section

Each network interface is configured with a Link Driver section. Network interfaces most commonly are LAN interface cards, but with TCP/IP, serial connections can also be established that count as network interfaces.

Options in the Link Driver section fall into two categories: options that specify hardware characteristics of the network interface and options that specify software characteristics of the network driver. Table 9.3 summarizes the options you will encounter in this book. Examples of most options are provided in the sample NET.CFG file presented earlier in the chapter.

	OPTION	PARAMETER VALUES	PURPOSE
TABLE 9.3 *Selected Link Driver Section Options*	DMA [#1|#2]	*channel*	Specifies the DMA channel the network interface is configured to use. Range: valid DMA for hardware.
	FRAME frame_type	frame_type	For interfaces that can support more than one frame type, this option configures the driver to support a particular frame type. When multiple frame types are to be supported, a separate FRAME option is included for each frame type. (Early Ethernet drivers defaulted to Ethernet_802.3; current drivers default to Ethernet_802.2.) Range: valid frame type for hardware.
	INT [#1|#2] irq *irq* or IRQ [#1|#2] *irq*		Specifies the IRQ (in decimal) for which the network interface is configured. Newer clients use the IRQ keyword but continue to accept the older INT keyword. Range: valid IRQ for hardware.

Continued

	OPTION	PARAMETER VALUES	PURPOSE
TABLE 9.3 Continued	MEM [#1|#2] start_address [length]	start_address	Specifies the starting memory address (in hex) of an area of memory reserved for use by this network interface.
		[length]	Optionally specifies the length of the memory range.
	PORT [#1|#2] start_address [ports]	start_address	Specifies the starting memory address (in hex) of a port, an area of memory used by this network interface for input/output.
		ports	A port size of up to 16 bytes can be specified by including a ports parameter, indicating the number of ports in hex.
	PROTOCOL name protocol_id frametype	name	Specifies a protocol name for which a protocol number and frame type are to be declared. Example: IPX. (See the section "Specifying Protocol Frame Types" for more information.)
		protocol_id	Specifies a number in hex that identifies a protocol.
		frametype	Specifies a frame type that is valid for the protocol.
	SLOT number	number	On slot-based systems, such as systems with EISA buses, specifies the slot in which the network interface hardware resides. The driver obtains network interface settings from the system configuration.

The Protocol Section

Each protocol can be configured by options in a Protocol section. The specific options depend on the protocol being configured. Table 9.4 summarizes the options used to configure the TCP/IP protocols. As you examine these parameters, you'll begin to realize why the operations of IP and TCP were covered so thoroughly in Chapters 4 and 5.

TABLE 9.4	OPTION	PARAMETER	PURPOSE
Protocol TCPIP Section Options	ARP_AGING_ TIMEOUT *Number*	*number*	Specifies the number of seconds an entry is kept in the ARP cache. Range=1–7200. Default=300.
	ARP_CACHE_ MAX *number*	*number*	Range=8–256 entries. Default=64 entries.
	ARP_ TIMEOUT *number*	*number*	Specifies the number of seconds Client 32 waits to receive a response from ARP before the client times out. Range=1–120. Default=5.
	BIND *driver* [*#board frame_type network_name*]		Specifies a binding between a network interface and a protocol stack. This option is required if more than one interface driver will support a given protocol stack. If this parameter is not included, the TCPIP driver will bind using the Ethernet_II frame type.
		driver	Specifies the name of the ODI driver that is loaded for this board. If the MLID module is named NE2000.EXE, the driver parameter has the value NE2000.

Continued

TABLE 9.4	OPTION	PARAMETER	PURPOSE
Continued		#board	This optional parameter specifies the number of the board to be bound. This parameter matches the physical load sequence of the driver, and is required only when more than one logical interface is defined. If this value is 0, TCPIP binds to the first board that supports TCP/IP and the frame type specified in *frame_type* parameter.
		frame_type	Specifies the frame type to be used. This frame type is the same as the frame type specified in the Link Driver section for this driver.
		network_name	Specifies a logical name for this network connection. The parameter is used to identify the network for the BIND,
	IF_CONFIG-URATION static|bootp| dhcp|rarp [network_ name]		Specifies the source of the configuration of the network interface.
		static	The configuration is defined by keywords in NET.CFG. This is the default setting.
		bootp	The configuration is obtained from a BOOTP server.
		dhcp	The configuration is obtained from a DHCP server.
		rarp	The configuration is defined by keywords in the NET.CFG file, except that the IP address is obtained from a RARP server.
		network_name	Specifies a logical name for the network connection. The parameter is used to identify the network in several NET.CFG statements.

OPTION	PARAMETER	PURPOSE
IP_ BROADCAST *address*	*address*	Specifies the broadcast address used with the network interface. The default broadcast address is 255.255.255.255. (The documentation mistakenly states that the default is 0.0.0.0.)
IP_ADDRESS *address* [*network_ name*]		This option specifies the IP address assigned to a network interface.
	address	Specifies an IP address, expressed in dotted-decimal notation. If this parameter is omitted, or has the value 0.0.0.0, the protocol uses BOOTP or Reverse ARP to determine an IP address.
	network_name	Specifies a logical name for this network connection. The *network_name* parameter is used to identify the network in several NET.CFG statements.
IP_NETMASK *mask* [*network_ name*]		Specifies the subnetwork mask to be used with this network interface.
	mask	Specifies a subnet mask, expressed in dotted-decimal notation.
	network_name	Specifies a logical name for this network connection. The *network_name* parameter is used to identify the network in several NET.CFG statements.
IP_ REASSEMBLY TIMEOUT_ *Number*	*number*	Specifies how long TCP/IP waits for all pieces of a fragmented IP datagram to arrive.
IP_RIP [YES|NO]	YES or NO	Specifies whether RIP is enabled. The default is NO, RIP disabled.

Continued

TABLE 9.4	OPTION	PARAMETER	PURPOSE
Continued	IP_ROUTER ip_address [network_ name]	ip_address	Describes the IP address of the default router to be used when no specific route is defined for a destination network.
		network_name	Specifies a logical name for the network connection. The parameter is used to identify the network in several NET.CFG statements.
	IP_RTSW_ TRIGGER Number	number	Specifies the number of transmissions that will be attempted before trying another router. Also enables "dead router" detection. number can be in the range of 1 to TCP_RXMIT_LIMIT+1.
	IP_TTL Ttl	ttl	Specifies the time to live (TTL) value in hops for an IP packet. This value should be twice as long as the longest path that an IP datagram may need to travel. Range: 1–65535. Default: 128.
	PATH TCP_ CFG [drive:] path	drive:path	Specifies one or more directories that contain the TCP/IP database configuration files HOSTS, NETWORKS, PROTOCOL, SERVICES, and RESOLV.CFG. The default directory is \NET\TCP.
	NO_BOOTP		Specifies that RARP should be used to identify a host's IP address, even if a BOOTP server is available.

OPTION	PARAMETER	PURPOSE
ROUTE NET| HOST *ip_address* *router_address* [*mask*		Defines a static route to a network or host. Multiple entries can be included if necessary to define all required routes.
	NET or HOST	Specifies whether the entry defines a route to a network or a host.
	ip_address	Specifies the IP address of the route destination.
	router_address	Specifies the IP address of the router to be used to reach the destination.
	mask	Specifies the subnet mask that applies to the destination IP address.
TCP_ CONNECT_ RETRY *Number*	*number*	Specifies the number of times a client attempts to establish a TCP connection. Range: 1–256. Default: 5.
TCP_ KEEPALIVE YES|NO	YES or NO	Specifies whether the client issues TCP "keepalive" packets. Default: YES.
TCP_ MAXSEGSIZ *Number*	*number*	Specifies the maximum size of segments constructed by TCP. The number parameter specifies a maximum segment size of 8192 bytes.
TCP_ MINRXMIT *Number*	*number*	Specifies the minimum number of timeouts allowed for TCP. The number parameter can specify a value of 1 to 540, each timeout lasting 55 milliseconds.
TCP_ MAXRXMIT *Number*	*number*	Specifies the maximum number of timeouts allowed for TCP. The number parameter can specify a value from 1+TCP_MINRXMIT to 1080, with each timeout lasting 55 milliseconds.

Continued

T A B L E 9.4	OPTION	PARAMETER	PURPOSE
Continued	TCP_RCV_WINDOWSZ Number	*number*	Specifies the maximum TCP receive window in bytes. Range: 1-65,535 bytes. Default: 16,384 bytes.
	TCP_RELEASE_WAIT_TIME Number	*number*	Determines how long client waits for release of a TCP to ensure the remote TCP stack received acknowledgment of a connection termination request.
	TCP_RXMIT_MAXTIME Number	*number*	Specifies the maximum TCP packet retransmission interval in milliseconds. Range: TCP_RXMIT_MINTIME+1 to 240,000. Default: 120,000.
	TCP_RXMIT_MINTIME Number	*number*	Specifies the minimum TCP packet retransmission interval in milliseconds. Range: 2 to TCP_RXMIT_MAXTIME+1. Default: 110.
	UDP_CHECKSUM YES|NO	YES or NO	Specifies whether the client uses UDP checksums. Default: YES.

The TCP/IP Highway Is Complete

You now have a complete TCP/IP network environment, including servers, clients, and applications. That's not to say that you couldn't add quite a bit more. You could add an NFS server, for example, or use the printing utilities to set up TCP/IP print servers. But the infrastructure is in place. Network traffic is about the only thing left to add.

Before we proceed much further, we need to enable the TCP/IP network to grow. Right now, we are limited to a single network — which is indeed limiting. Now we need an internetwork that can span an enterprise or the world, and that brings us to the next chapter, where we take a detailed look at routing.

## CHAPTER 10

Internetworking NetWare TCP/IP

The preceding chapters have examined NetWare in the context of relatively simple networks. The most elaborate network thus far consisted of two network segments, with a single NetWare server performing all routing functions. Few TCP/IP networks conform to such a simple model, however. This chapter examines two subjects that you will probably confront when your NetWare network grows beyond a single segment: routing and IP tunneling.

Most of this chapter is devoted to putting into practice the routing theory that you examined in Chapter 4 (The Internet Layer). You will learn how to configure NetWare servers with the following routing technologies:

- Static routing

- RIP

- OSPF

- ICMP Router Discovery Protocol

After RIP and OSPF have been examined separately, you will examine techniques that enable RIP and OSPF to coexist on the same internetwork.

After we look at routing protocols, we will examine packet filtering. Typically a router does not discriminate among protocols in a protocol suite. If a router is configured to forward TCP/IP, it will forward datagrams for all protocols in the TCP/IP protocol suite, which isn't always a good thing. Consider, for example, a router connecting your local network to the Internet. If the router doesn't control traffic arriving from the Internet, it is a big, open door that permits any outsider to muck around in your network. A variety of techniques can be used to determine the width of that doorway. The simplest is *packet filtering*, a technique that configures the router to block specified protocols at a specified network interface. You could, for example, use filtering to block the Telnet protocol, preventing an outsider from using Telnet to attach to your local Telnet-configurable devices.

The final topic in this chapter is *IP tunneling*, a neat trick that enables NetWare to route IPX packets through TCP/IP networks. This technique is especially useful when your network includes wide-area connections configured only for TCP/IP. You could, for example, connect two remote sites via the Internet and use IP tunneling to transport IPX traffic between the sites. Because IP tunneling only comes into action on a routed network, let's first see how NetWare can be used to construct complex internetworks.

NetWare 5 Internetwork Support

NetWare 5 incorporates the Novell Internet Access Server (NIAS), a suite of tools that configures routing and wide-area network access. One of the components of NIAS is the Novell MultiProtocol Router (MPR), a sophisticated, software-based router that runs on the NetWare 5 server. MPR supports the IPX/SPX, TCP/IP, and AppleTalk protocol suites over a wide variety of LAN and WAN network links, including Ethernet, token ring, FDDI, frame relay, ISDN, ATM, and X.25. MPR also supports IPX/SPX and TCP/IP network protocols, supporting both vector-based and link-state routing protocols for both protocol suites. For dial-up connections, MPR supports the Point-to-Point (PPP) protocol over serial and ISDN lines. That's a lot of capability for a product that is now included free with NetWare.

Of course, this book concentrates on TCP/IP, and many of the capabilities of MPR must remain unexamined. This chapter explicitly focuses on routing, and some of MPR's WAN features will be addressed elsewhere.

Here are some of the TCP/IP communication enhancements that MPR brings to NetWare 5 (these features are also available in NetWare 4.11 and 4.2):

▶ ICMP Router Discovery Protocol support. This support enables servers to obtain updated routing information without using RIP or OSPF.

▶ RIP I and RIP II. RIP I, the version used by NetWare 3 and 4, has limited support for subnet masking and does not provide a mechanism that enables routers to authenticate routing packets received from other routers. RIP II supports subnet masking by including subnet masks in route advertisements, and also includes an authentication mechanism.

▶ OSPF protocol support.

▶ BOOTP forwarding. This feature enables routers to forward BOOTP address requests. BOOTP enables workstations to obtain their IP addresses from DHCP servers, and is discussed along with the NetWare 5 DHCP service in Chapter 12.

▶ IP filtering. This feature enables network administrators to restrict the categories of datagrams permitted to cross the router.

▶ Menu-based configuration of static routes.

If your network is running NetWare 3 or 4, you can obtain these enhancements by installing the Novell MultiProtocol Router 3.1 add-in product. MPR is bundled with intraNetWare 4.11. (For Pure IP, you will need to upgrade to NetWare 5.)

Configuring Static Routes

Static routes are defined by entries in the SYS:\ETC\GATEWAYS database file. This file is processed when the TCPIP.NLM module is loaded. TCPIP.NLM reads the route entries in the GATEWAYS file and stores them in the server's IP routing table. (NetWare 4 processes the GATEWAYS file with IPCONFIG.NLM, but that functionality moves to TCPIP.NLM in NetWare 5.)

The GATEWAYS file can include entries that define routes to remote hosts and networks. It can also contain one entry that defines a default route used when the routing table does not contain an entry for a destination. The default route is a special use of a network route entry that should appear only once in the GATEWAYS file. The formats used for entries in the GATEWAYS file were discussed in Chapter 8.

Contents of the GATEWAYS file can be modified in two ways:

▶ A text editor such as EDIT.NLM can be used to directly edit the file.

▶ INETCFG can be used to modify the file using menus and forms.

To see how static routing works, we will construct a routing table for a server on a sample network.

NOTE

Static routing is required only when a network is not running a dynamic routing protocol such as RIP or OSPF. A GATEWAYS file is not required when dynamic routing is employed.

Building a GATEWAYS File

Typically, static routes must be configured individually for each server. Figure 10.1 illustrates a somewhat artificial internetwork that illustrates several characteristics of database entries in the GATEWAYS file. The example makes use of subnetted and non-subnetted networks. Here is a GATEWAYS file configured for server FS1:

```
#SYS:\ETC\GATEWAYS

#Server FS1-128.1.0.10

#Default route

NET 0 GATEWAY 128.1.0.2


NET 128.2 GATEWAY 128.1.0.1 METRIC 2

HOST FS3 GATEWAY 128.1.0.1

HOST FS5 GATEWAY 128.1.0.2
```

Most entries in a GATEWAYS file will probably define routes to networks. These entries have the following syntax:

```
NET {netid | netname} GATEWAY routeraddress [METRIC cost]
[ACTIVE | PASSIVE]
```

Entries that define routes to hosts have this syntax:

```
HOST {ipaddress | hostname} GATEWAY routeraddress

[METRIC cost] [ACTIVE | PASSIVE]
```

The NET and HOST keywords are used to specify whether the address defines a netid or the IP address of a host. The keywords also specify whether names should be resolved using the NETWORKS or the HOSTS database file.

▶ · ◀

Network Illustrating Use of the GATEWAYS File

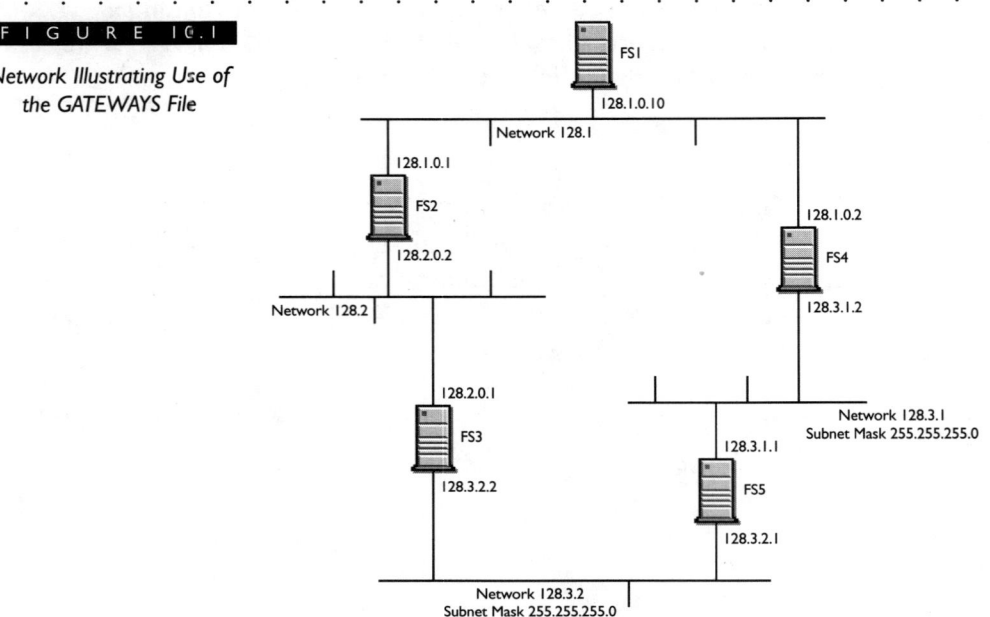

Each entry states, "To reach this remote destination, here is the next gateway to use." The HOST and NET keywords describe the type of address that the destination defines:

▶ For a HOST entry, the destination can be a host IP address, or it can be a host name defined in the HOSTS file.

▶ For a NET entry, the destination can be a netid (the network address portion only of the IP address), or it can be a network name defined in the NETWORKS file. To include a subnet mask with the netid, enter the address with the format *netid/mask*, for example: 10.1.0.0/255.255.0.0.

A NET entry for netid 0 defines a default route to be used for datagrams that don't match destinations defined in the router table. Because a default route is established through 128.1.0.2, the only required entries are for routes that do not have 128.1.0.2 as the next hop.

The *routeraddress* is the IP address of a router attached to a network that is local (directly attached) to this host. Any datagrams directed to the destination network or host will be forwarded to this IP address.

The optional cost represents the cost of this route. If a METRIC parameter is not specified, the default cost is 1.

By default, routes that the host receives from the GATEWAYS database are flagged as PASSIVE, which means that they do not expire. Routes flagged as ACTIVE must be refreshed through routing protocol messages (for example, RIP, OSPF, or ICMP) received from other routers. Active routes that are not refreshed by a routing protocol will expire eventually and be purged from the database. You should identify entries as PASSIVE when the route will not be advertised by a routing protocol.

If all routers are configured to advertise routes with ICMP, RIP, or OSPF, you should identify entries in the GATEWAYS file with the ACTIVE parameter. Passive entries are permanently loaded into the routing table and will not be adjusted as network conditions change.

Editing the GATEWAYS File

To edit the GATEWAYS file directly, enter the command **LOAD EDIT SYS:\ETC\GATEWAYS** at the server console. Make the required modifications and press Esc to save the changes. Separate the parameters with at least one space or tab character.

Managing the GATEWAYS File with INETCFG

You can use INETCFG to edit the GATEWAYS file. To manage static routes, do the following:

1. Start INETCFG by typing **LOAD INETCFG** at the server console.

2. Select the *Protocols* option in the Internetworking Configuration menu.

3. Select *TCP/IP* in the Protocol Configuration menu.

4. If the value of the *LAN Static Routing* field is *Disabled*, select the field and press Enter. In the LAN Static Routing menu, change the value to *Enabled*. (The value of this field determines the value of the Static= parameter in the LOAD TCPIP.NLM command executed when the system is started.)

5. Highlight the *LAN Static Routing Table* field in the TCP/IP Protocol Configuration form and press Enter to open the TCP/IP Static Routes list (see Figure 10.2).

FIGURE 10.2

TCP/IP Static Routes Displayed in INETCFG

6. To add an entry, press Insert to open the Static Route Configuration form shown in Figure 10.3. To modify an existing entry, select the entry and press Enter to open the Static Route Configuration form. To delete an entry, select the entry and press Delete.

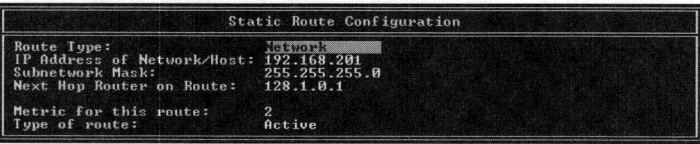

FIGURE 10.3

Defining a Static Route in INETCFG

7. In the *Route Type* field, press Enter and select a route type from the Route Type menu. The available choices are:

- *Default Route*. Specifies default route by creating a network route with a network ID of 0.

- *Host*. Creates a host route identified with the HOST keyword.

- *Network*. Creates a network route identified with the NET keyword.

8. If you selected *Host* or *Network* in the *Route Type* field, enter the address of the destination in the *IP Address of Network/Host* field. If subnetting is in use, enter the subnet mask in the *Subnetwork Mask* field. If a subnetwork mask is not specified, the route will use the default mask for the class of the address that was entered.

If you selected *Default Route* in the *Route to Network or Host* field, the *IP Address of Network/Host* and the *Subnetwork Mask* fields will be inactive.

9. In the *Next Hop Router on Route* field, enter the IP address of the interface that will be used for the next router hop. The interface must be connected to a network segment connected directly to this host.

10. In the *Metric for this route* field, specify a number between 1 and 16 to specify the cost of this route. A cost of 16 disables the route.

11. In the *Type of route* field, specify whether the route entry is Passive or Active. Passive routes are not advertised to other routers. Active routes are advertised if a routing protocol is configured and will be forwarded by other routers that receive router advertisements from this computer.

12. Press Esc and save the new entry.

Loading Static Routes

After the GATEWAYS file has been created, the static routes can be loaded into the server's router table, a function that is performed when TCPIP.NLM is loaded on the server. Changes made to the GATEWAYS file will not be reflected in the server's routing table until the next time TCPIP.NLM is loaded. You can use the INITIALIZE SYSTEM console command to reload the network protocols, including TCPIP.NLM, without restarting the server.

When to Use Static Routes

Why should you go to the trouble of configuring static routes when you could simply turn on a dynamic routing protocol such as RIP? On simple networks, static routes make a great deal of sense. RIP is an especially chatty protocol, and even OSPF has some network traffic overhead. Static routes aren't advertised and don't generate routing traffic. On a simple network that doesn't change often, the few minutes required to configure static routes are repaid by a quieter network. On a large network that often changes, however, the administration required to keep static routes current could be overwhelming.

Static routes are required when the network includes on-demand connections, such as routers connecting through demand-dial ISDN links. When dial-up links close their connections, their routes are no longer advertised. These routes will be timed out on network routing tables and the route to the dial-up link will be lost.

Using Default Routes

If your network is fairly simple and seldom changes, static routing can be a useful technique that reduces the processing overhead and network traffic required to sustain dynamic routing. As you saw in the earlier example of a GATEWAYS file, in many cases, a default route can eliminate the need to specify routes. The example file required a single NET routing specification to supplement the default route.

Unfortunately, default routes are inflexible and unthinking, and they can get you into trouble if you aren't careful. Let's examine some network configurations to see how default routes can cause problems. We'll also take a look at possible solutions.

Figure 10.4 illustrates a network with three segments and two NetWare servers configured as routers. It is possible for all the TCP/IP hosts to communicate using only the default routers. Let's examine some situations:

▶ When A needs to send a datagram to C, A is aware that C's IP address, 2.0.0.3, is not on A's local network; therefore, A sends the datagram to its default router at 1.0.0.1. B receives the datagram and determines that it is to be delivered to a network to which it is directly attached. Therefore, B can deliver the datagram to C.

▶ When A needs to send a datagram to E, the process begins the same way, with A sending the datagram to B. B determines that the destination is not on a network to which it is attached; therefore, it sends the datagram to its default router at 2.0.0.2. D receives the datagram and can complete the delivery.

▶ When C needs to send a datagram to A, C begins by sending the datagram to its default router at 2.0.0.2. D receives the datagram and cannot deliver it to a local network; therefore, D sends the datagram to its default router at

2.0.0.1. B receives the datagram and determines that the destination is on a network to which B is directly attached; therefore, B can deliver the datagram to A.

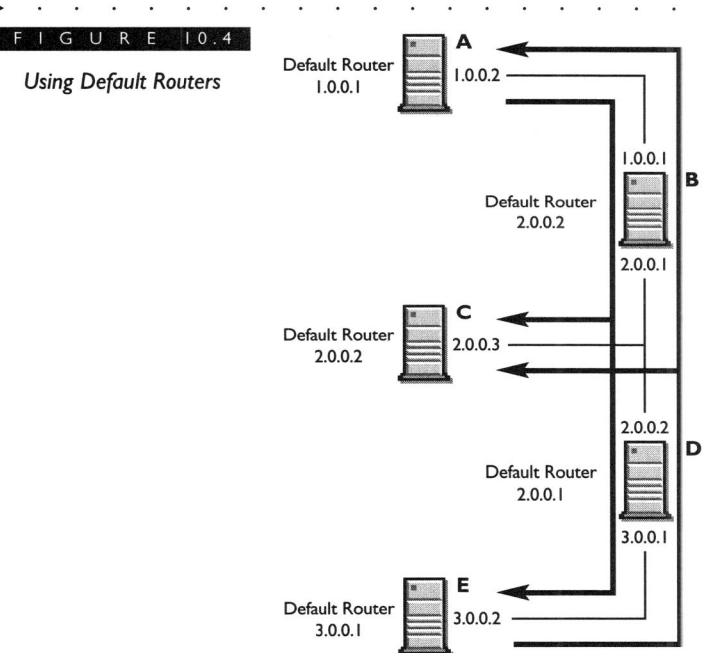

F I G U R E   10.4

Using Default Routers

If you examine each possible pair of hosts, you will see that delivery can be achieved using the default routes. The routing tables of these hosts do not require any other entries.

A small change to the network blows this theory cut of the water. Superficially, the network in Figure 10.5 looks like it should operate much like the network in Figure 10.4. That appears to be the case for datagrams that are moving down the figure. A, for example, can send datagrams successfully to any other host.

▶ . . . . ◀

FIGURE   10.5

A Larger Network with Only Default Routers

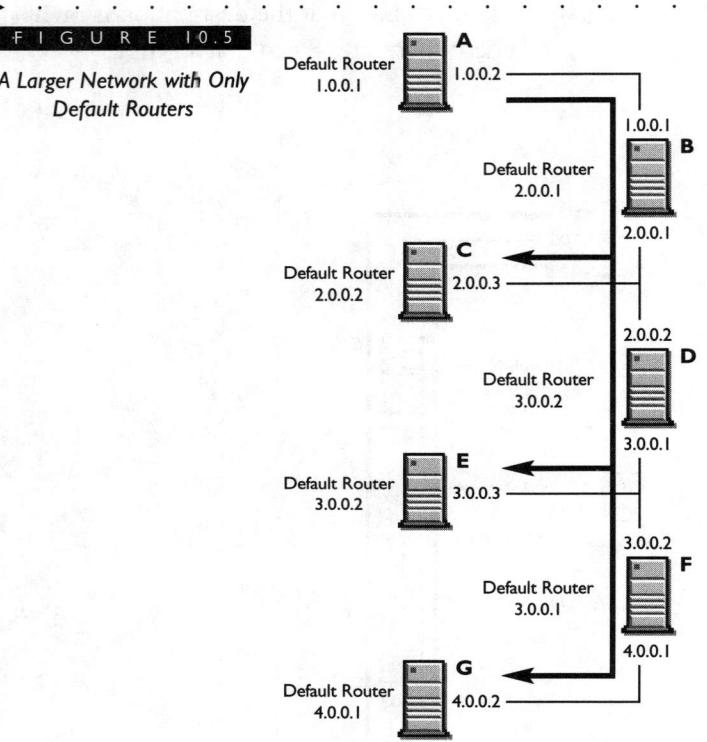

The problem becomes apparent when we look at what happens when G attempts to send a datagram to A (see Figure 10.6):

I. A is not on a network local to G; therefore, G sends the datagram to its default router address 4.0.0.1.

2. A is not on a network local to F; therefore, F sends the datagram to its default router address 3.0.0.1.

3. A is not on a network local to D; therefore, D sends the datagram to its default router address 3.0.0.2.

As you can see, a loop has developed, and the datagram will circulate between D and F until its time-to-live expires.

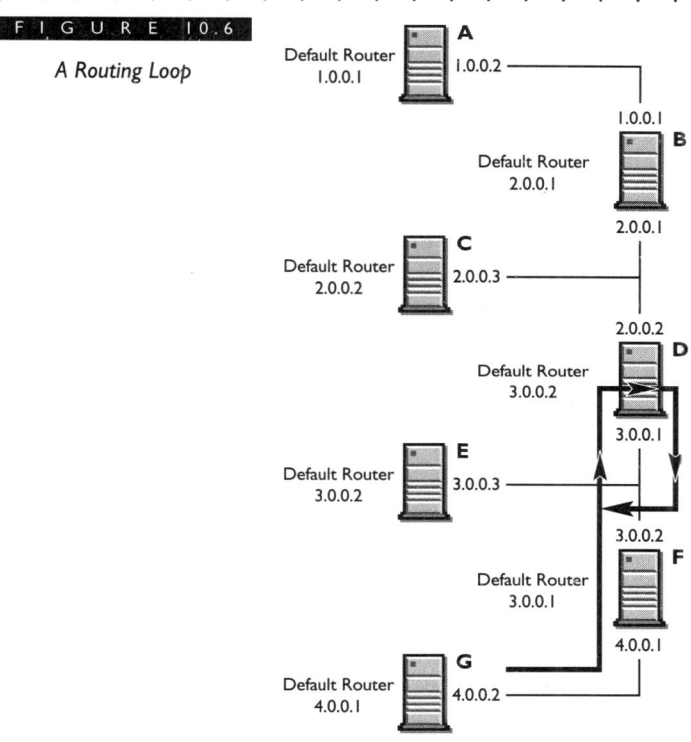

FIGURE 10.6

A Routing Loop

The loop develops because neither F nor D are aware of the location of Network 1.0.0.0. To correct the situation, the minimum fix is to add an entry to D's routing table by including the following line in its GATEWAYS file:

```
NET 1 GATEWAY=2.0.0.1
```

Static routing is not necessarily difficult to configure, but some caution obviously is needed. As you plan your network, try to "think like a router" to determine how datagrams will flow through the internetwork. Careful analysis will enable you to identify when additional static routes are required.

NOTE

The networks in Figures 10.5 and 10.6 are perfect candidates for static routing. A single route exists between any given pair of networks. If a connection between the networks breaks, all traffic ceases. Therefore, no benefit would be gained by implementing dynamic routing, because a dynamic routing algorithm could not converge on a new route.

Internetworks configured around backbones often conform to this single-path limitation. In these cases, the deciding factor on whether to use dynamic routing is how frequently the network configuration changes. A stable, single-path network benefits little from dynamic routing, but performance may improve if routing traffic is eliminated. That said, the decision to use static or dynamic routing is a fairly personal one that each network administrator will have to make on his or her own.

Configuring RIP

With the MPR, RIP is configured entirely by using the INETCFG utility. You don't have to muck around with manually-edited LOAD commands. That's a good thing, because MPR adds some features to RIP, including support for RIP II. These enhancements have added a number of configuration parameters, and the menu-driven nature of INETCFG makes it easy to deal with all of the possibilities.

Before you configure routing, you need to understand when routing is required and when a dynamic routing protocol should be enabled. There are two questions to ask: When should IP forwarding be enabled, and when should RIP be configured? You'll learn the answers to those questions in the next section.

When to Enable Routing

TCP/IP routing is enabled by parameters in the LOAD TCPIP and BIND IP commands. Immediately after NetWare 5 is installed, LOAD TCPIP and BIND IP statements will be found in the AUTOEXEC.NCF file where they can be manually edited. In most cases, however, you will configure TCP/IP using INETCFG and the LOAD commands will be moved into the NETINFO.CFG file, which is maintained by INETCFG. You should always use INETCFG to maintain NETINFO.CFG and should never edit the file manually.

Nevertheless, you may need to edit the LOAD TCPIP and LOAD IP commands in the AUTOEXEC.NCF of NetWare servers that don': have the MPR, and you will certainly want to examine the commands that INETCFG adds to the NETINFO.CFG file. As a result, we will begin to examine RIP by examining the parameters in LOAD TCPIP and LOAD IP relevant tc routing configuration. After reviewing the relevant options for the LOAD TCPIP command, we will examine the BIND IP options associated with IP routing.

LOAD TCP/IP Routing Options

Two LOAD TCPIP options control routing functions:

▶ *RIP=YES|NO*. Determines whether RIP is active or inactive. The default value for the RIP parameter is YES.

▶ *FORWARD=YES|NO*. Determines whether the server will forward IP datagrams. The default value of the FORWARD parameter is NO.

Settings for these parameters are determined by the role of the server and by other routing protocols in use on the network. Let's look at some situations to determine the most appropriate configurations.

A NetWare Server on a Single-Segment Network   A single-homed server (see Figure 10.7) cannot forward traffic, so forwarding should be disabled. Because all servers are attached to the same network segment, there is no need for a routing protocol that enables servers on different segments to exchange routing information. Therefore, the settings of all servers attached to a single-segment network can be configured with RIP and forwarding are both disabled using this command:

```
LOAD TCPIP RIP=NO
```

RIP is enabled by default, and the RIP=NO parameter is required if RIP is to be disabled. Forwarding is disabled by default and the FORWARD=NO parameter can be omitted.

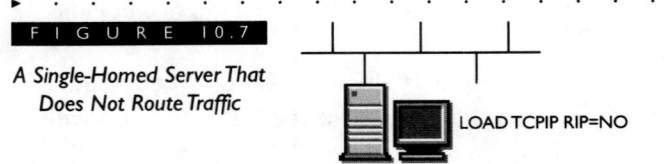

FIGURE 10.7

*A Single-Homed Server That
Does Not Route Traffic*

LOAD TCPIP RIP=NO

A Single NetWare Router on an Internetwork Any NetWare TCP/IP server
equipped with two network interface boards attached to different network
segments (see Figure 10.8) can forward IP traffic between the network segments.
If the server is the only router on the internetwork, it is unnecessary to run RIP,
because there are no other routers with which routing data can be exchanged.
Therefore, TCP/IP can be activated with this command, which enables forwarding
and disables RIP:

```
LOAD TCPIP RIP=NO FORWARD=YES
```

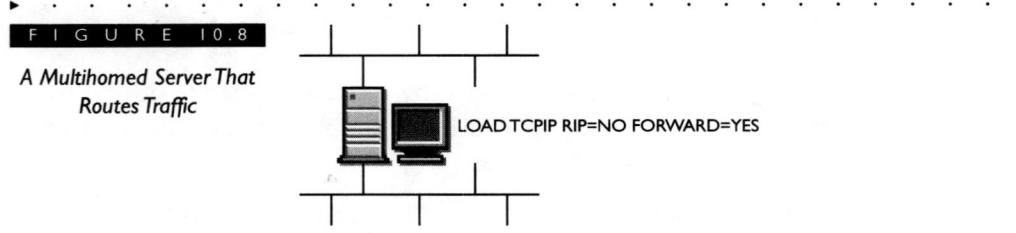

FIGURE 10.8

*A Multihomed Server That
Routes Traffic*

LOAD TCPIP RIP=NO FORWARD=YES

Multiple NetWare Routers on an Internetwork If any other routers are present
(see Figure 10.9), you must decide how the routers will be made aware of the
available routes. You could configure static routes, or if you prefer to have the
routers exchange dynamic routing information, you will need to enable RIP on all
routers. RIP is the only mechanism NetWare 3 provides for exchanging routes.
Under these circumstances, you would activate RIP by accepting the default value
of the RIP parameter, and TCP/IP would be loaded with the following command:

```
LOAD TCPIP FORWARD=YES
```

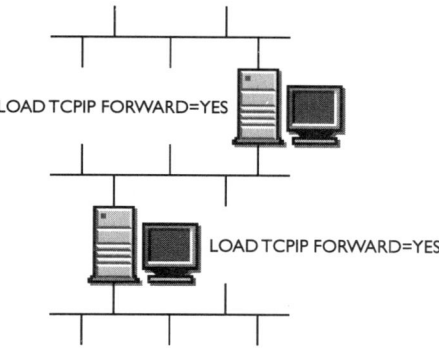

A Multihomed Server That
Operates a Routing Protocol

Single-Homed NetWare Servers on an Internetwork   Servers that do not forward datagrams may or may not benefit from participating in RIP broadcasts. Let's look at two situations.

In Figure 10.10, server S2 can reach remote networks only through a single path, via S1. If this path fails, S2 cannot learn another path. As a result, it is not necessary for S2 to run a routing protocol. It is sufficient to configure S2 with a single static route that defines S1 as the default router for S2; therefore, TCP/IP would be loaded with the following command:

```
LOAD TCPIP RIP=NO
```

Because S1 will not be exchanging RIP advertisements with other routers, RIP can also be deactivated on S1, as shown in Figure 10.10.

A Multisegment Network
That Does Not Require RIP

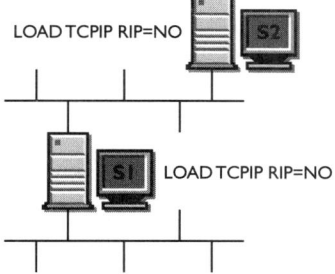

In Figure 10.11, server S5 has two paths to network NET2, via S3 and S4. If S3 is configured as the default router for S5 and S3 fails, S5 can only learn a new route if it is receiving RIP broadcasts. Therefore, even though S5 is not routing datagrams, the following command configures S5 with RIP enabled:

```
LOAD TCPIP
```

Servers S3 should be configured with RIP and forwarding active using the command:

```
LOAD TCPIP FORWARD=YES
```

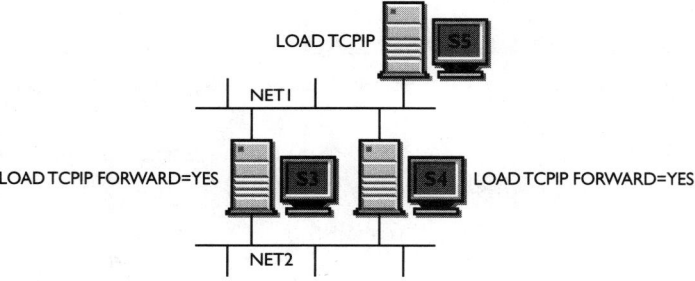

F I G U R E   10.11

Configuring Routers on an Internetwork with Multiple Routes

BIND IP Routing Options

Table 10.1 summarizes the options that can be used with the BIND IP command. Not all of the options are related to routing, but all have been included here for completeness. Four parameters are related to routing: GATE, DEFROUTE, COST, and POISON.

TABLE 10.1	PARAMETER	VALUE	PURPOSE
BIND IP Command Parameters	ADDR	IP address	Specifies the IP address to be associated with the interface being bound.
	MASK	Subnet mask	Specifies the IP network mask that applies to the network attached to the interface being bound.

PARAMETER	VALUE	PURPOSE
ARP	YES or NO	Specifies whether the Address Resolution Protocol will be used to resolve IP addresses to hardware addresses. When the value is NO, the host part of the IP address is mapped to the local hardware address. It is strongly recommended that the value of this parameter be set to the default value of YES.
BCAST	IP address	Specifies an IP address to be used for broadcasting messages on this network. By default, the broadcast is 255.255.255.255 (0xFF.0xFF.0xFF.0xFF).
COST	1–15 (decimal)	The cost of this interface in hops that will be advertised by RIP. The default value is 1.
DEFROUTE	YES or NO	If TCP/IP is loaded with the FORWARD=YES parameter, this parameter causes the server to announce this node through RIP as a default gateway. The default value is NO.
GATE	IP address	Specifies the IP address of a default gateway (router) for this interface. This parameter is not recommended when RIP is active on the server, in which case, the server can obtain all routing information from RIP.
POISON	YES or NO	If the value of this parameter is YES, poison reverse is active and split horizon is inactive. If this parameter is NO (the default), poison reverse is inactive and split horizon is active.

Using the COST Parameter   A router will have at least two interfaces, and each interface could be assigned its own COST parameter, which specifies the cost that RIP will advertise for this interface. To see how costs are advertised, examine Figure 10.12. In this figure, Router R1 is equipped with two interfaces:

▸ The interface on Network 1 is configured with a cost of 2.

▸ The interface on Network 2 is configured with a cost of 5.

The cost R1 advertises for a given network is the cost assigned to the interface attached to that network. Consequently, R1 has a route to Network 1, which is advertised to Network 2 with a cost of 2. Also, R1 has a route to Network 2, which is advertised to Network 1 with a cost of 5.

Host H1 receives a route advertisement from R1 indicating that R1's cost to reach Network 2 is 5. H1's cost to reach Network 1 is 1. H1 adds its cost to reach Network 1 to R1's cost to reach Network 2 and concludes that H1 can reach Network 2 with a cost of 6.

Host H2 receives a route advertisement from R1, indicating that R1's cost to reach Network 1 is 2. H2's cost to reach Network 2 is 1. H2 adds its cost to reach Network 1 to R1's cost to reach Network 1 and concludes that H2 can reach Network 1 with a cost of 3.

FIGURE 10.12

How COST Parameters Affect Route Advertisements

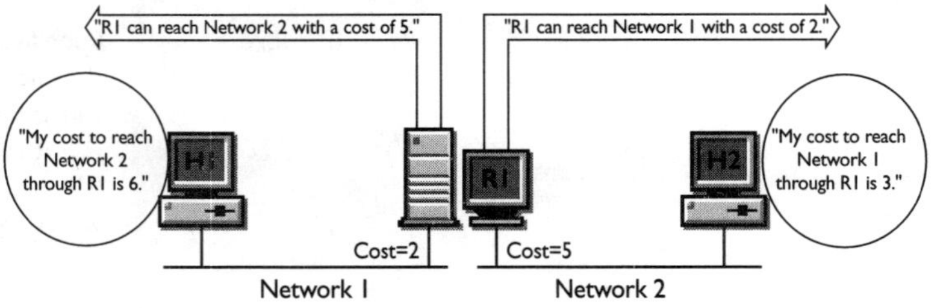

"R1 can reach Network 2 with a cost of 5."

"R1 can reach Network 1 with a cost of 2."

"My cost to reach Network 2 through R1 is 6."

"My cost to reach Network 1 through R1 is 3."

Cost=2   Cost=5

Network 1   Network 2

The COST parameter can be used to encourage or discourage the use of certain routes. Consider the network in Figure 10.13. R1 is a dedicated router that has been put in place to handle the bulk of traffic between Network 1 and Network 2. S1 is a NetWare server that has been configured as a router (RIP=YES

FORWARD=YES). The administrator wishes the majority of traffic to be routed through R1 to avoid loading down the server with routing duties. Therefore, when IP is bound on S1, the cost of the interface would be set to a value greater than 1, as in the following example:

```
BIND IP to NE2000_2_EII ADDR=2.0.0.1 COST=2
```

If the cost of R1 is 1, traffic normally will flow through R1. If R1 fails or is shut down for maintenance, hosts on Network 1 will begin to use S1 to reach Network 2.

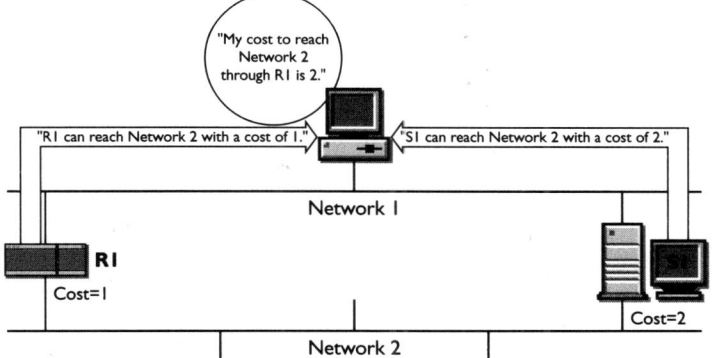

FIGURE 10.13

Using COST to Discourage Use of a Route

Using the DEFROUTE Parameter The DEFROUTE parameter takes effect only if the server is configured as a router by loading TCP/IP with the FORWARD=YES parameter. If the server is a router and the DEFROUTE=YES parameter is included with the BIND IP command, the server will advertise itself as a default router in RIP advertisements. That is to say, the server will advertise only the default route 0.0.0.0. Hosts that receive the default route announcement will add this server to their routing tables as a default router.

Careless use of the DEFROUTE parameter on multiple servers can result in network routing loops. As such, default route advertisements are very dangerous and should be used with extreme caution.

Using the GATE Parameter If RIP is not active on a server, the GATE parameter can be used to specify a default gateway. Figure 10.14 illustrates a situation in which a default gateway might be configured. Server S1 must be configured with a default gateway address that enables it to send datagrams to S2 for routing. This is accomplished by using a BIND IP command similar to the following on S1:

```
BIND IP TO NE2000_1_EII ADDR=10.0.0.10 GATE=10.0.0.1
```

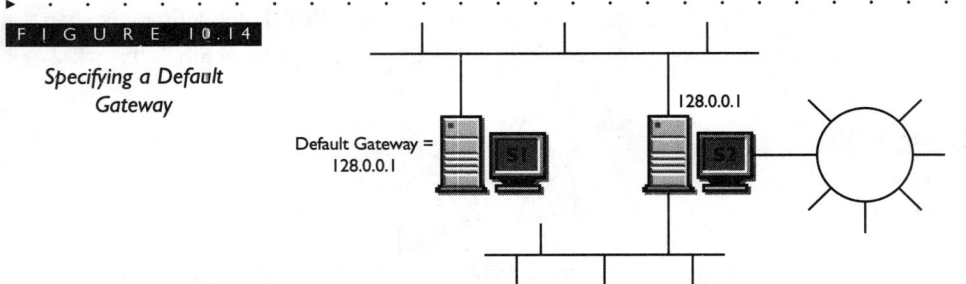

F I G U R E   10.14

Specifying a Default Gateway

As shown during the preceding discussion about static routing, a server that has only one possible routing path gains little by running a dynamic routing protocol. Use of the default gateway parameter can enhance performance in such situations.

Using the POISON Parameter   By default, NetWare routers are configured to use the split-horizon technique to limit the severity of the count-to-infinity problem. As you learned in Chapter 4, split-horizon breaks routing loops by preventing a router from advertising a route back to the interface from which the route was received.

Poison reverse is an alternative to split horizon that enhances network stability but increases network traffic. Routers configured to use poison reverse advertise a route back to the interface from which the route was received, but they advertise the route with a metric of 16, indicating that the destination is unreachable. In this way, poison reverse immediately notifies routers of invalid routes.

Enable poison reverse with the POISON=YES parameter when you wish to promote network stability at the cost of increased network traffic. By default, poison reverse is disabled (POISON=NO) and split horizon is enabled.

Example Routing Configurations

Here are two examples that illustrate the use of TCP/IP configuration parameters.

Configuring a Server as an End Node   A NetWare server is to be configured with the following characteristics:

► The IP address is 192.168.8.20.

► The server is an end node (no forwarding).

► RIP will not be active.

► The server will use 192.168.8.1 as a default router.

► The default subnet mask is used on this network.

To configure TCP/IP on this server, the following commands would be included in the AUTOEXEC.NCF file:

```
LOAD NE2000 FRAME=ETHERNET_II NAME=NE2000_1_EII other
parameters

LOAD TCPIP RIP=NO

BIND IP TO NE2000_1_EII ADDR=.192.168.8.20 GATE=192.168.8.1
```

Configuring a Server as a Router   A server will be configured as a router with the following characteristics:

► The server is a router with two interfaces.

► The IP address of the first interface is 10.1.1.2 with a cost of 2.

► The IP address of the second interface is 10.2.2.5 with a cost of 1.

► Both interfaces will be configured with the subnet mask 255.255.0.0.

► RIP will be active.

► Forwarding will be active.

► Poison reverse will be active.

The commands to configure TCP/IP on this server are as follows:

```
LOAD NE2000 FRAME=ETHERNET_II NAME=NE2000_1_EII other
parameters

LOAD NE2000 FRAME=ETHERNET_II NAME=NE2000_2_EII other
parameters

LOAD TCPIP FORWARD=YES

BIND IP TO NE2000_1_EII ADDR=80.1.1.2 MASK=255.255.0.0
POISON=YES COST=2

BIND IP TO NE2000_2_EII ADDR=80.2.2.5 MASK=255.255.0.0
POISON=YES
```

Router Configuration with INETCFG

The NetWare MultiProtocol Router component of NetWare 5 includes the INETCFG utility, which greatly simplifies configuration of routing parameters. The parameters for configuring RIP fall into two categories: TCP/IP load parameters and TCP/IP bind parameters. These groups of parameters are accessed through different menus in INETCFG.

Configuring TCP/IP Load Parameters for RIP

TCP/IP load parameters affect the settings of the RIP and FORWARD parameters in the LOAD TCPIP command.

To configure the TCP/IP load parameters for RIP, do the following:

1. Start INETCFG by typing **LOAD INETCFG** at the server console.

2. Select the *Protocols* option in the Internetworking Configuration menu.

3. Select *TCP/IP* in the Protocol Configuration menu to open the TCP/IP Protocol Configuration form shown in Figure 10.15.

4. If this server will be forwarding packets, set the value of the *IP Packet Forwarding* field to *Enabled ("Router")*. This setting adds the FORWARD=YES parameter to the LOAD TCPIP command.

If this server will not be forwarding packets, set the value of the IP Packet Forwarding field to *Disabled ("End Node")*. This setting adds the FORWARD=NO parameter to the LOAD TCPIF command.

5. To enable RIP on this server, set the value of the *RIP* field to *Enabled*. This setting adds the RIP=YES parameter to the LOAD TCPIP command.

To disable RIP on this server, set the value of the *RIP* field to *Disabled*. This setting adds the RIP=NO parameter to the LOAD TCPIP command.

6. After configuring these parameters, press Esc to exit the form. Choose Yes to update the TCP/IP protocol when prompted.

F I G U R E   10.15

TCP/IP Load Parameters

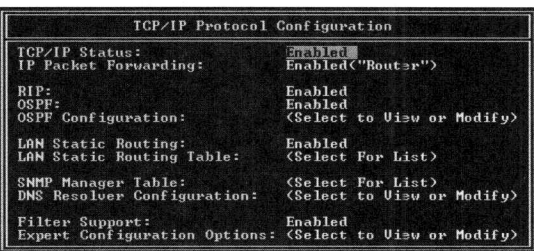

Configuring TCP/IP Bind Parameters for RIP

The TCP/IP bind parameters determine the parameters that configure individual interfaces when the BIND IP command is used. Some, but not all, parameters configured in INETCFG are reflected by parameters entered in the BIND IP command.

To configure TCP/IP bind parameters:

1. Start INETCFG by typing **LOAD INETCFG** at the server console.

2. Select the *Bindings* option in the Internetworking Configuration menu. This will open the Configured Protocol To Network Interface Bindings window, which lists bindings that have been configured.

3a. To add a new binding:

- Press Insert in the Configured Protocol To Network Interface Bindings window.

- Select *TCP/IP* from the list of configured protocols.

- Select a network interface from the list of configured network interfaces. When you press Enter, INETCFG will open the Binding TCP/IP to a LAN Interface window.

3b. To reconfigure an existing binding, select the binding in the Configured Protocol To Network Interface Bindings window. When you press Enter, INETCFG will open the Binding TCP/IP to a LAN Interface window.

4. Select the *RIP Bind Options* field in the Binding TCP/IP to a LAN Interface window. The RIP Bind Options window will be displayed (see Figure 10.16). The fields in this form are configured as follows:

- *Network Interface*. This is a read-only field that indicates which interface is being configured. The other fields are editable.

- *Interface Group*. If the interface specified in the *Network Interface* field is a member of a WAN interface group, the interface group name will appear in this field. This field cannot be modified.

- *Status*. This field indicates whether RIP is enabled or disabled for this interface. This value is automatically set to *Enabled* when RIP is enabled for the server in the TCP/IP Protocol Configuration form.

  You can enable or disable RIP for this interface by changing the value of the Status field. The effect of enabling or disabling RIP from this form depends on the TCP/IP load settings.

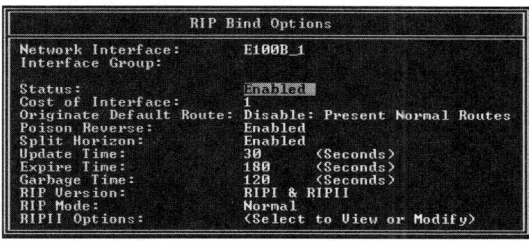

F I G U R E   10.16

Configuring RIP Bind Options in INETCFG

If the *IP Packet Forwarding* field is set to *Enabled ("Router")*, enabling RIP in the Status field configures this interface to participate in the exchange of RIP advertisements.

If the *IP Packet Forwarding* field is set to *Disabled ("End Node")*, enabling RIP in the *Status* field configures this interface to receive RIP advertisements from routers; however, this server will not generate RIP advertisements. This setting enables a non-routing host to update its routing table from RIP advertisements that it receives.

- *Cost of Interface.* This field specifies the cost that will be advertised for this interface. Enter a value between 1 and 16, where 16 indicates that routing is disabled for this interface. This parameter configures the COST parameter in the BIND IP command. See the section "Using the COST Parameter" for more information about how RIP advertises interface costs.

- *Originate Default Route.* This field determines whether this router will advertise itself as a default router.

  Set the value to *Disable: Present Normal Routes* to have this router send normal RIP advertisements. This setting adds the DEFROUTE=NO parameter to the BIND IP command.

  Set the value to *Enable: Present Default Route* to have this router advertise itself as a default router. This setting adds the DEFROUTE=YES parameter to the BIND IP command.

- *Poison Reverse.* This field determines whether this interface will use poison reverse to discourage routing loops. Set the value to *Enabled* to configure the interface to use poison reverse. Poison reverse can be enabled only if the *Split Horizon* field has also been configured with the value *Enabled.*

- *Split Horizon.* This field determines whether this interface will use split horizon to discourage routing loops. By default, the value of this field is set to *Enabled.* Poison reverse can be enabled only when split horizon is enabled.

- *Update Time.* This field specifies the interval between RIP advertisements. By default and by convention, RIP for IP advertises routes at 30-second intervals, and you should seldom need to modify this value.

- *Expire Time.* If an update for a route is not received within the interval specified by this field, the router will expire the route.

- *Garbage Time.* The router will retain an expired route for the time specified by this field before the route is discarded.

- *RIP Version.* This field has four possible values:

  RIPI configures the interface to use the RIP I only.

  RIPII configures the interface to use RIP II only. Choose this setting only if all routers on the network support RIP II.

  RIPI & RIPII configures the interface to operate with both levels of RIP.

  Send Only configures the interface to send RIP I packets announcing its routing table. Incoming RIP advertisements are discarded.

NOTE

The *Send Only* option is commonly used in environments that consist of OSPF and RIP routers. A router participating in OSPF routing can be configured to use Send Only mode so that it will announce its routing table to RIP routers on the network.

- *RIP Mode.* This field has three possible values:

  Normal. The router sends and accepts RIP updates. This is the default value.

  Receive Only. The router receives but does not send RIP updates. The router can learn routes from other routers. This mode is typically used to configure end nodes.

  Send Only. The router sends but does not accept RIP updates.

- *RIP II Options.* Selecting this field opens a RIP II Configuration form with two fields.

  The *Authentication* field determines whether RIP II authentication is enabled or disabled. The default value is *Disabled.* Change the value to *Enabled* if you wish RIP II routers to use an authentication key to verify messages.

  The *Authentication Key* field accepts a 16-byte string that functions as a password when authentication is enabled on the attached network.

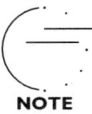

NOTE

Note that RIP authentication keys are formatted as ASCII text. Because they are not encrypted, they can be viewed using a protocol analyzer. Consequently, you should not rely on authentication keys to provide a high level of security.

After RIP routing has been configured in INETCFG, the changes must be activated. Because not all changes are activated by the REINITIALIZE SERVER command, it may be necessary to restart the server or execute the command INITIALIZE SERVER to activate the changes.

Configuring OSPF

Before you can make much sense out of OSPF, you need to be familiar with the alphabet scup that appears in OSPF verbiage. Otherwise, you'll never make sense out of expressions such as "connecting an OSPF AS to a RIP AS requires an ASBR that has an interface in each AS." You see the acronyms ASBR, ABR, and AS quite frequently because the full terms are such tongue twisters. How many times do you want to say "autonomous system boundary router" in one day?

Let's take a moment to define some OSPF terms. This summary focuses on the components of an OSPF routing system and how they are related. See Chapter 4 for a more theoretical discussion of how OSPF builds routing tables.

A Review of OSPF Terminology

Figure 10.17 shows a diagram of a network that uses OSPF routing. The diagram focuses on routers, and of course, many more TCP/IP hosts would appear on the networks that the routers join. Now, let's review the components of the network, with an emphasis on concepts that you must consider when configuring OSPF routers.

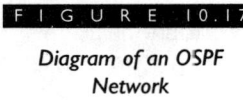

FIGURE 10.17

Diagram of an OSPF Network

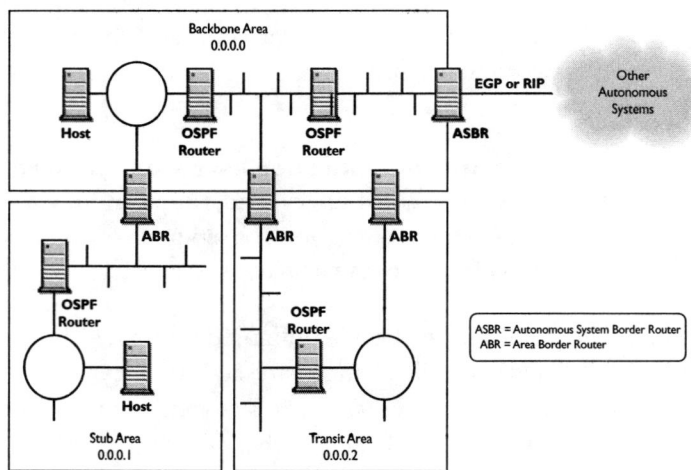

An *autonomous system* (AS) is a collection of networks that share a common routing protocol and fall under the same administrative jurisdiction. Figure 10.15 includes one OSPF AS.

Areas define groups of OSPF routers that share a common link-state database. OSPF advertises routes using *link-state advertisements* (LSAs), which are flooded throughout an area. *Flooding* describes the process of distributing LSAs to all OSPF routers in an area. On small-to-medium size networks, the entire AS can be configured as a single area.

One router in an area is identified as the *designated router* through an election process that can be configured by setting priorities for individual routers. The designated router is responsible for preparing LSAs for the area.

Within an area, OSPF routers communicate with *neighbors*, which are peer OSPF routers. On broadcast networks, OSPF routers can discover their peers using Hello packets. Only routers that exchange Hello packets establish themselves as neighbors. On non-broadcast networks, such as X.25 and frame relay, the addresses of neighbors must be added manually to the routers' configurations.

As areas grow in size, OSPF performance diminishes in two areas: it takes longer to recompute the new routes that result from link-state changes, and increasing amounts of network traffic are devoted to distributing link-state advertisements. Consequently, the design of OSPF accommodates partitioning the AS into multiple areas. This design has two advantages:

▶ Areas can be configured around organizational or geographical relationships, limiting the sharing of routing information and making the network more secure.

▶ The number of LSAs in the areas is reduced, and they are limited to the information users require most often.

 **Novell recommends limiting the size of an AS to 200 routers.**

NOTE

Areas must be organized hierarchically, with one area designated as a *backbone area*. All other areas must connect to the backbone area. Each area is identified by an *area ID*, a four-byte number, which is usually expressed in dotted-decimal form. These area IDs are not IP addresses and don't need to follow IP address restrictions. The backbone area is always assigned the area ID 0.0.0.0.

Areas must be configured out of contiguous groups of routers and networks. In other words, parts of an area may not be separated by another area. Because most areas typically support a localized subset of hosts, it is seldom a problem to configure areas out of contiguous components. Because only one backbone is permitted, however, it may be difficult to configure a backbone contiguously on a geographically dispersed network.

It is possible to partition the backbone area into multiple physical areas, and to enable the backbone partitions to communicate using a *virtual link* through another area. The area that supports the virtual link is called a *virtual-link transit area*. Be aware that, in Novell's words, virtual links are "complicated and error-prone." Figure 10.18 illustrates a backbone partitioned to span a large area. In such cases, a virtual link must be established to extend the backbone partition to the New York area. This approach enables Chicago and New York to share the same leased circuit between Chicago and Los Angeles.

FIGURE 10.18

Partitions of a Backbone Connected Through a Virtual Link

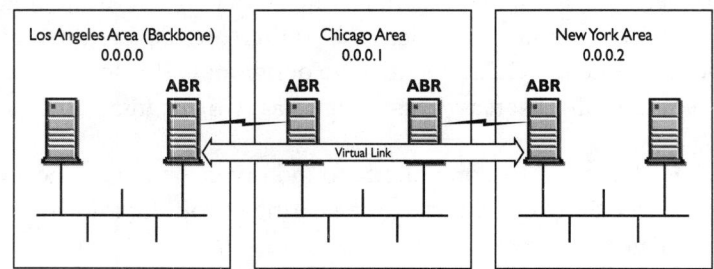

Area border routers (ABRs) connect areas and advertise destinations across area boundaries in the form of summary link advertisements.

Two types of areas can connect to the backbone area:

▶ *Stub areas* connect to the backbone through a single ABR. The ABR of a stub area does not advertise external routes. Instead, because all external traffic must go through the ABR, a single default route is advertised. Configuration of stub areas reduces the memory, processing, and bandwidth requirements of the ABR but obviously makes the area subject to a single point of failure.

▶ *Transit areas* connect to the backbone with more than one ABR. Processing, memory, and bandwidth requirements are higher for ABRs than for support transit areas.

Routing within an area, or *intra-area routing*, can take place without knowledge of external routes. Routing between areas, inter-area routing, requires ABRs to exchange routing information about their areas.

Autonomous system boundary routers (ASBRs) are responsible for routing traffic between the OSPF AS and ASs based on other routing protocols such as RIP or EGP. External routes are advertised through external link advertisements.

NOTE

OSPF gives different preferences to routes obtained from the local AS (internal routes) and from remote ASs (external routes). On a network that includes OSPF and RIP routers, for example, an OSPF router prefers a route that it learns internally from another OSPF router over a route that it learns externally from a RIP router. If you are configuring your network using only NetWare routers, you don't need to be concerned with the preferences. If, however, your network includes third-party routers in addition to NetWare routers, you need to ensure that all routers employ the same preferences. Consult the TCP/IP Reference manual for more information about OSPF protocol preferences.

OSPF Protocol Configuration

Setting up OSPF routing on a server involves the following steps:

1. Enabling OSPF protocol support

2. Configuring OSPF protocol settings

3. Configuring areas

4. Configuring virtual links (if applicable)

5. Configuring OSPF interface bindings

6. Activating the changes

These procedures are performed starting from the TCP/IP Protocol Configuration form in INETCFG. The following sections describe each procedure in detail.

Step 1. Enabling OSPF Protocol Support

Use the following steps to open the TCP/IP Protocol Configuration form:

1. Start INETCFG by typing **LOAD INETCFG** at the server console.

2. Select the *Protocols* option in the Internetworking Configuration menu.

3. Select *TCP/IP* in the Protocol Configuration menu. This will open the TCP/IP Protocol Configuration form shown in Figure 10.19.

To enable OSPF protocol support, set the value of the *OSPF* field to *Enabled*.

Step 2. Configuring OSPF Protocol Settings

Select the *OSPF Configuration* field in the TCP/IP Protocol Configuration form to open the OSPF Configuration form shown in Figure 10.19. Two settings are configured on this form:

▶ *Router ID*. This field uniquely identifies this router within the OSPF AS. The default value is *First IP Interface*, which identifies this router using the first IP address bound to an interface on the router.

Because each IP address on your internetwork should be unique, it can be used to identify your routers uniquely as well. If you wish, however, press Enter in the *Router ID* field and enter a router ID, using four-byte, dotted-decimal notation.

▶ *Autonomous System Boundary Router.* This field determines whether this router will serve as an ASBR. Any router on the backbone or in a transit area can function as an ASBR. Configuring a router as an ASBR increases the router's work and places greater demands on the router's memory and processing capabilities.

▶ *IP Load Sharing*. When load sharing is enabled, IP will divide traffic across routes that have equal costs. At most, four equal-cost routes can be configured for a given destination.

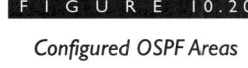

F I G U R E   10.19

Configuring the OSPF Protocol

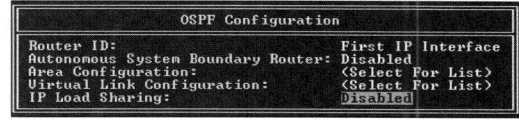

Step 3. Configuring Areas

To configure areas within the AS, select the *Area Configuration* field in the OSPF Configuration form. Then press Enter to open the OSPF Areas list shown in Figure 10.20, which shows all areas that have been defined. If you are creating the first area, INETCFG assumes it is the backbone area and presents the area ID 0.0.0.0 as a default.

F I G U R E   10.20

Configured OSPF Areas

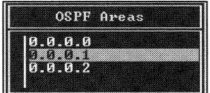

To modify an area, highlight the area in the list and press Enter to open the OSPF Area Configuration form shown in Figure 10.21. If you are configuring the first area in the AS, select the 0.0.0.0 entry and press Enter to configure the backbone area.

To add an area, press Insert to open the OSPF Area Configuration form. To delete an area, highlight the area ID and press Delete.

F I G U R E   10.21

Configuring an OSPF Area

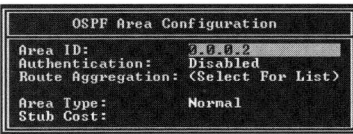

The OSPF Area Configuration form has five fields. Depending on the type of area being defined, some of the fields may be inactive. If, for example, you are configuring the backbone area by specifying 0.0.0.0 in the Area ID field, only the Area ID and Authentication fields will be active. The fields used to configure the OSPF area are as follows:

▶ *Authentication.* To activate authentication, change the value of this field to *Enabled.* When authentication is enabled, this router will accept only OSPF messages identified by an authentication key. The key is specified when OSPF is bound to a network interface. If authentication is activated, it must be activated for all routers in the area.

▶ *Area ID.* To configure a non-backbone area, edit the value of the *Area ID* field to specify a value other than 0.0.0.0, which can be assigned only to the backbone area. Assigning a non-zero value to the Area ID field will activate the *Area Type* field.

▶ *Route Aggregation.* Route aggregation is used to collect the network numbers of several networks that OSPF should advertise from a single area. To specify network numbers that are to be aggregated under this area, press Enter to open the Aggregated Networks form. Then press Insert and enter the network number and subnet mask of each network to be added to the aggregation. All subnets of the specified networks are automatically included.

▶ *Area Type.* To configure a transit area, leave the value of the *Area Type* field with the default value of Normal. To configure a stub area, change the value of the *Area Type* field to Stub. This will activate the *Stub Cost* field.

▶ *Stub Cost.* Enter a value in the range of 1 through 16777215 in this field. The value you enter will be used to advertise the stub cost when the summary link advertisement is prepared for the stub area. The stub cost represents the cost of all datagrams routed to the area.

When OSPF areas have been configured, press Escape to return to the OSPF Configuration form.

Step 4. Configuring Virtual Links

If the backbone is not contiguous, a virtual link must be specified to connect the backbone partitions. To configure virtual links, select *Virtual Link Configuration* in the OSPF Configuration form and press Enter to present the OSPF Virtual Links list shown in Figure 10.22.

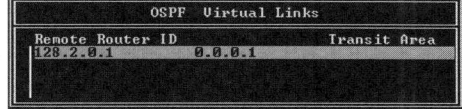

F I G U R E   10.22

Configured OSFF
Virtual Links

To add a virtual link, press Insert to open the OSPF Virtual Link Configuration form. To edit an existing link, select the link and press Enter to open the OSPF Virtual Link Configuration form. To delete an area, highlight the area ID and press Delete.

The OSPF Virtual Link Configuration form is shown in Figure 10.23. This form has five fields, which are configured as follows:

▶ *Router ID of Neighbor.* Specifies the IP address of the router at the other end of the virtual link. Press Insert in this field to present the list of host names defired in the HOSTS file, or enter an IP address.

▶ *Transit Area.* Specifies the area ID of the virtual link transit area that will support the virtual link.

▶ *Authentication Key.* This is an optional field. If authentication is enabled in the virtual link transit area, enter the eight-byte authentication key in this field

▶ *Hello Interval.* Specifies the time in seconds between transmission of Hello packets to the network interface specified in the *Router ID of Neighbor* field. The default value is 10 seconds. This value must be the same for all routers on this network or virtual link.

▶ *Router Dead Interval.* Specifies the time in seconds between Hello packets that a router will wait before declaring dead the router at the other end of the virtual link. This value must be the same for all routers on this network or virtual link.

When virtual links have been configured, press Escape to return to the OSPF Configuration form.

▶ · ◀

F I G U R E 10.23

*Configuring an OSPF
Virtual Link*

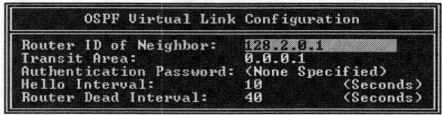

```
         OSPF Virtual Link Configuration
Router ID of Neighbor:    128.2.0.1
Transit Area:             0.0.0.1
Authentication Password:  <None Specified>
Hello Interval:           10          <Seconds>
Router Dead Interval:     40          <Seconds>
```

Step 5. Configuring OSPF Interface Bindings

When the OSPF protocol has been configured as discussed in Steps 1 through 4, OSPF can be bound to individual network interfaces as follows:

1. Start INETCFG by typing **LOAD INETCFG** at the server console.

2. Select the *Bindings* option in the Internetworking Configuration menu to open the Configured Protocols To Network Interface Bindings list.

3. Select an existing TCP/IP binding or, if necessary, create a binding as described in Chapter 8.

4. In the Binding TCP/IP to a LAN Interface form, select *OSPF Bind Options* and press Enter to open the OSPF Bind Options form shown in Figure 10.24. The fields in this form are completed as follows:

- *Network Interface.* Identifies the network interface for which OSPF is being configured (read-only).

- *Status.* When OSPF is enabled for the server, it is enabled for all interfaces on the server. To disable OSPF for a specific interface, change the value of this field to *Disabled*. When OSPF is disabled, this interface will not exchange route information with other OSPF routers.

- *Cost of Interface.* Specifies the cost OSPF associates with sending a datagram through this interface.

- *Area ID.* Specifies the OSPF area to which this router belongs. Areas must be defined in the OSPF Area Configuration form.

- *Priority.* Specifies the relative priorities that determine which router will be selected as the designated router for the area. Set the priority parameter to favor the selection of specific routers as the area designated router.

- *Authentication Password.* If authentication is enabled in this router's area, enter the eight-byte authentication string in this field.

- *Hello Interval.* Specifies the time in seconds between transmission of Hello packets to the network interface specified being configured. This value must be the same for all routers on this network or virtual link.

- *Router Dead Interval.* This field specifies the time in seconds between Hello packets that a router will wait before declaring a router dead. This value must be the same for all routers on this network or virtual link.

- *Neighbor List.* On broadcast networks such as Ethernet and token ring, routers can discover their neighbors dynamically using the Hello protocol. On non-broadcast networks such as X.25, frame relay, and PPP, neighbors must be added manually to the interface configuration. Select this field to open the OSPF Neighbors list and add the addresses of neighbors to the list.

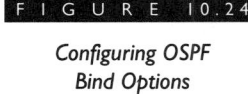

FIGURE 10.24

*Configuring OSPF
Bind Options*

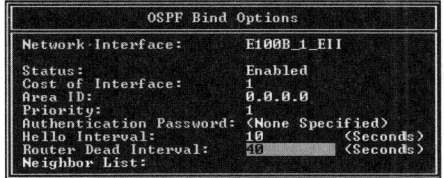

Step 6. Activating the Changes

After configuring OSPF, restart the server to activate the changes.

Managing OSPF

Here are a few tips for tuning OSPF:

- OSPF generates less network traffic than RIP. To achieve that economy, OSPF needs more processor and memory than RIP. In high-traffic areas, consider setting up dedicated routers using the MultiProtocol Router.

- Use areas to reduce the levels of LSA traffic.

▶ Use interface costs to favor the most efficient routes. Consider characteristics such as bandwidth and reliability when establishing interface costs.

In Chapter 13, you learn how to use TCPCON to inspect the configurations of TCP/IP computers. TCPCON also has an option that enables you to observe the configuration of OSPF. Figure 10.25 shows the OSPF Protocol Information screen in TCPCON. Take some time to explore the information that can be reached from this screen.

F I G U R E   10.25

*OSPF Protocol Information
in TCPCON*

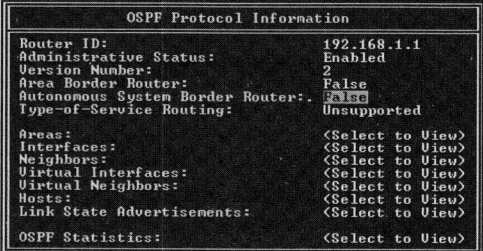

Here are highlights from a few of the more interesting possibilities.

Select the *Neighbors* field to view routers with which this router has established a neighbor relationship. All neighbors should indicate a State of "full," showing they are synchronized with this router.

You can view the link-state database by selecting the *Link State Advertisements* field. Each entry can be opened up to show its parameters, as shown in Figure 10.26. The *Contents* field shows a dump of the LSA in hexadecimal, which isn't particularly useful to most of us. However, all routers should be receiving identical LSAs from this router. You can verify this by examining the Checksum field, which should be the same on each router.

F I G U R E   10.26

*Examining the Link-State
Database*

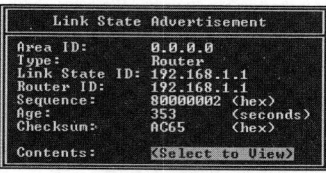

Running OSPF with RIP

A router running both RIP and OSPF does not necessarily forward routing information between the two environments. To enable OSPF to advertise routes derived from RIP, the OSPF router must be configured as an autonomous system border router (ASBR). The procedure is as follows:

1. Start INETCFG by typing **LOAD INETCFG** at the server console.

2. Select the *Protocols* option in the Internetworking Configuration menu to open the Protocol Configuration list.

3. Select *TCP/IP* in the Protocol Configuration list to open the TCP/IP Protocol Configuration form.

4. Select the *OSPF Configuration* field to open the OSPF Configuration form.

5. Change the value of the *Autonomous System Boundary Router* field to *Enabled*.

6. Press Escape to exit the form and save the changes.

Limit the number of routers configured as ASBRs. Functioning as an ASBR increases the processing overhead and memory requirement for the router. Also, each ASBR increases network traffic as the routers advertise the same routes. Novell recommends having at most two or three ASBRs between RIP and OSPF domains.

Configuring ICMP Router Discovery

If your TCP/IP network grows to significant size, you will probably have some NetWare servers and possible UNIX hosts that are not configured as IP routers. These hosts must be able to identify routers so that they can send datagrams to remote networks. What techniques are available for providing hosts with routing information?

One option is to configure the hosts with a default router address. However, that approach is inefficient in many cases. For example, in the network shown in Figure 10.27, A has several routes available to it. Router R1 is not always the most efficient route, and if Router R1 fails, A is dead in the water if it has only a default router with which to work.

▶ • ◀

*A Default Router Is
Inefficient on This Network*

Another approach is to configure A with RIP. OSPF routers can be configured to broadcast their routing tables to RIP, enabling A to obtain routing data. However, RIP broadcasts routing tables at 30-second intervals, which causes the traffic burden that we can avoid by using OSPF. Also, running RIP puts a load on A that may be undesirable.

A third approach is available if the host supports the ICMP Router Discovery Protocol. The ICMP Router Discovery Protocol has two types of messages that enable hosts to obtain the addresses of routers on the local network without running a full-blown routing protocol:

▸ *ICMP Router Advertisement Messages* are used by routers to advertise their presence on the network. These messages are broadcast or multicast to all hosts, and carry the IP address of the router and its preference level. Hosts use these messages to determine next-hop addresses. The router with the highest preference is selected as a default router.

▸ *ICMP Router Solicitation Messages* enable hosts to solicit router advertisements from all routers on the local network.

The ICMP Router Discovery Protocol is supported by NetWare 5/4.11/4.12, versions of NetWare configured with the NetWare MultiProtocol Router, and many UNIX implementations.

To configure the ICMP Router Discovery Protocol on a NetWare 5 server:

1. Start INETCFG by typing **LOAD INETCFG** at the server console.

2. Select the *Bindings* option in the Internetworking Configuration menu to open the Configured Protocols To Network Interface Bindings list.

3. Select an existing TCP/IP binding or, if necessary, create a binding as described in Chapter 8.

4. Select the *Expert TCP/IP Bind Options* field. Press Enter to open the Expert TCP/IP LAN Options window.

5. Select the *Router Discovery Options* field in the Expert TCP/IP LAN Options window to open the Router Discovery form shown in Figure 10.28.

Configuring ICMP Router Discovery

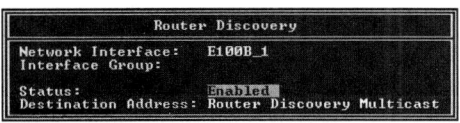

6. To enable router discovery, change the value of the *Status* field to *Enabled*.

7. On networks that support multicasting, set the value of the Destination Address field to *Router Discovery Multicast* (the default value).

If the network does not support multicasting, change the value of the Destination Address field to *Broadcast*, which configures the router discovery protocol to use the address 255.255.255.255.

8. Exit INETCFG, saving the configuration changes, and restart the server to activate the changes.

If IP packet forwarding and router discovery are both enabled, the server will send router discovery advertisements and respond to router advertisement requests. If IP packet forwarding is disabled and router discovery is enabled, the server sends router discovery requests to identify routers.

▶ · ◀

Filtering

Filtering enables you to determine which datagrams will be forwarded by a router. Under TCP/IP NetWare 5 supports filtering for RIP, EGP, OSPF, and packet forwarding. Filtering is configured using the FILTCFG NLM. You can apply filtering to routing protocols and to router packet forwarding. Because filtering is a router function, filters can be configured only on a multihomed NetWare server. Six categories of filters can be established:

▶ *Outgoing RIP Filters.* These filters restrict the routes that will be advertised by RIP. You can, for example, prevent a RIP router from advertising a route to a particular network or host.

▶ *Incoming RIP Filters.* These filters restrict the route advertisements that a RIP router will accept from other routers.

▶ *Outgoing EGP Filters.* When an EGP router learns a route from RIP, OSPF, or static routing tables, these filters determine whether the routes will be propagated to the router's EGP peers.

▶ *Incoming EGP Filters.* When an EGP router learns a route from an EGP peer, these filters determine whether the route will be added to the EGP router's routing table.

▶ *OSPF External Route Filters.* When an OSPF router learns a route from a non-OSPF domain (RIP or EGP), these filters determine whether the route will be propagated to the OSPF domain.

▶ *Packet Forwarding Filters.* Packet filters configure the router to block forwarding of specified types of packets.

Enabling Filter Support

Before you can specify filters for TCP/IP, you must enable filtering for the TCP/IP protocols. To enable filtering:

1. Start INETCFG by typing **LOAD INETCFG** at the server console.

2. Select the *Protocols* option in the Internetworking Configuration menu.

3. Select TCP/IP in the Protocol Configuration menu. This will open the TCP/IP Protocol Configuration form shown earlier in Figure 10.14.

4. Change the value of the *Filter Support* field to *Enabled*.

5. Exit INETCFG and enter the command **REINITIALIZE SERVER** to activate filtering.

Configuring Routing Protocol Filters

After filtering is enabled, use the FILTCFG.NLM to specify the filters you require. To specify filters for TCP/IP:

1. Start FILTCFG by typing **LOAD FILTCFG** at the server console.

2. The first menu displayed after entering the command LOAD FILTCFG enables you to specify whether you will enter filters for AppleTalk, IPX, TCP/IP, or Source Route Bridges. When TCP/IP is chosen, the form shown in Figure 10.29 is displayed. This form is used to enable or disable specific categories of filters. By default, all filter categories are disabled.

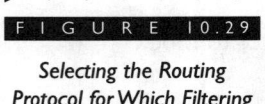

F I G U R E   10.29

Selecting the Routing Protocol for Which Filtering Is Being Configured

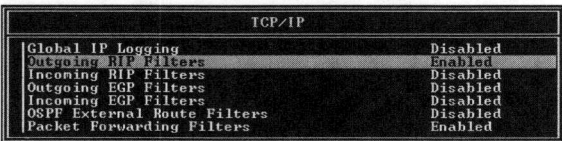

3. Select the RIP or OSPF filter option that you wish to configure and press Enter to open a Filters form similar to the one shown in Figure 10.30.

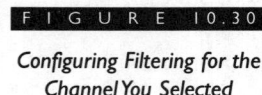

F I G U R E   10.30

Configuring Filtering for the Channel You Selected

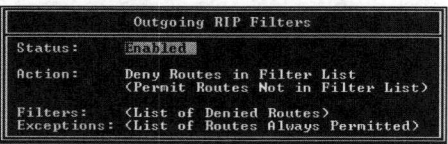

4. Select the *Status* field and change the value to *Enabled* to activate filtering.

5. By default, the value of the *Action* field is *Deny Routes in Filter List*. When this value is selected, you must explicitly specify the routes that will be filtered. Any routes that are not specified will not be filtered.

If desired, you can change the value of the *Action* field to *Permit Routes Not in Filter List*. When this value is selected, all routes are filtered out except for routes that you specify in the *Filters* field. If no routes are specified in the *Filters* field, all routes are filtered and no datagrams will be forwarded through this protocol.

6. Select the *Filters* field and press Enter to open a form similar to Figure 10.31. This form specifies filters that have been defined for this protocol. Notice that the highlighted filter is described in the top description box. Forms will differ somewhat depending on the protocol for which filtering is being configured.

▶ · ◀

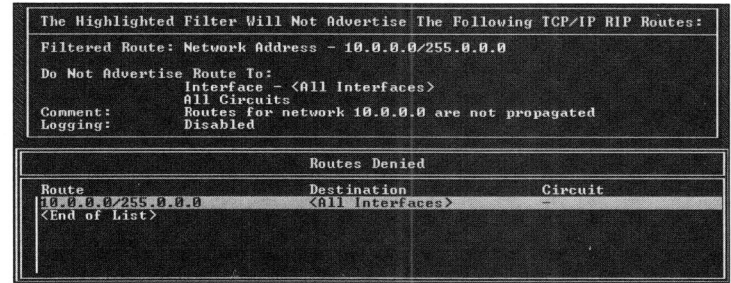

FIGURE 0.31

*Filters Defined
for a Protocol*

The Highlighted Filter Will Not Advertise The Following TCP/IP RIP Routes:

Filtered Route: Network Address — 10.0.0.0/255.0.0.0

Do Not Advertise Route To:
    Interface — <All Interfaces>
    All Circuits
Comment: Routes for network 10.0.0.0 are not propagated
Logging: Disabled

Routes Denied

Route	Destination	Circuit
10.0.0.0/255.0.0.0	<All Interfaces>	—
<End of List>		

7. To add a filter, press the INS key to open a Define Filter form similar to the one in Figure 10.32.

▶ · ◀

FIGURE 0.32

*Filters for RIP;
EGP Is Similar*

Define Filter

Filtered Route:
    Route to Network or Host: Network
    IP Address of Network/Host: 10.0.0.0
    Subnetwork Mask: 255.0.0.0

Do Not Advertise Route To:
    Destination Type:
    Destination: Interface
    Destination Circuit: <All Interfaces>

Advertised Hop Count:

Comment: Routes for network 10.0.0.0 are not propagated
Logging: Disabled

8. If you are specifying filtering for RIP or for EGP, the data entry fields in the Define Filter form are as follows:

- *Route to Network or Host*. This field specifies the routes that will be filtered and can have three values. Select *All Routes* to apply a filter routes for all hosts and all networks learned by this router. Select *Host* to apply a filter to routes to a specific host. Select *Network* to apply a filter to routes to a specific network.

- *IP Address of Network/Host*. If you are filtering for routes to a network or a host, enter the network or host IP address here.

- *Subnetwork Mask*. If you are filtering for a network or host, enter the subnet mask here.

- *Destination Type*. This field specifies the destination that will be filtered and can have two values. Select *Network* to filter routes destined for a specific network. Select *Interface* to specify the interface on this router for which the route is to be filtered; you can filter routes for a particular interface or for all interfaces.

- *Destination*. Press Enter in this field to open a form where you can specify the destination for which the filter is defined. If the destination is a network, press Enter to specify the IP address and subnet mask of the destination for this filter. If the destination is an interface, press Enter to select the interface to which the filter applies or to specify *All Interfaces* if desired.

- *Comment*. Enter an explanation of the filter if desired. Because the purposes of some filters can be obscure, it is a good idea to document the filter.

- *Logging*. When logging is enabled, the headers of packets that match the filters or exceptions will be logged to a BTRIEVE database located in SYS:\SYSTEM\CSLIB. Logging slows performance and should be enabled only when testing a router to ensure that the filter configuration is correct.

9. If you are specifying filtering for OSPF, the data entry fields in the Define Filter form are as follows:

- *Route to Network or Host.* This field has the same values as discussed in Step 8 for the RIP and EGP protocols.

- *IP Address of Network/Host.* If you are filtering for routes to a network or a host, enter the network or host IP address here.

- *Subnetwork Mask.* If you are filtering for a network or host, enter the subnet mask here.

- *Comment.* Enter an explanation of the filter if desired. Because the purposes of some filters can be obscure, it is a good idea to document the filter.

10. If you are specifying filters for packet forwarding, you are shown the Define Filters form shown in Figure 10.33. The data entry fields in this form are as follows:

- *Source Interface Type.* Select *Interface* to specify a specific interface as the source interface for the packet filter. Select *Interface Group* to specify a predefined interface group as the source interface for the packet filter.

- *Source Interface.* Select the interface or interface group that is the source of packets to be filtered. (Selecting *All Interfaces* prevents the router from forwarding all packets for the protocol you specify.)

- *Destination Interface Type.* Select *Interface* to specify a specific interface as the destination interface for the packet filter. Select *Interface Group* to specify a predefined interface group as the destination interface for the packet filter.

- *Destination Interface.* Select the interface or interface group that is the source of packets to be filtered. (Selecting *All Interfaces* prevents the router from forwarding all packets for the protocol you specify.)

- *Packet Type.* This field specifies the types of packets to be filtered. Press Enter to open a list from which packet types can be selected. The list contains entries for a wide range of TCP/IP protocols. Select *<ANY>* to filter packets for all TCP/IP services.

- *Protocol.* When you select a protocol in the *Packet Type* field, the transport protocol is indicated in this field.

- *Destination Port(s).* When you select a protocol in the *Packet Type* field, the port number associated with the protocol is indicated in this field.

- *Source Port(s).* When you select a protocol in the *Packet Type* field, the source port number associated with the protocol is indicated in this field.

- *Source Address Type.* Select *Any Address*, *Host*, or *Network* to specify the type of address that originates packets affected by this filter.

- *Source TCP/IP Address.* If *Host* or *Network* is selected in the *Source Address Type* field, enter the IP address here.

- *Destination Address Type.* Select *Any Address*, *Host*, or *Network* to specify the type of destination address for packets that will be affected by this filter.

- *Destination TCP/IP Address.* If *Host* or *Network* is selected in the *Destination Address Type* field, enter the IP address here.

- *Comment.* Enter an explanatory comment.

- *Logging.* When logging is enabled, the headers of packets that match the filters or exceptions will be logged to a BTRIEVE database located in SYS:\SYSTEM\CSLIB. Logging slows performance and should be enabled only when testing a router to ensure that the filter configuration is correct.

FIGURE 10.33

Filters for Packet Forwarding

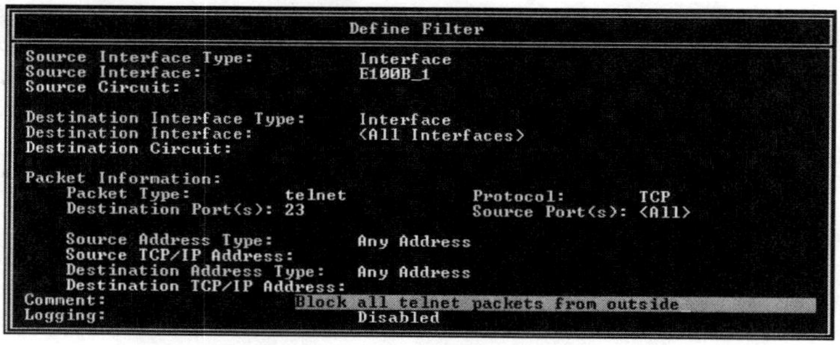

```
                                    Define Filter
Source Interface Type:              Interface
Source Interface:                   E100B_1
Source Circuit:

Destination Interface Type:         Interface
Destination Interface:              <All Interfaces>
Destination Circuit:

Packet Information:
      Packet Type:        telnet              Protocol:       TCP
      Destination Port(s): 23                 Source Port(s): <All>

      Source Address Type:          Any Address
      Source TCP/IP Address:
      Destination Address Type:     Any Address
      Destination TCP/IP Address:
Comment:              Block all telnet packets from outside
Logging:                            Disabled
```

11. After defining filters, press ESC to return to the Route Filters form. Select the *Exceptions* field and press Enter to specify any filters that are exceptions to the rule defined in the Action field.

- If the value of the *Action* field is *Deny Routes in Filter List*, use the *Exceptions* field to specify routes that are always permitted.

- If the value of the *Action* field is *Permit Routes in Filter List*, use the *Exceptions* field to specify routes that are always denied.

12. Exit FILTCFG when all filters have been defined.

Do not let this filtering capability lull you into a false sense of security. Filtering is primarily a means of limiting network traffic. A NetWare router is not a firewall, however. Dedicated TCP/IP intruders can hack their way around simple filters, particularly filters based on IP addresses. If your network connects to a public network such as the Internet, you should install a third-party firewall to protect your network from outside intruders.

Big Network, Big Trouble

Now you know how to build a really big network. Well, bad news: Big networks are susceptible to problems that you'll never see on a simple LAN. For one thing, internetworks can get really big. That possibility raises all sorts of issues about how to assign and manage IP addresses and host configurations, as well as how to provide names that make sense out of all those hosts. Fortunately, you'll learn some tricks about host names and host configuration in the next two chapters, which discuss DNS and the Domain Host Configuration Protocol (DHCP).

However, big networks can also malfunction. Data can be misrouted, damaged, or lost. Network segments can become overloaded. One piece of flaky hardware can upset the entire network. It's not enough to just build a big network — you also have to manage it, which means getting SNMP up and running. The Simple

Network Management Protocol is the standard protocol for monitoring and managing TCP/IP networks. Nearly all NetWare products can be configured as agents in an SNMP management system, and some basic SNMP management tools are included with NetWare. Network management is the subject of Chapter 13.

## CHAPTER 11

Managing the Domain Name Service (DNS)

DNS, as you learned in Chapter 6, is the TCP/IP service that matches "friendly" host names to hosts' IP addresses. If your network consists only of NetWare 5 servers and clients, it isn't essential for you to implement a DNS service. NetWare 5 uses SLP and DHCP to inform NetWare 5 clients about server names and the services they offer. However, there are many cases when you will find DNS practically indispensable. For example:

▸ When non-NetWare 5 users need to access services in your network, such as World Wide Web or TCP/IP-based e-mail services.

▸ When your users need to access outside TCP/IP services, such as services on the Internet.

▸ When you want to assign names to devices other than NetWare 5 servers, such as Windows NT servers, UNIX servers, or Windows clients that are sharing resources using peer-to-peer networking.

It takes a bit of time and planning to set up a DNS system. You need to understand the architecture of Novell's DNS service, but it also helps to understand how other services are managed. First we'll briefly review HOSTS files. Then we'll take a long look at the NetWare 5 DNS server. Finally, so that you can integrate with other popular DNS implementations, we'll examine the database structure for BIND, the most popular DNS server on the Internet.

NOTE

Features of DNS are defined in over a dozen RFCs. Of that group, I recommend that you examine the following RFCs. RFC 1033 (*Domain Administrators Operations Guide*) includes a good discussion of essential DNS concepts and examines most of the resource record types. RFCs 1034 and 1035 describe the DNS standard.

It will be easier to discuss DNS if we have an example network in mind. Figure 11.1 shows a simple network for the company Pseudo Corp, which has the Internet domain name `pseudo-corp.com`. The figure includes a sampling of the servers, routers, and end-user hosts.

The Pseudo Corp. network includes three types of components: name servers, hosts, and mail exchangers. NetWare servers not supporting DNS are classified as ordinary hosts. A mail exchanger is a DNS-aware mail server. Three hosts, `eng1.eng.pseudo-corp.com`,   `woody.eng.pseudo-corp.com`,   and `blythe.eng.pseudo-corp.com`, are placed in the eng subdomain of `pseudo-corp.com`. One host has two identities. `pseudo2.pseudo-corp.com` will be accessed as a NetWare server. It will also be a World Wide Web server with the name `www.pseudo-corp.com`.

Network for Pseudo Corp.

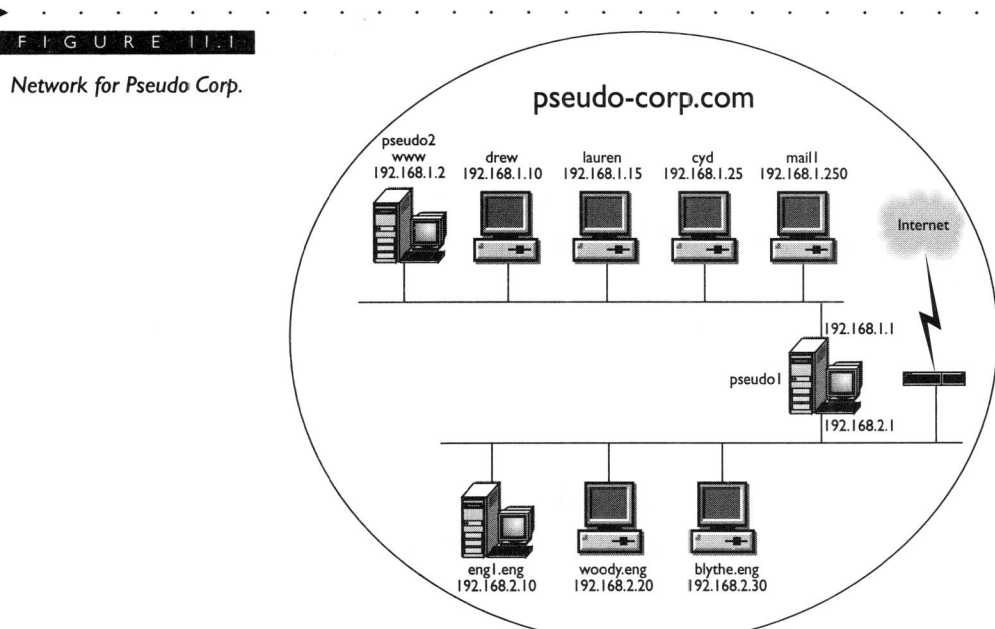

HOSTS Files

It is somewhat easier to understand DNS if you are comfortable with HOSTS files. A HOSTS file is simply a text file placed on each TCP/IP host that contains entries that map IP addresses to host names. Here is a HOSTS file that supports the sample network shown in Figure 11.1:

```
#IP Address Aliases

127.0.C.1    localhost loopback lb      #this host

192.16E.1.1  pseudo1.pseudo-corp.com pseudo1

192.16E.1.2  pseudo2.pseudo-corp.com pseudo1 www.pseudo-
corp.ccm

192.16E.1.10 drew.pseudo-corp.com drew

192.16E.1.15 lauren.pseudo-corp.com lauren

192.16E.1.25 cyd.pseudo-corp.com cyd

192.16E.1.250     mail1.pseudo-corp.com mail1

192.16E.2.10 eng1.eng.pseudo-corp.com drew

192.16E.2.20 woody.eng.pseudo-corp.com woody eng1

192.16E.2.30 blythe.eng.pseudo-corp.com blythe eng2
```

Each entry in the HOSTS file consists of an IP address, followed by one or more names that can be used to refer to the host. For each host, I have included a DNS FQDN and a host nickname for the convenience of users who wish to access local hosts. The first line of the example above is a *comment*, as indicated by the # character at the start of the line. Comments are informational only and are not used to resolve names.

On NetWare servers, HOSTS files are placed in the SYS:\ETC directory. The default location for HOSTS on Windows 95/98 is in C:\WINDOWS\. On Windows NT systems, the file is stored in %systemroot%\System32\drivers\etc (by default C:\Winnt\system32\drivers\etc).

HOSTS files are static. That is, entries in a HOSTS file are not dynamically updated as the network is reconfigured. An administrator must manually edit the text file whenever a change is required. Then a copy of the HOSTS file must be copied to every host on the network. While the copy process can be automated (for example, by putting a copy command in a user's network login script), users' HOSTS files will be updated infrequently at best. Because each user's computer has its own HOSTS file, it is possible for users' files to get out of sync. And, because LANs reconfigure constantly as users log in and out and as devices are added, deleted, and moved, it is very difficult to keep HOSTS files current with the network. Another drawback is that HOSTS files do not contain the information required to identify hosts on outside networks such as the Internet. Consequently, although basic naming functions can be performed using only HOSTS files, you will find DNS on nearly every TCP/IP network (except perhaps the smallest).

DNS Concepts

DNS was designed to handle the naming requirements for the Internet. Even when DNS was first envisioned, it was clear to planners that naming for the entire Internet could not be handled by a single name server. What the Internet needed was a way to distribute the Internet name database across large numbers of name servers, with each name server responsible for a small bit of the DNS *name space*, the overall Internet name database.

Delegation of Authority

A DNS server is responsible for one or more *zones*, where each zone contains the database for one or more DNS domains. We say that a DNS server "has authority for" or "is authoritative for" the zones and domains that it supports. On a private network, a single DNS server may be authoritative for all of the domains in the name space. But on larger networks such as the Internet, many name servers will be established, each responsible for one or more domains in the name space hierarchy. Therefore, on large networks, there must be a scheme for apportioning authority for different domains to the appropriate name server.

Figure 11.2 shows how a large name space might be organized into parent and child domains. In this case, we are looking at a small portion of the Internet name space. At the top of the name space hierarchy is the "root" domain. On the Internet, there are currently thirteen *root name servers*.

Below the first-level domains are second-level domains, each associated with the organization that has registered the domain name on the Internet. One or more name servers must be authoritative for each domain. In some cases, a name server can be authoritative for more than one domain. On the Internet, for example, the root name servers have authority for the root domain and for some of the first-level domains, such as com and org. Other first-level domains, such as mil, gov, and the various international domains have their own name servers. The root name servers are not authoritative for second-level domains, and each second-level domain must be associated with its own name servers. An organization can operate its own name servers, or it can rely on its Internet service provider to host the organization's domain on the ISP's name servers.

▶ · ◀

FIGURE II.2

Name Servers and the
Internet Name Space

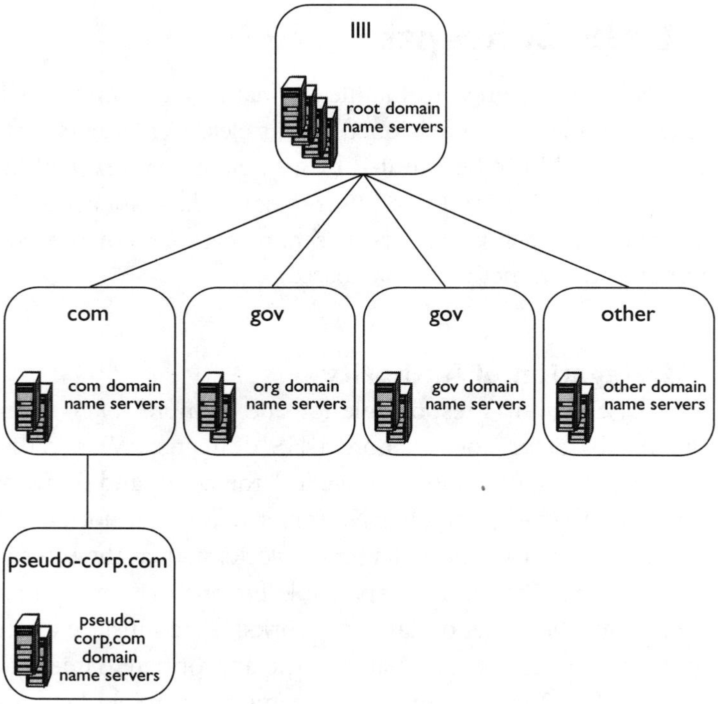

Each host is configured with the IP address of a name server to which the host sends its requests for name resolutions. When a host queries for a host name, say `drew.pseudo-corp.com`, the name server will attempt to resolve the name from information it already has, which may be in database files or in a memory cache that retains recently-resolved names. If the local name server cannot resolve the name, it refers the request to another name server that should be able to resolve at least part of the host name. In most cases, the query is referred to name servers for the root domain. The Internet root name servers are authoritative for the `com`

domain as well as the root domain, and can identify name servers that are authoritative for the second-level domains under com. When the root name servers receive a request to resolve drew.pseudo-corp.com, they refer the request to a name server that is authoritative for the pseudo-corp.com domain.

One way of looking at the relationship between the com domain and the pseudo-corp domain is that the com domain has *delegated* the authority for the pseudo-corp.com domain to the pseudo-corp.com domain name servers. The com domain name servers know that the pseudo-corp.com domain exists, but they hold other name servers responsible for resolving names in the pseudo-corp.com domain. Name servers in the com domain know the names of all the second-level domain names, such as pseudo-corp. However the com name servers do not know the names of any of the names under pseudo-corp.com. They only know the IP addresses of the name servers that are authoritative for pseudo-corp.com.

Domains and sub-domains in DNS are frequently referred to as *parent* and *child* domains. When a child domain is established, the parent domain must delegate authority to the child domain. This is done by placing information in the name servers for the parent domain that enables the parent name servers to locate name servers authoritative for the child domain. With this information, the parent domain name servers can refer name queries to the child domain name servers as required.

The example network in Figure 11.1 includes hosts on the sub-domain eng.pseudo-corp.com. The same name server can be authoritative for both pseudo-corp.com and eng.pseudo-corp.com, or the eng.pseudo-corp.com child domain could be delegated to a separate group of name servers. The network administrators have a variety of options. They can delegate subdomains to separate name servers, or they can support multiple domains with a single name server.

Primary and Secondary Name Servers

It is never a good idea to have one of anything, particularly when supporting a network service as critical as naming. Consequently, it is common practice to configure at least two DNS servers to perform name resolution for a zone. With most DNS implementations, there will a *primary DNS server*, which is the principle repository for zone records, and there will be one or more *secondary DNS servers* that contain replicas of the zone database.

The primary DNS server contains the master database files. With most name servers, such as BIND, the database files are text files that are manually edited by an administrator. These database files are loaded into the name server, typically once a day, so that changes can take effect.

A secondary DNS server obtains zone data by performing a *zone transfer* from a *DNS master*, which can be a primary DNS server or another secondary DNS server that supports the same zone. The secondary DNS server will periodically query the primary name server to determine whether changes have been recorded for the zone. If changes have been made, the secondary name server requests a copy of the revised zone database.

Figure 11.3 illustrates the relationship between the master and secondary name servers. Notice that a secondary name server can obtain its copy of the zone database by performing zone transfers from a primary name server or from another secondary name server. The choice is up to the DNS administrator.

Under this system, all changes to the zone database are made at the primary name server. The changes then migrate out to secondary name servers via zone transfers. If the primary name server is down, the zone database cannot be modified. Secondary name servers can continue to function because they record a copy of the latest zone data in a local database file, enabling the secondary name server to shut down and restart if necessary. But changes can be made to the domain database only when the primary name server's functionality is restored.

It is important to realize that a given name server can be the primary name server for some zones and a secondary name server for other zones. The DNS administrator has considerable freedom to allocate zones to name servers in a way that balances processing loads and achieves the best levels of performance and fault tolerance.

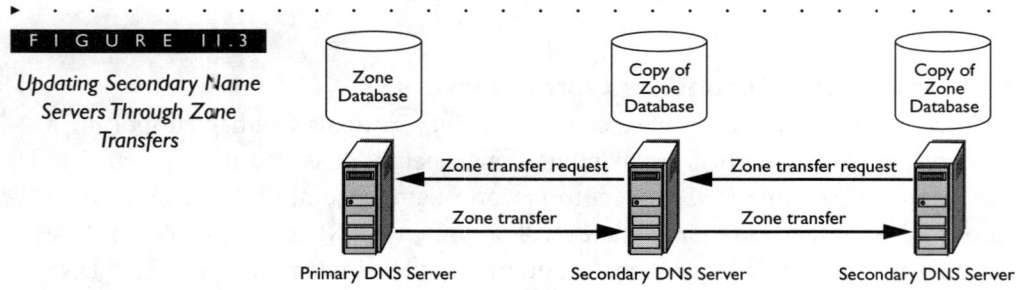

FIGURE II.3

Updating Secondary Name Servers Through Zone Transfers

NetWare 5 Name Servers

The NetWare 5 DNS service has several unique characteristics. Instead of storing zone databases on specific name servers, the database records are stored as objects in NDS. NDS, as you know, is a distributed database. It can be replicated across multiple NetWare servers, and it can be partitioned so that a given NetWare server may store part or all of the overall NDS database. The NDS database is available to all NetWare servers and clients that can access the tree.

The unique nature of NDS has enabled the designers of NetWare 5 DNS to take a fresh look at how name servers are organized. When a name server starts up, it loads its zone databases from NDS, as shown in Figure 11.4, not from local configuration files or from another DNS server. Consequently, the distinction between primary and secondary DNS servers disappears. All NetWare 5 DNS servers that support a given domain are peers and are configured as primary name servers. (NetWare 5 DNS servers can also be configured as secondary name servers if the primary name server for a zone is a non-NetWare 5 DNS server.)

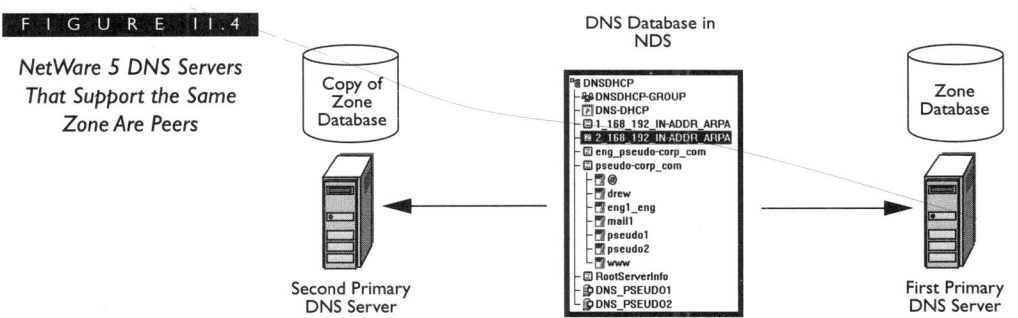

Because the zone data are stored in NDS, the NetWare 5 DNS service has unprecedented protection against data lost. If your NDS tree is properly partitioned and if partitions are properly replicated, the loss of a single NDS server will result in little or no loss of NDS zone data.

There is only one time when NetWare 5 DNS servers function specifically in a secondary role; that is, when zone data are transferred into the NetWare 5 DNS service from an outside DNS server. In that case, one of the NetWare 5 DNS servers supporting the zone must be designated as a secondary server for the zone.

The secondary NetWare 5 DNS server will populate the NDS database with zone data obtained from the outside primary name server. Other NetWare 5 DNS servers for the zone obtain zone data from NDS.

Reverse-Naming Zones

Until now, we have looked at DNS from the perspective of a client that knows a host's name and needs to learn the host's IP address. That is the most common type of DNS query, but there are also times when a client's IP address is known and we want to learn the client's DNS name. To enable DNS to perform address-to-name lookups, DNS supports *reverse-naming* zones. Reverse naming is based on a name hierarchy where nodes in the hierarchy receive their names from IP addresses.

Figure 11.5 shows a part of the tree used to perform reverse-name lookups on the Internet. The figure depicts the lookup for `drew.pseudo-corp.com`, with an IP address of 192.168.80.53. Starting at the top of the hierarchy, it is possible to quickly determine the host name that matches any IP address. Here's what happens when DNS performs a reverse-lookup for 192.168.80.53:

1. The lookup begins at the root of the tree and proceeds to the `arpa` subdomain followed by the `in-addr` subdomain. These are by convention the first- and second-level domains in the reverse-naming tree. (Recall that ARPA the Advanced Research Projects Agency of the United States Department of Defense, was the original backer of the Internet.)

2. Next, DNS looks for the domain that matches the first octet of the IP address, in this case 192.

3. Below the 192 subdomain, DNS looks for the second octet of the IP address, 168.

4. At the next level, DNS looks for the third octet of the IP address, 80.

5. Finally DNS looks for the fourth octet of the IP address, 53. The value of this node is the name of the host with the IP address 192.168.80.53.

▶ · ◀

Determining a Host Name Through a DNS Reverse Lookup

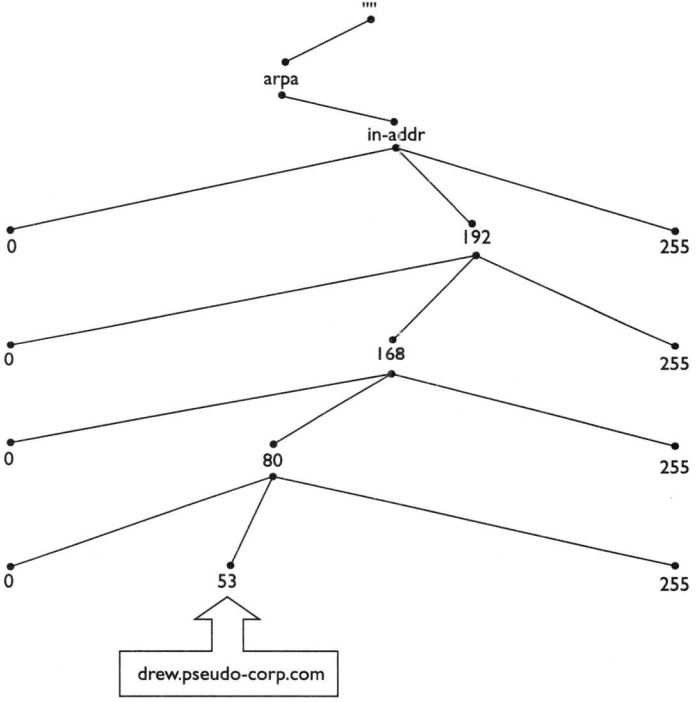

Zones in DNS hierarchies are named by listing the domain names between the lowest-level domain and the root. With forward-naming domains, zones names correspond to the fully qualified domain name of the domain. With reverse-naming domains, zones are named starting with the last octet of the network address, working up from the bottom of the tree. The zone 80.168.192.in-addr.arpa contains the reverse-naming record for host 192.168.80.53.

Because all reverse lookup zone names end with in-addr.arpa, they are commonly referred to as "in-addr.arpa" zones.

Forwarding Name Servers

DNS servers can resolve name queries using information from three sources:

▶ Resource records in zones for which the DNS server has authority.

. . . . .

► Cached name resolution information retrieved from other name servers.

► Referrals to other name servers.

If a name server cannot resolve a name query locally (using local resource records or data cached on the server), it will refer the request to another name server. In the majority of cases, the name server will forward the request to a root name server, which initiates name resolution from the root of the name space hierarchy.

A large organization may have many name servers on the local network. Figure 11.6 illustrates such an organization that is connected to the Internet. The problem with this network is that all the name servers are working independently. In a large organization, it is quite possible that several users will be requesting the same Internet host names. Because the name servers do not coordinate their efforts, they may be making the same name resolution requests. That wastes precious WAN bandwidth.

Figure 11.7 shows a better approach. Whenever local name servers cannot resolve a name query using information in their resource records or in their name cache, they refer the unresolved query to a special name server called a *forwarder* that in turn forwards the request to the Internet. The advantage of this scheme is that, if two users request the same name, it is much more likely that the forwarder will have the data in its cache because it is responsible for all name queries made through the WAN link.

FIGURE 11.6

An Organization with
Multiple Local Name
Servers

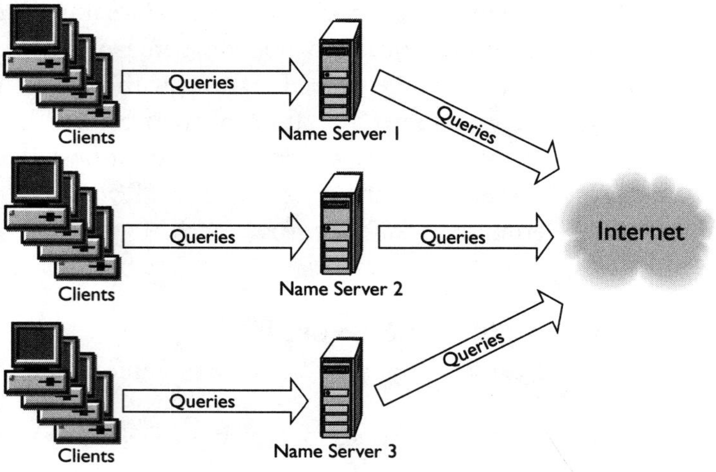

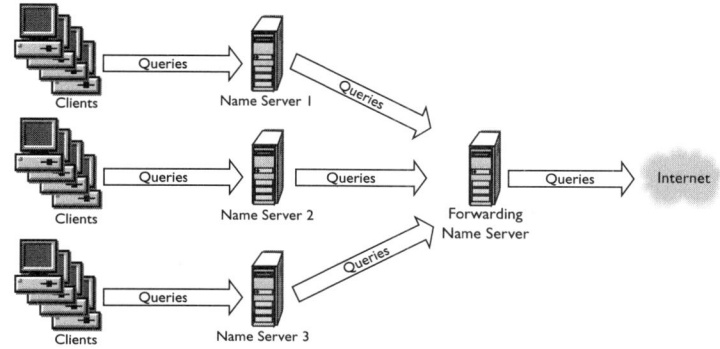

FIGURE 11.7

Improving Outside Name Queries Using a Forwarding Name Server

In some instances, it is useful to configure intermediate name servers as *cache-only* name servers. A cache-only name server is not authoritative for any domains and does not have any data files of its own. However, it does have a cache and when it facilitates a DNS name query through a forwarder, the cache-only name server remembers the result. If another client requests a lookup for the same name, the cache-only name server can satisfy the query from its cache memory. As a result, the cache-only name server reduces the work that must be performed by the forwarding name server but it requires very little configuration or maintenance.

Resource Records

Names in the DNS hierarchy identify two types of entities: domains and hosts. Domain names identify the nodes that define the hierarchy tree, but they do not necessarily identify hosts. In Pseudo Corp.'s network, for example, you will not find a host with the name `pseudo-corp.com`. Both `pseudo-corp.com` and `eng.pseudo-corp.com` are names of domains and do not correspond to any particular network device. Domain name nodes may contain sub-domains and hosts.

A host name on the DNS tree is an end-point. In DNS, a host's full name is constructed by appending the host's name to the names between the host name and the root domain. The complete name is knows as the *fully qualified domain name* or *FQDN*. An example of a FQDN in Figure 11.1 is `lauren.pseudo-corp.com`.

Figure 11.8 shows the organization of the domain name space for Pseudo Corp. The organization's second-level domain name is `pseudo-corp.com`, which appears in the context of the Internet name space. The `pseudo-corp.com` domain is defined in a zone database. The zone database consists of records that define the detailed characteristics of the domain and of the hosts in the domain.

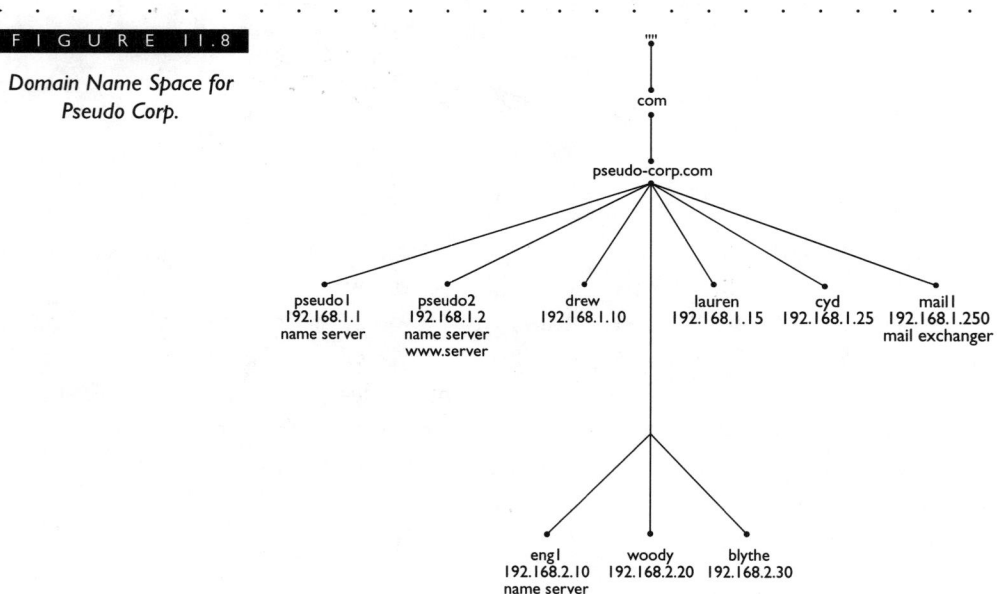

FIGURE 11.8

Domain Name Space for Pseudo Corp.

Now let's see how the various entities are described in the DNS database.

An entry in a DNS zone database is called a *resource record*. A zone database supports many types of resource records, but only the following ones will be discussed in detail in this chapter:

▶ **Start of Authority (SOA).** An SOA record declares the domain for which this name server is authoritative. In NDS, the SOA record is represented by detail parameters for the Zone object.

▶ **Address (A).** An A record matches a host name with an IP address. These records are used by resolvers to derive IP addresses from host names. In NDS, the A record is represented by an Address Resource Record object.

▸ **Canonical Name (CNAME).** A CNAME record provides an alias name for an IP address. NDS represents a CNAME record as a CNAME Resource Record object.

▸ **Mail Exchanger (MX).** Each mail server for a domain is identified by an mx record, enabling hosts in the domain to identify which hosts should receive mail destined for that domain. NDS represents an MX record as an MX Resource Record object.

▸ **Name Server (NS).** An NS record specifies a name server that is authoritative for a domain. On NetWare 5, an NS object is stored as a DNS Server NDS object.

In the course of this chapter, you will learn how these resource records are used and how they are entered into the DNS database. Before we can get our hands dirty, however, we need to install some NDS schema extensions and the DNS/DHCP Management Console.

Dynamic DNS

DNS was created before LANs and private workstations became widespread. In the early days of DNS, most TCP/IP hosts were multiuser computers. These computers seldom moved or changed their identities, and it wasn't a problem to update the DNS database by manually editing static database files.

A modern LAN environment is an entirely different ball game, however. For one thing, LAN hosts move, sometimes frequently. That makes it difficult to keep DNS current. In addition, there are many more hosts on a typical LAN than you would find on an average network in the 1980s. With large numbers of hosts it is convenient to configure their IP addresses automatically using DHCP. But DHCP doesn't always assign the same IP address to a given client. And, if a client moves to a different subnet, its IP address will change. DHCP can cope with the move, but now DNS is out of date.

Novell's scheme for coordinating DHCP and DNS is *Dynamic DNS* (DDNS). NetWare 5 DHCP can be configured to update the DNS database as clients obtain and lose IP addresses assigned by DHCP. If a client moves to a different subnet, for example, DHCP can remove the client's old resource record and add a new one that reflects the client's new IP address.

When DDNS is configured to update resource records in a zone, you must designate one of the zone's DNS name servers as a Dynamic DNS Server. The designated DDNS server performs all of the communication with DHCP and adds the DNS records to the NDS database. Other NetWare 5 DNS servers obtain the updated resource records from NDS.

Adding the DNS and DHCP Schema Extensions to NDS

To operate the DNS and DNCP services, several extensions must be added to the NDS schema. You can add the DNS and DHCP schema extensions to NDS while installing NetWare 5. In the *Additional Products and Services* dialog box, select *Novell DNS/DHCP Services*. On some systems, you may find that the DNS/DHCP Services do not install properly during the installation of NetWare 5. In such cases, you will need to use the DNIPINST.NLM utility to add the required schema extensions.

To add the DNS and DHCP services after NetWare 5 has been installed use the NWCONFIG utility. The procedure is as follows:

1. Insert the NetWare 5 Operating System CD-ROM and enter the command CDROM to mount the CD-ROM volume.

2. Load NWCONFIG and select **Product Options**.

3. Accept the file pathname that is offered.

4. When ConsoleOne is displayed, check **Novell DNS/DHCP Services** in the Additional Products and Services dialog box and click **Next**.

5. Follow the prompts to install the services.

In rare instances, it may be necessary to add or remove the NDS schema extensions after the DNS/DHCP Services have been installed. DNIPINST.NLM is used to add or remove the schema extensionse. By default, the command LOAD

DNIPINST adds the DHS and DHCP schema extensions. You can remove the schema extensions with the command LOAD DNIPINST –R.

WARNING **The DNIPINST –R option should be used with caution because it deletes *all* DNS and DHCP objects from the NDS database. You will need to configure both services from scratch if the –R option is used.**

When you are installing the DNS/DHCP Services, you have the option of designating a separate container as a repository for several objects that are added to NDS. The objects added to NDS are as follows:

▶ **DNS/DHCP Locator object.** This object contains global default values, DHCP options, lists of DNS and DHCP servers, DHCP subnets, and DNS zones. The DNS/DHCP Management Console can display DNS and DHCP objects without having to use the DNS/DHCP Locator object to search the tree.

▶ **DNS/DHCP Group object.** DNS and DHCP objects use this object to gain rights to DNS and DHCP data stored in NDS. When DNS/DHCP Management Console creates Server objects, the Server objects are given the rights required to access data.

▶ **RootSrvrInfo Zone object.** This DNS Zone objects contains a list of the name servers that have authority for the root domain in the Internet.

Only one each of the above objects is required. None of these objects requires any maintenance with the possible exception of the RootSrvrInfo Zone object, which may require updating should the Internet root domain name servers change.

In my examples, I created the container OU=DNSDHCP.O=PSEUDO in which I placed all DNS and DHCP objects. When you execute DNIPINST, you will be shown a dialog box (see Figure 11.9) where you can designate the containers in which DNIPINST will place the objects it creates. Actually, the containers of the DNS/DHCP Locator and Group objects aren't all that important. You should place the RootSrvrInfo Zone object in a container available only to DNS administrators.

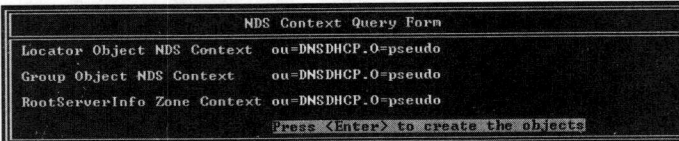

FIGURE 11.9

Specifying the Location in which DNS and DHCP Objects Will Be Created

You can create additional containers in the future as you define your DNS zones. Create a container for each set of zones that is to be managed by a different group of administrators. Also, to enable you to control replication traffic, create containers for zones supported by name servers at remote sites that are connected through a WAN link. Replicate those containers only at the remote site to reduce replication traffic that transits the WAN.

Be sure to install the NetWare 5 Support Pack 1, which includes many improvements that affect the DNS and DHCP services.

NOTE

Installing the DNS/DHCP Management Console

Your principal tool for managing the DNS and DHCP services is the DNS/DHCP Management Console, which requires the following resources on the client:

► Windows 95/98 or Windows NT with NetWare 5 client software.

► 12.5MB of free disk space.

► 64MB of memory. (Although the documentation states that 64MB are recommended and 32MB are minimum, I have experienced difficulties with less than 48MB of RAM and consider 64MB the practical minimum.)

To install the DNS/DHCP Management Console exit all running programs. Then execute the SETUP.EXE program, which is installed in SYS:PUBLIC\DNSDHCP. Restart the computer to complete the installation. Then launch the DNS/DHCP Management Console by double-clicking the new DNSDHCP icon that SETUP added to the desktop.

Managing the DNS Service

As explained earlier, the NetWare 5 DNS service is neatly integrated into Novell's NDS network directory. As you configure DNS, you are configuring objects in the NDS database. Some object management tasks are performed using the familiar NetWare Administrator utility. For example, you use NWADMIN to create containers for DNS objects, create management groups, assign trustee rights, and so forth. However, you do not create the DNS objects, or manage their parameters, using NWADMIN. DNS objects (and DHCP objects, as you will see in the next chapter) are managed with a new NetWare 5 utility, the DNS/DHCP Management Console. After laying some groundwork, we will dive into DNS configuration using the DNS/DHCP Management Console.

Earlier in the chapter, I listed the most common DNS resource records. Let's see how the resource records appear in NDS and look at the NDS objects in more detail. The DNS object types are:

- **DNS Server object.** Each NetWare server that will run the DNS service must be defined in a DNS Server object. Two DNS Server objects will be created for this network, associated with NetWare servers PSEUDO1 and PSEUDO2. DHCP Server objects are leaf objects and can be contained in any O, OU, C, or L object.

- **Zone object.** Every DNS zone is described by a Zone object, which describes the zone and serves as a container for the Resource Records in the zone. Two Zone objects will be created in this chapter: pseudo-corp.com, and eng.pseudo-corp.com. Zone objects are container objects that can be contained in any O, OU, C, or L object.

▶ **Resource Record Set (RRSet) objects.** A Resource Record Set object isn't an NDS container object, but it serves as an anchor point for all the Resource Record objects associated with a given domain name. Actually, resource records are attributes of the RRSet object and don't appear as distinct objects in NDS. You don't directly create an RRSet object. When you create a Resource Record object, the appropriate RRSet object is created first. Then the Resource Record object is created and is associated with the RRSet object. You will see how it all works when we create some Resource Record objects later in the chapter. RRSet objects are leaf objects and must be created within a Zone container object.

▶ **Resource Record (RR) object.** All DNS resource records are stored in Resource Record (RR) objects. Although RR objects look like objects in DNS/DHCP Management Console, they are not stored as distinct NDS objects. Each RR object is stored as a property of an RRSET object. In some cases, multiple RR objects may be associated with a given RRSet object. For example, a computer that is a name server will also have an address resource record. RR objects are not visible in NWAdmin, and can only be viewed in the DNS/DHCP Management Console. RR objects must be created in a Zone container object.

Figure 11.10 shows a representative sampling of DNS objects as viewed in DNS/DHCP Management Console. Figure 11.11 shows the same objects in the NetWare Administrator utility. Notice that I have collected the DNS objects in a container named ou=DNSDHCP.o=pseudo. Novell recommends that you place DNS and DHCP objects in their own containers. This strategy has two advantages: you can easily determine who will manage DNS and DHCP objects by assigning trustee rights to appropriate containers; and you can also establish partitions and configure replicas so that copies of the replicas are store locally on the name servers that must have access to the objects. Partition configuration is particularly important when your network includes WAN links and you wish to minimize WAN traffic related to NDS access and replication.

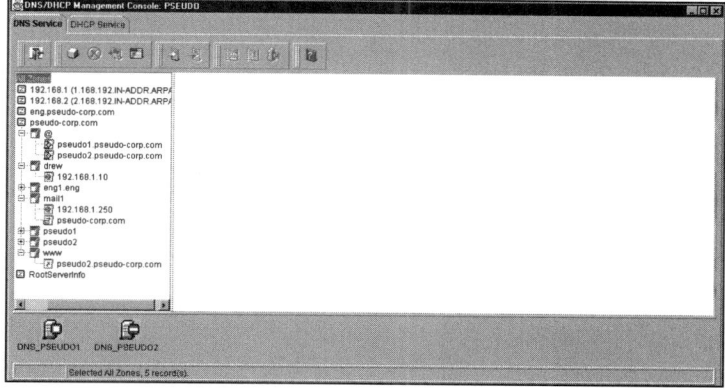

FIGURE 11.10

Representative DNS Objects in DNS/DHCP Management Console

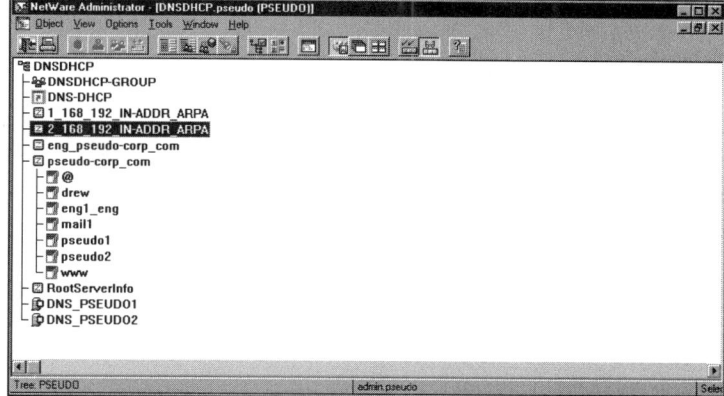

FIGURE 11.11

Representative DNS Objects in NetWare Administrator

Let's take a brief tour through the DNS/DHCP Management Console interface. At the top of the DNS/DHCP Management Console window are two tabs labeled *DNS Service* and *DHCP Service.* You will, of course, select the tab that corresponds to the service you wish to manage. In Figure 11.10, I have selected the *DNS Service* tab. (I probably didn't need to tell you that — it would be rather silly to select the *DHCP Service* tab in a chapter about DNS.) The DNS/DHCP Management Console consists of four distinct areas:

▸ **The "object hierarchy" pane** on the left displays most of the objects you will manage and shows the hierarchical relationships of the objects.

▸ **The "detail" pane** on the right shows detail parameters for the object currently selected.

▸ **The "server" pane** at the bottom shows an icon for each DNS Server object that has been created. DNS Server objects do not appear in the object hierarchy pane because a DNS server can support several zones.

▸ **The toolbar** at the top contains the command buttons. There are no pull-down menus in DNS/DHCP Management Console. All commands are executed from the toolbar. Different buttons are illuminated depending on the object selected. Figure 11.12 shows the buttons in the toolbar.

F I G U R E   11.12

*Buttons in the DNS
Server Toolbar*

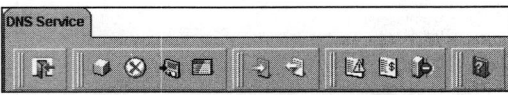

All of the features of the DNS/DHCP Management Console will be explained as we create and manage DNS servers and objects in the remainder of this chapter.

You now know how DNS works in general and the philosophy behind Novell's NetWare 5 DNS implementation. It is time to put that knowledge to work by setting up some NetWare 5 DNS servers. Before you can jump in, however, you need to ensure that the DNS and DHCP schema extensions have been installed in NDS. If DNS/DHCP Management Console refuses to run, review the preceding section "Adding the DNS and DHCP Schema Extensions to NDS" in this chapter.

Although objects can be created in various orders, I'm going demonstrate the process following a particular sequence:

1. First, we will create DNS Server objects.

2. Next we will create Zone objects. Zone objects will be associated with previously-defined DNS Server objects.

3. Third, we will create Resource Record objects as required. As RR objects are created, Resource Record Set objects are automatically created by DNS/DHCP Management.

In each case, the procedure has two distinct steps:

1. Creating the object.

2. Configuring options for the object.

Managing DNS Server Objects

Before a NetWare 5 server can run the DNS Server service, it must be described by a DNS Server object in NDS. Creating a DNS Server object is a good place to start when initially creating the DNS service. After the DNS Server objects are established, you can easily reference them in the configurations of the Zone objects.

Creating DNS Server Objects

To create a DNS Server object, do the following:

1. Log in using an account that has the Supervisor right for the container in which the DNS Server object will be created. (DNS Server objects are created in the same container as the corresponding NetWare server object, but can be moved to any container using NWADMIN.)

2. Start DNS/DHCP Management Console and select the *DNS Service* tab.

3. Select any object in the object hierarchy pane and click the *Create* button in the toolbar.

4. Select *DNS Server* in the *Create New NDS Record* dialog box.

5. Complete the *Create New DNS Server* dialog box (see Figure 11.13) as follows:

- **Select Server Object.** Enter the full NDS name of the NetWare 5 server that will be running the DNS Server service, or click the NDS browse button to select a server from the NDS tree.

- **Host Name.** Enter the DNS host name of the NetWare 5 server specified in the *Select Server Object* field. This may or may not be the same as the server's NetWare name.

- **Domain.** Enter the DNS domain name of the NetWare 5 server specified in the *Select Server Object* field. If you have already created a zone object for the domain, you can pull down the list box and select the desired domain from the list.

- **Define Additional Properties.** Check this box if you wish to define other properties of this object after you click the *Create* button.

6. Click *Create*.

FIGURE 11.13

Creating a DNS Server Object

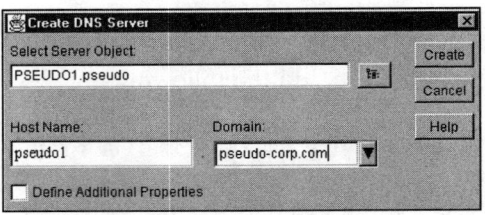

Figure 11.14 shows DNS/DHCP Management Console after two DNS Server objects have been defined. Server objects appear in the bottom pane of the DNS/DHCP Management Console and are not listed in the DNS object hierarchy in the left-hand pane. In fact, at this time, the only object that appears in the object hierarchy is a Zone object named RootServerInfo. You will learn about this Zone object when we discuss Zone objects in greater detail.

When the DNS/DHCP Management Console creates NDS objects for the DNS servers, it appends `DNS_` to the NetWare server's name (for example, `DNS_PSEUDO1`). It is important to realize that this name is the name of the DNS server's NDS object, not the name server's name in DNS. At present, in fact, neither of the DNS servers has a DNS domain name. Their domain names will not exist until an address (A) record has been created for the host, and the A record cannot be created until a Zone object has been defined for the servers' DNS domain. In other words, another couple of steps are required before these servers are fully defined in DNS.

When the DNS/DHCP Management Console cannot communicate with a DNS server, the DNS Server object icon is marked with a red slash, as shown with DNS_PSEUDO2 in Figure 11.14. At present, the DNS Server service (NAMED.NLM) has not been started on the PSEUDO2 NetWare 5 server. After the DNS server is configured, start the DNS Server service by loading NAMED.NLM on the server. NAMED.NLM is discussed in detail in the following section "Managing the DNS Server Service." The DNS Server service has been loaded and is running on DNS_PSEUDO1.

▶ · ◀

FIGURE 11.14

DNS Server Icons Depicting Server Status

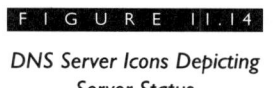 

Configuring DNS Server Objects

Several DNS Server parameters can be configured after the DNS Server object has been created. When you select a DNS Server icon, the right details pane of the DNS/DHCP Management Console contains four dialog tabs where you can view and modify the DNS Server object configuration.

After you change the detail parameters of a DNS Server object, you must store the changes in NDS. This does not happen until you do one of the following:

▶ Select a different object, in which case you will be prompted to save changes made to the object.

▶ Click the *Save Data to NDS* button in the toolbar.

The Zones Tab   Most of the fields in the *Zones* tab are informational. You can edit the contents of the *Comments* box, but the other information is determined by parameters in other dialog boxes. Specifically:

▶ The entries in the *Zone List* list box are determined by options associated with Zone objects.

▶ The entries in the *DNS Server IP Address* are established when the DNS Server object is created. You must delete the DNS Server object and re-create it to change this value.

▶ The *DNS Server Domain Name* parameter is established when the DNS Server object is created. You must delete the DNS Server object and re-create it to change this value.

The Forwarding List Tab   The preceding section "Forwarding Name Servers" explained the use of forwarding name servers and how they can reduce name resolution traffic through WAN links. To add a name server to the forwarding list, click *Add* and enter the appropriate IP address.

The No-Forward List Tab   This tab is used to prevent the name server from resolving name queries for specified domains. You might, for example, want to prevent resolution of the domain name xxx.com. To add a domain to the no-forwarding list, click *Add* and enter the appropriate domain name.

The Options Tab   This tab configures event and audit trail logging. The following options can be used to configure the Event Log behavior:

▶ **None.** This option suppresses all event log entries. Typically, it is not a good idea to entirely turn off these functions.

▶ **Major Events.** This option will log only significant events and is generally the preferred setting.

▶ **All.** This option generates verbose event logs. This level of messaging is desirable only when you are troubleshooting system problems.

If you check *Enable Audit Trail Log*, the DNS server records entries in the audit trail log.

Viewing the Logs

You must load CSATPXY.NLM on the target server to enable DNS/DHCP Management Console to retrieve logs from the DNS server. In most cases, you will want to add the command **LOAD CSATPXY** to your AUTOEXEC.NCF file.

The Events Log records events such as server startups and shutdowns. To view the events and alerts, select a DNS server and click the *View Events/Alerts* button in the toolbar. Then specify a time period that you wish to view. Figure 11.15 shows an example of an events/alerts log. Click the *Display Options* button to open a dialog box where you can specify the types of events that will be recorded in the Events Log.

F I G U R E   I I . I 5

The Events/Alerts Log for a DNS Server

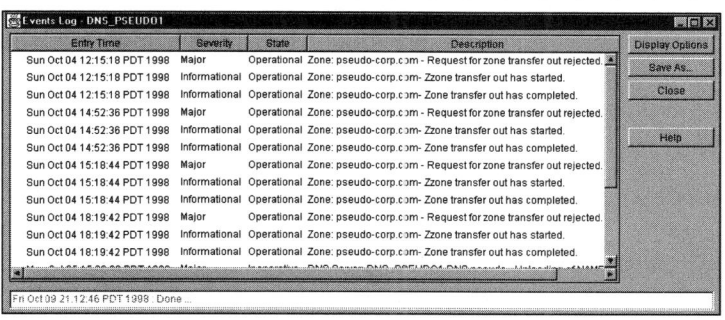

The Audit Trail Log records a history of DNS configuration events. To view the audit trail log, select a server and click the *View Audit Trail Log* button in the toolbar. Then specify a time period that you wish to view. Figure 11.16 shows an example of an audit trail log. Click the *Display Options* button to open a dialog box where you can specify the types of events that will be recorded in the Audit Trail Log.

An Audit Trail Log for a DNS Server

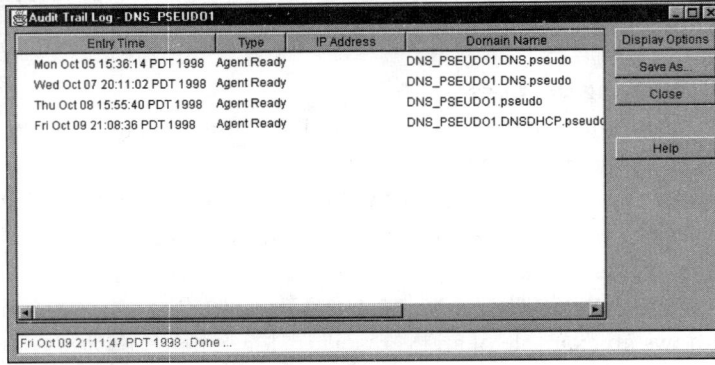

Managing Zone Objects

A Zone object is used to grant authority for a DNS domain to a DNS server. Zone objects also determine whether a DNS server functions as a primary or a secondary server for the zone. As you learned earlier, NetWare 5 DNS servers function as peers in the NetWare 5 environment, and aren't distinguished as primary and secondary name servers. However, when NetWare 5 DNS servers are receiving zone transfers from an outside DNS server, a secondary zone must be configured, and one of the NetWare 5 DNS servers must be designated as the zone-in server that will receive the zone transfer from the outside zone. You'll learn how DNS server roles work as we examine Zone object configuration.

As you have seen, DNS has two types of zones. Forward-naming zones are used to resolve domain names to their corresponding IP addresses. Reverse-naming zones, also known as IN-ADDR.ARPA zones, resolve IP addresses to their corresponding domain names. The Zone object type is declared when the Zone object is first created, so we need to examine separately the procedures for creating different types of Zone objects.

Creating Primary, Forward-Naming Zone Objects

Most of the Zone objects you create will be used for forward-naming purposes. The procedure is as follows:

1. Log in using an account that has the Supervisor right for the container in which the DNS Server object will be created. (DNS Server objects are created in the same container as the corresponding NetWare server object, but can be moved to any container using NWADMIN.)

2. Start DNS/DHCP Management Console and select the *DNS Service* tab.

3. Click the *Create* icon in the toolbar. Any object can be selected.

4. Select *Zone* in the *Create New DNS Record* dialog box to open the *Create Zone* dialog box shown in Figure 11.17.

5. Select the *Create New Zone* radio button to specify creation of a forward-naming zone.

6. Select the *Primary* radio button.

7. Complete the other fields in the *Create Zone* dialog box as follows:

- **NDS Context.** Specify the NDS container in which the Zone object is to be created. If desired, click the NDS browse button and select the container in the *Select NDS Object* dialog box.

- **Zone Domain Name.** Specify the full name of the domain associated with this zone.

- **Assign Authoritative DNS Server.** You can specify the name of an authoritative NetWare 5 DNS server when the Zone object is created or at a later time. If the DNS Server object has already been defined, select the DNS server that is authoritative for this zone. If you select an existing NetWare 5 DNS server, the *Host Name* and *Domain* fields will be completed with the FQDN of the server.

- **Host Name.** Specify the host name of the DNS server identified in the *Assign Authoritative DNS Server* field.

- **Domain.** Specify the domain name of the DNS server identified in the *Assign Authoritative DNS Server* field. If the domain has been defined in a Zone object, pull down the box to select the domain name from a list.

- **Define Additional Properties.** Check this box if you wish to specify other properties of the Zone object after you click the *Create* button.

8. Click *Create*.

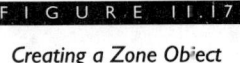

FIGURE 11.17

Creating a Zone Object

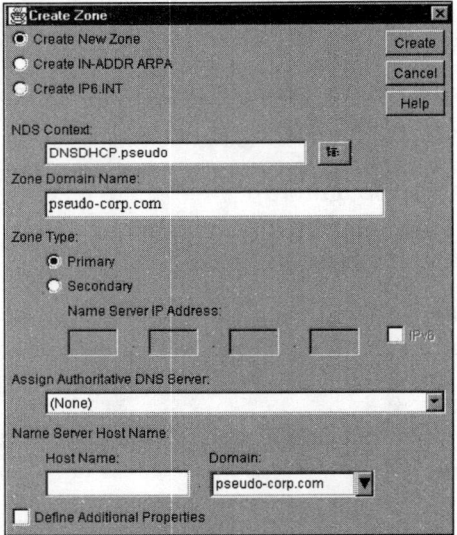

After you create a zone, an information box is displayed. It informs you that the zone has been created. It also reminds you to create the A (address) and PTR (pointer) records for the name server. Neither of those records is created automatically. You will see how to add the required records in the sections regarding managing resource records.

Figure 11.18 shows the DNS/DHCP Management Console after a Zone object has been created. When the Zone object is selected, the detail pane displays the configurable options for the Zone object. These options will be discussed in the section "Configuring Zone Objects."

In Figure 11.18, I expanded the hierarchy under the new Zone object so that you can see what DNS/DHCP Management Console creates with a new zone. The @ record is a Resource Record Set object. The @ name is a DNS shorthand. In any DNS resource record, the character @ refers to "this zone" or "the zone being defined here." So, appearing under the pseudo-corp.com Zone object, @ is synonymous with the pseudo-corp.com zone.

Appearing below the @ RRSet object is a name server (NS) Resource Record object. Every name server that is authoritative for a zone is declared in an NS resource record. You will learn more about NS and other resource records later in the chapter. The NS record is constructed using the name you enter in the *Host Name* and *Domain* fields.

The NS record by itself does not enable a server to provide name services for a zone. The name server must also be made authoritative for the zone. Only an authoritative name server will retrieve zone resource records from DNS and respond to queries made to the zone. When the Zone object is created, you can declare one authoritative name server in the *Assign Authoritative DNS Server* field. You can add or remove authoritative name servers for a zone using the Zone object's *Attributes* tab, which is described later in the chapter.

▶ · ◀

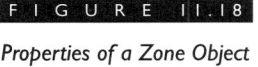

FIGURE 11.18

Properties of a Zone Object

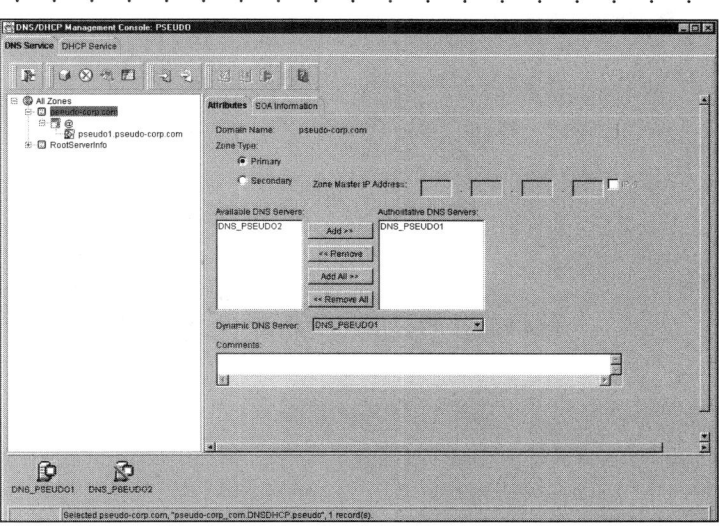

Creating Primary, Reverse-Naming Zone Objects

Create reverse-naming zones before you start adding host address resource records. If the appropriate in-addr.arpa zone exists, the reverse-naming resource records will be entered automatically when the host address resource record is created. The procedure for creating an in-addr.arpa zone is as follows:

1. Log in using an account that has the Supervisor right for the container in which the Zone object will be created.

2. Start DNS/DHCP Management Console and select the *DNS Service* tab.

3. Click the *Create* icon in the toolbar. Any object can be selected.

4. Select *Zone* in the *Create New DNS Record* dialog box to open the *Create Zone* dialog box.

5. Select the *Create IN-ADDR.ARPA* radio button to specify creation of a reverse-naming zone. The *Create Zone* dialog box will take on the appearance shown in Figure 11.19.

6. Select the *Primary* radio button.

7. Complete the other fields in the *Create Zone* dialog box as follows:

   • **NDS Context.** Specify the NDS container in which the Zone object is to be created. If desired, click the NDS browse button and select the container in the *Select NDS Object* dialog box.

   • **Zone Domain Name.** Specify the network address of the zone in normal address order. DNS/DHCP Management Console will reverse the address octets to form the IN-ADDR.ARPA domain name.

   • **Assign Authoritative DNS Server.** You can specify the name of an authoritative NetWare 5 DNS server when the Zone object is created or at a later time. If the DNS Server object has already been defined, select the DNS server authoritative for this zone. If you select an existing server, the *Host Name* and *Domain* fields will be completed with the FQDN of the server.

- **Host Name.** Specify the host name of the DNS server identified in the *Assign Authoritative DNS Server* field.

- **Domain.** Specify the domain name of the DNS server identified in the *Assign Authoritative DNS Server* field. If the domain has been defined in a Zone object, pull down the box to select the domain name from a list.

- **Define Additional Properties.** Check this box if you wish to specify other properties of the Zone object after you click the *Create* button.

8. Click *Create*.

▶ · ◀

F I G U R E   1 1 . 1 9

Creating an IN-ADDR.ARPA Zone Object

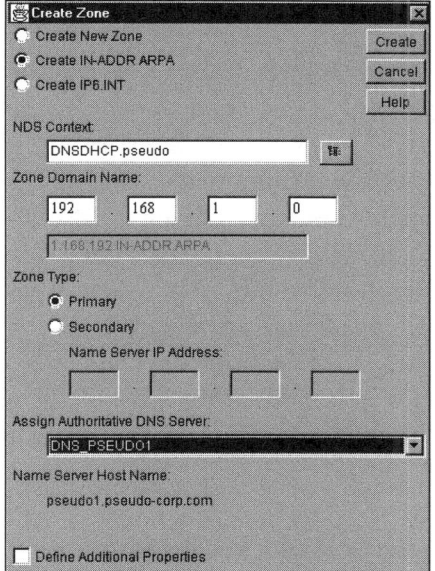

When an IN-ADDR.ARPA Zone object is selected, the detail pane of DNS/DHCP Management Console displays detail parameters for the object. The options are similar to those for a forward-naming Zone object and will be discussed in the section "Configuring Zone Objects."

NOTE

IN-ADDR.ARPA domains ignore subnetting and can only be defined for class A, B, and C network addresses. If you are working with a CIDR address assigned by an ISP, your netid probably does not end on an 8-bit boundary. If that is the case, you will not be able to host your IN-ADDR.ARPA zones on your local name servers. You will need to arrange with your ISP to place your reverse-naming resource records in the appropriate IN-ADDR.ARPA zones on their DNS servers. If you have subnetted a network address internally, you will need to configure in-addr.arpa zones based on even, 8-bit address boundaries. Suppose, for example, that your network is based on the class C network 192.168.5.0. Although you may subnet this address, you will configure a single zone named 5.168.192.in-addr.arpa to support all reverse-naming for the network address range.

Creating Secondary Zone Objects

As you know, the concept of primary and secondary zones is meaningless on a pure NetWare 5 network. All NetWare 5 DNS servers in a given NDS tree receive their data from NDS and all zones supported on NetWare 5 are primary zones.

It is necessary to create a secondary zone only if NetWare 5 DNS servers are performing zone transfers to retrieve zone data from a non-NetWare 5 server or from a NetWare 5 DNS server in another NDS tree. In such cases, a secondary zone is created in NetWare 5 and one NetWare 5 DNS server is designated as the *zone-in* server for the zone. The zone-in server will perform the zone transfer to retrieve the zone data and will then populate NDS with the required objects. Other NetWare 5 DNS servers in the same NDS tree that are authoritative for the zone obtain zone data from NDS. The procedure to configure a secondary zone is as follows:

1. Log in using an account that has the Supervisor right for the container in which the Zone object will be created.

2. Start DNS/DHCP Management Console and select the *DNS Service* tab.

3. Click the *Create* icon in the toolbar. Any object can be selected.

4. Select *Zone* in the *Create New DNS Record* dialog box to open the *Create Zone* dialog box.

5. Select the *Create Primary* or *Create IN-ADDR.ARPA* radio button as appropriate for the zone you are creating.

6. Select the *Secondary* radio button. The *Name Server IP Address* fields will be activated, as shown in Figure 11.20.

7. Check the *IPv6* checkbox if the name server IP address will be specified in IP Version 6 format.

8. In the *Name Server IP Address*, specify the IP address of the master name server from which zone data will be transferred. This can be a primary or secondary name server that is authoritative for the zone. The source name server must be aware that it will be performing zone transfers to this DNS server.

9. Complete the remaining fields in the *Create Zone* dialog box appropriately.

10. Click *Create*.

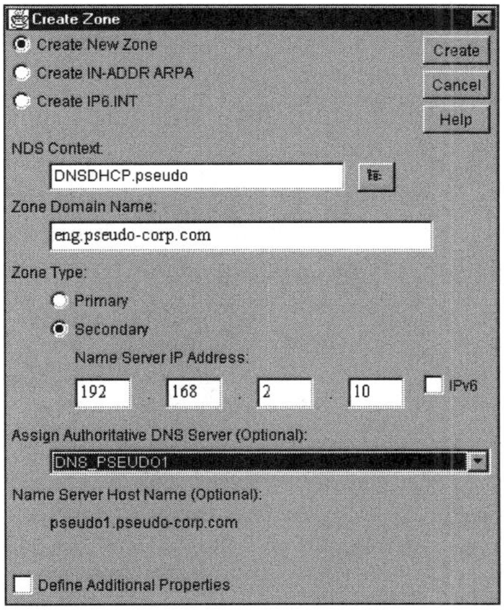

FIGURE 11.20

Creating a Secondary Zone

Configuring Zone Objects

When you select a Zone object, two tabs appear in the detail pane of DNS/DHCP Management Console. The next two sections review the data found on the detail tabs.

After you change any detail parameters of a Zone object, you must store the changes in NDS. Changes are not stored in NDS until you do one of the following:

▶ Select a different object, in which case you will be prompted to save changes made to the object.

▶ Click the *Save Data to NDS* button in the toolbar.

To ensure that the change will propagate to the DNS servers, remember to increment the *Serial Number* fields on the *SOA Information* tab of the Zone object. At periodic intervals, name servers check the zone serial numbers of the zones for which they have authority. If the zone serial number has changed, the name server will obtain an updated copy of the zone database.

The Attributes Tab   Figure 11.21 shows the *Attributes* tab for a Zone object. This tab contains the following fields:

▶ **Domain Name.** This field contains the domain name associated with the Zone object. You cannot change the domain name after the Zone object is created. To change the domain name, you must delete the Zone object and re-create it.

▶ **Zone Type.** The *Primary* and *Secondary* radio buttons determine whether the Zone object defines a primary or a secondary zone. If you select the *Secondary* radio button, you must complete the *Zone Master IP Address* fields with the IP address of the DNS server from which zone records will be transferred.

▶ **Available DNS Servers.** This box lists DNS servers that are defined in NDS but are not authoritative for the zone. To make a DNS server authoritative for the zone, select the server name and click *Add*. To make all known DNS servers authoritative for the zone, click *Add All*.

▶ **Authoritative DNS Servers.** This box lists NetWare 5 DNS servers authoritative for the zone. To revoke the authority of a DNS server, select the server name and click *Remove*. To revoke the authority of all NetWare 5 DNS servers, click *Remove All*.

▶ **Dynamic DNS Server.** If this zone's address records will be updated by DDNS, you must designate one of the DNS servers for the zone as the Dynamic DNS Server. The designated DDNS server will receive all address record changes from DHCP and will update NDS as required.

▶ **Comments.** This is a good place to keep a record of changes made to the zone.

The servers that appear in the *Authoritative DNS Servers* list are the working name servers for the zone. Only DNS servers that appear in this list will retrieve zone records from DNS and respond to DNS queries for the zone.

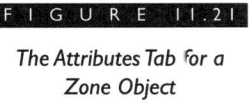

F I G U R E   11.21

The Attributes Tab for a
Zone Object

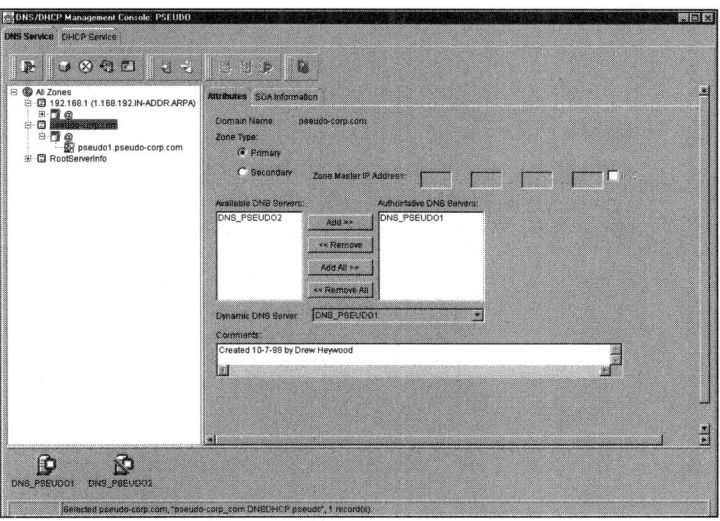

When you add a name server to the Authoritative DNS Servers list, DNS/DHCP Management Console creates an NS resource record under the @ RRSet object for the zone. The NS resource record is informational-only. It does not enable a computer as an authoritative name server. To be authoritative for a zone, a DNS server must appear in the *Authoritative DNS Servers* list and in an NS record under the @ RRSet object for the domain.

When a DNS server is removed from the *Authoritative DNS Servers* list, DNS/DHCP Management Console does not delete the server's NS record. You must manually remove the NS record.

The SOA Information Tab   Figure 11.22 shows the *SOA* tab for a Zone object. Fields in this tab correspond to the SOA (Start of Authority) resource record in the zone definition. The SOA resource record declares the DNS domain for which the zone has authority. It also specifies several parameters that affect zone behavior. This tab contains the following fields:

▶ **Zone Master.** This field specifies the name of the zone. Although this information can be modified, I recommend that you do not change it after the Zone object is created.

▶ **E-mail Address.** Here you should record the e-mail address of the primary contact person for the zone. Note that the DNS record format does not permit an @ to appear in the e-mail address. (The @ character has a special use in DNS database records, as you will see when we discuss the format of the BIND database files.) To record the e-mail address blythe@pseudo-corp.com, enter blythe.pseudo-corp.com in the *E-mail Address* field.

▶ **Serial Number.** Together, the *Year, Month, Date,* and *Revision Number* fields form a serial number that must be updated each time the zone database changes. A change in the serial number notifies NetWare 5 DNS servers that are authoritative for a zone that the DNS server must obtain updated resource records from NDS. The serial number is also used during zone transfers. A secondary DNS server checks the serial number of the DNS master server from which it obtains zone updates. If the serial number has incremented, the secondary DNS server initiates a zone transfer.

NOTE

You must update the *Serial Number* fields whenever you make a change to the zone database. Increment the *Revision Number* field if more than one update occurs in a given day. Otherwise, adjust the date fields. NetWare 5 servers periodically check the serial numbers of the zones for which they have authority and retrieve changed resource records only if the serial number has changed. Similarly, a secondary name server will initiate a zone transfer only if it detects a change in the serial number. DDNS presents an exception to the need to edit the serial number manually. When DDNS modifies the resource records for a zone, it automatically increments the zone serial number. Consequently, changes made by DDNS will be propagated to all name servers without administrative intervention.

▶ **Refresh.** This value specifies the interval in minutes at which a secondary name server checks its source name server to determine whether a zone transfer is required. The secondary name server uses the serial number to determine whether zone records have changed. The default refresh interval is 180 minutes.

▶ **Retry.** This value specifies the time in minutes that a secondary name server waits after a failed zone transfer before it re-attempts the zone transfer. The default retry interval is 60 minutes. If you shorten the refresh interval, you should also shorten the retry interval. If your refresh interval is 60 minutes, consider a retry interval of 20 minutes.

▶ **Expire.** This value determines the maximum number of hours that a secondary name server will persist in attempts to perform a zone transfer. If the secondary name server cannot perform a successful zone transfer before this time expires, the secondary name server discards data for the zone.

▶ **Minimum TTL.** When a DNS server for zone responds to a query, it includes this TTL with the response. This value specifies how long the other DNS server can keep the zone records in its cache.

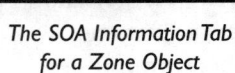

FIGURE 11.22

The SOA Information Tab
for a Zone Object

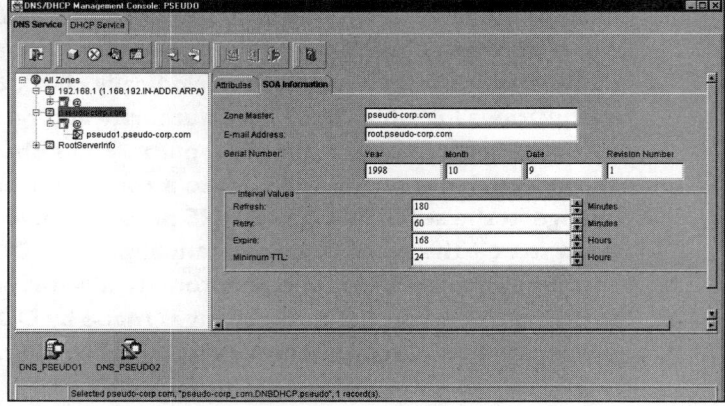

Managing Resource Records

Resource records contain the bulk of the data stored in DNS. Name servers and zones change infrequently once they are defined, but resource records are in a constant state of flux as hosts are added, moved, and removed. There are many types of resource records, but we are going to focus on the ones that you will encounter most frequently: name server, address, mail-exchanger, and cname. The Start of Authority (SOA) is also a resource record, but on the NetWare 5 DNS server, the SOA record is managed along with the other detail parameters of a Zone object. Therefore the SOA record does not appear as a distinct Resource Record (RR) object in the DNS/DHCP Management Console.

Apart from resource records that get special treatment, such as the SOA record, resource records are stored in Resource Record Set (RRSet) objects in NDS. All resource records for a given hostname are stored in the same RRSet object. To see how it all works, we need to create an object or two.

Creating the First Resource Record for a Host

All resource records are created under a Zone object. If a host has not yet been defined in any RRs, a RRSet object does not yet exist for that host. As a first resource record, let's create a host Address RR. The procedure is as follows:

1. Log in using an account that has the Supervisor right for the container of the Zone object under which the resource record will be created.

2. Start DNS/DHCP Management Console and select the *DNS Service* tab.

3. Select the Zone object under which the RR object will be created. Address records are created only in forward-naming zones. (The appropriate Zone object must be created before you can define the RR object. It is also best to create the applicable IN-ADDR.ARPA zone before adding a new address RR.)

4. Click the *Create* icon in the toolbar.

5. Select *Resource Record* in the *Create New DNS Record* dialog box to open the *Create Resource Record* dialog box shown in Figure 11.23.

6. To create an address RR, select the *A* radio button and complete the *Create Resource Record* dialog box as follows:

- **Host Name.** Enter the host name of the host associated with the RR.

- **Domain.** Enter the name of the domain in which the host resides. If you initiated the procedure by selecting a Zone object, this field will be pre-filled with the name of the domain associated with the Zone object.

- **IP Address.** Enter the IP address associated with the host.

7. Click *Create*.

8. If this is the last change you will be making to the zone, edit the *Serial Number* fields on the *SOA Information* tab for the Zone object containing the resource record.

▶ · ◀

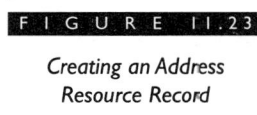

F I G U R E   11.23

Creating an Address Resource Record

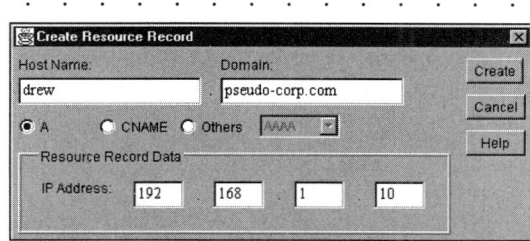

Figure 11.24 shows the DNS/DHCP Management Console after an address resource record has been created. I expanded the tree to show all the objects created when I added an Address resource record for `drew.pseudo-corp.com`. In the `pseudo-corp.com` zone, an RRSet object was added for the host name `drew`. Under the RRSet object, DNS/DHCP Management Console created an Address Resource Record object that provides a mapping to the IP address 192.168.1.10.

If the appropriate IN-ADDR.ARPA zone has been created, DNS/DHCP Management Console will also add the appropriate reverse-naming resource records. In the 1.168.192.IN-ADDR.ARPA zone, DNS/DHCP Management Console added a RRSet object with the name 10, which corresponds to the hostid part of the host's IP address. Under the RRSet object is a new pointer record. When we examine pointer records later on, you will see how a pointer record points from an IP address to a host's domain name.

NOTE

I'm going to take the liberty of repeating myself. Whenever you make a change to a zone, you must update the *Serial Number* field on the Zone object's *SOA Information* details tab. DNS servers will pull in changes only if they notice that the serial number has changed.

▶ · ◀

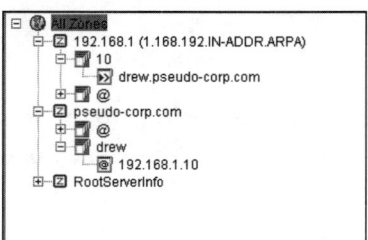

FIGURE 11.24

Resource Records Created for a Host Address

Adding a Resource Record for a Host That Already Has an RRSet Object

As mentioned earlier, some hosts may be associated with multiple resource records. For example, a mail exchanger must be described in a mail exchanger (MX), but it also must be referenced in an address record. All resource records for a given host are stored under the same RRSet object.

The procedure for adding a resource record to an RRSet object isn't all that different from creating the first resource record. You can begin by selecting the zone that will contain the resource record, or you can select the RRSet object that will contain the resource record. In either case, DNS/DHCP Management Console will store the RR object under the appropriate RRSet object. Figure 11.25 shows a Resource Record Set object for the host `mail1.pseudo-corp.com`. Under the mail1 RRSet object are two Resource Record objects. The top one is the Address RR object. The lower RR object is a mail exchanger record.

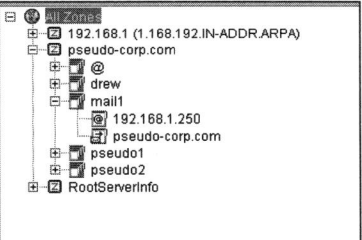

F I G U R E   11.25

Multiple Resource Record Objects Can Be Subordinate to the Same Resource Record Set Object

Address Resource Records

Address resource records are the workhorse records for DNS. Every host addressed by name must be defined by at least one address record. You have already seen an example of an address record. The form for creating one is shown in Figure 11.23. Typically, each host will be defined in a single Address resource record, but there are other possibilities as well.

Some hosts, particularly routers, have multiple interfaces. If the host should always be contacted through the same interface, you would create a single Address RR. However, there are times when you may want to create an Address RR for each interface. You may, for example, want to be able to ping each interface by name. In the sample network (Figure 11.1), the NetWare server PSEUDO1 is configured as a router. You could define the following Address RRs to simplify router management:

► route1-1.pseudo-corp.com for interface 192.168.1.1

► route2-2.pseudo-corp.com for interface 192.168.2.1

As you have seen, multiple Address records can be defined for a single interface, enabling users to address the host by multiple names. (CNAMEs are typically the preferred tools when an interface must have more than one name.) On the other hand, it is possible for the same host name to be linked to multiple interfaces. Let's see why that strategy might be valuable.

Suppose that your company's Web server has become busy to an uncomfortable degree. You want to add a second Web server that has exactly the same content. Users should access both Web servers about equally so that their loads are balanced. DNS provides a simple mechanism that makes this possible. Simply define an Address RRs for each host using the same host name. For example, you might define two Address RRs for host www.pseudo-corp.com, one for IP address 192.168.1.20 and one for IP address 192.168.2.15. As users submit name resolution requests for www.pseudo-corp.com, DNS will respond to the requests in round-robin fashion, alternating between the two IP addresses assigned to the requested host name.

CNAME Resource Records

CNAME ("canonical name") resource records are used to assign aliases to hosts. Suppose that you have already created an address record for a NetWare server named pseudo2.pseudo-corp.com. Now you want to run a World Wide Web server on the same computer and you want users to be able to access it using the name www.pseudo-corp.com. How would you go about giving the computer a dual identity?

Well, you could create two Address Resource Records for the same computer, one for each name. There is nothing preventing you from using that approach, which will solve your problem. However, there is a minor drawback. Suppose that the server's IP address changes. Now you have two address records that must be updated to contain the new IP address. If the server has still other services, you must update an address record for each service.

A CNAME, as we noted above, establishes an alias for a host name. Where an address resource record maps a host name to an IP address, a CNAME resource record maps an alias name to a host name defined in a separate Address resource record. So, we can create the alias simply by creating a CNAME record that maps www.pseudo-corp.com to pseudo2.pseudo-corp.com. The procedure for creating a CNAME record is as follows:

1. Log in using an account that has the Supervisor right for the container of the Zone object under which the CNAME resource record will be created.

2. Start DNS/DHCP Management Console and select the *DNS Service* tab.

3. Create the Address RR for the host that will be referenced by the CNAME.

4. Select the Zone object under which the CNAME RR object will be created. *Do not select the RRSet object under which the host's address RR is found.* CNAME records can be created in forward-naming and IN-ADDR.ARPA zones.

5. Click the *Create* icon in the toolbar.

6. Select *Resource Record* in the *Create New DNS Record* dialog box to open the *Create Resource Record* dialog box.

7. Select the *CNAME* radio button and complete the *Create Resource Record* dialog box (Figure 11.26) as follows:

- **Host Name.** Enter the alias host name.

- **Domain.** Enter the name of the domain in which the alias name resides.

- **Domain Name of Aliased Host.** Enter the FQDN of a host that can be referenced with the alias you are creating.

8. Click *Create*.

9. If this is the last change you will be making to the zone, edit the *Serial Number* fields on the *SOA Information* tab for the Zone object containing the RR object.

When you create a CNAME RR object, you are adding a new host name to the zone database. Consequently, a new RRSet object is created for the new host name and the CNAME RR object is created under the new RRSet object.

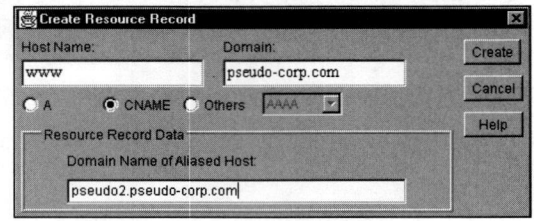

FIGURE 11 26

Creating a CNAME
Resource Record

Pointer Resource Records

Pointer (PTR) records are found only in reverse-naming (IN-ADDR.ARPA) zones. A PTR record maps an IP address to its associated host name. In many cases, DNS/DHCP Management Console will create PTR records automatically as you create Address RRs. DNS/DHCP Management Console can do this only if the appropriate IN-ADDR.ARPA zone was previously created. You may, however, need to create PTR records manually. Here is the procedure:

1. Log in using an account that has the Supervisor right for the container for the Zone object to contain the Pointer resource record.

2. Start DNS/DHCP Management Console and select the *DNS Service* tab.

3. Select the IN-ADDR.ARPA Zone object under which the RR object will be created.

4. Click the *Create* icon in the toolbar.

5. Select *Resource Record* in the *Create New DNS Record* dialog box to open the *Create Resource Record* dialog box, which appears in Figure 11.27. Notice that the *Create Resource Record* dialog box for an IN-ADDR.ARPA zone differs from the dialog box for a forward-naming zone.

6. Select the *PTR* radio button and complete the *Create Resource Record* dialog box (Figure 11.27) as follows:

   • **IP.** The network ID portion of the IP address is completed for you, as determined by the IN-ADDR-ARPA zone that you selected in Step 3. Enter the host ID portion of the IP address in the blank field.

- **Host Name.** Enter the host name part of the host's FQDN.

- **Domain.** Enter the domain name part of the host's FQDN.

7. Click *Create.* DNS/DHCP Management Console creates the PTR Resource Record object, naming it after the host's host ID.

8. If this is the last change you will be making to the zone, edit the *Serial Number* fields on the *SOA Information* tab for the Zone object containing the RR object.

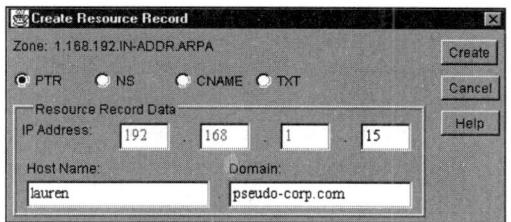

Creating a PTR Resource Record

Mail Exchanger Resource Records

The DNS term for an e-mail server is *mail exchanger.* If your network incorporates an TCP/IP-based electronic mail system such as *sendmail,* you should add appropriate Mail Exchanger (MX) resource records to the zone database file.

By including MX resource records, you make it easier for outsiders to send e-mail into your domain. E-mail can be addressed simply to `blythe@pseudo-corp.com`, for example. There's no need to address the message to `blythe@mail.pseudo-corp.com`. When an outside mail exchanger needs to send mail to `blythe@pseudo-corp.com`, it queries DNS to identify MX resource records for the `pseudo-corp.com` domain. In the case of the sample network, an MX record will identify `mail1.pseudo-corp.com` as a mail exchanger for the `pseudo-corp.com` domain.

Incoming mail is routed to the available mail exchanger according a preference parameter in the MX resource record. E-mail for a domain will be routed to the mail exchanger with the lowest active preference number, that is, a preference of 1 indicates the most preferred server. In other words, if mail1 and mail2 are both active with preferences of 10 and 20 respectively, e-mail will be routed to mail1. The numeric parameter simply specifies the priority order. Priorities of 2 and 7 would have exactly the same result as priorities of 10 and 20.

If two mail exchangers have the same priority, DNS will respond to outside queries in round-robin fashion, alternating among the available mail exchangers. This approach is often used to balance mail-processing loads across two or more mail exchangers in a busy domain.

In the sample network, the mail server is running on the host `mail1.pseudo-corp.com`. To create the MX resource record, do the following:

1. Log in using an account that has the Supervisor right for the container for the Zone object to contain the Mail Exchanger resource record.

2. Start DNS/DHCP Management Console and select the *DNS Service* tab.

3. Create an Address resource record for the mail exchanger host.

4. Select the Zone object or the RRSet under which the MX resource record object will be created.

5. Click the *Create* icon in the toolbar.

6. Select *Resource Record* in the *Create New DNS Record* dialog box to open the *Create Resource Record* dialog box.

7. Select the *Others* radio button, and select *MX* in the list of resource record types.

8. The *Create Resource Record* dialog box for an MX resource record is shown in Figure 11.28. Complete the fields as follows:

   - **Host Name.** Enter the host name of the mail exchanger. If you began to create the MX object by selecting the host's RRSet object, this field will be completed for you.

   - **Domain.** Enter the domain name part of the host's FQDN.

- **Preference.** Enter the preference associated with this mail exchanger. Preferences are explained later in this section. (In the first release of the DNS/DHCP Management Console, this field is mistakenly labeled "Reference." The error is corrected in NetWare 5 Service Pack 1, which was unavailable when I prepared the screen shot.)

- **Exchange.** Enter the domain name serviced by this mail exchanger.

7. Click *Create*. DNS/DHCP Management Console creates the PTR Resource Record object, naming it after the host's host ID.

8. If this is the last change you will be making to the zone, edit the *Serial Number* fields on the *SOA Information* tab for the Zone object containing the RR object.

▶ · ◀

F I G U R E   11.28

Creating a Mail Exchanger Resource Record

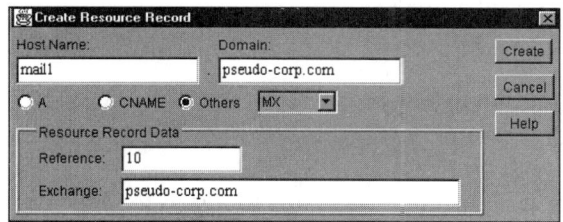

Remember that a mail exchanger must be defined by an Address resource record and by an MX resource record. A mail exchanger can support multiple exchanges, and more than one MX resource record might be defined for the same mail exchanger.

Name Server Resource Records

Name Server (NS) resource records are required in both forward- and reverse-naming zones. Each name server that is authoritative for a zone must be defined in an NS for the zone. Typically, DNS/DHCP Management Console creates NS resource records as you specify the authoritative name servers for a zone, as discussed earlier in the section "Configuring Zone Objects." However, there are two situations when you will be required to create NS resource records manually:

▶ When a non-NetWare server will function as a secondary name server for a zone that uses NetWare 5 DNS servers as the primary name servers. This situation is considered in the following section "Configuring a Non-NetWare 5 Secondary Name Server."

▶ When a parent DNS zone is configured to forward name resolution requests to a child DNS zone. See the section "Delegating Authority to a Child Zone" for more information.

NOTE

Remember that a name server must be defined by an Address resource record as well as a Name Server resource record. DNS/DHCP Management Console creates Name Server Resource Record objects when you define a DNS name server, but Address resource records are not automatically created. You must add an Address resource record to the appropriate zone after creating the DNS Server object.

Modifying Resource Records

The data for a resource record is split into two components:

▶ The host identification, which is found in the Resource Record Set object.

▶ The resource record parameters, which are found in the Resource Record object.

Figure 11.29 shows the detail parameters for a RRSet object. You can modify two fields:

▶ **Associated NDS Object.** This optional field can be used to specify the NDS object associated with this host. You can specify a NetWare Server object, for example, or the User object associated with the primary user of a host. This information has no function and is used only to document the relationship.

▶ **Comments.** This free-form field can be used to record any notes about the RRSet object, such as the date of its creation and a record of any changes.

Each Resource Record object has its own set of detail parameters. Some detail parameters cannot be modified. For example, you cannot change the IP address of an Address resource record. You must delete the Address Resource Record object and re-create it to change the IP address.

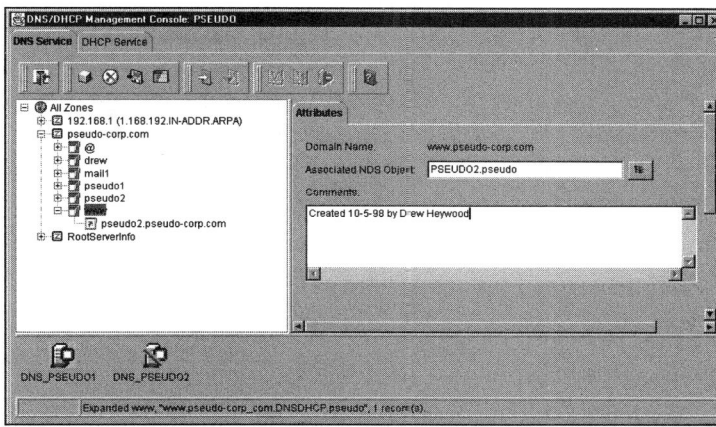

F I G U R E   11.29

Details for a Resource Record Set Object

The detail parameters of some Resource Record objects can be modified after the object is created. Figure 11.30 shows a CNAME object as an example. Note that the *Domain Name of Aliased Host* field can be edited.

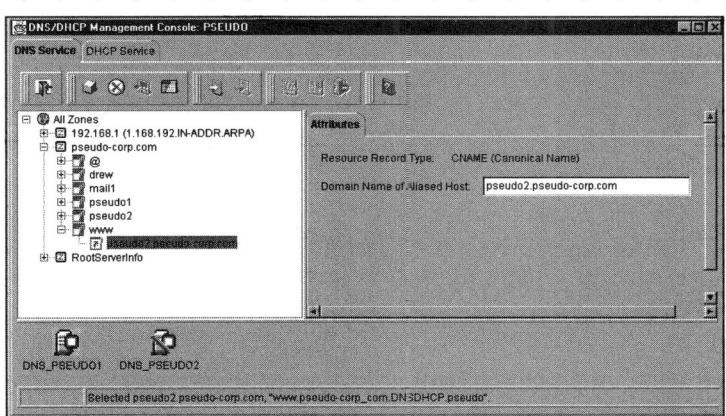

F I G U R E   11.30

Editing Detail Parameters of a CNAME Object

After you change the detail parameters of a RRSet or RR object, you must store the changes in NDS. Changes are stored when you do one of the following:

▸ Select a different object, in which case you will be prompted to save changes made to the object.

▸ Click the *Save Data to NDS* button in the toolbar.

Also, to ensure that the change will propagate to the DNS servers, remember to increment the *Serial Number* fields on the *SOA Information* tab of the Zone object.

Configuring a Cache-Only Name Server

Cache-only name servers were described earlier in this chapter in the section "Forwarding Name Servers." It is very simple to configure a cache-only name server. Just do the following:

1. Create a DNS Server object for the name server.

2. On the *Forward List* tab of the detail parameters for the DNS Server object, add the IP address of the DNS forwarding name servers to which this name server will forward name resolution requests.

3. Load NAMED.NLM on the NetWare 5 server.

DNS configuration tasks don't get much simpler than that!

Configuring a Non-NetWare 5 Secondary Name Server

You may find yourself managing DNS on a network that contains various types of DNS servers. Many organizations already have BIND name servers running on UNIX systems, for example, and may be reluctant to abandon well-established DNS platforms. However, BIND doesn't offer an equivalent of DDNS. As a result, you may want to implement some NetWare 5 name servers so that DDNS can update DNS based on IP address assignments made by DHCP. Whatever the reason, if you find yourself managing a mixed bag of DNS servers, you need to know how to configure primary and secondary name servers that are of different types.

Okay, you've already set up some NetWare 5 DNS servers and discover that you need to implement secondary copies of some of your zones on other types of name servers. The procedure has three steps:

1. Configure DNS on the secondary name server.

2. In the primary zone, add an address (A) record for the secondary name server.

3. In the primary zone, add a name server (NS) record for the secondary name server.

First, you need to configure the secondary zones as required on the non-NetWare 5 name servers. Later in this chapter, you will get an introduction to BIND that shows you how to set up a BIND name server with a secondary zone. Most name servers require the following:

▶ The name of the zone.

▶ The name of a data file where the secondary name server stores a copy of the zone data. This file name does not affect the zone transfer. It is used only on the secondary name server and defines a local file in which the BIND server stores a copy of the zone database.

▶ The IP address of a DNS master server from which the zone can be transferred. This can be the IP address of any of the DNS servers that are authoritative for the zone.

Second, add an A resource record for the secondary name server to the zone. If the primary zone database is stored on NetWare 5, use DNS/DHCP Management Console to add the Address resource record to the appropriate Zone object.

Finally, add an NS record to the primary zone for the secondary name server. On NetWare 5 DNS, this NS record is added to the @ RRSet object for the zone. The procedure is as follows:

1. Log in using an account that has the Supervisor right for the container of the Zone object that will contain the NS resource record.

2. Start DNS/DHCP Management Console and select the *DNS Service* tab.

3. Select the @ RRSet object in the Zone that will be supported by the secondary DNS server.

4. Click the *Create* icon in the toolbar.

5. Select *Resource Record* in the *Create New DNS Record* dialog box to open the *Create Resource Record* dialog box.

6. Select the *Others* radio button.

7. Select *NS* in the Resource Records list box. The *Create Resource Record* dialog box will resemble Figure 11.31.

8. In the *DNS Server Domain Name* field, enter the FQDN of the secondary name server. The *Host Name* and *Domain* fields cannot be modified.

9. Click *Create*. DNS/DHCP Management Console creates the PTR Resource Record object, naming it after the host's host ID.

<table>
<tr>
<td>

FIGURE 11.31

Creating a Name Server Resource Record for a Non-NetWare 5 Secondary Name Server

</td>
<td>

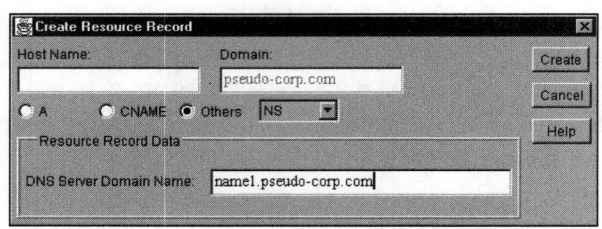

</td>
</tr>
</table>

After these preparations are completed, start the name service on the secondary name server. It should initialize its zone database by performing a zone transfer from the designated name server.

NOTE

When a non-NetWare 5 DNS server is configured with a secondary zone, it uses the zone serial number to determine whether changes have been made to the zone, and requests a zone transfer only if the serial number has changed. After editing records in the primary zone, remember to edit the *Serial Number* field in the zone *SOA* detail parameters.

Naming Hosts in Child Domains

Many organizations will organize their DNS name space into parent and child zones. Child zones may be used to organize host names by geographic region, department, or subsidiary, for example. Everything we have seen to this point assumes that all host name are in the same zone. Now we need to see how to delegate authority for child zones.

The sample network (Figure 11.1) includes three hosts that are in the eng sub-domain of pseudo-corp.com. We can support names in the eng child domain in two ways. One approach adds the host names in the child domain to the parent domain's zone. Another approach creates a separate child zone. Both approaches have advantages and disadvantages.

Including Child Domain Host Names in the Parent Zone

Even on a small network, you may want to use child domains to organize your host names into logical groups. But if your organization is small, you don't want to make administration any more difficult in the process. Adding a zone for each child domain might needlessly complicate administration.

However, a new zone isn't required. The RRs for the users in the child domain can be stored with the RRs for the parent domain in a single zone. Suppose you want to add a resource record for woody.eng.pseudo-corp.com. In the pseudo-corp.com zone, you simply use enter woody.eng in the *Host Name* field of the *Create Resource Record* dialog box, as shown in Figure 11.32. Because this RR is in the pseudo-corp.com zone, the RR object defines a resource record for woody.eng.pseudo-corp.com. Simple, huh?

▶ • ◀

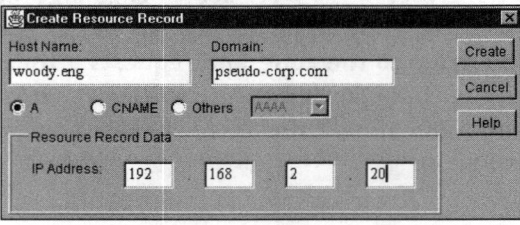

F I G U R E   I . 3 2

Creating an Address RR for a Host in a Child Domain

If it's so simple, why not do that for all child domain host records? The chief drawback is administrative. If you create different zones, you can place the zone objects in different NDS containers, enabling you to establish different administrators for each zone. All objects in a given zone will be placed in the same container and will typically be administered by the same people.

Additionally, if you configure multiple zones, the zones can be supported by separate name servers. This may be a necessity on a large private network where a single name server could be overwhelmed if it needed to resolve names for all the company's domains. It certainly is a necessity on the Internet.

Delegating Authority to a Child Zone

If you choose to delegate authority for the child domain to a separate zone, the first step is to create the child zone. On NetWare 5, follow the procedure described earlier in the section "Creating Primary, Forward-Naming Zone Objects." The Create Zone dialog box in Figure 11.33 shows the information required to create the sub-zone eng.pseudo-corp.com. The administrator must assign the desired name servers to the child zone and populate the child zone with the desired resource records. It is necessary to assign at least one name server that is authoritative for the zone. This may be a name server that is authoritative for the parent zone, or it may be a separate name server.

The parent zone needs to be informed of two items: that the child exists, and what the name servers are for the child zone. Doing so requires two records for each name server supporting the child zone — sometimes referred to as "glue" records because they establish a connection between a parent and a child zone:

▶ An A record that declares the name of the child zone's name server and its IP address.

> ▶ An NS record that identifies the host identified in the A record as a name
> server and specifies for which child zone the name server is authoritative.

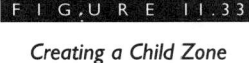

Creating a Child Zone

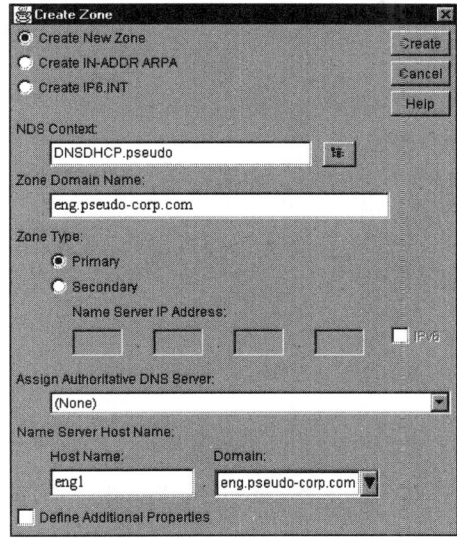

For the name server eng1.eng.pseudo-corp.com, the A record is configured
as shown in Figure 11.34.

*Address Record for a Name
Server in a Child Zone*

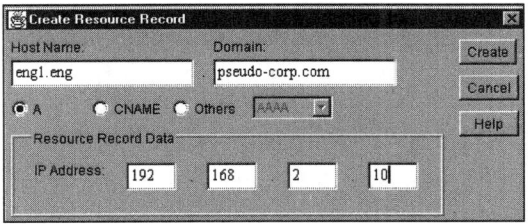

When enabling support for a child zone, the NS record is configured somewhat
differently than an NS record for a name server in the local zone. The procedure
is as follows:

1. Log in using an account that has the Supervisor right for the container in which the parent zone is located.

2. Start DNS/DHCP Management Console and select the *DNS Service* tab.

3. Select the Zone object corresponding to the parent zone.

4. Click the *Create* icon in the toolbar.

5. Select *Resource Record* in the *Create New DNS Record* dialog box to open the *Create Resource Record* dialog box.

6. Select the *Others* radio button.

7. Select *NS* in the Resource Records list box. The *Create Resource Record* dialog box will resemble Figure 11.35.

8. In the *DNS Server Domain Name* field, enter the following information:

   - **Host Name.** Enter the host name of the name server.

   - **Domain.** Enter the domain name of the child domain. Combined, the *Host Name* field and the *Domain* field must specify the FQDN of the name server.

   - **DNS Server Domain Name.** Enter the name of the domain for which the name server has authority.

9. Click *Create*. DNS/DHCP Management Console creates the PTR Resource Record object, naming it after the host's host ID.

10. If this is the last change you will be making to the zone, update the *Serial Number* fields on the *SOA Information* tab for the Zone object containing the RR object.

The child zone is defined in the same way as the parent zone. Child zones don't require any records that reference the parent zone. As a result, the eng.pseudo-corp.com zone would be created using the same procedures we have seen for defining the pseudo-corp.com zone.

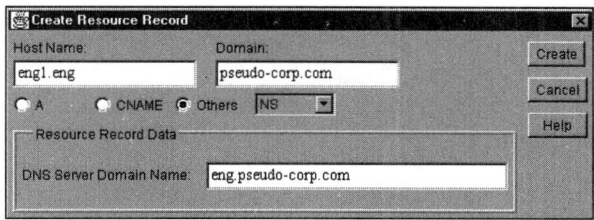

*Defining the NS Record
for a Name Server of a
Child Zone*

DNS Objects and NDS

All DNS objects are stored in NDS, but the hierarchy of DNS objects in the NDS database does not reflect the hierarchical relationships of the DNS objects with one another. Figure 11.36 shows some of the DNS objects required for the example network shown in Figure 11.1. All these objects were created in (or moved to) the context ou=DHSDHCP.o=pseudo. Let's see how the DNS hierarchy is and is not reflected in the NDS tree.

Zone objects are container objects. All the Resource Record Set objects associated with a zone are stored in the Zone container object. As you can see, Zone objects and Resource Record Set objects share a hierarchical relationship in DNS and in NDS.

DNS Server objects do not share hierarchical relationships with Zone objects, even though the DNS server may be authoritative for the zone. The authority relationship is defined as a property of the Zone object, and not by a hierarchical relationship between the Zone object and the DNS Server object.

Resource Record Set objects are not container objects and do not contain Resource Record objects. In fact, Resource Record objects do not appear in NDS and do not qualify as NDS objects. Resource Records entered in DNS/DHCP Management Console are stored as parameters of RRSet objects.

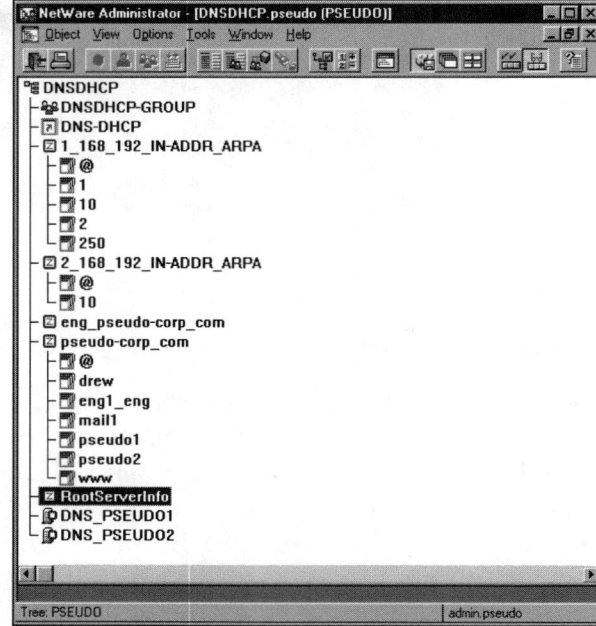

DNS Object Relationships
As Shown in NetWare
Administrator.

DNS Service Design Guidelines

The DNS service can have a significant impact on network traffic. In addition
to name resolution traffic, network traffic is generated by zone transfers and by
NDS partition replication. You need to consider both DNS and NDS in the design
of your DNS service.

Optimizing DNS Service Performance

There are two areas of concern: network traffic impact and responsiveness to
client requests.

Network traffic impact is particularly important when the network includes WAN links, either to the Internet or to other sites in your own organization. Your goal is to configure DNS so that it resolves as many names as possible without needing to transmit name resolution requests through the WAN.

Ideally, a client's primary DNS name server will be located at the local site. DNS servers employ caching to retain recently resolved names, enabling the DNS server to resolve frequently requested names locally without needing to send a request through a WAN connection. In some cases, you may wish to implement forwarders to concentrate cached names on a small number of name servers. Cache-only name servers can improve name resolution responsiveness and can reduce processing demand on forwarders by providing an intermediate level of caching, thereby reducing the number of name queries that reach the forwarding name server.

If DNS server performance is unacceptable, consider one of the following strategies to improve responsiveness:

▶ Deploy dedicated DNS servers

▶ Upgrade server hardware

▶ Subdivide your local name space into parent and child zones and assign different name servers to each zone

▶ Deploy multiple DNS servers and configure clients to use different DNS servers as their primary name servers

NDS Design Guidelines

Novell recommends that you create containers specifically to hold DNS and DHCP objects, enabling you to define administrators easily for these services. If necessary, DNS objects can be placed in multiple containers, enabling you to establish more than one group of administrators. If, for example, your organization has several locations, each of which has local network administrators, you may want to define separate containers that could be used to group the DNS objects and assign trustee rights to the appropriate personnel. In this example, I have grouped the DNS objects under the OU DNSDHCP.

If your network includes WAN connections, you need to take the WAN connections into account when defining the containers that will hold the DNS objects. This isn't the place to give you a thorough discussion about how to optimize your NDS tree design, but here are some basic guidelines:

▶ So that they will not generate excess WAN traffic, clients should be serviced by local DNS servers. Each location should have at least one DNS server, and preferably should have a NetWare server as well. The second NetWare server can provide NetWare file and print services, support a replica of the DNS NDS partition, and be configured as a second DNS server.

▶ Define a container object for each location and place the DNS objects needed for that location in the local container. For example, the local DNS servers and the local zones should be defined in a container replicated only at the local site.

▶ Establish an NDS partition for each local DNS container and replicate the partition only on local servers. This eliminates replication traffic that could clog the WAN link.

Managing the DNS Server Service

The DNS Server service (NAMED.NLM) enables a NetWare server to act as a DNS server. NAMED.NLM is loaded and unloaded at the server console, but can be paused and restarted from DNS/DHCP Management Console.

Loading and Unloading NAMED.NLM

Before starting NAMED.NLM on a NetWare server, you must define the server in a DNS Server object using DNS/DHCP Management Console. When you load NAMED, the DNS Server service checks NDS to determine for which zones it has authority, if any. It will load the records for those zones as it initializes. By default, NAMED will detect and load new zones while it is running.

When you have created a DNS Server object, DNS server configuration is complete. Start the DNS Server service by executing the command LOAD NAMED on the NetWare server. The NetWare console dialog is as follows:

```
PSEUDO1: load named

Loading module NAMED.NLM

  Novell DNS Server DNIPV136

  Version 5.00         July 29, 1998

  Copyright 1997-98, Novell Inc.  All rights reserved.


10-7-1998  8:11:01 pm:    NAMED-5.0-4

        DNS Server Ready to receive data on port 53

10-7-1998  8:11:01 pm:    NAMED-5.0-8

        Starting service for Primary zone 1.168.192.in-
addr.arpa

10-7-1998  8:11:01 pm:    NAMED-5.0-8

        Starting service for Primary zone pseudo-corp.com
```

You can, of course, unload the service with the command UNLOAD NAMED.

NAMED.NLM accepts several command line options, which are described in Table 11.1.

TABLE 11.1	OPTION	PURPOSE
Command Options	-a	Activates auto-detect of new zones. This is the default setting.
	-b	Turns off auto-detect of new zones.
	-f *file* [*context*]	Reads the file specified by *file*, which must be a text file in BIND boot file format. The boot file specifies zones to be created in an NDS context specified by the *context* parameter.

Continued

T A B L E 11.1	OPTION	PURPOSE
Continued	-h	Displays the command syntax and options.
	-l	Enables a DNS server to log in as an administrator, enabling it to obtain rights needed to create and delete zones from the command line.
	-m *file* [*context*]	Creates a new primary zone as specified in the file specified by the *file* parameter, where the data file is a BIND-format zone database file. Zone objects are placed in the context specified by *context*. This option can be used to import a zone from a BIND server when moving support for the zone to a NetWare 5 DNS server.
	-q	Disables verbose messages on the debug display. This is the default setting.
	-r *zone*	Deletes the zone specified by *zone*.
	-rp *characters*	For host names generated dynamically by DDNS, specifies characters to be replaced by a dash (-) character.
	-s [zone]	Displays status information. A zone name can be optionally specified.
	-u *file*	Updates an existing primary zone as specified in the file specified by the *file* parameter, where the file is a BIND-format zone database file.
	-v	Enables verbose messages on the debug display.
	-zi *zone*	Forces a zone-in transfer for a specified zone.

You can load NAMED repeatedly with different parameters to invoke different options. The DNS Server service is loaded re-entrantly to activate the new parameters

NAMED records messages on a debug screen which you can reach through Ctrl-ESC or Alt-ESC at the NetWare 5 console. The debug screen logs DNS Server activity. Use the –q and –v command-line parameters for NAMED.NLM to disable and enable verbose messaging.

Stopping and Starting the DHCP Server

Operation of the DNS Server service can be suspended and restarted from the DNS/DHCP Management Console. When the DNS Server service is restarted, it will initialize its zone databases by reading the zone resource records from NDS. Or, if the DNS Server service is supporting a secondary zone, the DNS server will initiate a zone transfer to obtain current zone resource records.

It should seldom be necessary to stop and restart the DNS Server service manually, however. By default, the DNS Server service checks NDS and will automatically detect new zones for which it has authority. Automatic detection of new zones is disabled by loading NAMED with the –b parameter.

The DNS Server service monitors the serial number in the SOA record of a zone to determine whether zone data have changed. If the serial number has been modified, the DNS Server will read the zone data from NDS to pull changes into its local database. DDNS automatically increments the zone serial number so that dynamic address records are promptly activated on the zone name servers.

To stop a running DNS server, select the server icon in DNS/DHCP Management Console and click the *Start/Stop Service* button in the toolbar. A dialog box prompts you to confirm that the server should be stopped. When the server has been stopped, the server icon will be flagged in the DNS/DHCP Management Console, as for DNS server DNS_PSEUDO2 in Figure 11.37.

*DNS/DHCP Management
Console Icon for a Server
That Has Been Suspended*

To resume operation of the DHCP service, select the server icon in the DNS/DHCP Management Console and click the *Start/Stop Service* button. After confirming your choice, the service will resume operation on the server. The DHCP icon in DNS/DHCP Management Console resumes its normal appearance.

▶ · ◀

Establishing Your Domain on the Internet

After you have configured your DNS servers with the required zones and resource records, you need to inform the Internet name servers of the names of your DNS servers. At the time I am writing this chapter, Internet domain registration services are managed by Network Associates. You can research and register domain names at www.internic.net. When you register your domain, you must supply the IP addresses of at least two name servers. Because the details change frequently, this book cannot provide precise information about the registration procedure.

▶ · ◀

Configuring DNS Clients

Both Windows 95/98 and NT can be configured as DNS clients. Chapter 9 discusses the details of configuring TCP/IP protocol support on these clients.

To configure a Windows 95/98 client to obtain its TCP/IP configuration from DHCP, do the following:

1. Open the *Network* applet in the Control Panel.

2. Select the *Configuration* tab.

3. Select the TCP/IP entry that binds to your network adapter.

4. Click *Properties*.

5. Select the *DNS Configuration* tab.

6. Configure the following fields:

- **Host.** Specify the computer's DNS host name, which may or may not be the same as its NetBIOS name.

- **Domain.** Specify the computer's DNS domain name.

- **DNS Server Search Order.** Add the IP addresses of up to three DNS name servers. The client will attempt to access the name servers according to the order in which they appear in the list.

7. Close the *Network* applet and restart the computer.

To configure a Windows NT client to obtain its TCP/IP configuration from DHCP, do the following:

1. Open the *Network* applet in the Control Panel.

2. Select the *Protocols* tab.

3. Select TCP/IP in the *Network Protocols* list.

4. Click *Properties*.

5. Select the *DNS* tab of the *Microsoft TCP/IP Properties* dialog box.

6. Configure the following fields:

- **Host.** Specify the computer's DNS host name, which may or may not be the same as its NetBIOS name.

- **Domain.** Specify the computer's DNS domain name.

- **DNS Server Search Order.** Add the IP addresses of up to three DNS name servers. The client will attempt to access the name servers according to the order in which they appear in the list.

7. Close the *Network* applet and restart the computer.

DNS name servers can also be specified in DHCP options, a procedure described in the next chapter. If a client is obtaining the IP address of a DNS server from DHCP, leave the *Domain* fields blank in the client DNS configuration dialog boxes. Otherwise, the local, static parameter will override the DNS server address specified by DHCP.

Configuring BIND Database Files

The DNS server that you will encounter most frequently is the Berkeley Internet Name Domain (BIND). BIND has been ported to most UNIX platforms and to other platforms as well. All of the root name servers on the Internet use BIND. Due to the popularity of BIND, Novell has enabled the NetWare 5 DNS server to import BIND databases and to export zone data to BIND database files. It is likely, therefore, that you will want to know a bit about how BIND works.

BIND servers are configured using static data files, which are standard text files. With the exception of the boot file, there is no hard-and-fast format for BIND data file names I'm using one common convention. You will encounter the following types of data files:

- ▶ **boot.** This file is the master configuration file. It declares all the various files used to initialize the DNS server.

- ▶ **cache.** This file contains host information that establishes basic DNS connectivity. Principally, this file defines the addresses of the root name servers for the DNS.

- ▶ **0.0.127.** This file includes reverse-lookup data for IP numbers on the 127 (loopback) network, such as localhost.

- ▶ *reverse-netid*.**in-addr.arpa.** For each netid managed by the DNS server, a reverse-lookup file is required to specify address-to-name mappings.

- ▶ *domain.* For each domain managed by the DNS server, a forward-lookup zone database file is required to specify name-to-address mappings.

The rest of this discussion explains how the BIND data files are formatted.

The BOOT File

The BOOT file is responsible for the following tasks:

- ▶ Specifying the location of the directory that contains the DNS configuration files, if the location differs from the default directory.

▶ Declaring the zones for which the server is authoritative, and the data file that describes each zone.

▶ Specifying the name and location of the file that identifies the DNS root name servers.

Here is a possible BOOT file for the sample network shown in Figure 11.1:

```
;   DNS BOOT FILE


cache     .                           cache.dns


primary  pseudo-corp.com             db.pseudo-corp.com
primary  1.168.192.in-adr.arpa       db.1.192.168.in-
addr.arpa

primary  2.168.192.in-adr.arpa       db.2.168.192.in-
addr.arpa

primary  0.0.127.in-adr.arpa         db.0.0.127.in-addr.arpa
```

The BCOT file has two directives: primary and cache. (A secondary directive appears in BOOT files for secondary DNS servers.)

The primary directives declare the zones for which this server is authoritative, as well as the data file that contains data for each zone. This server is authoritative for four zones:

▶ **pseudo-corp.com**. The file db.pseudo-corp.com contains the name-to-address mappings for the pseudo-corp.com domain.

▶ **1.168.192.in-adr.arpa**. The file db.1.168.192.in-addr.arpa.dns contains address-to-name mappings for this reverse-lookup domain.

▶ **2.168.192.in-adr.arpa**. Another reverse-lookup zone serviced by the file cb.2.168.192.in-addr.arpa.

▶ `0.0.127.in-adr.arpa`. This is a reverse-lookup zone associated with the loopback address, supported by the file `db.0.0.127.in-addr.arpa`.

A `primary` directive is required for each of these zones. Each DNS server is authoritative for the loopback zone (127.0.0) so that attempts to resolve loopback addresses are not propagated beyond the local DNS server.

The `cache` directive specifies the file that is authoritative for the root domain. Unlike files specified by `primary` directives, which are searched during the name resolution process, entries in the cache file are held in cache memory to make them immediately available.

You may encounter two other directives in BOOT files. The `forwarders` directive defines one or more servers at your site that serve as forwarders — DNS servers that take can be delegated to take responsibility for DNS queries. Forwarders are discussed earlier in this chapter. A directive that uses the `forwarders` keyword looks like this:

```
forwarders 172.16.32.10 192.168.8.5
```

If you have set up forwarders, you may want to restrict other DNS servers so that they won't even try to connect with the Internet. You do that by configuring the server as a slave. A slave server answers queries from its authoritative data and cache, but relies entirely on forwarders to resolve unknown names. To configure the DNS server as a slave, add the `slave` directive, as in this example:

```
forwarders 172.16.32.10 192.168.8.5

slave
```

Zone Database Files

Each zone for which a DNS server is authoritative must be described in a database file. The `db.pseudo-corp.com.` database file for `pseudo-corp.com` is as follows:

```
@                    IN  SOA  haydn.pseudo-corp.com.
peters.pseudo-corp.com. (

                10          ; Serial Number

                10800       ; Refresh after 3 hours
```

```
              3600        ; Retry after 1 hour

              604800      ; Expire after 1 week

              86400     ) ; Minimum TTL of 1 day



@                 IN  NS  pseudo1


@                 IN  MX  10  mail1.

ftp               IN  CNAME  pseudo2.

pseudo1           IN  A  192.168.1.1

pseudo1           IN  A  192.168.2.1

pseudo2           IN  A  192.168.1.2

drew              IN  A  192.168.1.10

lauren            IN  A  192.168.1.15

cyd               IN  A  192.168.1.25

mail1             IN  A  192.168.2.250

router            IN  CNAME  pseudo1.

router1           IN  A  192.168.1.1

router2           IN  A  192.168.2.1

eng1.eng          IN  A  192.168.2.10

woody.eng         IN  A  192.168.2.20

blythe.eng        IN  A  192.168.2.30
```

The following sections examine each of the sections in the domain database. Only a few of the possible resource record types appear in this example. Other resource records are defined in the DNS RFCs.

The Start of Authority Record

A Start of Authority (SOA) resource record is found at the beginning of each zone database file. This block of information declares the host that is most authoritative for the domain, contact information, and some DNS server parameters. (This is the same information that the NetWare 5 DNS service places in the *SOA Information* detail tab of a Zone object.)

An @ symbol at the beginning of the SOA header declares that this file defines members of the domain associated with the file in the BOOT file. Recall this entry in BOOT:

```
primary   pseudo-corp.com              db.pseudo-corp.com
```

As a result of that declaration, @ refers to the domain `pseudo-corp.com`. Consequently, when the `pseudo-corp.com.dns` file declares an entry for the host `pseudo1`, the directive is defining information for pseudo1 in the `pseudo-corp.com` domain. That is, the directive is defining `pseudo1.pseudo-corp.com`. Because the domain is implied by the context established by the boot file, the structure of the database file is simplified, requiring less administrative effort. The `IN A` entry for pseudo1 could have been entered as follows with exactly the same effect:

```
pseudo1.pseudo-corp.com.           IN   A   192.168.1.1
```

Notice that `pseudo1.pseudo-corp.com.` is terminated with a period, indicating that its origin is the root domain. Without the period indicating the origin in the root domain, DNS would understand the name as `pseudo1.pseudo-corp.com.pseudo-corp.com`, because it would be understood in the context of the `pseudo-corp.com` domain.

Improper use of trailing periods is a common cause of error in BIND database files, and it is worth emphasizing the point:

▶ Omit the trailing period if the host name falls within the domain defined by this database file (which is nearly always the case).

▶ Include the trailing period if the record fully specifies the domain name of the host being defined; that is, if the record specifies the fully-qualified domain name of the host.

The IN directive unsurprisingly stands for Internet, one class of data that can appear in the database files. Following IN, the SOA directive declares this as a Start of Authority header.

Following the SOA directive are two Internet names:

▸ The first, pseudo1.pseudo-corp.com., is the domain name of the name server host that is most authoritative for this domain.

▸ The second, drew.pseudo-corp.com., is the e-mail address of the primary contact for this name server. The actual e-mail address is "drew@pseudo-corp.com". The @ has been replaced with a period because the @ is a special-purpose character in DNS data files and cannot appear in this context. This e-mail name enables people to send messages when they have trouble with the name server.

Following the e-mail name are five parameters that set the operational characteristics of the DNS server, enclosed in parentheses to enable the parameters to span several lines, thereby permitting a comment to label each parameter. A comment begins with a semicolon (;) and extends to the end of the line. All comment text is for human consumption and ignored by the computer.

Note that the closing parenthesis immediately follows the final parameter, not the comment for the parameter. A parenthesis in the body of the comment would be ignored.

Without comments, the SOA record could have been entered like this:

```
@ IN SOA pseudo1.pseudo-corp.com. drew.pseudo-corp.com.(8
3600 600 86400 3600)
```

You probably agree that the comments make interpreting the record much easier. The five numeric parameters are as follows:

▸ **Serial.** A serial number that indicates the revision level of the file. The serial number must be incremented each time the zone database is modified. Secondary name servers will initiate zone transfers only when they detect a change in the serial number.

▸ **Refresh.** The interval in seconds at which a secondary name server checks in to download a copy of the zone data in the primary name server.

▶ **Retry.** The time in seconds a secondary name server waits after a failed download before it tries to download the zone database again.

▶ **Expire.** The period of time in seconds that a secondary name server continues to try to download a zone database. After this time expires, the secondary name server discards data for the zone.

▶ **Minimum.** The minimum Time To Live in seconds for a resource record. This parameter determines how long a DNS server retains an address mapping in cache. After the TTL expires for a record, the record is discarded. Short TTL values enable DNS to adjust to network changes more adroitly, but also increase network traffic and loading on the DNS server. A short TTL may be appropriate in the early days, while a network evolves, but you may want to extend the TTL as the network stabilizes.

Name Server Records

A name server (NS) record must declare each primary and secondary name server that is authoritative for the zone. Name servers are declared by IN NS records. Notice that the domain servers terminate with periods, indicating that the name originates with the root.

NS records might begin with the @ specifying "the domain for this database" or the @ might be omitted, in which case the domain is implied. If the @ is omitted, the IN should not occupy the first column of the line. In other words, the following declarations are equivalent in this context:

```
pseudo-corp.com. IN NS  pseudo1.pseudo-corp.com.

@               IN NS  pseudo1.pseudo-corp.com.

                IN NS  pseudo1.pseudo-corp.com.
```

Address Records

Each host name that DNS resolves must be specified using an address (A) resource record — unless the name will be resolved through WINS. One example from the pseudo-corp.com.dns database file is the following:

```
Pseudo1        IN  A  192.168.1.1
```

Multihomed hosts may require an address declaration for each network adapter, as with the host pseudo1 in the example database file. When users request name resolution for a multihomed host, DNS returns the IP address from the resource record that appears first in the zone database file.

Aliases

Many networks employ aliases. In most cases, aliases are declared using CNAME ("canonical name") resource records. On the pseudo-corp.com network, host pseudo2 will be configured as a World Wide Web server. So that users can access this server with the name www.pseudo-corp.com, it is necessary to establish an alias as follows:

```
www                 IN   CNAME   pseudo2
```

A more complex case is presented by multihomed computers. The aliases section of the sample database file includes three declarations related to the host haydn.edu:

```
router            IN   CNAME   pseudo1.

router1           IN   A   192.168.1.1

router2           IN   A   192.168.2.1
```

The CNAME declaration defines router as an alias for the multihomed host pseudo1. DNS queries for router or pseudo1 are resolved to the first IP address in the configuration of pseudo1. A CNAME declaration maps to a canonical name, however, not to a specific network interface of the multihomed host.

Usually, applications don't care about the address of a host to which they resolve. When troubleshooting a network, however, you may prefer to be able to diagnose a specific interface, which is why two IN A declarations are included. router1 and router2 enable an administrator, for example, to ping by name a specific network attachment of pseudo1.

The advantage of coding aliases using CNAME is that the actual IP address of the host appears in one place only. If the IP address changes, a single edit updates both the primary address map and the alias. A CNAME record specifies a host, not a particular interface. That is why, on a multihomed host, you must use A records to establish a name for each specific interface. If the address for pseudo1 changes, the CNAME records automatically reference the new IP address. However, it is also necessary to edit the A records manually for papa250 and papa190 as well as the A record for pseudo1.

E-mail Server Records

If your network incorporates an TCP/IP-based electronic mail system such as *sendmail*, you should add appropriate records to the zone database file.

In the sample network, the mail server is running on the host `mail1.pseudo-corp.com`. The following resource records support this host:

```
@                       IN  MX 10  mail1.

mail1                   IN  A  192.168.2.250
```

The A record simply specifies the IP address for `mail1.pseudo-corp.com`.

The MX record specifies that mail1 is an e-mail server for the `keystone.com` domain (specified by the @ character). If the domain is supported by more than one e-mail server, each is specified in an MX record:

```
@                       IN  MX  10  mail1

@                       IN  MX  20  mail2
```

The numbers following the MX keywords specify the priority for each mail server. E-mail will be routed to the server with the lowest active priority number; that is, 1 indicates the most preferred server. (In other words, if mail1 and mail2 are both active, e-mail will be routed to mail1.) The numeric parameter simply specifies the priority order. Priorities of 2 and 7 would have exactly the same result as priorities of 10 and 20.

By including MX resource records, you make it easier for outsiders to send e-mail into your domain. E-mail can be addressed simply to `blythe@pseudo-corp.com`, for example. There's no need to address the message to `blythe@mail1.pseudo-corp.com`. Incoming mail is routed to the available server that has the highest priority.

Reverse-Matching Database Files

A reverse-matching (address-to-name matching) database file is required for each network ID for which the DNS server is authoritative. Recall that the file named `db.192.168.1` is the database for network 192.168.1, which appears in the reverse database tree as `1.168.192.in-addr.arpa`.

The db.1.168.192.in-addr.arpa.dns file is constructed as follows:

```
@ IN SOA mozart.pseudo-corp.com.  peters.pseudo-corp.com. (
                    10          ; Serial Number
                    10800       ; Refresh after 3 hours
                    3600        ; Retry after 1 hour
                    604800      ; Expire after 1 week
                    86400     ) ; Minimum TTL of 1 day


@               IN  NS  pseudo1.pseudo-corp.com.


;addresses mapped to canonical names
1               IN  PTR  pseudo1.pseudo-corp.com.
2               IN  PTR  pseudo2.pseudo-corp.com.
10              IN  PTR  drew.pseudo-corp.com.
15              IN  PTR  lauren.pseudo-corp.com.
25              IN  PTR  cyd.pseudo-corp.com.
250             IN  PTR  mail1.pseudo-corp.com.
```

Similarly, the db.2.168.192.in-addr.arpa database file is constructed as follows:

```
@ IN SOA mozart.pseudo-corp.com.  peters.pseudo-corp.com. (
                    1       ;serial
                    10800   ;refresh after 3 hours
                    3600    ;retry after 1 hour
                    691200  ;expire in 8 days
                    86400)  ;minimum TTL 1 day
```

```
@                   IN  NS  mozart.pseudo-corp.com.


;addresses mapped to canonical names

10                  IN  PTR  eng1.eng.pseudo-corp.com.

20                  IN  PTR  woody.eng.pseudo-corp.com.

30                  IN  PTR  blythe.eng.pseudo-corp.com.
```

The reverse-naming files use the same Start of Authority header as the domain database file. As before, @ means "the domain specified in the BOOT file." Also, all host names are to be understood in the context of the domain name. Therefore, "10" in the IN PTR record refers to host 192.168.1.10 (which is 10.1.168.192.in-addr.arpa. in the reverse-naming database tree).

NS records declare the name servers that are authoritative for this domain.

PTR (pointer) records provide reverse mappings between IP addresses and host names. Notice that host names must be fully specified from the root domain.

The Localhost Database File

The db.0.0.127.in-addr.arpa file includes a reverse mapping for the localhost host name. It resembles the formats of the other reverse mapping files:

```
@ IN SOA pseudo1.pseudo-corp.com.  drew.pseudo-corp.com. (

                    10            ; Serial Number

                    10800         ; Refresh after 3 hours

                    3600          ; Retry after 1 hour

                    604800        ; Expire after 1 week

                    86400     ) ; Minimum TTL of 1 day


;name servers

@                   IN  NS  mozart.pseudo-corp.com.
```

```
;addresses mapped to canonical names

1                       IN  PTR localhost.
```

The Cache File

The cache file declares name-to-address mappings to be cached in the DNS server. Essentially, cached entries define the DNS servers that are authoritative for the root domain.

If you are establishing a private TCP/IP network, then the root domain will be supported by DNS servers running on your network. The records in cache will reflect this and will declare entries for local DNS servers authoritative for the root domain.

In the case of pseudo-corp.com, however, the network will be connected to the Internet, and the cache file will identify the Internet root name servers. These root name servers change from time to time, and a DNS administrator should periodically check the related information files to make sure the local cache database is kept up to date. The official root name server list can be obtained via FTP. Obtain the file /domain/named.root from FTP.RS.INTERNIC.NET.

The named.root file can be used unmodified as the cache database file, although you may want to rename the file to reflect local database file-naming conventions. The named.root file consists of entries such as the following, each of which describes a root domain server:

```
.                        3600000  IN  NS   A.ROOT-
SERVERS.NET.

A.ROOT-SERVERS.NET.      3600000      A    198.41.0.4

.                        3600000      NS   B.ROOT-
SERVERS.NET.

B.ROOT-SERVERS.NET.      3600000      A    128.9.0.107

.                        3600000      NS   C.ROOT-
SERVERS.NET.
```

Each host is declared in two directives:

▸ **NS directive.** Declares the server by name as a name server for the root domain.

▸ **A directive.** Declares the server name-to-address mapping.

The NS and A directives include an additional parameter in the cache file. In early versions of DNS, a numeric parameter (here 3600000) indicated how long the data should remain in cache. In current versions of DNS, the root name server entries are retained indefinitely. The numeric parameter remains a part of the file syntax but no longer serves a function.

Creating the cache file completes configuration of the DNS database files.

Setting Up a Secondary Name Server

The example files examined to this point have configured the primary name server pseudo1. They have also anticipated establishment of a secondary name server on pseudo2 that this section addresses. The distinction between the primary and secondary name servers is found in the structure of the BOOT file.

The DNS directory of the secondary name server needs copies of the following files:

▸ BOOT

▸ cache

▸ db.0.0.127.in-addr.arpa

The cache and db.0.0.127.in-addr.arpa files are identical on all DNS servers, and you do not need to create them. A cache file is created on each server when Microsoft DNS Server is installed.

The BOOT file would be modified for the secondary server on pseudo2 as follows:

```
;   DNS BOOT FILE
```

```
cache          .          cache


secondary    pseudo-corp.com              192.168.1.1  db.pseudo-
corp.com

secondary    1.168.192.in-adr.arpa        192.168.1.1
db.1.168.192.in-addr.arpa

secondary    2.168.192.in-adr.arpa        192.168.1.1
db.2.168.192.in-addr.arpa

primary      0.0.127.in-adr.arpa          db.0.0.127.in-addr.arpa
```

pseudo2 is a secondary name server for three zones, specified in the secondary directives. In the three secondary directives, an IP address is added to the syntax. This IP address specifies the computer that serves as the repository for the database file. pseudo2 loads pseudo-corp.com from pseudo1 (IP address 192.168.1 1). During operation, pseudo2 makes backup copies of the database files in its local DNS directory, which enables pseudo2 to start up if pseudo1 goes down.

A name server can be a primary for some zones and a secondary for others. The role of a name server is specified by the use of the primary and secondary directives in the BOOT file.

pseudo2 is a primary only for the reverse-naming 0.0.127.in-addr.arpa zone. Because this information is the same on all servers, there is no sense including the records in the zone transfer.

Because the information in the cache file is identical for all DNS servers, there is no sense in performing zone transfers for root name server data. Each DNS server is configured with a local cache file.

In addition to customizing the BOOT file for the secondary server, you need to add NS records for the secondary server to the database files on the primary DNS server. On the sample network, you would need to add the following resource record to the db.pseudo-corp.com, db.1.168.192.in-addr.arpa, and db.2.168.192.in-addr.arpa files:

```
@                        IN   NS   schubert.pseudo-corp.com.
```

▶ . . . . ◀

Exchanging DNS Databases

The NetWare 5 DNS server can import and export standard BIND format zone files, enabling you to exchange zone configuration data with most types of DNS name servers.

Two procedures can be used to import BIND database files:

▶ To import a file from the DNS/DHCP Management Console, select the *All Zones* icon in the objects tree and click the *Import DNS Database* button in the toolbar. You will be asked to supply the name of a file in BIND database format that includes the zone data to be imported.

▶ To import a file from the NetWare 5 console, load NAMED with the –m parameter to create a new zone or the –u parameter to update a zone. These parameters are described in the section "Loading and Unloading NAMED.NLM" earlier in this chapter.

To export a zone to a BIND database file, select the zone in the DNS/DHCP Management Console and click the *Export DNS Database* button in the toolbar.

To import data from a BIND BOOT file, load NAMED with the –f parameter. This parameter is described in the section "Loading and Unloading NAMED.NLM" earlier in this chapter.

▶ . . . . ◀

Enough Boring Stuff

DNS can be pretty boring. It is a technology that enables other things to function, but doesn't do anything exciting in and of itself. But you've got to have it, and I've tried to present DNS administration as simply as possible.

Paired with DNS on NetWare 5 is the Domain Host Configuration Protocol, or DHCP. You've probably noticed that DNS/DHCP Management Console is used to manage the DNS and DHCP services. Since we're so close, this is a fitting time to segue over to DHCP, another important infrastructure component that you will almost certainly want to set up on your network.

## CHAPTER 12

The Dynamic Host Configuration Protocol

By this time, it has probably dawned on you that a considerable part of a TCP/IP administrator's time can be devoted to configuring clients with IP addresses and other parameters. IP addresses can be a real nuisance to manage manually. When IP addresses are manually assigned, considerable bookkeeping is required so that you know which address is assigned to a particular client. You must ensure that no two clients obtain the same IP address. And you must assign a new IP address to any client that moves to a different network. Clients that move frequently are particular headaches.

The Dynamic Host Configuration Protocol (DHCP) was designed to automate the task of assigning IP addresses to clients. As an added benefit, DHCP can be used to configure a wide variety of client parameters. Suppose, for example, that the IP address of a router changes. DHCP makes it unnecessary to visit each client computer to change a statically-defined default gateway. With DHCP, you can change one parameter on a central server and the new value will be distributed to each DHCP client automatically.

Like the NetWare 5 DNS server discussed in Chapter 11, the new DHCP server is nicely integrated with NDS. The DHCP database is stored in NDS. Partition replication promotes fault-tolerance and enables the database to be distributed throughout the network. NDS also enables you to secure DHCP resources easily so that they can be managed only by authorized individuals.

NOTE

DHCP is defined in RFC 2131, which obsoletes RFC 1541. The new RFC adds several new features to DHCP, including the option of using a client identifier field as a substitute for using the MAC identifier. At present, clients supported by NetWare 5 (MS-DOS/Win 3.x, Windows 95/98, and Windows NT 4.0) conform to RFC 1541 and cannot take advantage of some of the newer features. Other new features enable DHCP to function as a configuration database that DHCP clients can consult at any time. On a Pure IP network, DHCP clients can obtain service information from DHCP.

After discussing how clients obtain their configurations from DHCP, we will examine the management of the NetWare DHCP server.

DHCP Concepts

DHCP configuration information is maintained on *DHCP servers*, which provide network configurations to *DHCP clients*. Clients can be assigned IP addresses either permanently or in the form of limited-duration *leases*. Figure 12.1 illustrates the architecture of a network that supports DHCP host configuration. In this network, the DHCP server is providing leases to clients on two networks. In fact, a single DHCP server can support as many networks and subnets as you wish, although on large networks it is preferable to have multiple DHCP servers to share the demand and provide a degree of fault tolerance.

When a DHCP client first enters a network, it has not yet been assigned an IP address. To obtain an IP address, it must communicate with a DHCP server. To send a request to a DHCP server, the new client issues a broadcast message that includes the client's hardware address. The DHCP server responds to the client by sending a message directly to the client's hardware address. Several DHCP operations are dependent on the use of broadcast messages, which somewhat complicates matters because broadcast messages are not forwarded to routers. The new client must communicate with the server via a broadcast message, but if the DHCP server is on a remote subnet, the broadcast message stops at the router.

To get around this difficulty, DHCP makes use of BOOTP forwarding. As mentioned, DHCP is essentially an expanded BOOTP and uses similar message formats. Routers configured to forward BOOTP messages can also forward DHCP broadcast messages. If a BOOTP forwarder receives a client's broadcast DHCP request, it reformats the request in a unicast message that it then sends to the DHCP server. One contribution of the BOOTP forwarder is to keep track of the subnet on which the DHCP client resides. When a client DHCP request must cross a router, the BOOTP forwarder includes its own IP address, which identifies the network on which the request originated. This enables the DHCP server to assign an IP address that is appropriate for the network on which the client resides.

DHCP servers maintain pools of addresses for each subnet that supports DHCP address assignment. On NetWare 5, these pools of addresses are stored as Subnet objects in the NDS database. Each subnet address pool consists of a range of IP addresses together with the TCP/IP characteristics clients receive when they are granted an address for the subnetwork. The client receives the address assignment in the form of a *lease*.

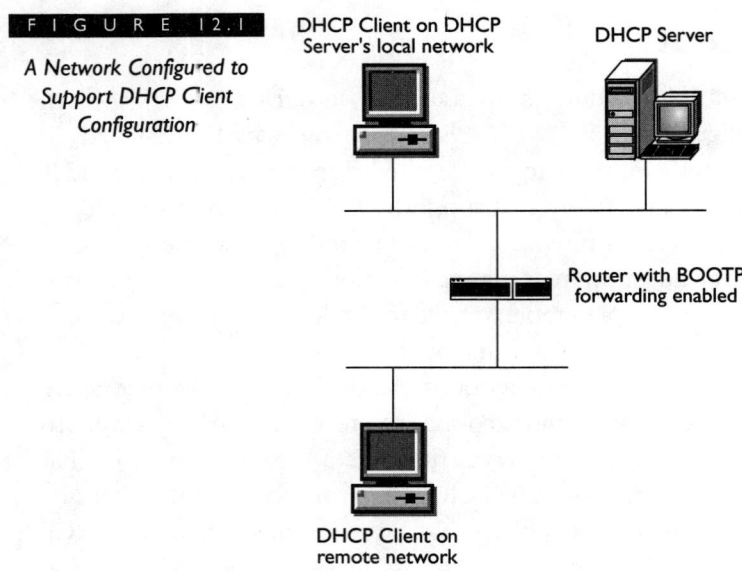

FIGURE 12.1

A Network Configured to Support DHCP Client Configuration

DHCP Client on DHCP Server's local network

DHCP Server

Router with BOOTP forwarding enabled

DHCP Client on remote network

DHCP Lease Management

You need to understand how leases are maintained to configure and manage DHCP. In the majority of cases, DHCP allocates IP addresses for a limited period of time by granting a lease for the address to the client. A lease conveys permission to use a particular IP address and typically has a limited duration. When the lease approaches expiration, it must be renewed by the client or the IP address is returned to the pool of available addresses for the subnetwork, after which the address can be assigned to other clients.

Figure 12.2 shows how a DHCP client communicates with a DHCP server to obtain a lease. Figure 12.3 shows the life cycle of the lease, which works like this:

1. When a DHCP client enters the network, it enters an *initializing state* and broadcasts a DHCPDISCOVER message on the local network. If this network is part of an internetwork and the routers are configured with BOOTP forwarding, the discover message will be forwarded to DHCP servers on other networks.

2. Every DHCP server that receives the discover message and is configured with a subnetwork profile matching the network on which the message originated responds with a DHCPOFFER message that includes an IP address and associated configuration information.

3. After sending its initializing message, the DHCP client enters a *selecting state* in which it examines any DHCPOFFER messages that it receives.

4. The DHCP client selects one of the DHCPOFFER messages and enters a *requesting state* in which it sends a DHCPREQUEST message to the DHCP server requesting a lease for the offered configuration.

5. If the DHCP server can still grant the request, it generates a DHCPACK (acknowledgment) message that puts the IP address and configuration information in the form of a lease to use the configuration for a specified period of time. The duration of the lease is configured by the network administrator.

6. When the DHCP client receives the acknowledgment message, it enters a *bound state* in which it configures itself with the parameters specified by the lease. (A node in a bound state has a network address and can communicate with other IP nodes.) The client retains this lease for the specified duration. If the client is restarted, it again communicates with the DHCP server and attempts to obtain access to its active lease.

7. When the lease time approaches an interval designated as the T1 interval, the client attempts to renew the lease by sending a unicast DHCPREQUIEST message to the DHCP server that the lease. The T1 interval is typically in the neighborhood of fifty percent of the lease duration, as determined by client default settings or by parameters received from DHCP.

8. If the server that granted the lease does not respond with a lease renewal within the T1 interval, the client continues to use the lease until a T2 interval is reached. At this time, the client reenters a *rebinding state* and attempts to solicit a lease from all available DHCP servers by broadcasting

DHCPREQUEST messages. If a new lease is granted, the client surrenders its current lease, which is returned to the available address pool. The client rebinds with the new IP address and enters a bound state.

If the client does not receive any DHCPOFFER messages by the time its lease is scheduled to expire, or if it receives a DHCPNACK (negative acknowledgment) during the rebinding interval, it loses its IP address lease and returns to an initializing state in which it must begin the DHCP discovery process again.

The backstage gimmickry of DHCP is pretty involved, but users are ordinarily quite unaware of the dynamics of the lease process, and no intervention is required on their parts. Only if the lease process breaks down at some point do users become aware that their IP addresses are unavailable.

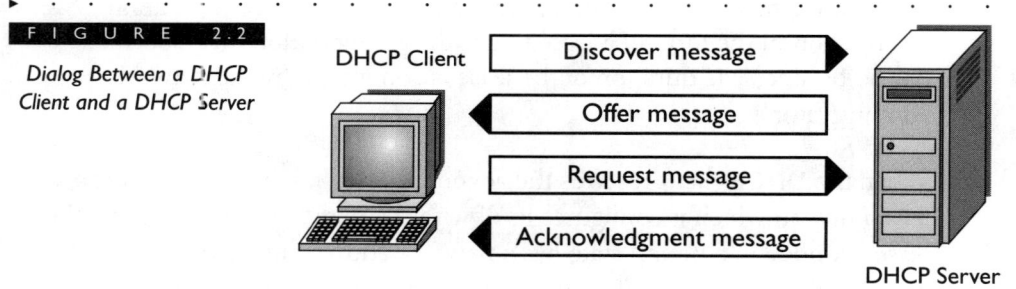

FIGURE 2.2

Dialog Between a DHCP Client and a DHCP Server

In some cases it is useful to configure more than one DHCP server to offer address leases for a subnet. When this is done, DHCP clients are able to choose among the leases offered by the various servers. Further, if one DHCP server is down, an alternative server can remain available to offer leases on the network. There is a catch, however, in that DHCP servers do not communicate to share their lists of active leases. Suppose that two DHCP servers are configured to offer IP addresses in the same address range. If one server assigns the IP address 192.68.10.33 to a client, the other server has no way of knowing that the address is in use. Consequently, the second server may make the address available to a different client, and communication conflicts are inevitable. So, while multiple DHCP servers are often useful, it is up to the network administrator to ensure that each subnetwork profile has a unique range of IP addresses.

▶ • ◀

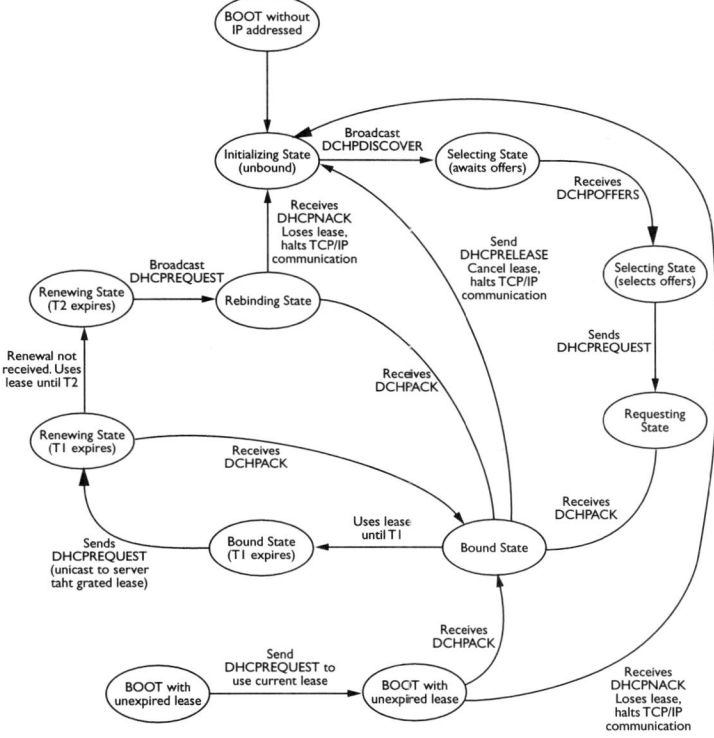

FIGURE 12.3

Life Cycle of a DHCP Lease

Many types of hosts require fixed IP addresses so that their identities do not change. Routers are good examples of devices that need fixed IP addresses, because hosts typically include a default router parameter in their configurations. DNS servers are other examples. Even hosts named in DNS may require fixed IP addresses. Ordinarily, DNS is not a dynamic database and must be manually updated whenever a host receives a new IP address. (NetWare 5 includes dynamic DNS, and the NetWare 5 DHCP server can notify DNS as IP addresses are assigned and released, enabling DNS to maintain a dynamic database of DHCP clients. Unfortunately, there is no standard for dynamic DNS, and you cannot use dynamic DNS with another vendor's DNS server.)

Hosts that require fixed IP addresses can be configured conventionally and their IP addresses can be excluded from the addresses assigned by DHCP. Alternatively, administrators can specify fixed DHCP address assignments tied to hosts' MAC addresses. A fixed DHCP address can still convey configuration information, enabling the administrator to manage host configurations centrally even when fixed IP addresses are necessary.

NOTE

Typically, DHCP is used to assign IP addresses dynamically to DHCP clients. In most cases, therefore, DHCP clients do not have fixed IP addresses. But as you learned in Chapter 11, the DNS database is static. An administrator enters an A resource record that matches an IP address with a hostname. DHCP is dynamic and DNS is static. Does that mean that an administrator must manually update DNS each time a DHCP client receives a new IP address? Fortunately, the answer to that question is no. Novell's DHCP service can dynamically update DNS to reflect the clients that it configures. As clients enter, leave, and move around the network, Dynamic Update keeps DNS current on the changes. Dynamic Update is easy to implement and will be covered in this chapter.

BOOTP Support

DHCP is an extension of the "bootstrap protocol" BOOTP, and was designed to overcome some of the limitations of the older protocol. BOOTP does not support dynamic address assignment, provides only limited client-configuration support, and does not implement the concept of client leases. IP addresses obtained from BOOTP are permanently assigned to the client.

BOOTP remains in use because — with a few other compact protocols (ARP and TFTP) — it enables a complete boot configuration to be implemented in ROM. This capability enables diskless workstations and other machines without non-volatile storage to obtain IP addresses and boot configurations from a network server. Often BOOTP clients use information obtained from BOOTP to obtain a boot image file used to complete the boot process initiated by the ROM routines.

The NetWare 5 DHCP service can supply addresses to BOOTP clients. But unlike BOOTP, which requires an administrator to match IP addresses manually to hardware addresses before IP addresses are distributed to BOOTP clients, NetWare 5 DHCP can assign IP addresses drawn from a dynamic pool. Because BOOTP does not implement a mechanism that limits the lease duration of an IP address assignment, IP addresses obtained through BOOTP are permanently assigned. Therefore, IP addresses allocated through BOOTP cannot be reused until they are manually deallocated.

Managing the DHCP Service

Before you can configure the DHCP service, you must install the DNS and DHCP schema extensions to NDS, a procedure described in the section "Installing the NDS Schema Extensions" in Chapter 11. You must also add an icon for the DNS/DHCP Management Console to your Start Menu or desktop, a procedure that also is described in the preceding chapter.

I've mentioned that the DHCP service is tied into NDS, so you can probably anticipate the next topic of discussion: the NDS object types associated with DHCP. As we discuss the various object types, examine Figure 12.4, which illustrates how the objects relate to the network. (The Subnet Pool object will be considered later in the chapter.) The DHCP object types are:

- **DHCP Server object.** Each server that will run the DHCP service must be defined in a DHCP Server object. Two DHCP Server objects will be created for this network, associated with the NetWare servers PSEUDO1 and PSEUDO2. DHCP server objects are leaf objects and can be contained in any O, OU, C, or L object.

- **Subnet object.** A Subnet object is created to describe each subnet for which DHCP will be assigning addresses. The Subnet object describes the entire range of IP addresses on the subnet but does not allocate any addresses for dynamic address assignment. Two Subnet objects will be defined for this network, one each for subnets 192.168.1.0 and 192.168.2.0. Subnet objects serve as container objects for Subnet Address Range and IP Address objects. Subnet objects can be contained in any O, OU, C, or L object.

- **Subnet Address Range object.** Subnet Address Range objects specify the addresses on a given subnet that are available for dynamic assignment. You must define a Subnet Address Range object for each subnet that supports dynamic IP address assignment. Subnet Address objects are leaf objects and can be created only in a Subnet container object.

▸ **IP Address object.** An IP Address object describes a specific host address assignment. IP Address objects can be used to assign a particular IP address to a given host, either manually or dynamically. They can also be used to exclude a particular IP address from DHCP assignment. For example, to reserve their IP addresses, IP Address objects will be created for servers PSEUDO1 and PSEUDO2, which have fixed IP addresses. IP Address objects are leaf objects and can be created only in a Subnet container object.

▸ **Subnet Pool object.** A Subnet Pool object can be used to support multiple subnets through a DHCP or BOOTP forwarder by identifying a pool of subnets for IP address assignment. We will see how subnet pools work later in this chapter. Subnet Pool objects are leaf objects and can be contained in any O, OU, C, or L object.

All DHCP objects must be managed by the DNS/DHCP Management Console. Figure 12.5 shows the DHCP Service tab of the DNS/DHCP Management. To preview a complete DHCP configuration, I have created a variety of DHCP objects in the left-hand pane of the window. We'll see how these objects are created and managed in the following sections.

All operations on the DHCP tab are initiated by clicking buttons in the toolbar. Figure 12.6 shows the toolbar and identifies the functions of the buttons. We will illustrate the use of each function in the course of this chapter.

Figure 12.7 illustrates the appearance of the DHCP objects in the NetWare Administrator utility. As with the DNS examples in the previous chapter, I have chosen to create the DHCP objects in a separate container, which is Novell's recommended practice. By placing DHCP objects in separate OUs, you can easily designate DHCP managers and distribute the NDS replication of DHCP objects to appropriate sites on your WAN. In many cases, you will not want all administrators to have the ability to change the DHCP configuration, and you can easily create a separate group to administer the DNS and DHCP services.

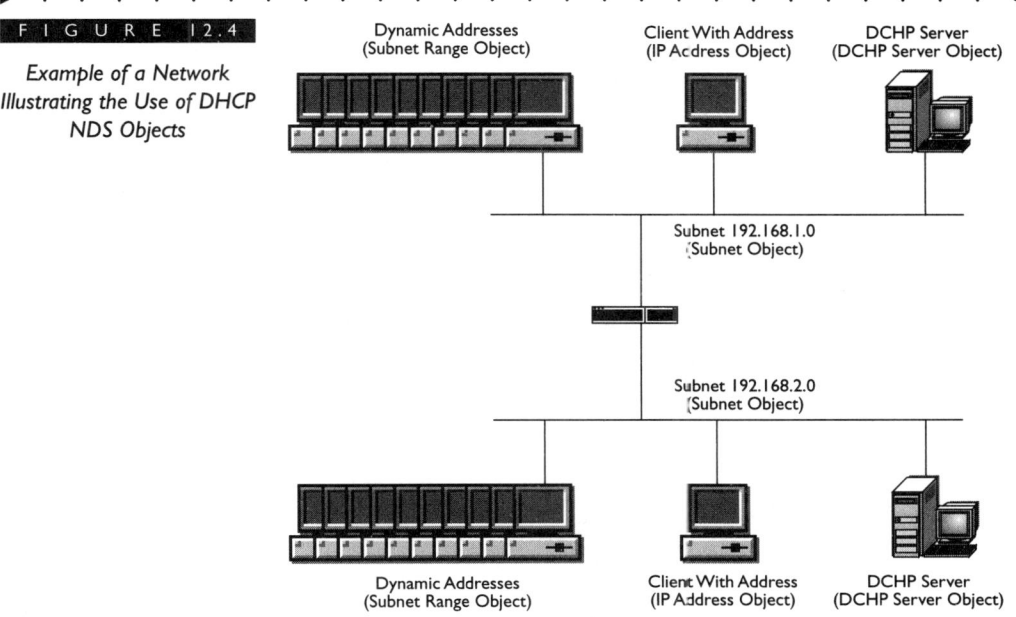

Example of a Network Illustrating the Use of DHCP NDS Objects

Dynamic Addresses
(Subnet Range Object)

Client With Address
(IP Acdress Object)

DCHP Server
(DCHP Server Object)

Subnet 192.168.1.0
(Subnet Object)

Subnet 192.168.2.0
(Subnet Object)

Dynamic Addresses
(Subnet Range Object)

Clienc With Address
(IP Address Object)

DCHP Server
(DCHP Server Object)

Although objects can be created in various orders, I'm going demonstrate the process following a particular sequence:

1. First, we will create Server objects.

2. Second, we will create Subnet objects to define the network infrastructure. Subnet objects will be associated with previously-defined Server objects.

3. Third, we will create Subnet Address Range objects to designate addresses available for dynamic address assignment.

4. Fourth, we will create IP Address objects to define IP address assignments for particular machines.

5. Finally, we will create Subnet Pool objects.

FIGURE 12.5

The DHCP Tab of the
DNS/DHCP Management
Console

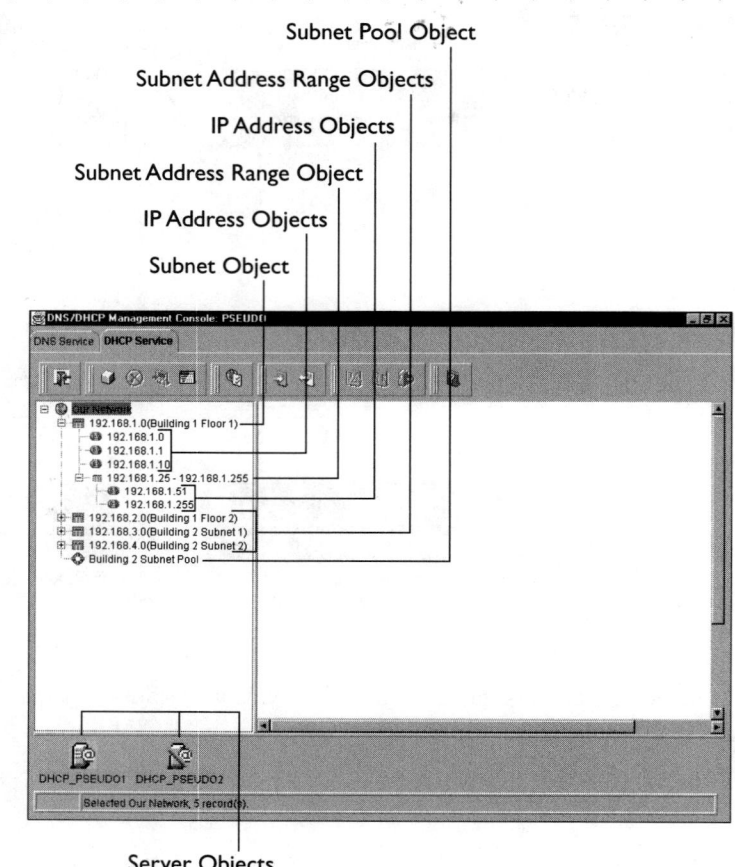

Subnet Pool Object

Subnet Address Range Objects

IP Address Objects

Subnet Address Range Object

IP Address Objects

Subnet Object

Server Objects

In each case, the procedure has two distinct steps:

1. Creating the object.

2. Configuring options for the object.

Managing DHCP Server Objects

Before a NetWare server can run the DHCP Server service, it must be described by a DHCP Server object in NDS. Creating your Server objects is a good place to start when initially configuring the DHCP service. After the Server objects are established, you can easily reference them in the configurations of the Subnet objects.

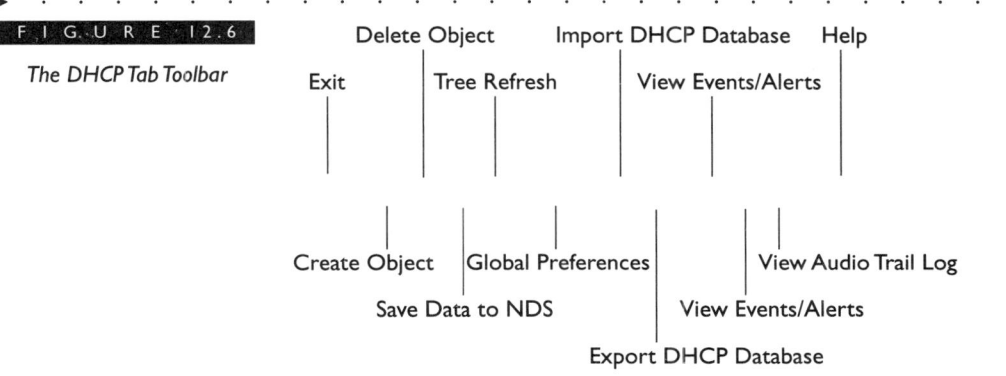

F I G U R E 12.6

The DHCP Tab Toolbar

Delete Object   Import DHCP Database   Help

Exit   Tree Refresh   View Events/Alerts

Create Object   Global Preferences   View Audio Trail Log

Save Data to NDS   View Events/Alerts

Export DHCP Database

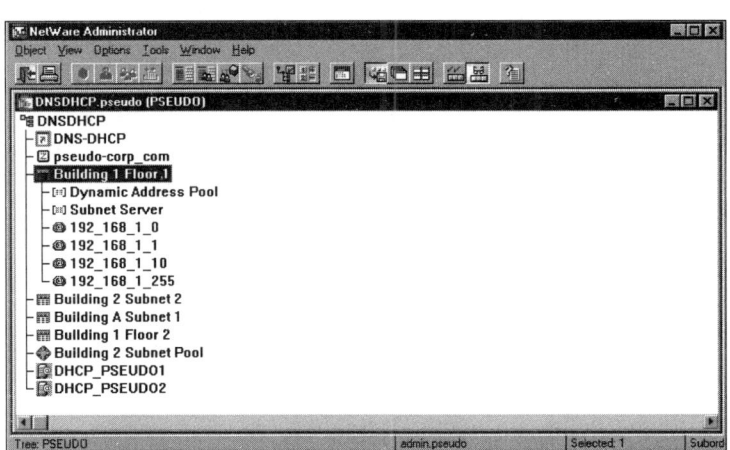

F I G U R E 12.7

DHCP Objects As Seen in NetWare Administrator

Creating Server Objects

To create a Subnet object, do the following:

1. Start DNS/DHCP Manager and select the *DHCP Service* tab.

2. Select *Our Network* in the left-hand pane.

3. Click the *Create* button in the toolbar.

4. Select *DHCP Server* in the *Create New DHCP Record* dialog box.

5. In the *Create DHCP Server* dialog box (Figure 12.8), specify the full NDS name of the server that will be running the DHCP Server service. You can click the NDS browse button to browse the NDS tree for the desired server.

6. Check *Define Additional Properties* if you wish to define other NDS properties for this DHCP Server object after closing the *Create DHCP Server* dialog box. When this box is checked, the object you are creating is selected after you click the *Create* button. The detail parameters for the object are then displayed.

7. Click *Create*.

NOTE

DHCP Server objects are leaf objects and are created in the context that contains the NetWare server object with which they are associated. If desired, you may move the DHCP Server object to any O, OU, C, or L container.

FIGURE 12.8

Creating a DHCP Server Object

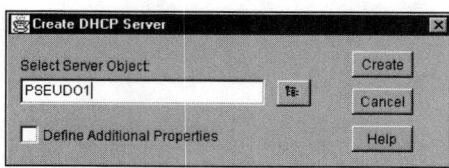

Figure 12.9 shows DNS/DHCP Management Console with two Server objects. Server objects appear in the bottom pane of the DNS/DHCP Management Console and are not listed in the DHCP object hierarchy in the left-hand pane.

When the DNS/DHCP Management Console cannot communicate with a DHCP server, the DHCP Server icon is marked with a red slash, as with DHCP_PSEUDO2 in Figure 12.9. At present, the DHCP Server service has not been started on the DHCP_PSEUDO2 NetWare server. After the DHCP server is fully configured, start the DHCP Server service by loading the DHCPSRVR.NLM on the server. DHCPSRVR.NLM is discussed in detail later in this chapter in the section "Managing the DHCP Server Service." The DHCP Server service has been loaded and is running on DHCP_PSEUDO1.

F I G U R E   12.9

The Server Tab for a Server Object

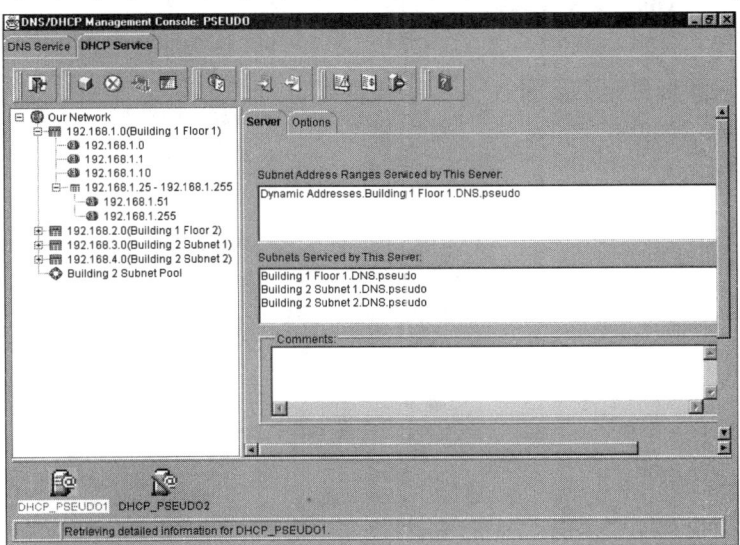

Configuring DHCP Server Options

Several DHCP Server parameters can be configured after the Server object has been created. When you select a DHCP Server icon, the right pane of DNS/DHCP Management Console contains two dialog tabs where you can view and modify the DHCP Server configuration.

The Server Tab   The Server tab is shown in Figure 12.8. To illustrate typical contents for this tab, I have created Subnet and Subnet Address Range objects and assigned them to the Server object. This tab is primarily informational. You can edit the contents of the *Comments* box, but the other information is determined in other dialog boxes. Specifically:

▶ The entries in the *Subnet Address Ranges Serviced by This Server* are determined by options associated with Subnet Address Range objects.

▶ The entries in the *Subnets Serviced by This Server* are determined by options associated with Subnet objects.

The Options Tab   Figure 12.10 shows the *Options* tab for a server object.

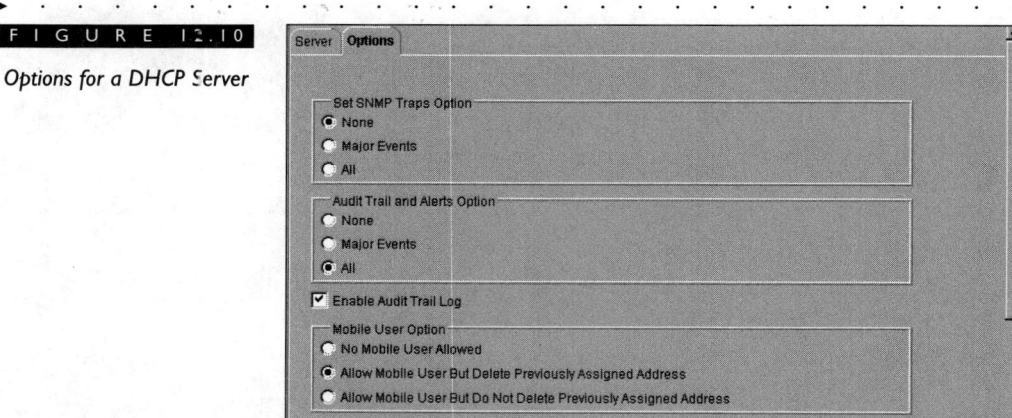

FIGURE 12.10

Options for a DHCP Server

Set SNMP Traps Option determines the type and number of SNMP traps that will be generated by the DHCP Server service. The following options are available:

▶ **None.** Select this option if your network is not monitored by an SNMP management console.

▶ **Major Events.** If your network is monitored by an SNMP management console, you should probably select this option.

▶ **All.** Select this option only if you are encountering problems with DHCP operation. Under normal circumstances, this option will generate unacceptable levels of network traffic.

Audit Trail and Alerts Option determines the detail of the audit trails and the number of administrative alerts that will be generated. The options are as follows:

▶ **None.** This option suppresses all audit trail entries and alerts. Typically, it is not a good idea to turn off these functions entirely.

▶ **Major Events.** This option will generate alerts in response to significant events and is generally the preferred setting.

▶ **All.** This option generates verbose audit trail entries and alerts. This level of messaging is desirable only when you are troubleshooting system problems.

Enable Audit Trail Log. The DHCP server records entries in the audit trail log only if this option is checked.

Mobile User Option. In DHCP terms, a *mobile user* is one that moves to different subnets. For such users, you have three options that regulate the handling of their IP addresses:

▶ **No Mobile User Allowed.** A user who has been assigned an IP address on one subnet will not be permitted to obtain an IP address for another subnet. This is also known as a "no duplicate" policy because it does not permit more than one IP address to be assigned to the same DHCP client.

▶ **Allow Mobile User But Delete Previously Assigned Address.** This option conserves IP addresses, but a computer may be assigned a different IP address each time it connects to a given subnet. This is known as a "delete duplicate" policy because, although it permits a client to change its IP address, it deletes the old IP address record when a new IP address is assigned.

▶ **Allow Mobile User But Do Not Delete Previously Assigned Address.**
The mobile computer will obtain the same IP address each time it connects
to a given subnet. This option uses IP addresses less efficiently because it
reserves IP addresses that are not currently in use. This is known as an
"allow duplicate" policy because it permits more than one IP address to be
assigned to the same DHCP client.

Ping Enabled. If this option is checked, the DHCP server will ping the network
to see if an IP address is in use before assigning the address to a client. This
prevents DHCP from assigning duplicate addresses but results in higher levels of
network traffic. If in doubt, enable this option, which protects you from any
misconfigured devices that conflict with addresses being assigned by the DHCP
server. If you can carefully control the network address configuration of your
network and are blessed with users who don't try to "tune" their computers by
adjusting network settings, you may be able to disable the ping test safely. But
pinging IP addresses before they are assigned can prevent numerous problems at
the cost of a moderate amount of network traffic overhead.

NOTE

**After editing the parameters for any object, you must commit the
changes to NDS in one of the following ways: (1) Click the *Save Data
to NDS* button in the toolbar, which is activated when any object
parameters are modified; (2) Select any other object. You will be
prompted with a *Save Record* dialog box. Click *Yes* to commit the
changes to NDS.**

Viewing the Logs

DNS/DHCP Management Console must be able to communicate with a server
to review its events, alerts, and audit trails. You must start the DHCP Server service
by loading DHCPSRVR.NLM. See the section "Managing the DHCP Server
Service" for details.

NOTE

**In addition to DHCPSRVR.NLM, you must load CSATPXY.NLM on
the target server to enable DNS/DHCP Management Console to
retrieve logs from the DHCP server. Add the command LOAD
CSATPXY to your AUTOEXEC.NCF file if you wish it to be enabled
when the NetWare server starts.**

The Events Log records events such as server startups and shutdowns. To view the events and alerts, select a server and click the *View Events/Alerts* button in the toolbar. Then specify a time period that you wish to view. Figure 12.11 shows an example of an events/alerts log.

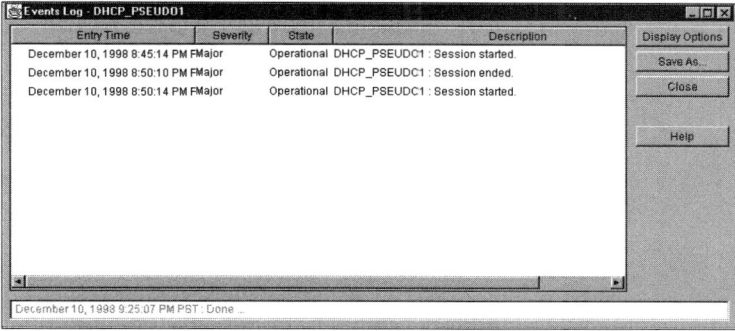

FIGURE 12.11

The Events/Alerts Log for a DHCP Server

The Audit Trail Log records DHCP client configuration events. To view the audit trail log, select a server and click the *View Audit Trail Log* button in the toolbar. Then specify a time period that you wish to view. Figure 12.12 shows an example of an audit trail log.

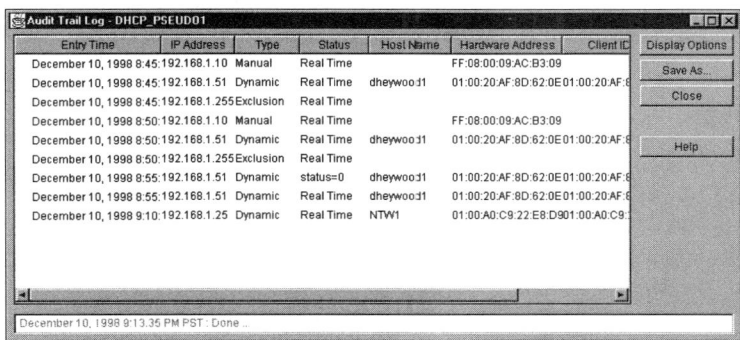

FIGURE 12.12

An Audit Trail Log for a DHCP Server

Managing Subnet Objects

You must create a Subnet object for each subnetwork that contains hosts to be configured through DHCP. A subnet is defined by a network address along with the relevant subnet mask. Let's look at two examples:

▶ The network address 192.168.1.0 with a subnet mask of 255.255.255.0 defines a class C subnet that supports 254 hosts (remember that hostids 0 and 255 are not available).

▶ The network address 10.54.0.0 with a subnet mask 255.255.0.0 describes a subnet of a class A network. In this case, the subnet mask indicates that only a portion of the class A address space is available on this subnet. Specifically, available hostids on this subnet range from 0.1 through 255.254.

The following sections explain how to create and modify Subnet objects.

 **Subnet objects are container objects and may be contained in an O, OU, C, or L.**

NOTE

Creating Subnet Objects

To create a Subnet object, do the following:

1. Open DNS/DHCP Manager and select the DHCP Service tab.

2. Select *Our Network.*

Or:

If you have already created a Server object that will support this subnet, select the DHCP Server object. Doing so automatically configures the DHCP server to support the subnet you are defining.

3. Click the *Create* button in the toolbar.

4. Select *Subnet* in the *Create New DHCP Record* dialog box.

5. Complete the *Create Subnet* dialog box (Figure 12.13), as follows:

- **Subnet Name.** Enter a descriptive name for the subnet. This name will appear with the Subnet object icon in the DNS/DHCP Management Console.

- **Select NDS Context.** Specify the NDS context in which the Subnet object is to be created. You can click the NDS browse button to browse the NDS tree for the desired context.

- **Subnet Address.** Enter the dotted-decimal network address for the subnet described by the Subnet object. Keeping with convention, the hostid portion of the network address is completed with zeros.

- **Subnet Mask.** Enter the dotted-decimal subnet mask for the subnet described by the Subnet object.

- **Default DHCP Server.** If Server objects have been defined, you can select the server that will support this subnet.

- **Define Additional Properties.** Check this box if you wish to define other properties for this Subnet object after closing the *Create Subnet* dialog box.

6. Click *Create* to create the object.

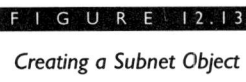

F I G U R E 1 2 . 1 3

Creating a Subnet Object

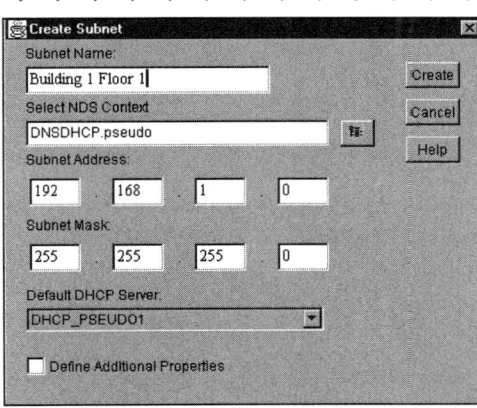

Figure 12.14 shows DNS/DHCP Management Console after a Subnet object has been created. When the Subnet object is selected, the right pane displays the configurable options for the Subnet object. These options will be discussed later in the chapter in the section "Configuring DHCP Options."

NOTE

As you learned in Chapter 4, certain IP addresses are invalid for use as host addresses. Specifically, the hostid portion of the IP address cannot be all 0s or all 1s. DNS/DHCP Management Console automatically excludes invalid IP addresses from subnet and subnet address ranges by defining appropriate IP Address objects. Later in the chapter, you will learn how IP Address objects are used.

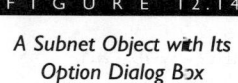

FIGURE 12.14

A Subnet Object with Its Option Dialog Box

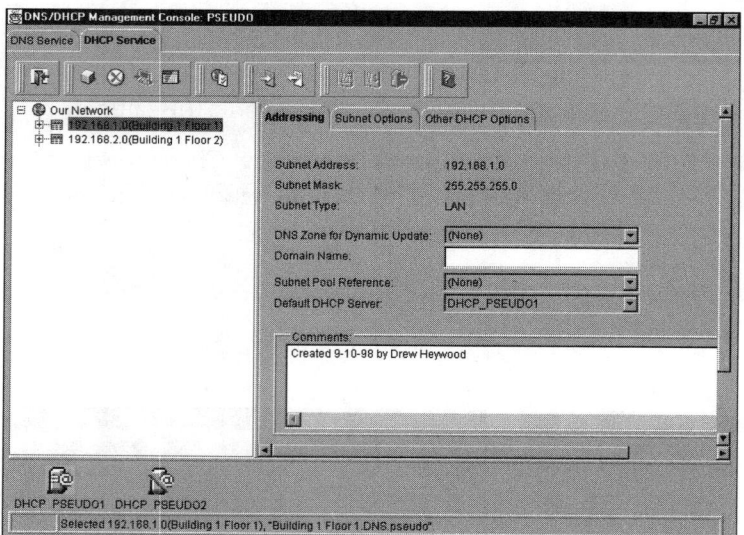

Configuring Subnet Options

Three tabs define the options associated with a Subnet object. You can edit these options at any time by selecting the Subnet object in DNS/DHCP Management Console.

The Addressing Tab   Figure 12.14 shows the *Addressing* tab, which is used to establish the relationship between the DHCP Server object and other objects and services. This tab contains the following fields:

▸ **Subnet Address.** This field contains the subnet address associated with the Subnet Object. This value cannot be modified after the Subnet object has been created.

▸ **Subnet Mask.** This field contains the subnet mask associated with the Subnet Object. This value cannot be modified after the Subnet object has been created.

NOTE
You cannot change the IP network address or subnet mask after a Subnet object has been created. If you need to change these values, you must delete the Subnet object and create a new one with the desired values.

▸ **DNS Zone for Dynamic Update.** If you wish to update the DNS database with IP address assignments made by DHCP, specify the DNS zone where the address records should appear.

▸ **Domain Name.** This field is optional. It is used to specify the value of the Domain Name DHCP option (option number 15). You can use it to specify a domain name that will be concatenated to the hostname supplied by the client. For example, if the domain name is pseudo-corp.com and the hostname is blythe, the value of the Domain Name option is blythe.pseudo-corp.com.

If Dynamic DNS is used, the domain name specified must be the same as or a subdomain of the DNS zone specified in the previous field. DDNS will add the host blythe.pseudo-corp.com to the DNS database.

▸ **Subnet Pool Preference.** This field is optional. Use it to specify a subnet pool with which this subnet will be associated. See the section "Managing Subnet Pool Objects" for more information about subnet pools.

▶ **Default DHCP Server.** This field specifies the DHCP server that will be assigning addresses to this subnet. The DHCP server specified will be the only one that will respond to BOOTP requests for this subnet.

▶ **Comments.** This field is optional. Use it to record any desired comments concerning the subnet. This is a good place to log any changes made to the subnet configuration.

The Subnet Options Tab   Figure 12.15 shows the *Subnet Options* tab for a Subnet object. This tab configures lease behavior and support for BOOTP address assignment.

Two options can be used to configure the lease type:

▶ **Permanent.** Select this option if leases obtained from DHCP are assigned permanently to clients.

▶ **Timed.** Select this option to establish a lease duration for DHCP leases assigned on this subnet. Three days is typically a good lease duration, resulting in reasonably timely updates without generating excessive amounts of network traffic.

The remaining options on this tab configure support for BOOTP configuration of diskless workstations:

▶ **Set Boot Parameter Option.** If this box is checked, support for BOOTP is enabled. You must complete the remaining fields to enable the BOOTP client to locate a boot file.

▶ **Server Address.** Specify the IP address of the server that has the boot file.

▶ **Server Name.** Specify the name of the server that has the boot file.

▶ **Boot File Name.** Specify the filename of the boot file.

Lease Assignment Strategy

Permanent lease assignments are usually not desirable. In addition to IP addresses, DHCP clients can obtain configuration options such as the addresses of DNS servers and default routers. Clients with permanent leases are not forced to renew periodically and will not learn about configuration changes.

If lease durations are too short, network traffic will be increased. A minimum time of three days is a good compromise lease time, enabling clients to learn of option changes within, at most, three days of when they occur.

If you know in advance that a network configuration change will occur, you can manipulate DHCP leases so that all clients will update on the critical day. Two days before the planned update, change the lease time to two days. On the day before, change the lease time to one day. This will force all clients to renew their leases with DHCP on the critical day, enabling them to obtain the new configuration parameters.

It may be advantageous to have a short lease duration when you have large numbers of transient users. Suppose that you have 50 sales staff who are usually out making sales calls and therefore do not need to be assigned permanent IP addresses. You can conserve IP addresses by setting up a subnet with a short lease duration, perhaps four hours. When a salesperson leaves the office, his or her lease will quickly expire and the IP address will be freed up for use by another staff member.

The Other DHCP Options Tab   The *Other DHCP Options* tab is used to specify DHCP options that apply to this subnet. DHCP options can be assigned at several levels in the DHCP hierarchy, so I have included a separate section that discusses the details. Options that apply to this subnet are listed in the *Other DHCP Options* tab shown in Figure 12.16. To modify the options, click the *Modify* button to open the *Modify DHCP Options* dialog box, which is discussed in the section "Configuring DHCP Options" later in the chapter.

FIGURE 12.15

The Subnet Options Tab for a DHCP Subnet Object

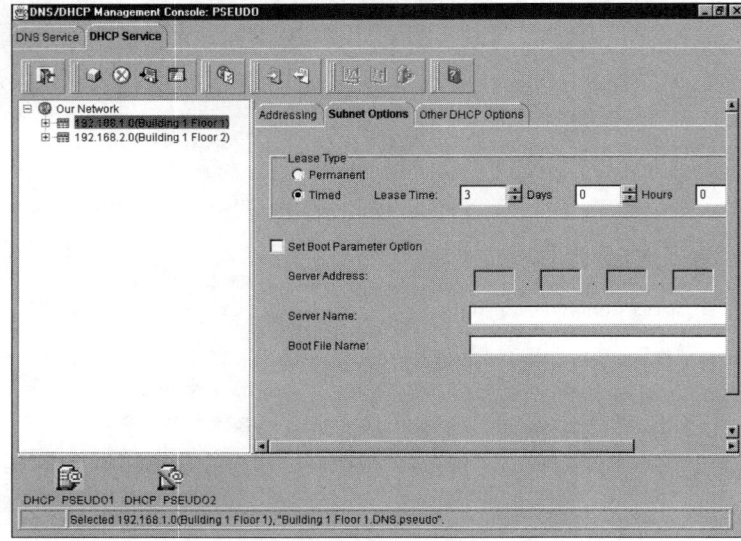

FIGURE 12.16

The Other DHCP Options Tab for a DHCP Server Object

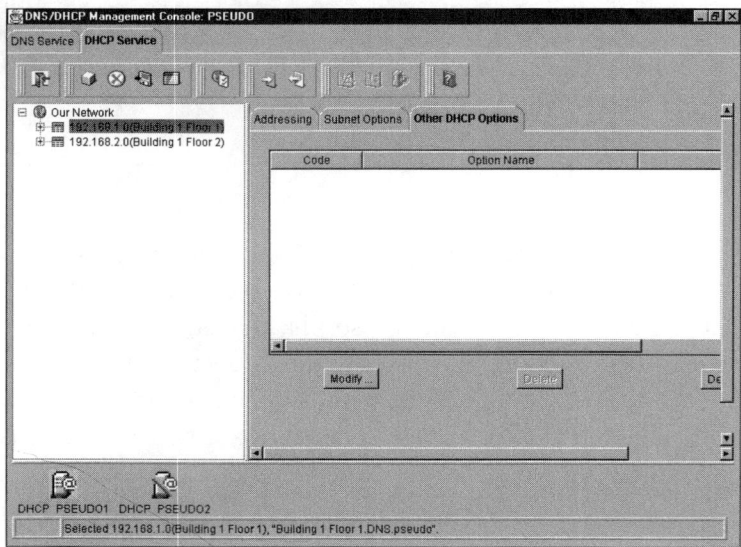

When a Subnet Is Too Large

As you have seen, some DHCP configuration parameters, such as lease duration, are configured at the subnet level. Suppose that you have a class C subnet and you want to configure clients with a variety of lease times. Altogether you have 280 users who share the subnet, too many for your class C address to handle. But many of the users work afield and spend little time in the office. You would like to configure a pool of 30 IP addresses with short lease times so that they can be shared among your 100 mobile users. But using short lease times would inconvenience staff who were permanently assigned to the office. If they took the afternoon off, they could start the next day with a different IP address.

You may be able to solve your problem by subnetting the class C address range. A subnet mask of 255.255.255.224 establishes seven subnets with 30 available hostids per subnet. These need not be physically separate subnets. You can bind multiple subnets to the same network adapter on a server by executing multiple BIND statements. Turn forwarding on and the NetWare server will route traffic among the virtual subnets.

Once established, each of the subnets can be configured with individual DHCP subnet options. Clearly, this approach sacrifices a significant portion of your class C address space, and should therefore be implemented only if short lease times are unacceptable.

Managing Subnet Address Range Objects

Subnet Address Range objects reserve ranges of IP addresses on a subnet for automatic address assignment. Until at least one Subnet Address Range object has been created, none of the addresses on a subnet can be automatically assigned to DHCP clients. Because Subnet Address Range objects always define a range of addresses on a particular subnet, Subnet Address Range objects must always be created below a Subnet object in the DHCP object hierarchy.

NOTE **Subnet Address Range objects are leaf objects and must be created in the context of the Subnet object that defines the Subnet Address Range's address block.**

Creating Subnet Range Objects

To create a Subnet object, do the following:

1. Open DNS/DHCP Manager and select the *DHCP Service* tab.

2. Select the Subnet object that contains the IP addresses in the subnet range you are defining.

3. Click the *Create* button in the toolbar.

4. Select *Subnet Address Range* in the *Create New DHCP Record* dialog box.

5. Complete the *Create Subnet Address Range* dialog box (Figure 12.17), as follows:

- **Subnet Address Range Name.** Enter a descriptive name for the subnet address range. This name will appear with the Subnet Address Range object icon in the DNS/DHCP Management Console.

- **Start Address.** Specify the first IP address in the address range. The default value is the first available IP address on the subnet.

- **End Address.** Specify the last IP address in the address range. The default value is the last available IP address on the subnet.

- **Define Additional Properties.** Check this box if you wish to define additional NDS properties for this object.

6. Click *Create* to create the object.

NOTE

As with Subnets, DNS/DHCP Management Console automatically manages IP Address objects to exclude invalid IP addresses from subnet address ranges. Notice in Figure 12.18 that the IP Address object 192.168.1.255 is now subordinate to the new subnet range in the hierarchy. IP Address objects are discussed later in this chapter.

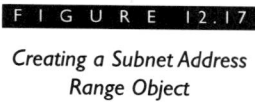

FIGURE 12.17

*Creating a Subnet Address
Range Object*

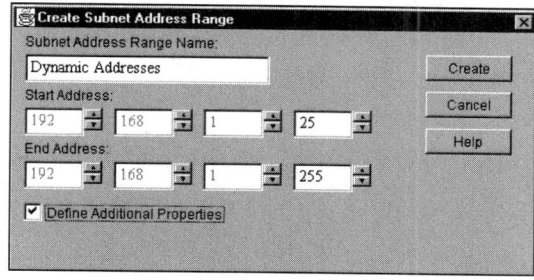

Figure 12.18 shows a newly-created Subnet Address Range object. Notice that the new object is indented under the Subnet object under which it was created. A Subnet Address Range object will always fall below a Subnet object in the DHCP tree.

FIGURE 12.18

*Configuration Options for a
Subnet Address Range
Object*

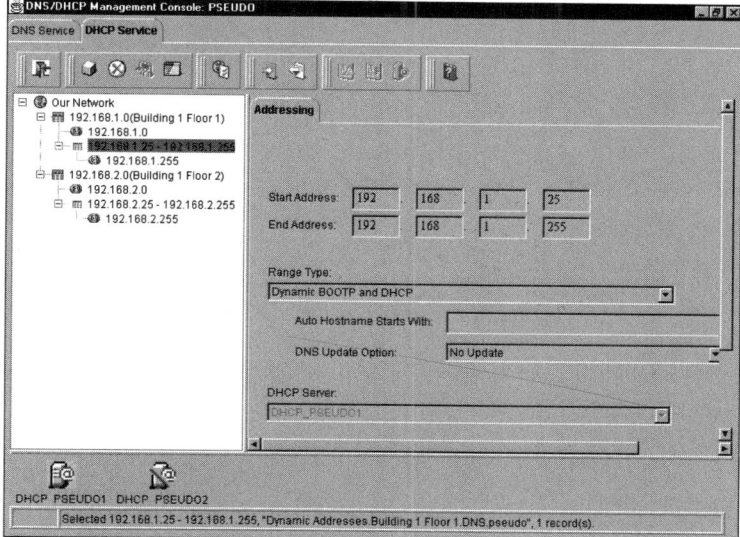

Configuring Subnet Address Range Options

In Figure 12.18, a Subnet Address Range object is selected to display the *Addressing* option tab. The fields on this tab are as follows:

▶ **Start Address** and **End Address.** These fields specify the address range defined by the Subnet Address Range object. These fields cannot be edited. To change the IP address range, you must delete the Subnet Address Range object and re-create it with the desired addresses.

▶ **Range Type.** This field determines which clients will be assigned addresses from this address range. Expand this list box to select one of the following options:

  • **Dynamic BOOTP and DHCP.** Select this option only if BOOTP clients must be serviced in addition to DHCP clients.

  • **Dynamic DHCP with Automatic Hostname Generation.** Select this option if you want DHCP to automatically generate hostnames for clients that receive DHCP leases. The automatic hostname is included in Dynamic DNS updates and is available to the client in DHCP option 12 (Host Name). Dynamic DNS is possible, and the *DNS Update Option* field is activated.

  • **Dynamic DHCP.** Select this option if you do not wish hostnames to be automatically generated. Dynamic DNS is possible, and the *DNS Update Option* field is activated.

  • **Excluded.** Selecting this option effectively disables this subnet address range. No IP address leases will be granted from this address range.

▶ **Auto Hostname Starts With.** This field is active if you have selected *Dynamic DHCP with Automatic Hostname Generation.* DHCP will generate a unique hostname for each client by appending a unique integer to the hostname you specify in this field. The automatic hostname will be used whenever a client does not include a hostname in its request for a DHCP lease. Windows 3.*x*, 95/98, and NT clients send their NetBIOS names to DHCP.

▶ **DHCP Server.** This field is active if the range type specifies that the subnet address range supports DHCP address assignment. Select the DHCP server that will assign IP addresses from this subnet address range.

▶ **Comment.** Record any comments concerning the subnet address range. This is a good place to record a history of any changes made to the Subnet Address Range object configuration.

Managing IP Address Objects

IP Address objects are used for three reasons:

▶ **To exclude an IP address from assignment.** Addresses may be excluded so that they remain available for future use or to ensure that DHCP cannot assign an IP address that has been statically configured on a host such as a NetWare server, which at this time must have a static IP address. Addresses are also excluded if they correspond to illegal IP addresses, such as addresses with the all 0s hostid or the all 1s hostid.

▶ **To assign an IP address manually to a specific host.** Manual assignment enables you to use DHCP to configure some clients that must have fixed IP addresses. If a host is statically defined in DNS, for example, manual address assignment ensures that the host will always receive the same IP address.

▶ **To record dynamic IP address leases.** As DHCP assigns and expires leases for IP addresses, it creates and removes IP Address objects in the Subnet container. You cannot directly create dynamic IP Address objects, but you can view their object parameters. See the section "Managing Dynamic IP Address Objects" later in the chapter for further discussion.

You can directly create IP Address objects that exclude IP addresses from assignment and manually assign IP addresses to hosts. These two types of IP address objects are sufficiently different that we should examine them separately.

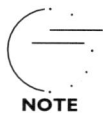

NOTE

IP Address objects are leaf objects and must be created in the context of the Subnet object that defines the address block that contains the IP address. If the desired address falls within a defined subnet address range, you must create the IP Address object under the Subnet Address Range object.

Creating an Exclusion IP Address Object

To create an IP Address object that excludes a specific IP address from assignment, do the following:

1. Open DNS/DHCP Manager and select the *DHCP Service* tab.

2. Select the Subnet object or the Subnet Address Range that contains the IP address you wish to exclude.

3. Click the *Create* button in the toolbar.

4. Select *IP Address* in the *Create New DHCP Record* dialog box.

5. Complete the *Create IP Address* dialog box, shown in Figure 12.19, as follows:

- **IP Address.** Enter the dotted-decimal IP address to be excluded.

- **Assignment Type.** Select *Exclusion.*

- **Define Additional Properties.** Check this box if you wish to define additional NDS properties for this object.

6. Click *Create.*

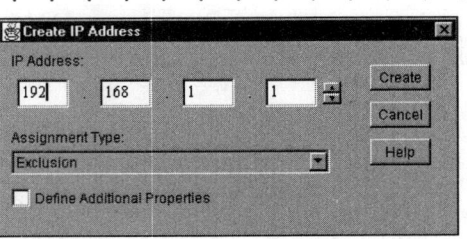

F I G U R E   12.19

Creating an Exclusion IP Address Object

Figure 12.20 shows a newly created exclusion IP Address object. Notice that the new object is indented under the Subnet object under which it was created. An IP Address object will always fall below a Subnet object in the DHCP tree. If the excluded IP address falls in the range defined by a Subnet Address Range object, the IP Address object is indented under the Subnet Address Range object.

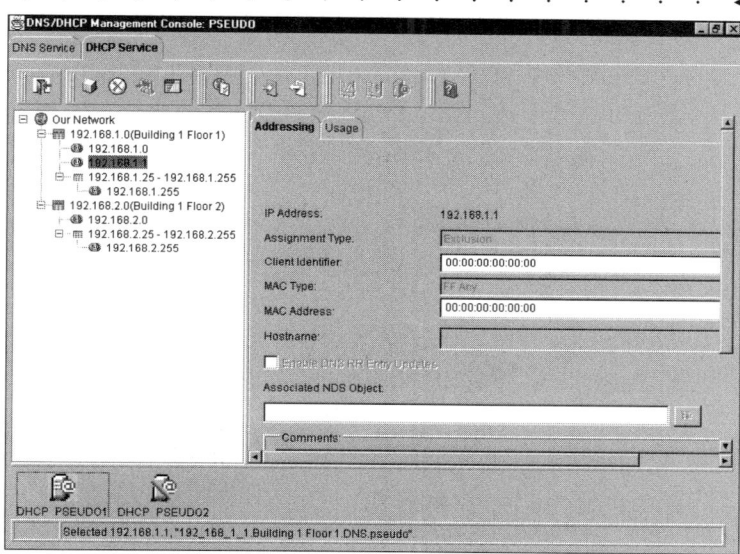

FIGURE 12.20

Configuration Options for an
Exclusion IP Address Object

Creating a Manual IP Address Object

To create an IP Address object that manually assigns a specific IP address to a specific machine, do the following:

1. Open DNS/DHCP Manager and select the *DHCP Service* tab.

2. Select the Subnet object that contains the IP address you wish to exclude.

3. Click the *Create* button in the toolbar.

4. Select *IP Address* in the *Create New DHCP Record* dialog box.

5. Complete the *Create IP Address* dialog box (Figure 12.21) as follows:

• **IP Address.** Enter the dotted-decimal IP address to be assigned.

- **Assignment Type.** Select *Manual.* The Create IP Address dialog box will expand as shown in Figure 12.21 to offer the additional fields required to define a manual IP address.

- **Define Additional Properties.** Check this box if you wish to define additional properties for this object.

- **Client Identifier.** Clients that conform to RFC 2131 may optionally be configured to send a client identifier instead of a MAC address to identify themselves to DHCP. The client identifier can be a MAC address, a hostname, or other unique identifier. The client must use the same client identifier each time it contacts the DHCP server. Windows 95, 98, and NT 4.0 do not support the extensions introduced with RFC 2131 and cannot be configured to send a client identifier. If the client will be identified by a client identifier as defined in RFC 2131, enter the client identifier.

- **MAC Type.** Specify the MAC type associated with the client's network. The default entry is FF Any, but you can select other network types by pulling down this list box as shown in Figure 12.22.

- **MAC Address.** If the client is identified by its MAC address, enter that address here in colon-delimited hexadecimal form. Figure 12.23 shows an example of a correctly formatted MAC address. At present, all NetWare clients are identified by their MAC addresses.

NOTE

On Windows 95 and 98 clients, execute the WINIPCFG utility to determine the client's MAC address. On Windows NT clients, execute the command ipconfig /all **to determine the client's MAC address.**

   6. Click *Create.*

Figure 12.23 shows a newly created manual IP Address object.

FIGURE 12.21

Creating a Manual IP
Address Object

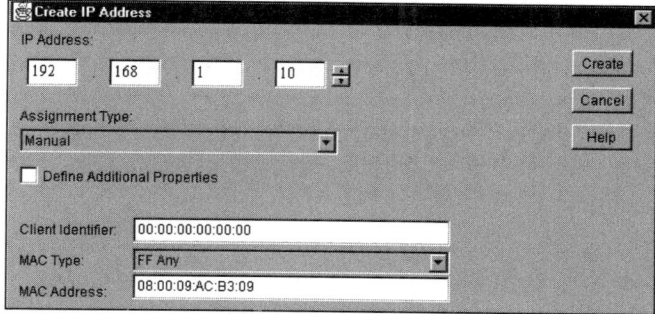

FIGURE 12.22

Examples of MAC Types
Available for Manual IP
Address Objects

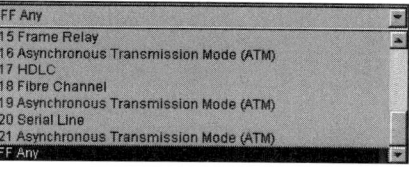

FIGURE 12.23

Options for an IP Address
Object

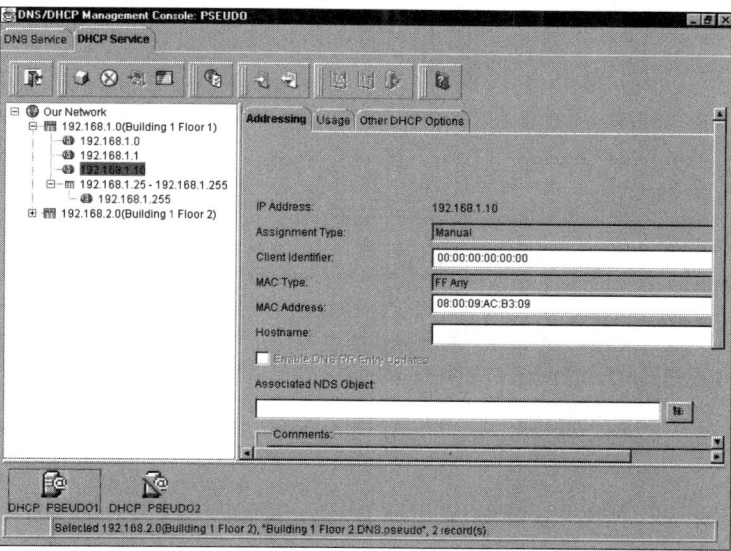

Configuring IP Address Objects

In Figure 12.23, an IP Address object is selected to display the *Addressing* option tab. The fields on this tab are as follows:

► **IP Address.** This field cannot be modified. To change the IP address, you must delete the IP Address object and re-create it with the desired IP address.

► **Assignment Type.** This field has the values Manual or Exclusion. If the value is Manual, you can change the value to Exclusion. However, you cannot change the value from Exclusion to Manual.

► **Client Identifier.** You can edit this field on IP Address objects with the type Manual. If the client will send an RFC 2131 client identifier, enter the identifier here. At this time, all NetWare clients (MS-DOS/Win 3.x, Windows 95/98, and Windows NT) send their MAC address for use as a unique identifier. The MAC Address field is used to identify all current Novell clients.

► **MAC Type.** You can edit this field on IP Address objects with the type Manual. Specify the MAC type associated with the client's network. The default entry is FF Any, but you can select other network types by pulling down this list box as shown in Figure 12.22.

► **MAC Address.** You can edit this field on IP Address objects with the type Manual. Use the MAC address as the host identifier with all current Novell clients (MS-DOS/Win 3.1, Windows 95/98, and Windows NT 4.0).

► **Comment.** This is a good place to describe the purpose of the IP Address object and to keep a long on any changes you may make.

IP Address objects also have a *Usage* tab, an example of which is shown in Figure 12.24. For IP Address objects with exclusion and manual assignment types, the *Permanent* radio button will be selected in the *Lease Expiration Time* field. The date and time shown in the *Expire* fields simply show the time at which you select the IP Address object in the DNS/DHCP Management Console.

FIGURE 12.24

*Usage Parameters for a
Manual IP Address Object*

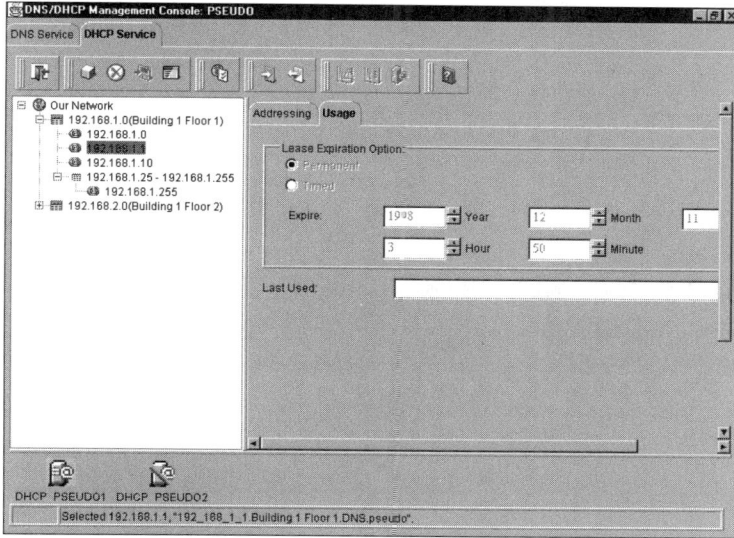

Dynamic IP Address Objects

Each time DHCP grants an IP address lease to a DHCP client, DHCP adds an object to NDS to record the parameters of the lease. Figure 12.25 shows the *Addresses* tab for a dynamically-assigned IP address. The fields are completed as follows:

▸ **IP Address.** This field records the IP address assigned to the DHCP client and cannot be modified.

▸ **Assignment Type.** This field has the value `Dynamic`.

▸ **Client Identifier.** If the client has supplied an RFC 2131 client identifier, it will appear here. If the client is identified by its MAC address, a client identifier is generated based on that MAC address.

▸ **MAC Type.** This field records the type of the network on which the client resides.

▶ **MAC Address.** This field records the MAC address by which the client is identified.

▶ **Hostname.** This field records the hostname received from the client. Windows 95/98 and NT clients send their NetBIOS computer names to DHCP.

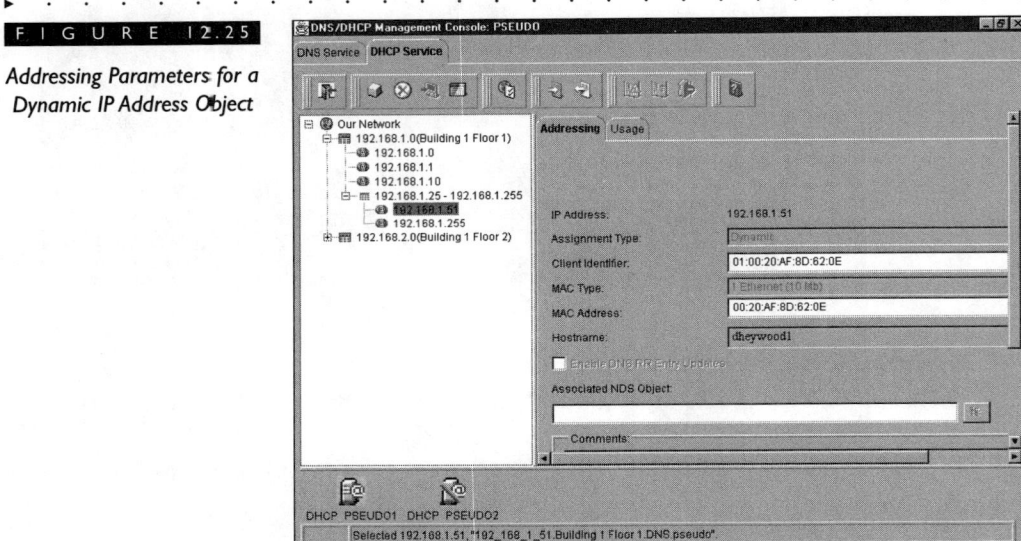

FIGURE 12.25

Addressing Parameters for a Dynamic IP Address Object

Figure 12.26 shows an example of the *Usage* tab for a dynamic IP Address objects. The fields are completed as follows:

▶ **Lease Expiration Option.** The *Timed* radio button is selected. This value cannot be modified.

▶ **Expire.** The values in the date and time fields record the time when the lease will expire. These values cannot be directly modified.

▶ **Last Used.** This field records the last time the client connected using this lease.

► • ◄

FIGURE 12.26

*Usage Parameters for a
Dynamic IP Address Object*

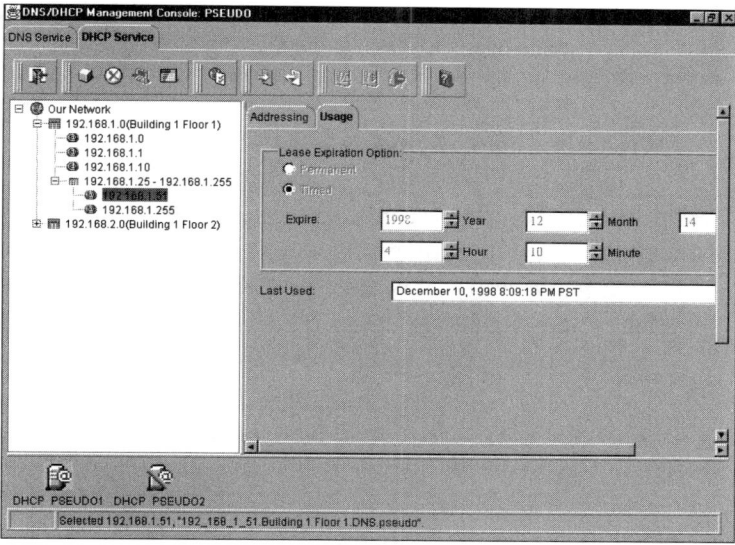

You cannot directly modify any of the parameters of an active dynamic lease. You can, if necessary, delete the IP Address object if the client no longer needs the address, but you should be careful not to delete an IP Address object associated with a lease currently in use by a client. The IP address is immediately made available to be leased to another client, introducing the possibility of a conflict when two hosts attempt to communicate using the same IP address. To prevent the possibility of such conflicts, select *Ping Enabled* in the configuration parameters of the DHCP server.

Managing Subnet Pool Objects

Many networks will not be required to use Subnet Pool objects. A Subnet Pool object is a logical group of related Subnet objects of the same type. Subnet Pools are used to enable a BOOTP forwarder to identify a pool of subnets for remote LAN address assignments.

Subnet Pool objects are used to support virtual LANs (VLANs) that consist of multiple subnets treated as a homogeneous network. To understand when Subnet Pool objects are required, let's look at some examples of networks which require and do not require Subnet Pool objects.

NOTE

Subnet Pool objects are leaf objects and may be created in the context of an O, OU, C, or L.

When Are Subnet Pool Objects Required?

As you learned in Chapter 4, it is very difficult to obtain a class B IP address from InterNIC, and you can forget entirely about obtaining a class A address. So what you will get from InterNIC or from your ISP is one or more class C addresses. A class C network ID, of course, supports only 254 clients. So what do you do if you have more than 254 devices on a network segment? You create a virtual LAN.

A virtual LAN exists when more than one IP address is bound to a router interface. Figure 12.27 shows a simple example. This network has 350 clients on a local network segment. To support these clients, two class C address ranges are assigned to the local interface on the server. On a NetWare server, this is accomplished simply by executing a BIND statement for each address range, using commands similar to the following:

```
BIND IP TO E100B_1_EII ADDR=192.168.3.1 MASK=255.255.255.0

BIND IP TO E100B_1_EII ADDR=192.168.4.1 MASK=255.255.255.0
```

These BIND statements establish the router with IP addresses on networks 192.168.1.0 and 192.168.2.0.

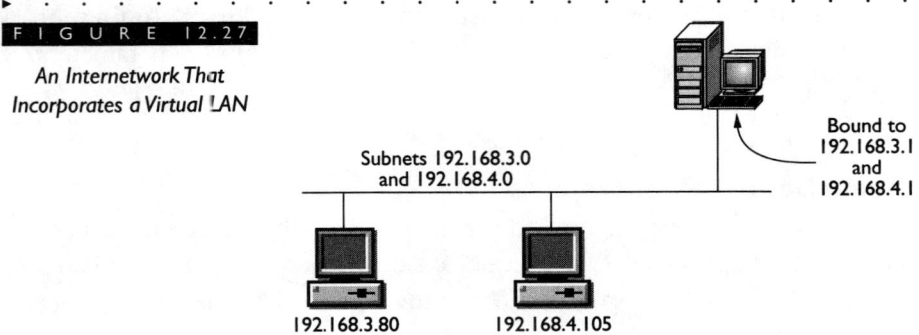

FIGURE   12.27

An Internetwork That Incorporates a Virtual LAN

Subnets 192.168.3.0 and 192.168.4.0

Bound to 192.168.3.1 and 192.168.4.1

192.168.3.80   192.168.4.105

Suppose that the NetWare server in Figure 12.27 is also a DHCP server. As clients on the local network secure IP address leases, DHCP begins by handing out

IP addresses defined by Address Range objects for the first subnet bound to the network interface. In this example, DHCP will begin allocating addresses defined in any Subnet Range objects associated with subnet 192.168.3.0. What happens when the available addresses on 192.168.3.0 are exhausted? Because the interface is local to the server, NetWare has full knowledge of all the bindings on the interface. Therefore, DHCP knows that the interface is also bound to subnet 192.168.4.0, and DHCP can therefore apportion addresses associated with Subnet object 192.168.4.0. In this simple case, there is no need to define Subnet Pool objects.

A simple change to the network dramatically alters things, however. In Figure 12.28, the VLAN is separated from the DHCP server by an intervening router — either a NetWare server or a dedicated third-party router. The router is configured to forward DHCP requests to the DHCP server using a BOOTP forwarder. To understand the difficulty, we need to examine how the BOOTP forwarder works.

When the BOOTP forwarder receives a request from a client on the VLAN, it forwards the request to the DHCP server. In the forwarded request, the BOOTP forwarder includes the IP address of the interface from which the BOOTP forwarder received the DHCP request. The DHCP server uses the IP address in the forwarded request to prepare a response that provides an IP address for the correct subnet.

The router connects to the VLAN through a network interface that has a dual identity. Because initially a DHCP client does not have an IP address, it must broadcast a request for an IP address, and the broadcast packet does not really arrive from either of the IP subnets that make up the VLAN. Therefore, the BOOTP forwarder assumes that all requests arrive through its first bound network. In this example, it assumes that all requests arrive on interface 192.168.3.1, and it is that address that is included when the request is forwarded to the DHCP server.

Now consider what happens when the DHCP server has granted leases for all available IP addresses on 192.168.3.0. The DHCP server does not know that network 192.168.4.0 is also on the VLAN, so it's stuck. It is out of addresses.

That's where Subnet Pool objects come in. A Subnet Pool object can be configured to inform the DHCP server that networks 192.168.3.0 and 192.168.4.0 are part of a VLAN. When addresses on 192.168.1.0 are exhausted, the Subnet Pool object lets the DHCP server know that it can also assign IP addresses from subnet 192.168.3.0 to clients whose requests are associated with network 192.168.4.0.

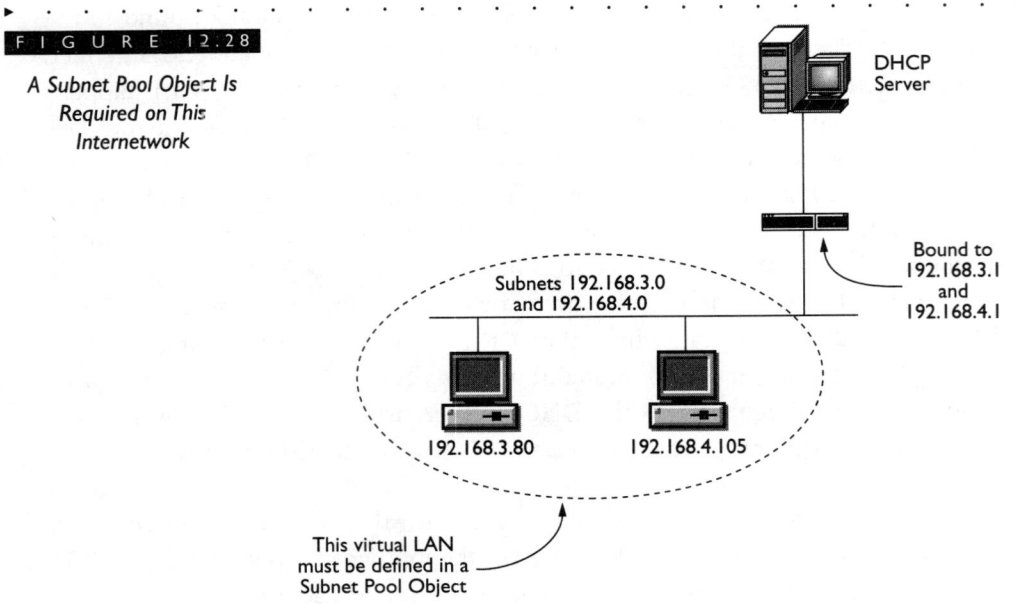

A Subnet Pool Object Is Required on This Internetwork

Let's look at one more example to see when a Subnet Pool object is not required. In Figure 12.29, the network changes in one small way. Networks 192.168.1.0 and 192.168.2.0 still are attached to a remote router, but they now connect through individual interfaces.

In such situations, Subnet Pool objects are not required. DHCP requests from clients on network 192.168.1.0 are tagged with the IP address 192.168.1.1, the interface on which the BOOTP forwarder received the request. DHCP requests from network 192.168.2.0 will be tagged with the IP address 192.168.2.1. Requests from the two subnets are distinctly identified, and the DHCP server can respond to each appropriately. No Subnet Pool objects are required.

Virtual LANs are also encountered in the world of switched hubs. Sophisticated switched hubs enable administrators to define multiple distinct subnets among the network segments that connect to the hub. If it is necessary to communicate between these virtual subnets, a router must be configured to forward the traffic. Depending on the configuration of the switched virtual LANs, you may or may not be required to configure Subnet Pool objects.

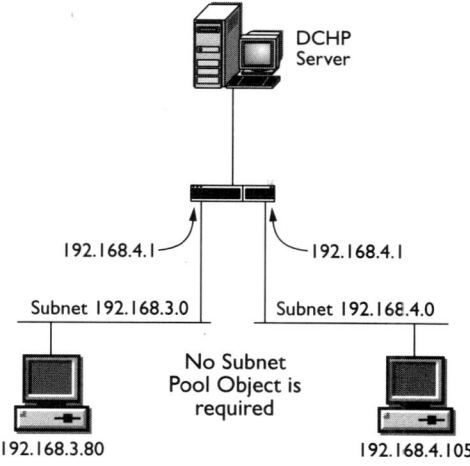

▶ • ◀

F I G U R E 12.29

No Subnet Pool Objects Are Required on This Internetwork

DCHP Server

192.168.4.1

192.168.4.1

Subnet 192.168.3.0

Subnet 192.168.4.0

No Subnet Pool Object is required

192.168.3.80

192.168.4.105

Creating a Subnet Pool Object

To create a Subnet Pool object:

1. Open DNS/DHCP Manager and select the *DHCP Service* tab.

2. Create the Subnet objects to be grouped by the Subnet Pool.

3. Click the *Create* button in the toolbar.

4. Select *Subnet Pool* in the *Create New DHCP Record* dialog box.

5. Complete the *Create Subnet Pool* dialog box (Figure 12.30) as follows:

• **Subnet Pool Name.** Enter a descriptive name for the subnet pool.

• **Select NDS Context.** Specify the NDS context in which the Subnet Pool object is to be created. Click the NDS browse button to browse for the desired context.

• **Define Additional Properties.** Check this box to define additional NDS properties for the Subnet Pool object.

6. Click *Create*.

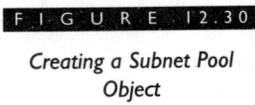

FIGURE 12.30

Creating a Subnet Pool Object

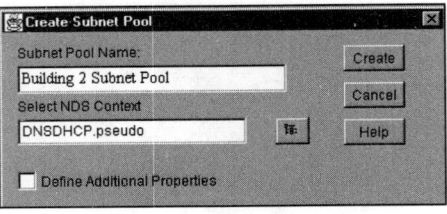

Figure 12.31 shows a Subnet Pool object. No entries will appear in the subnet list for a newly created object. To prepare the figure, I have added some sample entries.

Configuring a Subnet Pool Object

Subnet Pool objects contain lists of subnets. To add an entry to the Subnet Pool object's subnet list, do the following:

1. Open DNS/DHCP Manager and select the *DHCP Service* tab.

FIGURE 12.31

The Subnet List for a Subnet Pool Object

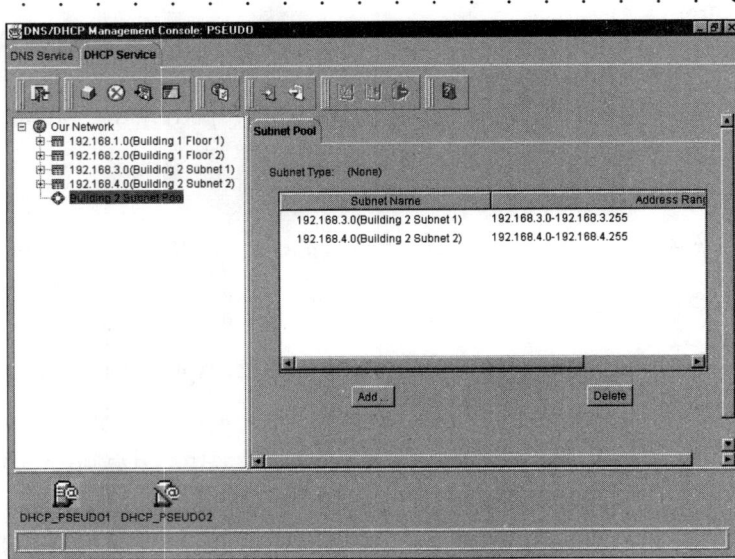

2. Define any required Subnet objects as described in the section "Managing Subnet Objects."

3. Create the Subnet Pool object as described in the previous section.

4. Select the Subnet Pool object in the DHCP object tree.

5. Click *Add* to open the *Select Subnet* dialog box shown in Figure 12.32.

6. Select a subnet and click *OK*.

7. Repeat Steps 5 and 6 for each subnet to be included in the subnet pool.

To remove a subnet from a subnet pool:

1. Open DNS/DHCP Manager and select the *DHCP Service* tab.

2. Select the Subnet Pool object in the DHCP object tree.

3. Select a subnet in the *Subnet Pool* tab.

4. Click *Delete*.

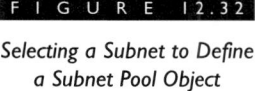

F I G U R E   12.32

Selecting a Subnet to Define a Subnet Pool Object

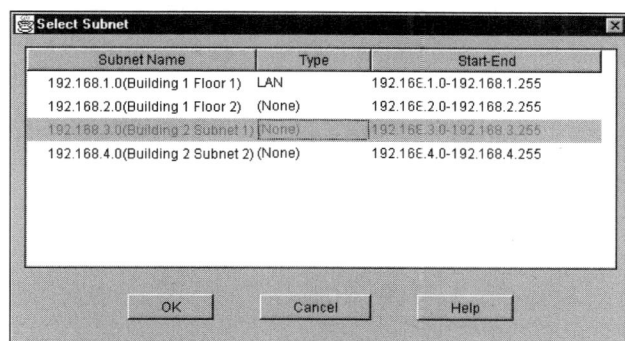

DHCP Objects and NDS

All DHCP objects are, as mentioned previously, recorded in the NDS database. However, the hierarchy of DHCP objects in the NDS tree structure is not necessarily related to the hierarchical relationships of DHCP objects to one another.

In Figure 12.33, I have arranged the DHCP objects created in the earlier examples. All were created in the context of OU=DNSDHCP.O=PSEUDO. Let's see how the DHCP hierarchy is and is not reflected in the NDS tree.

Subnet objects such as Building 1 are container objects. All Subnet Address Range and IP Address objects related to a subnet are created in the context of the Subnet object that defines the subnet. As you can see, these objects share a hierarchical relationship both in DHCP and in NDS.

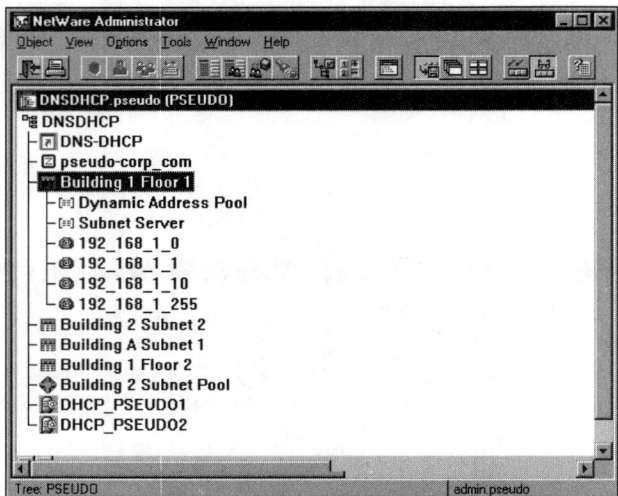

F I G U R E   12.33

DHCP Objects Relationships
As Displayed in NetWare
Administrator.

A Subnet is associated with a particular DHCP server. Note in Figure 12.33, however, that the Building 1 Subnet object is not subordinate to the DHCP_PSEUDO1 DHCP server object. Their relationship is defined by parameters in the Building 1 Subnet object, not by a hierarchical relationship in NDS. Of course, both Subnet and DHCP Server objects are leaf objects, so a hierarchical relationship is not possible.

A similar situation exists between IP Address objects that fall within a subnet address range and the Subnet Address Range object that defines the subnet address range. The relationship between the IP Address object and the Subnet Address Range object can be determined only by examining their configurations in the DNS/DHCP Management Console.

Managing the DHCP Server Service

The DHCP Server service (DHCPSRVR.NLM) enables a NetWare server to act as a DHCP server. DHCPSRVR.NLM is loaded and unloaded at the server console, but can be paused and restarted from DNS/DHCP Management Console.

Loading and Unloading DHCPSRVR.NLM

Before starting DHCPSRVR.NLM on a NetWare server, you must define the server in a DHCP Server object using DNS/DHCP Management Console. Also configure the Subnet, Subnet Range, IP Address, and Subnet Pool objects that affect the configuration of the DHCP server.

When DHCP server configuration is complete, start the DHCP Server service by executing the command **LOAD DHCPSRVR** on the NetWare server. The NetWare console dialog is as follows:

```
PSEUDO1: load dhcpsrvr-d1

Loading module DHCPSRVR.NLM

  DHCP Server (DNIPV129)

  Version 3.00t   July 24, 1998-09-12

  Copyright (c) 1991-1998 Novell, Inc.  All Rights Reserved

DHCPSRVR-3.00-1: Loading Initiated at 9-12-1998 1:45:22 pm.

DHCPSRVR-3.00-21: Logger thread to update NDS is started.
```

```
9-12-1998   1:45:23 pm:    DHCPSRVR-3.0-0

   IP Database loaded.
```

DHCPSRVR-3.00-20: Main thread for UI and Lease Expiration processing started.

DHCPSRVR-3.00-17: DHCP Server is ready at 9-12-1998 1:45:23 pm.

You can, of course, unload the service with the command **UNLOAD DHCPSRVR**. DHCPSRVR.NLM accepts several command-line options, which are described in Table 12.1.

T A B L E 12.1	OPTION	PURPOSE
DHCPSRVR Command Options	-d1	Activates a background screen log of DHCP packets.
	-d2	Activates a background screen log listing Debug statements and DHCP packets.
	-d3	Activates a background screen log listing Debug statements and DHCP packets. The log is also written to the file \ETC\DHCPSRVR.LOG.
	-h	Displays the command syntax and options.
	-s	Forces the DHCP Server service to read and write to the master replica.

The —d1 option is extremely useful when you are first configuring your DHCP service. By switching to the DHCP log screen, you can monitor the activity of the service to ensure that client requests are being received and filled. Of course, any logging is a drain on server performance, and you should load DHCPSRVR.NLM without logging unless it is necessary to troubleshoot or monitor its operation.

Stopping and Starting the DHCP Server

Operation of the DHCP Server service can be suspended and restarted from the DNS/DHCP Management Console. This enables you to pull configuration changes into the DHCP server without unloading and reloading DHCPSRVR.NLM.

To stop a running server, select the server icon and click the *Start/Stop Service* button in the toolbar. A dialog box prompts you to confirm that the server should be stopped. When the operation is successful, the server icon will be flagged in the DNS/DHCP Management Console as shown in Figure 12.34. Also, a console message such as the following will be displayed at the server:

```
DHCPSRVR-3.00-83: SUSPEND DHCP service command received from
the DNS/DHCP management utility at 9-1-1998 10:08:03 am


9-09-1998  10:08:03 am:      DHCPSRVR-3.0-0

    DHCPSRVR termination initiated


DHCPSRVR-3.00-84: DHCP service has been suspended at 9-1-1998
10:08:03 am on the request of the DNS/DHCP management
utility.
```

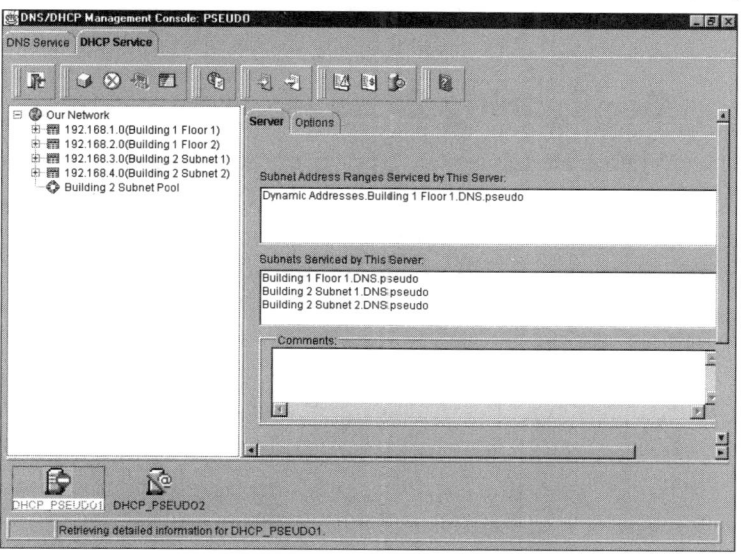

FIGURE 12.34

DNS/DHCP Management Console Icon for a Server That Has Been Suspended

To resume operation of the DHCP service, select the server icon in the DNS/DHCP Management Console and click the *Start/Stop Service* button. After confirming your choice, the service will resume operation on the server. The DHCP icon in DNS/DHCP Management Console resumes its normal appearance and the NetWare server confirms the operation with a console message similar to the following:

```
DHCPSRVR-3.00-64: START DHCP service command received from
the DNS/DHCP management utility at 9-1-1998 10:14:01 am


9-09-1998  10:14:01 am:    DHCPSRVR-3.0-0

    IP Database loaded.


DHCPSRVR-3.00-84: DHCP service successfully restarted at 9-1-
1998 10:14:01 am
```

Configuring BOOTP Forwarding

When a DHCP server is not connected to the same subnet as a DHCP client, DHCP messages must be routed. DHCP is an extension of BOOTP, and DHCP requests can be directed to DHCP servers by the same forwarders used for the BOOTP protocol. This requires installation of a BOOTP forwarding process on the router. Figure 12.35 shows how BOOTP forwarding works.

In the figure, two routers separate the DHCP client from the DHCP server. The DHCP client initiates the process of obtaining an IP address by broadcasting a DHCPDISCOVER message. But broadcasts cannot cross routers, so the original message cannot reach the DHCP server. To bridge the communication gap, the BOOTP forwarder receives the broadcast DHCPDISCOVER message and formulates a unicast DHCPDISCOVER message that can be routed to the server.

▶ . . . . ◀

FIGURE 12.35

An Internetwork with
BOOTP Forwarding

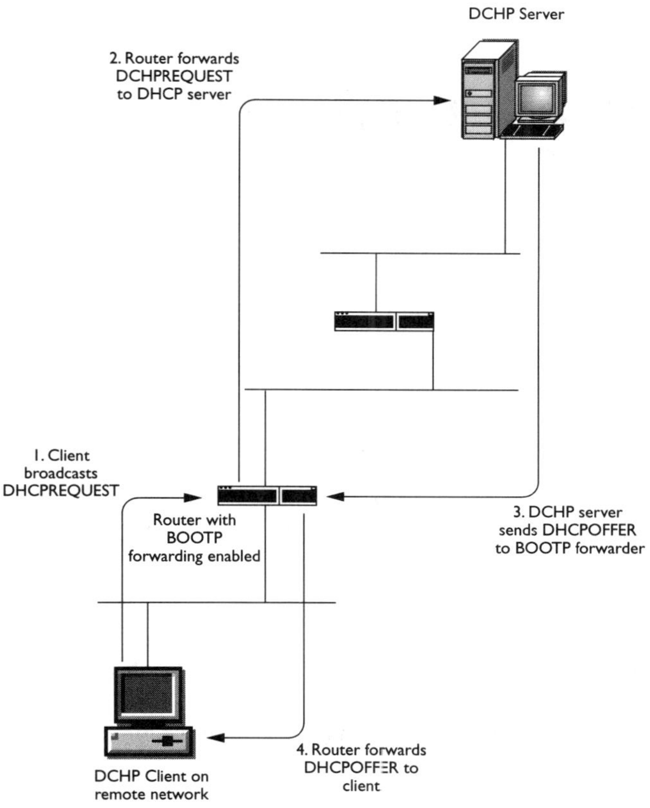

DCHP Server

2. Router forwards
DCHPREQUEST
to DHCP server

1. Client
broadcasts
DHCPREQUEST

Router with
BOOTP
forwarding enabled

3. DCHP server
sends DHCPOFFER
to BOOTP forwarder

DCHP Client on
remote network

4. Router forwards
DHCPOFFER to
client

The server must send a DHCPOFFER message to the client, a task complicated by the fact that *the client does not yet have an IP address*. Therefore, normal IP addressing techniques cannot be used. Until the client has an IP address, all messages must be directed to the client's MAC address, using the IP address of the BOOTP forwarder to enable the response to reach the client's network.

To enable its BOOTP requests to get to the DHCP server, the router on the client's network must have BOOTP forwarding enabled. On a NetWare server, BOOTP forwarding is enabled by loading the BOOTPFWD NLM. When it is loaded, the IP address of the DHCP server is declared like this:

```
LOAD BOOTPFWD 192.168.1.10
```

The LOAD BOOTPFWD command accepts four options, which should follow the IP address. These options are described in Table 12.2.

TABLE 12.2	OPTION	PURPOSE
BOOTPFWD Command Options	SERVER=*ipaddress*	Specifies the address of a remote DHCP server to which **BOOTPFWD** is to forward BOOTP and DHCP requests.
	LOG={YES | NO}	Specifies whether forwarding activity should be logged to the screen or a file.
	FILE=*filename*	Specifies the name of a log file. If no filename is specified the log file is SYS:ETC\BOOTP.LOG.
	INFO	Displays current operational statistics.

If the server is running NetWare 4, NetWare 5, or the MultiProtocol Router, configure BOOTP using INETCFG with this procedure:

1. Load INETCFG.

2. Select *Protocols* in the *Internetworking Configuration* menu.

3. Select *TCP/IP* in the *Protocol Configuration* menu.

4. Select *Expert Configuration Options* in the *TCP/IP Protocol Configuration* form.

5. Select *BOOTP Forwarding Configuration* in the *TCP/IP Expert Configuration* form. This will open the *BootP Configuration Options* form shown in Figure 12.36.

▶ . . . . ◀

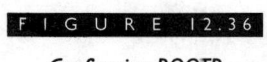

FIGURE 12.36

Configuring BOOTP Forwarding in INETCFG

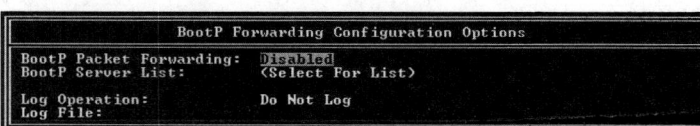

6. Select *BootP Servers List* to display a list of BOOTP server IP addresses. Press Insert to add an IP address to the list. At least one BOOTP server must be configured before BOOTP packet forwarding can been enabled.

7. Change the *BootP Packet Forwarding* field to *Enabled* to have BOOTP loaded on the server.

8. The Log Operation file accepts three values:

- **Do Not Log** disables logging. Logging should not be necessary unless troubleshooting is required.

- **Log to BootP Screen** logs messages to the BOOTP protocol monitor screen.

- **Log to File** logs messages to a file.

9. If messages will be logged to a file, the Log File field specifies the path name of the log file. The default is SYS:\ETC\BOOTP.LOG.

Save changes to TCP/IP and restart the server to activate BOOTP forwarding.

. . . .

Configuring DHCP Options

IP addresses are not the only things clients can receive from DHCP. Along with a DHCP lease, a client can receive a wide variety of configuration parameters, such as default router addresses, DNS server addresses, subnet masks, and dozens of others. Options are handed out with address leases, and when a client renews its lease, it also receives updates to its DHCP options.

Even if you don't want to assign IP addresses dynamically, you may want to use DHCP to configure your clients. Suppose that you are changing the IP address of the default router on a network segment. Without DHCP, you must manually visit each client on the segment to make static changes to its TCP/IP configuration. With DHCP, you can change one central parameter and all your DHCP clients will learn of the change when they must renew their leases.

Supported Options

The current list of registered DHCP options is documented in RFC 2132. Nearly all of these options are supported by the NetWare 5 DHCP server. Novell has defined some options specific to the NetWare environment that do not appear in the RFC. These options are documented in *Novell's DNS/DHCP Administrator's Guide*.

NOTE

DHCP options provide a versatile way for clients and DHCP servers to exchange information. Some of the options enable the client to send information to the server. For example, the Host Name option is used by the client to send its name to the server. That is how the hostname is communicated through DHCP to DDNS. To understand fully how DHCP options are used, you will need to thoroughly digest RFCs 2131 and 2132.

Not all of the options will be used in the NetWare environment. However, you may find yourself configuring non-NetWare hosts through DHCP, and it is nice to know that the NetWare 5 DHCP server is versatile enough to enable you to send almost any options to clients. Table 12.3 describes some of the options you are most likely to encounter.

TABLE 12.3	OPTION CODE	NAME	DESCRIPTION
Common DHCP Options	3	Router	A list of IP addresses of routers to be used by the client in order of preference.
	6	Domain Name Server	A list of IP addresses of DNS servers to be used by the client in order of preference.

OPTION CODE	NAME	DESCRIPTION
44	NetBIOS over TCP/IP Name server	A list of IP addresses of NetBIOS name servers (WINS servers) in order of preference.
45	NetBIOS over TCP/IP Node Type	Configures the client NetBIOS node type as follows: 0x1 b-node, 0x2 pnode, 0x4 m-node, 0x8 h-node).
62	NetWare/IP Domain Name	The client's NetWare/IP domain name.
63	NetWare/IP Information	All NetWare/IP infor-mation except the domain name.
78	Directory Agent	Specifies a list of SLP directory agents to be used by the client. See Chapter 14 for a description of SLP directory agents and SLP client configuration.
79	Service Scope	Specifies a list of SLP scopes with which an SLP client is to communicate. See Chapter 14 for a description of SLP scopes.
85	NDS Server	A list of IP addresses of NDS servers.
86	NDS Tree Name	The client's NDS tree name.
87	NDS Context	The client's initial NDS context.

Option 63 is a particularly significant one in the Novell world because it is used to configure a variety of sub-options related to IPX compatibility support in NetWare 5 Sub-options 1 through 11 are associated with NetWare/IP and are documented in RFC 2242. Three new sub-options are used to support IPX compatibility on NetWare 5. These sub-options are described in Table 12.4. Chapter 15 explains the configuration and use of the IPX compatibility mode.

T A B L E 12.4	SUB-OPTION	DESCRIPTION
NetWare 5 IPX Compatibility Sub-Options for DHCP Option 63	12	Identifies the network number of the virtual IPX network created by the IPX Compatibility feature.
	13	Specifies the minimum interval in minutes (the *IPX stale time*) that must expire before clients attempt to refresh their Migration Agent addressing information.
	14	Specifies a list of addresses for Migration Agent servers used by IP nodes to communicate with IPX nodes.

The use of the IPX compatibility sub-options will be described in Chapter 15, where we will examine the IPX Compatibility mode and the Migration Agent.

Levels of Option Assignment

Options can be assigned at three levels:

- **Global** options apply to all subnets unless they are overridden by subnet or IP address options.

- **Subnet** options apply to all clients on a subnet unless they are overridden by options assigned to a specific IP address.

- **IP Address** options apply only to the client described by a particular IP Address object.

This layered approach is very versatile, enabling you to manage options easily for large groups of users while retaining the ability to define options at the level of the individual computer.

NOTE

RFC 1541, the first iteration of DHCP, defined a message format with a fixed-size option field of 312 bytes. RFC 2131 defines a DHCP message format with a variable-length option field. Because current Microsoft clients were written with RFC 1541 in mind, it is uncertain what will happen if they receive a DHCP message with more than 312 bytes of options. For the time being, you should keep options for Microsoft clients within the previous 312 byte limit.

Viewing the Global DHCP Options

The best place to start when working with options is to view the DHCP Options Table, which is a tab under Global Preferences. This table is shown in Figure 12.37. It lists three critical bits of information about the options:

▶ The option numbers, including the sub-option numbers for option 63

▶ The format of the data accepted for the option

▶ The RFC name of the option

To view the DHCP Options Table:

1. Open DNS/DHCP Management Console.

2. Select the *DHCP Services* tab.

3. Click the *Global Preferences* button in the toolbar.

4. Select the *DHCP Options Table* tab.

This is the only place you can see all this information in a nice, neat list. Before you configure an option for the first time, you may want to review its entry in the DHCP Options Table. You should also read up on the option in RFC 2132.

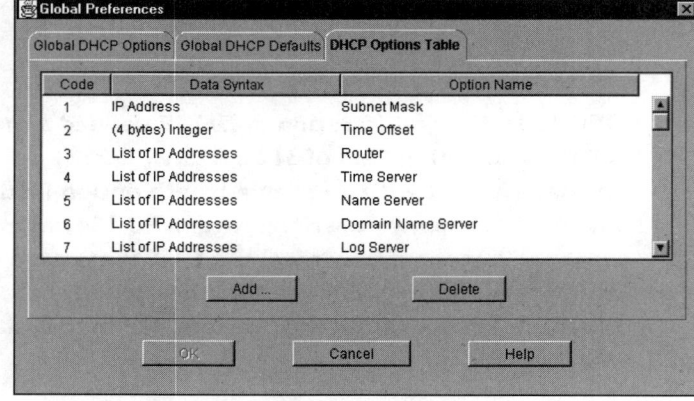

F I G U R E   12.37

The List of DHCP Options in the DHCP Options Table

Configuring DHCP Options

Whether you are entering global, subnet, or IP address DHCP options, the procedure is much the same:

1. Open DNS/DHCP Management Console.

2. Select the *DHCP Services* tab.

3. To specify global options, click the *Global Preferences* button in the toolbar and select the *Global DHCP Options* tab.

Or:

To specify options for a subnet, select a Subnet object and select the *Other DHCP Options* tab in the right pane of the DNS/DHCP Management Console.

Or:

To specify options for an IP address, select a manual-address IP Address object and select the *Other DHCP Options* tab in the right pane of the DNS/DHCP Management Console.

4. Any of the procedures in Step 3 will produce a dialog box similar to the one in Figure 12.38. This dialog box lists options currently in effect at the level being defined.

To modify the options, click the *Modify* button to open the *Modify DHCP Options* dialog box shown in Figure 12.39.

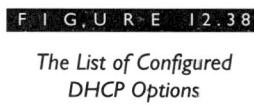

F I G U R E 12.38

The List of Configured DHCP Options

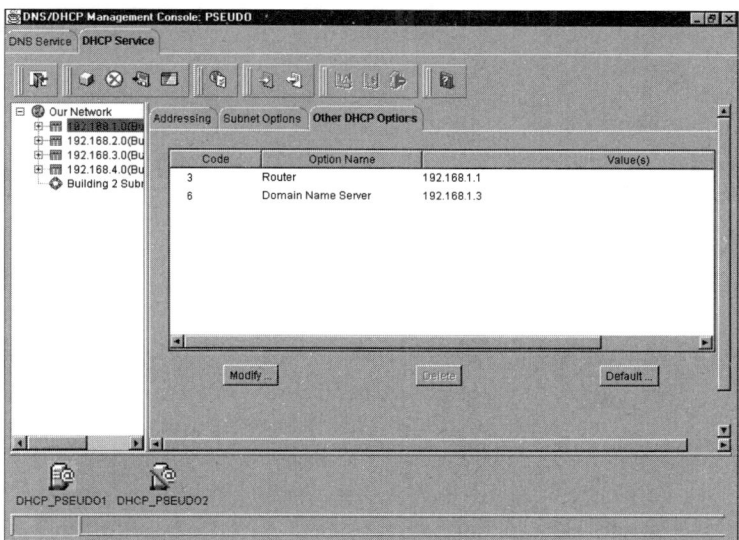

5. The *Available DHCP Options* list box contains the options that have not been added to the global, subnet, or IP address configuration with which you are working.

To add an option, select the option and click *Add*.

To add all options, click *Add All*.

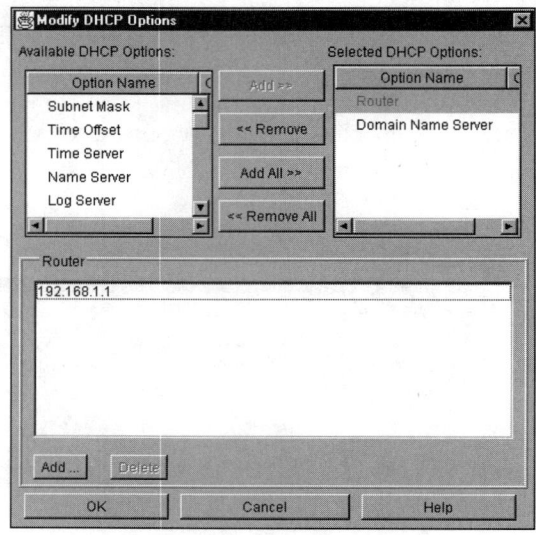

FIGURE 12.39

The Modify DHCP Options
Dialog Box

NOTE

DHCP options are most commonly referred to by number. You can view the DHCP option numbers in the *Available DHCP Options* and *Selected DHCP Options* lists by scrolling the windows left.

6. The *Selected DHCP Options* list box contains the options that have been added to the global, subnet, or IP address configuration with which you are working.

To remove an option, select the option and click *Remove.*

To remove all options, click *Remove All.*

7. Most options accept configurable parameters. For a description of the data format of the parameters, view the option in the Global DHCP Options list as described in the previous section.

To configure the parameters for an option, select the option in the *Selected DHCP Options* list. The bottom part of the *Modify DHCP Options* dialog box will mutate into an entry form tailored to the data requirements for the selected option. Figure 12.39 illustrates the parameters for the Router option, which configures a list of default routers. You can use the *Add* and *Delete* buttons to add and remove entries in the Router list.

8. Click *OK* to accept the changes you have made to the options.

9. You must suspend and restart the DHCP server to activate the changes you have made. See the section "Stopping and Starting the DHCP Server" for the procedure.

There are several things to keep in mind when defining DHCP options:

▸ Not all options apply to all types of clients. For example, a UNIX host wouldn't have any use for the address of a Microsoft NetBIOS name server. Options that don't apply will be ignored by the client.

▸ Some options are sent to clients only if the client requests them.

▸ Some options will be overridden by static configuration parameters on the client.

Consequently, you must make yourself familiar with the characteristics of the clients you are supporting so that you can anticipate their reactions to options they receive from DHCP. In particular, you must be familiar with the techniques for configuring Windows 95/98 and NT clients, which will probably constitute the bulk of the clients you will configure through DHCP.

Optimizing DHCP Service Performance

When planning your DHCP service configuration, you need to take two things into account: the performance of the DHCP servers and the impact of DHCP on your network.

Optimizing DHCP Server Performance

The primary consideration when planning DHCP server deployment is performance. There are two areas of concern: network traffic impact and responsiveness to client requests.

Ideally, a DHCP server will be located on each subnet so that client requests can be serviced locally. However, it is not necessary to go to that extreme on a local area network. DHCP requests can be easily routed by configuring BOOTP forwarders between the subnets. On a LAN, therefore, the primary impact on performance is the number of clients and objects that a DHCP server must support. If your internetwork includes WAN segments, however, you should locate DHCP servers locally with the clients they serve to reduce the impact of DHCP on limited WAN bandwidth.

Although lease renewals tend to be staggered, there will nevertheless be times of high demand (for example, at the beginning of the workday, when many machines are booted and must reacquire their IP addresses). If DHCP server performance is unacceptable, consider one of the following strategies to improve responsiveness:

- Deploy dedicated DHCP servers.

- Upgrade server hardware. A minimum server configuration should have a 200MHz Pentium processor and at least 64MB of memory, although additional memory will typically improve performance, particularly on larger networks.

- Deploy multiple DHCP servers and distribute support for the subnets across the various servers.

- For best performance, Novell recommends that you have no more than 2,048 DHCP objects on a single subnet.

Novell recommends that you create containers specifically to hold DNS and DHCP objects, enabling you to define administrators easily for these services. If necessary, DHCP objects can be placed in multiple containers, enabling you to establish more than one group of administrators. If, for example, your organization has several locations, each of which has local network administrators, you may wish to define separate containers that could be used to group the DHCP objects and assign trustee rights to the appropriate personnel. In this example, I have grouped the DHCP objects under the OU DNSDHCP.

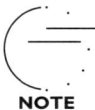

NOTE

An unfortunate limitation of DHCP is that DHCP servers cannot determine which IP addresses have been assigned by other DHCP servers. This prevents you from configuring two DHCP servers that service the same IP address range, because the DHCP servers are likely to assign the same IP address to different hosts. DNS/DHCP Management Console will not permit you to create two Subnet objects that service the same address range, but it is possible for conflicts to exist between NetWare 5 DHCP servers and other vendors' DHCP servers.

NDS Design Guidelines

If your network includes WAN connections, you need to take the WAN connections into account when defining the containers that will hold the DHCP objects. This isn't the place to give you a thorough discussion about how to optimize your NDS tree design, but here are some basic guidelines:

▶ So that they will not generate excess WAN traffic, clients should be serviced by local DHCP servers. Each location should have at least one DHCP server, and preferably should have a NetWare server as well. The second NetWare server can provide NetWare file and print services, support a replica of the DHCP NDS partition, and be rapidly configured as a backup DHCP server if the primary DHCP server fails.

▶ Define a container object for each location and place the DHCP objects needed for that location in the local container.

▶ Establish an NDS partition for each local DHCP container and replicate the partition only on local servers. This eliminates replication traffic that could clog the WAN link.

Configuring DHCP Clients

Both Windows 95/98 and NT can be configured to accept their TCP/IP configurations from DHCP. Chapter 9 discusses the details of configuring TCP/IP protocol support on these clients.

To configure a Windows 95/98 client to obtain its TCP/IP configuration from DHCP, do the following:

1. Open the *Network* applet in the Control Panel.

2. Select the *Configuration* tab.

3. Select the TCP/IP entry that binds to your network adapter.

4. Click *Properties*.

5. Select the *Obtain an IP address automatically* radio button.

6. If the client will obtain a DNS configuration from DHCP:

- ▸ Select the *DNS Configuration* tab.
- ▸ Select the *Enable DNS* radio button.
- ▸ Enter the computer's hostname in the *Host* field.
- ▸ Leave the *DNS Server Search Order* list blank.
- ▸ Enter the client's DNS domain name in the *Domain* field.
- ▸ Optionally, add entries to the *Domain Suffix Search Order* list.

7. If the client will receive router addresses from DHCP:

- ▸ Select the *Gateway* tab.
- ▸ Remove all entries from the Installed gateways list.

8. If the client will receive its WINS configuration from DHCP:

- ▸ Select the *WINS Configuration* tab.

> ► Select the *Use DHCP for WINS Resolution* radio button.

9. Close the *Network* applet and restart the computer.

To configure a Windows NT client to obtain its TCP/IP configuration from DHCP, do the following:

1. Open the *Network* applet in the Control Panel.

2. Select the *Protocols* tab.

3. Select TCP/IP in the *Network Protocols* list.

4. Click *Properties*.

5. On the *IP Address* tab, select the *Obtain an IP address automatically* radio button.

6. If the client will receive its routing configuration from DHCP:

> ► On the *IP Address* tab, click the *Advanced* button to open the *Advanced IP Addressing* dialog box.
>
> ► Remove all entries in the *Gateways* list.
>
> ► Close the *Advanced IP Addressing* dialog box.

7. If the client will obtain a DNS configuration from DHCP:

> ► Select the *DNS* tab.
>
> ► Enter the computer's hostname in the *Host Name* field.
>
> ► Leave the *DNS Server Search Order* list blank.
>
> ► Enter the client's DNS domain name in the *Domain* field.
>
> ► Optionally, add entries to the *Domain Suffix Search Order* list.

8. If the client will receive its WINS configuration from DHCP:

> ► Select the *WINS Address* tab.

> ▸ Clear the *Primary WINS Server* and *Secondary WINS Server* fields.

9. Close the *Network* applet and restart the computer.

In the above procedures, it was necessary to clear various properties to enable those parameters to be obtained from DHCP. DHCP does not override properties that have been statically configured on the local computer. You must remove local configuration entries for router, DNS, and WINS properties to have the properties configured through DHCP.

All DHCP lease activity is initiated from the client. On Windows 95/98 clients, you can use the WINIPCFG graphic utility to manage DHCP leases. Figure 12.40 illustrates WINIPCFG for a DHCP client. I clicked the *More Info* button to expand the display, because some of the DHCP information does not appear on the initial window. WINIPCFG has four buttons that are used to manage the DHCP lease:

> ▸ **Release.** Releases the lease for the selected network adapter.

> ▸ **Release All.** Releases the leases for all network adapters.

> ▸ **Renew.** Renews the lease for the current network adapter.

> ▸ **Renew All.** Renews the leases for all network adapters.

On Windows NT, you use the IPCONFIG command-line utility to view and manage DHCP leases. To view the network configuration of a Windows NT computer, enter the following command:

```
ipconfig /all
```

To release the DHCP lease for an adapter, enter the following command:

```
ipconfig /release adapter
```

WINIPCFG for a DHCP
Client

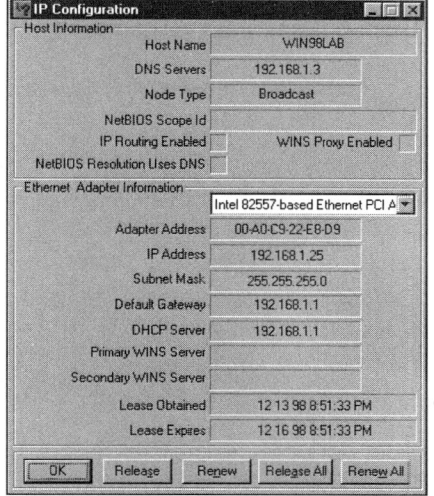

where *adapter* is the name of the adapter to be managed. You can learn the name of the adapter by executing the `ipconfig /all` command. If the computer has a single network adapter, you can omit the *adapter* parameter.

To renew the DHCP lease for an adapter, enter the following command:

```
ipconfig /renew adapter
```

The *adapter* parameter is treated as with the `ipconfig /release` command.

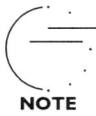

NOTE

Some clients do not behave particularly well when they are moved to a new subnet. Windows 95/98 clients, for example, will try to renew their old IP addresses with a DHCP server. If they are unable to renew the leases, which they should not be able to do on a new subnet, they continue to use their old addresses! To move the client, you must manually use WINIPCFG to release the old lease. Then use the renew request to obtain a lease on the new subnet.

DHCP — Better than Antacids

DHCP is one of the most important tools we have as TCP/IP network administrators. Without DHCP, host configuration can be a never-ending task, sucking up your time and energy. With DHCP, host configuration becomes, if not fun, at least manageable.

But DHCP is evolving into more than a mere labor-saving aid. DHCP is one more way for clients to obtain information they need from the network. Now, network services can use DHCP as a data repository that DHCP clients can access as needed. That, in fact, is exactly what Novell has done in the Pure IP environment. In Chapter 15, you learn how DHCP can be used to reduce or eliminate SLP traffic. The more you work with DHCP, the more you will like it.

## CHAPTER 13

Managing NetWare TCP/IP

The major pieces of your internetwork — servers, routers, and clients — are now in place. So, how's the network doing? Are there any performance bottlenecks? Are all devices functioning? Are any devices generating excessive errors? What? You don't know? One of your responsibilities as a LAN administrator is to answer these and other important questions about your network's health. That's where the *Simple Network Management Protocol* (SNMP) comes in. SNMP agents are built into all NetWare platforms that support TCP/IP. SNMP is easy to configure and monitor with tools that NetWare provides. NetWare 5 includes the TCP/IP Console (TCPCON), a server-based utility for monitoring and managing TCP/IP nodes on your network.

NOTE

The SNMP protocol is not exclusive to the TCP/IP protocol suite, and Novell has configured SNMP consoles to manage other NetWare-supported protocols. Similar utilities are available for managing SNMP over IPX (IPXCON) and AppleTalk (ATCON). These management consoles provide very basic SNMP management capabilities. For networks that require a more powerful network management capability, Novell also offers ManageWise, a separate product with more powerful network management capabilities. Among its many capabilities, ManageWise is a full-function SNMP network management console.

This chapter first examines how to configure SNMP agents so that we have something to monitor and manage. After that task, we will examine TCPCON.

Configuring SNMP Agents

SNMP managers communicate with SNMP agents, and an SNMP agent must be configured on each host to be managed. Configuration of an agent involves several activities:

▶ Loading the agent software

▶ Configuring SNMP communities

▶ Configuring SNMP node information

▶ Specifying trap destinations

This section examines the procedures required to activate and configure SNMP agents on NetWare servers, NetWare 5 DOS clients, and NetWare 5 Windows 95/98 clients.

NOTE

The NetWare 5 client for Windows NT does not include an SNMP agent. Managewise includes enhanced SNMP agents for a variety of platforms, including Windows NT.

Configuring SNMP Agents on NetWare Servers

On a server that has the MultiProtocol Router component (including NetWare 5 and NetWare 4.11/4.2), INETCFG is used to configure the SNMP agent.

Loading the Agent Software

NetWare server-based protocols incorporate SNMP agents as standard features. Consequently, you don't need to do anything specific to load an SNMP agent on the server. The module SNMP.NLM provides SNMP agent functionality and is loaded for all server-based protocols.

The SNMP agent can be configured with three SNMP *community names*, that determine which SNMP nodes will communicate to exchange management information and traps.

▶ The *monitor community* name grants Read access to an agent's MIB. Any SNMP manager that provides the correct monitor community name will be granted Read-only access to the MIB. By default, the monitor community name is set to "public."

▶ The *control community* name grants Read/Write access to an agent's MIB. An SNMP manager that supplies the correct control community name can modify some information in an agent's MIB. By default, the control community name is disabled.

▸ The *trap community* name is attached to all trap messages that an agent generates. An SNMP manager will receive only those trap messages identified by a specific trap community name. By default, the trap community name is set to "public."

With NetWare 5 (or any NetWare equipped with the NetWare MultiProtocol Router), you will configure SNMP communities using INETCFG. To configure SNMP communities:

1. Load INETCFG.

2. Select *Manage Configuration* from the Internetworking Configuration menu.

3. Select *Configure SNMP Parameters* from the Manage Configuration menu to open the SNMP Parameters form shown in Figure 13.1.

Each of the *State* fields can be opened into a menu with three or four options. Press Enter to open the menu and select a configuration setting from the menu. The options for each of the *State* fields are described in the following steps.

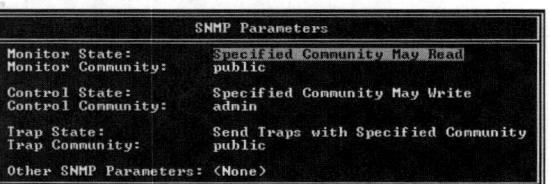

FIGURE 13.1

SNMP Parameters Configuration Form

4. Select one of the following settings in the *Monitor State* field:

- *Any Community May Read.* It will be unnecessary to specify a monitor community name.

- *Leave as Default Setting.* The monitor community name will be "public."

- *No Community May Read.* No community will have Read access to the MIB.

- *Specified Community May Read.* You must specify a community name in the *Monitor Community* field.

5. If you selected *Specified Community May Read*, enter a monitor community name in the *Monitor Community* field.

6. Select one of the following settings in the *Control State* field:

- *Any Community May Write.* It will be unnecessary to specify a control community name.

- *Leave as Default Setting.* Write access will be disabled.

- *No Community May Write.* Write access will be disabled.

- *Specified Community May Write.* You must specify a community name in the *Control Community* field.

7. If you selected *Specified Community May Write*, enter a monitor community name in the *Control Community* field.

8. Select one of the following settings in the *Trap State* field:

- *Do not send traps.* It will be unnecessary to specify a control community name.

- *Leave as Default Setting.* Traps will be sent to "public."

- *Send Traps with Specified Community.* You must specify a community name in the *Trap Community* field.

9. If you selected *Send Traps with Specified Community*, enter a monitor community name in the *Trap Community* field.

10. Two parameters can be entered in the *Other SNMP Parameters* field. These parameters are entered in the same manner that they would be entered on the LOAD SNMP command line:

- **VERBOSE.** VERBOSE alone or VERBOSE=YES enables SNMP parameter configuration messages to the console. This parameter is enabled by default. VERBOSE=NO disables these messages

- **AUTHENTICATION TRAPS.** Enter AUTHENTICATION TRAPS=YES to send traps to trap targets when authentication failure occurs in GET, GET-NEXT, or SET operations. Trap targets are specified in the file SYS:\ETC\TRAPTARG.CFG.

11. After configuring SNMP communities, press Esc. Complete any other required information before quitting INETCFG.

Configuring SNMP Node Information   SNMP node information is descriptive information that enables managers to identify a node, its characteristics, and the person responsible for the node. This information is optional but can be handy when you are managing a large network with many nodes. Node information is specified using INETCFG as follows:

1. Load INETCFG.

2. Select *Manage Configuration* from the Internetworking Configuration menu.

3. Select *Configure SNMP Information* from the Manage Configuration menu to open the SNMP Parameters form shown in Figure 13.2.

▶ . . . . ◀

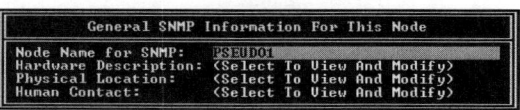

4. If desired, enter a node name in the *Node Name for SNMP* field. By default, the SNMP node name will be the same as the file server name specified in the AUTOEXEC.NCF file.

5. The *Hardware Description*, *Physical Location*, and *Human Contact* fields can be selected to open forms that can be used to describe this node. Figure 13.3 shows the form produced by selecting the *Human Contact* field.

The information you enter in these forms is up to your discretion. Ideally, when planning the LAN, you should define standard formats for this information. If uniform formats are maintained on all computers, it will be much easier for managers of large networks to remain informed about the network configuration.

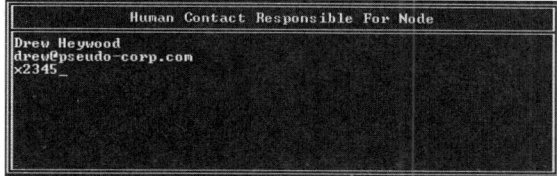

F I G U R E   13.3

SNMP Information Describing the Human Contact

6. When the node information has been completed, press Esc. Complete any other required information before quitting INETCFG.

Configuring Trap Addresses   The final parameters to configure are the addresses to which this host will send trap messages. If the *Trap Settings* field in the SNMP Parameters has been configured with the setting "Do not send traps," it is unnecessary to specify trap addresses. In the majority of cases, however, trap messages will be generated and addresses should be configured. To specify TCP/IP trap addresses:

1. Load INETCFG.

2. Select *Protocols* from the Internetworking Configuration menu.

3. Select *TCP/IP* from the Protocol Configuration menu.

4. Select the *SNMP Manager Table* field to open the SNMP Manager Table window shown in Figure 13.4.

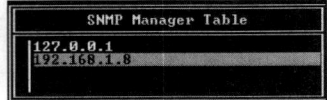

FIGURE   3.4

SNMP Manager Table Window

> By default, a NetWare server will send trap messages to the loopback address 127.0.0.1, thereby sending trap messages to the server's local SNMP trap log. If a remote SNMP manager should receive trap messages, this address should be added to the list.

5. To delete an address from the SNMP Manager Table window, highlight the address and press Delete. Choose Yes to confirm the deletion when you are prompted "Delete current entry from list?"

6. To add an address to the SNMP Manager Table window, press Insert. In the IP Address of Manager window, enter the IP address of an SNMP manager. Press Enter to add the address to the SNMP Manager Table window.

7. After the desired addresses have been deleted or added, press Esc. Complete any other required information before quitting INETCFG.

Remember that configuration changes made in INETCFG do not take effect until the server has been restarted or the REINITIALIZE SERVER command has been executed from the server console.

NOTE

Configuring SNMP Agents on NetWare DOS Clients

An SNMP agent is included with the Novell Client for DOS and Windows 3.1*x*. Two options in the client installation program support the SNMP agent:

> ► *Simple Network Management Protocol (SNMP)*. This option installs a multiprotocol SNMP agent that functions with IPX or IP. This component is also referred to as *Desktop SNMP*.

▸ *Host Management Information Base (MIB).* This optional component enables an SNMP console to poll the agent to determine resources configured on the client.

When you install Simple Network Management Protocol, two dialog boxes prompt you for SNMP client information. The first dialog box prompts for the following information:

▸ *Your Computer's Name.* Enter a descriptive name for the computer.

▸ *Your Computer's Location.* Enter a description of the computer's location.

▸ *Your Name.* Enter the name of the primary contact person for this computer.

The second SNMP configuration dialog box, shown in Figure 13.5, is used to specify the addresses of SNMP management consoles to receive traps generated by this computer. You can add IPX or IP addresses to the lists.

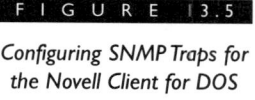

F I G U R E   13.5

Configuring SNMP Traps for the Novell Client for DOS

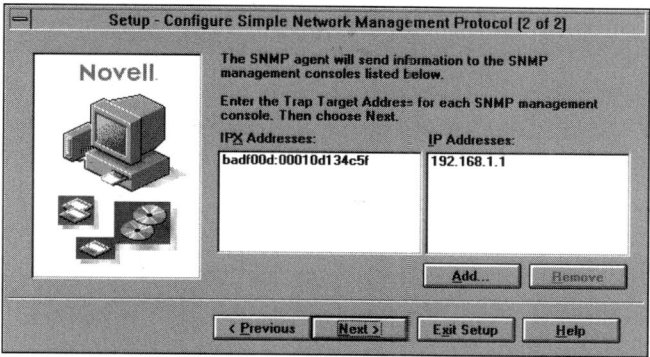

When you install the Host Management Information Base, two dialog boxes prompt you for information about your computer's hardware and software inventory. The first dialog box, shown in Figure 13.6, lists modems, printers, and tape drives installed on the client. To add a hardware item to the list, click Add to open the dialog box shown in Figure 13.7. Select the type of hardware (Printer, Modem, or Tape Drive) along with a brief description of the device.

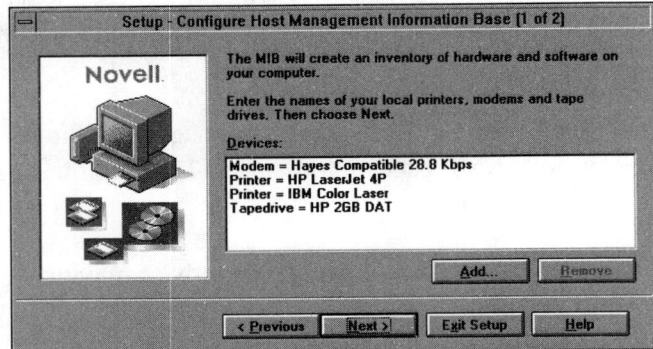

F I G U R E   13.6

*Hardware Specifications
That Are Added to the
Client's MIB*

F I G U R E   13.7

*Editing a Hardware
Specification for a
Client MIB*

The second dialog box that configures the client MIB specifies directories to be searched to identify programs installed on the client. Click Add to add directories to the search list. The depth of the search is determined by the value of the *Maximum Directory Levels to Search from Root* field. If this value is 1, only the root directory will be automatically searched. If this value is zero (0), no directories will be automatically searched.

Individual directories can be added to those defined by the *Maximum Directory Levels to Search from Root* field. To add a directory to those that will be catalogued by the client MIB, click Add and enter the directory path. Terminate the directory path with "*" if you want to also search subdirectories of the directory you specify.

Then edit the STARTNET.BAT file to load the required NLMs. The following code example includes the required LOAD commands. The new lines required for SNMP are shown in bold type. Commands required to enable SNMP over IPX are included as remarks.

```
REM ***************************************
REM this section is not to be modified manually
```

```
@ECHO CFF

C:\NOVELL\CLIENT32\ISINPATH C:\NOVELL\CLIENT32

if errcrlevel 1 goto skippath

PATH=C:\NOVELL\CLIENT32;%PATH%

:skippath

SET NWLANGUAGE=ENGLISH

C:

CD C:\NOVELL\CLIENT32


C:\NOVELL\CLIENT32\NIOS.EXE

LOAD C:\NOVELL\CLIENT32\NBIC32.NLM

LOAD C:\NOVELL\CLIENT32\LSLC32.NLM

LOAD C:\NOVELL\CLIENT32\CMSM.NLM

LOAD C:\NOVELL\CLIENT32\ETHERTSM.NLM

rem LOAD C:\NOVELL\CLIENT32\E100B.LAN FRAME=Ethernet_802.2
SLOT=3

LOAD C:\NOVELL\CLIENT32\E100B.LAN FRAME=Ethernet_II SLOT=3

LOAD C:\NOVELL\CLIENT32\SNMP.NLM

LOAD C:\NOVELL\CLIENT32\TCPIP.NLM

LOAD C:\NOVELL\CLIENT32\TRANNTA.NLM

rem LOAD C:\NOVELL\CLIENT32\IPX.NLM

rem LOAD C:\NOVELL\CLIENT32\SNMPIPX.NLM

LOAD C:\NOVELL\CLIENT32\SNMPUDP.NLM

LOAD C:\NOVELL\CLIENT32\SRVLOC.NLM

rem LOAD C:\NOVELL\CLIENT32\SPX_SKTS.NLM

LOAD C:\NOVELL\CLIENT32\CLIENT32.NLM
```

```
LOAD C:\NOVELL\CLIENT32\HOSTMIB.NLM

REM *****************************************
```

The following modules support SNMP on the DOS TCP/IP client:

▸ **SNMP.NLM.** Enables the client to be monitored and controlled by an SNMP management console. Implements the system, interfaces, and SNMP groups of MIB-II. This component is also referred to as Desktop SNMP.

▸ **SNMPUDP.NLM.** Implements a UDP transport provider for SNMP. Monitors the SNMP port to receive SNMP request messages and sends SNMP reply messages. (The module SNMPIPX.NLM implements an IPX transport provider for SNMP.)

▸ **HOSTMIB.NLM.** Enables the client to be managed over SNMP using the Host Resources MIB database format. This component is optional.

The SNMP.NLM module is configured in the Desktop SNMP section in the NET.CFG file. The fields that appear in the Desktop SNMP section are summarized in Table 13.1. Here is an example of a Desktop SNMP section:

```
Desktop SNMP

    ENABLE MONITOR COMMUNITY ANY

    ENABLE CONTROL COMMUNITY SPECIFIED

    CONTROL COMMUNITY        ADMIN

    SYSCONTACT               Blythe Heywood

    SYSNAME                  BHeywood

    SYSLOCATION              Building A Room 105
```

TABLE 13.1	PARAMETER	VALUES	PURPOSE
Parameters for SNMP.NLM	Enable Control Community	off|any|specified	If the value is "off," no control community can access this computer. If the value is "any," any control community can access this computer. If the value is "specified," a control community must be specified by the Control Community parameter.
	Enable Monitor Community	off|any|specified	If the value is "off," no monitor community can access this computer. If the value is "any," any control community can access this computer. If the value is "specified," a control community must be specified by the Monitor Community parameter.
	Enable Trap Community	off|any|specified	If the value is "off," no trap community can access this computer. If the value is "any," any control community can access this computer. If the value is "specified," a control community must be specified by the Trap Community parameter.
	Control Community	32-character	The community name that permits (not case-sensitive) Read/Write access to the MIB. Control community access is enabled only when the Enable Control Community parameter is set to "specified."

Continued

T A B L E 13.1	PARAMETER	VALUES	PURPOSE
Continued	Monitor Community	32-character	The community name that permits (not case-sensitive) Read-only access to the MIB. The default value is "public." Monitor community access is enabled only when the Enable Monitor Community parameter is set to "specified."
	Trap Community	32-character	The community name used for (not case-sensitive) traps. Trap community access is enabled only when the Trap Control Community parameter is set to "specified."
	snmpEnable-AuthenTrap	on|off	If the value of this parameter is "on," SNMP sends an alert when unauthorized SNMP access is attempted.
	sysContact	text	The name of the primary contact person for this host.
	sysName	text	Typically the primary contact's e-mail name, including the domain name.
	sysLocation	text	A description of the location of the host.

The HOSTMIB.NLM module enables an SNMP management console to determine hardware and applications installed on the client. It is configured in the Host MIP section in the NET.CFG file. The fields that appear in the Host MIP section are summarized in Table 13.2. Here is an example of a Host MIB section (note use of the "=" characters):

```
Host MIB

    Modem = Hayes Compatible 28.8 Kbps

    Printer = HP LaserJet 4P

    Printer = Epson Stylus Color

    Tapedrive = HP 2GB DAT

    SWDirectorySearch-Depth =2

    SWDirectory-Search = C:\APPS
```

Notice that, as with the Printer parameter in the example, multiple devices can be specified by including multiple instances of the parameter.

TABLE 13.2	PARAMETER	VALUES	PURPOSE
Parameters for HOSTMIB.NLM	Modem	*"text"*	Enter a text description of any modems installed on the client.
	Printer	*"text"*	Enter a text description of any printers installed on the client.
	Tapedrive	*"text"*	Enter a text description of any tape drives installed on the client.
	SWDirectory Search-Depth	*number*	Specifies how many directory v levels will be searched by the Host Resources MIB in an effort to catalog software on the client. Software searches start from the root directory. If this value is 1, only the root directory will be automatically searched. If this value is zero (0), no directories will be automatically searched.
	SWDirectory Search	*"path [path]"*	Use this field to specify search paths in addition to those allowed by the value of SWDirectorySearch-Depth. Enter one or more directory paths.

Trap addresses are specified in SNMP Transport Provider sections, as in these examples:

```
SNMP TRANSPORT PROVIDER IPX
    TRAP TARGET badf00d:00010d134c5f


SNMP TRANSPORT PROVIDER IP
    TRAP TARGET 192.168.1.12
```

Configuring SNMP Agents on Novell Windows 95/98 Clients

When you install the Novell Client for Windows 95/98, you can select the following optional components to configure SNMP agent support:

▶ *Novell SNMP Agent.* This option installs a multiprotocol SNMP agent that functions with IPX or IP. This component is also referred to as Desktop SNMP.

▶ *Host Resources MIB for the Novell Client.* This optional component enables an SNMP console to poll the agent to determine resources configured on the client.

Both components are added to the list of installed components in the Control Panel's Network applet. These, like all installed components, are configured by selecting the component and clicking the Properties button.

The configuration dialog box for the Novell SNMP Agent is shown in Figure 13.8. The fields in this dialog box are as follows:

▶ *Enable monitor community.* Select one of three values to specify support for SNMP read access to the client through use of the GET and GET NEXT operations. Select "off" to disable read-only access. Select "any" to permit read-only access by SNMP consoles that are members of any monitor community. Select "specified" to limit read-only access to a particular community as defined in the *Monitor community* field.

▶ *Monitor community.* This field is enabled if the value of the *Enable monitor community* field is "specified." Enter the name of the monitor community to be given read-only access to the SNMP client.

▶ *Enable control community.* Select one of three values to specify support for SNMP read-write access to the client through use of the SET operation. Select "off" to disable read-write access. Select "any" to permit read-write access by SNMP consoles that are members of any control community. Select "specified" to limit read-write access to a particular community as defined in the Control community field.

▶ *Control community.* This field is enabled if the value of the *Enable control community* field is "specified." Enter the name of the control community to be given read-write access to the SNMP client.

▶ *System name.* Enter a text description of the system.

▶ *System location.* Enter a text description of the system location.

▶ *System contact.* Enter the name of the person responsible for this system.

▶ *Enable authentication traps.* If this field is checked, the SNMP agent will generate a trap message if an attempt is made to access it using an unauthorized community name.

The Host Resources MIB configuration dialog box is shown in Figure 13.9. Information entered in this dialog box describes devices and applications that can be cataloged by an SNMP console. Three types of devices can be specified:

▶ *Local Printers.* This entry appears on the *Printers and Modems* tab. Enter text descriptions of any printers supported by this client. For example: "HP LaserJet 4P."

▶ *Local Modems.* This entry appears on the *Printers and Modems* tab. Enter text descriptions of any modems connected to this client. For example: "Hayes Compatible 28.8Kbps."

▸ *Local Tape Drives.* This entry appears on the *Tape Drives* tab. Enter text descriptions of any tape drives connected to this client. For example: "HP 2GB DAT."

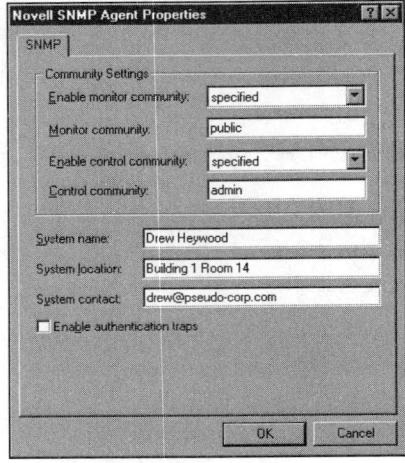

F I G U R E 13.8

Configuration of the Windows 95/98 SNMP Agent

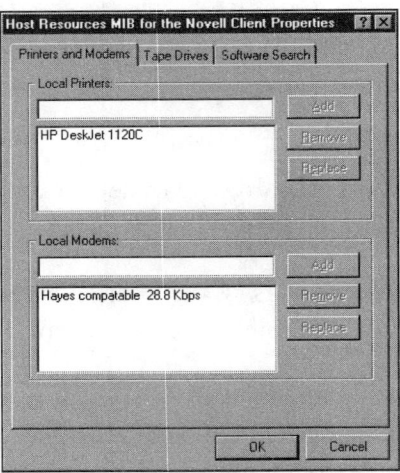

F I G U R E 13.9

Configuration Device Information for the Host Resources MIB

An SNMP management console can use the SNMP agent to catalog software on the client. You must specify which directories are to be searched using the fields on the *Software Search* tab, shown in Figure 13.10. Configure software search as follows:

▸ *Directory levels to search from root.* This value specifies how many directory levels will be searched by the Host Resources MIB in an effort to catalog software on the client. Software searches start from the root directory. If this value is 1, only the root directory will be automatically searched. If this value is zero (0), no directories will be automatically searched.

▸ *Additional Search Paths.* Use this field to specify search paths in addition to those allowed by the value of *Directory levels to search from root*. Enter a search path and click Add to insert the path in the list. Use the *Remove* and *Replace* keys to edit the list.

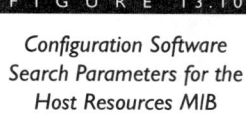
F I G U R E   13.10

*Configuration Software
Search Parameters for the
Host Resources MIB*

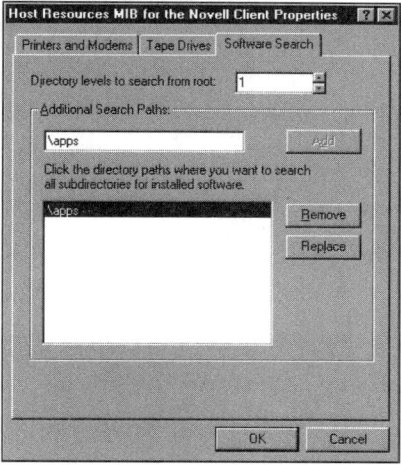

Using TCPCON

TCP/IP Console (TCPCON) can be used to monitor and manage the SNMP agents configured in the previous section. Many of the features of TCPCON are self-explanatory or described in the context-sensitive help. Press F1 to obtain a description of the current field in any window. This section is an orientation for TCPCON and highlights specific features.

NOTE

To enable a NetWare server to log SNMP trap messages, you must load the SNMPLOG NLM after loading the TCPIP NLM. SNMPLOG is a background process that collects trap messages and stores them in the file SYS:ETC\SNMP$LOG.BIN. This file can be read by TCPCON running on the local server. No size restrictions are placed on the SNMP$LOG.BIN file, and it will grow over time. If you are logging traps, you should monitor the size of this file and delete it periodically.

To start TCPCON, enter the command LOAD TCPCON at the server console. The TCP/IP Console main window is shown in Figure 13.11.

▶ · · · · · · · · · · · · · · · · · · ◀

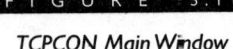

FIGURE 13.11

TCPCON Main Window

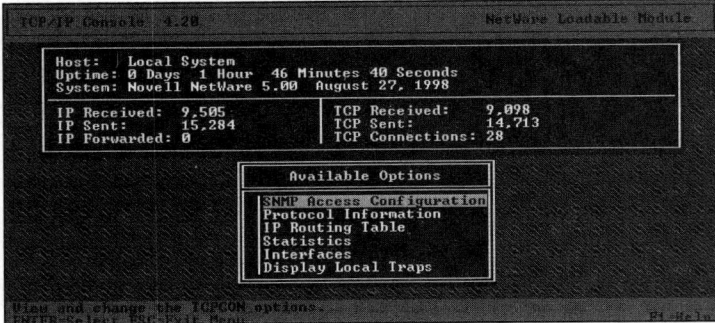

TCPCON can display data for a single host at one time. By default, TCPCON selects the local TCP/IP host, which is identified as the *Local System in the Host* field of the TCPCON main window. TCPCON displays some basic statistics for the selected host. The Available Options menu offers the following choices:

▶ *SNMP Access Configuration.* Selects the SNMP agent to be managed.

▶ *Protocol Information.* Displays and configures protocols on the managed node.

▶ *IP Routing Table.* Displays and configures the routing table on the managed node.

▶ *Statistics.* Enables you to observe protocol-related statistics on the managed node.

▶ *Interfaces.* Displays the network interface configuration of the managed node.

▶ *Display Local Traps.* Displays the traps that have been recorded in the local SNMP log file.

The following sections examine each of these functions briefly.

Selecting an SNMP Agent

The *SNMP Access Configuration* menu choice displays the window shown in Figure 13.12. This window is used to select the SNMP agent that will be managed and to set some management parameters.

▶ . . . . ◀

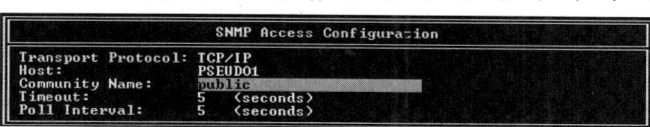

FIGURE 13.12

Setting the SNMP Access Configuration

```
                    SNMP Access Configuration
Transport Protocol: TCP/IP
Host:               PSEUDO1
Community Name:     public
Timeout:            5    (seconds)
Poll Interval:      5    (seconds)
```

The *Transport Protocol* field has three choices, revealed by selecting the field and pressing Enter:

▶ *Local System.* Configures TCPCON to manage the local server. If you pick this option, the *Host* field is inactive.

▶ *TCP/IP.* Configures TCPCON to manage the TCP/IP protocol stacks on computers running SNMP agents.

▶ *IPX.* Configures TCPCON to access the selected node's TCP/IP information using SNMP over IPX. (Configuration of SNMP over IPX is not covered in this book.)

If you select either TCP/IP or IPX in the *Transport Protocol* field, the *Host* field will be active. In that field, you can specify the name or address of the host to be managed. For TCP/IP, press Insert to display a list of hosts taken from entries in the HOSTS file.

The *Community Name* field should be configured with the community name that matches the actions you wish to take. Enter the monitor community name to obtain Read-only access to the agent's MIB. Enter the control community name to obtain Read/Write access to the MIB. When managing a remote node, the community name will be used to authenticate your SNMP messages.

The *Timeout* field determines the number of seconds (with a range of 0 to 120 seconds) that TCPCON waits for a response after polling for information. If a response is not received, TCPCON will repeat the poll.

The *Poll Interval* field determines the interval in seconds (with a range of 0 to 900 seconds) between polls. Specifying a poll interval of 0 seconds configures TCPCON to poll the target as frequently as possible.

After configuring options in this window, press Esc. TCPCON displays the prompt "Save TCP/IP Console Options?" Type **Yes** to save the changes you have made.

Displaying Protocol Information

After selecting the Protocol Information option in the TCPCON Available Options menu, you will be presented with a list of protocols on which TCPCON can report. The following protocols are listed:

► EGP

► ICMP

► IP

► OSPF

► TCP

► UDP

The next window you see will depend on the protocol you select. Figure 13.13 shows the window that displays information for IP. This window illustrates the two types of fields that TCPCON presents:

▶ Editable fields are identified by an extra dot to the right of the colon following the field label. These fields can be edited, and the changes can be saved to the MIP of the node being managed. IP Packet Forwarding is an example of an editable field.

▶ Non-editable fields do not have the extra dot. These fields are for display purposes only and cannot be altered. IP Addresses is an example of a non-editable field.

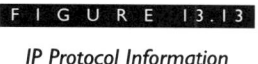

FIGURE 13.13

IP Protocol Information

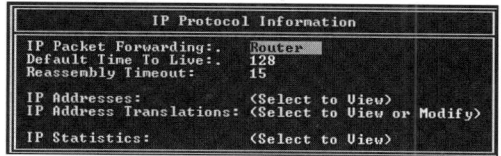

The *IP Packet Forwarding* field is significant because it allows you to enable and disable forwarding remotely on an IP router. This capability can be used to route traffic around a network segment that is generating errors or must be shut down.

Select the *IP Statistics* field to generate a statistics display for the selected protocol. Figure 13.14 shows statistics for the IP protocol on a NetWare server.

FIGURE 13.14

Statistics for the IP Protocol

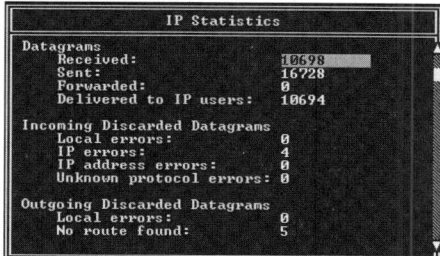

Be particularly attentive to the value increments in the *Local errors* field. These errors reflect datagrams that were discarded because of limited buffer capacity. Errors in this field may indicate a need to increase the MAXIMUM PACKET RECEIVE BUFFERS parameter (see Chapter 8).

Managing Routing Tables

Select the *IP Routing Table* choice in the TCPCON Available Options menu to view the routing table of the host being managed. The first form you see, shown in Figure 13.15, enables you to specify which routes will be displayed. The fields in the Route Selection Options form are as follows:

▶ *Proceed.* Select this field and press Enter when ready to view the routing table.

▶ *Mask.* Select this field and press Enter to see the list of currently configured masks. Masks in IP routing tables determine which bits in the destination address are significant. Routing table masks are configured like IP subnet masks. For example, for a route to a Class C network, the mask would be 255.255.255.0. If no masks appear in this list, all routes in the local routing table will be displayed. If masks are added to this list, TCPCON displays only routes with masks that match an entry appearing in the list.

▶ *Next Hop.* By default, this field value is "*" and next hop values are not filtered. To display only routes with a specific next hop, enter the IP address of the next hop in this field.

▶ *Protocol.* If this field value is All, TCPCON displays routes learned from all routing protocols. To restrict the list to routes learned from a specific protocol, press Enter in this field and select the desired protocol from the provided list.

▶ *Cost.* By default, all routes are displayed, regardless of cost. To display only routes with a specific cost, enter the cost metric in this field.

▶ *Interface.* By default, TCPCON displays routes for all interfaces. To select specific interfaces, select this field and press Enter. Mark the desired interfaces with an *X* in the Show column.

▶ *Flush All Routes.* Select this field and press Enter to flush routes and force the router to rebuild its routing table.

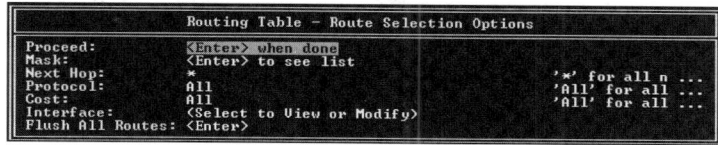

F I G U R E   13.15

Selecting Routes for Display

Figure 13.16 shows an example of a routing table for a multihomed server. This table includes one remote route, which was learned through RIP from another server. Other routes are direct; that is, they are routes to directly-attached networks.

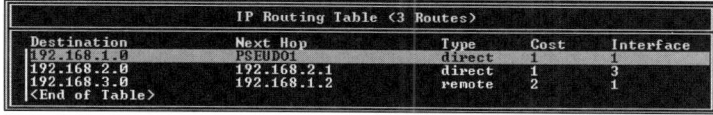

F I G U R E   13.16

Routing Table for a Multihomed Server

By default, the routing table will display host names, derived from the HOSTS file, as described in Chapter 8. In Figure 13.16, the hostname PSEUDO1 is mapped to 192.168.1.1 in the HOSTS file and is therefore identified by name. You can toggle between listing table entries by IP address or host name by pressing the Tab key. You can edit, delete, or add entries to routing table entries. To edit an entry, select the entry and press Enter. To add a new entry, press Insert. Figure 13.17 shows the IP Route Information form used to edit routing table entries.

Figure 13.17 also illustrates an example of detailed IP routing information, which is accessed by selecting a route and pressing Enter. You can use this form to view route specifics and make changes to entries in the routing table. Much of the information in this form can be used to refine filters when displaying routes, as explained in the discussion about Figure 13.15. The IP Route Information window contains the following fields:

▶ *Destination.* The address or name of the destination network or host. Names are taken from the NETWORKS and HOSTS database files. (Editable)

▶ *Mask.* The applicable subnet mask. (Editable) The example destination is a Class C network, with 24 significant addresses, as indicated by the mask of 255.255.255.0.

▶ *Next Hop.* The host name or IP address that is the next hop to the destination. If the route was learned from an interface attached to a broadcast medium, this field has the value of the agent's IP address for the interface. (Editable)

▶ *Type.* This field has the value "direct" if the route is associated with a directly attached network. The value will be "remote" if the route is associated with an indirectly attached network. (Editable)

▶ *Interface.* The logical interface number on the host associated with the route. Use the Interfaces option in the TCPCON Available Options menu to determine the interfaces configured on this host. (Editable)

▶ *Protocol.* The protocol from which the route was learned (for example, RIP or OSPF). For routes learned from local interfaces, the value will be "local." For routes entered manually, the value will be "netmgmt." (Not editable)

▶ *Age.* The elapsed time since the route was established. (Editable)

▶ *Cost.* The primary cost metric associated with the route. (Editable)

▶ *Metric 2* through *Metric 5*. Additional cost metrics for protocols supporting them. (Editable)

After entering route configuration parameters, press Esc. To save the route entry, respond Yes when TCPCON displays the prompt "Save IP Route Entry?" New routes will be displayed in the IP Routing Table.

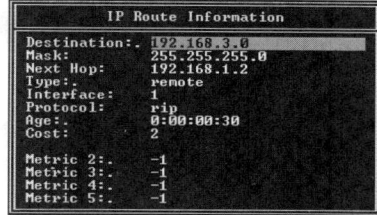

F I G U R E   13.17

*Detailed IP Route
Information*

Examining Protocol Statistics

The *Statistics* option in the TCPCON Available Options menu produces statistics displays for the supported protocols (see Figure 13.14). These are the same displays we examined in the preceding "Displaying Protocol Information" section.

Interfaces

Choose the *Interfaces* option in the TCPCON Available Options menu to display information about the interfaces configured on the managed host (see Figure 13.18).

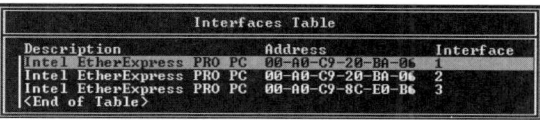

F I G U R E   13.18

*Displaying the Interfaces of
a Managed Node*

Select any interface and press Enter to obtain more information about the selected interface (see Figure 13.19). Note the *Type* field in this figure. The interface type is iso88023-csmacd, which is the international standard derived by the ISO from the IEEE 802.3 Ethernet.

FIGURE 13.19

Details of a Host Interface

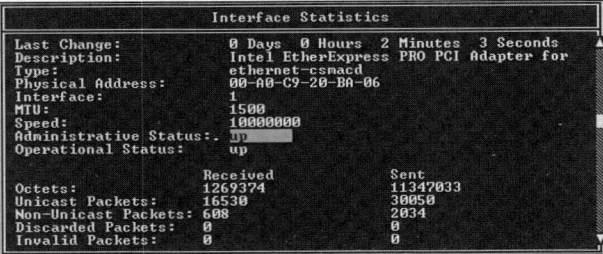

Interface Statistics		
Last Change:	0 Days 0 Hours 2 Minutes 3 Seconds	
Description:	Intel EtherExpress PRO PCI Adapter for	
Type:	ethernet-csmacd	
Physical Address:	00-A0-C9-20-BA-06	
Interface:	1	
MTU:	1500	
Speed:	10000000	
Administrative Status:	up	
Operational Status:	up	

	Received	Sent
Octets:	1269374	11347033
Unicast Packets:	16530	30050
Non-Unicast Packets:	608	2034
Discarded Packets:	0	0
Invalid Packets:	0	0

NOTE

The *Type* field in Figure 13.19 does not match the NetWare Ethernet_802.3 frame type. The interface was, in fact, configured for Ethernet_802.2 frames. The value of the *Type* field will be iso88023-csmacd **for all frame types based on IEEE 802.3 networks, including Ethernet_802.2, Ethernet_802.3, and Ethernet_SNAP. For an interface bound with the Ethernet_II frame type, the value of the *Type* field is be** ethernet-csmacd.

The *Administrative Status* field can be used to enable and disable interfaces. Press Enter to select one of the following values for this field:

- *Up.* The interface functions normally.

- *Down.* The interface is disabled.

- *Testing.* The interface will not pass any operational packets.

The *Operational Status* field indicates the current status of the interface.

TIP

You can use the *Administrative Status* field to disable an interface temporarily. Suppose that the *Invalid Packets* field for a router interface indicates that the router is receiving a high number of bad packets. If an alternate route exists, you can disable this interface on the router without completely disabling forwarding for the entire router. Simply set the value of the *Administrative Status* field to "down" until the problem is corrected. Other interfaces on the router will continue to function, and the router will still forward packets among its other interfaces.

Displaying Traps

Choose the *Display Local Traps* option in the TCPCON Available Options menu to display trap messages that have been captured in the local SNMP trap database. Figure 13.20 shows a local trap table containing two entries generated when binding parameters were altered for a TCP/IP interface. The traps were generated when the REINITIALIZE SYSTEM command was used to activate the changes on the server.

NOTE

You must load **SNMPLOG.NLM** to capture local traps.

F I G U R E   13.20

Examples of Messages in the Traps Database

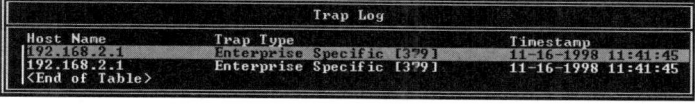

```
                              Trap Log

Host Name            Trap Type                    Timestamp
192.168.2.1          Enterprise Specific [379]    11-16-1998 11:41:45
192.168.2.1          Enterprise Specific [379]    11-16-1998 11:41:45
<End of Table>
```

Conclusion

This chapter finishes our discussion of installing, configuring, and managing TCP/IP on NetWare servers and clients. The next section addresses a variety of topics. First, we'll look more closely at the Service Location Protocol (SLP) that figures so prominently in Pure IP operation. Then, we'll examine strategies for migrating from IPX to Pure IP. Finally, we'll see how to implement a variety of TCP/IP services in NetWare 5 servers, including FTP, WWW, and NFS.

## PART III

Supporting TCP/IP Services

## CHAPTER 14

Locating Services on Pure IP Networks

When Novell worked to adapt NetWare to a Pure IP environment, they didn't want to give up any of the amenities we have come to expect on a NetWare network. One of those amenities is service location. NetWare client workstations have always been able to query the network to locate NetWare servers and NDS trees, for example. When you log in to your preferred NDS tree, your NetWare client software queries the network to identify a server that supports logins to that tree. The query and response are transparent to the user and work even if the client or server have changed networks or been configured with new network interface adapters.

In the IPX environment, NetWare has traditionally relied on SAP and RIP queries to locate servers and routes. While SAP and RIP make NetWare easy to configure and use, they exact a high cost because both protocols rely on periodic broadcast messages to get the word out concerning changes in service and route configurations. Broadcast messages may be okay on moderately-used LANs, but they are highly undesirable on heavily-used WANs. Novell did not adapt IPX SAP and RIP to the IP environment, in part, because of these protocols' reputations as network busters.

Another reason SAP and RIP won't port to the IP environment is that IP routers don't maintain Service Information Tables, as is the practice with IPX routers. When an IPX client issues a query for a service that can't be satisfied by a server on the local network segment, an IPX router can respond to the query using information it has gleaned from other networks. This enables service information to reach every IPX segment without needing to broadcast messages into the segments. However, that approach won't port into the IP world. It isn't realistic for Novell to add a proprietary service advertisement protocol that would be required on all routers that supported NetWare 5 Pure IP.

The day of proprietary protocols is passing, and Novell was fortunate in that a new Internet protocol does for IP what SAP has traditionally done for IPX: makes it possible for network services to be catalogued in ways that clients can query. This new protocol, called the *Service Location Protocol* (SLP; RFC 2165), substitutes for SAP without inheriting SAP's most irritating characteristic — its dependence on broadcast messages.

SLP brings two attributes: it uses multicast messaging to improve network efficiency, and it has a scaleable architecture that enables SLP to be tailored to small, medium, and large networks. On a small network, SLP requires practically no attention from administrators. It simply works. But as networks become larger, administrators need to get involved in configuration issues. So let's start simple and then see what happens when SLP is adapted to larger networks.

NOTE

Novell is very careful to point out that SLP is an optional protocol. Some organizations feel that service advertisements jeopardize security. Others don't want the network traffic that SLP generates. Besides SLP, there are three other ways to discover services on NetWare 5 networks: static configuration parameters, DHCP, and DNS. That's why this chapter isn't titled "Service Location Protocol," even though the bulk of its content targets SLP. In this chapter, you will also see how the alternative service location methods work.

SLP Agents

SLP relies on *agents* to catalog services and to originate and respond to queries. Three types of agents are employed: User Agents, Service Agents, and Directory Agents.

A *User Agent* (UA) is found on every SLP client and server. The UA receives requests for services from applications and queries Service Agents and Directory Agents to locate servers that can provide the requested service. NetWare 5 servers and clients are always configured with UAs.

A *Service Agent* (SA) is found on every device that advertises services through SLP. When a service is activated or deactivated, the service should communicate with the SA to register its change of state. UAs can direct multicast queries to SAs to locate desired services. Every NetWare 5 server is configured with an SLP SA process. Expect to see more servers sporting SAs as additional vendors bring out SLP-compatible products.

A *Directory Agent* (DA) collects service information from multiple SAs, building global service directories. If a DA is present on the network, a UA will query the DA. You won't see DAs on small networks, but they can be configured on large networks to reduce the amount of multicast traffic generated by SLP.

With those three types of agents in mind, let's see how SLP scales to different sizes of networks.

SLP Agents and Small Networks

On a small network that includes about 25 or fewer NetWare servers and does not incorporate a WAN, Directory Agents are not required. We simply allow the UAs and SAs automatically configured on the NetWare client and server to do their business.

Figure 14.1 shows a block diagram that illustrates how an SA supports queries. When a service is initialized, it makes itself known to the SA on the server. As a result, the SA is aware of all services running on its server. The SA does not actively advertise services. It makes services known by responding to explicit queries from UAs.

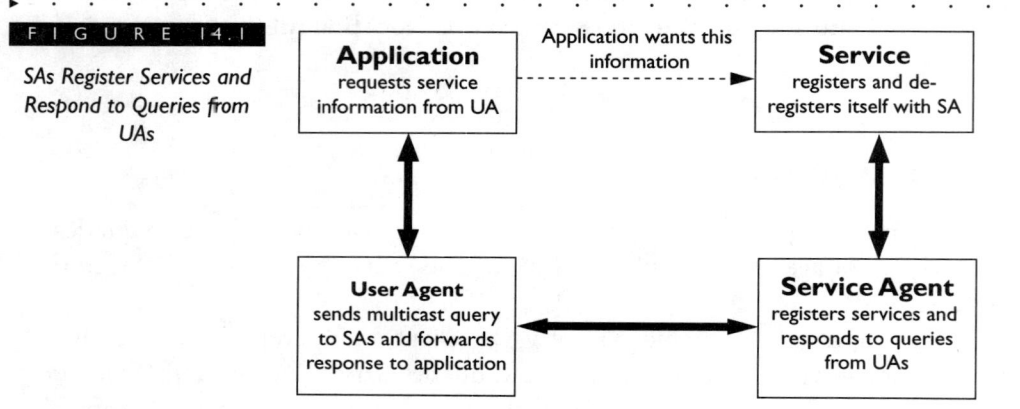

FIGURE 14.1

SAs Register Services and Respond to Queries from UAs

Figure 14.2 shows how a UA queries SAs to discover a service. When an application on a client needs to know the address of a service, it makes a request through the UA on the client. The UA multicasts a request seen by all SAs within a specified network radius. An SA responds to the client's UA if its server can provide the required service. The reply packet includes the IP address of the server, enabling the client to access the service.

On a NetWare 5 server, the primary service that a client needs to know about is NDS. Once the client knows how to access a desired NDS tree, the client uses NDS to locate services represented in the tree.

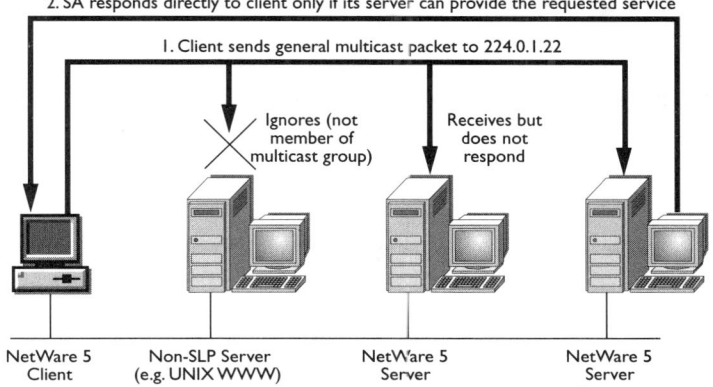

FIGURE 14.2

UAs Send Multicast Queries to SAs to Discover Services

2. SA responds directly to client only if its server can provide the requested service

1. Client sends general multicast packet to 224.0.1.22

Ignores (not member of multicast group)

Receives but does not respond

NetWare 5 Client

Non-SLP Server (e.g. UNIX WWW)

NetWare 5 Server

NetWare 5 Server

Recall from the discussions in Chapters 8 and 9 that we were able to set up a basic TCP/IP network without concerning ourselves about SLP. NetWare 5 servers are always configured with SAs, and NetWare 5 servers and clients are configured with UAs. Servers and clients configured to use SLP join the SLP multicast group (224.0.1.22), enabling UAs to address multicast queries to SAs. Everything is automatic and as invisible as SAP, but SLP does not generate nearly the levels of network traffic with which we are familiar on IPX LANs.

As servers are added to the network, however, eventually a point is reached where traffic begins to become bothersome. When too many active SAs are responding to client queries, it is time to move to the next level of SLP scaling and deploy one or more Directory Agents. Let's see how DAs work on larger networks.

SLP Agents and Larger Networks

When SLP servers and clients activate on the network, they automatically issue an SLP Directory Agent discovery packet to multicast group 224.0.1.35. If a DA responds, servers and agents alter their behavior to take advantage of its presence. Figure 14.3 shows the relationships among agents when a DA is available.

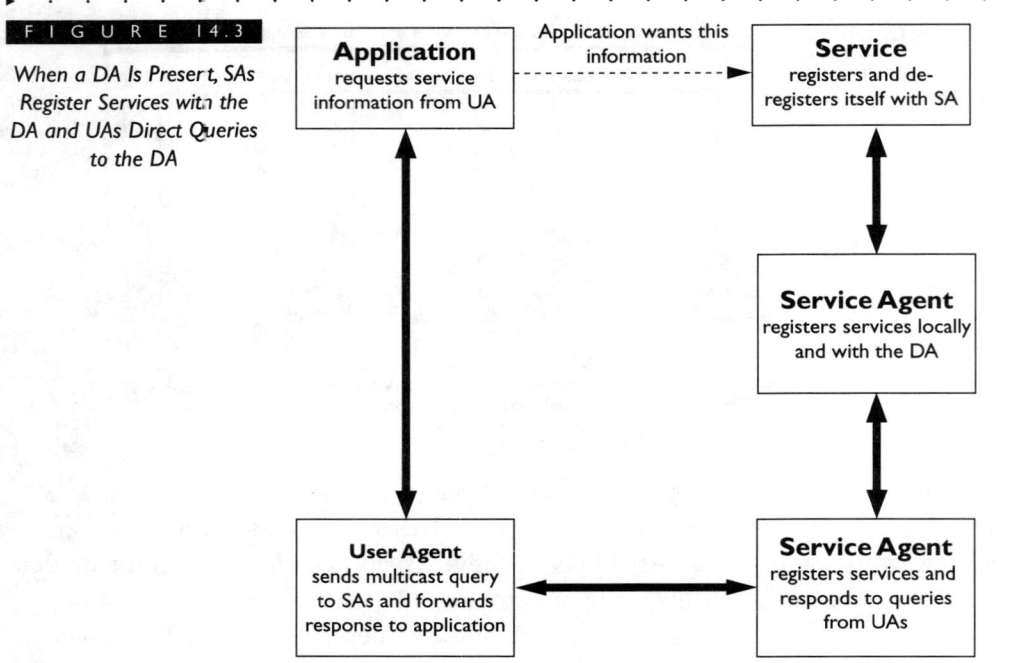

F I G U R E   14.3

When a DA Is Present, SAs Register Services with the DA and UAs Direct Queries to the DA

When a server discovers that a DA is present on the network, the server's SA communicates with the DA to register all services provided by the server. The DA keeps a central database of all the services it learns about from the SAs with which it communicates.

Because the DA has a complete database of services, UAs now have only one place to look when they need to discover a service. When a UA discovers that a DA is available, the UA ceases multicasting queries to SAs and instead directs all service queries to the DA. Figure 14.4 shows how the UA uses a DA to query services learned from multiple SAs. Recall that SAs provide only positive responses to UA queries; an SA will not respond if the service does not exist on the SA's server. A DA, on the other hand, responds to all queries, whether or not the DA has information about the service.

▶ . . . . ◀

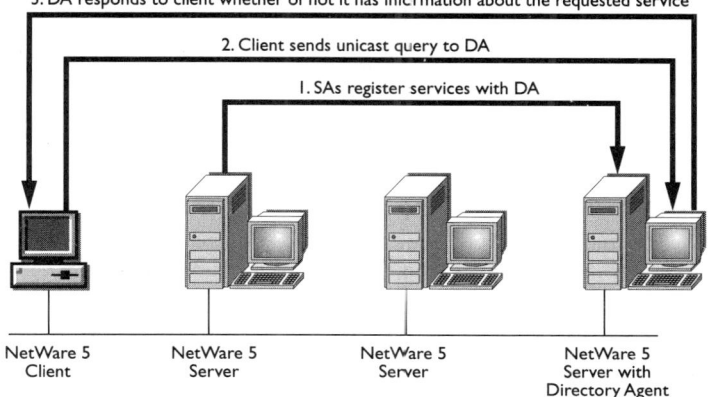

*A UA Can Direct All Service
Queries to a Single DA*

3. DA responds to client whether of not it has information about the requested service

2. Client sends unicast query to DA

1. SAs register services with DA

NetWare 5
Client

NetWare 5
Server

NetWare 5
Server

NetWare 5
Server with
Directory Agent

Prior to discovery of a DA, each UA must communicate with every SA on the network. Therefore, the UA must use broadcast or multicast messages. Multicasts are preferable to broadcasts, but both have the potential to generate more network overhead than a unicast message that goes straight from one node to another. Broadcasts generate processing on every host on the local network, and multicasts generate traffic on every network segment on which the multicast group is registered. Consequently, one big change made possible by the presence of a DA is that UAs and SAs now have a single DA with which they must communicate. After the DA is discovered, all subsequent communications use unicast messages.

UAs and SAs learn about DAs in several ways:

▶ By multicasting Directory Agent discovery packets

▶ From static configuration tables

▶ From DHCP

▶ From periodic "heartbeat" messages that are multicast by DAs

Suppose that a UA or SA attempts to contact a DA and fails. How can it know that the DA has returned to service? One approach would be to have each UA and SA periodically multicast a DA discovery packet. That could generate a lot of traffic if they attempted DA discovery too often. The alternative is for the DA to transmit

. . . . .

a periodic message that lets UAs and SAs know that it is alive. A NetWare 5 DA transmits a heartbeat packet at intervals that can be configured by the administrator. UAs and SAs listen for these heartbeat packets and begin to use the DA when they learn of its existence.

When a service is stopped in an orderly manner, as when a NetWare server is downed normally, the SA will communicate with the DA to de-register the service. When a service is stopped abnormally — when a server crashes, for example — the service will not be de-registered at the DA. Therefore, until the service's database entry expires, the DA may provide information for an unavailable service. In most circumstances, clients will be configured to cope with such failures.

A DA must be activated manually on a NetWare 5 network by loading SLPDA.NLM. The procedure for configuring a DA is discussed thoroughly in the section "Enabling a Directory Agent."

SLP Agents and Very Large Networks

When networks become very large, or when they span WAN links, it may be desirable to have multiple DAs and to localize SLP data and queries. SLP *scopes* enable you to configure groups of UAs, SAs, and DAs that work together. Figure 14.5 shows how scopes might be deployed. The company shown in the figure has two sites, connected via a WAN link.

Each location is configured with a separate SLP scope. For example, every host, server, and Directory Agent in Chicago is configured with the chicago scope. Similarly, every host, server, and Directory Agent in Boston is configured with the boston scope. Agents will communicate only with agents that share a common scope parameter. Consequently, scopes compartmentalize SLP communication.

In the example network, scopes are used to limit SLP traffic through the WAN. Scopes might also be useful in a campus environment. Suppose that you wish users to see only the services in their departments. Simply configure each department with a unique SLP scope so that clients in that department will be able to see only local services. Scopes don't provide added security, because any user can change the scope parameter on his or her workstation. (RFC 2165 discusses the capability of implementing SLP with encrypted scopes using digital certificates, but that feature is not currently implemented in NetWare 5.) However, scopes can reduce the confusion that users experience when confronted by too many service possibilities.

FIGURE 14.5

Scopes Can Be Used to Compartmentalize SLP Agents

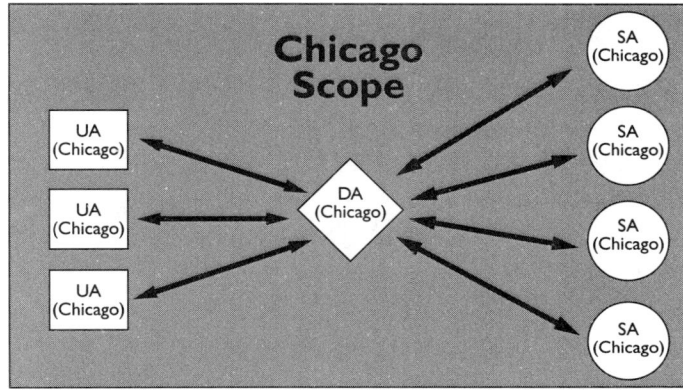

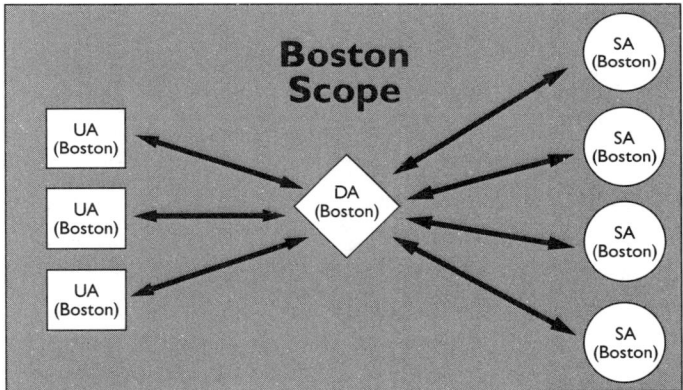

What happens if some clients need to access services in more than one scope? That's not a problem, because NetWare 5 clients can be configured with multiple scopes and the IP addresses of multiple DAs. You'll see how when we look at client configuration later in the chapter.

Enabling a Directory Agent

Directory Agents must be enabled manually by loading SLPDA.NLM on the NetWare server. Three types of NDS objects are associated with Directory Agents. Figure 14.6 shows the SLP objects in NWAdmin.

▸ **SLP Directory Agent** objects are leaf objects that configure a DA for a particular NetWare server and specify with which scopes the DA will be associated. The SLP Directory Agent object in Figure 14.6 is named PSEUDO1_SLPDA.

▸ **SLP Scope Unit** objects are container objects that define the scopes themselves. Figure 14.6 includes two SLP Scope Unit objects, appearing in the SLP_SCOPE container, named PSEUDO and UNNAMED.

▸ **SLP Service** objects are leaf objects that describe specific services in the scope. These objects are defined by the system as services that are registered and de-registered with the DA. In Figure 14.6, the tree has been expanded below the PSEUDO SLP Scope Unit object to show the SLP Service objects that are currently defined. See the sidebar titled "SLP Service Descriptors" for a discussion of the format.

FIGURE 14.6

This NDS Tree Includes Objects That Define an SLP Directory Agent

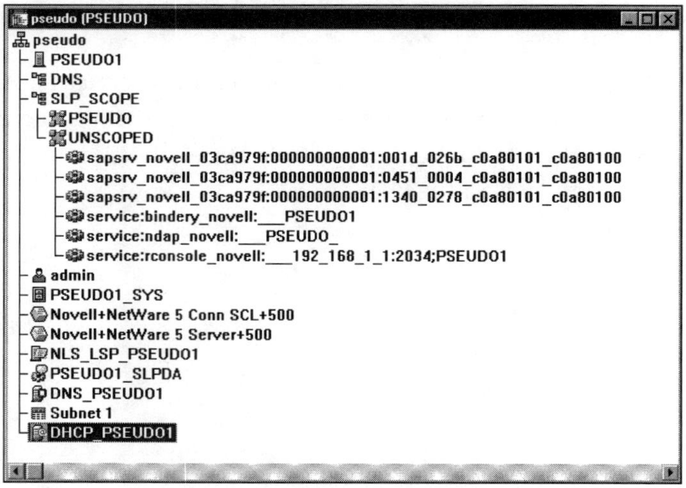

SLP Scope Descriptors

Services are described in SLP communication using a variation of the Uniform Resource Locator (URL) format (described in RFC 1738) with which you are familiar on the World Wide Web. The general format of a service URL is:

```
service:service_type[.name_authority]://[address_spec]
```

The elements of a service URL are as follows:

▶ `service:`. This label identifies the URL as a service descriptor. (Recall from the World Wide Web that the designation `http:` precedes each URL, indicating that the URL designates an object that is accessed via the Hypertext Transfer Protocol.)

▶ `service_type`. This string describes the type of service that is referred to by the URL. For example, an NDS server is described with the service type `ndap`.

▶ `name_authority`. This is an optional field that describes the entity that has authority for defining the service descriptor. The name authority for all NetWare services is `novell`.

▶ `address_spec`. This field describes the specific instance of the service. For an NDS service, the specification is the NDS tree name.

The following URL is a service descriptor for the NDS tree named PSEUDO:

```
service:ndap.novell:///PSEUDO
```

A NetWare bindery-emulation service incorporates an address specification that matches the name of the NetWare server, as in the following example:

```
service:bindery.novell:///PSEUDO1
```

Another example is the URL for a Remote Console service, such as the following:

```
service:rconsole.novell:///192.168.1.1:2034;PSEUDO1
```

Before a Directory Agent can be started, required SLP Directory Agent and SLP Scope Unit objects must be defined. These objects can be created manually using NWAdmin, or they can be created automatically the first time SLPDA.NLM is loaded.

Automatically Creating SLP Objects in NDS

If you load SLPDA.NLM and the required SLP objects are not present in NDS, NetWare presents the prompt Setup default configuration? If you respond N, SLPDA exits. If you respond Y, SLPDA creates the following objects in NDS:

- ► A SLP Directory Agent object with the name *servername*_SLPDA, where *servername* is the name of the NetWare server where SLPDA.NLM was loaded.

- ► An Organizational Unit container named SLP_SCOPE, which is the default container for SLP Scope Unit objects.

- ► An SLP Scope Unit object named UNSCOPED that is used when scopes are not explicitly defined. The *servername*_SLPDA SLP Directory Agent object is configured to service the UNSCOPED scope.

NOTE

DAs are the only SLP entities that store data in NDS. UAs and SAs store data they maintain in local memory caches.

After SLPDA.NLM has been loaded, the UNSCOPED SLP Service Unit container is populated with SLP Service objects that represent the services operating on the server. When SLPDA loads, it reports the Directory Agent and SLP Scope Unit objects that it is using, as in the following example:

```
Directory Agent Object is \T=PSEUDO\O=pseudo\CN=PSEUDO1_SLPDA

'unscoped' scope is using \T=PSEUDO\O=pseudo\OU=SLP_SCOPE\

SU\=UNSCOPED
```

After a few minutes, use NWAdmin to inspect the SLP Service objects placed in the SLP Scope Unit container. SLP Service objects are created and destroyed as services are registered and de-registered.

WARNING

Automatic SLP setup is possible only if a partition replica exists on the server where SLPDA.NLM will be loaded. If a partition replica does not exist on the server, the server does not have sufficient rights to set up the default container.

Managing SLP Objects with NWAdmin

You can configure all SLP objects manually using NWAdmin, both as a substitute for the automatic setup procedure just described and to modify existing SLP Directory Agent and SLP Scope Unit objects.

Managing SLP Directory Agent Objects

SLP Directory Agent objects can be created in any NDS container. When you create the object, the only data entry field requests a name for the SLP Directory Agent. I suggest that you include the name of the target NetWare server in the object name. Figure 14.7 shows the details dialog box for an SLP Directory Agent Object. Figure 14.7 shows the *Configuration* page, which has the following fields:

- ▸ *Status.* This field indicates the status of the DA service. The status may be UP (the service is running), DOWN (the service is not running), or UNKNOWN (the service has never been loaded).

- ▸ *Host server.* This field indicates the NetWare server that will operate the DA defined in this object. You can enter the NDS name of the server or click the NDS Browse button to select the NetWare Server object by browsing the NDS tree. This field cannot be modified if the *Status* field indicates that the server is up.

- ▸ *Clear.* Click this button to disassociate the SLP Directory Agent object with its current NetWare server. The *Host server* field will be cleared. This button is not active if the *Status* field indicates that the server is up.

- ▸ *Cache Limit.* This field determines the maximum size in kilobytes of the cache maintained by the DA. Increase the cache limit if the DA seems to be losing SLP services.

- ▸ *Start Purge Hour.* The DA purges its cache once a day starting at the time specified in this field.

▶ · ◀

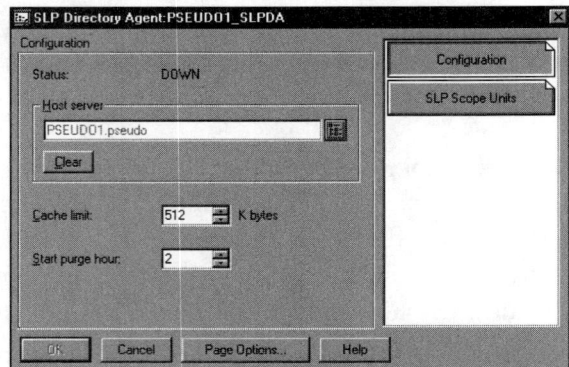

F I G U R E   14.7

The Configuration Details Page Specifies Operational Parameters for the Directory Agent

Figure 14.8 shows the *SLP Scope Units* page for an SLP Directory Agent object. The *Serviced scope units* list box should include the name of at least one SLP Scope Unit object, indicating which scopes are serviced by the DA. After an SLP Scope Unit object has been created, click the *Add* button to select an SLP Scope Unit object and add it to the list.

▶ · ◀

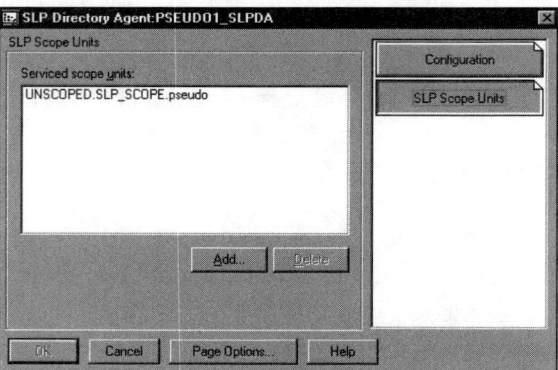

F I G U R E   14.8

The SLP Scope Units Details Page Lists the SLP Scope Unit Objects for Scopes Serviced by a DA

You may wish to place SLP Scope Unit objects in separate containers so that partitions can be defined and replicated as required. More than one DA can service a given scope, and you can use partition replication to place a copy of an SLP scope partition locally on a NetWare server on which a DA is configured.

Server SET Parameters Associated with SLP

A number of SET parameters can be used to configure SLP operation on a NetWare 5 server. These SET parameters are summarized in Table 14.1. To configure these parameters using MONITOR, select Server parameters ⇨ Service Location Protocol. These SET parameters can also be specified from the command line or placed in STARTUP.NCF.

TABLE 14.1	SET PARAMETER	FUNCTION
Set Parameters Asscciated With SLP	SLP Scope List	Specifies a comma-delimited list of scope names. The value has a maximum length of 184 characters. SAs and UAs operating on this server will use scopes specified by this parameter. DAs are configured by scopes specified in NDS SLP Directory Agent objects.
	SLP Close Idle TCP Connections Time	Specifies the time in seconds which idle TCP connections will be closed. Range: 0–86400.
	SLP DA Heart Beat Time	Each DA multicasts a periodic *heartbeat* packet to inform UAs and SAs that it is alive. This parameter specifies the interval in seconds between heartbeat packets. Range: 0–65535.
	SLP DA Event Timeout	Specifies the number of seconds to wait before timing out a DA packet request. Range: 0–120.
	SLP Event Timeout	Specifies the number of seconds to wait before timing out multicast packet requests. Range: 0–120.
	SLP SA Default Lifetime	Specifies the lifetime in seconds that a service registration remains in effect. Range: 0–65535.

Continued

T A B L E 14.1	SET PARAMETER	FUNCTION
Continued	SLP Retry Count	Specifies the maximum number of retries. Range: 0–120.
	SLP Debug	Configures SLP debug mode. This parameter is an 8-bit bit map where bits have the following functions: Bit 0x01 = COMM Bit 0x02 = TRAN Bit 0x04 = API Bit 0x08 = DA Bit 0x10 = ERR Bit 0x20 = SA These bits may be ORed together to enable multiple debug modes. By default, the value is 0 and debug mode is disabled. Range: 0–65535.
	SLP Rediscover Inactive Directory Agents	Specifies the time in seconds that SLP will wait between requests to rediscover inactive Directory Agents. Range: 0–86400.
	SLP Multicast Radius	Specifies the maximum multicast radius in hops. By default, the multicast radius is 32 hops. Range: 0–32.
	SLP DA Discovery Options	This parameter determines the methods that will be used to discover DAs. The parameter is an 8-bit map where bits have the following functions: Bit 0x01 = Use multicast DA advertisements Bit 0x02 = Use DHCP discovery Bit 0x04 = Use static file SYS:\ETC\SLP.CFG Bit 0x08 = Scopes are required.

SET PARAMETER	FUNCTION
	A value of 0 disables all DA discovery. These bits may be ORed together to enable multiple discovery methods. The default value is 7 (multicast, DHCP, and static methods are enabled; scopes are not required).
	If the SLP.CFG file method is selected, and the SLP.CFG file is modified, you must change the value to disable bit 0x04 and then change the value to re-enable bit 0x04 to force SLP to read the SLP.CFG file. Range: 0–15.
SLP MTU Size	Specifies the maximum transfer unit size. The default value is suitable for Ethernet networks.
SLP Broadcast	If the value is ON, SLP will use broadcast messages for SLP discovery. Broadcast messages are required on networks that do not support multicast messages. By default, this parameter is set to OFF and multicast messaging will be used. Range: ON or OFF.
SLP TCP	If this value is ON, SLP will use TCP instead of UDP. By default, the value is OFF and UDP is used. Range: ON or OFF.

Let me draw special attention to the SLP Multicast Radius parameter. You may wish to limit the multicast radius to limit the distribution of SLP multicast packets. You may limit the multicast radius to eliminate unnecessary multicast traffic on WAN links or on links between buildings or departments in a campus environment. Multicast messages are employed by UAs to discover SAs. They are also employed by UAs and SAs to discover DAs. If SAs or DAs on remote subnets are not being discovered, check the SLP Multicast Radius parameter to ensure that multicast messages are permitted to reach the target agents.

The SLP.CFG File

On a NetWare 5 server, DA addresses can be statically defined by including specifications in the text database file SYS:\ETC\SLP.CFG. A DA address specification in this file resembles the following:

```
DA IPV4, 196.168.1.1
```

In this instance, IPV4 specifies that the address is in IP Version 4 format.

The SLP.CFG file is utilized only when bit 0x08 is set in the SLP DA Discovery Options SET parameter described in Table 14.1. If the SLP.CFG file is modified, you must force NetWare to reload the file by changing the value of SLP DA Discovery Options to disable bit 0x08 and then changing the value again to re-enable the bit.

DHCP Service Location Options

For all its benefits, SLP isn't the preferred method for locating services on NetWare 5. When the client initializes, it initiates an SLP dialog that locates a server that can provide the NCP connection the client requires. Once the NCP connection is established, the client uses NCP calls to obtain service location information from NDS. For services that are defined in NDS, SLP is not required once a server for the required tree is located. As you can see, for NetWare 5, SLP's mission is a limited one.

NetWare 5 clients can use DHCP (Chapter 12) to obtain the required service location, thereby reducing their reliance on SLP. The NetWare 5 DHCP server includes three DHCP options that can be used to configure Pure IP clients:

► **NDS Servers** (option 85) supplies a list of the IP addresses of one or more NetWare servers that will accept an NDS logon from the client.

► **Directory Agent** (option 78) supplies a list of the IP addresses of one or more SLP Directory Agents. If this option is configured, it is unnecessary for a client to make multicast queries to locate DAs. Figure 14.9 shows the DHCP Options dialog box with the Directory Agent option selected.

DHCP Option 78 Configures
Clients with the IP Addresses
of One or More SLP
Directory Agents

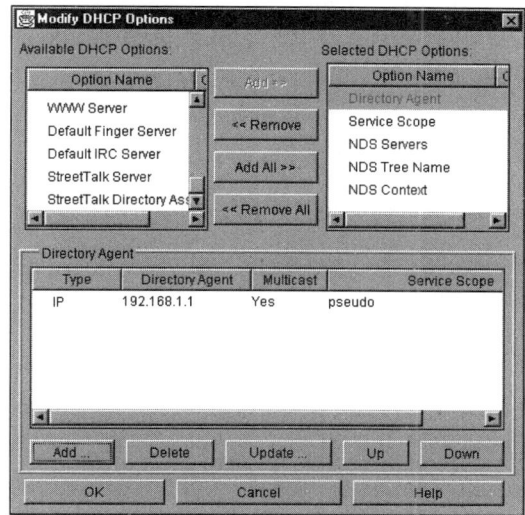

▸ **Service Scope** (option 79) supplies a list of SLP scopes in which the client participates.

Remember that static client parameters override options received from DHCP. If you want the client to obtain a parameter from DHCP, you must clear the relevant field in the Network applet of the Control Panel.

NOTE

Configuring SLP Clients

The NetWare 5 Client for DOS does not offer any configuration parameters. SLP is supported on the DOS client with the following restrictions:

▸ Scopes are not supported.

▸ DOS clients can identify Directory Agents only through multicast discovery.

▸ DOS clients cannot be configured statically with the IP addresses of DAs.

Remember that I warned you in Chapter 9 that Pure IP is not officially supported on the DOS client. If your network requires non-default SLP configuration, you will need to switch to a Windows 95/98 or Windows NT client.

SLP can be configured on NetWare 5 Windows 95/98 and Windows NT clients. The default configuration has the following characteristics:

▸ Directory agents are identified through multicast discovery.

▸ No scopes are enabled. Scopes may be discovered dynamically through Directory Agents. If no scopes are discovered, the client sends SLP requests to all DAs identified on the network.

Service Location Configuration Parameters

On the Windows 95/98 and Windows NT client, SLP is configured on the *Service Location* tab of the client configuration dialog box, as shown in Figure 14.10. To open the *Service Location Tab*, do the following:

1. Open the Network applet in the Control Panel.

2. On Windows 95/98, select the *Novell NetWare Client* entry in the list of configured network components and click *Properties*.

On Windows NT, select the *Services* tab. Then select *Novell Client for Windows NT* in the Network Services list and click *Properties*.

3. Select the *Service Location* tab of the Clients Properties dialog box.

Configuring Scopes

If *Scope List* is empty, the client does not include a scope name in its SLP service queries and will communicate only with SAs and DAs configured with an empty scope list. When no scopes are defined, client queries are sent unscoped, meaning that the client is not looking for a particular scope. If SLP scopes are used on the network, add one or more scope names to *Scope List*. If any scope names are added, the client will communicate only with SAs and DAs configured with the same scope.

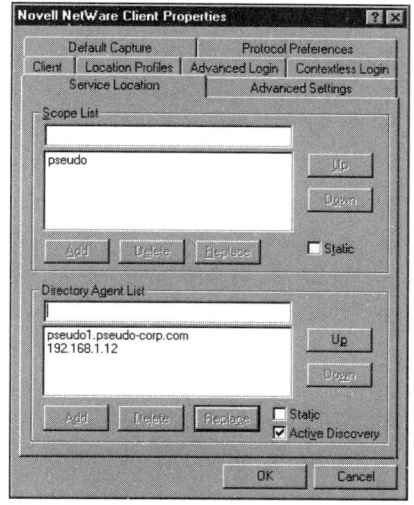

FIGURE 14.10

The Service Location Tab of the Network Applet Is Used to Configure Client Support for SLP

If the *Static* checkbox adjacent to *Scope List* is checked, the client will use only the scope names that appear in *Scope List* or are received from DHCP. If the *Static* checkbox is not checked, the client supplements statically-configured scopes with scopes it discovers dynamically based on responses received from Directory Agents.

Configuring Directory Agents

UAs and SAs attempt to discover Directory Agents by transmitting multicast messages to address 224.0.1.35, a process called *active discovery*. The active discovery process is relatively efficient, generating moderate amounts of network traffic, all of which is either multicast or unicast. Nevertheless, it may be preferable to configure clients with static lists of IP addresses that identify DAs. Statically-configured clients do not generate the multicast messages required to discover DAs and experience slightly less latency when initializing on the network.

To configure Windows 95/98 and Windows NT clients with static lists of DA addresses, add the IP addresses or DNS names of the DAs to the *Directory Agent List* box.

If DAs have been specified in the *Directory Agent List*, you can check the *Static* checkbox if you want SLP requests to be sent only to DAs specified in the list. If the *Static* checkbox is not checked, SLP sends requests to all DAs advertised on the network.

The *Active Discovery* checkbox is found only on Windows 95/98 clients. (On Windows NT clients, the parameter is configured on the *Advanced Settings* tab.) If this box is checked, SLP will attempt to discover SAs and DAs dynamically if it is unable to contact a statically-configured DA. This checkbox can be disabled only if at least one DA has been specified in·the *Directory Agent List*. However, it is usually preferable to leave active discovery enabled, particularly if the network has more than one DA. If a client's DA fails and another DA is available, the client can use active discovery to find the alternative DA, even though it is not listed in the client's static or DHCP configuration parameters.

Advanced Settings

Several parameters on the *Advanced Settings* tab (Figure 14.11) relate to SLP. These parameters are described in Table 14.2.

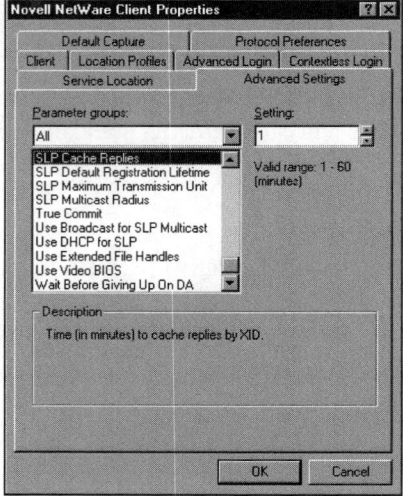

The Advanced Settings Tab of the Network Applet Includes Several SLP-Related Parameters

TABLE 14.2	ADVANCED SETTINGS PARAMETER	FUNCTION
Set Parameters Associated With SLP	Give Up on Requests to SAS	Specifies the time in seconds that the client waits for a response to an SA multicast query. Range: 1–60000.
	SLP Active Discovery	If this parameter value is ON, the client uses active discovery to identify SAs and DAs if it is unable to contact a statically-configured DA. This setting is found on Windows NT only. Windows 95/98 clients are configured using the Active Discovery checkbox on the Service Location tab. Range: ON or OFF.
	SLP Cache Replies	Specifies how long in seconds SLP will cache received replies. Increase this value to reduce the number of SLP queries that the client generates with the risk that the client is more likely to use an obsolete service address. Range: 1–60.
	SLP Default Registration Lifetime	Specifies the time in seconds that a service is registered with SLP. Range: 60–60000.
	SLP Maximum Transmission Unit	Specifies the maximum transfer unit size. The default value is suitable for Ethernet networks.
	SLP Multicast Radius	Specifies the maximum multicast radius in hops. By default, the multicast radius is 32 hops. Range: 0–32.

Continued

T A B L E 14.2	ADVANCED SETTINGS PARAMETER	FUNCTION
Continued	Use Broadcast for SLP Multicast	If the network does not support multicast messages, change this setting to ON. Range: OFF or ON.
	Use DHCP for SLP	If this setting is ON, the client uses DHCP to obtain SLP scope and DA configurations. Range: ON or OFF.
	Wait Before Giving Up on DA	Specifies the time in seconds the client waits for a response to a DA query before giving up and reverting to active discovery. Range: ON or OFF.
	Wait Before Registering on Passive DA	Specifies the time in seconds the client waits to register services following passive DA discovery. Range: 1–60000.

Examining the SLP Client

Both Windows 95/98 and Windows NT provide an SLPINFO command that can be used to examine the client's SLP configuration. On Windows 95/98, SLPINFO accepts no parameters and always generates a full report. On Windows NT, SLPINFO accepts the command options described in Table 14.3. The reports for Windows 95/98 and Windows NT contain similar information. Here is an example of the output produced on a Windows NT client with the command SLPINFO /A:

```
******************************************************

***          Novell Client for Windows NT          ***
```

```
***          Service Location Diagnostics          ***


*******************************************************


SLP Version:            1.0

SLP Start Time:         3:24:18pm    11/22/1998

Last I/O:               7:22:44pm    11/22/1998

Total Packets:          Out: 5          In: 10

Total Bytes:            Out: 170        In: 992


SLP Operational Parameters                  Values
_____                    _____


Static Scopes                               NO

Static Directory Agents                     NO

Active Discovery                            YES

Use Broadcast for SLP Multicast             NO

Use DHCP for SLP                            YES

SLP Maximum Transmission Unit               1400 bytes

SLP Multicast Radius                        32 hops


SLP Timers                                  Values
_____                    _____


Give Up on Requests to SAs                  15 seconds

Close Idle TCP Connections                  5 minutes

Cache SLP Replies                           1 minutes
```

SLP Default Registration Lifetime   10800 seconds

Wait Before Giving Up on DA   5 seconds

Wait Before Registering on Passive DA   1-2 seconds

Scope Name   Source(s)

_____   _____

PSEUDO   DA

DA IP Address   Source(s)   State   Local Interface
Scope(s)

_____-   _____-   __-   _____-   _____-

192.168.1.1   MCST   UP   192.168.1.51
PSEUDO

Local Interface   192.168.1.51

_____-

Operational State: UP

Operating Mode(s):   MCAST

Last I/O: 7:22:44pm   11/22/1998

Total Packets: Out: 5   In: 10

Total Bytes: Out: 170   In: 992

Last Addr Out: 224.0.1.35

Last Addr In: 192.168.1.1

TABLE 14.3	COMMAND SWITCH	FUNCTION
Command Options for SLPINFO on Windows NT Clients	/A	Displays all options
	/C or /O	Displays configured parameter settings
	/D	Display information about known DAs
	/H or /Help	Displays help
	/I	Displays local interface information
	/S	Displays known SLP scopes
	/T	Displays timer values

Putting It All Together

We now know that a Pure IP client has several available methods to locate service information. Let's summarize the sequence in which the client employs the available techniques. The client's first task is to discover a server for its preferred NDS tree. As it starts, it employs the following strategies:

1. If the client is statically configured, it queries any DAs specified in its *Directory Agent List*.

2. If the client is configured to use DHCP to obtain SLP configuration data (Use DHCP for SLP = ON), the client issues a request for information from a DHCP server. The DHCP server provides information included in the client's scope options.

3. If the client cannot identify a DA from static configuration data or from DHCP, the client issues a Directory Agent discovery multicast packet to multicast address 224.0.1.35.

4. If the client cannot identify a DA using any of the above techniques, it issues an SLP general multicast packet to multicast address 224.0.1.22. All SAs that have registered the requested service respond to the client.

If none of the above strategies results in an appropriate SLP reply, the client is unable to connect with its preferred tree. Because an SA is always enabled on all NetWare 5 servers, the server's SA should respond to UA queries while the server is active. If clients are unable to connect with a server, suspect the communication infrastructure. Verify that IP communication can take place between the client and server, and that the SLP multicast radius enables the client to communicate with the target server.

All of the above assumes that the client uses SLP to locate a server for its preferred NDS tree. However, it is possible to log in to the network without making SLP calls at all. In the *Novell Login* dialog box, instead of entering a tree name in the *Tree* field, you can enter the DNS name or the IP address of a server that can authenticate your login to the desired tree. If you look at traffic on the network when the client is so configured, no SLP traffic is generated during the process of connecting to the NetWare server. (Of course, an A record for the server must exist in DNS if the DNS name is to be used during login.)

As this book is being written, Novell is implementing updates for NetWare that will enable administrators to turn off SLP on the NetWare server. It may also become possible to disable SLP on the NetWare client. Without SLP, clients will remain able to log in using server IP addresses or DNS names, and will subsequently be able to use calls to NCP to locate services described in NDS. Thus, it is potentially feasible to eliminate SLP traffic from the network. However, SLP will remain necessary in two instances:

▶ If the network is using compatibility mode.

▶ If clients want to browse the network through the Network Neighborhood. Without SLP, resources cannot be identified by browsing, and clients will be unable to locate any services that are not defined in NDS.

Better Than SAP

SLP is a tremendous improvement on SAP. As you have seen, SLP generates modest amounts of network traffic, scales well, and is highly configurable. Clients actually rely on SLP very little. Once they can communicate with a NetWare server, most service queries are directed to NDS. NetWare 5 has retained the advantages of automatic service location while significantly reducing network overhead.

SLP is only one of the new techniques Novell included in NetWare 5 with the goal of ensuring a smooth transition to Pure IP. They also did a lot of work to ensure that the move from IPX was as uneventful as possible. In the next chapter, we will examine ways that NetWare 5 supports legacy IPX systems and enables you to execute a smooth segue from IPX to Pure IP.

## CHAPTER 15

Migrating to Pure IP

No matter how much we may like Pure IP, Novell wouldn't have won many points if it had abandoned its IPX legacy. We expect a lot from Pure IP. We expect it to interoperate with IPX network segments, support all our NetWare applications, and support a smooth transition from IPX to TCP/IP should we choose to migrate to single protocol suite. Those are stern marching orders considering the distinctions between the IPX and TCP/IP protocol suites, but Novell has actually fulfilled them. With NetWare 5, you can have any amount of TCP/IP support you require, from coexistence with IPX to TCP/IP homogeneity.

Figure 15.1 illustrates a network that connects IPX and IP network segments. The server that connects the segments is configured with both IPX and IP protocol stacks. Why, we may ask, can't the server merely extract the data in an IPX packet, stuff it into an IP datagram, and forward the data to the Pure IP segment? That process would enable raw communication to take place, but it does not enable NetWare services to function normally. The chief problem is that IPX servers and clients exchange service information using the Service Advertising Protocol (SAP), whereas Pure IP services are advertised using SLP. Consequently, services on the IPX servers are not advertised to clients on the IP segment, and IPX clients cannot learn about services offered by IP servers.

To support genuine integration between IPX and IP networks, Novell needed to enable the two environments to exchange service information. This is accomplished using a feature called *IPX Compatibility Mode*, which can be enabled on NetWare 5 servers and clients. IPX Compatibility Mode is supported by the Compatibility Mode Driver (CMD) and networks that support IPX Compatibility Mode are frequently referred to as CMD networks.

On the NetWare 5 server, the Compatibility Mode Driver actually has three distinct capabilities:

- The *CMD Server* enables IPX-dependent applications to function in a Pure IP network.

- The *Migration Gateway* enables communication to take place between IPX and IP network segments.

- The *Backbone Support Gateway* enables IPX traffic to tunnel through IP network segments.

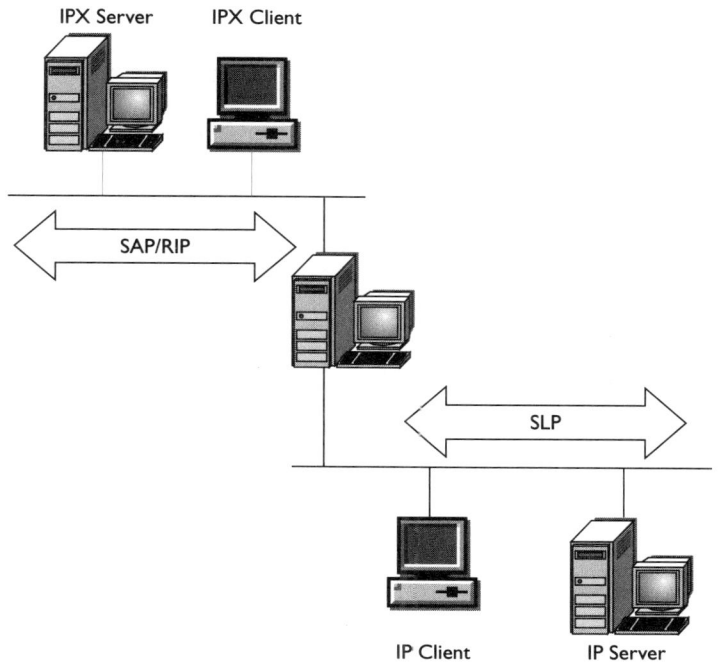

F I G U R E   15.1

IPX and IP Segments Cannot Communicate Directly Because They Use Different Service Advertisement Protocols

IPX Server   IPX Client

SAP/RIP

SLP

IP Client   IP Server

Of these three modalities, the CMD Server is the mode most commonly considered when discussing IPX Compatibility Mode. So let's look at that configuration first.

IPX Compatibility Mode

In Chapter 7, we discussed one of the chief concerns when migrating from IPX to TCP/IP: The existence of applications that cannot execute without access to IPX protocols. Some IPX-dependent applications make legitimate calls through NCP to features of the IPX protocol stack, such as packet burst mode or connection-oriented services provided by the SPX transport. Other IPX-dependent applications bypass NCP and utilize "dirty hooks" directly into the IPX protocol stack. But IPX-dependency doesn't mean that an application cannot be crucial to an organization.

Novell doesn't want legacy IPX applications to impede your transition to Pure IP and has included support for IPX Compatibility Mode with NetWare 5 servers and clients. IPX Compatibility Mode provides transparent, on-demand access to IPX services without compromising the Pure IP network environment. The Compatibility Mode drivers are automatically enabled on every NetWare 5 server configured to support Pure IP (that is, TCP/IP is enabled but IPX is not). And Compatibility Mode is easily enabled when installing the NetWare 5 clients for Windows 95/98 and Windows NT. Let's look at the Compatibility Mode server and client components.

Compatibility Mode on the Server

Figure 15.2 shows the communication architecture of a NetWare 5 server that is configured as a CMD Server. To enable the Pure IP server to function with complete protocol transparency, the server supports various types of communication as follows:

▶ Normal NCP communications are directed through the NCP/IP interface to the TCP/IP protocol stack. (Recall from Chapter 7 that all protocol dependencies have been removed from NCP, which now happily communicates directly through the TCP/IP protocol stack.)

▶ TCP/IP-specific traffic (WinSock 2.0, TLI/Streams, or BSD Sockets) is directed through the protocol interface to the TCP/IP protocol stack.

▶ Outgoing SAP announcements are redirected to SLP. From there, the information can be used to populate NDS and Bindery databases as appropriate.

▶ Incoming SLP traffic is translated to SAP and RIP as required to service requests from non-CMD clients (pre-NetWare 5 clients).

▶ Outgoing IPX packets encapsulated in UPD or TCP as appropriate before directing them to IP for delivery. Incoming packets containing encapsulated IPX are decapsulated and the IPX contents are directed to the IPX protocol stack.

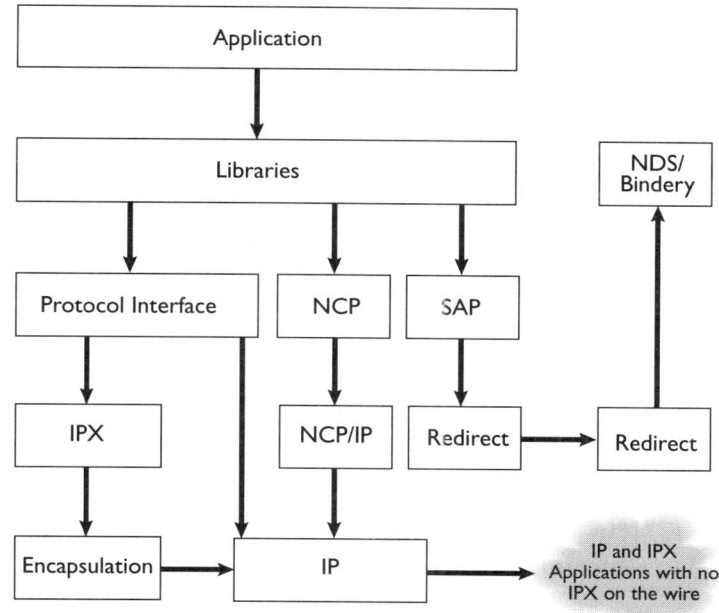

FIGURE 15.2

Compatibility Mode on the Server Redirects IPX-Dependent Traffic through Pure IP Protocols

Even though Compatibility Mode is sometimes forced to encapsulate IPX packets in IP, Pure IP is not comparable to the older NetWare/IP technology. Under NetWare/IP, *all* NCP communication is directed through the IPX protocol stack, and all IPX communication on the wire is encapsulated in IP. Pure IP resorts to encapsulation only when the application requires IPX communication. In all other cases, communication takes place through IP protocols. NCP communication takes place directly through the TCP/IP stack. SAP and RIP functions are performed by SLP.

Compatibility Mode on the Client

In Chapter 9, you saw how to install Compatibility Mode support on Windows 95/98 and Windows NT clients. The NetWare 5 Client for DOS does not support Compatibility Mode. You must configure DOS clients with dual protocol stacks if IPX applications must be supported.

A CMD client can communicate with services in the following environments:

▶ Pure IP servers on which Compatibility Mode is enabled

▶ IPX servers that communicate through a Migration Gateway

The Compatibility Mode client communicates as follows:

▶ Normal NCP communications are directed through the NCP/IP interface to the TCP/IP protocol stack.

▶ TCP/IP-specific traffic (WinSock) is directed through the protocol interface to the TCP/IP protocol stack.

▶ Outgoing SAP queries are redirected to SLP.

▶ Outgoing IPX packets are encapsulated in UPD or TCP as appropriate before directing them to IP for delivery. Incoming packets containing encapsulated IPX are decapsulated and the IPX contents are directed to the IPX protocol stack.

Configuring the CMD Server

The NetWare 5 INSTALL program configures support for the CMD Server on any server installed for Pure IP (IPX is not bound to any interface). The CMD Server is activated on the server by the command LOAD SCMD, which INSTALL adds to AUTOEXEC.NCF following the protocol LOAD and BIND statements.

You can verify the configuration of the CMD Server by entering the command CONFIG at the server console. The Compatibility Mode Driver section resembles the following:

```
Compatibility Mode Driver

     Version 1.04c   August 13, 1998

     Hardware setting: I/O Port A55h

     Node address: 7E01C0A80202
```

    Frame type: CMD

    Bcard name: CMD Server

    LAN protocol: IPX network FFFFFFFD

The CMD Server establishes a virtual IPX network within the Pure IP infrastructure. By default, the CMD network is assigned IPX network number FFFFFFFD, although other network numbers can be configured. The IPX router process (IFXRTR) is loaded with the IPX protocol stack and routes packets between the internal IPX network (also a virtual IPX network that is assigned node address 00000001) and the CMD network.

SCMD.NLM requires the IPX protocol stack and will load it if necessary. However, the IPX stack is not bound to an interface on a CMD server, and SCMD.NLM cannot be activated if IPX is bound to a network interface (unless it is configured as a Migration Gateway or with the Backbone Support option as described later in the chapter). When you reconfigure protocols on a server, remember the following guidelines:

▶ If you disable IPX protocol support and wish to enable the CMD Server, add the command LOAD SCMD to AUTOEXEC.NCF following the TCP/IP LOAD and BIND statements. If INETCFG is used to manage the server's network configuration, add the LOAD SCMD command after the statement SYS:ETC\INITSYS.NCF.

▶ If you enable IPX protocol support, remove or disable the LOAD SCMD command if it is present in AUTOEXEC.NCF.

The network number for the CMD network can be changed by including a /NET parameter as in the following example:

```
LOAD SCMD /NET=D00BD00
```

WARNING

All CMD servers and clients must be configured with the same CMD network number. Because Novell has standardized the CMD network number, I recommend that you reconfigure conflicting devices rather than selecting a different CMD network number.

Configuring the CMD Client

To enable Compatibility Mode support in a Windows 95/98 or Windows NT client, install the Novell client with the *IP with IPX Compatibility* option, as described in Chapter 8. By default, the Compatibility Mode Driver on the client is configured to obtain its configuration information from DHCP. CMD parameters can also be defined statically in the Network applet.

Configuring Windows 95/98 Clients

To change the CMD configuration on Windows 95/98 clients, select the *Compatibility Mode Driver (CMD)* entry in the Network applet *Configuration* tab and click *Properties* to open the Compatibility Mode Driver (CMD) Properties dialog box shown in Figure 15.3. The following entries can be configured:

▶ **Use DHCP.** If this box is checked, the CMD obtains its configuartion parameters from DHCP. This box is checked by default. If the check is removed, the CMD obtains its configuration from SLP or from static entries in the CMD property page.

▶ **IPX Compatibility Scope.** This field can be used to specify an SLP scope for the client. SLP scopes are discussed in Chapter 14.

▶ **Network Number (Hex).** This field specifies the IPX network number of the CMD network used by the client. This number must match the CMD number configured on the servers used by this client. This value defaults to FFFFFFFD, the CMD network number configured by default on the server.

▶ **Agent List Stale Time.** This setting is used only when the client is configured to discover Migration Agents dynamically. It specifies the minimum time the client must wait before attempting to refresh its Migration Agent addressing information. A setting of 0 disables the timeout so that the client does not attempt to refresh Migration Agent addressing information. If the setting is too high, the client will have difficulty recovering when a Migration Agent becomes unavailable. If the setting is too low, the client may generate excessive network traffic.

▶ **Migration Agents.** This field can be used to list up to ten Migration Agents that can be used by the client. Migration Agents can be specified by dotted-decimal IP address, fully-qualified DNS host name, or by a name that appears in the client's HOSTS file. If this field is blank, the client uses SLP to discover Migration Agents.

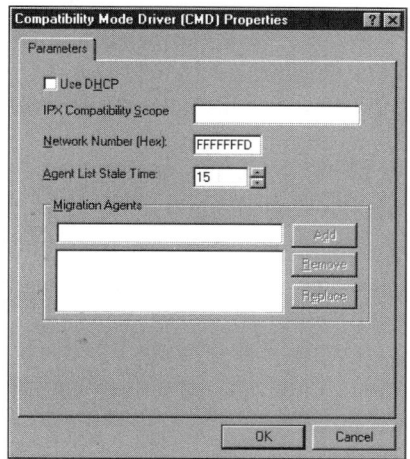

Configuring Compatibility Mode on a Windows 95/98 Client

Configuring Windows NT Clients

On Windows NT clients, open the Network applet and select the *Adapters* tab. Select the *Novell IPX Compatibility Adapter* entry and click *Properties* to open the Novell IPX Compatibility Adapter Dialog box shown in Figure 15.4. This dialog box has the following configurable properties:

▶ **Server Resolution Time.** The compatibility client will first attempt to connect with a server using an IP connection, even though the server is known by its IPX address. After the Server Resolution Time expires, the client will revert to a CMD connection using IPX encapsulated in IP. This setting is used when IPX applications request that the client establish a NetWare connection or when the user wants to connects to an IPX server.

▶ **IPX Compatibility Scope.** Optionally specifies an SLP scope that contains only Compatibility Mode information. If a scope is specified, the same scope must be specified on all nodes that use Compatibility Mode. It is usually unnecessary to define an IPX Compatiblity scope. If a scope is not specified, the client uses the SLP scope specified in the Service Location tab of the Novell Client Configuration property page.

▶ **Adapter.** This box selects the adapter being configured. If the computer has multiple network adapters, each can be configured with separate settings. Parameters defined for the `Default Settings` adapter apply to all adapters for which the *Use Default Settings* checkbox is checked.

▶ **Use DHCP.** If this box is checked and the client is configured to use DHCP, the client will obtain its IPX Compatibility configuration from DHCP options. If the box is not checked, the client will obtain its configuration from SLP. This box is checked by default.

▶ **Use Default Settings.** If a network adapter is selected in the *Adapter* field (`Default Settings` is not selected) and this box is checked, the adapter will be configured with properties assigned to the `Default Settings` adapter.

▶ **Enabled.** If this box is checked, IPX Compatibility Mode is enabled for the adapter selected in the *Adapter* field. Remove the check mark to disable Compatibility Mode support for the selected adapter. On a computer with multiple network adapters, use this field to determine which adapter will provide Compatibility Mode support.

▶ **Network Number (Hex).** This field specifies the IPX network number of the CMD network used by the client. This number must match the CMD number that is configured on the servers used by this client.

▶ **Agent List Stale Time.** This setting is used only when the client is configured to discover Migration Agents dynamically. It specifies the minimum time the client must wait before attempting to refresh its Migration Agent addressing information. A setting of 0 disables the timeout so that the client does not attempt to refresh Migration Agent addressing information. If the setting is too high, the client will have difficulty recovering when a Migration Agent becomes unavailable. If the setting is too low, the client may generate excessive network traffic.

▶ **Migration Agents.** This field can be used to list up to ten Migration Agents that can be used by the client. Migration Agents can be specified by dotted-decimal IP address, fully-qualified DNS host name, or by a name that appears in the client's HOSTS file. If this field is blank, the client uses SLP to discover Migration Agents.

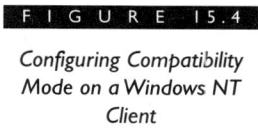

F I G U R E   15.4

Configuring Compatibility Mode on a Windows NT Client

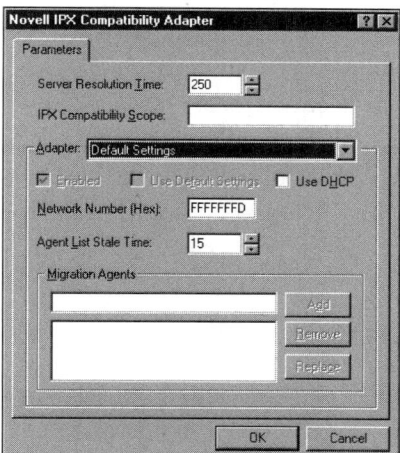

Configuring DHCP Clients

It is often most convenient to configure CMD clients through DHCP. The following DHCP options pertain to client CMD configuration:

▶ **IPX Network Number** (Option 63-12) specifies the IPX network number of the CMD network.

▶ **IPX Stale Time** (Option 63-13) specifies a minimum time in minutes that must expire before the client attempts to renew its Migration Agent address information. This option applies when the client is configured to discover Migration Agents dynamically.

> ▸ **Migration Agents** (Option 63-14) specifies a list of IP addresses that identify Migration Agents available to the client. If the client is not explicitly configured with the IP addresses of one or more Migration Agents, the client uses dynamic discovery to identify Migration Agents.

Recall that static configuration parameters take precedence over parameters learned from DHCP. If a feature will be configured through a DHCP option, leave the corresponding field in the Network applet blank.

Identifying IPX-Dependent Applications

Compatibility Mode is not a particularly costly service because it functions only when IPX services are in use. The Compatibility Mode Drivers exact some system memory overhead, but have little or no impact on network traffic unless activated by IPX-dependent services or client requests.

If your organization does not use any IPX-dependent applications, it is possible to disable the CMD network by unloading SCMD.NLM on the server and by installing the Novell client for IP-only operation.

How do you determine whether you have IPX-dependent applications? The documentation may not tell you because, until NetWare 5, developers could safely assume that IPX would be present on the server. Consequently, the applications may make direct calls to IPX without that fact being mentioned in the documentation. A good test is to enable the application on a NetWare 5 server configured to support CMD. Then unload SCMD.NLM and see if the application continues to function. If the application fails, you need to either enable Compatibility Mode or update the application if possible to eliminate IPX dependencies.

You can try this test using the IPX Remote Console. Enable a Pure IP server and an IP client, both with CMD support. Load the remote console server (LOAD RSPX) and ensure that the client can connect using RCONSOLE. Then unload SCMD.NLM. The Remote Console will cease to communicate with the client.

The Compatibility Mode Migration Gateway

If you are converting a large internetwork from IPX to Pure IP, you probably want to complete the migration in discrete steps, perhaps reconfiguring a single network segment at a time. The Migration Gateway is a CMD configuration that enables IPX and IP network segments to interoperate so that clients in one protocol environment can communicate with servers in the other environment. Figure 15.5 shows a network that incorporates a Migration Gateway, along with some of communication types that the Migration Gateway facilitates.

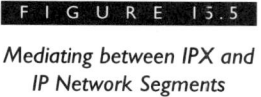

FIGURE 15.5

Mediating between IPX and IP Network Segments

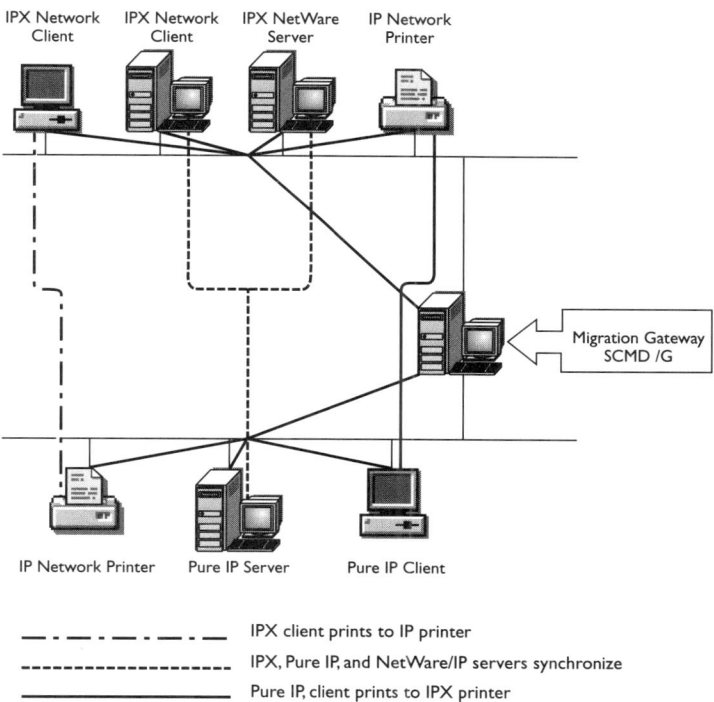

The Migration Gateway (also referred to as a Migration Agent) mediates between the IPX and IP logical networks, exchanging service information and serving as a protocol gateway. The Migration Agent registers as a Service Agent on the IP network, enabling it to translate SAP and RIP packets received from the IPX network into SLP packets. Similarly, SLP packets received from the IP network are forwarded to the IPX network as SAP and RIP packets.

IP clients that communicate with IPX servers do so using Compatibility Mode. The client encapsulates IPX packets in IP for delivery to the Migration Gateway. The gateway extracts the IPX packets and forwards them to servers on the IPX network. IPX packets received by the Migration Gateway are encapsulated in IP for delivery on the IP network. Because IPX encapsulation is performed on the IP network, clients and servers on the IP network must be configured to support Compatibility Mode.

The Migration Gateway can also interface IPX and IP servers on the same network segment. Figure 15.6 shows a network that includes a mixture of IPX and IP clients and servers. The Migration Gateway server is configured with dual protocol stacks (IPX and IP) so that it can serve as a communication portal between the two environments. As you will see later in the chapter, this technique can be very useful when you want to migrate an IPX network to Pure IP in discrete stages.

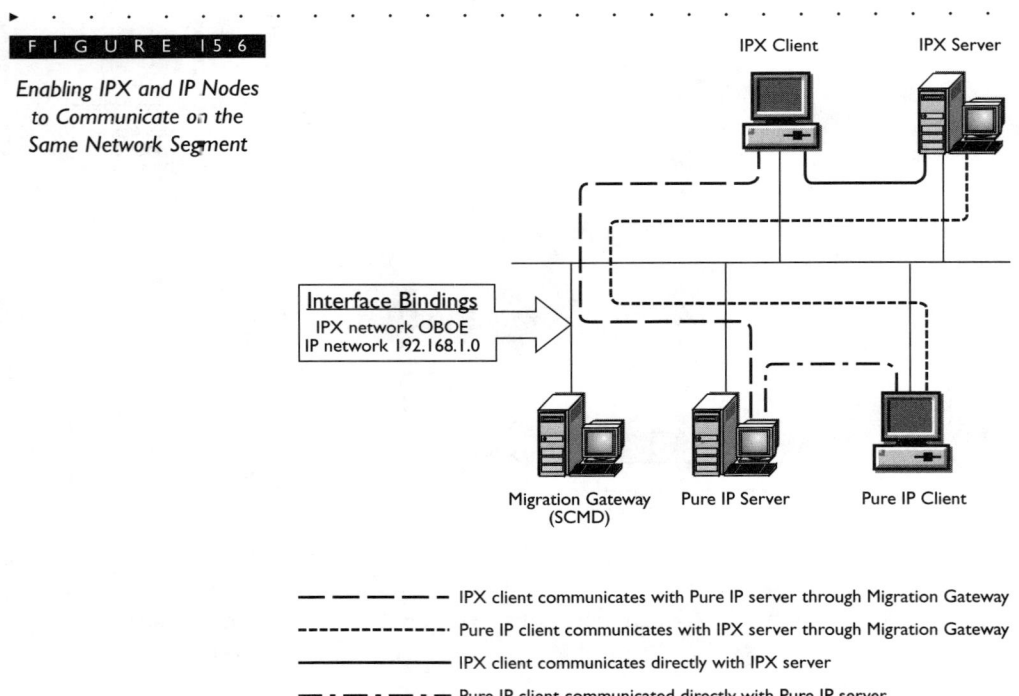

FIGURE 15.6

Enabling IPX and IP Nodes to Communicate on the Same Network Segment

IPX Client   IPX Server

Interface Bindings
IPX network OBOE
IP network 192.168.1.0

Migration Gateway   Pure IP Server   Pure IP Client
(SCMD)

— — — — — IPX client communicates with Pure IP server through Migration Gateway

- - - - - - - - - - Pure IP client communicates with IPX server through Migration Gateway

———————— IPX client communicates directly with IPX server

— - — - — - — Pure IP client communicated directly with Pure IP server

Configuring Migration Gateway Servers

A Migration Gateway server must be configured with both IPX and TCP/IP protocol stacks, which may be bound to the same or to different network interfaces. Chapter 8 explains how to enable, configure, and bind TCP/IP. Similar procedures are used to set up an IPX interface. Figure 15.7 shows the status of the Configured Protocol To Network Interface Bindings window in INETCFG for a server configured with IPX and TCP/IP bindings on separate network interfaces.

▶ · ◀

FIGURE 15.7

Configuring with Both TCP/IP and IPX Protocol Stacks

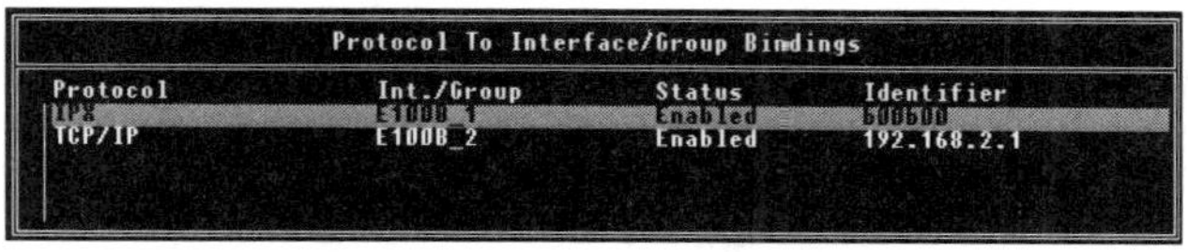

After binding both protocol stacks to network interfaces, enable the Migration Gateway with the following command:

```
LOAD SCMD /G
```

SCMD.NLM can be loaded re-entrantly to enable the gateway feature. To disable the Migration Gateway, you must unload SCMD.NLM and reload it without the /G parameter.

To verify that the Migration Gateway is enabled, enter the CONFIG command and examine the Compatibility Mode Driver section of the report. The Board Name parameter reads as follows for a server configured with the Migration Gateway feature:

```
Board name: Migration Agent
```

Servers communicate with Migration Gateways using multicast messages. If a server is separated from its preferred Migration Gateway by routers that do not propagate multicast packets, the server must be configured statically with a list of available Migration Gateways. This is done using the SET parameter PREFERRED MIGRATION AGENT LIST. The following example specifies two Migration Gateways:

```
SET PREFERRED MIGRATION AGENT LIST: 192.168.2.1;172.31.3.5/
```

IP addresses in the parameter lists are separated by semicolons (;) and the list is terminated with a slash (/). You must unload and reload SCMD.NLM to put configuration changes into effect.

Configuring Migration Gateway Clients

Configuration of the CMD client is described in the discussion associated with Figure 15.3. CMD clients can use SLP multicasts to discover Migration Agents. Also, CMD clients can be configured with static lists of IP addresses that identify available Migration Agents, in which case they will not attempt to discover Migration Agents dynamically.

It is necessary to configure the IP addresses of Migration Agents statically if the client is separated from the Migration Agent by routers that do not propagate multicast messages. In such cases, include the IP address or the DNS name of the Migration Agent in the *Migration Agents* list in the Compatibility Mode Driver configuration dialog box.

NOTE

Notice that IPX clients require no special configuration to enable them to communicate through the Migration Gateway. This enables you to configure a Migration Gateway between a legacy IPX network and a Pure IP network without needing to upgrade clients on the IPX network segment.

Compatibility Mode Backbone Support

The Compatibility Mode Drivers can be configured to tunnel IPX packets through IP network segments. This capability is most often used to enable IPX servers to communicate through a TCP/IP backbone. Hence, the capability is referred to as *backbone support*.

Figure 15.8 illustrates a network that takes advantage of CMD Backbone Support mode. In this instance, no servers are hosted on the TCP/IP backbone. Servers on the IPX segments communicate with one another, but do not need to communicate with any nodes on the backbone.

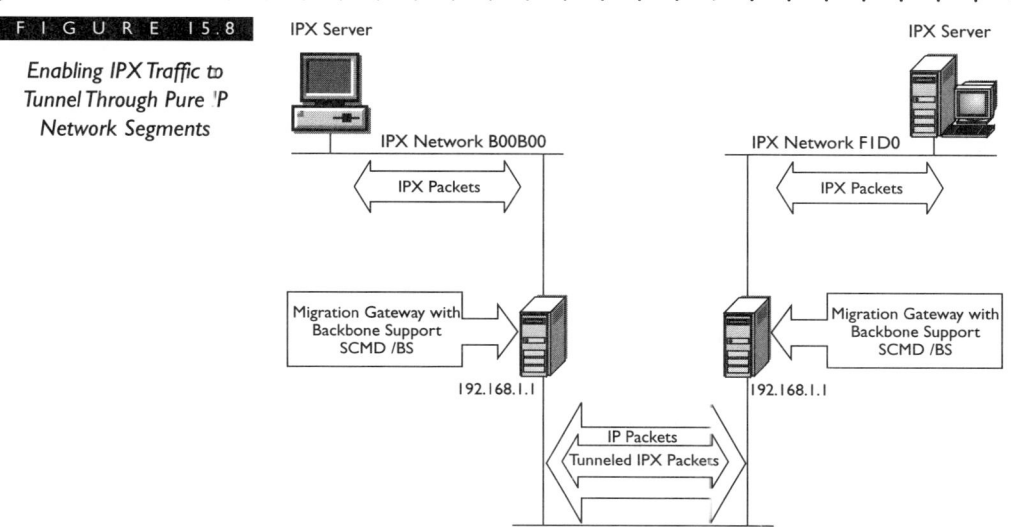

Enabling IPX Traffic to Tunnel Through Pure IP Network Segments

A Migration Gateway is enabled whenever Backbone Support is enabled on the routers. This combination is particularly useful when performing a phased migration from IPX to IP. The Migration Gateway feature ensures that Pure IP segments will not become islands that cannot communicate with IPX. The Backbone Support mode ensures that IPX segments can communicate even though there may be intervening Pure IP network segments.

The capability shown in Figure 15.8 is a particularly impressive demonstration of the migration support offered by NetWare 5. The entire network is visible to clients on the IPX segment, even though the clients have not been upgraded in any way. Similarly, servers on the IPX segments function without modification. Only the servers that interface IPX and IP segments have been upgraded to NetWare 5. Amazingly, despite this complex environment, users can still browse all servers in the Windows Network Neighborhood.

Backbone Support can also be configured on Migration Agents that are not configured as routers. Figure 15.9 illustrates an example of a network with this configuration, which is useful when dedicated routers are being used. Because the routers are not NetWare servers, they cannot be configured as Migration Agents.

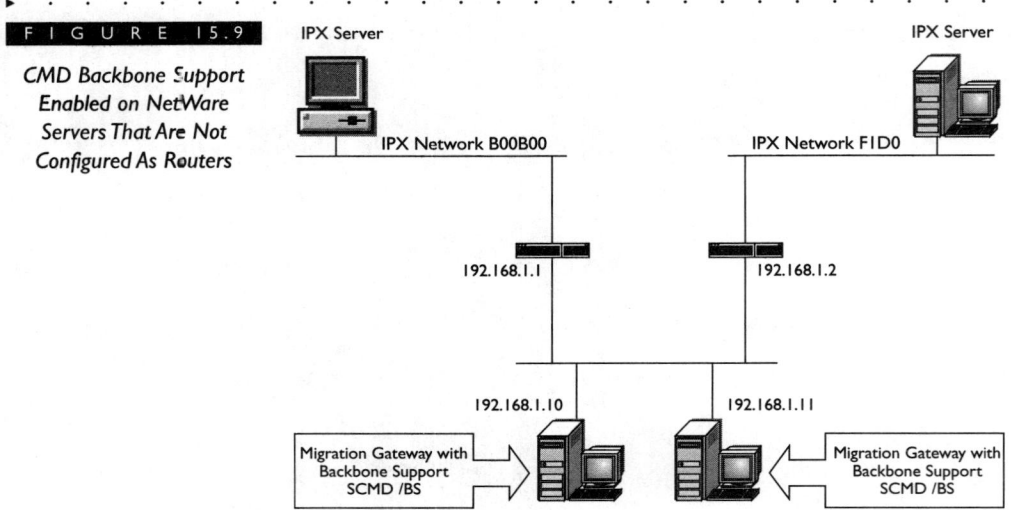

F I G U R E   15.9

CMD Backbone Support
Enabled on NetWare
Servers That Are Not
Configured As Routers

Configuring CMD Backbone Support Servers

Backbone Support servers interface IPX and TCP/IP networks. Both protocol stacks must be enabled and bound to the appropriate interface. At least two servers must be configured with the Backbone Support feature to enable the IPX tunnel to function.

Backbone Support is configured with the following command:

```
LOAD SCMD /BS
```

SCMD can be loaded re-entrantly to enable Backbone Support on a server configured as a CMD Server. If the server is currently configured as a Migration Gateway, you must unload SCMD before enabling Backbone Support mode.

All Migration Agents communicating through the backbone must have NLSP routing enabled and be configured with the same CMD network number.

To verify that Backbone Support is enabled, enter the CONFIG command and examine the Compatibility Mode Driver section of the report. The board name parameter reads as follows for a server configured with the Backbone Support feature:

```
Board name: Migration Agent BS
```

NOTE

The IP part of the internetwork shown in Figure 15.9 could actually consist of multiple IP segments or an IP internetwork, perhaps the Internet. The intervening IP network must propagate IP multicasts. When multicasts do not have end-to-end support on the IP segment, you must configure a multicast tunnel between the Migration Agent servers. See Chapter 10 for the required procedures.

CMD Network Design Guidelines

As mentioned earlier, the CMD network forms a virtual IPX network with the default IPX network number FFFFFFFD. This CMD network is virtualized throughout the Pure IP network infrastructure, and is oblivious to the IP routing architecture. Because a single CMD network is established throughout the Pure IP internetwork, some issues arise regarding the placement of Migration Gateways.

Consider the network in Figure 15.10. Migration Gateways are placed on network Segments A and C. A CMD client on network C uses the Migration Gateway to communicate with the IPX-only server on Segment B. Because the CMD network forms a unified virtual network, as far as the IPX server is concerned, routers 1 and 2 represent equally good routes to the CMD network, with which it can communicate through either Migration Gateway. Consequently, the IPX server may choose the less efficient return route shown in Figure 15.10.

To alleviate the problem, it is necessary to add a Migration Gateway to Segment B, as shown in Figure 15.11. The IPX server will identify the local Migration Gateway as the most efficient route to the CMD network. The Migration Gateway communicates with the client via IP, and IP routing ensures that packets travel between the Migration Gateway and the client using the most efficient route.

Figure 15.12 shows another network where placement of the Migration Gateway is at issue. Because the only available Migration Gateway is on a remote network segment, communication between the CMD client and the IPX server must be routed, even though client and server are on the same network. If a Migration Gateway is added to the local network, communication follows the more efficient path shown in Figure 15.13.

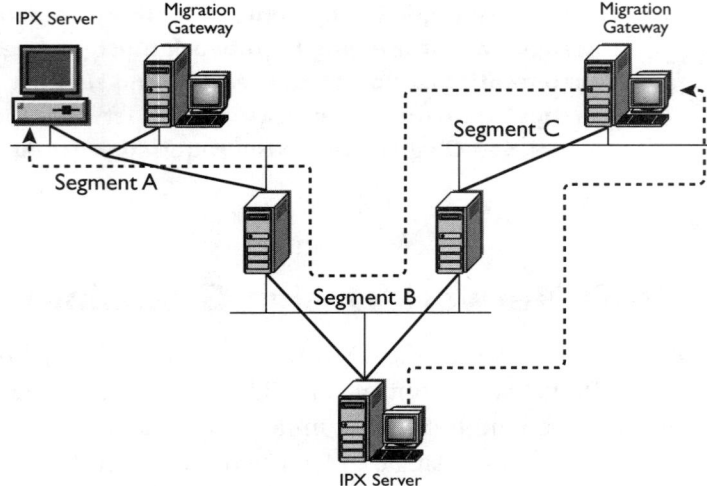

FIGURE 15.10

The IPX Server May Reply through an Indirect Route on This Internetwork.

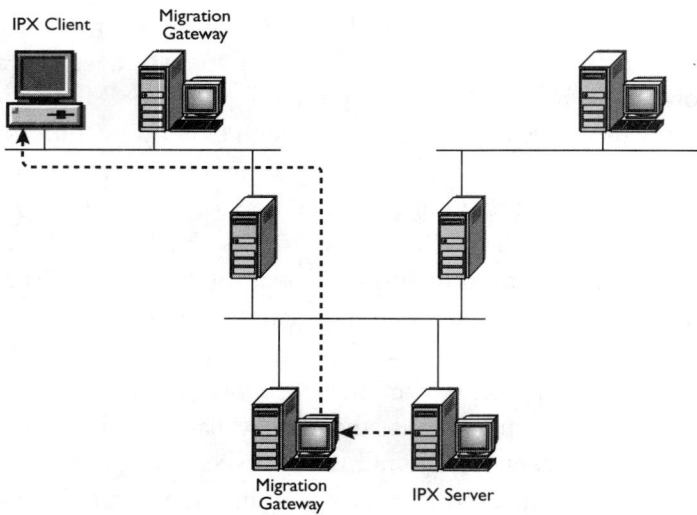

FIGURE 15.11

A Local Migration Gateway Results in More Efficient Routing

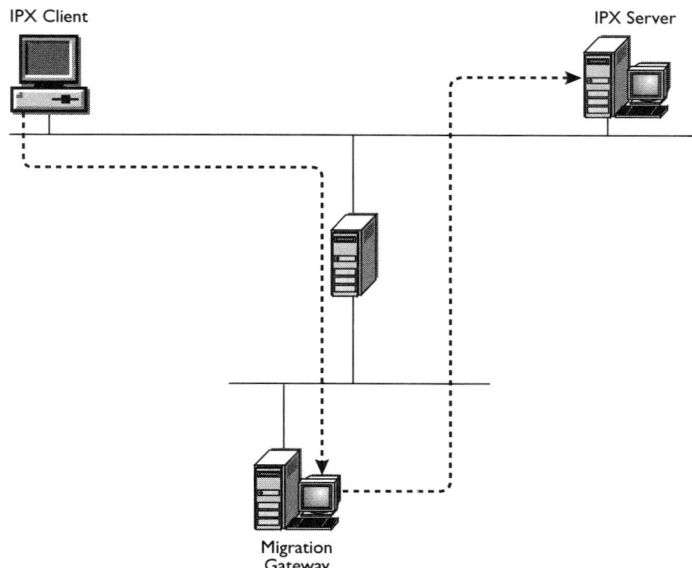

FIGURE 15.12

All Communication Between the CMD Client and the IPX Server Must Be Routed through the Remote Migration Gatewcy.

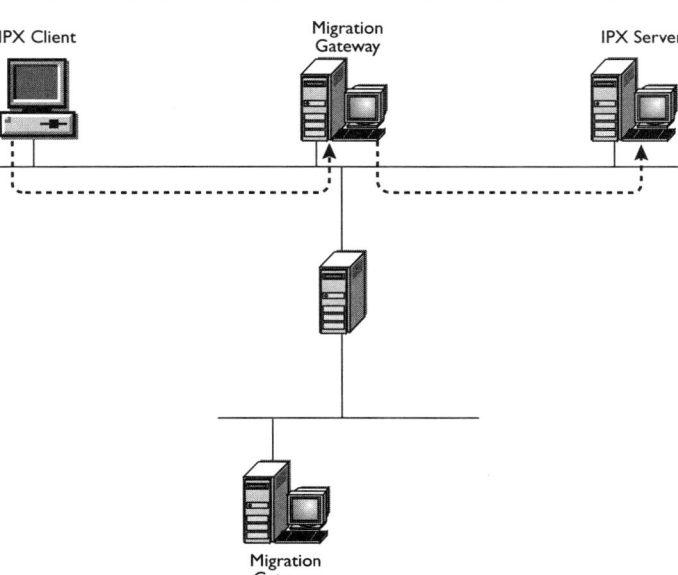

FIGURE 15.13

A Local Migration Gateway Enables Communication to Take Place without Routing.

Migration Strategies

There are a variety of configurations that enable clients to communicate with NetWare servers and with TCP/IP services. Here are a few of the possibilities:

▶ Clients are configured with both IPX and TCP/IP protocol stacks. They can use IPX to communicate with NetWare servers and use IP to communicate with the Internet and local TCP/IP services.

▶ Clients and servers are configured with NetWare/IP. Clients communicate with NetWare servers using IPX encapsulated in IP. Clients communicate with TCP/IP services using TCP/IP.

▶ Clients are configured with IPX. NetWare servers are configured with IP Compatibility Mode. A Migration Gateway enables IPX clients to communicate with the NetWare servers.

▶ Clients are configured with IP Compatibility Mode. NetWare servers are IPX. A Migration Gateway enables clients to communicate with the NetWare server.

▶ Clients and servers are configured with IP Compatibility Mode. Clients use Pure IP to communicate with NetWare servers and with TCP/IP services.

I'm sure we could come up with a few more possible variations. The idea behind the list is that multiple strategies exist for getting from one protocol configuration to another.

If you are not planning to upgrade all your NetWare servers to NetWare 5, you are stuck with a hybrid network. NetWare 3 and 4 servers can be configured with NetWare/IP. NetWare 2 servers can only use IPX. You can use the Migration Gateway to support communication between your legacy IPX servers and NetWare 5 servers configured with Pure IP.

But let's assume that you have a NetWare network configured only with IPX and that you want to migrate it to Pure IP. How would you go about it? Let's go through a simple scenario that involves a single network first. Then we'll look at more complex scenarios that involve internetworks.

Migrating a Simple Network

Suppose you have the network shown in Figure 15.14. It is a one hundred percent IPX network that you want to convert to Pure IP. Here is one strategy that limits the risk of service disruption:

1. Upgrade Servers A, B, and C to NetWare 5. Configure them with both IPX and IP protocols. Make sure that the network operates normally before you add IP to the protocol mixture. Test IP communication by PINGing the various interfaces. Clients continue to communicate with servers using IPX.

2. Identify Server A as a Migration Gateway and load SCMD with the Migration Gateway feature (LOAD SCMD /G).

3. Identify Server B as a Migration Gateway and load SCMD with the Migration Gateway feature (LOAD SCMD /G). To provide fault tolerance, at least two Migration Gateways should be enabled.

4. Unbind IPX from the network adapter on Server C. Add the command LOAD SCMD to AUTOEXEC.NCF. When you restart the server, Server C will function as a Pure IP server with support for Compatibility Mode. Ensure that IPX clients can communicate with Server C through the Migration Gateways. All applications hosted by the server should function normally.

5. Upgrade a client to the NetWare 5 client, selecting *IP with IPX Compatibility* as the installation option. Ensure that the client can communicate with all NetWare servers.

6. Upgrade remaining clients to the NetWare 5 client as described in Step 5. All clients now communicate with the NetWare servers using IP with CMD.

7. Disable the Migration Gateway feature on the Servers A and B. (Remove the /G option from the LOAD SCMD command.)

8. If tests do not detect any IPX-dependent applications, you may choose to disable CMD support on the servers and clients.

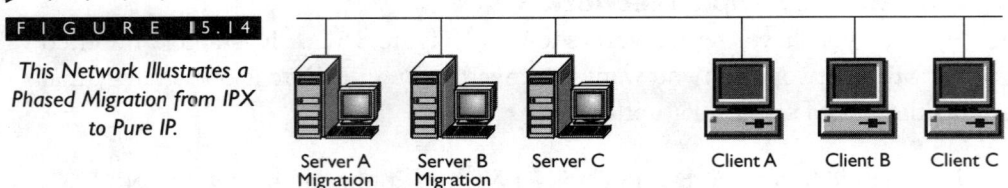

F I G U R E   15.14

This Network Illustrates a
Phased Migration from IPX
to Pure IP.

Server A
Migration
Gateway

Server B
Migration
Gateway

Server C

Client A

Client B

Client C

NOTE

It is possible to load SCMD.NLM as a Migration Agent on a NetWare 4.11 or 4.2 server. If your network supports NetWare/IP, you may wish to configure Migration Agents on existing NetWare 4.11/4.2 servers so that it is unnecessary to enable NetWare/IP support on a NetWare 5 server. The Migration Agent treats NetWare/IP network segments as IPX network segments.

Migrating an Internetwork

Figure 15.15 depicts an IPX internetwork. In this case, all routers are NetWare servers. This enables us to use the routers as Migration Gateways. Here is one strategy for migrating the network in discrete phases:

1. Upgrade all routers to NetWare 5. Configure all interfaces with IPX and IP. Use existing network numbers on the IPX interfaces. Ensure that the IPX communication infrastructure functions as before and that IP communications function from end-to-end.

2. Enable each NetWare 5 router with Migration Gateway support (LOAD SCMD /G).

3. Migrate Segment A as described in the section "Migrating a Simple Network." All clients should be able to communicate with all servers on the internetwork.

4. Migrate Segment B as described in Step 3.

5. Migrate Segment C as described in Step 3. All clients now communicate with all servers using IP with CMD.

6. Disable Migration Gateway support on the routers and unbind IPX from the router interfaces.

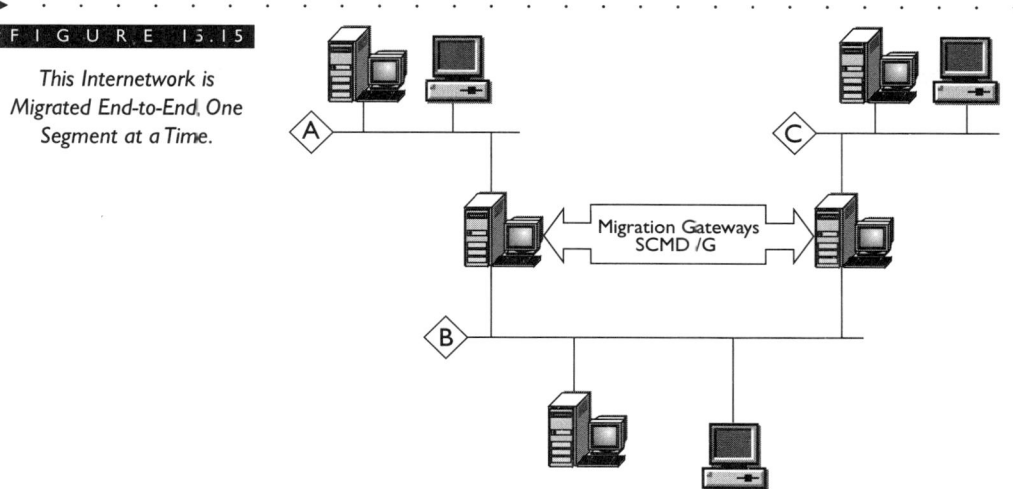

This Internetwork is Migrated End-to-End, One Segment at a Time.

Migrating the Backbone First

In the preceding example, the network segments formed a neat chain and I could migrate them from one end to another. This approach ensured that migration didn't interrupt communication at any of the network interfaces.

But large networks are typically configured in a backbone configuration where one network — often a high-performance network — serves as a central communication hub between leaf networks that provide service to client nodes. Figure 15.16 illustrates a network architected with a backbone segment. Backbone migrations are complicated by several factors:

▶ The backbone may serve as a communication hub only. There may be no NetWare servers on the backbone that can be configured as Migration Gateways.

▶ Typically, third-party routers are used to connect leaf networks to the backbone. Routers based on the NetWare MultiProtocol Router typically do not provide the performance required for a backbone configuration. Consequently, the routers cannot be configured as Migration Gateways.

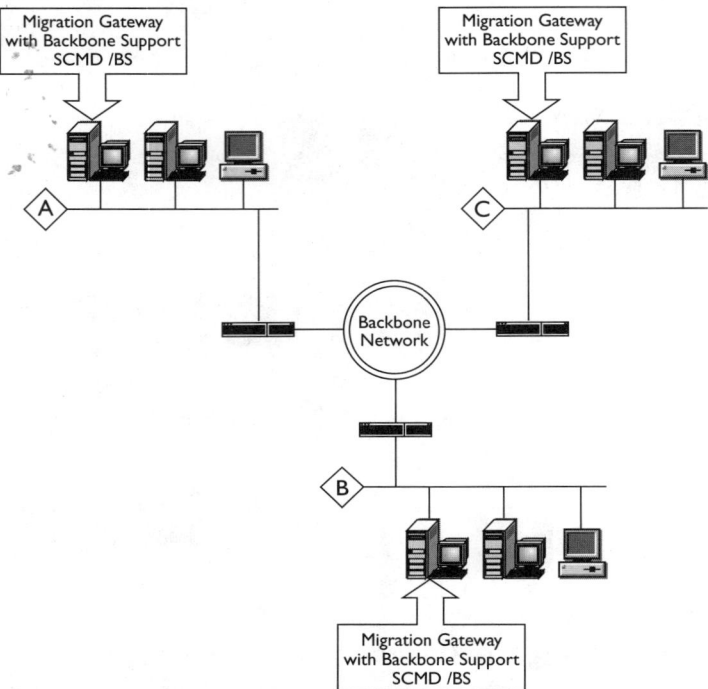

FIGURE   5.16

This Internetwork is Migrated Starting with the Backbone and Proceeding to Leaf Segments.

▶ It is important not to create a communication hole on the backbone that prevents communication between the leaf segments.

▶ There may be so many servers that we don't want to migrate them all at once It may be necessary to leave IPX servers in place for some time.

NOTE

Many of these same concerns apply to internetworks that incorporate a WAN link. There are no servers on the WAN, and hence no Migration Gateways. Also, the routers connecting LANs to WANs are typically dedicated routers that cannot host Migration Gateways. Simply picture a WAN link in the place of the backbone network segment and you will see how this example applies to WANs as well.

Let's assume that your immediate goal is to remove IPX from the backbone. Here are two benefits to removing IPX from the backbone first:

► If your organization is using third-party routers, you are probably paying for each protocol stack supported by the router. IPX support can be costly.

► Converting the backbone to IP eliminates IPX housekeeping traffic such as SAP and RIP broadcasts. SLP eats up much less network bandwidth.

Because the routers cannot be configured as Migration Gateways, we need to employ a strategy such as the following:

1. Enable IP on all router interfaces.

2. Identify the first leaf segment to be migrated. We will migrate Leaf Segment A first.

3. Install NetWare 5 with Migration Gateway support for one server on Segment A. Configure the server with IPX and IP protocol stacks and enable SCMD with the Backbone Support feature (LOAD SCMD /BS).

4. Install a Migration Gateway with Backbone Support on Leaf Segment C as described in Step 3.

5. Disable IPX on the backbone routers. This may disrupt service, and you should schedule network down time for this test. Thoroughly test communication among the gateways. All servers should appear in the output of the DISPLAY SERVERS command, for example. (IPX-only servers are not discovered by the DISPLAY SLP SERVICES command.) Then test clients to ensure that they can connect to all NetWare servers. If all tests are successful, IPX can be permanently removed from the backbone routers.

6. Migrate Leaf Segment A as described in the section "Migrating a Simple Network." The Migration Gateways may be disabled when all IPX clients and servers are upgraded to Pure IP.

7. Migrate Leaf Segments B and C as described in Step 6.

▶ · ◀

One Protocol At Last

This is as close as we get to network nirvana: a homogeneous network on which all communication utilizes a common protocol. Because the Internet revolution forces us to add TCP/IP connections to most of our LANs, single protocol networks have been rare. We have had to make IPX and IP co-exist. As you can see, however, dual protocols are no longer required on NetWare networks. No, migrations aren't easy, but I think you will agree that Pure IP is a worthy goal.

This is the last chapter that addresses core NetWare support. From now on, we can address the configuration of two quintessential TCP/IP services: FTP and the World Wide Web. NetWare 5 includes solid FTP and Web servers, and in just a bit you will know how to support both services.

## CHAPTER 16

Managing an FTP Server

Even with the advent of the World Wide Web, FTP remains the primary method of data transfer among TCP/IP hosts. To enable NetWare servers to support FTP, Novell has included the Novell FTP Services with NetWare 5. The FTP Service is bundled with several other services in the UNIX Print Services.

Novell FTP Services have some special advantages that apply specifically to the NetWare environment. A user who FTPs into the NetWare FTP server can use it as a gateway to reach other NetWare servers regardless of whether they are running FTP services. Novell FTP Services also support NDS. Users can use NDS directory maps to access directories anywhere on the NDS tree.

This chapter will cover the basic procedures for installing, managing, and using the Novell FTP server. Before we can get to FTP, however, we need to take a couple of side trips. You will need to become familiar with UNICON, the NetWare server utility used to manage all of the UNIX-related services. Also, you will need to understand the Network Information System, a naming database used with the FTP server.

Introduction to UNICON

The NetWare DNS server is administered using the UNICON server utility, as are many of the TCP/IP services that run on NetWare servers. UNICON is installed when you install UNIX Print Services. During the first installation of UNICON, it is necessary to designate UNICON administrators with various levels of privileges.

NOTE **When UNICON is created, two NCF files are installed that can be used to start and stop UNICON with all its elements. Execute UNISTART.NCF to start UNICON, and execute UNISTOP.NCF to stop the services UNICON supports. When any service installs UNICON, the command UNISTART.NCF is added to the AUTOEXEC.NCF file so that services supported by UNICON are started when the server boots.**

UNICON is started with the command LOAD UNICON. The main menu of UNICON is shown in Figure 16.1. Although any user can start UNICON, he or she must be given specific rights to perform certain UNICON functions.

▶ · ◀

The UNICON Main Menu

When UNICON is installed, four group objects are created that convey different sets of UNICON capabilities. These groups are:

- ▶ **UNICON MANAGER.** Membership in this group enables full use of the UNICON utility and access to all menu options. (However, users must be members of the UNICON HOST MANAGER group to manage hosts in the DNS database.)

- ▶ **UNICON SERVICES MANAGER.** Membership in this group gives the user access to the Start/Stop Services and Manage Services menu options, enabling the user to start, stop, and manage services.

- ▶ **UNICON HOST MANAGER.** Membership in this group gives the user access to the Manage Global Objects and Manage Hosts menu options, enabling the user to create, delete, and modify host entries.

- ▶ **UNICON USER/GROUP MANAGER.** Membership in this group enables the user to manage UNICON users and groups.

To assign specific UNICON capabilities to users, use NWAdmin to assign the appropriate group memberships to their User objects.

Because UNICON is used to manage several services, no attempt is made here to cover all its features. In this chapter, we will look only at features required to manage the FTP service.

▶ · ◀

Planning for Installation

Installation and management of the Novell FTP Server is not difficult, but you should take some time to do some planning before you begin. This section discusses several areas you should consider prior to installation.

User Accounts

One decision you must make is how you will secure user access to the FTP server. Will you support anonymous FTP? Will you permit users to log in using their NetWare accounts?

By far the most common approach is to support anonymous logins. When users log in anonymously to the Novell FTP Services, they are not required to enter a valid password. Anonymous users are usually given strictly defined access to strictly limited areas of the server.

If you choose, you can require users to log in to the FTP server with a valid user account and password. Security and file management for the Novell FTP Services are tied into normal NetWare procedures. Users can log in to the NetWare FTP server using their standard NetWare user accounts and passwords, in which case their access to resources is regulated by their trustee assignments and group memberships. In other words, you don't need to learn new security procedures to support an FTP server.

But there is a downside to using users' NetWare accounts to secure FTP access. The FTP login procedure transmits user accounts and passwords in clear text that can be read by anyone equipped with a network protocol analyzer. This is particularly a problem on the Internet, which can be snooped with readily available software. Because a surprisingly large number of potential intruders are equipped with all they need to see your passwords, requiring passwords for FTP logins may actually reduce your system security by giving intruders the passwords they need to gain access to your server. If you will use passwords to control access to FTP, create separate NetWare user accounts for use with FTP and carefully set the rights for those accounts so that they cannot be used to jeopardize the security of your system.

In summary, closely controlled support for anonymous FTP may leave the fewest doors open to your network. Be careful to tie the anonymous user account up with tight security restrictions.

Directories

You need to give careful consideration to the directories that will be available to FTP clients, particularly if your FTP server can be accessed from the Internet. In many cases, you will want to set up a separate directory for access by FTP clients. User access should be restricted to the FTP directory and its subdirectories.

Particularly if your server will be connected to the Internet, it is a bad idea to permit FTP users freedom to roam the server. Even users who are limited to scanning directories can learn a great deal about your system.

Installation Context

When you install the UNIX Print Services, a number of objects are added to the NDS tree. These objects will be added to the default NDS context, which is determined as follows:

1. If the bindery context is set, that context is used. When NetWare 5 is installed, the server object is placed in a container object, and the container object is established as the bindery context. The bindery context can be changed with the SET BINDERY CONTEXT command.

2. If a bindery context is not set, the NetWare servers location in the NDS tree is used as the default NDS context, which is the container where the server's own NDS object is located. For a server with the full name .CN=pseudo1.O=pseudo, the default context will be O=pseudo.

3. The default NDS context can be set manually by editing the NDS_CONTEXT parameter in the file SYS:ETC\NWPARAMS.

Before you install UNIX Print Services, you should determine the context in which installation will take place and change it if desired.

You should also review the TCP/IP configuration on the computer where UNIX Print Services will be installed. Ensure that IP addresses are properly configured. Also, verify that the IP address of at least one DNS server has been configured on the DNS Resolver Configuration fields. A DNS server should be configured and made operational before attempting to install the UNIX Print Services.

Network Information System

The *Network Information System* (NIS) is a name database used by several of the NetWare-based UNIX services, including NetWare-to-UNIX printing and the Network File System (NFS). The primary use of NIS is to provide mappings between NetWare and UNIX user accounts so that users can access services transparently using the account information under which they are currently logged in.

FTP has its own login and user authentication procedures and does not make use of NIS. However, you will be asked to provide some NIS configuration information when you install the UNIX Print Services. Unless NIS is already operating on your network, simply configure a local NIS server as described in the installation procedures. You can always reconfigure NIS at a later time.

Installing UNIX Print Services

To install Novell FTP Services on IntranetWare:

1. Install and configure TCP/IP protocol support on the NetWare server.

2. Insert the NetWare 5 Operating CD-ROM in a drive on the NetWare 5 server.

3. Enter the command **CDROM** to mount the Novell FTP Services CD-ROM.

4. Load NWCONFIG.

5. Select *Product options* in the Installation Options menu.

6. Move the cursor up to highlight *Install Unix Print Services* and press Enter.

7. Press Enter to confirm the path to the installation files.

8. For the purposes of this chapter, you can ignore the README.TXT file, but you should examine it at a later time.

9. Next you are prompted *Enter the drive and/or path for booting NetWare*. Enter the drive letter and directory in which SERVER.EXE is installed (C:\NWSERVER by default).

10. After files are copied to the server, you are required to log in. Enter a username and password for an account with administrator access to the displayed context.

11. Next, you must specify the location of your NIS server. Choose *Local NIS* or *Remote NIS*. If NIS is not operational on your network, select *Local NIS* and configure NIS with default information.

12. If you specify *Local NIS*, you will see the Setup (Local NIS) Name Service form (shown in Figure 16.2) where you specify the names and addresses of the remote servers as follows:

- **NIS Domain.** Enter the name of the NIS domain to be created. This may be the same as an existing DNS domain, but the name can also be unique to NIS. The default NIS domain name is the name of the server on which the installation is performed.

- **NIS Server.** This field specifies the IP address of the NIS server and must match one of the interfaces on the server. For a local NIS server installation, this field cannot be modified.

- **DNS Domain.** Enter the DNS domain in which host names will be placed. The default domain is the domain specified in the DNS Resolver Configuration fields of the NetWare server's TCP/IP protocol configuration.

- **DNS Server.** This field matches the IP address of the DNS server specified in the DNS Resolver Configuration fields of the NetWare server's TCP/IP protocol configuration. The value cannot be modified.

FIGURE 16.2

Setting Up Local Access to Name Services

13. If you specified *Remote NIS* service, you must be prepared to manage hosts, UNIX users, and UNIX groups on the remote name server. Management of UNIX hosts, users, and groups on UNICON will be read-only. You will see the Setup (Remote NIS) Name Service form, which is similar to the one shown in Figure 16.2. Specify the names and addresses of the remote servers as follows:

- **NIS Domain.** Enter the name of the NIS domain created on the remote NIS server.

- **NIS Server.** This field specifies the IP address of the remote NIS server.

- **DNS Domain.** Enter the DNS domain in which host names are placed. The default domain is the domain specified in the DNS Resolver Configuration fields of the NetWare server's TCP/IP protocol configuration.

- **DNS Server.** Enter the IP address of the remote DNS server. The default is the IP address of the DNS server specified in the DNS Resolver Configuration fields of the NetWare server's TCP/IP protocol configuration.

14. If NIS is being installed locally, the installation program attempts to import data to NIS from any hosts, password, or group files available in the SYS:\ETC or SYS:\ETC\DBSOURCE\NIS.

15. After you see the message *Product Initialization Complete*, press ESC until you return to the NWCONFIG Other Installation Actions menu.

All required modules are loaded when the UNIX Print Services are installed. There is no need to execute the UNISTART command at this time. You can immediately begin to manage the supported services using UNICON.

Managing the FTP Service

The FTP service is managed using UNICON, which will be installed with the FTP service if it is not already present on the host server. To administer the FTP service, you must log in with an account that is a member of the UNICON MANAGERS group.

Starting and Stopping the FTP Service

After installing the UNIX Print Services, use UNICON to start and stop the FTP service as follows:

1. Load UNICON and log in with a user account that is a member of the UNICON MANAGER group.

2. Select *Start/Stop Services* in the Main Menu to open the Running Services list.

3. To start the DNS server, press Insert. Select *FTP Server* from the Available Services list and press Enter. The service will be added to the Running Services list.

4. To stop the DNS server, select *FTP Server* in the Running Services list and press Delete. At the *Stop Service* prompt, choose Yes to confirm that the service should be stopped.

Configuring FTP Server Parameters

Several parameters can be adjusted to configure operation of the FTP service. The procedure is as follows:

1. Load UNICON and log in with a user account that is a member of the UNICON MANAGER group.

2. Select *Manage Services* in the Main Menu to open the Manage Services list.

3. Select *FTP Server* in the Manage Services list to open the FTP Administration menu shown in Figure 16.3

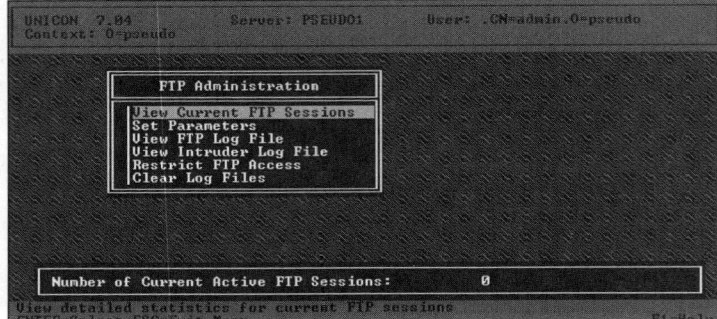

The FTP Administration Menu

4. Select *Set Parameters* to open the FTP Server Parameters form shown in Figure 16.4. The fields in this form are as follows:

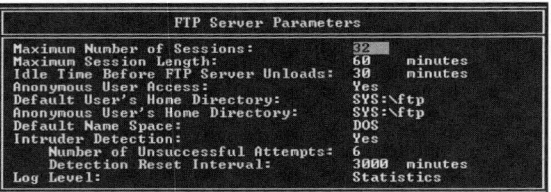

Configuring FTP Server Parameters

- **Maximum Number of Sessions.** This parameter determines the number of connections the FTP server will support. Your server hardware and the speed of the network connection will determine how many sessions the server can support without service degradation. This parameter has a range of 1–64 sessions.

- **Maximum Session Length.** This parameter enables you to limit the duration of a connection. A value of –1 establishes unlimited session length.

- **Idle Time Before FTP Server Unloads.** If no connections are established with the FTP server in the time interval specified, the server will unload. A setting of –1 disables the idle timeout.

- **Anonymous User Access.** If this value is *Yes*, the server permits users to log in with the username anonymous. If this value is *No*, anonymous login is disabled. If this value is *Yes*, UNICON creates an NDS user account named "anonymous," which is used to define anonymous access.

- **Default User's Home Directory.** If a user logs in using an account that does not have a home directory, the user will be connected to this default directory along with the FTP service. Select this field to open a form (similar to Figure 16.5) where you can specify the volume and directory path for the default user's home directory.

- **Anonymous User's Home Directory.** If a user logs anonymously, the user will be connected to this directory. (See the following section "Supporting Anonymous Logins.") Select this field to open a form (similar to Figure 16.5) where you can specify the volume and directory path for the anonymous user's home directory.

- **Default Name Space.** This parameter determines whether the user will see files and directories in a DOS or NFS (UNIX) style. Although the default name space is DOS, most FTP servers provide a UNIX name space.

- **Intruder Detection.** If intruder detection is enabled, the server records unsuccessful login attempts in the Intruder Log File. Also, SNMP alert messages are sent to the SNMP management console.

- **Number of Unsuccessful Attempts.** If intruder detection is enabled, this parameter determines how many unsuccessful login attempts can be made before a login failure is logged.

- **Detection Reset Interval.** If intruder detection is enabled, this parameter determines how long the FTP server keeps a record of an unsuccessful login attempts. Login failures must exceed the Number of Unsuccessful Attempts within the Detection Reset Interval before a login failure is logged.

- **Log Level.** This field determines the level of detail for information recorded in the FTP log file. The following options are available:

  None. No information is logged.

  Logins. Only login information is logged.

  Statistics. Log records record the number of files copied to and from the FTP server, and also records login information.

  File. All FTP transactions are logged, including login activity and statistics.

5. Press Escape to exit the FTP Server Parameters form, saving any changes that have been made.

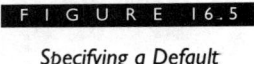

FIGURE 16.5

Specifying a Default Directory

Supporting Anonymous Logins

The FTP server uses an anonymous user account that requires no password when connecting. (Earlier versions of the NetWare FTP service required the configuration of a separate anonymous NetWare user account.) The home directory for anonymous FTP users is specified in UNICON as follows:

1. Load UNICON and log in with a user account that is a member of the UNICON MANAGER group.

2. Select *Manage Services* in the Main Menu to open the Manage Services list.

3. Select *FTP Server* in the Manage Services list to open the FTP Administration menu.

4. Select *Set Parameters* to open the FTP Server Parameters form.

5. If necessary, change the value of the *Anonymous User Access* field to *Yes*.

6. Select the *Anonymous User's Home Directory* field and press Enter to open the form shown in Figure 16.5.

7. Specify the volume name in the *Volume Name* field.

8. Specify the directory path in the *Directory Name* field. If the directory does not already exist, you can direct UNICON to create it.

9. Press Escape to exit.

When the value of the *Anonymous User Access* field is changed to *Yes*, UNICON creates an NDS User object named "anonymous." This account is given the RWCEMF and A rights to the directory that is specified in the *Anonymous User's Home Directory*. These default rights enable the user to both read files from and write files to the anonymous user's home directory. In most cases, however, anonymous users are permitted only to read files from the FTP server. Unless you require write access for anonymous users, you may wish to revoke the Erase, Write, Modify, and Access Control trustee rights for the anonymous user account.

Unlike other user accounts, anonymous users cannot access directories above their home directory.

If you wish to permit anonymous users to upload files, you may wish to establish a directory with the Create permission alone, enabling the user to create files in the directory but not to delete or modify files already in existence.

Because the anonymous user account does not require a password, anonymous users will not be prompted for a password when connecting to the FTP server. As a result, operation of the Novell FTP Server is a bit at variance with normal FTP practice. On most FTP servers, anonymous users are prompted for a password, but any text the user enters is accepted. The convention is that users should enter their e-mail addresses when asked for a password.

Restricting FTP Access

The file SYS:ETC\RESTRICT.FTP is an editable configuration file that defines FTP access. This file is installed with the FTP Server and must be present; otherwise, no access is permitted to the FTP server.

You can edit RESTRICT.FTP as follows:

1. Load UNICON and log in with a user account that is a member of the UNICON MANAGER group.

2. Select *Manage Services* in the Main Menu to open the Manage Services list.

3. Select *FTP Server* in the Manage Services list to open the FTP Administration menu.

4. Select *Restrict FTP Access* to edit RESTROCT.FTP.

5. Edit the file following standard NetWare editing procedures. The editor is shown in Figure 16.6.

6. Press Escape to save changes.

▶ · ◀

FIGURE 16.6

Editing the Access Control File

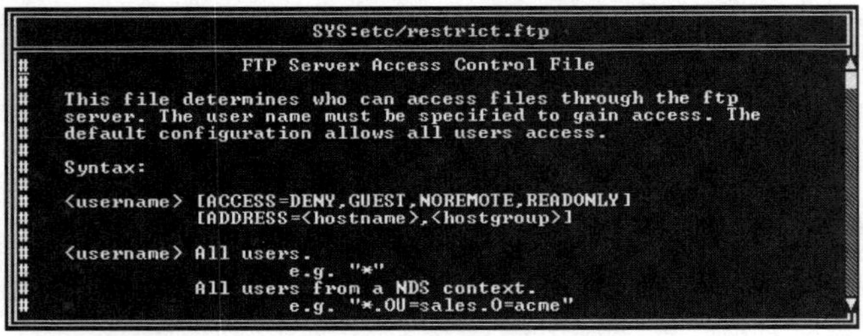

Initially, RESTRICT.FTP contains only one active record, which is simply an asterisk (*) that indicates that all users are permitted and that no restrictions are applied. All other lines in RESTRICT.FTP are preceded by a # character that indicates the lines are comments.

If you wish to define specific access characteristics, first add a # to the beginning of the line containing * to deactivate that line. Then add the desired entries to the file as described below.

Entries to define FTP server access have the following format:

```
username [ACCESS=GUEST, READONLY, NOREMOTE, DENY, NORMAL]

    [ADDRESS=hostname,ipaddress]
```

The variable *username* describes one or more users to which the entry applies. The following types of entries are accepted:

- A * by itself matches all users.

- A * in an NDS context matches all users in the context (for example, *.ou=corp.o=jazziz matches all users in the container ou=corp.o=jazziz).

- A username without a context identifies the user of that name in the default context.

- A complete pathname identifies a specific user (for example, .cn=charlie.o=jazziz).

The ACCESS parameter defines the type of access that is permitted. When appropriate, more than one argument can appear, with the arguments separated by a | character. The arguments are as follows:

- GUEST restricts the user to his or her home directory and its subdirectories. The user cannot access directories above the home directory.

- READONLY restricts the user from copying files.

- NOREMOTE restricts the user from accessing files on other NetWare servers. The user can access files only on the FTP server.

- DENY prevents this user from logging in to the server.

- NORMAL imposes no restrictions on the user. This is the default setting, and is applied when an ACCESS section is not present in the user definition.

The ADDRESS parameter specifies the hosts affected by this access control entry. If the ADDRESS parameter is absent, the entry applies to all hosts. The following arguments can be included with the ADDRESS parameter:

▶ *hostname* specifies a specific TCP/IP host by name.

▶ *ipaddress* specifies a host by IP address.

The following access restriction applies to the user JIM, restricts him to guest access, and prevents him from downloading files:

```
JIM ACCESS=GUEST|READONLY
```

This access restriction applies to all users, preventing them from accessing remote servers:

```
* ACCESS=NOREMOTE
```

Here is an entry that permits all users from .OU=CORP.O=JAZZIZ to access the file server, but restricts them to access from the host DIZZY:

```
*.OU=CORP.O=JAZZIZ ADDRESS=DIZZY
```

Finally, here is an entry that prevents the user ADMIN from accessing the FTP server, which may be desirable given the power of ADMIN and the poor security of FTP:

```
.ADMIN.O=JAZZIZ ACCESS=DENY
```

FTP Server Log Files

Two log files record FTP server events:

▶ FTPSERV.LOG is the FTP Service log file and contains an activity record for FTP sessions.

▶ INTRUDER.FTP contains records of failed login attempts.

The FTP Service Log File

To view the FTP Service log file, do the following:

1. Load UNICON and log in.

2. Select *Manage Services* in the Main Menu to open the Manage Services list.

3. Select *FTP Server* in the Manage Services list to open the FTP Administration menu.

4. Select *View FTP Log File*. Figure 16.7 shows an example of a record in the FTP log file.

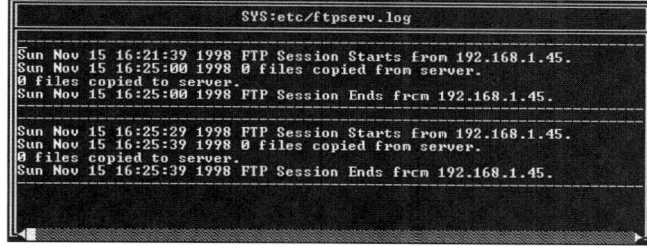

FIGURE 16.7

The FTP Log File

The Intruder Log File

If intruder detection is enabled on the FTP Server Parameters form, UNICON maintains an intruder log. The intruder log file records the following information for failed login attempts:

▸ Time of the attempt

▸ Login name of the user attempting access

▸ Incorrect password

To view the FTP Service log file, do the following:

1. Load UNICON and log in.

2. Select *Manage Services* in the Main Menu to open the Manage Services list.

3. Select *FTP Server* in the Manage Services list to open the FTP Administration menu.

4. Select *View Intruder Log File*. If intruder logging is enabled, the intruder log will list the IP address, username, and password used for any user whose failed login attempts exceed the configured thresholds.

Clearing the Log Files

Log files can grow quite large, and you should clear them periodically. To clear the log files:

1. Load UNICON and log in with a user account that is a member of the UNICON MANAGER group.

2. Select *Manage Services* in the Main Menu to open the Manage Services list.

3. Select *FTP Server* in the Manage Services list to open the FTP Administration menu.

4. Select *Clear Log Files*.

5. Select *FTP* or *Intruder* to specify which log should be cleared.

6. At the *Delete Log File* prompt, select *Yes* to confirm the operation.

Managing Active Sessions

You can view a list of active sessions and close sessions if necessary. To manage active FTP sessions, do the following:

1. Load UNICON and log in with a user account that is a member of the UNICON MANAGER group.

2. Select *Manage Services* in the Main Menu to open the Manage Services list.

3. Select *FTP Server* in the Manage Services list to open the FTP Administration menu.

4. Select *View Current FTP Sessions*. Figure 16.8 shows an FTP server with one active session.

5. To close an active session, select the session and press Delete. When prompted, confirm that the session should be deleted.

FIGURE 16.8

Viewing Active FTP Sessions

User	Remote Address
.CN=ANONYMOUS.O=pseudo	192.168.1.45

Using the Novell FTP Server

Chapter 6 discussed using FTP, so the only concerns here regard special features of the Novell FTP Server. Three such features are:

- ▶ Accessing remote NetWare servers

- ▶ Using the STAT command

- ▶ Using the SITE command

Accessing Remote NetWare Servers

Users who have NetWare accounts can use the NetWare FTP Server as a gateway, enabling them to access files available to them on other NetWare servers, even if the remote NetWare servers are not running the FTP Service.

To enable users to access remote NetWare servers, execute the following command at the console of the NetWare server running the FTP service. This command can be added to the AUTOEXEC.NCF file if desired:

```
SET REPLY TO GET NEAREST SERVER=ON
```

After a user logs on to the server running the FTP server, files on remote NetWare servers can be specified using the following syntax:

```
//remoteserver/volume/pathname
```

where

- *remoteserver* is the name of a remote NetWare server.

- *volume* is the name of a volume on the remote server.

- *pathname* is the directory path and filename of the file to be accessed, expressed in UNIX format with forward slashes.

Here is an example of a remote file specification that identifies the file JUNE96.DOC in the REPORTS directory of the DATA1 volume on the WIDGETS server:

```
//WIDGETS/DATA1/REPORTS/JUNE98.DOC
```

There are a few restrictions that affect remote file access:

- Anonymous users cannot access remote files.

- Remote files cannot be renamed or moved between servers.

- Only the DOS name space is supported on the remote servers, even though the NFS name space may have been added to the volume.

- The / character specifies the root directory of the local FTP server. Entering the command **cd /** changes the current working directory to the root directory of the FTP server.

- The SITE command, described below, is not supported on remote servers.

Using the STAT Command

The STAT command reports the status of the current connection or the status for a file or directory. The syntax is as follows:

```
QUOTE STAT [pathname]
```

The following dialog shows an example of the data reported by the STAT command:

```
ftp> quote stat
211-Status on WIDGETS
        Client node:           128.1.0.50
        Client name:           .CN=ANONYMOUS.O=PSEUDO
        UNIX U++++++-er Name:       No UNIX User Account
        UNIX UID:              User assumes NetWare Rights
        Directory:             /
        Type:                  Ascii Non-Print
        Structure:             File
        Mode:                  Stream
        Namespace:             DOS
        NDS Context:           O=jazziz
211-End of Status.
```

Notice that the directory is reported as /. The default directory for the user ANONYMOUS is PSEUDO_SYS:FTP, but as far as the user is concerned, this is the root directory.

The SITE Command

The SITE command accesses features specific to the Novell FTP Server. The syntax is as follows:

```
QUOTE SITE [HELP | CX | DOS | NFS | OU | PATH | SERVER | SLIST]
```

Options for the SITE command are as follows:

▶ **HELP.** Displays a description of the SITE command with its syntax.

▶ **CX.** Enables users to change the NDS context. The CX parameter alone reports the current NDS context of the FTP client. To change the current context, the CX parameter is followed by the full or relative name for the new context.

▸ **DOS.** Changes the current name space to DOS. Filenames and directories are displayed and accessed using the DOS format.

▸ **NFS.** Changes the current name space to NFS. Filenames and directories are displayed and accessed using the UNIX format.

▸ **OU.** Displays the NDS organizations (containers) below the current NDS context.

▸ **PATH.** Lists available NetWare directory maps in the user's current context with their descriptions.

▸ **SERVER.** Displays all NetWare servers in the current context.

▸ **SLIST.** Lists NetWare servers identified both in NDS and the Bindery.

For the PATH, SERVER, and SLIST parameters, a name template can be used to limit the listed objects. For example, the command QUOTE SERVER ABC* lists servers in the current context whose names begin with ABC.

That's One Down

In this short chapter, you have learned to add one of the most important TCP/IP applications to your network. As you have seen, setting up an FTP server requires little effort, but it can be a significant enhancement to any network. Now your users can access files on your server, or even send you files, via the Internet. That's a lot easier than dialing up long-distance.

Now, let's move on to the second application you will learn to support: a World Wide Web server. In the next chapter, you will see that a Web server also can be easily added to your NetWare network.

## CHAPTER 17

Building a Web Server

I don't need to preach to you about the World Wide Web. If your organization doesn't already have Web servers on the Internet or on its private network, you know with near certainty that your future includes Web server administration. Fortunately, NetWare 5 includes the Netscape FastTrack Server for NetWare, a product resulting from the Novonyx partnership between Novell and Netscape Communications.

FastTrack is an easily administered Web server that runs on the Novell platform. It is so easy to manage that you can use it immediately after installation, without needing to change a single parameter. Simply add your Web content to the appropriate directory and your Web server is up and running. But FastTrack has some advanced features as well: features that enhance its versatility and may be all you need in a Web server. This chapter will cover the essential details you need to know about the installation, configuration, and management of the FastTrack Web server.

My goal in this chapter is to cover the basics of the FastTrack Web server. FastTrack is a pretty elaborate piece of software, and I can't cover everything you need to know about Web server administration in a single chapter. I've tried to identify the essential tasks so that you can get a fast start with FastTrack.

Installing FastTrack

The FastTrack server runs on a NetWare 4.11 or later server and is installed from a Windows client. The installation procedure is quite straightforward, and little planning is required.

Requirements for the FastTrack server are as follows:

► NetWare Version 4.11 or higher.

► NetWare 4 must include CLIB 4.11J or later.

► NetWare 4 must have long filename support. The installation program adds long filename support if necessary. NetWare 5 has long filename support as a standard feature.

- If you want to integrate users and groups with NDS via the administration server, NetWare 4 must have the NLDAP gateway installed, available from www.novell.com.

- At least 32MB RAM with 64MB recommended.

- 100MB free on the SYS: volume.

Requirements for the client used to install FastTrack are as follows:

- Windows 95/98 or Windows NT 4.0.

- 32-bit NetWare client.

- Netscape 3.x browser (or later version).

- CD-ROM drive or a connection to a networked CD-ROM drive (the CD-ROM could be mounted on the target NetWare server).

- 100MB free on hard disk (used temporarily during installation).

To begin installation, mount the NetWare 5 Operating System CD-ROM on the Windows workstation and execute the program \Products\ Webserv\ Setup.exe. I won't walk you through the entire installation process, which is controlled by an easily understood Wizard, but here are some highlights:

- Configure DNS prior to installation and include appropriate Address records for the target NetWare server. (See Chapter 11.)

- Know the IP address and DNS name of the target server. You may wish to add a CNAME entry to DNS so that the Web server can be accessed by the convention of www.yourdomain (for example, www.pseudo-corp.com).

- Prior to installation, determine the server port that will be used by the Web server. The default port is 80. Users must specify the port in URLs if a different port is configured.

▶ Before you start, you must be logged in to the target NetWare server and have a drive mapped to the root of the SYS: volume. You are required to specify the mapped drive letter to identify the installation target drive. You cannot specify the directory in which FastTrack will be installed.

▶ You can update or overwrite an existing FastTrack installation.

▶ During installation, you will specify a port used to access the FastTrack administration server. The setup program will test the port you specify to verify that the port is not already in use on the target server. Remember this port. You cannot administer the server without this port number.

▶ During installation, you specify a username and password that will be used as the SuperUser account for the administration server. Remember this information. You cannot administer the server without it.

After installation is complete, Setup starts the server and launches Netscape Communicator to display the default page for the new Web site. The Web server is now operational. Actually, two Web servers are operational:

▶ The main Web server, on port 80, is the Web server that serves Web objects to users.

▶ The administration server is used by administrators and users to configure the Web server and manage user access. The administration server is associated with the port specified during FastTrack installation.

FastTrack server setup creates the directory SYS:\Novonyx and installs all Web server support files and directories there. Specific directories that you need to know about will be mentioned during this chapter.

▶ · ◀

Configuring the FastTrack Administration Server

There are three levels of access to the FastTrack server administration capabilities:

▶ **SuperUser.** This is the user account you specified when FastTrack was installed. Information for this user is stored in `SYS:\Novonyx\admin serv/config/admpw`. The SuperUser has full access to all FastTrack administrative features except for the Users & Groups forms. If the users and groups database is local, the SuperUser always has access to the database. If the users and groups database is maintained on an LDAP server, the SuperUser must also have a valid account on an LDAP server. If the NDS is used as the users and groups database, the SuperUser must have appropriate rights in NDS.

▶ **Administrators.** Administrators are users designated by the SuperUser to perform limited management tasks and can make changes that affect other users, such as adding users and changing access control.

▶ **End users.** End users have limited capability to change information specific to their own FastTrack accounts. For example, end users can change their passwords and other personal information.

All FastTrack functions are administered remotely using a Web browser. When you installed FastTrack, you specified a port number for the administration server. This port number must be specified in the URL when accessing the administration server. For an Administration Server configured on port 2468, you would enter a URL similar to the following:

```
http://www.pseudo-corp.com:2468/
```

Figure 17.1 shows the first Web page displayed by the administration server. This page has links that enable you to configure the administrative server. The following elements are found on the page:

- ▸ Five buttons under the *General Administration* heading access options for configuring the administration server.

- ▸ The off/on button starts and stops the FastTrack server processes.

- ▸ Buttons enable you to select a public Web server to be administered.

FIGURE 17.1

This Is the Home Page for the FastTrack Administration Server

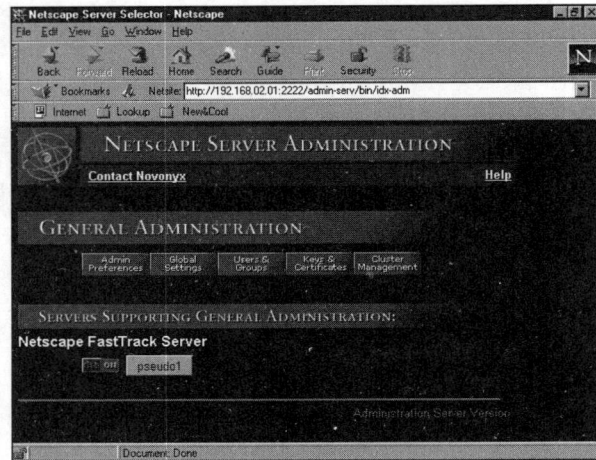

There are five buttons under the *General Administration* heading that open forms used to configure the administrative server itself:

- ▸ Admin Preferences

- ▸ Global Settings

- ▸ Users & Groups

- ▸ Keys & Certificates (not covered in this chapter)

- ▸ Cluster Management (not covered in this chapter)

As previously mentioned, we aren't delving into Web server security in this introduction to FastTrack, so we won't be looking at the Keys & Certificates forms. Apart from that, we'll examine most of the available configuration forms in the following sections.

Admin Preferences

Figure 17.2 shows the Admin Preferences form on which I have selected the *SuperUser Access Control* option. I have scrolled the page to show the buttons at the bottom. The *OK* button saves changes, as you probably suspected. To activate many changes made in the General Administration forms, you must stop and restart the administrative server and all the Web servers it supports. You will be prompted when a shutdown is necessary. Click *Reset* to cancel changes made in the form.

To return to the Server Administration page, click the *Server Administration* button at the top of the General Administration page. The following functions can be performed on the Admin Preferences page:

▸ Stopping and Starting the Administration Server

▸ Changing the Administration Server Port

▸ Editing SuperUser Access Controls

▸ Enabling and Disabling Secure Socket Level Security (not covered in this chapter)

▸ Configuring and Viewing Log files

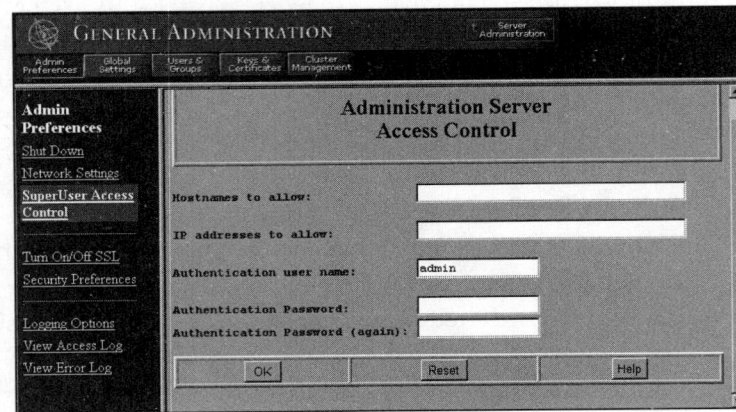

FIGURE 7.2

Administration Server:
Admin Preferences,
SuperUser Access Control

Stopping and Starting the Administration Server

You can stop and start the Administration Server without affecting operation of the public Web server. You might want to shut down the Administration Server as a security precaution to reduce the likelihood that an intruder could gain access.

To stop the Administration Server remotely, do the following:

1. Select Admin Preferences ⇨ Shut Down.

2. Click the button labeled "Shut down the administrative server!"

To stop the Administration Server at the NetWare console, unload ADMSERV.

To start the Administration Server at the NetWare console, load ADMSERV.

Changing the Administration Server Port

The port number for the Administration Server is established when FastTrack is installed You may need to change the port if it conflicts with a port being used by another process. To change the port:

1. Select Admin Preferences ⇨ Network Settings.

2. Change the number in the *Admin server port* field and click OK.

3. Stop the Administration Server and restart it as described in the previous section.

Editing SuperUser Access Controls

Although SuperUser access is restricted by a username and password, you can establish other access controls as well. Figure 17.2 shows the Administration Server Access Control page, which is displayed by selecting Admin Preferences ⇨ SuperUser Access Control.

You can restrict access to particular hostnames. When a user attempts to connect to the Administration Server, a DNS reverse lookup is performed to match the IP address in the connection request to a host name. A connection is permitted only if the host name appears in the *Hostnames to allow* field. You can use wildcard patterns as host names. For example, the name `*.pseudo-corp.com` allows access from all hosts in the `pseudo-corp.com` domain. Additional wildcard patterns are described in Table 17.1. Examples of the use of wildcard patterns are found in Table 17.2. You can include one or more host name patterns in the *Hostnames to allow* field.

Access can also be restricted according to IP address by adding the IP addresses to the *IP addresses to allow* field. Wildcard patterns can be employed in IP address strings.

To change the name and password for the SuperUser, edit the *Authentication user name* and *Authentication Password* fields.

NOTE   **The SuperUser name and password are stored in the file SYS:\Novonyx\suitespot\admin-serv\config\admpw. The password is stored in encrypted form and cannot be read. However, if you forget the password, you can edit the file to delete the encrypted password. Then use the Administrative Server to enter a new password.**

TABLE 17.1	PATTERN	USAGE
Resource Name Wildcard Patterns	*	Matches zero or more occurrences of any characters.
	?	Matches one occurrence of any character.

Continued

T A B L E 17.1	PATTERN	USAGE
Continued	|	Establishes an *or* expression. The substrings must appear in parentheses separated by | characters; for example, *(expr1|expr2|expr3)*. A match occurs when a match is found with one or more of the expressions.
	$	Matches the end of the string.
	[abc]	Matches one occurrence of any of the characters in the list.
	[a-z]	Matches one occurrence of any character in the specified range.
	[^ac]	Matches any characters except *a* and *c*.
	*~	Removes any pattern found in an expression that follows.

T A B L E 17.2	PATTERN	MATCHES
Wildcard Pattern Examples	*.pseudo-corp.com	Any string ending with the characters "pseudo-corp.com".
	192.168.1.???	Any string that begins with 192.168.1 and ends with any three characters (not necessarily numbers).
	.	Any string that includes a period.
	~pseudo-corp	Any string that does not begin with "pseudo-corp".
	.pseudo-corp.com~widgets.pseudo-corp.com	Any name that ends with "pseudo-corp.com" except "widgets.pseudo-corp.com".
	(widgets|blivets).pseudo-corp.com	Matches "widgets.pseudo-corp.com" or "blivets.pseudo-corp.com".
	.com*~pseudo-corp.com	Any host in the COM domain except hosts in the pseudo-corp.com domain.

Configuring and Viewing Log Files

The FastTrack server maintains two logs that record Web server accesses and errors. The following operations are available:

▸ To specify the file and pathnames of the log files, select Admin Preferences ⇨ Logging Options.

▸ To view the Access Log, select Admin Preferences ⇨ View Access Log. FastTrack does not record an access log unless you enable the access log as described in the section "Configuring Log Preferences" later in this chapter.

▸ To view the Error Log, select Admin Preferences ⇨ View Error Log.

Configuring the Directory Server

The Global Settings page only has one menu option, as shown in Figure 17.3. In the figure, I have selected the *LDAP Directory Server* option. The Configure Directory Service page enables you to specify which directory service will be used by FastTrack to authenticate users and groups who log in to the Web server. You have three choices: Local Database, LDAP Directory Server, and Novell Directory Services.

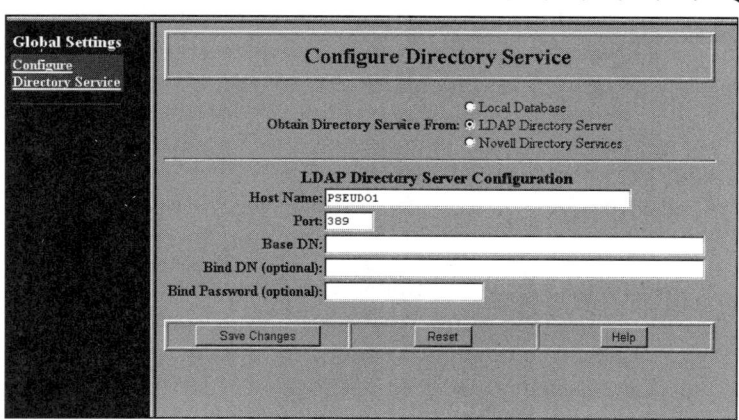

Selecting a Local Directory Server Database

When the *Local Database* option is selected, users and groups are maintained in a database managed by FastTrack. The FastTrack local directory supports an X.500-style organizational hierarchy, which is similar to the hierarchy used by NDS with minor differences in notation. The *Base DN* field accepts a distinguished name that is appended as a suffix to usernames entered in the local directory, establishing a default point at which name lookups take place. An example suffix could be o=pseudo-corp, c=US. If the *Base DN* field is left empty, a null string is used as the suffix and all searches begin from the root of the directory. Click *Save Changes* when finished. Then shut down and restart the Administration Server and all Web servers to activate the changes.

Selecting an LDAP Directory Server

If your organization operates a *Lightweight Directory Access Protocol* (LDAP; RFC 1777, 1778) server as its name service, you can use LDAP as the directory server for FastTrack. If you select this option, you must administer names through LDAP and can no longer manage them through the FastTrack server manager. Although NetWare 5 includes a service that enables LDAP clients to query NDS, there seems little point in using that facility with FastTrack because you can configure FastTrack to access NDS directly.

WARNING

Novell Directory Services and LDAP do not permit anonymous access to the Web service. All users must be authenticated through the selected name service before they are permitted access. If you wish to permit anonymous access, select *Local Database* in the *Configure Directory Service* form.

If you select *LDAP Directory Server*, the following fields are presented:

- **Host Name.** Enter the FQDN of the LDAP server.

- **Port.** Enter the protocol port number used to access the LDAP server. The default port is 389. If communication with the LDAP directory server takes place via SSL, enter the port number used for SSL communication. The default SSL port is 636.

▶ **Base DN.** Enter a distinguished name to be appended as a suffix to usernames entered in the local directory, establishing a default point at which name lookups take place. An example suffix could be `o=pseudo-corp`, `c=US`. If the *Base DN* field is left empty, a null string is used as the suffix and all searches begin from the root of the directory.

▶ **Bind DN.** Enter the Bind DN name used to gain initial read and search access to the directory server. Because the directory server cannot be administered through FastTrack, write access is not required. The Bind DN name and password are sent as clear text and can be easily viewed with a protocol analyzer. Therefore, anonymous access can be used. You should not specify the directory servers unrestricted (Root DN) username. This field is optional.

▶ **Bind Password.** Enter a password associated with the name specified in the *Bind DN* field. This field is optional.

Click *Save Changes* when finished. Then shut down and restart the Administration Server and all Web servers to activate the changes.

Selecting Novell Directory Services

The FastTrack Web server included with NetWare 5 has the special capability of using NDS as its directory service. If you select *Novell Directory Services*, you cannot administer Web users through the FastTrack administrative server. Instead, you must use native NDS administration tools such as NWAdmin to manage users. Figure 17.4 shows the form used to configure access to NDS.

The NDS tree that will be used by FastTrack is established when the Web server is installed, according to the tree membership of the user account used to install the product. The *Search Contexts List* specifies one or more contexts in the tree that will be examined by FastTrack when looking for usernames. Configure the list as follows:

▶ To add a context to the list, click *Insert Context* and enter a context in the *New NDS Context* field that is presented.

▶ To remove a context, select the context and click *Remove Context*.

▶ Names appear in the *Search Contexts List* according to priority, starting with the first context that FastTrack will query. To raise the priority of a context, select the context entry and click the *Float Context* button.

Click *Save Changes* when finished. Then shut down and restart the Administration Server and all Web servers to activate the changes.

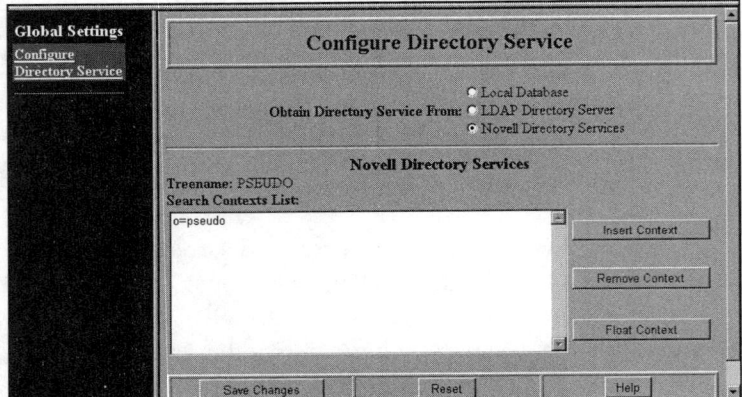

FIGURE 17.4

You Can Select NDS As the FastTrack Directory Service

Managing Users & Groups

Users and groups are available only if FastTrack has been configured with the *Local Database* setting on the *Configure Directory Service* form. If FastTrack is configured to use an LDAP or NDS directory, users and groups must be configured on the LDAP or NDS name service.

Because we are discussing the FastTrack server as installed on a NetWare platform, I am assuming that you will be using NDS as your directory service. If you wish instead to use FastTrack's own directory service, please consult the online help screens for guidelines.

Configuring a Web Server

This section explains how to manage the Web server accessed by end users, which I refer to as the *public Web server* to distinguish it from the *administrative Web server*. The FastTrack server actually enables you to configure multiple virtual Web servers, each of which can be accessed as if it is an independent Web server. This feature enables an organization to offer multiple Web sites while operating a single copy of FastTrack. Virtual servers are often used by ISPs who host Web servers for their clients, but are useful in other situations as well. For example, virtual servers enable separate departments in an organization to have their own virtual Web servers on the organization's intranet.

To administer the public Web server, return to the Netscape Server Administration Web page (Figure 17.1). If you are currently at the General Administration page (Figure 17.2) click the *Server Administration* button to return to the Netscape Server Administration page.

To administer a Web server, click its button under the *Netscape FastTrack Server* heading to open the Server Preferences page shown in Figure 17.5. I will refer to the pages used to manage an individual server as the Server Manager in the following sections.

Let's examine some of the most important Web server administration tasks.

F I G U R E   17.5

Server Preferences Are Used to Administer a Public Web Server

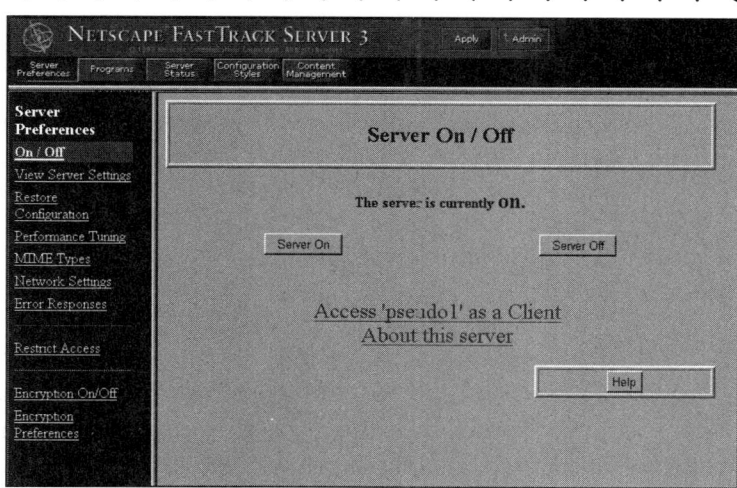

Stopping and Starting the Web Server

You must stop and start the Web server to activate changes made to its configuration. The Web server can be stopped and started remotely. To access the Server On/Off form, select Server Manager ⇨ Server Preferences ⇨ On/Off. The Server On/Off form reports the server status and provides *Server On* and *Server Off* buttons that can be used to change the status of the Web server. These actions do not actually start or stop processes running on the server (no NLMs are unloaded or loaded), as when you stopped and started the Administration Server. Consequently, no events are reported on the NetWare console.

If you click *Server Off* after making changes to the Web server's configuration, you must confirm that you want to activate the new configuration parameters. FastTrack displays a form titled Save and Apply Changes. Scroll to the bottom and make one of the following selections:

- **Save and Apply** saves the changes and activates the configuration change.

- **Save** saves the change but does not activate the configuration change. The change is activated the next time the Web server is started.

- **Undo** backs out all changes you have made since the last time changes were saved.

You will encounter the Save and Apply Pages form repeatedly. It is used to commit most changes made to a Web server.

NOTE

You can also stop and start the Web server using the *On* and *Off* buttons on the Netscape Server Administration home page (Figure 17.1). At the NetWare server, stop the Web server by entering the command NSHTTP. Start the Web server with the command NSWEB.

Viewing Server Settings

Select Server Manager ⇨ Server Preferences ⇨ View Server Settings to open the server settings form shown in Figure 17.6. You can edit these setting values by clicking the appropriate link. FastTrack servers are stored in files with the filename extension `.conf`, which are stored in various subdirectories under the `\Novonyx` root directory. These files are text files that can be viewed and modified using a text editor. To avoid introducing syntax errors to the files, however, I recommend that you perform most modifications using the FastTrack server administrator.

This form provides a central place where you can view most of the Web server settings. However, most of the settings shown on this page are modified using other forms — clicking the setting links to the appropriate page. We will review the configurable settings in the appropriate sections.

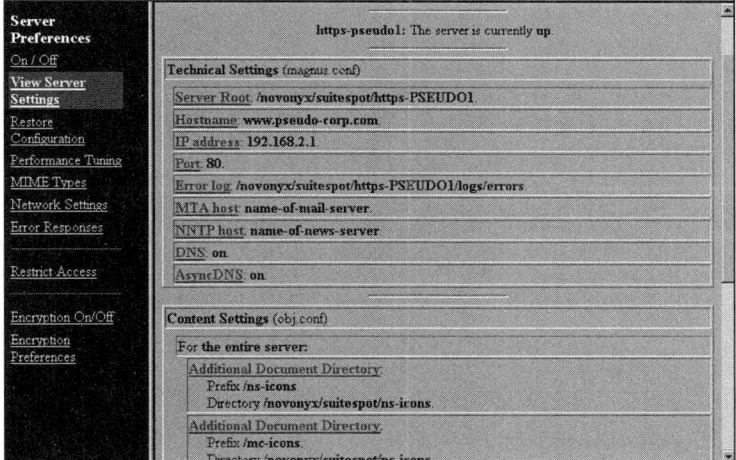

FIGURE 17.6

View Server Settings Displays a Variety of Server Configuration Settings

Restoring the Server Configuration

Access the *Restore Configuration* form (Figure 17.7) by selecting Server Manager ➪ Server Preferences ➪ Restore Configuration. This form enables you to back out changes made to the server configuration. Simply click any of the *Restore to* buttons to restore all configuration files to their state on that date and time.

Click the appropriate *Restore* button to back out changes made after the specified time stamp.

Click the *View* button to view the contents of the appropriate configuration file as it was at the specified date and time.

In the field *Set number of sets of backups*, specify how many generations of server configurations you want to retain. Click the *Change* button to commit a change to this parameter.

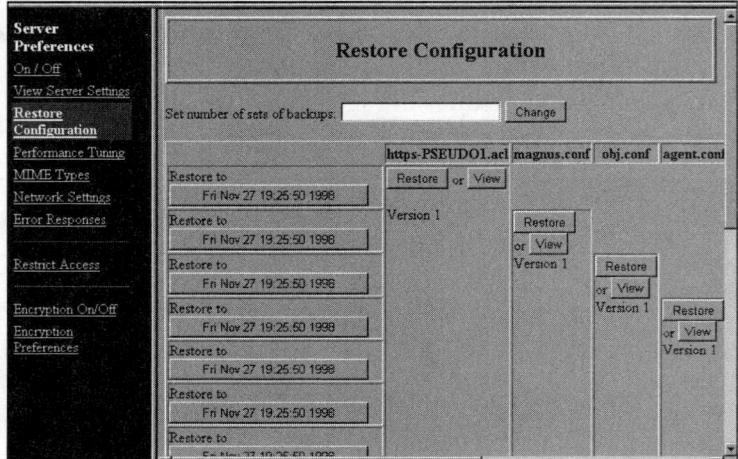

F I G U R E   7.7

The Restore Configuration Page Enables You to Revert to an Earlier Web Server Configuration

Performance Tuning

Access the *Performance Tuning* form (Figure 17.8) by selecting Server Manager ⇨ Server Preferences ⇨ Performance Tuning. This form contains settings for a variety of Web server parameters. These settings are grouped together because they can affect server performance. In most cases, the settings result in trade-offs between functionality and performance. After changing any settings, scroll to the bottom of the page and click *OK* to save the changes. Click *Reset* to cancel changes.

The available settings are:

► **Maximum Simultaneous Requests.** Most Web server requests are fulfilled quickly, and this value need not equal the number of users that can be serviced simultaneously. In theory, the Web server can function with only one available request. In practice, however, many user requests are not completed and the server must wait 30 seconds for open requests to time out. This value must be set to ensure that requests are available to users. Increasing the value increases memory demand. The default value is 48, which is adequate for a Web server that experiences moderate demand. Increase this values if users frequently report an inability to connect with the Web server.

▶ **Enable DNS.** If this setting is enabled, the Web server performs a reverse DNS lookup for each user who connects with the Web server and records the DNS name in the FastTrack server log. DNS lookups may improve the utility of logs but can have a significant impact on performance.

Hostname access restrictions work only when DNS reverse lookup is enabled.

NOTE

▶ **Enable Async DNS.** DNS lookups produce multiple serialized process threads to be scheduled for execution. Enabling asynchronous DNS may improve server performance. This feature can be enabled only if DNS lookups are enabled.

▶ **Cache DNS entries.** If DNS lookups are enabled, the server can maintain a cache of recently-resolved DNS names. If a DNS cache is enabled, specify the number of entries that will be maintained in the DNS cache, with a default value of 512 entries and a range from 32–32,768 entries. Specify the time that entries remain in cache in the *Expire entries (sec)* field, where the default value is 1200 seconds and the range is 1 second to 1 year. A DNS cache reduces the frequency of DNS reverse lookups.

Listen Queue Size. The listen queue size specifies the number of incoming connections the Web server will accept for a given socket. Increasing the listen queue size may actually degrade the performance of an overloaded server by queueing up more requests than the server can handle. In general, you should not change the default value of this parameter.

▶ **HTTP Persistent Connection Timeout.** HTTP 1.1 connections can be configured to be persistent. A persistent connection timeout releases connections not released by the client in a reasonable time. It should seldom be necessary to change the default value.

▶ · ◀

F I G U R E   7 . 8

The Performance Tuning Page Configures Several Performance-Related Parameters

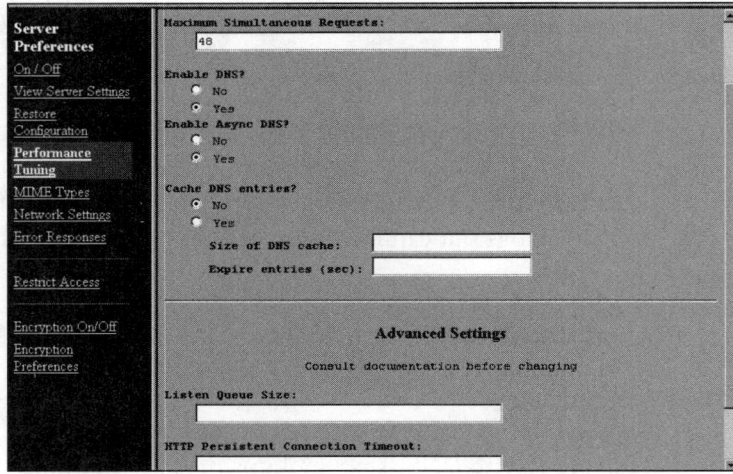

Configuring MIME Types

Web servers can provide a variety of media types, including text, graphics, sound, and application-specific formats. When the Web server sends an object to a client, it includes a Multipurpose Internet Mail Extension (MIME) type that enables the browser to know which application should be used to display the data. The MIME type is determined by the filename extension of the object supplied by the Web server. For example, objects with the filenames jpeg, jpg, and jpe are JPEG graphics files.

FastTrack is installed configured with a large number of MIME types. Depending on the content you add to the Web server, you may need to add, edit, or remove MIME types using the Global MIME Types form shown in Figure 17.9. Access this form by selecting Server Manager ⇨ Server Preferences ⇨ MIME Types.

FIGURE 17.9

The Global MIME Types Form Lists MIME Types That Are Currently Configured on the Web Server

Configuring Network Settings

To access the Network Settings form (Figure 17.10), select Server Manager ⇨ Server Preferences ⇨ Network Settings. Options on this form establish the following network settings:

- **Server Name.** This field specifies the name that users will use to access the Web server and should match an Address or CNAME entry in DNS.

- **Server Port.** This field specifies the protocol port number for the Web server. If the default port of 80 is not used, users must specify the port number in the URL used to access the Web server.

- **Bind To Address.** This field specifies the IP address bound to the Web server.

- **MTA Host.** This field specifies the DNS name of an SNMP mail transfer agent that can used by this Web server.

- **NNTS Host.** This field specifies the DNS name of a Network News Transfer Protocol server that can be used by this Web server.

After changing any of these fields, click *OK* to save the change or *Reset* to reject the change. After selecting *OK*, you must click the *Save and Apply* button to save and activate the changes.

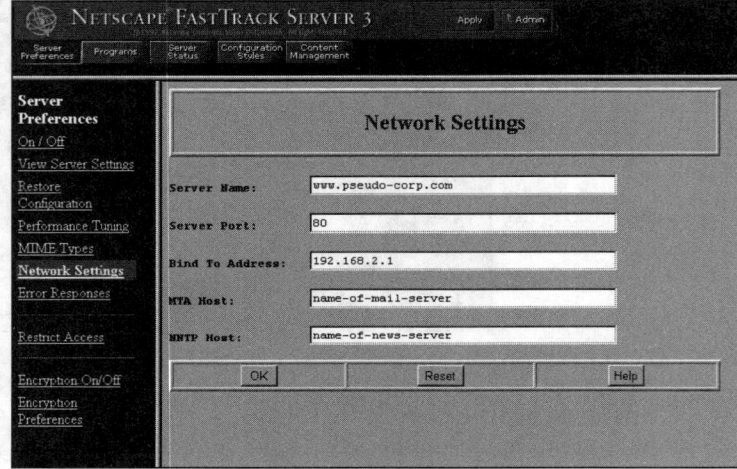

F I G U R E   17.10

This Form Configures
Various Web Server
Network Settings

Customizing Error Responses

The Web server generates error responses under the following conditions:

- ▸ **Unauthorized.** The user does not have the access permissions required to access an object protected by access control. The object might be sent upon receipt of user authentication information.

- ▸ **Forbidden.** The server does not have the permissions required to access the requested object.

- ▸ **Not Found.** A requested object cannot be found, or the server has been instructed to deny the existence of an object.

- ▸ **Server Error.** The server is improperly configured to access the requested object, or a catastrophic server failure occurs.

HTTP errors are characteristically cryptic. Using the Custom Error Responses form (Figure 17.11), you can provide two types of custom error responses for each of the error types listed. Access this form by selecting Server Manager ⇨ Server Preferences ⇨ Error Responses. The options to configure an error response are as follows:

▸ **File.** Supply the name of an HTML file to be sent to the user.

▸ **CGI**. Check this box if the file specified is a CGI program file.

You can select a filename to edit. Click *Browse* to select a file from a browse list. Click *Wildcard* to specify a filename that contains a wildcard pattern. (See Tables 17.1 and 17.2 for more information on wildcards.)

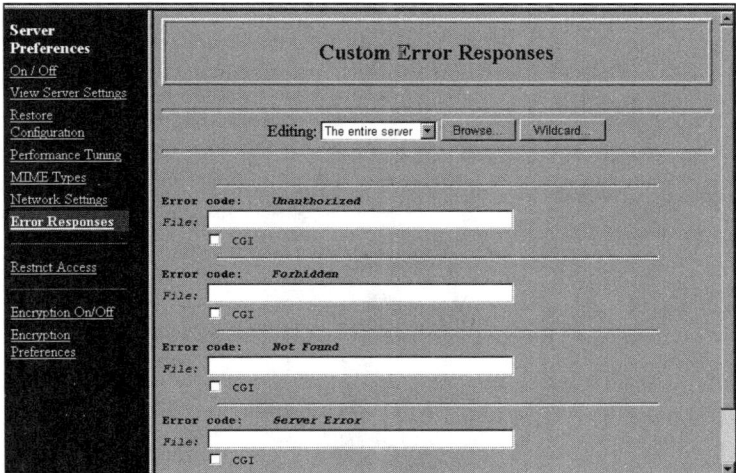

FIGURE   7.11

You Can Provide Custom Error Messages for Standard Error Conditions

Reviewing Server Operations

You can review activity on the FastTrack server in a number of ways. FastTrack maintains several logs, and you can examine server statistics in real time. An error log is always maintained. You must activate an access log to monitor client access activity.

Configuring Log Preferences

The Log Preferences form (Figure 17.12) is used to configure server logging. Access this form by selecting Server Manager ⇨ Server Status ⇨ Log Preferences. The following log options can be configured:

▶ **Log client accesses?** By default, a client access log is not maintained.

▶ **Log File.** If you activate the client access log, specify a filename here. The file will be stored in logs directory in the server root (by default, SYS:Novonyx). You can specify a full pathname to store the log file in a different directory or a relative pathname to store the log file in a subdirectory of the logs directory.

▶ **Record.** Log files can identify users by domain names or IP addresses. Domain name identification can be used only if DNS reverse lookup is activated in the *Performance Tuning* form. See the preceding section "Performance Tuning" in this chapter for more information.

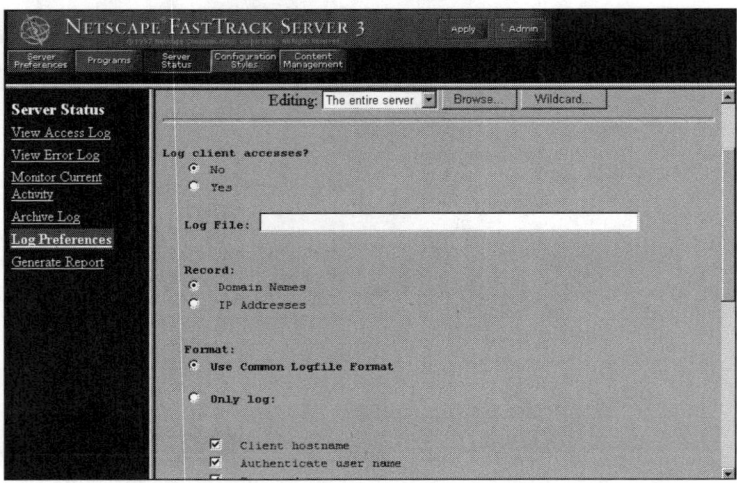

Use This Form to Activate the Client Access Log and Configure Log Preferences

You can select one of three log file format options:

▸ **Use Common Logfile Format.** If you select this option, the log will be maintained using a standard, widely-accepted format.

▸ **Only log.** If you select this option, you can specify the information to be logged by checking the desired options.

▸ **Custom format.** If you select this format, you can specify the exact log file format. See the online help for assistance with log file configuration.

If logging is enabled, you may want to specify certain hosts whose activities will not be logged. If that is the case, you can specify hosts in two ways:

▸ **Hostnames.** Specify a hostname or wildcard name that is not to be logged. For example, enter `*.pseudo-corp.com` if you do not want to log any activity from users in the domain `pseudo-corp.com`. A hostname can be used only if DNS reverse lookup is activated in the *Performance Tuning* form. See the preceding section "Performance Tuning" in this chapter for more information.

▸ **IP Addresses.** Specify an IP address that is not to be logged. A wildcard pattern can be used if desired. For example, the pattern `192.168.*` matches all IP addresses beginning with 192.168.

Viewing the Logs

To view the Access Log, select Server Manager ⇨ Server Status ⇨ View Access Log.

To view the Error Log, select Server Manager ⇨ View Error Log.

The forms used to review logs are similar. Figure 17.13 shows the View Error Log form. Access this form by selecting Server Manager ⇨ Server Status ⇨ View Error Log. You can configure logging in two ways:

▸ **Number of entries/errors to view?** Specify the number of log entries to be displayed.

▶ **Only show entries with:** You can limit the errors displayed by entering a string in this field. Only entries that contain the string will be displayed. For example, enter `Warning` to display only messages that contain that text.

Click *OK* to activate a change to these fields. Click *Reset* to cancel a change that has not been committed with *OK*.

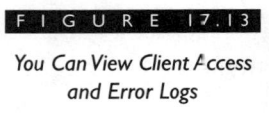

FIGURE 17.13

You Can View Client Access and Error Logs

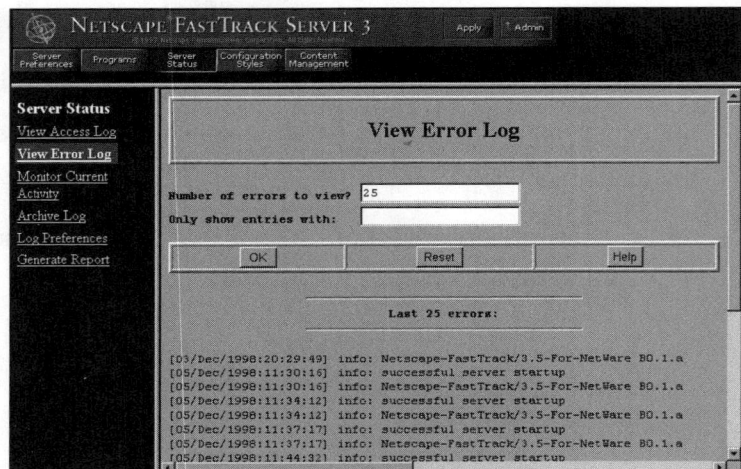

Monitoring Server Activity

You can view real-time server statistics by selecting Server Manager ⇨ Server Status ⇨ Monitor Current Activity to open the Server Monitor. My lab server doesn't generate a lot of traffic, so I can't show you what to expect on a busy Web server, but Figure 17.14 shows some features of the Server Monitor. The following activity categories are logged:

▶ **Bytes transferred.** Total activity by bytes transferred.

▶ **Total requests.** Total activity by requests.

▶ **Bad requests.** Bad requests handled by the server.

▶ **2xx.** Total status code 200–299 handled by the server.

▶ **3xx.** Total status code 300–399 handled by the server.

▶ **4xx.** Total status code 400–499 handled by the server.

▶ **5xx.** Total status code 500–599 handled by the server.

▶ **xxx.** Total of all status codes the server handled, minus timeouts and errors that returned an HTTP error code.

▶ **200.** The number of transactions handled successfully.

▶ **302.** The number of URL status codes handled.

▶ **304.** The number of requests where the server told the client to use a local copy of a URL rather than retrieving it from the server.

▶ **401.** The number of unauthorized requests handled by the server.

▶ **403.** The number of forbidden URL status codes handled by the server.

F I G U R E   17.14

The Server Monitor Provides Real-Time Server Performance Data

Server Monitor for port 80

Totals				
Bytes transferred	100%	34266		34266
Total requests	100%	19		19
Bad requests	0%	0		19
2xx	78%	15		19
3xx	10%	2		19
4xx	10%	2		19
5xx	0%	0		19
xxx	0%	0		19
200	78%	15		19
302	10%	2		19
304	0%	0		19
401	0%	0		19
403	0%	0		19

Producing Reports

To reach the Generate Report form, select Server Manager ⇨ Server Status ⇨ Generate Report. This form can generate reports in HTML or plain text, and can be customized to a considerable degree. These reports enable you to summarize usage in a variety of ways. The Generate Report form is practically self-explanatory. The important point is that there won't be any user data to report unless you enable Access Logs as described in "Configuring Log Preferences" earlier in this chapter.

Configuring CGI Program Support

Common Gateway Interface (CGI) programs can be written in a variety of programming languages including the UNIX Bourne Shell, Perl script language, C++, or Windows batch files. On NetWare servers, CGI programs can be written in NetBasic, PERL, or LCGI. The common factor among CGI programs is that they accept and return data in the same manner. This isn't a programming book, so I can't go into details. If you want more information, one place to start is:

```
http://developer.netscape.com/library/documentation/
```

The important thing from an administrator's standpoint is that CGI programs must be stored in certain ways so that FastTrack knows what they are. There are two ways to identify CGI programs:

▶ By placing them in directories that contain only CGI programs. All files in these directories are run as programs, regardless of the file extensions. The advantage of this approach is that access to CGI directories can be controlled, enabling the administrator to set up access restrictions for specific users or groups.

▶ By declaring file extensions that identify CGI programs. On NetWare servers, the administrator might specify that files with the extensions .cgi, .exe, .nlm, or .bat are treated as programs. Files with these extensions can be located in any directory that the server can access. This approach is easier to manage and permits any user to add CGI files to FastTrack server directories.

Let's look at the tasks involved in managing both approaches.

Defining CGI Directories

To reach the CGI Directory form shown in Figure 17.15, select Server Manager ⮕ Programs ⮕ CGI Directory. Scroll this form down to see a list of CGI directories that are currently configured.

To add a CGI directory, complete the following fields:

▸ **URL Prefix.** Enter the URL prefix to be used to access this directory. For example, if you enter `cgi-bin` for the Web server `www.pseudo-corp.com`, these CGI programs are accessed with the URL `http://www.pseudo-corp.com/cgi-bin/program_name`.

▸ **CGI Directory.** Enter the full pathname of the directory. This directory need not be a subdirectory of the Web server root.

Click *OK* after completing these fields. Then click *Save and Apply* to activate the changes.

To modify a CGI directory, scroll down on the CGI Directory form and click the appropriate *Edit* or *Remove* button.

▸ · ◀

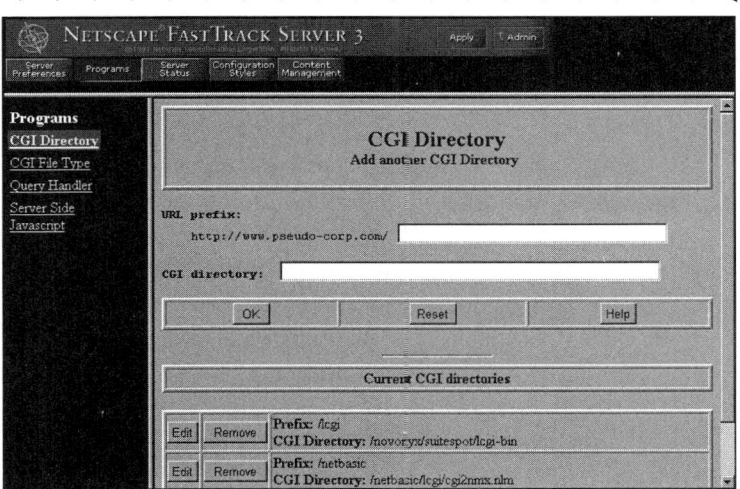

F I G U R E   17.15

Use the CGI Directory Form to Add, Modify, or Remove CGI Directories

Defining CGI File Types

To reach the CGI File Type form shown in Figure 17.16, select Server Manager ⇨ Programs ⇨ CGI File Type. On NetWare servers, files with the extensions .exe, .cgi, .nlm, or .bat are treated as programs. By default, CGI is declared as a file type for the entire server. You can use the CGI Directory form to disable CGI as a file type if desired.

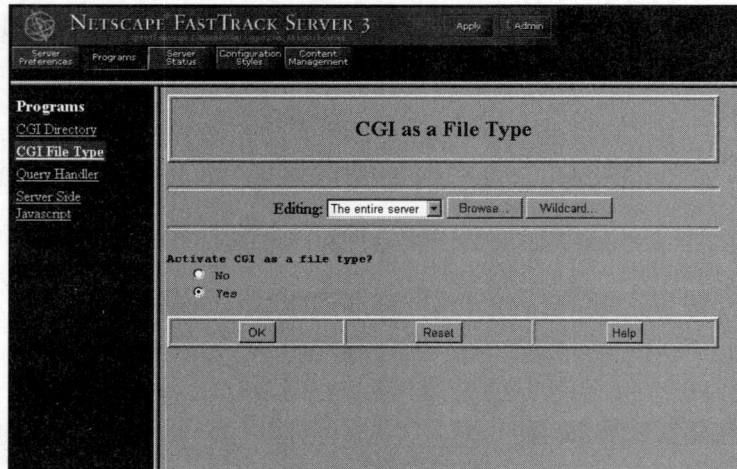

F I G U R E 17.16

Use the CGI As a File Type Form to Specify Whether CGI Is Treated As a File Type

A disadvantage of using .exe files as CGI files is that users cannot download .exe files as executables. There are several solutions to this:

▶ Compress the file. This will improve download times and change the filename extension.

▶ Edit the FastTrack servers obj.conf file to specify a download directory. Files in this directory are not treated as executables and are downloaded automatically. This procedure is described in a technical note at:

    http://help.netscape.com/kb/server/960513-130.html

Managing Server Content

Server content options describe the locations of server content and define how users will access that content. They also enable you to define virtual servers.

Defining the Primary Document Directory

Often, a single directory is used to store all content. In any case, a primary document directory is specified. This is the directory accessed by the default URL for the Web server. The Primary Document Directory form is shown in Figure 17.17. To reach this form, select Server Manager ⇨ Content Management ⇨ Primary Document Directory.

To change the primary document directory, edit the *Primary directory* field and click *OK*. Then click *Save and Apply* to activate the change.

Specifying Additional Document Directories

You may wish to declare additional document directories. In fact, several extra document directories are included in the default server installation. The Additional Document Directory form is shown in Figure 17.18. To reach this form, select Server Manager ⇨ Content Management ⇨ Additional Document Directories.

▶ · ◀

FIGURE 17.17	
You Can Change the Server's Primary Document Directory	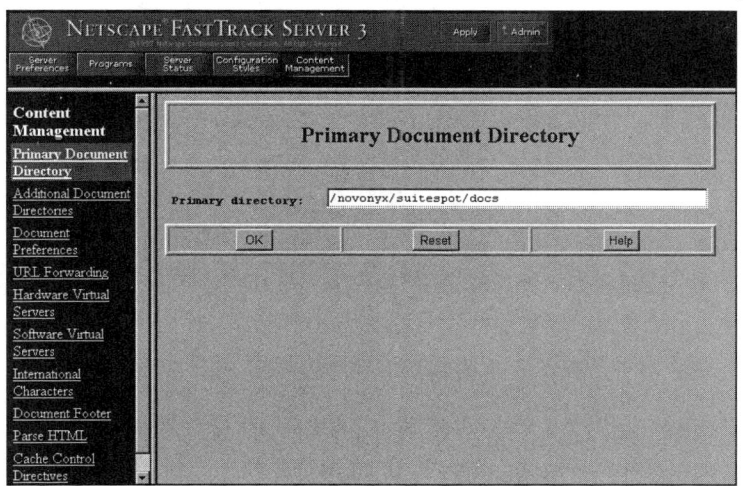

To add a document directory, complete the following fields:

▶ **URL Prefix.** Enter the URL prefix to be used to access this directory. For example, if you enter `widgets` for the Web server `www.pseudo-corp.com`, files in the specified directory are accessed with a URL like `http://www.pseudo-corp.com/widgets/file_name`.

▶ **Map to Directory.** Enter the full pathname of the directory. This directory need not be a subdirectory of the Web server root.

Click *OK* after completing these fields. Then click *Save and Apply* to activate the changes.

To modify a Document directory, scroll down on the CGI Directory form and click the appropriate *Edit* or *Remove* button.

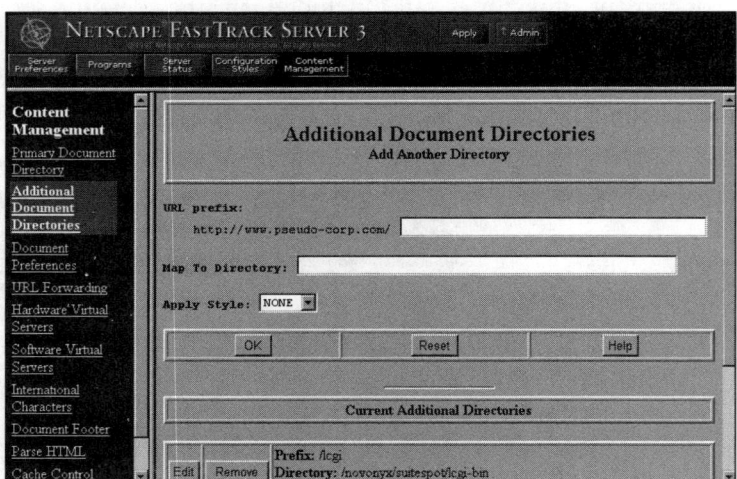

F I G U R E   17.18

Use This Form to Define Additional Document Directories

Specifying Document Preferences

The Document Preferences form (Figure 17.19) defines several document characteristics. Reach this form by selecting Server Manager ⇨ Content Management ⇨ Document Preferences.

After making changes to this page, scroll down and click the *OK* button. Then click *Save and Apply* to activate the changes.

▶ · ◀

FIGURE 17.19

*Use This Form to Define
Document Preferences*

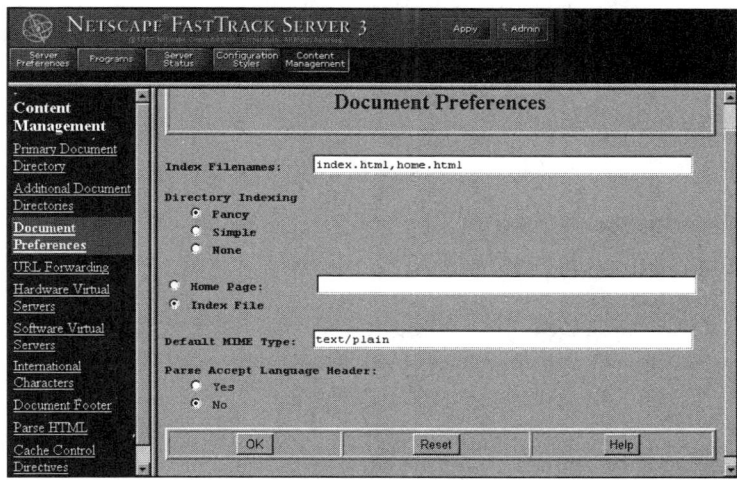

Index Filenames   If the Web server receives a URL that does not specify a filename, it has to be able to send *something* to the user. If a filename is not specified by the URL, FastTrack looks for the filenames specified in the *Index Filenames* field, searching for documents in the order they appear in the list. Suppose that you access the Web with the URL http://www.pseudo-corp.com. If the first filename in *Index Filenames* is index.html, FastTrack looks for a file with that name in the Web server's default document directory. If it can't find index.html, it looks for additional files that may be specified in the *Index Filenames* list. You can add other filenames to this field if desired.

Index Styles   If FastTrack can't find any of the filenames specified in the *Index Filenames* list, it can serve up an index that it generates. You can select one of the following formats for the server-generated index:

▶ **Fancy.** This option generates a detailed index. Each file entry includes a graphic that matches the file type and is identified with the date the file was last modified and the file size.

▶ **Simple.** This option provides a plain index that takes less time to generate.

· · · · ·

> **None.** With this option, FastTrack does not automatically generate an index. If the server does not find an index file, it returns an error message to the user.

In many cases, you do not want users browsing files and therefore should not enable indexing.

The Home Page   When users access the Web server, you may want to return a specified home page. You have two options for specifying the home page:

> **Index File.** If this option is selected, FastTrack looks for the files identified in the *Index Filenames* field.

> **Home Page.** If this option is selected, FastTrack looks for the filename that you specify.

The Default MIME Type   When FastTrack sends a document to a client's Web browser, it tags the document with a MIME type that informs the browser how to display the document. If FastTrack cannot determine the correct MIME type by examining the filename extension, it will use MIME type specified in the *Default MIME Type* field. This value matches the standard HTML file format and should seldom need to be changed.

Parsing the Language Header   Clients using HTTP 1.1 can send header information describing languages that they accept. If your server supports multiple languages, enable the *Parse Accept Language Header* option.

Configuring Virtual Servers

Virtual servers enable a single Web server to support multiple virtual Web sites. There are two ways to identify virtual Web servers:

> **Hardware virtual servers** are each identified by a unique IP address.

> **Software virtual servers** have different DNS names but do not need to have different IP addresses.

Let's see how both of these options work.

Hardware Virtual Servers

Each hardware virtual server is identified by a unique IP address and a unique DNS name. Before enabling the virtual server in FastTrack, do the following:

▶ In INETCFG, add a TCP/IP binding for each IP address that will identify a virtual server. A BIND statement will be created for each IP address. Activate the changes with the REINITIALIZE SERVER command.

▶ Create a directory that will be the document root directory for the virtual server.

▶ After binding all the desired IP addresses, configure DNS with an Address resource record for each IP address. Each address should be associated with a unique DNS name.

To add a hardware virtual server to the FastTrack configuration, open the Hardware Virtual Servers form (Figure 17.20) by selecting Server Manager ⇨ Content Management ⇨ Hardware Virtual Servers. The following fields define a hardware virtual server:

▶ **IP Address.** This is an IP address that identifies the hardware virtual server. This must be an IP address bound to a local interface.

▶ **Document Root.** Each virtual server has its own root directory. Specify the complete pathname of the document root directory.

After the virtual server has been defined, click *OK*. Then click *Save and Apply* to activate the changes.

You can scroll down on the Hardware Virtual Servers form to examine and modify currently-defined virtual servers. Click *Edit* to modify the virtual server. Click *Remove* to remove the virtual server from the configuration.

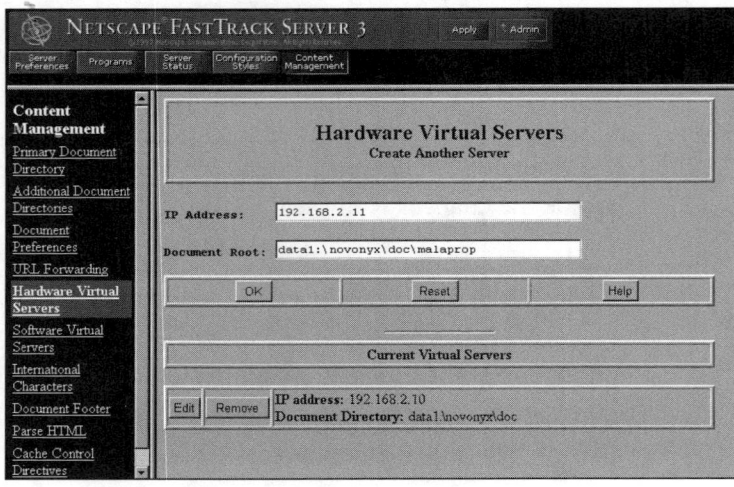

Software Virtual Servers

Software virtual servers share an IP address. However, each software virtual server is defined by a unique DNS name. For example, you could configure DNS so that www.pseudo-corp.com and www.malaprop.com both map to the same IP address. Then you could configure software virtual servers for the following URLs:

    http://www.pseudo-corp.com/

    http://www.malaprop.com/

The interesting thing is that both URLs map to the same Web server. To enable the Web server to determine which Web site to access, the Web browser must include an HTTP host header. Not all browsers supply the HTTP host header, and I have not seen a comprehensive list of browsers that support the feature. Because they depend on a browser feature, software virtual servers are a bit less universal than hardware virtual servers. If you will be using software virtual servers, test them with the browsers you will support so that you can let your users know which platforms are supported.

Before enabling the software virtual server in FastTrack, do the following:

► Configure DNS with an Address resource record for each Web site. Each address should be associated with the same IP address.

▸ Create a directory under the docs directory that will be used as a primary document directory for the software virtual server.

To add a software virtual server to the FastTrack configuration, open the Hardware Virtual Servers form (Figure 17.21) by selecting Server Manager ⇨ Content Management ⇨ Software Virtual Servers. The following fields define a software virtual server:

▸ **URL host.** Enter the software virtual server's DNS name.

▸ **Home Page.** If you specify a full pathname, the path you specify will be used. If you specify a relative pathname, FastTrack will use a subdirectory of the docs directory. Enter a pathname that defines the software virtual server's default document directory and home page.

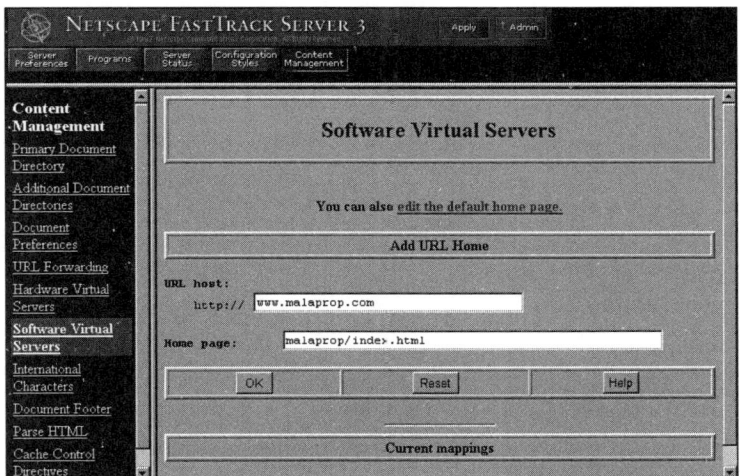

After the virtual server has been defined, click OK. Then click *Save and Apply* to activate the changes.

You can scroll down on the Software Virtual Servers form to examine and modify currently-defined virtual servers. Click *Edit* to modify the virtual server. Click *Remove* to remove the virtual server from the configuration.

In Conclusion

A Web server adds a final touch to the TCP/IP network we have labored to produce in this book. As you can see, there isn't much to basic Web administration, although there are a lot of fine points you will want to examine as you become comfortable with the technology. The primary task of mounting a Web site isn't server management, however. With Web sites, most of the work concerns providing content, but that is a subject far too big for this book.

It is the end of the book, and you are no longer a TCP/IP novice. You will no doubt find that there is much more to learn about TCP/IP; this book should give you a good start. Thanks for staying the course, and good luck in your career.

Understanding Decimal, Binary, and Hexadecimal Numbers

How most human societies settled on a numbering system based on multiples of 10 is lost in history. The probable explanation, of course, is that 10-based numbering came about as a natural extension of the way we kept track of livestock and pots, counting them on our fingers. But whatever the explanation, decimal numbers, the system called "base 10," is the system with which most humans are comfortable.

Humans abandoned counting with fingers long ago because ten fingers just isn't enough to deal with the real world. Ten grains of wheat isn't a lot of wheat, for example. The problem of representing really large numbers was solved by Arab mathematicians who introduced the concept of zero, a hole that stood for an empty place. Combining the use of zero with multiples of ten produced the decimal numbering system we use today, which capable of representing values of any magnitude.

However the digits in digital computers aren't the same as the digits we call fingers. Computers count in a very different way from us, using large arrays of switches that are either on or off. As a result, they are called *binary computers* because of this two-state operation. Yes, these switches could have been used to count like fingers, with each switch in a bank of ten representing a finger that was counted in sequence, but that wouldn't have permitted computers to handle large numeric values. Instead, the developers of computers needed a numbering system that was as natural to computers as base 10 is to us.

The branch of mathematics that became the foundation for computer operation was established in 1854 by George Boole. *Boolean algebra*, as it came to be called, is based on binary logic (true/false, on/off, yes/no) and fits quite nicely with the on/off character of digital computers. For the pioneers of digital computers, mathematical geniuses all, boolean algebra was mother's milk. They had no trepidations whatsoever in using binary boolean logic to solve complex problems.

That leaves us network administrators with a headache, because few of us were math majors. However, we have no choice but to accept the computer for what it is and learn a bit of its binary logic. Fortunately, if you take it in small steps, the process isn't difficult. Before looking at the binary and hexadecimal numbering systems closely allied with computers, let's take a refresher course on decimal numbers.

How Decimal Numbers Work

The decimal numbering system is based on powers of ten. For example:

```
10⁰ = 1 (any integer to the 0 power = 1)
10¹ = 10 × 1 = 10
10² = 10 × 10 = 100
10³ = 10 × 10 × 10 = 1,000
10⁴ = 10 × 10 × 10 × 10 = 10,000
```

The position of a digit in a decimal number determines its magnitude in powers of ten. For the number 6,812, the digits represent the following values:

```
6 represents 6 × 10³ = 6 × 10 × 10 × 10 = 6 × 1000 = 6000
8 represents 6 × 10² = 6 × 10 _ 10 = 6 × 100 = 800
1 represents 1 × 10¹ = 1 × 10 = 1 × 10 = 10
2 represents 2 × 10⁰ = 2 × 1 = 2
```

That's enough for grade-school arithmetic. Let's see how binary numbers follow the same principle.

How Binary Numbers Work

Base 10 (decimal) numbers use digits 0 through 9 to represent digits. Base 2 (binary) digits are restricted to the values 1 and 0. As with base 10 numbers, the values of base 2 numbers are associated with powers of the base. The first few powers of 2 are as follows:

```
2⁰ = 1
2¹ = 2 × 1 = 2 decimal
2² = 2 × 2 = 4 decimal
2³ = 2 × 2 × 2 = 8 decimal
2⁴ = 2 × 2 × 2 × 2 = 16 decimal
```

These powers of 2 can be used to evaluate binary numbers. This example evaluates the binary number 1101:

1 represents $1 \times 2^3 = 1 \times 2 \times 2 \times 2 = 1 \times 8 = 8$

1 represents $1 \times 2^2 = 1 \times 2 \times 2 = 1 \times 4 = 4$

0 represents $0 \times 2^1 = 0 \times 2 = 0 \times 2 = 0$

1 represents $1 \times 2^0 = 1 \times 1 = 1$

Therefore, 13 is the decimal equivalent of the binary number 1101.

Binary digits (bits) are typically organized in terms of groups of eight, comprising the familiar *byte*, also referred to as an *octet* in some network standards. A byte can range in value from 0 through 11111111 binary, equivalent to a range of 0 through 255 decimal. That's how dotted-decimal IP address representation (discussed in Chapter 4) works—each group of eight bits is represented by a decimal value from 0 through 255.

How Hexadecimal Works

Decimal representation is used as a way to make binary numbers more palatable to humans. Which of these numbers is easier for you to comprehend:

0100111011001110111110101100010001 binary

or

78.206. 251.71 dotted-decimal

The act of converting binary to decimal and back isn't something we can all do in our heads. Unless you're very good at head math, you'll probably resort to a conversion table (such as the one in Appendix B) or to a scientific calculator. That's why the hexadecimal numbering system is more commonly used as an alternate to binary representation. Hexadecimal looks weird and foreboding, but it's really an easier way to go if you work a lot with computer numbers.

Hexadecimal, or *hex*, has a base of 16. Because a hex digit can have one of 16 values, letters are used to represent the hex digits equivalent to decimal 10 through 15. The digits used in hex with their decimal equivalents are shown in Table A.1:

TABLE A.1	HEX DIGIT	DECIMAL EQUIVALENT
Hex Digits with Decimal Equivalents	0	0
	1	1
	2	2
	3	3
	4	4
	5	5
	6	6
	7	7
	8	8
	9	9
	A	10
	B	11
	C	12
	D	13
	E	14
	F	15

The values represented by digits in a hex number are determined by powers of 16. Here are the first few powers of 16:

$$16^0 = 1 \ (2^0)$$
$$16^1 = 16 \times 1 \qquad\qquad = 16 \text{ decimal } (2^4)$$
$$16^2 = 16 \times 16 \qquad\qquad = 256 \text{ decimal } (2^8)$$
$$16^3 = 16 \times 16 \times 16 \qquad = 4,096 \text{ decimal } (2^{16})$$
$$16^4 = 16 \times 16 \times 16 \times 16 = 65,536 \text{ decimal } (2^{32})$$

Here is how the hex number E40A evaluates:

E represents $E \times 16^3$ = $E \times 16 \times 16 \times 16$

= $E \times 4,096$ = 57,344 decimal

4 represents 4×16^2 = $4 \times 16 \times 16$ = 4×256

= 1,024 decimal

0 represents 0×16^1 = 0×16 = 0×16 = 0 decimal

A represents $A \times 16^0$ = $A \times 1$ = 10 decimal

As a result, 58,378 (57,344 + 1,024 + 10) is the decimal equivalent of the hex number E40A.

Converting Binary to Hex

As things develop, it is a piece of cake to convert binary numbers to hex in your head.

Take the binary number 1111, which is decimal 15. Referring to the list of hex digits presented a couple paragraphs ago, it becomes clear that binary 1111 represented in hex is F. Therefore, any four-bit binary number can be represented by a single hex digit as shown in Table A.2:

TABLE A.2	FOUR-BIT BINARY NUMBER	HEX DIGIT EQUIVALENT
Binary Numbers with Hex Equivalents	1	1
	10	2
	11	3
	100	4
	101	5
	110	6
	111	7
	1000	8
	1001	9
	1010	A
	1011	B

FOUR-BIT BINARY NUMBER	HEX DIGIT EQUIVALENT
1100	C
1101	D
1110	E
1111	F

To convert longer binary numbers to hex, just break the binary number into groups of four bits, and represent each group with a hex digit. For example:

    0100 1110   1100   1110   1111   1011   0001   0001
      4   E   C   E   F   B   1   1

As you can see, if you can memorize just 16 bit patterns and their hex equivalents, you can convert binary to hex and back without a net.

Most commonly, hex numbers are organized in groups of two digits, with each group representing one byte. You may see the above number written something like this:

    4E CE FB 11

However, hex numbers can easily look like decimal. Is the number 1025 decimal or hex? So it is important to have a way of unambiguously identifying hex numbers.

Representing Hex Numbers

In Chapter 4, you learn about subnet masks and discover that it is extremely important to consider the bit pattern that the subnet mask represents. Subnet masks are often shown in dotted-decimal form (for example: 255.255.240.0). To make it easier to convert subnet masks to their binary forms, however, you will often see subnet masks represented in hex. 255.255.240.0 in hex may be written as:

    0xFF.0xFF.0xE0.0x0

The 0x stuff is taken from the C programming language, which identifies a hex digit with the 0x prefix. Hex numbers are also frequently identified with a lowercase letter ·h, for example: 4Eh. Expect to see both forms as you read about TCP/IP.

Decimal, Binary, and Hexadecimal Equivalents

TABLE B.1

DECIMAL	BINARY	HEX	DECIMAL	BINARY	HEX
0	0	0	26	11010	1A
1	1	1	27	11011	1B
2	10	2	28	11100	1C
3	11	3	29	11101	1D
4	100	4	30	11110	1E
5	101	5	31	11111	1F
6	110	6	32	100000	20
7	111	7	33	100001	21
8	1000	8	34	100010	22
9	1001	9	35	100011	23
10	1010	A	36	100100	24
11	1011	B	37	100101	25
12	1100	C	38	100110	26
13	1101	D	39	100111	27
14	1110	E	40	101000	28
15	1111	F	41	101001	29
16	10000	10	42	101010	2A
17	10001	11	43	101011	2B
18	10010	12	44	101100	2C
19	10011	13	45	101101	2D
20	10100	14	46	101110	2E
21	10101	15	47	101111	2F
22	10110	16	48	110000	30
23	10111	17	49	110001	31
24	11000	18	50	110010	32
25	11001	19	51	110011	33

T A B L E   B . I

DECIMAL	BINARY	HEX	DECIMAL	BINARY	HEX
52	110100	34	79	1001111	4F
53	110101	35	80	1010000	50
54	110110	36	81	1010001	51
55	110111	37	82	1010010	52
56	111000	38	83	1010011	53
58	111010	3A	84	1010100	54
59	111011	3B	85	1010101	55
60	111100	3C	86	1010110	56
61	111101	3D	87	1010111	57
62	111110	3E	88	1011000	58
63	111111	3F	89	1011001	59
64	1000000	40	90	1011010	5A
65	1000001	41	91	1011011	5B
66	1000010	42	92	1011100	5C
67	1000011	43	93	1011101	5D
68	1000100	44	94	1011110	5E
69	1000101	45	95	1011111	5F
70	1000110	46	96	1100000	60
71	1000111	47	97	1100001	61
72	1001000	48	98	1100010	62
73	1001001	49	99	1100011	63
74	1001010	4A	100	1100100	64
75	1001011	4B	101	1100101	65
76	1001100	4C	102	1100110	66
77	1001101	4D	103	1100111	67
78	1001110	4E	104	1101000	68

TABLE B.1

DECIMAL	BINARY	HEX	DECIMAL	BINARY	HEX
105	1101001	69	131	10000011	83
106	1101010	6A	132	10000100	84
107	1101011	6B	133	10000101	85
108	1101100	6C	134	10000110	86
109	1101101	6D	135	10000111	87
110	1101110	6E	136	10001000	88
111	1101111	6F	137	10001001	89
112	1110000	70	138	10001010	8A
113	1110001	71	139	10001011	8B
114	1110010	72	140	10001100	8C
115	1110011	73	141	10001101	8D
116	1110100	74	142	10001110	8E
117	1110101	75	143	10001111	8F
118	1110110	76	144	10010000	90
119	1110111	77	145	10010001	91
120	1111000	78	146	10010010	92
121	1111001	79	147	10010011	93
122	1111010	7A	148	10010100	94
123	1111011	7B	149	10010101	95
124	1111100	7C	150	10010110	96
125	1111101	7D	151	10010111	97
126	1111110	7E	152	10011000	98
127	1111111	7F	153	10011001	99
128	10000000	80	154	10011010	9A
129	10000001	81	155	10011011	9B
130	10000010	82	156	10011100	9C

TABLE B.1

DECIMAL	BINARY	HEX	DECIMAL	BINARY	HEX
157	10011101	9D	183	10110111	B7
158	10011110	9E	184	10111000	B8
159	10011111	9F	185	10111001	B9
160	10100000	A0	186	10111010	BA
161	10100001	A1	187	10111011	BB
162	10100010	A2	188	10111100	BC
163	10100011	A3	189	10111101	BD
164	10100100	A4	190	10111110	BE
165	10100101	A5	191	10111111	BF
166	10100110	A6	192	11000000	C0
167	10100111	A7	193	11000001	C1
168	10101000	A8	194	11000010	C2
169	10101001	A9	195	11000011	C3
170	10101010	AA	196	11000100	C4
171	10101011	AB	197	11000101	C5
172	10101100	AC	198	11000110	C6
173	10101101	AD	199	11000111	C7
174	10101110	AE	200	11001000	C8
175	10101111	AF	201	11001001	C9
176	10110000	B0	202	11001010	CA
177	10110001	B1	203	11001011	CB
178	10110010	B2	204	11001100	CC
179	10110011	B3	205	11001101	CD
180	10110100	B4	206	11001110	CE
181	10110101	B5	207	11001111	CF
182	10110110	B6	208	11010000	D0

T A B L E   B.I

DECIMAL	BINARY	HEX	DECIMAL	BINARY	HEX
209	11010001	D1	233	11101001	E9
210	11010010	D2	234	11101010	EA
211	11010011	D3	235	11101011	EB
212	11010100	D4	236	11101100	EC
213	11010101	D5	237	11101101	ED
214	11010110	D6	238	11101110	EE
215	11010111	D7	239	11101111	EF
216	11011000	D8	240	11110000	F0
217	11011001	D9	241	11110001	F1
218	11011010	DA	242	11110010	F2
219	11011011	DB	243	11110011	F3
220	11011100	DC	244	11110100	F4
221	11011101	DD	245	11110101	F5
222	11011110	DE	246	11110110	F6
223	11011111	DF	247	11110111	F7
224	11100000	E0	248	11111000	F8
225	11100001	E1	249	11111001	F9
226	11100010	E2	250	11111010	FA
227	11100011	E3	251	11111011	FB
228	11100100	E4	252	11111100	FC
229	11100101	E5	253	11111101	FD
230	11100110	E6	254	11111110	FE
231	11100111	E7	255	11111111	FF
232	11101000	E8			

Internet Top-Level Domains

The following table lists the country codes for country domains in the Internet domain name space. These codes were obtained from www.ietf.org on January 12, 1999.

TABLE C.I
Internet Top-Level Domains for Countries

COUNTRY	DOMAIN
AFGHANISTAN	AF
ALBANIA	AL
ALGERIA	DZ
AMERICAN SAMOA	AS
ANDORRA	AD
ANGOLA	AO
ANGUILLA	AI
ANTARCTICA	AQ
ANTIGUA AND BARBUDA	AG
ARGENTINA	AR
ARMENIA	AM
ARUBA	AW
AUSTRALIA	AU
AUSTRIA	AT
AZERBAIJAN	AZ
BAHAMAS	BS
BAHRAIN	BH
BANGLADESH	BD
BARBADOS	BB
BELARUS	BY
BELGIUM	BE
BELIZE	BZ
BENIN	BJ
BERMUDA	BM
BHUTAN	BT

COUNTRY	DOMAIN
BOLIVIA	BO
BOSNIA AND HERZEGOVINA	BA
BOTSWANA	BW
BOUVET ISLAND	BV
BRAZIL	BR
BRITISH INDIAN OCEAN TERRITORY	IO
BRUNEI DARUSSALAM	BN
BULGARIA	BG
BURKINA FASO	BF
BURUNDI	BI
CAMBODIA	KH
CAMEROON	CM
CANADA	CA
CAPE VERDE	CV
CAYMAN ISLANDS	KY
CENTRAL AFRICAN REPUBLIC	CF
CHAD	TD
CHILE	CL
CHINA	CN
CHRISTMAS ISLAND	CX
COCOS (KEELING) ISLANDS	CC
COLOMBIA	CO
COMOROS	KM
CONGO	CG
CONGO, DEMOCRATIC REPUBLIC OF THE	CD
COOK ISLANDS	CK
COSTA RICA	CR
COTE D'IVOIRE	CI

Continued

TABLE C.1	COUNTRY	DOMAIN
Continued	CROATIA (local name: Hrvatska)	HR
	CUBA	CU
	CYPRUS	CY
	CZECH REPUBLIC	CZ
	DENMARK	DK
	DJIBOUTI	DJ
	DOMINICA	DM
	DOMINICAN REPUBLIC	DO
	EAST TIMOR	TP
	ECUADOR	EC
	EGYPT	EG
	EL SALVADOR	SV
	EQUATORIAL GUINEA	GQ
	ERITREA	ER
	ESTONIA	EE
	ETHIOPIA	ET
	FALKLAND ISLANDS (MALVINAS)	FK
	FAROE ISLANDS	FO
	FIJI	FJ
	FINLAND	FI
	FRANCE	FR
	FRANCE, METROPOLITAN	FX
	FRENCH GUIANA	GF
	FRENCH POLYNESIA	PF
	FRENCH SOUTHERN TERRITORIES	TF
	GABON	GA
	GAMBIA	GM
	GEORGIA	GE
	GERMANY	DE

COUNTRY	DOMAIN
GHANA	GH
GIBRALTAR	GI
GREECE	GR
GREENLAND	GL
GRENADA	GD
GUADELOUPE	GP
GUAM	GU
GUATEMALA	GT
GUINEA	GN
GUINEA-BISSAU	GW
GUYANA	GY
HAITI	HT
HEARD AND MC DONALD ISLANDS	HM
HOLY SEE (VATICAN CITY STATE)	VA
HONDURAS	HN
HONG KONG	HK
HUNGARY	HU
ICELAND	IS
INDIA	IN
INDONESIA	ID
IRAN (ISLAMIC REPUBLIC OF)	IR
IRAQ	IQ
IRELAND	IE
ISRAEL	IL
ITALY	IT
JAMAICA	JM
JAPAN	JP
JORDAN	JO

Continued

COUNTRY	DOMAIN
KAZAKHSTAN	KZ
KENYA	KE
KIRIBATI	KI
KOREA, DEMOCRATIC PEOPLE'S REPUBLIC OF	KP
KOREA, REPUBLIC OF	KR
KUWAIT	KW
KYRGYZSTAN	KG
LAO PEOPLE'S DEMOCRATIC REPUBLIC	LA
LATVIA	LV
LEBANON	LB
LESOTHO	LS
LIBERIA	LR
LIBYAN ARAB JAMAHIRIYA	LY
LIECHTENSTEIN	LI
LITHUANIA	LT
LUXEMBOURG	LU
MACAU	MO
MACEDONIA, THE FORMER YUGOSLAV REPUBLIC OF	MK
MADAGASCAR	MG
MALAWI	MW
MALAYSIA	MY
MALDIVES	MV
MALI	ML
MALTA	MT
MARSHALL ISLANDS	MH
MARTINIQUE	MQ
MAURITANIA	MR
MAURITIUS	MU

COUNTRY	DOMAIN
MAYOTTE	YT
MEXICO	MX
MICRONESIA, FEDERATED STATES OF	FM
MOLDOVA, REPUBLIC OF	MD
MONACO	MC
MONGOLIA	MN
MONTSERRAT	MS
MOROCCO	MA
MOZAMBIQUE	MZ
MYANMAR	MM
NAMIBIA	NA
NAURU	NR
NEPAL	NP
NETHERLANDS	NL
NETHERLANDS ANTILLES	AN
NEW CALEDONIA	NC
NEW ZEALAND	NZ
NICARAGUA	NI
NIGER	NE
NIGERIA	NG
NIUE	NU
NORFOLK ISLAND	NF
NORTHERN MARIANA ISLANDS	MP
NORWAY	NO
OMAN	OM
PAKISTAN	PK
PALAU	PW
PANAMA	PA

Continued

TABLE C.1	COUNTRY	DOMAIN
Continued	PAPUA NEW GUINEA	PG
	PARAGUAY	PY
	PERU	PE
	PHILIPPINES	PH
	PITCAIRN	PN
	POLAND	PL
	PORTUGAL	PT
	PUERTO RICO	PR
	QATAR	QA
	REUNION	RE
	ROMANIA	RO
	RUSSIAN FEDERATION	RU
	RWANDA	RW
	SAINT KITTS AND NEVIS	KN
	SAINT LUCIA	LC
	SAINT VINCENT AND THE GRENADINES	VC
	SAMOA	WS
	SAN MARINO	SM
	SAO TOME AND PRINCIPE	ST
	SAUDI ARABIA	SA
	SENEGAL	SN
	SEYCHELLES	SC
	SIERRA LEONE	SL
	SINGAPORE	SG
	SLOVAKIA (Slovak Republic)	SK
	SLOVENIA	SI
	SOLOMON ISLANDS	SB
	SOMALIA	SO
	SOUTH AFRICA	ZA

COUNTRY	DOMAIN
SOUTH GEORGIA AND THE SOUTH SANDWICH ISLANDS	GS
SPAIN	ES
SRI LANKA	LK
ST. HELENA	SH
ST. PIERRE AND MIQUELON	PM
SUDAN	SD
SURINAME	SR
SVALBARD AND JAN MAYEN ISLANDS	SJ
SWAZILAND	SZ
SWEDEN	SE
SWITZERLAND	CH
SYRIAN ARAB REPUBLIC	SY
TAIWAN, PROVINCE OF CHINA	TW
TAJIKISTAN	TJ
TANZANIA, UNITED REPUBLIC OF	TZ
THAILAND	TH
TOGO	TG
TOKELAU	TK
TONGA	TO
TRINIDAD AND TOBAGO	TT
TUNISIA	TN
TURKEY	TR
TURKMENISTAN	TM
TURKS AND CAICOS ISLANDS	TC
TUVALU	TV
UGANDA	UG
UKRAINE	UA

Continued

· · · · ·

T·A·B·L·E C·I	COUNTRY	DOMAIN
Continued	UNITED ARAB EMIRATES	AE
	UNITED KINGDOM	GB
	UNITED STATES	US
	UNITED STATES MINOR OUTLYING ISLANDS	UM
	URUGUAY	UY
	UZBEKISTAN	UZ
	VANUATU	VU
	VENEZUELA	VE
	VIETNAM	VN
	VIRGIN ISLANDS (BRITISH)	VG
	VIRGIN ISLANDS (U.S.)	VI
	WALLIS AND FUTUNA ISLANDS	WF
	WESTERN SAHARA	EH
	YEMEN	YE
	YUGOSLAVIA	YU
	ZAMBIA	ZM
	ZIMBABWE	ZW

Index

(continued)

(continued)

(continued)

Q

Notes

Notes

Notes

Notes

Notes

Notes

Notes

Notes

Notes

Notes

Notes

Notes

Notes

Notes

Notes

Notes

Notes

Notes

Notes

Notes

Notes

Notes

Notes

Notes

Notes

Notes

Notes

Notes

WE WROTE THE BOOK
ON NETWORKING

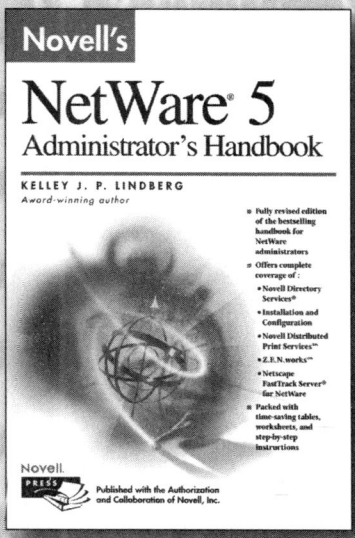

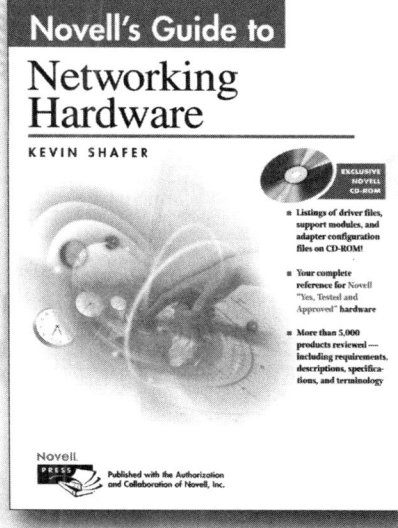

MORE BOOKS FROM NOVELL PRESS™

my2cents.idgbooks.com

Register This Book — And Win!

Visit **http://my2cents.idgbooks.com** to register this book and we'll automatically enter you in our fantastic monthly prize giveaway. It's also your opportunity to give us feedback: let us know what you thought of this book and how you would like to see other topics covered.

Discover IDG Books Online!

The IDG Books Online Web site is your online resource for tackling technology — at home and at the office. Frequently updated, the IDG Books Online Web site features exclusive software, insider information, online books, and live events!

10 Productive & Career-Enhancing Things You Can Do at www.idgbooks.com

- Nab source code for your own programming projects.

- Download software.

- Read Web exclusives: special articles and book excerpts by IDG Books Worldwide authors.

- Take advantage of resources to help you advance your career as a Novell or Microsoft professional.

- Buy IDG Books Worldwide titles or find a convenient bookstore that carries them.

- Register your book and win a prize.

- Chat live online with authors.

- Sign up for regular e-mail updates about our latest books.

- Suggest a book you'd like to read or write.

- Give us your 2¢ about our books and about our Web site.

You say you're not on the Web yet? It's easy to get started with IDG Books' *Discover the Internet*, available at local retailers everywhere.